乱序版
TOEFL词汇
词根+联想
记忆法

俞敏洪 ● 编著

西安交通大学出版社

XI'AN JIAOTONG UNIVERSITY PRESS

图书在版编目(CIP)数据

TOEFL 词汇词根＋联想记忆法：乱序版 / 俞敏洪编著
. —2 版. —西安：西安交通大学出版社，2013.8
ISBN 978-7-5605-5589-8

Ⅰ. ①T⋯　Ⅱ. ①俞⋯　Ⅲ. ①TOEFL—词汇—记忆术—
自学参考资料　Ⅳ. ①H313

中国版本图书馆 CIP 数据核字(2013)第 196841 号

书　　名	TOEFL 词汇词根＋联想记忆法：乱序版	
编　　著	俞敏洪	
责任编辑	黄科丰	
封面设计	大愚设计	
出版发行	西安交通大学出版社	
地　　址	西安市兴庆南路 10 号(邮编：710049)	
电　　话	(010)62605588　62605019(发行部)　(029)82668315(总编室)	
读者信箱	bj62605588@163.com	
印　　刷	北京慧美印刷有限公司	
字　　数	664 千	
开　　本	720mm×960mm　1/16	
印　　张	37.5	
版　　次	2013 年 10 月第 1 版　2013 年 10 月第 1 次印刷	
书　　号	ISBN 978-7-5605-5589-8/H・1563	
定　　价	58.00 元	

　　词汇向来是英语学习的基础，更是应对所有英语考试的关键。如果把英语学习比作构建大厦，词汇便是深埋于地下的基石，虽不浮于表面，但决定了这座语言大厦的坚固与否。词汇量的匮乏严重影响并制约着一个人听、说、读、写等各方面能力的发展，更会成为各种英语考试的障碍。托福考试注重考查考生对英语的实际运用能力，对词汇的掌握和运用更是提出了挑战。

　　学习词汇至关重要的一步在于选择一本好的词汇书。那么何谓"好的词汇书"呢？简而言之，一本好的词汇书应该具备科学的词汇学习理念与方法、合理的编排和设计、全面而实用的内容，以及轻松有趣的记忆方法。经广大考生多年实践证明，"词根＋联想"记忆法是一种科学且高效的学习方法。因此，本书以词根、词缀记忆法为主体，利用单词的拆分、谐音和形近词的比较等，并配合幽默的插图形成了一套高效实用、生动有趣的记忆方法，帮助考生掌握托福考试必备词汇，轻松应对托福考试。本书特色如下：

一、收词全面，重点词汇"一网打尽"

　　经过对托福考试和官方指南的深入研究，本书在以往"TOEFL词汇红宝书"的基础上，精析近期考试，甄选最新词汇，共收录约4500个核心词汇，并补充大量的同义词、派生词、形近词和同源词，总计约8000词汇量，将托福考试重点单词"一网打尽"。尤其值得注意的是，本书以*标注已考同义词，帮助考生备考。

　　本书突破了从A到Z按字母顺序排列单词的方式，所有单词采取"乱序"编排，打破单词常规记忆模式，帮助考生自由灵活地理解和记忆单词，从而在最短的时间内攻克托福词汇。

二、"词根＋联想"，词汇障碍一扫而光

　　如果没有科学的记忆方法，单词记忆将是个效率低下、枯燥乏味的过程。实践证明，"词根＋联想"记忆法能够在最大程度上提升单词记忆的趣味性和考生背单词的成就感。

与汉字的偏旁部首类似，英文单词由大量的词根、词缀构成。掌握常见的词根、词缀，考生即可以此为支点，举一反三，用"四两拨千斤"的巧力构建自己的词汇大厦，短时间内记忆海量单词。例如：

词根：scrib = to write(写)

inscribe = in(进入) + scrib(写) + e → 写进去 → (在某物上)写、题、铭刻

prescribe = pre(在…前面) + scrib(写) + e → 预先写好 → 规定；指示；开处方

transcribe = tran(= trans 穿过) + scrib(写) + e → 用另一种方式来写 → 抄录；改编

subscribe = sub(在…下面) + scrib(写) + e → 在下面写上名字 → 订阅，订购

考生在掌握了词根scrib后，结合常见的词缀in-, pre-, tran-, sub-就可以推出上述单词的意思。而且，考生在学习或考试中遇到含有词根scrib的单词，也能从其结构推出词义。因此，通过词根、词缀的学习，记忆单词将不再单调乏味，而是妙趣横生的"拼词游戏"。

联想记忆法主要是通过单词的拆分、形近词对比、同音词，以及联想电影名等有趣的方式，激发考生的想象力，帮助考生强化记忆。发音记忆法主要利用英文单词与中文的谐音，帮助考生巧妙记忆单词。这些灵活有趣的记忆方法把考生从记忆单词的枯燥劳役中解放出来，帮助考生克服背诵单词的畏惧心理，提高学习效率。

三、幽默插图，开启轻松记忆之旅

除文字助记方法外，本书为单词配备约350幅生动有趣的插图，为考生营造一个轻松的学习环境。一张幽默的插图往往能抵上千言万语，帮助考生变抽象记忆为形象记忆，在愉悦的氛围中学习单词。例如：

| hover
[ˈhʌvər] | *vi.* 徘徊，彷徨(wander)；(鸟等)翱翔，盘旋
记 联想记忆：在爱人(lover)身边徘徊(hover)
例 The criminal is *hovering* between life and death. 这个罪犯在生死之间徘徊。
参 hovercraft(*n.* 气垫船) |  |

四、原汁原味例句，模拟考试语境

与大多数国内英语考试相比，托福考试中出现的句子(尤其是阅读文章中的句子)在难度和长度上都更具挑战性。针对这一特点，本着符合考试情境、紧贴考试内容的原则，本书精心编写了大量与真实考试难度相当以及与历次考试内容相关的例句，并对这些例句进行录音，便于考生在学习单词时，熟悉真实考试环境，了解考查要点，为备考托福打下坚实的基础。

五、返记菜单，反复自查

不少考生在记忆单词时一味追求效率，忽视了效果，往往等到一本单词书学完，最先学习的单词已经忘得差不多了。本书在页面最下方设置了"返记菜单"，帮助考生随时检查记忆效果。

本书得以顺利出版，要感谢世纪友好的编辑们，是他们的辛苦工作使得本书能够及时与读者见面。

对还在备考托福之路上奋进的各位考生，我无法相助其他，唯有通过本书为考生铺就托福备考之路，祝各位取得理想的成绩，顺利进入自己理想的大学。

新东方教育科技集团
董事长兼总裁

单元前的词根、词缀预习表帮助考生掌握常用词根、词缀，迅速扩大词汇量。

配有 670 分钟录音，对英文主词及例句进行朗读，考生通过听录音能有效提高对单词的理解程度和记忆效果，扫描二维码即可收听。

幽默有趣的插图将单词含义形象化，辅助记忆的同时增加学习的趣味性。

音频

Word List 13

词根、词缀预习表

fin	最后	finance n. 财政，金融	spect	看	retrospect n. 回顾，反顾
vis	看	supervise vt. 监督	vacu	空的	evacuate v. 疏散，撤离
sanct	神圣的	sanction vt./n. 同意，许可	lingu	语言	bilingualism n. 双语现象
hanc	高的	enhance vt. 提高；增强	tent	测试	tentative a. 试验性的
pend	悬挂	append vt. 附加	agon	挣扎	agonize vi. 苦苦思索

---

systematic
[ˌsɪstəˈmætɪk]

a. 系统的，体系的(methodic)

记 来自 system(*n.* 系统)

例 While Edison's approach to invention was often cut-and-try, it was highly *systematic*. 虽然爱迪生用于发明的方法经常是试验性的，但这个方法却极具系统性。

派 systematize(*vt.* 使系统化，使制度化)

client
[ˈklaɪənt]

n. 委托人，当事人；顾客(customer)

例 Social workers must always consider the best interests of their *clients*. 社会工作者必须时刻考虑其当事人的最佳利益。

把猫干掉

client

dye
[daɪ]

n. 颜料，染料 *v.* 染色

记 联想记忆：劣质染料(dye)会致人死亡(die)

例 I want to *dye* my hair blonde. 我想把头发染成金黄色。

turtle
[ˈtɜːtl]

n. 龟，海龟

记 发音记忆："特逗" → 龟(turtle)的样子特逗 → 龟

finance
[ˈfaɪnæns]

vt. 给…提供资金(*subsidize) *n.* 财政，金融；[常 *pl.*]财务情况

记 词根记忆：fin(最后) + ance → 最后起作用的东西 → 财政，金融

例 The troupe is *financed* by the elders. 剧团由老年人提供资金。

派 financing(*n.* 融资，财务)；financial(*a.* 财政的，金融的)；financier(*n.* 金融家)

□ systematic   □ client   □ dye   □ turtle   □ finance

采用《牛津高阶英语词典（第 8 版）》中的音标体系，帮助考生熟悉单词发音。

真题例句以及大量难度适当的例句帮助考生记忆单词，熟悉考试难度。

借助英文单词与中文的谐音，灵活记忆单词。

以*标注已考同义词，复习时更加有的放矢。

丰富派生词，横向扩充词汇量。

提供词根记忆法，考生可举一反三，达到事半功倍的效果。

补充丰富的形近词、近义词、反义词以及同源词等，帮助考生串联记忆，提高效果。

supervise
[ˈsuːpərvaɪz]
vt. 监督(oversee)；指导
记 词根记忆：super(在…上面) + vis(看) + e → 在上面看 → 监督
例 The National Academy of Design for the painters *supervised* the incorporation of new artistic techniques. 为画家而开设的国家设计研究院指导新艺术技巧的融合。
派 supervision(*n.* 监督)；supervisor(*n.* 主管；监督员)

tariff
[ˈtærɪf]
n. 关税(tax, duty)；(旅馆、饭店等的)价目表，收费表
例 The regulations keep *tariffs* high. 这些规定使关税一直居高不下。

copious
[ˈkoʊpiəs]
a. 丰富的，富饶的
记 联想记忆：copi(看做copy，复制) + ous → 能不断复制的 → 丰富的
例 Scientists support the theory of relativity with *copious* evidence. 科学家们用大量证据支持相对论。

exposure
[ɪkˈspoʊʒər]
n. 暴露，显露；曝光；面临，遭受(危险或不快)
记 来自expose(*vt.* 暴露，显露；揭露；使面临，使遭受)
例 Vaccines for some rare diseases are given only to persons who risk *exposure* to the diseases. 某些罕见疾病的疫苗只供有可能接触这些疾病的人使用。
参 extension(*n.* 延长)；expansion(*n.* 扩充)

substance
[ˈsʌbstəns]
n. 物质；主旨，实质(matter)；根据；重要性(significance)
记 词根记忆：sub(在…下面) + st(站) + ance → 站在下面的东西 → 实质
例 The Moon isn't much like the Earth in terms of *substance*. 从物质方面来看，月亮不太像地球。// Nothing of any *substance* was achieved in the meeting. 会议没有取得任何实质性成果。

neoclassical
[ˌniːoʊˈklæsɪkl]
a. 新古典主义的
例 The *neoclassical* sculptors seldom held a mallet or chisel in their own hands. 新古典主义雕塑家很少亲自手持槌棒或凿子。
派 neoclassicism(*n.* 新古典主义)

array
[əˈreɪ]
n. 一系列(series)；阵列 *vt.* 布置，排列；部署
记 联想记忆：ar + ray(光线) → 像光线一样 → 一系列
例 Glasses of all shapes and sizes were *arrayed* on the shelves. 架子上整齐地排列着大大小小各式各样的玻璃杯。

counselor
[ˈkaʊnsələr]
n. (尤指针对私人问题的)顾问(advisor)；律师
例 She worked as a marriage guidance *counselor*. 她是一名婚姻指导顾问。

sanction
[ˈsæŋkʃn]
vt. 同意，许可；惩罚，实施制裁 *n.* 同意，许可；约束；制裁
记 词根记忆：sanct(神圣的) + ion → 神圣之物，原指教会的法令，后引申为"同意，许可" → 同意，许可
搭 sanction against 制裁，处罚
例 Based on previous experience, the government will not *sanction* such a bill. 根据之前的经验，政府不会批准这种法案的。

□ supervise　□ tariff　□ copious　□ exposure　□ substance　□ neoclassical
□ array　□ counselor　□ sanction

归纳常考词组和搭配，帮助考生迅速抓住考试重点。

页面底部设置返记菜单，考生结束每页学习后可以及时进行复习和自测，有助于巩固对单词的掌握。

通过单词的拆分、谐音和词与词之间的联系将难词化简、联词成串，轻松高效地记忆单词。

目 录

词根、词缀预习表

ess	存在	essence n. 本质，精髓	deca	十	decade n. 十年，十年期
cult	种植；培养	cultivate vt. 耕种；培养	vag	漫游	vagrant n. 无业游民
stit	站立	substitute v. 代替	clin	倾斜	incline v. (使)倾斜
naiss	出生	renaissance n. 再生	nown	名字	renown n. 名望
form	形状	conform vi. 符合	liter	文字	obliterate vt. 消灭

essence [ˈesns]	*n.* 本质，精髓(*basic nature) 记 词根记忆：ess(存在) + ence → 存在的根本 → 本质，精髓 搭 of the essence 非常重要的，不可缺少的 例 This constant reshaping and recreation is the *essence* of folk music. 这种不断的重塑和再创造是民间音乐的精髓。
pastel [pæˈstel]	*a.* 彩色蜡笔的；柔和的(bland, soft) *n.* 彩色蜡笔(画) 记 词根记忆：past(生面团) + el → 用糊状物制作的粉笔 → 彩色蜡笔的 搭 pastel shades 柔和的色彩 例 *Pastel* colors are always restful to our eyes. 柔和色总能让我们的眼睛得到休息。 派 pastelist(*n.* 彩色蜡笔画家)
cultivate [ˈkʌltɪveɪt]	*vt.* 耕种；培养(bring up, foster) 记 词根记忆：cult(种植；培养) + iv + ate(动词后缀) → 耕种；培养 例 Expressive leaders *cultivate* a personal relationship with staff in the group. 富有表现力的领导能与小组成员建立一种私人关系。 派 cultivation(*n.* 耕种；培养)
recover [rɪˈkʌvər]	*v.* 复原，恢复(renew)；重新获得；收回 记 联想记忆：re(再，又) + cover(包括) → 重新获得 例 After taking some medicine, she has almost *recovered* from her cough. 吃了些药后，她的咳嗽快好了。 派 recovery(*n.* 恢复；重获)
substitute [ˈsʌbstɪtuːt]	*n.* 代替者，代替品(replacement) *v.* 代替(replace) 记 词根记忆：sub(在…下面) + stit(=stat 站立) + ute → 站在下面 → 代替 例 Radio is a *substitute* for newspapers in people's homes. 在人们家中，广播是报纸的一种替代品。 派 substitution(*n.* 代替，替换)

renaissance
[ˈrenəsɑːns]

n. [the R-] (欧洲 14 至 16 世纪的)文艺复兴, 文艺复兴时期; 复兴, 再生 (renewal, revival)

记 词根记忆: re(再, 又) + naiss(=nasc 出生) + ance → 再生

例 The *Renaissance* was more than a "rebirth". It was also an age of new discoveries, both geographical and intellectual. 文艺复兴不仅仅是一次"新生", 也是一个重新发现的时代, 既包括地理上的新发现, 又包括智力上的新发现。

sweat
[swet]

n. 汗; 一身汗 *v.* (使)出汗

记 联想记忆: 辛勤的汗水(sweat)过后是甜蜜的(sweet)果实

搭 sweat gland 汗腺

例 I woke up in a *sweat*. 我醒来时浑身是汗。

派 sweaty(*a.* 出汗的; 吃力的); sweater(*n.* 毛衣; 厚运动衫)

参 sweatshirt(*n.* 运动衫); sweatshop(*n.* 血汗工厂)

underscore
[ˌʌndərˈskɔːr] *vt.* 强调(stress, emphasize, underpin); 在…之下画线

[ˈʌndərskɔːr] *n.* 底线

记 组合词: under(在…下面) + score(画线) → 在下面画线以示重要 → 强调

例 These excesses *underscore* a feature of residential expansion related to the growth of mass transportation. 这些多出的部分强调了住宅扩展的特点, 这一扩展与大规模运输的发展有关。

conform
[kənˈfɔːrm]

vi. 遵守, 服从(comply); 符合(agree); 适应(adapt)

记 词根记忆: con(共同) + form(形状) → 形状相同 → 符合

例 They should be designed to *conform* to the topography of the area. 它们的设计应该符合该地区的地貌。

派 conformity(*n.* 符合, 一致); nonconformity(*n.* 不墨守成规)

husk
[hʌsk]

n. (果类、谷物等的)外壳, 外皮(shell, outer covering) *vt.* 去壳, 削皮

例 How can we remove the *husk* of the grains? 我们怎样去掉谷物的外皮?

tide
[taɪd]

v. 涨落 *n.* 潮, 潮汐; 潮流, 趋势(trend)

记 联想记忆: 潮(tide)起潮(tide)落, 岁月(time)如歌

搭 tide sb. over 帮助某人渡过难关

例 Could I borrow a twenty to *tide* me over till payday next Thursday? 你能借我 20 块钱帮我渡过难关吗? 下周四就发工资了。

派 tidal(*a.* 潮汐的; 潮流的)

参 tidy(*a.* 简洁的, 整齐的)

decade
[ˈdekeɪd]

n. 十年, 十年期

记 词根记忆: deca(十) + de → 十年, 十年期

例 The last *decade* is a dream *decade* for the country's economic growth. 过去的十年是该国经济飞速发展的十年。

decade

pluralism [ˈplʊrəlɪzəm]	*n.* 多元化，多元性；多元主义 记 来自 plural(*a.* 复数的) 搭 cultural pluralism 文化的多元性 例 Don't pursue *pluralism* too much, or you will accomplish nothing instead. 不要过于强调多元性，否则你将一事无成。
vagrant [ˈveɪɡrənt]	*n.* 无业游民，流浪者 *a.* 漂泊的 记 词根记忆：vag(漫游) + rant → 无业游民，流浪者 例 Sophie met a band of *vagrants* at the door of the coffee shop. 索菲在咖啡店门口遇到一群流浪汉。
incline 	[ɪnˈklaɪn] *v.* (使)倾斜；(使)倾向于 [ˈɪnklaɪn] *n.* 斜坡，斜面(slope) 记 词根记忆：in(向内) + clin(倾斜) + e → 向内斜 → (使)倾斜 例 They have come back from their trip to Europe; they *inclined* to take a rest for a couple of days. 他们刚从欧洲旅行回来；这几天想休息一下。
grievous [ˈɡriːvəs]	*a.* 令人忧伤的；极严重的(serious) 记 词根记忆：griev(=gra 重的) + ous → 心情沉重的 → 令人忧伤的 例 The report said that was a *grievous* waste. 报道称，那真是一种令人悲痛的浪费。
saucy [ˈsɔːsi]	*a.* 无礼的；俏皮的；漂亮的 例 She was tall, slim, with fair skin and large *saucy* eyes. 她高个子，苗条，皮肤白皙，有一双漂亮的大眼睛。
disproportionate [ˌdɪsprəˈpɔːrʃənət]	*a.* 不成比例的 例 *Disproportionate* emphasis on examinations may bring about serious consequences. 对考试的过分重视会造成严重的后果。
withhold [wɪðˈhoʊld]	*vt.* 拒绝给，不给(refuse)；抑制(prevent)；忍住 记 联想记忆：with(有) + hold(拿着) → 自己拿着，就是不给 → 拒绝给 例 There are some parents who might *withhold* sweets from their children as a form of punishment. 有些父母会不给孩子糖果，以示惩罚。
nosy [ˈnoʊzi]	*a.* 爱管闲事的，好打听的(inquisitive) 记 来自 nose(*n.* 鼻子) 例 Tom says it's *nosy* to ask others about their private lives. 汤姆说询问及他人的私生活是爱管闲事的表现。
stumble [ˈstʌmbl]	*vi.* 绊脚；蹒跚而行；(说话等时)结巴 记 联想记忆：stum(看做 stump, 树桩) + ble → 绊脚之物 → 绊脚 搭 stumble across/on/upon 意外发现，偶然遇见；stumble into 无意间涉足 例 Be careful not to *stumble* against that table, or you'll break the glasses on it. 当心不要撞上那张桌子，否则会打翻上面的玻璃杯的。
imaginative [ɪˈmædʒɪnətɪv]	*a.* 富有想象力的；创新的 例 That famous artist who was seen as the father of painting is full of *imaginative* ideas. 那位被奉为绘画之父的知名艺术家有着丰富的想象力。

chaotic [keɪˈɑːtɪk]	*a.* 混乱的，无秩序的 记 联想记忆：chao(看做 chaos，混乱) + tic → 混乱的 例 Inherent complexity is the true cause of *chaotic* systems. 内在的复杂性是系统混乱的真正原因。// The traffic in the city is *chaotic* in the rush hour. 在高峰时间，城市的交通混乱不堪。
renown [rɪˈnaʊn]	*n.* 名望，声誉(reputation) 记 词根记忆：re(再，又) + nown(=nom 名字) → 名字被一再提及 → 名望 例 Seldom has a city as New York gained such world *renown*. 很少有哪个城市能像纽约这样在世界上享有如此盛名。
scroll [skroʊl]	*n.* 卷轴；纸卷，画卷；名册 例 Look at this; it's a Chinese vertical *scroll* painting. 来看看这个，这是一幅中国垂直式卷轴画。
embrace [ɪmˈbreɪs]	*v.* 拥抱；包含；欣然接受 *n.* 拥抱(hug) 记 词根记忆：em(使…) + brac(胳膊) + e → 使在胳膊里 → 拥抱 例 Not everyone *embraced* the new population plan which was proposed by the President. 并非每个人都拥护总统提出的这个人口计划。// He held her in a warm *embrace*. 他热烈地拥抱着她。
obliterate [əˈblɪtəreɪt]	*vt.* 覆盖；消灭；忘却 记 词根记忆：ob(去掉) + liter(文字) + ate(动词后缀) → 去掉文字 → 消灭 例 The government official was eager to *obliterate* his mistake. 这名政府官员急于掩盖自己的过错。
colonization [ˌkɑːlənəˈzeɪʃn]	*n.* 殖民地化 记 来自 colonize(*v.* 殖民化，殖民地化) 例 This treaty ends the *colonization* of the two islands. 该条约结束了这两个岛屿的殖民化历史。
affiliate	[əˈfɪlieɪt] *vt.* 使隶属于 [əˈfɪliət] *n.* 分公司 记 词根记忆：af(接近) + fil(儿子) + iate → 形成近乎和儿子一样的关系 → 使隶属于 例 The next item on the agenda is to discuss the *affiliating* program. 会议议程的下一项是讨论联盟计划。 派 affiliation(*n.* 隶属关系；隶属)
rancorous [ˈræŋkərəs]	*a.* 怨恨的，满怀恶意的 记 来自 rancor(*n.* 怨恨) 例 Ever since the family has been characterized by a *rancorous* bitterness. 从此，这个家庭充满了仇恨与痛苦。
subculture [ˈsʌbkʌltʃər]	*n.* (某群体所特有的)亚文化行为观念，次文化 例 It is obvious that foreign culture here belongs to a *subculture*. 很明显，外来文化在这里属于一种亚文化。

forum [ˈfɔːrəm]	*n.* 论坛；讨论会 记 词根记忆：for(门，户外) + um → 在室外(进行公开讨论) → 论坛 例 The on-line *forum* provides a platform for people to voice their opinions. 在线论坛为人们提供了一个表达自己观点的平台。
participant [pɑːrˈtɪsɪpənt]	*n.* 参与者；参赛者 记 词根记忆：part(部分) + i + cip(拿，取) + ant(表人，名词后缀) → 只拿住部分的人 → 参与者 例 That black man was a leading *participant* in the movement to end slavery. 这位黑人是结束奴隶制运动的一位重要参与者。
strain [streɪn]	*n.* 拉力，压力，张力；扭伤 *vt.* 扭伤(sprain)；使紧张；拉紧 记 本身为词根，意为"拉紧" 例 These repayments are putting a *strain* on our finances. 偿还这些债务给我们的财务状况带来了压力。// You might *strain* your shoulder. 你可能会扭伤你的肩膀。
vary [ˈveri]	*v.* 改变，变化(change, alter) 例 Orthoclases *vary* in color from white to pink to red. 正长石颜色不一，从白色到粉色再到红色都有。 派 varied(*a.* 各式各样的)；various(*a.* 不同的，多种多样的)
mediate [ˈmiːdieɪt]	*v.* 调解，调停，斡旋(reconcile, compose) 记 词根记忆：medi(中间) + ate → 在矛盾双方中间 → 调解，调停 例 The National Academy of Design *mediated* conflicts between artists. 国家设计研究院调解了艺术家们之间的冲突。
sensitive [ˈsensətɪv]	*a.* 敏感的；灵敏的(delicate) 记 词根记忆：sens(感觉) + itive → 敏感的 例 Ants can be extremely *sensitive* to these signals. 蚂蚁会对这些信号极其敏感。 派 hypersensitive(*a.* 非常敏感的)；sensitivity(*n.* 灵敏性；敏感)
exposition [ˌekspəˈzɪʃn]	*n.* 展览会，博览会(exhibition)；阐释 记 词根记忆：ex(出) + pos(放) + ition → 放出来(让人看) → 展览会，博览会 例 The city will host the country's biggest flower *exposition*. 这个城市将主办国内最大的花博会。
sphere [sfɪr]	*n.* 球(体)(ball, globe)；范围，领域；阶层 记 词根记忆：spher(球) + e → 球(体) 搭 the political sphere 政界 例 This area was formerly within the *sphere* of French influence. 这一地区先前属于法国人的势力范围。 派 spherical(*a.* 球状的)

discharge	[ˈdɪstʃɑːrdʒ] *n.* 流出物；放电
	[dɪsˈtʃɑːrdʒ] *v.* 释放(release)；放(电)；解雇；清偿；履行
	记 联想记忆：dis(分离) + charge(电荷) → 放电
	例 Are you in any pain or is there any *discharge* in your ears? 你感觉到痛吗？耳朵里有分泌物吗？// If too much volcanic heat is *discharged*, the crater's ice pack will melt away entirely. 如果释放出过多的火山热量，火山口的冰层就会完全融化。
giant [ˈdʒaɪənt]	*a.* 巨大的(immense)；超群的(outstanding) *n.* 巨大的动物(或植物)；才智超群的人
	记 联想记忆：gi + ant(蚂蚁) → 蚂蚁虽小，但团结起来力量却很大 → 巨大的
	例 A galaxy is a *giant* family of many millions of stars. 星系是由数百万颗恒星组成的一个大家族。
melt [melt]	*v.* (使)融化，(使)熔化；(使)溶化(dissolve, liquefy)；(使)消散
	例 If clay contains too much iron it will *melt* when fired. 黏土中如果含有过多的铁就会在烧制过程中熔化。
solicit [səˈlɪsɪt]	*v.* 恳请(entreat)；乞求(beg)；征求；勾引；招揽(生意)
	记 词根记忆：soli(=sole 唯一，全部) + cit(引出) → 全力引出某人做事 → 恳请；乞求
	例 Bill *solicited* my opinion. 比尔征求了我的意见。
	派 solicitor(*n.* 事务律师，诉状律师)；solicitous(*a.* 关怀的；热切的)
leisure [ˈliːʒər]	*n.* 空闲，闲暇(rest, spare time)
	搭 at leisure 闲散，悠闲；leisure pursuits 休闲活动
	例 She doesn't have much *leisure*. 她没有太多空闲时间。
unravel [ʌnˈrævl]	*v.* 澄清(*discover)；解体，瓦解；解开
	记 联想记忆：un(解开) + ravel(纠缠) → 解开纠缠 → 澄清
	例 Genetic engineering helps researchers *unravel* the mysteries of previously incurable diseases. 遗传工程帮助研究人员揭开此前那些不治之症的谜团。
nail [neɪl]	*n.* 指甲，爪；钉 *vt.* 将…钉牢，钉住
	搭 as hard/tough as nails 像钉子一样硬，坚强；a nail in sb.'s/sth.'s coffin 导致失败的事物；nail down 将…固定；达成一致
	例 She hammered the *nail* in. 她把钉子敲了进去。
	参 hail(*n.* 冰雹)；mail(*n.* 邮件)；snail(*n.* 蜗牛)
attain [əˈteɪn]	*vt.* 达到(*reach)；获得(*achieve, gain)
	记 词根记忆：at + tain(拿住) → 稳稳拿住 → 获得
	例 Mango trees grow rapidly and can *attain* heights of up to 90 feet. 芒果树长得很快，高度可达 90 英尺。
	派 attainment(*n.* 达到；成就)

melt

□ discharge   □ giant   □ melt   □ solicit   □ leisure   □ unravel
□ nail   □ attain

constitute [ˈkɑːnstətjuːt]	*v.* 组成(make up)；设立(set up, establish)；制定(enact) 记 词根记忆：con(共同) + stit(站立) + ute → 站在一起 → 组成；设立 例 Governments should be *constituted* by the will of the people. 政府应依人民的意志而设立。 参 institute(*n.* 学会)；substitute(*n.* 代替品)
unsubstantiated [ˌʌnsəbˈstænʃieɪtɪd]	*a.* 未经证实的，无事实根据的(*unverified) 记 来自 substantiate(*vt.* 证实) 例 There are numerous *unsubstantiated* reports. 有无数未经证实的报告。
stylized [ˈstaɪlaɪzd]	*a.* (绘画、写作等手法)非写实的；程式化的 记 来自 stylize(*vt.* 使风格化) 例 In her versions the figures became more *stylized* and the landscapes less naturalistic. 在她的版本里，人物更加脸谱化，风景也不再那么写实。
intrepid [ɪnˈtrepɪd]	*a.* 勇敢的，无畏的(fearless) 记 词根记忆：in(不) + trep(害怕) + id → 不害怕的 → 勇敢的，无畏的 例 Nellie gained a reputation as a daring, *intrepid* journalist. 内莉赢得了勇敢无畏的记者的美名。 intrepid
nominee [ˌnɑːmɪˈniː]	*n.* 被提名者，被任命者 例 Both political parties wanted Dwight D.Eisenhower as their presidential *nominee.* 两个政党都想让德怀特·D.艾森豪威尔当他们的总统候选人。
panic [ˈpænɪk]	*n./v.* 惊慌(alarm) 记 来自 Pan(潘)，希腊神话中的山林、畜牧之神。它的怪叫声使人产生极大的恐惧感，panic 指 Pan 出现时给人们带来的恐惧感 搭 in panic 惊慌；panic sb. into doing sth. 使某人仓促做某事 例 The class presentation started half an hour ago and I was just beginning to *panic.* 半个小时前，课堂报告开始了，我就开始惊慌了起来。
lure [lʊr]	*vt.* 吸引，诱惑(*attract, tempt) *n.* 诱惑力；诱饵 记 联想记忆：纯(pure)属诱惑(lure) 例 Many adults were *lured* to the cities by promises of steady employment. 很多成年人被稳定的就业所吸引，纷纷来到城市。 lure
routine [ruːˈtiːn]	*n.* 例行公事；惯例，常规(convention) *a.* 例行的；常规的(regular) 记 联想记忆：例行公事(routine)就是按常规路线(route)走 例 Farmers relieved the burden of the daily *routine* with such relaxation as hunting. 农民以诸如狩猎等娱乐活动来缓解日常劳作的艰辛。// The fault was discovered during a *routine* check. 这个错误是在一次常规检查中发现的。 派 routinely(*ad.* 例行公事地)

solution [səˈluːʃn]	*n.* 溶液(liquor); 解答，解决(办法) 记 词根记忆: solu(解开; 溶解) + tion → 让其充分溶解 → 溶液 例 Attempts to find a *solution* have failed. 找到解决方法的种种努力均以失败告终。
revere [rɪˈvɪr]	*vt.* 尊敬，敬畏(*respect) 记 联想记忆: 我们都很敬畏(revere)这位严厉(severe)的老师 例 The movement *revered* craft as a form of art. 这场运动把工艺尊为一种艺术。 派 reverent(*a.* 尊敬的，虔诚的); reverently(*ad.* 尊敬地，虔诚地)
idealize [aɪˈdiːəlaɪz]	*vt.* 将…理想化(transfigure) 记 来自ideal(*n.* 理想 *a.* 理想的) 例 This is how Thomas Jefferson *idealized* the farmers at the beginning of the 19th century. 这就是托马斯·杰斐逊在 19 世纪初如何把农民理想化的。 派 idealization(*n.* 理想化)
flash [flæʃ]	*n.* 闪光; 闪现(flare, sparkle) *vi.* 闪光; 反射(flare, glare, sparkle) 记 联想记忆: 网络词汇"闪客"就是 flash 搭 in a flash 转瞬间; flash by 一闪而过 例 *Flashes* of light were followed by an explosion. 阵阵闪光之后就是一声爆炸的巨响。
secrete [sɪˈkriːt]	*vt.* 分泌(excrete); 藏匿，躲藏 记 联想记忆: 他把那封秘密(secret)信件藏(secrete)在角落里 例 This substance is *secreted* from cells in the intestinal walls. 这种物质是从肠壁的细胞中分泌出来的。 派 secretion(*n.* 分泌; 分泌物); secretin(*n.* 分泌素)
issue [ˈɪʃuː]	*n.* 问题，争论点; 发行; (报刊的)一期 *vt.* 颁布; 发行 例 He and Dr. Johnson disagreed on basic economic *issues*. 他和约翰逊博士在基本的经济问题上无法达成共识。// No silver coins were *issued* until 1794. 直到 1794 年才发行银币。
aria [ˈɑːriə]	*n.* 独唱曲，咏叹调 例 An *aria* in music was originally any expressive melody, usually, performed by a singer. 在音乐中，咏叹调最初是指任何形式的抒情曲调，通常由一位歌唱家来表演。
facilitate [fəˈsɪlɪteɪt]	*vt.* 推动，促进(impulse) 记 词根记忆: fac(做) + ilit + ate(使…) → 使做事更便利 → 推动 例 Government's trade policies *facilitated* the exporting of agricultural products. 政府的贸易政策推动了农产品的出口。
electricity [ɪˌlekˈtrɪsəti]	*n.* 电; 电流 例 The hydroelectric station began generating *electricity* in the mid-1980s. 该水电站于 20 世纪 80 年代中期开始发电。 派 electric(*a.* 电动的，电的); electrical(*a.* 有关电的); electrician(*n.* 电工)

□ solution □ revere □ idealize □ flash □ secrete □ issue
□ aria □ facilitate □ electricity

progressive [prə'gresɪv]	*a.* 进步的(ascensive)；逐步的，渐进的(gradual)；【语】进行时的 记 来自 progress(*n.* 进步) 例 Although based on feudal models, the colony of Pennsylvania developed a reputation for a *progressive* political and social outlook. 尽管基于封建模式，宾夕法尼亚殖民地却因进步的政治和社会观点而颇受好评。 派 progressively(*ad.* 逐渐地)；progressivism(*n.* 进步主义)
reef [ri:f]	*n.* 礁，暗礁 搭 a coral reef 珊瑚礁
president ['prezɪdənt]	*n.* 总统，(大学)校长，(大会)主席 例 The *President's* visit promoted the cooperation between the two countries. 总统的访问促进了两国间的合作。 派 presidential(*a.* 总统的)
feeble ['fi:bl]	*a.* 虚弱的，衰弱的，无力的(weak, frail) 记 联想记忆：fee(费用) + ble → 需要花钱看病 → 虚弱的 例 The national government made a *feeble* attempt to make larger holdings available to homesteaders. 国民政府试图给自耕农更大的股份，但收效甚微。
influx ['ɪnflʌks]	*n.* 注入，涌入(*arrival) 记 词根记忆：in(内) + flu(流) + x → 涌入 例 The rapid growth of Boston during the mid-nineteenth century coincided with a large *influx* of European immigrants. 随着大量欧洲移民的涌入，波士顿在 19 世纪中期得到迅速发展。
receptacle [rɪ'septəkl]	*n.* 容器(container)；插座 记 词根记忆：re(再，又) + cept(拿，取) + acle → 能一再拿住 → 容器 例 The seas have been used as a *receptacle* for a range of industrial toxins. 海洋成了各种有毒工业废料的容器。
accent	['æksent] *n.* 重音(stress)；口音；重音符号 [æk'sent] *vt.* 重读 记 词根记忆：ac(表加强) + cent(歌唱) → 大声歌唱 → 强调 → 重音 搭 a strong/broad accent 浓重的口音 例 Anyone with a foreign *accent*, even a child, was discriminated against in the district. 有外国口音的人，哪怕是孩子，在这个地区都会受到歧视。
kernel ['kɜːrnl]	*n.* (硬壳果)仁；(谷物去核后的)粒；核心，要点 记 词根记忆：kern(=corn 谷粒) + el → 仁；粒 例 Squirrels bite through the shells to get at the nutritious *kernels*. 松鼠咬开果壳，吃里面营养丰富的果仁。

secure [sə'kjʊr]	*a.* 安全的，有保障的(*safe)；可靠的；确定的；稳固的 *vt.* 获得(*obtain, *acquire)；确保 记 联想记忆：se(看做 see，看) + cure(治愈) → 亲眼看到治愈，确定其是安全的 → 安全的 例 Agriculture made possible a more stable and *secure* life. 农业使更加稳定且更有保障的生活成为可能。// The girl *secured* herself a place at business school. 那个女孩在商学院获得了一席之地。 派 securely(*ad.* 安全地)；security(*n.* 安全，保障)
electron [ɪ'lektrɑːn]	*n.* 电子 派 electronic(*a.* 电子的)；electronics(*n.* 电子学) 参 electrocardiogram(*n.* 心电图)
segment ['seɡmənt]	*n.* 音段；段，部分(part, section) 记 词根记忆：seg(=sect 切割) + ment → 段，部分 例 Social atomization affected every *segment* of society. 社会分化影响了社会的各个部分。
nourish ['nɜːrɪʃ]	*vt.* 滋养；养育(rear) 记 词根记忆：nouri(=nutri 滋养，孕育) + sh → 滋养；养育 例 The rain *nourished* the crops. 雨水滋养了庄稼。 派 nourishment(*n.* 营养品)；nourishing(*a.* 有营养的)
engulf [ɪn'ɡʌlf]	*vt.* 吞没(merge) 记 联想记忆：en(进入) + gulf(海湾；深渊) → 进入深渊 → 吞没 例 The movie star was *engulfed* by a crowd of his fans. 那个电影明星被他的粉丝团团围住。
bedrock ['bedrɑːk]	*n.* 基础，根基(foundation, basis)；基岩 例 Honesty is the *bedrock* of any healthy relationship. 诚实是建立一切良好关系的基础。
due [duː]	*a.* 到期的；预期的(scheduled)；应得的；恰当的，适当的；应支付的 搭 due to 由于；due date 到期日，支付日 例 I can't remember the *due* date for our final paper. 我不记得论文的截止日期了。
unprecedented [ʌn'presɪdentɪd]	*a.* 空前的(unexampled) 记 联想记忆：un(不) + precedent(先例) + ed → 空前的 例 These innovations in manufacturing boosted output and living standards to an *unprecedented* extent. 这些生产创新把产量和生活标准提高到了前所未有的程度。
expel [ɪk'spel]	*vt.* 开除；驱逐；排出(discharge) 记 词根记忆：ex(出) + pel(推) → 推出去 → 开除；排出 例 When you sneeze, you *expel* air from your lungs. 打喷嚏时会排出肺部的空气。 参 impel(*vt.* 推动，推进)；compel(*vt.* 强迫，驱使)；repel(*vt.* 击退)；dispel(*vt.* 驱散)

□ secure　　　□ electron　　　□ segment　　　□ nourish　　　□ engulf　　　□ bedrock
□ due　　　□ unprecedented　□ expel

verbal [ˈvɜːrbl]	*a.* 口头的(oral, spoken)；言辞的；动词的 记 词根记忆：verb(言语) + al → 言辞的 搭 verbal agreement 口头协议 例 They were too excited to give a *verbal* description of what the success of the Moon landing meant. 他们太兴奋了，以至于无法用语言表达登月成功意味着什么。
deadline [ˈdedlaɪn]	*n.* 最后期限，截止时间 记 组合词：dead(死) + line(线) → 最后期限 例 If you can't meet a *deadline* for an essay, you should go and see your lecturers. 如果不能按时提交论文，就应该去找你们的导师(说明情况)。
tolerate [ˈtɑːləreɪt]	*vt.* 忍受(*endure, withstand)；容许，承认 例 I won't *tolerate* your foolish behavior anymore. 我再也无法容忍你愚蠢的行为了。
identity [aɪˈdentəti]	*n.* 身份(status)；特征，特性(characteristic)；同一性 记 联想记忆：i + dent(牙齿) + ity(表性质，名词后缀) → 通过牙齿来确定身份 → 身份 例 The *identity* of the author is unknown. 这名作者的身份不为人所知。// The hardness of the mineral often gives a clue to its *identity*. 矿物的硬度常常是了解其特性的线索。
seep [siːp]	*v.* 漏出，渗漏(pass through slowly, ooze) 记 联想记忆：啤酒(beer)渗出(seep)发出哔哔声(beep) 例 Some parts of this country are dry because rainwater *seeps* quickly through sandy soils and into the rock below. 该国的一些地区非常干燥，因为雨水很快渗入砂土，进入下面的岩石层。 派 seepage(*n.* 渗漏；渗漏的量)
patriarch [ˈpeɪtriɑːrk]	*n.* 家长，族长(master, chief) 记 词根记忆：patri(父亲) + arch(统治) → 男性统治者 → 家长，族长
engage [ɪnˈgeɪdʒ]	*v.* (使)从事于，(使)忙于；吸引；(使)订婚；聘用(employ) 记 联想记忆：en(使…) + gage(挑战) → 使接受挑战 → (使)从事于 搭 engage in (doing) sth. 从事于某事 例 How are we going to classify a typical politician or business person who *engages* in unethical practices? 我们如何区分那些做事不道德的典型政客或商人呢？ 派 engaged(*a.* 忙碌的)；engagement(*n.* 婚约；雇用)
constrain [kənˈstreɪn]	*vt.* 束缚，限制(confine, limit) 记 词根记忆：con(表加强) + strain(拉紧) → 使劲拉紧 → 束缚，限制 例 Their species' genetic makeup *constrains* them to be insects. 它们的物种基因对它们构成了限制，使它们只能成为昆虫。 派 constraint(*n.* 约束，强制)

□ verbal □ deadline □ tolerate □ identity □ seep □ patriarch
□ engage □ constrain

innocent

[ˈɪnəsnt]

a. 天真的(naive); 清白的; 无恶意的(harmless)

记 词根记忆: in(无) + noc(伤害) + ent → 无害人之心的 → 天真的

例 The man was found *innocent* of any crime. 该男子获判无罪。// It was a perfectly *innocent* remark. 那只不过是一句毫无冒犯之意的话。

派 innocence(*n.* 天真, 无知; 清白)

Today is the first day of the rest of my life, I wake as a child to see the world begin. On monarch wings and birthday wonderings, want to put on faces, walk in the wet and cold. And look forward to my growing old, to grow is to change, to change is to be new, to be new is to be young again, I barely remember when.

——美国乡村歌手 约翰·丹佛(John Denver)

音频

词根、词缀预习表

hydr	水	dehydrate v. (使)脱水	nomin	名称	nominal a. 名义上的
sinu	曲线	sinuous a. 蜿蜒的	cert	确信	certitude n. 确定
cip	拿，取	anticipate v. 预见	hom	人	homage n. 敬意
crit	判断	critic n. 评论家，批评家	fatu	傻瓜	infatuate vt. 使糊涂
ortho	正	orthodox a. 正统的	pos	放	oppose v. 反对，对抗

interior [ɪnˈtɪriər]	*a.* 内部的(inner)；内地的 *n.* 内部；[the ~]内陆(inland) 记 词根记忆：inter(在…之间) + ior → 内部的 搭 interior design 室内设计；in the interior of 在…内部 例 If a volcano erupts, some of the Earth's *interior* heat escapes to the surface. 如果火山喷发，地球内部的一些热量就会逃逸到地表。
constitution [ˌkɑːnstəˈtuːʃn]	*n.* 宪法，章程；体质；构成 记 词根记忆：con + stit(站立) + ution → 国无法不立 → 宪法 例 The student studied the genetic *constitution* of cells hard. 这个学生努力学习细胞的基因构成。 派 constitutional(a. 章程的，宪法的)；constitutionally(ad. 按照宪法)
freeze [friːz]	*v.* (使)结冰，(使)凝固 搭 freeze over 冰封；freeze up (机器、引擎等中的水)结冰 例 Jack caught a fish and dropped it beside him on the ice and it *froze* solid. 杰克捉到一条鱼，将其随手扔在身旁的冰上，结果鱼冻得硬邦邦的。// I was really happy to be writing a detective story. But after the first few pages, I sort of *froze* up mentally. 我很高兴能写侦探小说。但是只写了几页，我的脑子就不转了。
dehydrate [diːˈhaɪdreɪt]	*v.* (使)脱水(dry, desiccate) 记 词根记忆：de(分离) + hydr(水) + ate(使…) → (使)脱水 例 The little girl's body had *dehydrated* dangerously with the high temperature. 那个小姑娘的体温很高，严重脱水。 派 dehydration(n. 脱水，干燥)
sinuous [ˈsɪnjuəs]	*a.* 蜿蜒的(winding)；迂回的 记 词根记忆：sinu(曲线) + ous → 弯曲的 → 蜿蜒的 例 They walked along the *sinuous* course of the river. 他们沿着弯弯曲曲的河道散步。

alarm [əˈlɑːrm]	*n.* 闹钟；警报(alert) *vt.* 使惊恐(startle)；使担心 记 联想记忆：al + arm（武器）→ 用武器来惊吓 → 使惊恐 搭 a burglar alarm 防盗警报；alarm call 叫醒电话；告警声 例 She never wakes up before her *alarm* goes off. 闹钟不响她就醒不来。// Ecologists would probably be *alarmed* by the scientists' findings. 科学家们的发现可能会让生态学家们感到惊恐。 派 alarming(*a.* 令人担忧的)；alarmist(*n.* 危言耸听者)

RING RING RING!

alarm

machinery [məˈʃiːnəri]	*n.* 〈总称〉机器，机械(machines in general)；机构(organization) 记 来自machine(*n.* 机器，机械) 例 The use of farm *machinery* continued to increase. 农机工具的使用在继续增加。
expect [ɪkˈspekt]	*v.* 预期，期望，指望(anticipate) 例 I wonder where the books I ordered are. I *expected* to receive the package several days ago. 我不知道我订购的书到哪里了。我本来指望几天前收到包裹的。// Economists *expect* the global economy to drop by 2% this year. 经济学家预期今年全球经济将下降 2%。 参 inspect(*v.* 检查)；aspect(*n.* 方面)
anticipate [ænˈtɪsɪpeɪt]	*v.* 预见，预期(*look forward to, foresee, expect)；先于…行动 记 词根记忆：anti(在…之前) + cip(拿，取) + ate → 预先取得 → 预见 例 The test was much harder than he had *anticipated*. 测验比他预期的要难得多。 派 anticipation(*n.* 预期，预料)
critic [ˈkrɪtɪk]	*n.* 评论家，批评家；吹毛求疵者(detractor) 记 词根记忆：crit(判断) + ic → 作出判断 → 评论家，批评家 搭 a music critic 乐评人 例 The coal industry has been targeted by *critics* as a significant contributor to the greenhouse effect. 煤炭业被评论家指责为是造成温室效应的罪魁祸首。 派 criticism(*n.* 评判；批评)；criticize(*v.* 批评；评论)
instinctual [ɪnˈstɪŋktʃuəl]	*a.* 本能的 例 We must completely understand and be aware of its *instinctual* behavior. 我们必须充分理解和意识到它的本能行为。
uncanny [ʌnˈkæni]	*a.* 神秘的(weird)；易乎寻常的(unusual) 记 联想记忆：un(不) + can(能) + ny → 不能理解的 → 异乎寻常的 例 The magician says it doesn't end here, and the *uncanny* part is yet to come. 魔术师说，魔术到此并未结束，神秘的还在后头。

□ alarm　　　□ machinery　　□ expect　　□ anticipate　　□ critic　　□ instinctual
□ uncanny

arrest [əˈrest]	*n./vt.* 逮捕, 拘留; 停止, 阻止; 吸引 记 联想记忆: ar(表加强) + rest(休息) → 让人休息 → 拘留; 停止 例 The suspect was put under *arrest* by the police. 嫌疑犯被警察逮捕了。
sprinkle [ˈsprɪŋkl]	*v.* 撒, 洒, 喷 *n.* 少量 记 联想记忆: sprin(看做 spring, 春天) + kle → 春天的阳光洒在身上很舒服 → 洒 例 *Sprinkle* some pepper on the dish when it's done. 菜出锅后, 在上面撒点胡椒粉。
orthodox [ˈɔːrθədɑːks]	*a.* 传统的; 正统的 记 词根记忆: ortho(正) + dox(观点) → 正统观点的 → 正统的 例 The *orthodox* Thanksgiving dinner must have turkey and pumpkin pie. 传统的感恩节晚餐必须有火鸡和南瓜派。
preliterate [ˌpriːˈlɪtərət]	*a.* 文字出现以前的, 没有文字的 记 词根记忆: pre(在…前面) + liter(文字) + ate → 文字出现以前的 例 In *preliterate* societies oral literature was widely shared; it saturated the society and was as much a part of living as food, clothing, shelter, or religion. 在文字出现以前, 口头文学被广泛传播。口头文学遍布社会, 与食物、衣服、住处或宗教一样, 是生活的重要组成部分。
nominal [ˈnɑːmɪnl]	*a.* 名义上的; (费用等)微不足道的 记 词根记忆: nomin(名称) + al → 名义上的 搭 nominal assets 名义资产 例 Frank is only a *nominal* chairman; the real work is done by others. 弗兰克只是名义上的主席, 实际工作是其他人做的。
certitude [ˈsɜːrtɪtuːd]	*n.* 确定, 确信; 必然性(certainty) 记 词根记忆: cert(确信) + it + ude(表状态, 名词后缀) → 确定 搭 moral certitudes 道德信念 例 The old man told me with absolute *certitude* there was a shoeshop on the corner. 那个老人十分确定地告诉我街角就有一家鞋店。
hustle [ˈhʌsl]	*n.* 忙碌 *vt.* 猛推; 催促 搭 hustle and bustle 熙熙攘攘 例 I hate the *hustle* and bustle of the city life. 我讨厌城市熙熙攘攘的生活。
fake [feɪk]	*a.* 冒充的 *n.* 假货; 骗子 *v.* 伪造; 伪装 记 联想记忆: 打击造(make)假(fake) 例 This e-mail is *fake*. I'm sure it's not sent by Mark. 这封邮件是假的, 我确信不是马克发的。 // All the paintings proved to be *fakes*. 所有的画最后被证实都是赝品。

engrave [ɪnˈɡreɪv]	*vt.* (在…上)雕刻；铭刻 记 联想记忆：en(进入) + grave(坟墓) → 进入坟墓也要记着，真是刻骨铭心 → 铭刻 例 The teacher told us to *engrave* these rules on our minds. 老师告诉我们要把这些规则熟记于心。
prohibit [prəˈhɪbɪt]	*v.* 禁止，阻止(prevent) 记 词根记忆：pro(在…之前) + hibit(拿住) → 提前拿住 → 禁止 例 The government introduced a new law to *prohibit* smoking in public. 政府推出一项新法律以禁止在公众场所吸烟。
homage [ˈhɑːmɪdʒ]	*n.* 尊敬，敬意 记 词根记忆：hom(人) + age(集体名词后缀) → 敬意 例 Many people came to pay *homage* to those soldiers who died in the war. 很多人前来向在战争中牺牲的士兵致敬。
dramatize [ˈdræmətaɪz]	*v.* 改编成戏剧；(使)戏剧化，戏剧性地表现 记 来自 drama(*n.* 戏剧) 例 He intended his novel to *dramatize* the relationship between sense and sensibility. 他想在小说里戏剧化地描写理智与情感的关系。
infatuate [ɪnˈfætʃueɪt]	*vt.* 使迷恋；使糊涂(confuse) 记 词根记忆：in + fatu(傻瓜) + ate(使…) → 使成为傻瓜 → 使糊涂 例 The part that makes people *infatuate* Barbie the most is her countless beautiful clothes. 最使人们痴迷于芭比的是她有着数不清的漂亮衣服。
exclusive [ɪkˈskluːsɪv]	*a.* 独占的；除外的，排他的；奢华的 *n.* 独家新闻 记 词根记忆：ex(出) + clus(关闭) + ive(形容词后缀) → 把其余的都关在门外 → 独占的 搭 exclusive of 除…外，不计算在内 例 The two options are not mutually *exclusive*. 这两个选择并不互相排斥。// That is one of the most *exclusive* clubs in this city. 那是这个城市最高档的俱乐部之一。
cynical [ˈsɪnɪkl]	*a.* 愤世嫉俗的，冷嘲热讽的(sardonic) 记 来自 cynic(*n.* 愤世嫉俗者) 例 With a *cynical* view, the young man is easily to go to extremes. 这个年轻人持有愤世嫉俗的观点，很容易走极端。
discriminate [dɪˈskrɪmɪneɪt]	*v.* 区别；歧视(differentiate) 记 词根记忆：dis(分开) + crimin(分开) + ate → 分开对待 → 区别；歧视 搭 discriminate between 区别；discriminate against 歧视 例 You must learn to *discriminate* right from wrong. 你必须学会明辨是非。

associate	[əˈsoʊʃieɪt] *v.* 结交(*consort); 关联(relate)
	[əˈsoʊʃiət] *a.* 副的; 合伙的 *n.* 伙伴(companion, partner)
	记 词根记忆: as(表加强) + soci(结交, 同伴) + ate → 关联; 伙伴
	例 I don't like you *associating* with those boys. 我不喜欢你和那些男孩混在一起。// The young girl is closely *associated* in the public mind with horror movies. 在公众的心目中, 那个年轻女孩总是和恐怖电影紧密联系在一起。
	派 associated(*a.* 关联的; 联合的); association(*n.* 协会; 联合)
spare [sper]	*vt.* 抽出(时间等); 免除 *a.* 备用的; 空闲的(free) *n.* 备用品(reserve)
	例 I don't know if I could *spare* the time. 我不知道能否抽出空来。// We arrived at the airport with ten minutes to *spare*. 我们赶到机场时还剩十分钟。
database [ˈdeɪtəbeɪs]	*n.* 数据库
	记 组合词: data(数据) + base(基地) → 数据库
	例 You can't use the figures from the *database*, because it is flawed. 这个数据库有缺陷, 你不能用里面的数据。
proclaim [prəˈkleɪm]	*v.* 宣布, 声明(declare, announce); 显示(display)
	记 联想记忆: pro(在…前面) + claim(叫, 喊) → 在前面大叫大喊 → 宣布
	例 Advocates of organic foods frequently *proclaim* that such products are safer and more nutritious than others. 有机食品的支持者经常宣称这些产品比其他食品更加安全, 更有营养。
	参 exclaim(*v.* 惊呼); reclaim(*vt.* 要求归还)
level [ˈlevl]	*n.* 水平; 高度(altitude); 级别 *a.* 平坦的(plain); 等高的 *vt.* 夷平, 使平坦
	搭 level off/out (经过急剧的涨落后)保持平稳发展
	例 I just had to get his signature to take an upper *level* seminar. 我必须得到他的签名, 才能参加高水平的研讨会。// The mountains were *leveled* and their debris dumped into the oceans. 山脉被夷平, 岩屑注入了海洋。
controversy [ˈkɑːntrəvɜːrsi]	*n.* 争论, 辩论(dispute, argument)
	记 词根记忆: contro(反) + vers(转) + y → 因反对而转向另一方 → 争论, 辩论
	搭 arouse/cause controversy 引起争论
	例 Peary's claim was surrounded by *controversy*. 皮尔里的声明饱受争议。// There was a bitter *controversy* over his latest novel. 关于他最新的小说, 存在着激烈的争论。
	派 controversial(*a.* 有争议的; 好争论的)
oppose [əˈpoʊz]	*v.* 反对, 对抗(object, resist)
	记 词根记忆: op(反) + pos(放) + e → 反着放 → 反对, 对抗
	例 Politicians rarely *opposed* the government's generous support of business owners. 政客们很少反对政府对企业家的慷慨支持。
	派 opposed(*a.* 反对的); opposing(*a.* 反向的; 相反的)

地心说 日心说

controversy

□ associate　　□ spare　　□ database　　□ proclaim　　□ level　　□ controversy
□ oppose

toxic [ˈtɑːksɪk]	*a.* 有毒的(poisonous); 中毒的 记 发音记忆: 逃(一)个是(一)个 → 酒里有毒, 赶快逃 → 有毒的 例 Some plant tissues contain a diverse array of *toxic* or potentially *toxic* substances. 某些植物组织含有各种有毒或可能有毒的物质。 派 toxicity(*n.* 毒性)
lead [liːd]	*v.* 领导, 引导; 领先, 占首位; 通向, 导致, 引起 *n.* 带领, 引导 搭 lead to 导致; 通向; lead the way 带路, 引路 例 For some students, these part-time jobs could *lead* to full-time work after graduation as they may offer experience in their own fields. 对一些学生而言, 这些兼职为他们在各自的领域提供经验, 帮助他们在毕业后找到全职工作。// What probably *leads* people to choose gourmet coffees over regular brands? 什么可能使人们选择极品咖啡而非普通品牌的咖啡呢? // A: I can't believe that Prof. Lawrence is going to retire. B: He's still going to *lead* a seminar each semester though. A: 我不敢相信劳伦斯教授就要退休了。 B: 不过他还是会每个学期组织一次研讨会。 参 head(*n.* 头)
rustproof [ˈrʌstpruːf]	*a.* 不锈的 记 组合词: rust(铁锈; 生锈) + proof(防…的) → 防止生锈的 → 不锈的 例 Stainless products are so popular because they are *rustproof*. 不锈钢产品不会生锈, 所以大受欢迎。
sunlit [ˈsʌnlɪt]	*a.* 阳光照射的 记 联想记忆: sun(太阳) + lit(light 的过去分词, 照亮) → 阳光照射的 例 Icebergs are graceful, stately, inspiring in calm, *sunlit* seas. 在阳光照射的平静海洋上, 冰山优雅壮观, 令人鼓舞。
profession [prəˈfeʃn]	*n.* 职业(occupation); 同行; 专业(specialty); 宣称 搭 enter/go into a profession 从事/加入一个行业 例 She was a teacher by *profession*. 她的职业是教师。
hay [heɪ]	*n.* 干草(stover) 搭 hay stack 干草堆
vegetarian [ˌvedʒəˈteriən]	*n.* 素食者 *a.* 素食者的 搭 vegetarian principles 素食主义; a vegetarian restaurant 素食饭馆 例 Obtaining enough protein in the diet is especially important for *vegetarians*. 对素食者而言, 从膳食中获得足够的蛋白质尤其重要。
column [ˈkɑːləm]	*n.* 专栏(文章); 圆柱, 支柱(pillar); 纵队 例 I always read his *column* in the magazine. 我一直读他在杂志上的专栏文章。// The temple is supported by marble *columns*. 这座庙宇由大理石柱支撑着。

hay

□ toxic □ lead □ rustproof □ sunlit □ profession □ hay
□ vegetarian □ column

microbe
['maɪkroʊb]

n. 微生物，细菌(bacteria, germ)

记 词根记忆：micro(微小的) + be(=bio 生命) → 微生物

例 *Microbes* are one of the oldest forms of life on Earth. 细菌是地球上最古老的生命形式之一。

派 microbial(*a.* 由细菌引起的); microbiology(*n.* 微生物学)

homestead
['hoʊmsted]

n. 家宅，农庄；宅地

例 The original *Homestead* Act was signed into law by President Abraham Lincoln in 1862. 《宅地法》最早于 1862 年由亚伯拉罕·林肯总统签署成为法律。

派 homesteader(*n.* 农场所有人；自耕农)

canyon
['kænjən]

n. 峡谷

例 The Grand *Canyon* was considered a barrier to travelers. 人们认为大峡谷是旅行者的一个障碍。

参 crayon(*n.* 蜡笔)

portraiture
['pɔːrtrətʃər]

n. 画像技法；肖像，画像

例 Many innovations in the various forms of *portraiture* evolved during this fertile period. 在这个多产的时期，各种画像技法都得到大量创新。

参 landscape(*n.* 风景画)

alloy

['ælɔɪ] *n.* 合金 [ə'lɔɪ] *vt.* 使成合金

记 联想记忆：all(所有的) + oy → 把所有金属混在一起 → 合金

例 Brass is an *alloy* of copper and zinc. 黄铜是铜锌合金。

microscopic
[ˌmaɪkrə'skɑːpɪk]

a. 用显微镜可见的；极小的

记 词根记忆：micro(微小的) + scop(看) + ic → 小得看不清的 → 极小的

搭 a microscopic creature 微生物；a microscopic analysis 显微镜分析

例 Compared with a mountain, the rock is *microscopic*. 与大山相比，石头显得极其微小。

verse
[vɜːrs]

n. 诗歌(poetry)；韵文(rhyme)；诗节

记 词根记忆：vers(转) + e → 诗歌的音节百转千回 → 诗歌

例 Walt Whitman originated a distinctive form of free *verse*. 沃尔特·惠特曼创造了一种独特的自由诗体。

credential
[krə'denʃl]

n. 证书(certificate)；文凭(diploma)；资格(qualification)

记 词根记忆：cred(相信) + ential → 让人相信的东西 → 证书

例 None of the people who applied for the job has the required *credentials*. 申请这份工作的人都不具备所需的证书。

towering
['taʊərɪŋ]

a. 高耸的(topping)；杰出的

记 联想记忆：tower(塔) + ing → 像塔一样的 → 高耸的

例 *Towering* skyscrapers cast long shadows at dusk. 耸入云霄的摩天大楼在黄昏时分投射出长长的影子。

pervasive [pərˈveɪsɪv]	*a.* 普遍深入的；遍及的，弥漫的 记 来自 pervade(*vt.* 弥漫，遍及) 例 The basic fact has been the most *pervasive* influence in determining the social arrangements and cultural practices of the people. 这一基本事实已最普遍深入地影响着人们的社交安排和文化习俗。
lush [lʌʃ]	*a.* 茂盛的(flourishing) 例 Severin began to paint large, *lush* still lifes of flowers, fruit, or both. 塞弗兰开始创作花卉、水果或两者兼而有之的大幅葱翠静物写生。 派 lushness(*n.* 草木茂盛) 参 blush(*v./n.* 脸红)；slush(*n.* 烂泥)
igneous [ˈɪɡnɪəs]	*a.* 火的，似火的；火成的，火成岩的 记 词根记忆：ign(火) + eous → 火的 例 Intrusive *igneous* rocks are formed from magma that cools and solidifies within the crust of a planet. 侵入火成岩由在行星表面冷却并凝固的岩浆形成。
salient [ˈseɪlɪənt]	*a.* 显著的，突出的(distinct, outstanding) 记 词根记忆：sal(跳) + ient → 跳出来的 → 突出的 例 He pointed out the *salient* features of the new design. 他指出了新设计的几个显著特征。
rescue [ˈreskjuː]	*vt./n.* 营救，搭救(save) 记 联想记忆：res(看做 rest，休息) + cue(线索) → 放弃休息紧追线索，进行营救 → 营救 例 We only try to *rescue* the most valuable first-edition books in our collection. 我们只尽力抢救收藏中最珍贵的首版书。 rescue HELP!
acquire [əˈkwaɪər]	*vt.* 获得，取得(*obtain, gain) 记 词根记忆：ac(表加强) + quir(追求) + e → 不断寻求才能获得 → 获得 例 They have just *acquired* a starting capital of $900,000. 他们刚刚获得90万美元的启动资金。 派 acquired(*a.* 后天习得的，已获得的)；acquisition(*n.* 获得，习得) 参 require(*vt.* 需要)；inquire(*v.* 询问)
geometry [dʒiˈɑːmətri]	*n.* 几何，几何学 记 词根记忆：geo(地) + metr(测量) + y → 测量地表的学科 → 几何学 例 I had the wrong date for my *geometry* test. 我记错几何测试的日期了。 派 geometric(*a.* 几何的，几何图案的)；geometrically(*ad.* 几何学上)；geometrician(*n.* 几何学者)
inner [ˈɪnər]	*a.* 内部的；内心的 *n.* 内部；内心 记 词根记忆：in(在…里面) + ner → 内部的；内心的 例 The drama reflected the *inner* frustrations of the dramatist. 这部戏剧反映了剧作家内心的挫败感。 派 innermost(*a.* 最里面的)

combine [kəmˈbaɪn]	*v.* (使)联合，(使)结合(*fuse, unite) 记 词根记忆：com(共同) + bi(两个) + ne → 使两个在一起 → (使)结合 例 In public ceremonies singing is *combined* with dancing and with music from a variety of instruments. 在公共仪式上，歌唱与舞蹈以及各种乐器演奏的音乐结合在一起。
shrivel [ˈʃrɪvl]	*v.* (使)枯萎 记 联想记忆：sh(音似：使) + rivel(看做 river，河流) → 天气干旱使河流无水，树木枯萎 → (使)枯萎 例 The hot weather had *shriveled* the leaves on the plants. 天气炎热，植物的叶子都蔫了。 派 shriveled(*a.* 干巴的；枯萎的)
infancy [ˈɪnfənsi]	*n.* 幼年(babyhood)；(发展或生长的)初期(beginning) 记 来自 infant(*n.* 婴儿，幼儿) 搭 in one's infancy 处于初创期 例 In the Earth's *infancy*, its surface was warm enough for life. 地球形成初期，其表面很温暖，能维持生命。
syrup [ˈsɪrəp]	*n.* 糖浆 记 联想记忆：sy + rup(看做 cup，杯) → 一杯一杯地喝糖浆 → 糖浆 例 The *syrup* may also be sugar-free. 糖浆也可以是无糖的。
hemp [hemp]	*n.* 大麻(纤维)；由大麻制成的麻醉药 例 It is illegal to grow *hemp* in the United States, although some related medicines are legally imported. 在美国种植大麻是非法的，尽管与其相关的药物可以合法进口。
ethical [ˈeθɪkl]	*a.* 道德的(moral) 例 In his positive *ethical* viewpoint, George tries to support the opinion that human beings should live in harmony with nature. 乔治具有积极的道德观，他尽力支持人类应该与自然和谐共处的观点。 参 ethnic(*a.* 人种的，种族的)
weed [wiːd]	*n.* 杂草；水草 记 联想记忆：种子(seed)在杂草(weed)中顽强生长 例 The yard was overgrown with *weeds*. 庭院里杂草丛生。
trend [trend]	*n.* 趋势，倾向(*tendency) 记 联想记忆：倾向(tend)加 r 还是倾向(trend) 搭 economic trend 经济趋势 例 Other *trends* and inventions had also helped make it possible for Americans to vary their daily diets. 其他趋势和发明也使得美国人改变日常膳食成为可能。

motivate [ˈmoʊtɪveɪt]	*vt.* 激励(*stimulate, impel); 激发(inspire) 记 词根记忆: mot(移动) + iv + ate(使…) → 激励; 激发 例 The students need to be *motivated*. 学生需要激励。 派 motivated(*a.* 有动机的; 由…推动的); motivation(*n.* 动机; 刺激)

motivate
连续工作240小时奖励: $1000000

dilate [daɪˈleɪt]	*v.* (使)膨胀, 扩大(expand); 详述 记 词根记忆: di(分开) + lat(搬运) + e → 分别搬运 → (使)膨胀 搭 dilate on/upon 详述 例 The doctor told me red wine could help to *dilate* my blood vessels. 医生告诉我说, 红葡萄酒有助于扩张血管。 参 dilute(*vt.* 冲淡, 稀释)
peak [piːk]	*a.* 最高的, 高峰的 *n.* 最高点, 顶峰(*maximum, summit) 记 发音记忆: "匹克" → 奥林匹克的精神之一就是挑战极限, 到达顶峰 → 顶峰 例 After the *peak* year of 1957, the birth rate in Canada began to decline. 加拿大的出生率在 1957 年达到顶峰, 之后开始下降。
homing [ˈhoʊmɪŋ]	*a.* 有返回原地本能的 搭 homing pigeon 信鸽 例 Many birds have a remarkable *homing* instinct. 很多鸟类都具有了不起的返回原地的本能。
flagellum [fləˈdʒeləm]	*n.* [*pl.* flagella] 鞭毛 记 词根记忆: flagell(鞭子) + um → 鞭毛 例 Many bacteria lack *flagella* and cannot move about by their own power. 很多细菌没有鞭毛, 不能靠自身的力量移动。
intricate [ˈɪntrɪkət]	*a.* 错综复杂的(*complex) 记 词根记忆: in(在…里面) + tric(小障碍物) + ate → 里面有小障碍物的 → 错综复杂的 例 A city is more *intricate* than a village. 城市比村庄更加错综复杂。
tournament [ˈtɜːrnəmənt]	*n.* 比赛(game, match); 锦标赛(title match) 记 联想记忆: 这样巡回(tour)参加比赛(tournament)真是个折磨(torment) 例 I almost forgot to tell you about the all-day volleyball *tournament* going on. 我差点忘了告诉你现在全天都在举行排球锦标赛。
advocate	[ˈædvəkeɪt] *vt.* 提倡(recommend publicly) [ˈædvəkət] *n.* 倡导者(*proponent) 记 词根记忆: ad(表加强) + voc(叫喊) + ate → 大声呼喊 → 提倡 例 They *advocate* the use of masonry in the construction of skyscrapers. 他们提倡在建造摩天大楼时使用石工技术。 派 advocacy(*n.* 拥护, 支持)

□ motivate　　□ dilate　　□ peak　　□ homing　　□ flagellum　　□ intricate
□ tournament　　□ advocate

crush
[krʌʃ]

vt. 碾碎（grind）；使变形；镇压

记 联想记忆：碰撞（crash）后被碾碎（crush）

例 The weight of a tornado can *crush* a building's roof when it passes overhead. 龙卷风经过时能将建筑物的屋顶摧毁。

参 crash（*v./n.* 碰撞）

---

ingredient
[ɪnˈɡriːdiənt]

n. 成分，要素（element）；（烹调的）原料

记 词根记忆：in（里，内）+ gred（=grad 进入）+ ient → 构成物体的内部物质 → 成分

例 The weather map became an essential *ingredient* in the redesign of the American newspaper. 气象图成为美国报纸改版的基本要素。// You can get all the *ingredients* at any supermarkets. 你可以在任何超市买到所有原料。

---

terminal
[ˈtɜːrmɪnl]

n. 终点站（destination）；终点；航站楼 *a.* 末端的（endmost）

记 词根记忆：termin（边界）+ al → 末端的

搭 passenger terminal 客运枢纽站

例 You'd be better off calling the *terminal* for a new schedule. 你最好给终点站打电话索取新的时刻表。

参 terminus（*n.* 终点站）；terminate（*v.* 终止，结束）

---

rub
[rʌb]

n./v. 擦，摩擦

记 rubber（*n.* 橡皮）就是来自这个词

例 If you *rub* some soap on that drawer, it might stop sticking. 如果你在抽屉上擦点肥皂，抽屉可能就不会再卡住了。

---

mighty
[ˈmaɪti]

a. 强有力的（powerful）；巨大的

例 This circumstance was mitigated by the *mighty* river and lake systems. 强有力的河流和湖泊系统减轻了这种状况。

---

accident
[ˈæksɪdənt]

n. 意外事件，事故

记 词根记忆：ac（向）+ cid（落，掉）+ ent → 东西从天而降落向某人 → 意外事件

例 According to the new statistics, one in seven *accidents* is caused by drunken drivers. 最新统计数据表明，七起事故中就有一起是由醉酒驾驶造成的。

accident

派 accidental（*a.* 意外的，偶然的）；accidentally（*ad.* 意外地，偶然地）

---

inflammation
[ˌɪnfləˈmeɪʃn]

n. 炎症，发炎

例 The connection between *inflammation* and heart disease, arthritis, and other chronic ailments has become increasingly clear. 炎症与心脏病、关节炎及其他慢性病之间的关系已变得越来越清晰。

☐ crush ☐ ingredient ☐ terminal ☐ rub ☐ mighty ☐ accident
☐ inflammation

shield [ʃiːld]	*n.* 防护物(defense)；盾 *vt.* 保护(*protect, defend) 例 The mountains surrounding Los Angeles effectively *shield* the city from the heat. 周边的山脉有效地使洛杉矶这个城市免受酷热之苦。
mammoth [ˈmæməθ]	*a.* 巨大的(enormous, huge) *n.* 猛犸，毛象 记 发音记忆：原指古代的猛犸象，十分巨大 例 The *mammoth* statue known as the Statue of Liberty is located in New York. 那广为人知的巨大雕像——自由女神像就位于纽约。
nightmare [ˈnaɪtmer]	*n.* 噩梦；无法摆脱的恐惧；可怕的事 例 The journey turned into a *nightmare* when they lost their wallet. 他们的皮夹子丢了，这次旅游成了一场噩梦。// A: Why are you leaving so early? The movie doesn't start till seven. B: I don't want to be at the traffic there. It's a *nightmare* on the express way during rush hour. A: 你为什么走这么早？电影7点才开始。 B: 我不想堵在路上。高峰时段在高速路上简直是个噩梦。
accord [əˈkɔːrd]	*n.* 协议，条约 *v.* 与…一致，符合(agree) 记 词根记忆：ac + cord(心) → 双方达成一条心 → 协议，条约 搭 in accord with 与…一致，符合；of one's own accord 自动地 例 An *accord* with the labor union was reached at about midnight. 约在午夜时分，与工会达成了一致。 参 concord(*n.* 和睦；公约)
versus [ˈvɜːrsəs]	*prep.* 对，对抗；与…相对，与…相比 记 词根记忆：vers（转）+ us → 转向→ 与…相对；常缩写成 vs 例 It is England *versus* Brazil in the final. 决赛是英格兰队对巴西队。// When the scientists looked at the shoot *versus* the root surface, they found that the shoot surface, with all of its leaves, had a total surface area of about five square meters. 科学家们对比芽部和根部的表面时发现，将所有叶片面积计算在内，芽部的总表面积约为五平方米。
musician [mjuˈzɪʃn]	*n.* 音乐家，乐师 例 Even great *musicians* require constant practice. 伟大的音乐家也需要不断练习。

Word List 3

音频

词根、词缀预习表

pli	满，填满	compliment vt./n. 赞美	trig	小障碍物	intrigue n. 阴谋
gen	出生	genius n. 天赋	not	知道	connote v. 暗示
put	想	repute v. 认为	ced	走	secede vi. 正式脱离
mort	死亡	mortality n. 死亡率	sol	安慰	console vt. 安慰，抚慰
vis	看	visual a. 视觉的	men	引导	amenable a. 顺从的

---

dwarf
[dwɔːrf]

vt. 使显得矮小，使相形见绌(outshine) a. 矮小的 n. 侏儒，矮人
搭 dwarf star 矮星
例 Cotton became the main American export, *dwarfing* all other products.
棉花超过所有其他产品，成为美国主要的出口商品。

---

classic
['klæsɪk]

a. 经典的；典型的(typical) n. 经典作品；[pl.]古典文学
例 The girl displayed the *classic* symptoms of depression. 那个女孩表现出了忧郁症的典型症状。// The novel may become a *classic*. 这部小说可能会成为经典。

---

muggy
['mʌgi]

a. (天气)闷热的(fuggy)
例 I was expecting another hot, *muggy* day, but the wind's cooled things off. 我本以为这又是炎热潮湿的一天，但是风已经使天气凉爽了。

---

skyscraper
['skaɪskreɪpər]

n. 摩天楼
记 联想记忆：sky(天) + scrape(摩擦) + r → 楼高得可以擦到天 → 摩天楼
例 *Skyscrapers* became popular in this country during the 1990s. 20 世纪 90 年代摩天楼在该国开始流行起来。

---

compliment

['kɑmplɪment] vt. 赞美，称赞
['kɑmplɪmənt] n. 赞美(praise)；[常 pl.]问候(regards)
记 词根记忆：com(共同) + pli(满，填满) + ment (名词后缀) → 一起满足某人的愿望 → 赞美
例 The young man *complimented* her on her good table manners. 那个年轻男子夸奖她得体的餐桌礼仪。// Thanks for your *compliments*. 谢谢你的赞誉。
派 complimentary(a. 赞赏的)
参 complement(vt. 补充)；implement(n. 工具 vt. 实现)

compliment

□ dwarf   □ classic   □ muggy   □ skyscraper   □ compliment   25

pest [pest]	*n.* 害虫;令人讨厌的人(或物)(nuisance) pest killer 记 发音记忆:"拍死它" → 见到害虫就拍死它 → 害虫 例 The boy is being a real *pest*. 那个小男孩真是 讨厌。 参 pesticide(*n.* 杀虫剂);insect(*n.* 昆虫);bug (*n.* 小虫,臭虫)
genius ['dʒiːniəs]	*n.* 天才(talent);天赋(endowment) 记 词根记忆:gen(出生) + ius → 天生具有的才能 → 天赋 例 They insisted that *The Iliad* and *The Odyssey* could have been the work of a single poetic *genius*. 他们坚持认为《伊利亚特》和《奥德赛》是一位天才诗 人的作品。
repute [rɪ'pjuːt]	*v.* (被)称为,认为(consider) *n.* 名声,名誉(reputation) 记 词根记忆:re(再,又) + put(想) + e → 反复想 → 认为 例 The hotel was *reputed* to be the best in the country. 这家酒店据说是该 国最好的。// My father is a writer of international *repute*. 我父亲是一位享 有国际声誉的作家。 派 reputation(*n.* 名誉);reputedly(*ad.* 据说);disrepute(*n.* 丧失名誉)
fauna ['fɔːnə]	*n.* 动物群 记 来自 Faunus(潘纳斯,罗马神话中的动物之神) 例 The region's rich *fauna* attracts frequent visits of large vertebrates, such as whale sharks and dolphins. 该地区丰富的动物群吸引鲸鲨、海豚 等大型脊椎动物经常来访。 参 flora(*n.* 植物群)
healthful ['helθfl]	*a.* 有益健康的 例 The old man lived to 84 years old with little illness, largely due to his *healthful* living habits. 那个老人活到 84 高龄,而且少病痛,很大程度上要 归功于其健康的生活习惯。
sympathetic [ˌsɪmpə'θetɪk]	*a.* 感应的,交感的;有同情心的;体谅的 记 词根记忆:sym(共同) + path(感觉) + et + ic → 有着共同感觉的 → 感应 搭 sympathetic vibration 共振 例 He is *sympathetic* and understanding. 他富有同情心,善解人意。
mortality [mɔːr'tæləti]	*n.* 死亡率 记 词根记忆:mort(死亡) + al + ity(表性质,名词后缀) → 死亡率 例 *Mortality* from lung cancer is still increasing. 死于肺癌的人数仍在增长。
wanna ['wɔːnə]	*v.* (=want to)想要 例 Hey, Larry. *Wanna* meet a few of us for coffee in a little while? 你好, 拉里。一会儿想和我们几个喝点咖啡吗?

predecessor ['predəsesər]	*n.* 前辈(*antecedent)；前任；(被取代的)原有事物 记 词根记忆：pre(在…前面) + de + cess(走) + or(表人，名词后缀) → 走在前面的人 → 前辈 例 The eighteenth century houses showed great interior improvements over their *predecessors*. 18 世纪的房屋内部改进很大，胜过之前的房屋。
scrub [skrʌb]	*v.* 擦洗；取消(计划等) *n.* 灌木丛(shrub)；丛林地带 记 联想记忆：走过灌木丛(scrub)，腿上被擦破(rub)好几处 例 Mom is *scrubbing* the floor in the kitchen. 妈妈正在厨房里擦地板。
check [tʃek]	*n.* (=cheque)支票；账单；检查 *v.* 检查；制止 搭 check in 登记，报到；check out 付账后离开；查证；check up on 核实，查证 例 A mass of foreign tourists cash *checks* at the big bank. 很多外国游客在这家大银行把支票兑换成现金。// I have to get a *check* cashed to pay my bookstore bill. 我得兑现一张支票来支付书店的账单。// *Check* your work before handing it in. 交作业前先检查一遍。
dive [daɪv]	*vi./n.* 跳水；潜水(submerge) 例 The main purpose of my holiday to Greece was to go *diving*. 我去希腊度假的主要目的就是去潜水。 派 diver(*n.* 潜水员；跳水运动员) dive
rough [rʌf]	*a.* 粗糙不平的(coarse)；粗暴的(tough)；艰难的 *n.* 高低不平的地面 例 Life in nineteenth century forts was very *rough*. 19 世纪要塞里的生活非常艰苦。 派 roughness(*n.* 粗糙；粗暴)
stain [steɪn]	*v.* 沾污；留下污渍 *n.* 污点，污渍(spot) 记 联想记忆：一下雨(rain)，到处都是污点(stain) 例 The events had *stained* her reputation unfairly. 这些事件使她背上了不该有的恶名。 派 stained(*a.* 满是污渍的；着色的)
multiple ['mʌltɪpl]	*a.* 多样的；多重的(various, manifold) *n.* 倍数 记 词根记忆：multi(多的) + ple(折叠) → 多样的；多重的 例 Glass can be decorated in multiple ways. 玻璃可以通过多种方式进行装饰。
visual ['vɪʒuəl]	*a.* 视觉的 记 词根记忆：vis(看) + ual → 视觉的 搭 visual arts 视觉艺术；visual image 可视图像 例 Without Julie's photograph, no *visual* record of the work would exist. 如果没有朱莉的照片，这个作品就不存在视觉记录了。 派 visualize〔 *v.* 想象，(使)形象化〕；visually(*ad.* 视觉上)

□ predecessor □ scrub □ check □ dive □ rough □ stain
□ multiple □ visual

rationality [ˌræʃəˈnæləti]	*n.* 理性；合理性 记 来自 rational (*a.* 合理的；理性的) 例 The professor tells us: use your *rationality* not your experiences to deal with it when you confront a problem like this. 教授告诉我们：当遇到这种问题时，要用自己的理性来解决问题，而不是诉诸经验。
tout [taʊt]	*v.* 吹捧；兜售 记 联想记忆：t + out(在外面) → 去外面兜售商品 → 兜售 例 Passengers should avoid the mini-cabs that *tout* for business. 旅客应离兜售商品的小车远点。
stubborn [ˈstʌbərn]	*a.* 顽固的，倔强的；难对付的 记 联想记忆：生来(born)倔强(stubborn) 例 The *stubborn* mayor finally agreed to have a dialogue with the strike workers. 固执的市长最终同意与罢工工人进行对话。
outrage [ˈaʊtreɪdʒ]	*n.* 暴行；愤慨 *vt.* 激怒 记 组合词：out(在外面) + rage(狂怒) → 过分狂怒 → 愤慨 例 Teachers responded with *outrage*, saying it was against the purpose of education. 老师们愤怒地回应，称这种做法违反了教育的宗旨。
intrigue 	[ˈɪntriːg] *n.* 阴谋，诡计 [ɪnˈtriːg] *v.* 密谋；迷住 记 词根记忆：in(进入) + trig(=tric 小障碍物) + ue → 在里面放小障碍物 → 搞阴谋诡计 → 阴谋 例 This *intrigue* has been going on for centuries. 这一阴谋已持续了数世纪。
connote [kəˈnoʊt]	*v.* 意味着；暗示 记 词根记忆：con(with) + not(知道) + e → 有含义 → 暗示 例 The term "Third World" very soon comes to *connote* poverty. 很快，"第三世界"这个词就意味着贫穷。
persistent [pərˈsɪstənt]	*a.* 坚持的，百折不挠的；持续的 记 词根记忆：per(贯穿) + sist(站立) + ent → 始终站着的 → 坚持的；持续的 例 Be *persistent* and you will get the opportunity you desired. 坚持下去，你就会得到你所梦寐以求的机会。
secede [sɪˈsiːd]	*vi.* 正式脱离，退出(组织等) 记 词根记忆：se(分开) + ced(走) + e → 走开，脱离 → 正式脱离 例 The country won't allow the state to *secede* from it and become an independent nation. 该国绝对不允许这个州脱离它而成为独立的国家。
disquiet [dɪsˈkwaɪət]	*v.* (使)不安，(使)忧虑 *n.* 不安，忧虑(unease) 记 联想记忆：dis(不) + quiet(安静的) → 不安 例 I must say that bad news *disquieted* him a lot. 我得说这个坏消息使他很不安。
bode [boʊd]	*vi.* 预示 搭 bode well/ill (for sb./sth.) (对某人/某事)是吉兆/凶兆 例 The figures nonetheless *bode* well for the future. 这些数字对将来并不意味着吉兆。

□ rationality   □ tout   □ stubborn   □ outrage   □ intrigue   □ connote
□ persistent   □ secede   □ disquiet   □ bode

folkway [ˈfoʊkˌweɪ]	*n.* 社会风俗 记 组合词: folk(民间) + way(方式) → 民间的行事方式 → 社会习俗 例 The next day, we visited the *folkway* museum of my hometown. 第二天，我们参观了我家乡的民俗博物馆。
console [kənˈsoʊl]	*vt.* 安慰，抚慰 记 词根记忆: con + sol(安慰) + e → 安慰，抚慰 例 We tried to *console* her when her father died, but she didn't listen to us. 她父亲去世时我们尽力安慰她，但她不听我们的。 派 consolation(*n.* 安慰，慰藉之事)
overrun [ˌoʊvəˈrʌn]	*v.* 超过，溢出；泛滥；横行 *n.* 泛滥；超出的部分 记 联想记忆: over(过度) + run(跑) → 跑过了头 → 超过；泛滥 例 His speech was boring and *overran* the time limit. 他的演讲很枯燥，而且超时了。
turmoil [ˈtɜːrmɔɪl]	*n.* 骚动，混乱(disorder, turbulence)；焦虑 例 He came back after three years of political *turmoil*. 他在三年的政治动乱之后归来。
amenable [əˈmiːnəbl]	*a.* 顺从的，服从劝导的；有服从义务的 记 词根记忆: a(向) + men(引导) + able(能…的) → 能往某个方面引导的 → 顺从的 例 All the citizens are *amenable* to the law. 所有公民都有义务遵纪守法。
interrelate [ˌɪntərɪˈleɪt]	*v.* (使)相互关联，紧密联系 记 联想记忆: inter(在…之间) + relate(有联系) → 互相有联系 → (使)相互关联 例 It is suggested by the study that crime and poverty are *interrelated*. 研究发现犯罪与贫穷是密切相关的。
nude [nuːd]	*a.* 裸体的 记 联想记忆: 有人认为裸体(nude)是不礼貌的(rude) 例 Some *nude* scenes have been deleted from the movie. 电影中的一些裸露镜头已经被剪掉了。
redundant [rɪˈdʌndənt]	*a.* 多余的；累赘的 记 词根记忆: red(=re 再，又) + und(波动) + ant(形容词后缀) → 反复波动，反复出现 → 多余的 例 You used too many *redundant* words in this passage. 你在这篇文章里用了太多不必要的词。
inverse [ˌɪnˈvɜːrs]	*a.* 相反的，反向的 *n.* 反面(reverse)；倒数 记 词根记忆: in(反) + vers(转) + e → 反转 → 相反的，反向的 例 A person's happiness is often in *inverse* proportion to his age. 一个人的幸福感经常与其年龄成反比。 // Sometimes when the direct method fails, you should try the *inverse* one. 有时当直接做法失败时，你应该尝试相反的做法。

console

revive [rɪ'vaɪv]	*v.* 恢复；(使)苏醒；重新利用 记 词根记忆：re(再，又) + viv(生命；生活) + e → 恢复；(使)苏醒 例 The economy is beginning to *revive*. 经济开始复苏。// The doctors couldn't *revive* the little boy. 医生无法使那个小男孩苏醒过来。
insulin ['ɪnsəlɪn]	*n.* 胰岛素 记 词根记忆：insul(岛) + in → 胰岛素 例 *Insulin* injection is used to control blood sugar in people who have type I diabetes. 胰岛素注射被用于控制 I 型糖尿病患者的血糖。
explore [ɪk'splɔːr]	*v.* 探索，勘探；探险（adventure）；探究（*probe for, search） 记 词根记忆：ex(出) + plor(哭泣，流泪) + e → 使流泪 → 探索 例 We'll *explore* through lecture and discussion what prominent political thinkers had to say about the topic. 我们将通过讲座和讨论的方式来探究著名政治思想家们对这个话题的看法。 派 explorer(*n.* 探险家); exploration(*n.* 探索); exploratory(*a.* 探险的，探测的)
cart [kɑːrt]	*n.* 运货马车(wagon)；手推车 *vt.* 用车装运 例 The rubbish is then *carted* away for recycling. 垃圾接着被运去进行回收处理。
pertinent ['pɜːrtnənt]	*a.* 相关的(*relevant)；恰当的，贴切的 记 词根记忆：per(始终) + tin(拿住) + ent → 始终拿着 → 相关的 例 The *pertinent* considerations that will be affected by each decision are listed. 会受到每个决定影响的相关考虑因素都被列了出来。
mercy ['mɜːrsi]	*n.* 宽恕(*condone)；仁慈(sympathy)；恩惠，幸运 搭 at the mercy of 受⋯支配；mercy killing 安乐死 例 Our pilots are at the *mercy* of the winds, so who knows where they'll drift off to. 我们的飞行员受制于风，谁知道他们会飘到哪里呢。// It's a *mercy* he wasn't seriously hurt. 幸运的是他伤势不重。
rebellious [rɪ'beljəs]	*a.* 反叛的，叛逆的；叛乱的 记 来自 rebel (*v.* 反叛) 例 It is hard to control those rebellious teenagers. 那些叛逆的青少年很难管教。
barrel ['bærəl]	*n.* 桶 记 联想记忆：bar(横木) + rel → 用横木围一个桶 → 桶 例 We got through two *barrels* of beer. 我们喝了两桶啤酒。 派 barrelful(*n.* 一桶之量)
transition [træn'zɪʃn]	*n.* 过渡，过渡时期；转变(change, conversion) 记 词根记忆：trans(穿过) + it(走) + ion → 穿过一地走到另一地 → 转变 例 The *transition* to settled life also has a profound impact on the family. 向稳定生活的转变对这个家庭也有着深远的影响。 派 transitional(*a.* 过渡期的)

☐ revive ☐ insulin ☐ explore ☐ cart ☐ pertinent ☐ mercy
☐ rebellious ☐ barrel ☐ transition

lyric [ˈlɪrɪk]	*a.* 抒情的 *n.* 抒情诗；[常 *pl.*]歌词 记 联想记忆：ly(看做lying, 躺) + ric → 躺在星空下 → 抒情的 例 Margaret wrote the *lyrics* for 21 children's records. 玛格丽特为 21 张儿童唱片创作了歌词。 派 lyrically(*ad.* 抒情地)；lyricism(*n.* 抒情)
adorn [əˈdɔːrn]	*vt.* 装饰，装扮(*decorate, beautify) 记 词根记忆：ad + orn(装饰) → 装饰，装扮 例 Children *adorned* themselves with beads. 儿童用珠子装扮他们自己。 派 adornment(*n.* 装饰)；unadorned(*a.* 未装饰的，朴实的) 参 ardor(*n.* 热情)；adore(*v.* 崇拜)
questionnaire [ˌkwestʃəˈner]	*n.* 问卷，调查表 记 来自 question(*n.* 问题) 例 The professor wants them to fill in a research *questionnaire*. 教授想让他们填写一份研究调查表。
minority [maɪˈnɔːrəti]	*n.* 少数(fewness)；少数民族 记 来自 minor(*a.* 较少的) 例 Unfortunately, based on the general response, you and I are definitely in the *minority*. 不幸的是，基于一般人的反应，你我肯定属于少数派。
entitle [ɪnˈtaɪtl]	*vt.* 使…有权；给(书等)题名 记 联想记忆：en(使…) + title(头衔；权利) → 使…有权；给(书等)题名 例 Most students buy meal contracts, which *entitle* them to twenty meals a week at any of the cafeterias. 大多数学生购买饭票契约，这使他们能够每周在任意一个餐厅用餐 20 次。 派 entitled(*a.* 有资格的；名为…的)
renew [rɪˈnjuː]	*vt.* 使…续期；重新开始(resume)；重申(repeat)；修复(restore) 例 I'd like to *renew* these library books. 我想续借这几本图书馆的书。 派 renewable(*a.* 可再生的；可续订的)；renewal(*n.* 更新；复兴)
consistent [kənˈsɪstənt]	*a.* 一致的(coherent)；稳定的(sustained)；调和的(compatible)；始终如一的(*constant) 例 Now, keep in mind that a theory of the Moon's origin has to be *consistent* with two important facts. 现在请记住，有关月球起源的理论必须与两个重要事实保持一致。// The quality of the cooking at Sullivan's is *consistent*. 苏利文的烹饪水平始终如一。 派 consistency(*n.* 一致性；坚固性)；inconsistent(*a.* 不一致的，矛盾的)
quotation [kwoʊˈteɪʃn]	*n.* 引文，引语，语录；报价 记 来自 quote(*v.* 引用) 例 His *quotation* for repairing my car was too high. 他为修理我的汽车索价太高。

□ lyric　　　　□ adorn　　　　□ questionnaire　□ minority　　　■ entitle　　　□ renew
□ consistent　　□ quotation

so-called [ˌsoʊˈkɔːld]	*a.* 所谓的(commonly named) 例 How have those *so-called* improvements helped the local community? 这些所谓的进步对当地社会有什么帮助?
magnitude [ˈmægnɪtjuːd]	*n.* 巨大; 重要性; 星等, 星球的亮度 记 词根记忆: magn(大) + it + ude(表状态, 名词后缀) → 巨大 例 The star has a *magnitude* of 2. 那颗恒星的亮度等级为2。
rectangle [ˈrektæŋgl]	*n.* 长方形, 矩形 记 词根记忆: rect(直的) + angl(角) + e → 四个角都为直角 → 长方形 例 My garage is in the shape of a *rectangle*. 我的车库形状是矩形。 派 rectangular(*a.* 长方形的, 矩形的)
telescope [ˈtelɪskoʊp]	*n.* 望远镜 记 词根记忆: tele(远) + scop(看) + e → 往远处看所借助的工具 → 望远镜 例 I looked at the stars through a *telescope*. 我用望远镜观察星星。 派 telescopic(*a.* 望远镜的; 能望见远处的)
lightning [ˈlaɪtnɪŋ]	*n.* 闪电 *a.* 闪电般的, 快速的 记 联想记忆: light(光) + ning → 极强的光 → 闪电 例 Although thunder and *lightning* are produced at the same time, light waves travel faster than sound waves do. 尽管雷鸣和闪电同时产生, 但光波传播速度要快于声波。
utensil [juːˈtensl]	*n.* (家庭)用具(appliance); 器皿 记 词根记忆: ut(用) + ensil → (家庭)用具 搭 cooking utensils 炊具; kitchen utensils 厨房用具 例 During the middle ages, mined metal was scarce and expensive, therefore was rarely used in the manufacture of household *utensils*. 中世纪时, 挖掘出的金属稀少且昂贵, 所以它们很少用于制造家庭用具。
kennel [ˈkenl]	*n.* 狗窝; 养狗场 记 词根记忆: ken(=can 犬) + nel → 狗窝; 注意不要和 kernel(*n.* 核; 核心)相混 例 When the dog escaped, the bird went into the *kennel* and ate its food. 这条狗逃跑之后, 鸟钻进狗窝吃了它的食物。
liquid [ˈlɪkwɪd]	*a.* 液体的, 液态的, 流体的; 清澈的; 流畅的 *n.* 液体; 液态 记 联想记忆: liqu(液体) + id → 液体; 液态 例 The energy is used to convert *liquid* water to water vapor. 这个能量是用来把液态水转化为水蒸气的。
remark [rɪˈmɑːrk]	*v.* 评论(comment); 谈论; 察觉 *n.* 评论, 评语; 注释 记 联想记忆: re(再, 又) + mark(做标记) → 一再做标记 → 评论 例 The customer agreed, and after drinking it, *remarked* how good it tasted. 这位顾客同意了, 而且饮用之后还评价说味道相当不错。

principal [ˈprɪnsəpl]	*a.* 主要的，最重要的（*major, *main）*n.* 校长；资本；主角 记 词根记忆：prin（第一）+ cip（拿，取）+ al → 需要第一位选取的 → 主要的，最重要的 例 Coal became the *principal* source of electricity in the United States. 煤成了美国电力的主要来源。 参 principle（*n.* 原则）
hide [haɪd]	*v.* 躲藏；掩藏（conceal）；掩盖（cover）*n.* 兽皮（skin） 例 She couldn't *hide* her excitement. 她无法掩饰自己的兴奋之情。
spoil [spɔɪl]	*v.* 破坏（damage, destroy, ruin）；宠坏，溺爱；变质（decay） 记 联想记忆：破坏（spoil）土地（soil），损人不利己 例 The bad weather *spoiled* our camping trip which we had longed for. 糟糕的天气破坏了我们期待已久的露营旅行。// The bread can be stored a long time without *spoiling*. 面包可以存放很长时间而不变质。 派 spoilage（*n.* 变质，腐败）
internship [ˈɪntɜːrnʃɪp]	*n.* 实习期 例 Why might the summer *internship* be a good opportunity for Jenise? 为什么暑期实习对詹尼斯而言可能是个好机会？ 参 membership（*n.* 会员身份）
polish [ˈpɑːlɪʃ]	*v.* 磨光，擦亮（burnish, gloss）；修改，润色 *n.* 上光剂 记 联想记忆：波兰的（Polish）上光剂（polish） 例 The statement was carefully *polished* and checked before release. 这项声明是经仔细润色检查后才发表的。// The shoe *polish* doesn't match the shoes. 鞋油与鞋子不匹配。 派 polished（*a.* 磨光的，光亮的；娴熟的）
starch [stɑːrtʃ]	*n.* 淀粉（fecula）；[*pl.*]淀粉类食物 记 联想记忆：star（星星）+ ch → 星星碎了，洒落下来成了淀粉 → 淀粉 例 There is too much *starch* in his diet. 他的饮食中淀粉含量太高。
assimilation [əˌsɪməˈleɪʃn]	*n.* 同化；吸收 记 词根记忆：as + simil（相同）+ ation → 使相同 → 同化 例 I felt confusion and fun during my *assimilation* into American culture. 在吸收美国文化的过程中，我感到既困惑又有趣。
detest [dɪˈtest]	*v.* 憎恶（hate） 记 联想记忆：de + test（考试）→ 学生一般都憎恶考试 → 憎恶 例 My sister *detests* rock music. 我妹妹讨厌摇滚乐。 参 attest（*v.* 证明）；testify（*v.* 证实）；contest（*v.* 争论，争辩）
gigantic [dʒaɪˈɡæntɪk]	*a.* 巨大的，庞大的（*huge, *enormous） 记 词根记忆：gigant（=giant 巨人）+ ic → 巨大的 例 Scientists speculate it might be a *gigantic* hurricane. 科学家们推测那可能是一场大型飓风。

实习医生？ internship

□ principal　　□ hide　　□ spoil　　□ internship　　□ polish　　□ starch
□ assimilation　　□ detest　　□ gigantic

convention [kənˈvenʃn]	*n.* (正式)会议；习俗，惯例(custom)；公约(agreement) 记 词根记忆：con(共同) + vent(来) + ion → 大家共同来到 → (正式)会议；惯例；公约 例 Have you any idea who will attend the *convention*? 你知道谁会参加会议吗? // In last week's films, we saw how Graffith ignored both these limiting *conventions*. 在上周的电影里，我们看到了格拉菲斯是如何忽视这些限制性惯例的。 派 conventional(*a.* 传统的；惯例的；常见的) 参 intervention(*n.* 干预，介入)
diagonal [daɪˈægənl]	*a.* 斜线的，对角线的 *n.* 斜线，对角线 记 词根记忆：dia(穿过) + gon(角) + al → 穿过中心的角 → 斜线，对角线 搭 diagonal stripes 斜纹 例 He told me how to measure the length of the *diagonal* line of a square. 他教我如何测量正方形的对角线长度。
absenteeism [ˌæbsənˈtiːɪzəm]	*n.* 旷课；旷工 记 联想记忆：absent(缺席的) + ee(表人) + ism(抽象名词后缀) → 旷课；旷工 例 Johnson was fired because of his habitual *absenteeism*. 约翰逊因经常旷工被开除了。
bacon [ˈbeɪkən]	*n.* 咸肉，熏肉 搭 bring home the bacon 成功；赚钱糊口 例 There is nothing I like better to get me started in the morning than a big breakfast. Eggs, *bacon*, home-fried potatoes… 没什么比一顿丰盛的早餐更能让我精力充沛地开始新的一天——鸡蛋、熏肉、家制的炸土豆……
silversmith [ˈsɪlvərsmɪθ]	*n.* 银匠；银器商人 例 Only a few *silversmiths* were available in New York or Boston in the late seventeenth century, but in the eighteenth century they could be found in all major colonial cities. 17 世纪晚期，在纽约或波士顿只有为数不多的银匠，但到了 18 世纪银匠的身影遍布所有主要的殖民城市。
cell [sel]	*n.* 细胞；基层组织；单人房间；电池 搭 blood cells 血细胞 例 The *cell* is the functional basic unit of life. 细胞是生命的基本功能单位。
digression [daɪˈgreʃn]	*n.* 离题，扯到枝节上；题外话，枝节内容 记 词根记忆：di(离开) + gress(行走) + ion → 走开 → 离题 例 Although this might seem to be a *digression*, the professor is using an example to explain why plants that are grown in water must have gas bubbled through the water. 表面看来这好像是题外话，实际上教授是在用这个例子来解释水生植物为何必须在水中产生气泡。

stake [steɪk]	*n.* 股份；赌注；利害关系 *vt.* 以…打赌，拿…冒险 搭 at stake 有风险，成败难料；stake out a claim 公开宣布对…的所有权 例 He has a personal *stake* in the success of the movie. 这部电影的成功与否对他个人有重大的利害关系。// The President *staked* out his position on the issue. 总统明确阐述了他在这个问题上的立场。
pesticide ['pestɪsaɪd]	*n.* 杀虫剂，农药 记 词根记忆：pest(瘟疫) + i + cide(杀) → 杀虫剂 例 The aim of this study was to investigate the nature and extent of *pesticide*-related illness. 这项研究旨在调查与农药相关的疾病的本质和影响范围。 参 pesticide-free (*a.* 无农药的)
conflict	[kənˈflɪkt] *vi.* 冲突(clash)；不一致(disagree)；争论(argue) [ˈkɑːnflɪkt] *n.* 冲突(clash)；争论(dispute) 记 词根记忆：con(共同) + flict(打，击) → 互相打 → 冲突 例 All the other work schedules *conflict* with his classes. 其他所有的工作安排都与他的课程相冲突。 conflict
accumulate [əˈkjuːmjəleɪt]	*v.* 积累，积聚，堆积(*build up, *collect) 记 词根记忆：ac(表加强) + cumul(堆积) + ate → 积累，积聚，堆积 例 The glacier had formed as layer upon layer of snow *accumulated* year after year. 一层层的积雪经年累月之后就形成了冰川。 派 accumulation(*n.* 堆积物；积聚) accumulate
eternal [ɪˈtɜːrnl]	*a.* 永恒的，不朽的(lasting) 记 联想记忆：外面(external)世界是永恒的(eternal)诱惑 例 They represent humans in an *eternal* struggle with the forces of nature. 他们代表着与自然力量进行持续斗争的人类。
sting [stɪŋ]	*v.* 刺，蜇；(使)感觉刺痛 *n.* (昆虫的)尾刺；刺痛 记 发音记忆："死叮" → 刺痛 例 I was *stung* on the face by a bee. 我的脸让蜜蜂蜇了一下。
extinct [ɪkˈstɪŋkt]	*a.* 灭绝的，不存在的；(火山)不再活跃的 记 词根记忆：ex(出) + tinct(刺) → 用针刺使没有 → 灭绝的 搭 an extinct species 已灭绝的物种；an extinct volcano 死火山 例 It is estimated that over 99 percent of all species that ever existed have become *extinct*. 据估计，99%以上过去存在的物种都已灭绝。 派 extinction(*n.* 灭绝)

respond [rɪˈspɑːnd]	vi. 回答，答复(reply)；作出反应；响应
	记 词根记忆：re(再，又) + spond(回答，约定) → 再次约定 → 回答，答复
	搭 respond to 回复；响应
	例 They don't *respond* to stress well. 他们不能很好地应对压力。
	派 respondent(n. 回答者)
sunset [ˈsʌnset]	n. 日落(时分)，傍晚(sundown)
	记 组合词：sun(太阳) + set(落，下沉) → 日落
	例 Every evening at *sunset* the little girl upstairs plays the piano. 每天日落 时分，楼上的小女孩都会弹钢琴。

Man errs so long as he strives.

人只要奋斗就会犯错误。

——德国诗人、剧作家 歌德

(Johann Wolfgang Goethe, German poet and dramatist)

Word List 4

音频

词根、词缀预习表

grav	重的	gravity *n.* 重力；严重性	laud	赞美，称赞	laudable *a.* 值得赞美的
sent	想法	assent *n./vi.* 同意	cur	跑	incur *vt.* 招致
ceit	拿	conceit *n.* 自负	plic	重叠	replica *n.* 复制品
qui	安静，平和	tranquil *a.* 安静的，平静的	rud	天然的	crude *a.* 天然的；粗糙的
inter-	在…之间	interim *n.* 过渡时期	mun	服务	community *n.* 社团

expertise
[ˌekspɜːˈtiːz]

n. 专门知识(或技能等)，专长(skill)

记 来自 expert(*n.* 专家)

例 The company provided professional *expertise* to help you run your own business. 该公司提供帮助你经营自己业务的专业知识。

blend
[blend]

v. (使)混合，(使)混杂 *n.* 混合(mix, combine)；混合物

记 发音记忆："不论的" → 不论什么东西都放在一起 → 混合物

例 Their music *blends* traditional and modern styles. 他们的音乐融合了传统和现代风格。// Many birds have feathers whose colors *blend* with their surroundings. 很多鸟羽毛的颜色与周围环境相混杂。

派 blended(*a.* 混合的)

blend 发明新饮料

fungus
[ˈfʌŋɡəs]

n. [*pl.* fungi]真菌；霉菌

记 联想记忆：fun(有趣的) + g + us(我们) → 我们去采了蘑菇，真有趣 → 真菌

例 The doctors still need to do much research on the basics of the disease, including research on transmission of the *fungus*, exactly how the *fungus* interacts with the bats' immune systems. 医生们仍需对这种疾病的本质进行大量研究，其中包括对霉菌传播的研究，确切地说是霉菌如何与蝙蝠的免疫系统互相作用。

参 fungicide(*n.* 杀真菌剂)

elasticity [ˌiːlæ'stɪsəti]	*n.* 弹力；弹性 例 This kind of material eventually lost its *elasticity*. 这种材料最终失去了弹性。
moisture ['mɔɪstʃər]	*n.* 潮湿，湿气(humidity) 例 This *moisture* is supplied by the passage of an airstream over a water surface. 气流经过水面，带来了这股湿气。
gravity ['grævəti]	*n.* 重力；严重性(seriousness)；严肃，庄严 记 词根记忆：grav(重的) + ity → 重力；严重性 例 There is more *gravity* on Mars than on the Moon. 火星上的重力比月球上的大。// He doesn't realize the *gravity* of the situation. 他没有意识到形势的严峻性。
stout [staʊt]	*a.* 结实的，强壮的(strong)；肥胖的；顽强的 记 联想记忆：st + out(出来) → 肌肉都鼓出来了 → 结实的 例 He put up a *stout* defence in court. 他在法庭上进行了顽强的辩护。// Crows have been seen to tear off *stout* green twig. 人们见过乌鸦扯掉结实的绿树枝。 stout
assent [ə'sent]	*n./vi.* 同意，赞成 记 词根记忆：as(向) + sent(想法) → 向他人表明自己的想法 → 同意 例 The manager gave his *assent* to the new project. 经理同意了新的工程项目。
bizarre [bɪ'zɑːr]	*a.* 奇形怪状的，古怪可笑的，怪诞的(weird) 记 联想记忆：集市(bazaar)上满是奇形怪状的(bizarre)货物 例 Watching the horror film alone is quite *bizarre*. 独自一人看恐怖片是件非常奇怪的事。
conceit [kən'siːt]	*n.* 自负，自大 记 词根记忆：con(表加强) + ceit(拿) → 全部拿到 → 自负 例 The young man was told to guard against *conceit*. 那个年轻人被告知要谨防骄傲自大。 派 conceited(*a.* 自负的，骄傲自大的)
husbandry ['hʌzbəndri]	*n.* 耕种，务农，农牧业 记 联想记忆：husband(丈夫) + ry → 男耕女织 → 耕种 例 The professor has an interesting theory about crop *husbandry*. 这位教授对于种植业有一套有趣的理论。
abysmal [ə'bɪzməl]	*a.* 深不可测的；极坏的，糟透的 记 词根记忆：a(没有，不) + bys(尽头) + m + al(形容词后缀) → 没有尽头的 → 深不可测的；极坏的 例 The boy took many courses to remedy his *abysmal* ignorance. 为弥补他极大的无知，这个男孩学了很多课程。

scorn [skɔːrn]	*n.* 轻蔑，鄙视（contempt）*v.* 轻蔑，鄙视（dismiss）；不屑于 记 联想记忆：考分（score）太低被鄙视（scorn）了 搭 pour/heap scorn on 嗤之以鼻，不屑一顾 例 She uses silence as her expression of *scorn*. 她用沉默来表示她的不屑。
tranquil [ˈtræŋkwɪl]	*a.* 安静的，平静的 记 词根记忆：tran（=trans 表加强）+ qui（安静，平和）+ l → 完全安静、平和的 → 安静的，平静的 例 My dream is to be with my family and lead a simple and *tranquil* life. 我的梦想是和家人一起过简单而平静的日子。
swoop [swuːp]	*n.* 突然行动 *v.* 猛扑；突然袭击 例 She even thought she might settle all the problems in a single *swoop*. 她甚至想一下子解决所有的问题。
punch [pʌntʃ]	*vt.* 拳打；打孔；按，压 *n.* 重拳击打；冲床，打孔机 例 He *punched* me on the nose and my nose started to bleed. 他一拳打在我的鼻子上，我的鼻子流血了。
mingle [ˈmɪŋɡl]	*v.* (使)混合；交往 记 联想记忆：铃声（jingle）混合（mingle） 例 It is not easy for Tina to *mingle* at the party because she is very shy. 蒂娜很害羞，因此在聚会上和人交往对她来说并不容易。
interim [ˈɪntərɪm]	*n.* 间歇，过渡期间 *a.* 暂时的，过渡的 记 词根记忆：inter（在…之间）+ im → 中间时期 → 过渡时期 搭 in the interim 在期间 例 I will go to visit London in the *interim* of Christmas. 我会在圣诞节期间去伦敦。
laudable [ˈlɔːdəbl]	*a.* 值得赞美的，值得称赞的 记 联想记忆：laud（赞美，称赞）+ able → 值得赞美的，值得称赞的 例 Though their aims were *laudable*, they may have missed the larger point. 尽管他们的出发点值得称赞，但或许漏掉了更重要的一点。
incur [ɪnˈkɜːr]	*vt.* 招致，招惹，遭受 记 词根记忆：in（在…里面）+ cur（跑）→ 在里面跑 → 招致 例 Smoking could *incur* a great danger to health. 吸烟对健康有极大的危害。
pretext [ˈpriːtekst]	*n.* 借口，托词（excuse） 记 联想记忆：pre（在…前面）+ text（文本）→ 预先想好的说法 → 借口 例 She used her being sick as a *pretext* for not going to work. 她以生病为借口而不去上班。
replica [ˈreplɪkə]	*n.* 复制品 记 词根记忆：re（再，又）+ plic（重叠）+ a → 一再重叠 → 复制品 例 This painting is not the authentic one, but a *replica* made by a young artist. 这幅画并不是真迹，而是一名年轻画家临摹出来的。

siege [siːdʒ]	*n.* 包围，围困；封锁 记 发音记忆："吸脂" → 吸脂让人逃离脂肪的包围 → 包围 例 After the news got exposed, dozens of journalists laid *siege* to his apartment. 自从新闻曝光后，许多记者包围了他的公寓。
lunge [lʌndʒ]	*vi./n.* 猛冲，猛扑 记 联想记忆：长途跋涉后，一看到休息室(lounge)就猛冲(lunge)过去 例 The dog *lunged* at the door suddenly. 那条狗突然向门冲去。
basement ['beɪsmənt]	*n.* 地下室，地窖(cellar)；建筑物的底部(basis) 记 联想记忆：base(底部) + ment(名词后缀) → 房子的底部 → 地下室 例 Wendy is in the *basement* trying to repair the washing machine. 温迪正在地下室试图修理洗衣机。
crude [kruːd]	*a.* 天然的，未提炼的 (unrefined)；粗糙的 (rough)；粗俗的(vulgar) 记 词根记忆：c + rud (天然的；粗糙的) + e → 天然的；粗糙的 搭 crude oil 原油；crude jokes 粗俗的笑话 例 Even now many species still lay eggs in this sort of *crude* nest. 甚至到现在，许多物种仍在这种粗糙的巢穴中产卵。 参 rude(*a.* 粗鲁的)
gibe [dʒaɪb]	*n./v.* (=jibe) 嘲弄，讥笑 搭 gibe at 嘲笑，嘲弄 例 She made several cheap *gibes* at her opponent during the interview. 在采访中她三番五次粗俗地对她的对手加以嘲弄。
community [kə'mjuːnəti]	*n.* 社会(society at large)；社团(corporation)；(动、植物的)群落；共同体 记 词根记忆：com(共同) + mun(服务) + ity → 为大家服务 → 社团 搭 community service 社区服务；sense of community 社区意识 例 The advocates of *community* participation firmly believe that it brings many lasting benefits to people instead of only a means of getting things done. 社区参与的提倡者坚信，社区参与给人们带来很多持久的益处，而不仅仅是一种做事方式。
speckle ['spekl]	*v.* 弄上斑点；点缀 *n.* 斑点；色斑 记 来自 speck (*n.* 斑点) 例 The cook's apron was *speckled* with oil. 厨师的围裙上油光点点。
beaver ['biːvər]	*vi.* 忙干 *n.* 海狸；海狸毛皮 例 Susan has been *beavering* away at her report all morning. 苏珊一上午都在忙着她的报告。
pollutant [pə'luːtənt]	*n.* 污染物质，有害物质 记 来自 pollute(*vt.* 污染) 例 These cars put no *pollutants* whatsoever into the atmosphere. 这些车不向大气排放任何污染物。

basement

40

sardonic [saːrˈdɑːnɪk]	*a.* 嘲笑的，讥讽的 例 Even though she didn't say anything, there was a *sardonic* expression on her face. 尽管她没说什么，但她脸上有嘲讽的表情。
practical [ˈpræktɪkl]	*a.* 实用的；实际的；现实的(realistic) 例 There are some obvious *practical* applications of the research. 这项研究有一些明显的实际用途。
circular [ˈsɜːrkjələr]	*a.* 圆形的，环形的(round)；循环的；绕行的 记 词根记忆：circ(圆，环形) + ular → 圆形的；循环的 例 He took a *circular* route to his office to avoid the traffic jam. 为了避开交通堵塞，他绕道去上班。
disappoint [ˌdɪsəˈpɔɪnt]	*v.* (使)失望，(使)扫兴 记 联想记忆：dis(不) + appoint(任命) → 没被任命，所以失望 → 使失望 例 Her latest novel *disappointed* her fans. 她最近发表的这部小说让她的粉丝们很失望。 派 disappointment(*n.* 失望，扫兴)
nomadic [noʊˈmædɪk]	*a.* 游牧的；流浪的 记 来自 nomad(*n.* 游牧民；流浪者) 例 Some hunters continued the old pastoral and *nomadic* ways. 一些猎户继续过着古老的游牧生活。
soft [sɔːft]	*a.* 柔软的(delicate)；柔和的(mild, gentle)；不强烈的；心肠软的；软性的 搭 soft drink 软饮料 例 A *soft* breeze rustled the trees. 微风吹拂，树叶沙沙作响。 派 soften[*v.* (使)变柔软]；softness(*n.* 柔和；柔软)
talent [ˈtælənt]	*n.* 天赋(gift)；才干(ability)；人才(intellectual) 记 联想记忆：tal(看做 tall，高的) + ent(表人) → 高人 → 人才 例 Bonnie has a *talent* for expressing her ideas. 邦妮非常善于表达自己的观点。 派 talented(*a.* 有才能的，天才的)
confer [kənˈfɜːr]	*v.* 授予(award)；协商，商讨 记 词根记忆：con(共同) + fer(带来) → 带着某物一起来 → 授予 例 In the family, traditional cultural patterns *confer* leadership on one or both of the parents. 在家庭中，传统文化模式把领导权授给父母中的一方或双方。
incessantly [ɪnˈsesntlɪ]	*ad.* 不断地(continually) 例 After his girlfriend left him, Tom asked himself *incessantly* "why does she leave me". 女友离开后，汤姆就不断地问自己"她为什么离开我"。
stadium [ˈsteɪdiəm]	*n.* 竞走场；运动场(playground) 记 词根记忆：stad(站立) + ium(表场所，名词后缀) → 参加走路比赛的地方 → 竞走场，后引申为"运动场" 例 The new national *stadium* was finally completed on the 10th of May. 新的国家运动场最终于 5 月 10 日竣工。

□ sardonic □ practical □ circular □ disappoint □ nomadic □ soft
□ talent □ confer □ incessantly □ stadium

budget [ˈbʌdʒɪt]	*n.* 预算 *v.* 做预算 *a.* 价格低廉的 搭 a budget deficit 预算赤字；education budget 教育预算 例 They should ask for an increase in the *budget*. 他们应该要求增加预算。
dominate [ˈdɑːmɪneɪt]	*v.* 支配，统治（*monopolize）；控制（control, rule）；盛行（*prevail） 记 词根记忆：domin（统治）+ ate（动词后缀）→ 统治；控制 例 The states *dominated* economic activity during this period. 在此期间，各州在经济活动中起主导作用。 派 dominant（*a.* 有统治权的，占优势的）；dominance（*n.* 优势；统治）
intelligence [ɪnˈtelɪdʒəns]	*n.* 智力，智慧；情报 记 来自 intelligent（*a.* 聪明的，有才智的） 搭 intelligence quotient 智商；an intelligence agent 情报员 例 Scientists think dolphins have a higher *intelligence* than ordinary mammals. 科学家认为海豚的智商比普通哺乳动物的要高。 派 intelligencer（*n.* 情报员）
ultimatum [ˌʌltɪˈmeɪtəm]	*n.* 最后通牒 记 词根记忆：ultim（最后的）+ atum → 最后通牒 例 If George misses one more meeting, we'd better give him an *ultimatum*. 如果乔治再错过一次会议，我们最好给他下个最后通牒。
personality [ˌpɜːrsəˈnæləti]	*n.* 个性（individuality）；性格（character）；名人 搭 personality cult 个人崇拜 例 A number of factors related to the voice reveal the *personality* of the speaker. 与声音有关的一些因素揭露了说话者的个性。
decrease	[dɪˈkriːs] *v.* 减少（diminish, reduce）[ˈdiːkriːs] *n.* 减少（量） 记 词根记忆：de（反）+ cre（生长）+ ase → 减少 例 He thinks clothing prices will *decrease* even further. 他认为服装的价格会进一步下跌。
milieu [miːˈljɜː]	*n.* 出身背景（background）；社会环境 例 His most recent novel goes even farther away from the *milieu* of his early work, tracing the politically charged homosexual romance between an upper-class writer and a working-class Communist. 他最近的一部小说更远地脱离了早期作品的社会环境，探讨了一位上层阶级作家和一名工人共产主义者之间充满政治色彩的同性恋爱情故事。
satiric [səˈtɪrɪk]	*a.* (=satirical) 讽刺的，嘲讽的（sarcastic） 记 来自 satire（*n.* 讽刺） 例 He published a *satiric* novel to provide an updated account of the politician's life. 他出版了一本讽刺小说，向人们揭露了那名政客最近的生活。

□ budget   □ dominate   □ intelligence   □ ultimatum   □ personality   □ decrease
□ milieu   □ satiric

alchemist [ˈælkəmɪst]	*n.* 炼金术士 记 联想记忆：al + chemist（化学家）→ 炼金术士
untamed [ˌʌnˈteɪmd]	*a.* 未驯服的，难驾驭的（wild） 记 联想记忆：un + tame（驯服）+ d → 未驯服的，难驾驭的 例 Robert S. Duncanson was considered a painter of the Hudson River School, which concentrated on scenes of America's *untamed* wilderness. 罗伯特·S. 邓肯森被认为是哈得孙河流派画家，这一画派专门描绘美国蛮荒之地的景色。
diffusion [dɪˈfjuːʒn]	*n.* 散布，扩散；传播 搭 air diffusion 空气扩散；cultural diffusion 文化扩散 例 A series of reaction *diffusion* system is involved in the new equipment. 新设备包括一系列反应扩散系统。
stream [striːm]	*v.* 涌（flow）*n.* 溪流（brook）；串，股（strand） 记 联想记忆：梦想（dream）是一条奔流不息的溪流（stream） 例 Approximately 23 million immigrants *streamed* to the United States. 大约 2300 万移民涌入了美国。
clipper [ˈklɪpər]	*n.* 快速帆船；剪刀 例 I am looking for a pair of hair *clippers*. 我想要一把理发剪刀。
equivalent [ɪˈkwɪvələnt]	*n.* 对等物（equal）；等价物 *a.* 相同的（identical）；相当的（*interchangeable*） 记 词根记忆：equi（相等）+ val（力量）+ ent → 力量相等的 → 相同的；相当的 例 American children's stories differed a lot from their British *equivalents*. 美国儿童故事与英国的儿童故事大不相同。
fray [freɪ]	*vi.* 磨损，磨破（rub, fret）；(使)烦躁，恼火 *n.* 争斗 记 联想记忆：f + ray（光线）→ 时光催人老 → 磨损，磨破 例 His woolen pants were sometimes fortified with buckskin to keep them from *fraying*. 为免磨破，他有时给羊毛裤子缝上鹿皮。// We were ready for the *fray*. 我们为斗争作好了准备。
prolific [prəˈlɪfɪk]	*a.* 多产的（*productive, *fruitful*）；富有创造力的 记 联想记忆：pro + lif（看做 life，生命）+ ic → 产生生命的 → 多产的 例 The beds of former lakes are also *prolific* sources of fossils. 过去湖泊的湖底也是化石形成的丰富来源。 派 prolifically（*ad.* 多产地；丰富地）
revolution [ˌrevəˈluːʃn]	*n.* 革命；巨变；旋转 记 词根记忆：re + volut（滚；卷）+ ion → 不断向前席卷而来的 → 革命 例 A *revolution* in information technology is taking place. 信息技术正在发生巨变。 派 revolutionary（*a.* 革命的 *n.* 革命者）；revolutionize（*vt.* 彻底改变）

4

equivalent

crab [kræb]	*n.* 蟹，螃蟹 记 联想记忆：cr(看做 cry，叫) + ab → 被螃蟹的两个钳子夹住了，痛得直叫 → 蟹 例 A *crab* nipped his toe. 一只螃蟹咬住了他的脚趾。 crab
inhabit [ɪnˈhæbɪt]	*vt.* 居住于，栖居于(*live) 记 词根记忆：in(在…里面) + hab(居住，生活) + it → 住在里面 → 居住于，栖居于 例 The archaeological evidence indicates that Native Americans first *inhabited* the area. 考古学证据显示，美洲土著人最初居住于该地区。 派 inhabitant(*n.* 居民；栖息的动物)；uninhabited(*a.* 无人居住的，杳无人迹的)；uninhabitable(*a.* 不适于人居住的)
tissue [ˈtɪʃuː]	*n.* [常 *pl.*]组织 搭 soft tissue 软组织 例 *Tissue* engineering is a multidisciplinary field incorporating the principles of biology, chemistry, engineering and medicine to create biological substitutes of native *tissues* for scientific research or clinical use. 组织工程学跨越多个学科，融合了生物学、化学、工程学和医学，旨在为科学研究或医用开发可用于取代人体组织的生物替代物。
precede [prɪˈsiːd]	*v.* 在…之前，先于(forerun) 记 词根记忆：pre(在…前面) + ced(走) + e → 走在前面 → 先于 例 The idea of sea-floor spreading actually *preceded* the theory of plate tectonics. 海底扩展理论实际上先于板块构造学理论。 派 preceding(*a.* 前述的；前面的)；unprecedented(*a.* 空前的) 参 proceed(*vi.* 进行，继续)
mushroom [ˈmʌʃrʊm]	*n.* 蘑菇(fungus) *vi.* 迅速成长 记 联想记忆：mush(软块) + room(房子) → 蘑菇的样子很像软软的小房子 → 蘑菇 例 We expect the market to *mushroom* in the next three years. 我们期望未来三年内市场会快速发展。
listless [ˈlɪstləs]	*a.* 倦怠的，没精打采的(downhearted, lethargic) 记 联想记忆：list(名单) + less → 榜上无名所以没精打采 → 没精打采的 例 The illness left her feeling *listless* and depressed. 那场病使她感到虚弱无力，提不起精神。
stretch [stretʃ]	*n.* 一段路程；延伸 *v.* 延伸，拉长(*extend) 搭 stretch out 伸展；开始大踏步走 例 The whole 150-mile *stretch* is influenced by tides from the Atlantic Ocean. 整段长达 150 英里的路程受到大西洋潮汐的影响。
recharge [ˌriːˈtʃɑːrdʒ]	*v.* 充电；休整；再装弹药 例 Swimming is a best way to relieve stress and *recharge* yourself. 游泳是缓解压力、养精蓄锐的最好办法之一。

□ crab □ inhabit □ tissue □ precede □ mushroom □ listless
□ stretch □ recharge

groom
[gruːm]

v. (给动物)刷洗；(给…)梳理毛发；培养，训练
n. 马夫；新郎
记 联想记忆：在房间(room)里梳头(groom)
例 Mother chimpanzees care for and *groom* their young. 黑猩猩母亲照顾子女，并给它们梳毛。// All trails have to be checked daily to make sure they are *groomed* probably. 所有道路都得每天检查以确保其已清理干净。

groom

---

dim
[dɪm]

a. 模糊的(faint)；暗淡的(pale)；朦胧的；不乐观的 *v.* (使)变暗淡；(使)变冷漠
例 This light is too *dim* to read by. 这光线太暗，无法看书。// My passion for writing never *dimmed* over the years. 这些年来我对写作的热情一直不减。
参 dime(*n.* 一角硬币)

---

quantify
['kwɑːntɪfaɪ]

vt. 以数量表示，量化
记 词根记忆：quant(数量) + ify(使…) → 使变成数字 → 以数量表示
例 Scientists have tried to *quantify* this proportion of the Sun's energy. 科学家们已经在努力量化太阳能的大小。
参 quantitative(*a.* 数量的；定量的)；quantity(*n.* 量，数量)

---

equitable
['ekwɪtəbl]

a. 公平的，公正的(just, fair)
搭 an equitable system 公正的制度
例 It may be the most *equitable* solution to the international issue. 这可能是解决国际争端最公正的方法。

---

appreciate
[ə'priːʃieɪt]

vt. 赏识(*recognize)；鉴赏，欣赏；感激
例 She's learned to *appreciate* the sculptures. 她已经学会了欣赏雕塑。// I *appreciate* your getting my books, Bill. 谢谢你帮我拿书，比尔。
派 appreciation(*n.* 欣赏；感激)；appreciative(*a.* 有欣赏力的；表示感激的)；appreciable(*a.* 值得重视的；可感知的)
参 depreciation(*n.* 贬值)

---

neuron
['nʊrɑːn]

n. 神经元，神经细胞
记 词根记忆：neur(神经) + on → 神经元
例 *Neurons* come in many different shapes and sizes. 神经细胞大小形状多种多样。

---

glare
[gler]

n. 耀眼的光(shine)；怒视，瞪眼 *v.* 怒目而视；发出刺眼的光
例 The *glare* was so intense even my sunglasses didn't help. 光太耀眼，墨镜都不管用了。

---

marsh
[mɑːrʃ]

n. 沼泽，湿地(swamp)
记 联想记忆：红军长征(march)过沼泽(marsh)
例 Cows were grazing on the *marsh*. 牛群在湿地上吃草。
派 marshy(*a.* 沼泽般的，沼泽的)

□ groom □ dim □ quantify □ equitable □ appreciate □ neuron
□ glare □ marsh

foul [faʊl]	*a.* 污秽的，肮脏的(disgusting, filthy)；充满脏话的，辱骂性的；邪恶的 记 联想记忆：邪恶的(foul)心灵(soul) 例 The teachers were all shocked by the boy's *foul* language and behavior. 老师们都被这个男孩的污言秽语和不良行径惊呆了。
eclipse [ɪˈklɪps]	*vt.* (月球、地球等)遮住(…的)光；使相形见绌 *n.* 日食，月食 记 词根记忆：ec(没有) + lip(离开) + se → 日月的光华溜走 → 日食，月食 搭 lunar/solar eclipse 月/日食 例 The desperate plight of the South has *eclipsed* the fact that reconstruction had to be undertaken also in the North. 南方极糟的情况掩盖了北方也需要重建这一事实。 参 ellipse(*n.* 椭圆，椭圆形)；lapse(*vi.* 失效)
incentive [ɪnˈsentɪv]	*n.* 刺激(stimulus)；动机(motive) 记 词根记忆：in(在里面) + cent(唱歌) + ive → 在内心里唱歌 → 刺激 例 There was *incentive* for American potters to replace the imports with comparable domestic goods. 美国制陶工人用与进口商品相当的国产商品替代进口商品是有一定动机的。 incentive
command [kəˈmænd]	*n./v.* 命令；指挥，统率(govern, control) 记 词根记忆：com(表加强) + mand(命令) → 命令；指挥 例 Who issued the *command* to fire? 是谁下令开枪的？ 派 commander(*n.* 司令官，指挥)；commandment(*n.* 戒律) 参 demand(*n./v.* 要求)
puncture [ˈpʌŋktʃər]	*v.* 刺穿(*pierce, penetrate)；(使)泄气，挫伤(某人的锐气) *n.* 小孔；刺伤 记 词根记忆：punct(刺) + ure → 刺穿 例 The tire *punctured* a mile from home. 在离家一英里处车胎被扎破了。
corrosive [kəˈroʊsɪv]	*a.* 腐蚀(性)的 例 Chlorine is a *corrosive* gas that has a sharp odor. 氯气是一种带有刺激气味的腐蚀性气体。
picky [ˈpɪki]	*a.* 挑剔的，难以取悦的(fussy) 例 The bees are *picky* about who comes to their family reunion. 蜜蜂对谁来参加它们的家庭聚会比较挑剔。 参 sticky(*a.* 黏的，黏性的)
raven [ˈreɪvn]	*a.* 乌黑光亮的 *n.* 渡鸦 例 The girl sitting beside me has *raven* hair. 坐在我身边的女孩有着乌亮的头发。
durable [ˈdʊrəbl]	*a.* 持久的，耐用的(*long-lasting, *lasting) 记 词根记忆：dur(持续) + able(能…的) → 持久的 例 Beads were probably the first *durable* ornaments humans possessed. 珠子可能是人类最先拥有的耐用装饰品。 派 durability(*n.* 持久，耐用)

approve [ə'pru:v]	*v.* 批准(pass, ratify); 赞成(assent) 记 联想记忆：ap + prove(证实) → 经过证实才能批准 → 批准; 赞成 例 The advisor has already *approved* the man's class schedule. 指导教师已经批准了此人的课程安排。// He doesn't *approve* of the dean's plan. 他不赞成院长的计划。 派 approval(*n.* 赞成; 批准); disapproval(*n.* 不赞成)
jot [dʒɑːt]	*vt.* 草草记下, 匆匆记下 搭 jot down 草草记下 例 I have *jotted* down your telephone number. 我已经记下了你的电话号码。 参 lot(*n.* 签); hot(*a.* 热的)
prudent ['pru:dnt]	*a.* 谨慎的(discreet); 深谋远虑的 记 词根记忆：pr(=pro 在…前面) + ud(=vid 看) + ent → 事先进行观察的 → 谨慎的 例 This was a colossal sum for those days but one that a *prudent* government could pay. 在那些日子里, 这是个巨额数目, 但对于一个谨慎的政府而言, 尚能支付。
ratify ['rætɪfaɪ]	*vt.* 正式批准, 使正式生效(approve) 记 词根记忆：rat(清点) + ify → 一一清点 → 正式批准 例 The treaty was *ratified* by all the member states. 这个条约得到了所有成员国的批准。
athlete ['æθliːt]	*n.* 运动员, 体育家 记 发音记忆："爱死你的" → 运动员体格健美, 让人喜爱 → 运动员 例 The seminar is recommended for coaches and/or *athletes* who already have a good working knowledge of hybrid training. 我们向那些在综合训练方面已经具备出色应用知识的教练和(或)运动员推荐这一研究班。 派 athletic(*a.* 运动的; 体格健壮的)
ideology [ˌaɪdi'ɑːlədʒi]	*n.* 思想体系; 意识形态 记 词根记忆：ideo(思想) + logy(…学) → 思想体系 例 Gradually, economic reality overcame *ideology*. 经济现实逐渐战胜了意识形态。
spur [spɜːr]	*n.* 刺激(物); 激励; 马刺 *vt.* 激励, 鼓舞; 刺激, 促进(urge, provoke) 记 联想记忆：美国 NBA 的马刺队(Spurs) 例 I phoned him up on the *spur* of the moment. 我一时心血来潮, 给他打了个电话。// I was *spurred* into action by your words. 你的话激励我行动了起来。
vice [vaɪs]	*n.* 恶行, 恶习; 副, 代理 例 Cigarettes are my only *vice*. 我唯一的罪过就是爱抽烟。
oyster ['ɔɪstər]	*n.* 牡蛎, 蚝 记 联想记忆：妹妹(sister)爱吃牡蛎(oyster) 例 The girl is as dumb as an *oyster*. 那个女孩寡言少语。

4

| **debatable**
[dɪ'beɪtəbl] | *a.* 有争议的(disputable, unsettled)
搭 debatable viewpoint 有争议的观点
例 It's *debatable* whether or not the policies have changed the messed-up situation. 这些政策是否改变了混乱局面，对此还存有争议。 |

Ordinary people merely think how they shall spend their time; a man of talent tries to use it.

普通人只想到如何度过时间，有才能的人设法利用时间。

——德国哲学家 叔本华(Arthur Schopenhauer, German philosopher)

词根、词缀预习表

psycho	灵魂，精神	psychology *n.* 心理学	cas	落，掉	casualty *n.* 伤亡事故
bell	美丽的	'embellish *vt.* 装饰；渲染	sip	扔	dissipate *v.* (使)消散；挥霍
verg	转	diverge *vi.* 分歧	ment	思想，心智	mental *a.* 精神的；智力的
press	压	repress *vt.* 克制；镇压	tamin	触摸	contamination *n.* 污染
thrus	刺	thrust *v./n.* 戳，刺	scrib	写	inscribe *v.* 铭刻

---

deposit
[dɪˈpɑːzɪt]

v. 沉淀(settle)；堆积(accumulate)；储蓄；寄存 deposit
n. 沉积物，堆积物；存款
记 词根记忆：de(向下) + pos(放) + it → 向下放
→ 沉淀；堆积
例 The sediments have been *deposited* over a comparable period of time. 沉淀物经过相当长的一段时间堆积了起来。// The *deposits* associated with present-day glaciers have been well studied. 对与当今冰河相关的沉淀物的研究已经很深入了。
派 deposition(*n.* 沉积物；沉积作用)；depositor(*n.* 存款人)

---

reunion
[ˌriːˈjuːniən]

n. 团圆，重聚
记 联想记忆：re(重新) + union(联合) → 重新联合在一起 → 团圆，重聚
例 Next Monday, we will have a family *reunion*. 下周一我们有个家庭聚会。

---

lay
[leɪ]

v. 产(卵)；放置；铺；筹划，设置；提出，提交
例 Turtles travel miles through the sea to *lay* eggs on an island. 为去岛上产卵，海龟在海里游数英里远。// They *laid* the injured woman down on the grass. 他们把受伤的女人平放在草地上。

---

occupy
[ˈɑːkjupaɪ]

vt. 占用；占据，占领(take up)；使忙于(做某事)
记 联想记忆：发生(occur)大事了，敌人占领(occupy)了该市
例 Wish I'd brought a book or something to *occupy* my time. 我真该带本书或一些别的东西来打发时间。
派 occupation(*n.* 职业；占有)；occupant(*n.* 居住者)；occupancy(*n.* 占用；居住)

---

envelop [ɪnˈveləp]	*vt.* 包围(*surround, encircle) 例 More dense atmosphere gradually *enveloped* Earth. 更多浓厚的大气逐渐笼罩了地球。 派 envelope(*n.* 塑料封皮；信封)
storage [ˈstɔːrɪdʒ]	*n.* 库房(warehouse)；贮藏；存储 记 来自 store(*vt.* 储存) 搭 storage space 储藏室；storage shed 仓库；storage battery 蓄电池 例 Some fungi can grow at 500℃, while others can grow at −5℃, so even food in cold *storage* may not be completely safe from them. 有些真菌能在 500 摄氏度的温度下生长，有些能在零下 5 摄氏度下生长，所以甚至冷藏的食品都不能完全免于真菌。
proactive [ˌprouˈæktɪv]	*a.* 积极主动的；先发制人的 记 联想记忆：pro(在…前面) + active(活动的) → 预先活动的 → 积极主动的 搭 proactive computing 预发式计算 例 My role is to help you take a more *proactive* approach to your life. 我的职责是帮助你对你的生活采取更加积极主动的态度。
fantasy [ˈfæntəsi]	*n.* 想象，幻想(imagination, illusion) 记 游戏《最终幻想》的英文名为 *Final Fantasy* 例 Science fiction is a mixture of science and *fantasy*. 科幻小说融合了科学和幻想。 参 fantastic(*a.* 极好的)
posit [ˈpɑːzɪt]	*vt.* 安排(arrange)；假定(assume, postulate) 记 联想记忆：po + sit(坐) → 坐下来 → 安排 例 Most religions *posit* the existence of life after death. 大多数宗教都假定人死后生命仍存在。
disguise [dɪsˈɡaɪz]	*vt./n.* 掩饰(mask)；伪装，假装(pretend) 记 联想记忆：dis(分离) + guise(外表) → 使看不到真实的外表 → 掩饰；伪装 例 These songs' origins cannot be *disguised* and therefore they belong primarily to the composer. 这些歌曲的起源不能被掩盖，它们主要属于这位作曲家。
psychology [saɪˈkɑːlədʒi]	*n.* 心理学；心理，心理特征(mentality) 记 词根记忆：psycho(灵魂，精神) + logy(…学) → 心理学 搭 clinical psychology 临床心理学 例 The scientific study of *psychology* has a long and illustrious history at this university. 该大学的心理学研究历史悠久，享誉盛名。 派 psychological(*a.* 心理的，精神上的)；psychologist(*n.* 心理学家)

embellish [ɪmˈbelɪʃ]	*vt.* 装饰(decorate)；对…添枝加叶，渲染(*exaggerate) 记 词根记忆：em(使…) + bell(美丽的) + ish → 使变美丽 → 装饰；渲染 例 Jimmy *embellished* the tale of his fishing trip to make it sound more exciting. 吉米给他的钓鱼之行添油加醋，使其听起来更加令人兴奋。
weird [wɪrd]	*a.* 怪异的，神秘的(strange, mysterious) 记 联想记忆：we(我们) + ird(看做 bird, 鸟) → 如果我们都变成鸟会很怪异 → 怪异的 例 Those modern sculptures over there are really *weird*. 那边的那些现代雕塑真是怪异。
diverge [daɪˈvɜːrdʒ]	*vi.* (道路、线条等)分开，叉开；(意见等)分歧；偏离 记 词根记忆：di(分开) + verg(转) + e → 分别转换方向 → 分歧 例 This is where our points of view *diverge* from each other. 这就是我们的意见产生分歧之处。
infuriate [ɪnˈfjʊrieɪt]	*vt.* 激怒(enrage) 记 联想记忆：in + furi(看做 fury, 狂怒) + ate → 激怒 例 Ross knew that some of his words might *infuriate* the fans of that singer. 罗斯知道他的一些言论会激怒那个歌星的粉丝。
spear [spɪr]	*v.* 刺，戳 *n.* 矛，枪；嫩叶 记 联想记忆：用 s 刺(spear)梨(pear) 例 Tom isn't good at table manners; he *spears* the cake and puts it on the plate. 汤姆不怎么懂餐桌礼仪，他把蛋糕叉起放在盘子上。
repress [rɪˈpres]	*vt.* 克制，抑制；镇压，压制 记 词根记忆：re(向后) + press(压) → 向后压 → 克制；镇压 例 It's not healthy to *repress* your anger. 压抑愤怒不利于身体健康。
conquer [ˈkɑːŋkər]	*vt.* 战胜，征服；克服(overcome) 记 词根记忆：con(全部) + quer(寻求) → 全部寻求到 → 征服 例 Very often, the most difficult thing is to *conquer* oneself. 很多时候，最难的事就是战胜自己。
thrust [θrʌst]	*v.* 挤，插；戳，刺 *n.* 戳，刺；要旨；驱动力 记 词根记忆：thrus(=trus 刺) + t → 戳，刺 搭 thrust at 戳，刺；thrust aside 置之不理 例 The little boy started to cry when a needle was *thrust* into his arm. 当注射针头扎进胳膊时，小男孩哭了。
casualty [ˈkæʒuəlti]	*n.* 伤亡事故；伤亡(人员) 记 词根记忆：cas(落，掉) + ualty → 掉落下来，造成事故 → 伤亡事故 搭 casualty insurance 意外保险 例 There has been no report of *casualty* or damage. 还没有人员伤亡或事物损毁的报道。

incidental [ˌɪnsɪˈdentl]	*a.* 偶然的；附带发生的，伴随而来的 例 The discovery was *incidental* to their main research. 这一发现是他们主要研究中的附带收获。
superb [suːˈpɜːrb]	*a.* 极好的，高质量的，上乘的；华丽的 记 联想记忆：super(上等的) + b → 极好的，高质量的 例 I was fascinated by their *superb* performances. 我被他们的精湛表演吸引住了。
bestow [bɪˈstoʊ]	*vt.* 赠与，授予，献给 记 联想记忆：best(最好的) + ow(看做 own，拥有) → 把自己所拥有的最好的拿出来 → 赠与 例 Some of the students would be *bestowed* honors and prizes upon at the graduation ceremony. 一些学生将在毕业典礼上被授予荣誉证书和奖金。
adventitious [ˌædvenˈtɪʃəs]	*a.* 偶然的，偶发的 记 来自 advent(*n.* 出现，到来) 例 I found this *adventitious* meeting with my friend was very lucky. 我觉得这次与朋友偶遇真是很幸运。
dissipate [ˈdɪsɪpeɪt]	*v.* (使)消散，(使)消失；挥霍，浪费(时间、金钱等) 记 词根记忆：dis(离开) + sip(扔) + ate → 扔出去 → (使)消散；挥霍 例 Don't *dissipate* your efforts over something so trivial. 不要把精力浪费在这些小事上。
resolute [ˈrezəluːt]	*a.* 坚决的，果断的 记 词根记忆：re(表加强) + solu(松开) + te → 完全松开的 → 坚决的 例 He has taken bold and *resolute* actions. 他已经采取了果断勇敢的行动。
cranial [ˈkreɪniəl]	*n.* 头盖骨的，颅骨的 例 These are usually benign tumors that often form near the cerebellum and in the *cranial* nerve. 这些通常是良性肿瘤，形成于小脑附近或颅神经内。
lineage [ˈlɪniɪdʒ]	*n.* 宗系，世系，血统(ancestry) 记 联想记忆：line(线) + age(年龄) → 区分年龄的线 → 宗系，血统 例 She traced her *lineage* back to the Tang Dynasty. 她的世系能追溯到唐朝。
balk [bɔːk]	*n.* 障碍 *v.* 畏缩；阻止(prevent)；妨碍(hinder) 记 联想记忆：畏畏缩缩(balk)，不敢前行(walk) 例 The high housing price is a *balk* to many young people working and living in big cities. 对在大城市工作和生活的年轻人来说，高房价是一个障碍。
irritate [ˈɪrɪteɪt]	*vt.* 激怒，使烦躁；刺激 记 词根记忆：irrit(痒) + ate → 激怒，使烦躁 例 You do not want to make any troubles to *irritate* your boss. 你并不想自找麻烦惹怒你的老板吧。

consolidate [kən'sɑːlɪdeɪt]	*v.* 巩固；(使)合并 记 联想记忆：con(共同) + solid(结实的) + ate → 联合在一起使更加结实 → (使)合并 例 But if they can succeed, it may encourage other companies to *consolidate*. 但如果他们能成功的话，或许会鼓励其他公司的合并。
intervening [ˌɪntər'viːnɪŋ]	*a.* 介于中间的，发生于期间的 记 词根记忆：inter(在…之间) + ven(来) + ing → 来到中间的 → 介于中间的 例 The *intervening* time between the TV series is full of commercials. 电视剧的中间空档充斥着商业广告。
corrosion [kə'roʊʒn]	*n.* 腐蚀(状态)，侵蚀 记 来自corrode(*v.* 腐蚀，侵蚀)；cor(表加强) + rod(咬) + e → 用力咬掉 → 腐蚀，侵蚀 例 If the beads are buried for long, the effects of *corrosion* can further change their outer appearance. 珠子埋藏时间长了，腐蚀作用会进一步改变其外观。
mental ['mentl]	*a.* 精神的(spiritual)；智力的(intellectual)；精神健康的 记 词根记忆：ment(思想，心智) + al(形容词后缀) → 精神的；智力的 搭 mental age 心理年龄，智力年龄 例 Do you have a *mental* picture of what it will look like? 在你脑子里它会是什么样子？ 派 mentally(*ad.* 智力上；精神上)；mentality(*n.* 心态)
plump [plʌmp]	*a.* 微胖的；丰满的 记 发音记忆："拨浪鼓" → 长着一张拨浪鼓一样圆圆胖胖的脸 → 微胖的；注意不要和plumb(*vt.* 深入了解)相混 例 The man is so short and *plump* that he has to be lifted up on his horse. 那个人又矮又胖，只得被抬上马。
readily ['redɪli]	*ad.* 欣然地(willingly)；容易地(*easily) 记 来自ready(*a.* 有准备的；情愿的) 例 It is made of wood not *readily* available. 它是由珍稀木材制成的。
cooperative [koʊ'ɑːpərətɪv]	*a.* 合作的，协作的；配合的 *n.* 合作企业 例 He is not *cooperative*. 他不是太合作。
pave [peɪv]	*v.* 铺(cover)；密布(densely cover) 例 The sky was *paved* with clouds. 天空乌云密布。
contamination [kənˌtæmɪ'neɪʃn]	*n.* 污染(pollution)；玷污 记 词根记忆：con(共同) + tamin(触摸) + ation → 共同触摸脏东西 → 污染 例 In the 1970s, the peregrine falcons almost disappeared as a result of the *contamination* of the food chain by the DDT in pesticide. 20世纪70年代，由于杀虫剂中的DDT污染了食物链，游隼几乎消失了。

shrink [ʃrɪŋk]	*v.* (使)收缩，缩小(dwindle); 退缩，畏缩 记 联想记忆：童话故事里，喝(drink)了巫婆的药水就能收缩(shrink)身体 搭 shrink from 畏避，回避(困难等) 例 The crystals *shrink* and become more compact. 晶体收缩后会变得更加紧凑。 派 shrinkage(*n.* 收缩；收缩程度)
pretentious [prɪ'tenʃəs]	*a.* 自负的(boastful) 记 词根记忆：pre(向前) + tent(伸展) + ious → 向前伸展的 → 自负的 例 Self-image can be indicated by a tone of voice that is confident, *pretentious*, shy, aggressive, or outgoing. 自我形象能够通过自信、做作、羞涩、挑衅或开朗的语气表现出来。
laser ['leɪzər]	*n.* 激光；激光器 记 发音记忆："镭射" → 激光 例 The bar codes on the products are read by *lasers*. 产品上的条形码是用激光读取的。
identify [aɪ'dentɪfaɪ]	*v.* 识别(*spot, recognize); 鉴定(judge); 找到，发现 搭 identify with sb. 与某人产生共鸣；谅解，同情；identify sb. with sth. 把某人视为 例 This odor allows ants to *identify* intruders. 借助于这种气味，蚂蚁能够识别入侵者。 派 identifiable(*a.* 可识别的); identification(*n.* 辨认，鉴别)
barter ['bɑːrtər]	*n./v.* 实物交易，以物易物(trade, deal) 记 联想记忆：bar(酒吧) + ter → 人们通常在酒吧谈交易 → 实物交易 例 Food could be *bartered* for other commodities long ago. 很久以前食物可用来换取其他商品。
cue [kjuː]	*n.* 暗示，提示(hint) 记 联想记忆：线索(clue)有提示(cue)作用 例 She stood in the wings and waited for her *cue* to go on. 她站在舞台侧面等待着出场的提示。
tenant ['tenənt]	*n.* 房客，承租人(dweller, occupant) *vt.* (作为租赁者)居住 记 联想记忆：ten(十) + ant(蚂蚁) → 十只蚂蚁来住店 → 房客 例 The *tenant* can use any space in the parking area. 房客可以使用停车区的任何空间。
medal ['medl]	*n.* 奖牌，奖章(medallion) 记 联想记忆：奖牌(medal)是用金属(metal)做的 例 The young girl won a gold *medal* in the Olympics. 那个年轻女孩在奥运会上赢得一枚金牌。

inscribe
[ɪnˈskraɪb]

v. (在某物上)写、题、铭刻(engrave); 铭记

记 词根记忆: in(进入) + scrib(写) + e → 写进去 → 铭刻

例 They *inscribed* vocabulary and other study aids on tables. 他们把单词和其他学习资料刻在了桌上。

派 inscription(n. 铭刻; 碑文)

flake
[fleɪk]

v. 使成薄片(chip); 雪片般落下 n. 薄片(slice)

记 联想记忆: f(看做 fly, 飞) + lake(湖) → 飞向湖面的薄片 → 雪片般落下

例 *Flake* the tuna and add it to the sauce. 把金枪鱼切成片, 然后加上调味汁。

concert
[ˈkɑːnsərt]

n. 音乐会, 演奏会(musicale); 一致(agreement)

记 联想记忆: 那位身患癌症(cancer)的音乐家举办了最后一场个人音乐会(concert)

搭 in concert with 与…合作, 同心协力

例 All their musical instruments were lost and they couldn't play at their *concert*. 他们所有的乐器都不见了, 所以无法在演奏会上表演。

派 concerted(a. 互相配合的, 同心协力的)

supreme
[suːˈpriːm]

a. 至高无上的(*most outstanding)

记 词根记忆: supre(=super 在…上面) + me → 在最上面的 → 至高无上的

搭 the Supreme Court 最高法院

例 It is an event in which she reigns *supreme*. 这个比赛项目她所向无敌。

派 supremacy(n. 至高无上, 霸权); supremely(ad. 至高无上地, 极其)

encounter
[ɪnˈkaʊntər]

vt./v. 偶然碰到(come across); 遭遇(meet)

记 联想记忆: en(使…) + counter(相反的) → 使从两个相反方面来 → 偶然碰到

例 Abstract art *encountered* much opposition in its early years. 抽象艺术在早期遭到了很多反对。

lease
[liːs]

n. 租约; 租期 vt. 出租

记 联想记忆: l + ease(安心) → 签了租约, 可以安心了 → 租约

例 Her *lease* ends after graduation. 她的租约毕业后到期。

downward
[ˈdaʊnwərd]

ad. 向下, 往下(down) a. 向下的

记 联想记忆: down(向下的) + ward(向…) → 向下的

例 Aristotle noted that when he released most objects, they would drop *downward*. 亚里士多德注意到, 大多数物体脱落后都会往下掉。

参 upward(a. 向上的 ad. 向上); forward(ad. 向前地)

courteous
[ˈkɜːrtiəs]

a. 谦恭的, 有礼貌的

记 联想记忆: court(向…献殷勤) + eous → 谦恭的

例 Please keep this in mind: introduce yourself in a *courteous* manner. 请记住一点: 介绍自己时要有礼貌。

5

evolve [iˈvɑːlv]	*v.* 发展(develop)；(使)进化 记 词根记忆：e(出) + volv(转，滚) + e → 转出来 → 发展；(使)进化 例 The techniques of pottery manufacture had *evolved* well before the Greek period. 制陶技术早在希腊时期就已经得到了很好的发展。 派 evolution(*n.* 进化)；evolutionary(*a.* 进化的)
jeopardize [ˈdʒepərdaɪz]	*vt.* 破坏，危及(endanger) 记 发音记忆："皆怕打死" → 当危及自身安全时，谁都怕死 → 危及 例 My boss keeps asking me to work overtime, but I always said no because I don't want to *jeopardize* my studies. 我的老板一直让我加班，不过我总说不行，因为我不想影响学业。
detergent [dɪˈtɜːrdʒənt]	*n.* 清洁剂 *a.* 净化的，清洁的 记 词根记忆：de(分离) + terg(擦) + ent → 擦掉脏东西 → 清洁剂 例 No *detergent* can remove these stains. 没有清洁剂能去掉这些污迹。
parking [ˈpɑːrkɪŋ]	*n.* 机动车停放；停车场 搭 parking sticker 停车许可证；parking lot 停车场；parking meter （投币式）计时停车计费器 例 We're organizing a rally on Thursday afternoon to get the administration to reconsider the *parking* lot plan. 我们正在组织周四下午的集会，让当局重新考虑停车场计划。
imprint	[ɪmˈprɪnt] *vt.* 使铭记，使牢记(engrave)；压印 [ˈɪmprɪnt] *n.* 印记，印痕(*trace)；持久的影响 记 联想记忆：im(进入) + print(印) → 印在内心深处 → 使铭记 例 The terrible scenes were deeply *imprinted* on my mind. 那些恐怖的场面深深地印在了我的脑海里。 // Did you see the deep *imprint* of the big toe? 你看到大脚趾所留下的深深的印痕了吗？
degree [dɪˈgriː]	*n.* 程度；度数；学位；等级(grade) 搭 to some degree 从某种程度上来说 例 Some studies done with mice indicate that mammals do inherit fearfulness to some *degree*. 用老鼠做的一些研究表明，哺乳动物的确在一定程度上遗传恐惧。
bulk [bʌlk]	*n.* 容积，体积；主体，大部分(majority) 例 Most of their *bulk* is hidden below the water. 它们的主体都藏在水中。 // Airmail began to constitute the *bulk* of the United States' mail. 航空邮件开始成为美国邮件的主要部分。

spontaneity [ˌspɑːntəˈneɪəti]	*n.* 自发性；自发行为 记 来自 spontaneous(*a.* 自发的) 例 In fact, the discernment which we are speaking of has an essential relationship with *spontaneity*. 实际上，我们所讲的这种洞察力与自发性有着固有的联系。
mast [mæst]	*n.* 船桅；旗杆；天线塔 例 The ship lost its *mast* in the gale. 大风刮走了那艘船的桅杆。
inanimate [ɪnˈænɪmət]	*a.* 无生命的；无生气的(dull) 记 词根记忆：in(无) + anim(生命) + ate → 无生命的 例 A fable is usually a short tale featuring animals or *inanimate* objects that can talk and think like humans. 寓言通常是关于能像人类那样说话和思考的动物或无生命物体的短小故事。
exhale [eksˈheɪl]	*v.* 呼出(气)(breathe out)；散发 记 词根记忆：ex(出) + hale(气) → 呼出(气) 例 A diver must ascend slowly, never at a rate exceeding the rise of the *exhaled* air bubbles, and must *exhale* during ascent. 潜水者必须缓慢上升，速度不能超过呼出气泡上升的速度，而且上升过程中还必须呼气。
comply [kəmˈplaɪ]	*vi.* 服从；遵守(conform, submit) 记 词根记忆：com(表加强) + ply(装满) → 完全装满 → 服从 例 A good citizen *complies* with the laws of the country. 好公民遵守国家的法律。
plantation [plænˈteɪʃn]	*n.* 种植园；人造林 记 来自 plant(*n.* 植物；种植) 搭 plantation economy 种植园经济 例 Back in the 17th and 18th century, African and American women wove the baskets to use in the rice *plantations*. 早在十七八世纪，非洲和美洲女性就编织篮子以供稻米种植园使用。
request [rɪˈkwest]	*n./vt.* 要求，请求 记 词根记忆：re(再，又) + quest(追求) → 要求，请求 例 People from the television station have *requested* the viewers to send in their suggestions. 电视台的工作人员要求观众把建议反馈给他们。
penetrate [ˈpenətreɪt]	*v.* 刺穿(*go through, pierce)；渗透；洞察(apperceive) 例 In a microwave oven, radiation *penetrates* food and is then absorbed primarily by water molecules, causing heat to spread through the food. 在微波炉里，热辐射穿透食物，然后主要被水分子吸收，从而使热量在食物中扩散。 派 penetrating(*a.* 刺鼻的；敏锐的)

diversion [daɪˈvɜːrʒn]	*n.* 消遣，娱乐(recreation, entertainment)；转移，转换 记 词根记忆：di(分离) + vers(转) + ion → 转移 搭 created a diversion 分散注意力，声东击西 例 Statistics showed that there was a *diversion* of funds from the manufacture to food industry in March. 统计数据显示，三月份有资金从制造业转向了食品业。
endure [ɪnˈdʊr]	*vt.* 忍受，忍耐(*tolerate, suffer)；持久，持续 记 联想记忆：end(结束) + ure → 坚持到结束 → 忍受，忍耐 例 I had to *endure* many painful shots because I'd been exposed to rabies. 我遭遇狂犬病，不得不忍受多次打针的疼痛。 派 enduring (*a.* 持久的，持续的)；endurance (*n.* 忍耐力；持久力) endure
reserve [rɪˈzɜːrv]	*n.* 储备(物)；自然保护区；谨慎；替补队员；后备部队 *vt.* 保留(save)；预订(book) 记 词根记忆：re(再，又) + serv(保持) + e → 保留 例 The *reserve* section of the library is due to close in one hour. 图书馆的预订区在一个小时后关闭。// She was asked to *reserve* a room. 她被要求预订一个房间。 派 reservation(*n.* 预订；保留意见)；reserved(*a.* 内向的) reserve 预订
overload	[ˌoʊvərˈloʊd] *vt.* 使超载，使过载；使(电路等)超负荷；给…增加负担 [ˈoʊvərloʊd] *n.* 超载(量)；超负荷 例 Car drivers usually *overload* their cars. 卡车一般都超载。
region [ˈriːdʒən]	*n.* (大气等的)层；地区，区域(district)；范围 记 词根记忆：reg(统治) + ion → 统治的地方 → 地区，区域 例 She earns somewhere in the *region* of $8,000. 她大约赚八千美元。 派 regional(*a.* 地方的，地域性的)；regionalism (*n.* 地域性；地方分权主义)；regionalization (*n.* 按地区安排)
absurd [əbˈsɜːrd]	*a.* 可笑的，荒唐的(ridiculous) 记 联想记忆：ab + surd(无道理的) → 不合理的 → 可笑的，荒唐的 例 Don Quixote makes chivalry seem *absurd*. 堂吉诃德使骑士精神显得荒唐可笑。 absurd

exemplary [ɪgˈzempləri]	*a.* 模范的；典型的 记 词根记忆：ex(外) + empl(拿) + ary → 从外拿(例子)的 → 模范的 例 The *exemplary* function of the hero in literary works seems to remain constant. 文学作品的主人公的模范作用似乎是持久的。
leftover [ˈleftoʊvər]	*n.* [常 *pl.*]残留物；吃剩的食物 *a.* 剩余的 例 There weren't many *leftovers* from yesterday. 昨天没剩下多少饭菜。
conservationist [ˌkɑːnsərˈveɪʃənɪst]	*n.* 自然环境保护论者 例 A British *conservationist* has become the first individual to view the extraordinarily beautiful bird for one year. 英国一位自然环境保护论者成为观察这种美丽非凡的鸟儿长达一年的第一人。
suspect	[səˈspekt] *v.* 怀疑，猜想(speculate) [ˈsʌspekt] *a.* 可疑的(questionable, suspicious)；不信任的 *n.* 嫌疑犯，可疑分子 记 词根记忆：su(s)(在…下面) + spect(看) → 在下面看一看 → 怀疑 例 Most paleontologists *suspect* that abrupt changes in climate led to the mass extinctions. 大多数古生物学家猜想气候的突然变化导致了大规模灭绝。// The phlogiston theory became *suspect*, and eventually was replaced by new ideas. 燃素理论遭到质疑，最终被新的概念所替代。
adhesive [ədˈhiːsɪv]	*n.* 胶合剂 *a.* 带黏性的 记 词根记忆：ad(表加强) + hes(=her 黏附) + ive → 胶合剂；带黏性的 例 It's considered one of the strongest *adhesives* in nature. 它被认为是大自然中最强的胶合剂。
gravitational [ˌɡrævɪˈteɪʃnl]	*a.* 重力的，万有引力的 记 来自 gravitation(*n.* 万有引力) 搭 gravitational force 引力，重力；gravitational field 引力场，重力场 例 Jupiter has a weaker *gravitational* force than the other planets. 木星的引力比其他行星弱。// Mars was captured by the *gravitational* field of the Sun. 火星被太阳的引力场捕获了。
hydrogen [ˈhaɪdrədʒən]	*n.* 氢 记 词根记忆：hydro(水) + gen(产生) → 参与生成水的物质 → 氢 例 *Hydrogen* has the potential to revolutionize transportation and, possibly, our entire energy system. 氢具有能让交通系统，甚至有可能是我们整个的能源体系发生根本性变革的潜能。
celebrate [ˈselɪbreɪt]	*v.* 赞美(proclaim)；庆祝(commemorate, observe) 例 He decided to *celebrate* his birthday some other time. 他决定在其他时间庆祝生日。

5

exemplary

学习雷锋好榜样

Word List 6

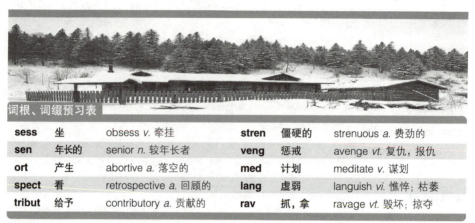

obsess [əb'ses]	**v. 迷住**(charm)**；牵挂** 记 词根记忆：ob(反，逆) + sess(=sit 坐) → 坐立不安 → 牵挂 例 Evans early was *obsessed* by the possibilities of mechanized production and steam power. 埃文斯早些时候对机械化生产和蒸汽动力的可能性很入迷。 派 obsession(n. 入迷；困扰) 参 obese(a. 肥胖的)
atomic [ə'tɑːmɪk]	**a. 原子的；原子能的**(nuclear) 记 来自 atom(n. 原子) 搭 atomic energy 原子能 例 Atoms that have different *atomic* numbers generally behave differently. 具有不同原子数的原子一般表现也不同。
senior ['siːniər]	**a. 地位较高的**(superior)**；较年长的 n. 较年长者**(elder)**；四年级学生** 记 词根记忆：sen(老的，年长的) + ior → 较年长者 例 He has ten years' experience at *senior* management level. 他有十年的高层管理经验。
finalize ['faɪnəlaɪz]	**vt. 使完成；把…最后定下来；定稿** 搭 finalize papers 论文定稿 例 We will meet tomorrow to *finalize* the terms of the treaty. 我们明天要见面确定条约的条款。 // A: Have you *finalized* your plans for spring break yet? B: I could visit some friends in Florida, or go to my roommate's home. It's a tough choice. A: 你春季休假的计划定下来没有？ B: 我可能会去佛罗里达看望朋友，或者去我室友家。很难取舍啊。

utter
[ˈʌtər]

vt. 出声；说（speak, express）*a.* 完全的（absolute）

例 He didn't *utter* a word during lunch. 吃午饭时，他一言不发。

派 utterance（*n.* 发声；言论）；utterly（*ad.* 完全地）

---

outrageously
[aʊtˈreɪdʒəsli]

ad. 令人不能容忍地；肆无忌惮地

例 These watches are *outrageously* expensive. 这些手表贵得离谱。

---

mammal
[ˈmæml]

n. 哺乳动物

记 联想记忆：mamma（妈妈）+ l → 靠吃妈妈的奶长大 → 哺乳动物

例 Desert-adapted *mammals* have the further ability to feed normally when extremely dehydrated. 适应了沙漠环境的哺乳动物在极度脱水时还能正常哺乳。

派 mammalian（*a.* 哺乳动物的，哺乳纲的）

---

bare
[ber]

a. 赤裸的（naked, bald）；光秃的，无遮盖的；最基本的 *vt.* 脱掉（衣服）；显露

例 I like to walk around in *bare* feet. 我喜欢光着脚走来走去。// We only have the *bare* essentials in the way of equipment. 我们只有最基本的设备。

派 barely（*ad.* 几乎不能）

哇！我衣服呢？

bare

---

sticky
[ˈstɪki]

a. 黏的，黏性的；（天气）闷热的；棘手的

记 来自 stick（*v.* 粘）

例 My fingers are *sticky* from that candy bar. 我的手指被巧克力条弄得黏糊糊的。

---

personnel
[ˌpɜːrsəˈnel]

n. 全体人员，员工（crew）

记 来自 person（*n.* 人）

例 The fungus infections afflicted many military *personnel*. 很多军事人员遭受着真菌感染的折磨。

参 personal（*a.* 个人的）

---

inclination
[ˌɪnklɪˈneɪʃn]

n. 爱好，意愿（*preference）；趋向，趋势（tendency）；倾斜度

记 词根记忆：in（向内）+ clin（倾斜）+ ation → 内心的倾向 → 爱好；趋向

例 They had neither the skills nor the *inclination* to become farmers. 他们既无当农民的技能，又不愿成为农民。

---

particle
[ˈpɑːrtɪkl]

n. 微粒，颗粒（fragment, grain）；【语】小品词

记 联想记忆：part（部分）+ icle（看做 article，物品）→ 物品的一部分 → 微粒，颗粒

例 The smoke *particles* are so small that they cool rapidly. 烟的微粒非常小，能迅速冷却。

---

notify
[ˈnoʊtɪfaɪ]

vt. 通报（inform）

记 词根记忆：not（知道）+ ify（使…）→ 使…知道 → 通报

例 I didn't *notify* them about camp registration. 我没有通知他们露营登记的事。

---

survey	[ˈsɜːrveɪ] *n.* 调查；概述 [sərˈveɪ] *v.* 调查；概述
	例 A *survey* is a study, generally in the form of an interview or a questionnaire. 调查是一种研究，通常采用采访或问卷的形式。
	派 surveyor(*n.* 测量员)
abortive [əˈbɔːrtɪv]	*a.* 落空的，失败的
	记 词根记忆：ab(离开) + ort(=ori 产生) + ive → 离开产生的地方 → 落空的
	例 Tom tried to unlock the door, but his attempt proved *abortive*. 汤姆企图把锁撬开，但失败了。
catholic [ˈkæθlɪk]	*a.* 广泛的，包罗万象的；[C-]天主教的 *n.* [C-]天主教
	例 One of the world's largest religions, Christianity, later split into *Catholic* and Protestant. 作为当时世界上最大的宗教之一的基督教，后分化为天主教和新教。
offset [ˈɔːfset]	*n.* 分支，补偿；抵消 *vt.* 补偿；抵消
	记 来自词组 set off(抵消)
	例 The good news is that international trade will provide an *offset*. 好消息是国际贸易将对其形成抵消。
stable [ˈsteɪbl]	*a.* 稳定的，安定的(steady, balanced)；牢固的；沉稳的 *n.* 马厩
	记 词根记忆：st(站) + able(能…的) → 能屹立不倒的 → 稳定的，安定的
	例 The patient's condition is becoming *stable* after injection. 打过针之后，病人的病情趋于稳定。
	派 stability(*n.* 稳定性)；stabilize(*vt.* 使稳定)；unstable(*a.* 不稳定的)
ambiguity [ˌæmbɪˈɡjuːəti]	*n.* 模棱两可的话；歧义(现象)
	例 I find that this word itself is full of *ambiguity*. 我发现这个词本身就充满歧义。
	参 ambiguous(*a.* 模棱两可的)
retrospective [ˌretrəˈspektɪv]	*a.* 回顾的，追想的；有追溯效力的
	记 词根记忆：retro(向后) + spect(看) + ive → 向后看的 → 回顾的
	例 I went to an exhibition that is a *retrospective* review of many famous artists' works. 我去看了一个展览，是对许多著名艺术家作品的回顾展。
overt [oʊˈvɜːrt]	*a.* 公开的，非秘密的
	记 联想记忆：covert(隐蔽的)去掉了帽子(c)就变成 overt(公开的)
	例 As the text reads, we should learn to fight the enemy in both *overt* and covert ways. 就像课本上说的那样，我们应该学会同敌人做公开的和隐蔽的斗争。
contributory [kənˈtrɪbjətɔːri]	*a.* 贡献的；捐助的；促进的
	记 词根记忆：con(完全) + tribut(给予) + ory → 无偿给予 → 贡献的；促进的
	例 Many factors were *contributory* to the failure of this project. 造成这个项目失败的因素很多。

strenuous [ˈstrenjuəs]	*a.* 费劲的，费力的，艰苦的；精力充沛的；奋力的 记 词根记忆：stren(=stern 僵硬的) + uous → 身体累得僵硬 → 费劲的 例 Regular exercises can adapt the body for *strenuous* activities. 坚持锻炼可使身体适应剧烈活动。
puff [pʌf]	*v.* 喘气，喘息；(使)喷出(烟等) *n.* 吸；(烟等的)一缕；喘息 记 联想记忆：pu(音似：噗) + ff(音似：呼) → 像呼气的声音 → 喘气，喘息 搭 out of puff 气喘吁吁；puff out 使膨胀，使肿胀；puff up 肿起，肿胀 例 I don't like smokers, who *puff* their cigarette smoke into my eyes. 我讨厌那些把烟往我的眼睛里喷的吸烟者。
instill [ɪnˈstɪl]	*vt.* 慢慢灌输；逐渐培养 记 词根记忆：in(进入) + still(掉) → 掉进去 → 慢慢灌输 例 Teachers try to *instill* some new ideas into students' minds. 老师们努力给学生们灌输一些新观念。
depress [dɪˈpres]	*vt.* 降低，削弱；使沮丧；使萧条 记 词根记忆：de(向下) + press(压) → 向下压 → 降低；使沮丧 例 It *depressed* me that nobody seemed to care about my absence. 似乎没人关心我的缺席，这让我很沮丧。 参 repress(*vt.* 抑制，镇压)
avenge [əˈvendʒ]	*vt.* 复仇，报仇；向⋯报仇 记 词根记忆：a(向) + veng(惩戒) + e → 向某人施惩戒 → 复仇，报仇 例 The girl was determined to *avenge* herself on the man who had betrayed her. 那个女孩决心报复那个负心男人。 参 revenge(*vt.* 复仇)
meditate [ˈmedɪteɪt]	*v.* 沉思，冥想；考虑；谋划 记 词根记忆：med(计划) + it + ate → 谋划 例 Some people *meditate* to improve their spiritual life, and others want to find inner peace. 有些人冥想是为了提升精神生活，有些人是为了寻求内心的平静。
ensure [ɪnˈʃʊr]	*vt.* 确保，担保，保证 记 联想记忆：en(使⋯) + sure(确定的) → 确保 例 What can we do to *ensure* that each staff get the medical insurance? 我们能做些什么来确保每位员工都能获得医疗保险呢？
gush [gʌʃ]	*v.* 滔滔不绝地说(话)；喷出，涌出 *n.* 喷出，涌出；进发，发作 例 Tom likes to *gush* out ideas to impress others. 汤姆喜欢滔滔不绝地阐述观点以给别人留下印象。
predispose [ˌpriːdɪˈspəʊz]	*v.* 事先(在某方面)影响某人；(使)易受感染(或患病) 记 联想记忆：pre(在⋯前面) + dispose(处理) → 预先处理，不然容易感染 → (使)易受感染(或患病) 搭 predispose to 易受感染 例 Too much stress can *predispose* people to heart attacks. 压力大容易诱发心脏病。

6

languish [ˈlæŋgwɪʃ]	*vi.* 憔悴；凋谢，枯萎；受煎熬 记 词根记忆：lang(虚弱) + uish → 变虚弱 → 憔悴；枯萎 例 Although we are living in the prosperous city, millions of people still *languish* in poverty. 尽管我们生活于繁华的城市，但仍有数百万人备受贫穷的煎熬。
ravage [ˈrævɪdʒ]	*vt.* 毁坏；(尤指军队等)抢劫，掠夺 记 词根记忆：rav(抓，拿) + age → 抢夺 → 毁坏；掠夺 例 The girl was in despair because of her *ravaged* face from the accident. 女孩陷入绝望之中，因为一场意外毁了她的面容。
exodus [ˈeksədəs]	*n.* 大批离去，成群外出 记 词根记忆：ex(出) + od(路) + us → 走上外出的道路 → 大批离去 例 Once the *exodus* begins, everyone may go through the same exit. 一旦人们开始大批离开，所有人可能都会走同一个出口。
compound 	[ˈkɑːmpaʊnd] *n.* 化合物，复合物 *a.* 化合的，复合的 [kəmˈpaʊnd] *vt.* 使恶化，使加重；混合 记 词根记忆：com(共同) + pound(放置) → 放到一起使合成 → 化合物 例 Kilns are used to dissolve iron *compounds*. 干燥炉用来分解铁化合物。// Not all insects have *compound* eyes. 并非所有昆虫都有复眼。
subject 	[ˈsʌbdʒɪkt] *n.* 主题(theme)；对象(object) *a.* 受…支配的(*susceptible to) [səbˈdʒekt] *vt.* 使服从(submit) 记 词根记忆：sub(在…下面) + ject(投，掷) → 被投掷在他人之下 → 受…支配的 例 Organic material trapped in sediments is slowly buried and *subject* to increased temperatures and pressures. 沉淀物中的有机物质慢慢被掩埋，继而会受到升温和增压的影响。 派 subjective(*a.* 主观的)
couple [ˈkʌpl]	*n.* (一)对，(一)双(pair)；夫妇，情侣；几个人，几件事 *vt.* 连接，结合 搭 a couple of 两个；几个 例 I have already had a *couple* of ideas about how to do this experiment. 我对怎么做这个实验已经有了一些想法。// Overproduction, *coupled* with falling sales, has led to huge losses for the company. 生产过剩加上销售下降使这家公司蒙受巨大损失。
downtown [ˌdaʊnˈtaʊn]	*a.* 市中心的 *ad.* 在市中心；往市中心 例 I just got back from the new art gallery *downtown*. 我刚从市中心新开的艺术画廊回来。
backlighting [bækˈlaɪtɪŋ]	*n.* 逆光 记 组合词：back(在后面) + lighting(灯光) → 逆光
mild [maɪld]	*a.* 轻微的(slight)；温和的(temperate)；随和的 记 联想记忆：温柔(mild)"美眉"有时也会很野蛮(wild) 例 The southwestern coastal region has a humid *mild* marine climate. 西南沿海地区是湿润温和的海洋性气候。

□ languish □ ravage □ exodus □ compound □ subject □ couple
□ downtown □ backlighting □ mild

consistency [kən'sɪstənsi]	*n.* 浓度，密度；一致性，协调；连接，结合 记 来自 consistent(*a.* 一致的；持续的) 搭 consistency of …的浓度；…的一致性 例 Unitarians stress the *consistency* of the character portrayed in the poetry. 一神论者强调诗歌中所描述的人物的一致性。
exalt [ɪg'zɔːlt]	*vt.* 高度赞扬，褒扬；提升，提拔(promote) 记 词根记忆：ex(出) + alt(高的) → 使高出他人 → 提升 例 He was *exalted* to the position of manager. 他获得提拔，当上了经理。
soluble ['sɑːljəbl]	*a.* 可溶的；可解决的 记 词根记忆：solu(解开；溶解) + ble(能…的) → 可溶的；可解决的 搭 soluble material 可溶性物质 例 Glucose is *soluble* in water. 葡萄糖可溶于水。 派 insoluble(*a.* 不溶解的)
academy [ə'kædəmi]	*n.* 学会，研究院；专科院校 记 哲学家柏拉图常在园林小径上对向他求教的学生边走边讲，这种讲学方式被称为 Academia，后代的教学机构沿用此名 例 The *Academy* was founded in March 2004 in response to demand for knowledge and skills in intellectual property training. 该学院成立于 2004 年 3 月，旨在提供知识产权培训方面的知识和技能。 派 academic(*a.* 学院的；学术的)；academician(*n.* 学者；学会会员)
prodigious [prə'dɪdʒəs]	*a.* 巨大的 记 来自 prodigy(*n.* 惊人的事物) 例 Desert animals can drink *prodigious* volumes of water in a short time. 沙漠动物可以在短时间内饮用大量的水。
brief [briːf]	*a.* 简短的，短暂的(fleeting, short)；简洁的 *vt.* 向…介绍基本情况 *n.* 指示；摘要 例 They are having a *brief* staff meeting. 他们正在开一个简短的员工会议。 派 briefing (*n.* 情况介绍会；详细指示)；briefly (*ad.* 简要地，简短地) 爸：钱。 儿 brief
optimistic [ˌɑːptɪ'mɪstɪk]	*a.* 乐观的(affirmative) 记 词根记忆：optim(最好的) + istic → 什么都往最好的一面想 → 乐观的 例 Few people are *optimistic* about the team's chances of winning. 很少有人对该队获胜的可能性持乐观态度。 参 optimization(*n.* 最优化) 天塌下来高个顶着 optimistic

marked [mɑːkt]	*a.* 显著的(*noticeable, pronounced); 有记号的; 被监视的 例 Crows have *marked* preferences for certain kinds of foods. 乌鸦对某些食物有明显的偏好。 派 markedly(*ad.* 显著地, 明显地) 参 marker(*n.* 标记; 里程碑)
typify ['tɪpɪfaɪ]	*vt.* 是…的典范; 成为…的特征 例 These houses which were popular in the early 1900s *typify* what's known as the unique style. 20 世纪初流行的这些房子是当时独特风格的典范。
imitation [ˌɪmɪ'teɪʃn]	*n.* 模仿, 仿效(mock); 仿制; 仿造品(fake) 记 来自 imitate(*vt.* 模仿, 仿效) 搭 in imitation of 为了仿效…; the illegal imitation 伪造 例 The increasing popularity of winter cycling can be attributed to the creation of mountain bike and its subsequent *imitations*. 冬季骑车的日趋流行要归因于山地车及随后其仿制品的出现。 imitation
gallery ['gæləri]	*n.* 画廊, 美术馆 搭 play to the gallery 哗众取宠 例 The *gallery* is a good place for the exhibition. 美术馆是举办这个展览的好场所。
compile [kəm'paɪl]	*vt.* 汇编(*put together); 编辑, 编纂(edit) 记 联想记忆: com(共同) + pile(堆) → 共同堆积 → 汇编 例 Computers can quickly *compile* and analyze this large volume of weather information. 计算机能快速收集并分析如此大量的气象信息。 派 compiler(*n.* 汇编者, 编著者)
propel [prə'pel]	*vt.* 推进, 驱使(push, drive); 激励 记 词根记忆: pro(向前) + pel(推) → 推进 例 The small plants and animals float about or weakly *propel* themselves through the sea. 小植物和动物要么漂浮着, 要么就在海中轻轻地推动自己前行。 派 propellant(*n.* 推进物)
hoe [həʊ]	*vt.* 用锄头锄 *n.* 锄头 记 联想记忆: 用锄头(hoe)挖洞(hole) 例 You should *hoe* the flower beds. 你应该给花坛除除草松松土。 参 harrow(*n.* 耙)
stride [straɪd]	*n.* 大步; 步法(pace); 进展 *vi.* 大步走 记 联想记忆: st + ride(骑自行车) → 走得像骑自行车一样快 → 大步走 搭 without breaking stride 步调不变, 阵脚不乱 例 They are making great *strides* in the search for a cure. 在探索治疗方法方面, 他们正不断取得重大进展。 stride

fade [feɪd]	*v.* 褪色；凋谢(wither)；逐渐消失(*disappear from, vanish) 搭 fade away 逐渐凋谢，慢慢减弱；衰弱 例 I've heard the printing really *fades* when you wash them. 我听说印花一洗真的会褪色。
tunnel [ˈtʌnl]	*n.* 隧道(tube)；地道 *v.* 开凿隧道；挖地道 记 联想记忆：海峡(channel)像条长长的地道(tunnel) 例 These caves form a labyrinth of *tunnels*. 这些洞穴形成迷宫般的隧道。
highlight [ˈhaɪlaɪt]	*vt.* 强调，突出(stand out)；以强烈光线照射 *n.* 最精彩部分 记 组合词：high(高的) + light(发光) → 突出；最精彩部分 例 The light *highlights* the figures of the sailors. 灯光突出了水手们的身影。
friction [ˈfrɪkʃn]	*n.* 摩擦；摩擦力；矛盾，冲突(clash, conflict) 记 联想记忆：润滑油的功能(function)是减小摩擦(friction) 例 The forward movement of a small animal is seriously reduced by the air *friction*. 小动物向前的运动因受到空气的摩擦而大幅减缓。
calm [kɑːm]	*a.* (天气、海洋等)平静的；镇静的，沉着的(tranquil; cool, composed) *vt.* 使平静，使镇定，平息(tranquilize, soothe) 记 联想记忆：她手(palm)心出汗，内心很不平静(calm) 例 A majority of people take investment in stock market seriously because the financial markets are still not *calm* at the moment. 鉴于目前金融市场仍不稳定，多数人在投资股市上都很谨慎。
wrinkle [ˈrɪŋkl]	*n.* 皱纹 *v.* (使)起皱纹 记 联想记忆：眯眼 (twinkle) 过多容易起皱纹(wrinkle) 例 There are fine *wrinkles* around her eyes. 她眼角出现了鱼尾纹。 // What Galileo has shown us is that Ganymede's surface is deeply *wrinkled* with ridges and fissures, a sign that it experiences some of the same dynamic forces that move continents and cause quakes on Earth. 伽利略向我们表明，木卫三表面布满山脊和裂缝，沟壑丛生，这标志着它上面存在着与地球上导致大陆漂移并引发地震的相同的动力。
cube [kjuːb]	*n.* 立方体；立方形的东西(尤指食物)；立方 记 联想记忆：和 tube(*n.* 管，显像管)一起记 例 Cut the meat into *cubes*. 把肉切成丁儿。
plank [plæŋk]	*n.* 木板(board)；政策要点，政纲的核心 记 联想记忆：计划(plan)用木板(plank)做条凳子 例 The central *plank* of the bill was urban development. 这一法案的核心是城市发展。

transfer [ˈtrænsˌfɜːr]	*v.* 转移(move)；转学；转让；换乘 *n.* 转移；转学；转让；换乘 记 词根记忆：trans(穿过，越过) + fer(带来) → 从一地带到另一地 → 转移 例 Pollen can be *transferred* by birds that come into contact with flowers. 花粉可以通过接触花朵的鸟来传播。
situated [ˈsɪtʃueɪtɪd]	*a.* 坐落在…的(located)；处于…境地的 例 If a city is well *situated* in regard to its hinterland, its development is much more likely to continue. 一座城市如果腹地位置不错，就更有可能持续发展。
eclecticism [ɪˈklektɪsɪzəm]	*n.* 折中主义 例 It is accompanied by a nostalgic impulse for the past and at the same time by an international cultural *eclecticism*. 与之相伴的是一种对过去的缅怀，同时还有一种国际文化折中主义。
piracy [ˈpaɪrəsi]	*n.* 海盗行为；抢劫行为；剽窃行为 记 来自 pirate(*vt.* 掠夺；盗版) 例 During periods of heavy *piracy* at sea, the amount of interest and the cost of the policy went up considerably. 在海盗活动猖獗期间，利益总数和政策成本显著增长。
deception [dɪˈsepʃn]	*n.* 骗局，诡计；欺骗，欺诈 记 词根记忆：de(分离) + cept(拿，抓) + ion → 拿走 → 欺骗 例 He was accused of obtaining property by *deception.* 他被指控骗取钱财。
blanket [ˈblæŋkɪt]	*n.* 毯子；覆盖物 记 联想记忆：blank(空的) + et(放在词尾表小玩意) → 毯子铺在一小块空地上 → 毯子 例 The trial was conducted under a *blanket* of secrecy. 审讯在高度保密状态下进行。
subtle [ˈsʌtl]	*a.* 细微的，微妙的(*slight)；精巧的，巧妙的；狡猾的；敏锐的 记 词根记忆：sub(在…下面) + tle → 暗藏于下面 → 微妙的 例 This interdependence is sometimes *subtle*, sometimes obvious. 这种相互依赖性有时不易察觉，有时显而易见。
dissenter [dɪˈsentər]	*n.* 不同意者，反对者(objector) 记 词根记忆：dis(分离) + sent(想法) + er(表人，名词后缀) → 没有相同想法的人 → 不同意者 例 It's important in building our organizational machines not to exclude the *dissenters*. 我们在建立组织机构时，不应将持异议者排拒在外，这一点很重要。 参 proponent(*n.* 支持者)

habit [ˈhæbɪt]	*n.* 习惯(custom); 习性, 脾性 记 词根记忆: hab(拥有) + it → 长期拥有的东西 → 习惯 搭 have a habit of doing 有做…的习惯 例 Professor Johnson, for my sociology project this term I'm thinking of interviewing all the residents in town on their TV viewing *habit*. 约翰逊教授，关于这个学期社会学的项目，我想着看电视的习惯采访镇里的所有居民。// I've heard that playing cards is a *habit* forming, and it's hard to kick it off. 我听说打牌会养成一种习惯，很难戒掉。
dictate [ˈdɪkteɪt]	*v.* 规定(regulate); 决定(*determine*); 口述; 支配 *n.* 命令, 规定 记 词根记忆: dict(讲话; 命令) + ate → 规定; 决定; 命令 例 The quality of the hinterland *dictated* the pace of growth of the cities. 腹地的特征决定了城市的发展速度。 参 abdicate(*v.* 退位, 卸任)
subway [ˈsʌbweɪ]	*n.* 地铁(underground) 记 联想记忆: sub(在…下面) + way(路) → 在下面的路 → 地铁 例 You can take the *subway* to get there. 你可以乘地铁去那。
aroma [əˈroʊmə]	*n.* 芳香, 香味; 气氛, 氛围 记 发音记忆: "爱罗马" → 最爱《罗马假日》中如雏菊般芳香四溢的赫本 → 芳香 例 The *aroma* of fresh pastry came to us from the kitchen. 我们闻到了从厨房飘来的新鲜糕点的香味。
niche [niːʃ]	*n.* 生态位; 壁龛 记 联想记忆: nice(好的)中间加 h → 比 nice 还多一点，更好更合适 → 生态位 例 Ancestral horse types moved from their forest *niche* out onto the grassy plains. 马的祖先离开了森林环境，来到了草原。
rush [rʌʃ]	*v.* (使)冲, (使)突进; 奔, 急速流动; (使)仓促从事; 突袭 *n.* 冲, 急速行进; 匆忙; (交通等的)繁忙 *a.* (交通)繁忙的 搭 rush hour 交通高峰期; rush through 使快速通过, 仓促处理 例 When gold was discovered in California in the mid-1800s, hundreds of people *rushed* in, hoping to get a part of the wealth. 19 世纪中叶在加州发现黄金之后，成百上千的人蜂拥而至，希望分得一杯羹。// I was running late this morning and had to *rush* to get here for the meeting. 我今天上午迟到了，只得匆匆赶过来开会。 派 rushed(*a.* 匆忙的) 参 bush(*n.* 矮树丛)
embody [ɪmˈbɑːdi]	*vt.* 表达, 体现(express); 含有(contain) 记 词根记忆: em(给予) + body(形体) → 给予形体 → 使有形 → 体现 例 That's a national team that *embodies* competitive spirit and skill. 那是一支体现了竞争精神和技能的国家队。

inviting [ɪnˈvaɪtɪŋ]	*a.* 动人的，诱人的(*attractive)；引人注目的 例 The regions have become increasingly *inviting* playgrounds for the growing number of recreation seekers. 这些地区已日益成为吸引越来越多娱乐探索者的活动场所。
elective [ɪˈlektɪv]	*a.* 选举的；可选择的；选修的(optional) 搭 elective system 选课系统 例 Students are required to take at least eight *elective* courses. 学生们至少需要上八门选修课。
benefit [ˈbenɪfɪt]	*n.* 益处，好处；恩惠；津贴 *v.* (使)受益(profit)；得益于 记 词根记忆：bene(善，好) + fit(做) → 益处，好处 例 He has *benefited* from the woman's help. 他得益于这个女子的帮助。

In order that people may be happy in their work, these things are needed: they must be fit for it; they must not do much of it; and they must have a sense of success in it.

为了使人们在工作时感到快乐，必须做到以下三点：他们一定要胜任自己的工作；他们不可做得太多；他们必须对自己的工作有成就感。

——英国作家 罗斯金 .J. (John Ruskin, British writer)

音频

词根、词缀预习表

pens	悬挂；支付	compensate *v.* 赔偿	**fa**	说话	affable *a.* 和蔼可亲的
card	心	cardinal *a.* 主要的	**duct**	拉	induct *vt.* 使正式就任
herb	草	herb *n.* 药草，香草	**anim**	生命；精神	animate *vt.* 赋予生命
aer	空气	aerial *a.* 空中的	**culmin**	顶点	culminate *vi.* 告终
charis	喜爱	charisma *n.* 超凡魅力	**quer**	询问	query *n.* 疑问

rhinoceros [raɪˈnɑːsərəs]	*n.* 犀牛 例 Among the most ancient animals, *rhinoceroses* thrived for millions of years before meeting their most deadly enemy: humans. 在大多数最古老的动物中，犀牛茁壮成长了数百万年，直到遇上它们最致命的死敌——人类。
herald [ˈherəld]	*vt.* 预示(foreshadow)；宣布，宣告(*announce) *n.* 信使(messenger)；预示，预兆 记 联想记忆：he(他) + rald(看做 raid，突然袭击) → 他带来敌人突然袭击的消息 → 信使 例 America's War of Independence *heralded* the birth of three modern nations. 美国的独立战争预示着三个现代国家的诞生。
affirm [əˈfɜːrm]	*v.* 断言，坚持声称(assert)；证实，确认 记 联想记忆：af + firm(坚定的) → 断言，坚持声称 例 The scholar *affirmed* Shakespeare's authorship of the plays. 这位学者坚持认为莎士比亚是这些剧本的作者。
modem [ˈmoʊdem]	*n.* 调制解调器 例 She hooks up her telephone *modem* connections. 她连接上电话调制解调器。
compensate [ˈkɑːmpenseɪt]	*v.* 赔偿，弥补(pay for, make up) 记 词根记忆：com(全部) + pens(悬挂；支付) + ate → 全部支付 → 赔偿 例 How do humans *compensate* for an underdeveloped sense of smell? 人类如何弥补不够发达的嗅觉？ 派 compensatory(*a.* 补偿性的)

这是公司的赔偿！

compensate

wax [wæks]	*v.* 给…打蜡；(月亮)渐满 *n.* 蜡；蜡状物 搭 wax and wane 兴衰荣枯，盛衰 例 My father *waxed* the wooden furniture. 我父亲给木头家具打上了蜡。 派 waxy(*a.* 蜡制的；光滑的)
psychoanalysis [ˌsaɪkoʊəˈnæləsɪs]	*n.* 心理分析，精神分析 记 联想记忆：psycho(灵魂，精神) + analysis(分析) → 精神分析 例 There are some good things, however, that have resulted from the method of *psychoanalysis* developed by Sigmund Freud more than a century ago. 然而西格蒙德·弗洛伊德于一个多世纪前所提出的心理分析方法也带来一些益处。 派 psychoanalyst(*n.* 心理分析学者，精神分析学家) 参 psychogenic(*a.* 心理的；精神的)
least [liːst]	*a.* 最小的；最少的；最不重要的 *ad.* 最小；最少；微不足道 搭 at least 最少；至少 例 She is the best employee, even though she has the *least* experience. 她虽然经验是最少的，却是最出色的员工。 参 feast(*n.* 节日，盛宴)
differentiate [ˌdɪfəˈrenʃieɪt]	*v.* (使)不同，区别(distinguish) 记 来自 different(*a.* 不同的) 例 Export merchants were *differentiated* from their importing counterparts. 出口商与进口商区别开来了。
cardinal [ˈkɑːrdɪnl]	*a.* 主要的，最重要的(main, essential) *n.* 红衣凤头鸟 记 词根记忆：card(心) + inal → 心一样的 → 主要的，最重要的 例 Respect for freedom is a *cardinal* principle of the country's law. 尊重自由是该国法律最重要的原则。
organism [ˈɔːrɡənɪzəm]	*n.* 生物，有机物(a living being)；有机体 记 联想记忆：organ(器官) + ism → 生物 例 All living *organisms* have to adapt to it when environment has changed. 所有活的生物都必须适应环境的变化。
refund	[ˈriːfʌnd] *n.* 偿还额；退款 [rɪˈfʌnd] *vt.* 退还(钱款)，偿付 记 联想记忆：re(向后) + fund(资金) → 返回资金 → 退还(钱款)；退款 例 It's too late for the woman to get a *refund.* 对这个女子而言，现在要回退款为时已晚。

herb [ɜːrb]	*n.* 药草，(调味用的)香草；草本植物 记 本身为词根，意为"草" 例 In the written record, the study of *herbs* dates back to the Sumerians, who described well-established medicinal uses for such plants as laurel, caraway, and thyme. 在书面记录中，药草学可追溯至苏美尔人，苏美尔记载了月桂、葛缕子和百里香等植物在药物上得到了广泛的使用。 参 herbicide(*n.* 除草剂); herbivore(*n.* 食草动物)
federal [ˈfedərəl]	*a.* 联邦的；联邦制的；联邦政府的 例 She is considered to be the first woman to hold a *federal* position. 她被认为是第一位担任联邦职务的女性。 派 federalist(*n.* 联邦制拥护者)
conceal [kənˈsiːl]	*vt.* 隐蔽；隐瞒；覆盖(*cover) 记 联想记忆：con + ceal(看做 seal，密封) → 密封起来 → 隐蔽；隐瞒 例 Those shallow puddles are often *concealed* by leaves. 这些浅水坑经常被树叶所覆盖。
otherwise [ˈʌðərwaɪz]	*ad.* 另样，用别的方法；在其他方面 *conj.* 要不然，否则 记 联想记忆：other(其他的) + wise(方面) → 在其他方面 例 My friends lent me money. *Otherwise*, I couldn't have afforded the trip. 朋友们借钱给我了，否则我可付不起这次旅费。// A: I'm looking for a gift for a friend of mine, any suggestions? B: Well, I have to know a little bit about your friend first. It's hard for me to say *otherwise*. A: 我想给一个朋友买礼物，有什么建议吗？ B: 我得先了解一下你的朋友。不然很难给出什么建议。 参 likewise(*ad.* 同样地)
steady [ˈstedi]	*a.* 牢固的(firm)；稳定的(constant, fixed)；沉稳的，可靠的 *v.* (使)平稳；稳定下来；使镇定 记 联想记忆：st + eady(看做 ready，有准备的) → 事先有准备，心里有底 → 稳定的 例 We are making slow but *steady* progress. 我们前进的步伐虽然缓慢，但却是在稳步前进。 派 steadily(*ad.* 稳定地)
ignore [ɪgˈnɔːr]	*vt.* 忽视(neglect)；不顾，不理 记 联想记忆：ig + nore(看做 nose，鼻子) → 翘起鼻子不理人 → 不理 例 The accomplishments of women are *ignored* in most historical documents. 大多数历史文献都忽略女性的成就。
originate [əˈrɪdʒɪneɪt]	*v.* 起源；发起(initiate, launch)；创立 记 来自 origin(*n.* 起源) 例 Life *originated* in the early seas less than a billion years after the Earth was formed. 地球形成之后不到十亿年，生命就形成于早期的海洋中。 派 origination(*n.* 起源); originator(*n.* 创始人；发明人)

7

aerial [ˈeriəl]	*a.* 空中的，地表以上的；从飞行器上的 *n.* 天线 记 词根记忆：aer(空气) + ial(形容词后缀) → 空中的 例 The banyan tree has *aerial* roots. 榕树有气根。
lipid [ˈlɪpɪd]	*n.* 脂质，类脂 例 *Lipids* are organic molecules that are insoluble in water. 类脂是不溶于水的有机分子。
interactive [ˌɪntərˈæktɪv]	*a.* 交互式的；合作的，互相配合的 搭 interactive systems 交互式系统 例 The school believes in *interactive* teaching methods. 这所学校相信互动教学法。 派 interactivity(*n.* 交互) 参 intercourse(*n.* 交往，交流)
charisma [kəˈrɪzmə]	*n.* 超凡魅力；感召力；号召力 记 词根记忆：charis(喜爱) + ma → 受到神眷顾，被赋予超凡魅力 → 超凡魅力 例 I don't have the *charisma* to attract so many people. 我没有这么大的魅力，能吸引这么多人。
affable [ˈæfəbl]	*a.* 和蔼可亲的，易于交谈的，友善的 记 词根记忆：af(=ad 近) + fa(说话) + (a)ble(能…的) → 能靠近说话的 → 和蔼可亲的 例 This conversation is joyous and *affable*. 这次谈话既愉快又友善。 派 affability(*n.* 和蔼可亲)
disconcert [ˌdɪskənˈsɜːrt]	*vt.* 使惊慌，使不安；使困惑(compound) 记 联想记忆：dis(不) + concert(一致) → 不一致 → 使惊慌 例 The things I'm about to say may *disconcert* others but not you. 我要说的事可能会让别人不安，但你不会。
induct [ɪnˈdʌkt]	*vt.* 使正式就任；使了解，传授；使入伍 记 词根记忆：in(内) + duct(拉) → 向里面拉 → 使正式就任 例 Many players form an organization, and *induct* other players to join in. 一群玩家组成一个组织并吸纳别的玩家加入。
wedge [wedʒ]	*n.* 楔子；楔形物 *vt.* 楔入，塞入 记 联想记忆：楔子(wedge)的边缘(edge)很尖锐 例 He hammered the *wedge* into the crack in the stone. 他用锤子把楔子砸入石缝里。
cohesive [koʊˈhiːsɪv]	*a.* 黏着的；使凝结的，使内聚的 记 词根记忆：co(共同) + hes(黏附) + ive → 黏在一起的 → 黏着的；使凝结的 例 Our team lacks *cohesive* force, and that's why we lost the game. 我们队缺乏凝聚力，这就是为什么我们输掉了比赛。

rape [reɪp]	*vt./n.* 强奸；肆意破坏 记 联想记忆：r + ape(猿) → 禽兽之举 → 强奸 例 He was charged with *rape*. 他被控犯了强奸罪。
animate [ˈænɪmət]	[ˈænɪmət] *a.* 活的，有生命的 [ˈænɪmeɪt] *vt.* 赋予生命，使有活力 记 词根记忆：anim(生命；精神) + ate → 赋予生命 例 The alarm clock is the only *animate* thing in this quiet room. 闹钟是这个安静的房间里唯一有生气的东西。
culminate [ˈkʌlmɪneɪt]	*vi.* 达到顶点；(以某种结果)告终；【天】到中天 记 词根记忆：culmin(顶点) + ate → 达到顶点 → (以某种结果)告终 搭 culminate in (以…)告终 例 The band's summer tour will *culminate* at a fabulous concert in New York. 这个乐队将在纽约举行精彩绝伦的演唱会，为夏季巡回演出画上句号。
predation [prɪˈdeɪʃn]	*n.* 掠夺；掠食 例 One of the explanations is defense from *predation*. 其中一个解释是对被捕食的防范。
gloss [ɡlɑːs]	*n.* 光泽，色泽；亮光漆；注解 *v.* (使)有光泽 记 联想记忆：总的(gross)来说，有光泽(gloss)的不都是金子 例 Repeat the last procedure and add another coat of *gloss*. 重复上述步骤，再上一层亮光漆。
adjoin [əˈdʒɔɪn]	*v.* 贴近，紧挨，毗连(abut) 记 联想记忆：ad(向) + join(连接) → 贴近 例 The city *adjoins* a well-known small-goods market. 那个城市毗邻全国闻名的小商品城。
shear [ʃɪr]	*v.* 剪(羊毛、头发等)；切断，剪切 记 联想记忆：sh(看做 she，她) + ear(耳朵) → 她剪了个齐耳短发 → 剪(头发等) 例 It was time for the sheep to be *shorn*. 是剪羊毛的时节了。
triumph [ˈtraɪʌmf]	*n.* 狂喜；胜利，成功 *v.* 获胜，成功 记 联想记忆：胜利(triumph)之后吹喇叭(trump) 例 The football team's victory was regarded as a major *triumph*. 足球队的胜利被认为是一个巨大的成功。
query [ˈkwɪri]	*n.* 疑问，问题 *v.* 向…提问；对…表示怀疑 记 词根记忆：quer(询问) + y → 疑问 例 I *query* whether his word can be trusted or not. 我怀疑他的话是否可信。
incredulous [ɪnˈkredʒələs]	*a.* 怀疑的，不轻信的(sceptical) 记 词根记忆：in(不) + cred(相信) + ul + ous(形容词后缀) → 怀疑的 例 People nowadays are *incredulous* about ghosts. 人们现在都不相信有鬼怪了。

7

puritanical [ˌpjʊrɪˈtænɪkl]	*a.* 极守道德的 记 联想记忆：puritan(清教徒) + ical → 如清教徒的 → 极守道德的 例 Mary was anything but *puritanical* in her behavior. 玛丽的行为根本不守道德。
anonymous [əˈnɑːnɪməs]	*a.* 匿名的，不具名的；无特色的，无个性特征的 记 词根记忆：an(无) + onym(名字) + ous(形容词后缀) → 匿名的 例 Susan received an *anonymous* letter. 苏珊收到了一封匿名信。
savage [ˈsævɪdʒ]	*a.* 凶残的；野蛮的，未开化的 *n.* 野蛮人，未开化的人 *vt.* 残害；激烈抨击 记 词根记忆：sav(森林) + age → 生活于丛林的(相对于城市而言，更不开化) → 未开化的 例 The blockbuster is mainly about a *savage*, bitter battle. 这部大片主要讲了一场残酷、激烈的战斗。
cider [ˈsaɪdər]	*n.* 苹果酒；苹果汁 例 I'd like a glass of *cider*. 我想要一杯苹果汁。
barn [bɑːrn]	*n.* 谷仓；牲口棚 记 联想记忆：这个酒吧(bar)是由谷仓(barn)改建而成的 例 They lived in a converted *barn*. 他们住在由谷仓改建的房子里。
uneven [ʌnˈiːvn]	*a.* 不平均的(unequal)；不平坦的；不规则的；(指竞争、比赛等)不势均力敌的；不公平的 例 Her hair has been badly cut and the ends are *uneven*. 她的头发剪得很糟，发端参差不齐。 派 unevenly(*ad.* 不平坦地；不均衡地)
awake [əˈweɪk]	*v.* 唤醒；醒(wake)；觉醒，醒悟 *a.* 醒着的；警觉的 记 联想记忆：a + wake(醒来) → 醒过来 → 醒着的 搭 stay awake 保持清醒；awake to sth. 察觉到，意识到 例 It took the young tiger some time to *awake* to the dangers of its situation. 过了一会儿那只小老虎才意识到处境危险。
stingy [ˈstɪndʒi]	*a.* 吝啬的，小气的 记 词根记忆：sting(刺) + y → 用针刺的 → 吝啬的 例 To my surprise, even though now Mary is rich, she is still *stingy*. 出乎我的意料，现在玛丽虽然有钱了，却还是那么吝啬。
bargain [ˈbɑːrɡən]	*n.* 特价商品，廉价货；协议；交易 *vi.* 讨价还价 记 联想记忆：bar(障碍) + gain(获得) → 高价是得到物品的障碍，所以要讨价还价 → 讨价还价 例 The *bargain* Frank got on his new stereo made him very happy. 弗兰克买的新音响很划算，他很高兴。// I've done what I promised and I expect you to keep your side of the *bargain*. 我已经履约，希望你也能遵守协议。// In the market dealers were *bargaining* with growers over the price of tea. 在市场上经销商们正和茶农就茶叶的价格进行商谈。

□ puritanical □ anonymous □ savage □ cider □ barn □ uneven
□ awake □ stingy □ bargain

exceed
[ɪk'siːd]

v. 超过，超出(*surpass, *go beyond)

记 词根记忆：ex(出) + ceed(走) → 走出去 → 超过

例 The circulation of weekly magazines *exceeded* that of newspapers in that period. 在那个时期，周刊的发行量超过了报纸。

派 exceeding(*a.* 超过的); exceedingly(*ad.* 非常)

forestall
[fɔːr'stɔːl]

vt. 预防，预先阻止；先发制人

记 联想记忆：fore(在…前面) + stall(拖延) → 在前面拖延时间 → 预防

例 Try to anticipate what your child will do and *forestall* problems. 尽量预见你的孩子会干什么，并预先阻止问题发生。

concave
[kɑːn'keɪv]

a. 凹的

记 词根记忆：con(表加强) + cav(空的) + e → 凹的

搭 a concave lens 凹透镜

例 A *concave* lens has two focal points — one on each side. 凹透镜有两个焦点，每面各有一个。

acknowledge
[ək'nɑːlɪdʒ]

v. 承认，确认(recognize, admit)；对…表示感谢(express gratitude)

记 联想记忆：ac + know (知道) + ledge → 大家都知道了，所以不得不承认 → 承认

例 Bill *acknowledged* his failure to complete the job. 比尔承认了未能完成工作。// I *acknowledged* Tom for all of his help with the project. 我对汤姆为这个项目提供的所有帮助表示了感谢。

boast
[boʊst]

v./n. 自我夸耀(brag)

记 联想记忆：面包师傅夸耀(boast)自己的面包烤(roast)得好

例 Anne made many *boasts* about her business. 安妮大肆夸耀自己的生意。

distribute
[dɪ'strɪbjuːt]

vt. 分配，分发 (parcel out)；散布(scatter, spread)

记 词根记忆：dis(分开) + tribut(给予) + e → 分开给 → 分配，分发

例 Professor Burke will *distribute* calendars to the students. 伯克教授将日历分发给学生。

派 distribution(*n.* 分发，分配); distributor(*n.* 发行人)

turnout
['tɜːrnaʊt]

n. (比赛、会议等的)出席人数；产量，产额(output)

例 Voter *turnout* is a fundamental quality of fair elections and is generally considered to be a necessary factor for a healthy democracy. 投票人数是公平选举的基本特征，其被广泛认为是健康民主的必备因素。

reinforce [ˌriːɪn'fɔːrs]	*vt.* 加固，加强(strengthen)；增援 记 联想记忆：re(再，又) + in(内) + force(力量) → 再次输入力量 → 加固，加强 例 I guess they wanted to *reinforce* the stuff we learned in school about history. 我猜他们想巩固我们在学校学过的历史知识。 派 reinforcement(*n.* 增援；加强)
jolt [dʒoʊlt]	*v.* (使)震动，颠簸；(使)震惊(*shock) *n.* 震动(shake)，颠簸；震惊；一阵强烈的感情等 记 联想记忆：防止颠簸(jolt)，用门闩(bolt)固定 例 The rate of species extinction in these environments *jolted* us into action. 这些环境里的物种灭绝率使我们猛然醒悟而行动起来。// The eel can produce a strong *jolt* of electricity to stun its prey. 鳗鱼可以产生一股强烈的电流来击昏猎物。
spiral ['spaɪrəl]	*vi.* 盘旋(coil, twist)；盘旋上升(或下降)；(物价等)急剧增长 *a.* 螺旋形的(helical) *n.* 螺旋形；螺旋式的上升(或下降) 搭 spiral galaxy 螺旋星系，旋涡星云；spiral thread 螺旋丝 例 Particles *spiral* back and forth between the Earth's magnetic poles. 粒子在地球磁极之间来回盘旋。
perspective [pər'spektɪv]	*n.* 展望；观点，看法；远景；透视图，透视法；前途 记 词根记忆：per(穿过) + spect(看) + ive → 透过某物看 → 展望 搭 perspective glass 透视镜 例 The cost has also made such plants less attractive from a purely economic *perspective*. 纯粹从经济角度考虑，其成本也使这种作物不那么有吸引力。
mask [mæsk]	*n.* 面具；面罩；假面具，伪装 *vt.* 掩饰，掩藏 记 联想记忆：准备化装舞会上用的面具(mask)真是项大任务(task) 例 The kids were all wearing animal *masks*. 孩子们都戴着动物面具。// The professor *masked* his anger with a smile. 教授用微笑来掩饰愤怒。
hitherto [ˌhɪðər'tuː]	*ad.* 迄今，至今 例 The weather, which had *hitherto* been sunny and mild, suddenly turned cold. 迄今为止还是晴朗温暖的天气忽然就变冷了。
comet ['kɑːmət]	*n.* 彗星 记 联想记忆：come(来) + t → 很多年才来一次的星星 → 彗星 例 He has been studying a *comet* for more than 20 years. 他已研究彗星长达20余年。

sociology

[ˌsəʊsɪˈɑːlədʒi]

n. 社会学

记 词根记忆：soci(同伴，结交) + ology(…学) → 社会学

例 The fascination of *sociology* lies in the fact that it makes us see in a new light the very world in which we have lived all our lives. 社会学的引人入胜之处在于它让我们从一个新的角度来观察我们一辈子都生活于其间的这个世界。

派 sociological(*a.* 社会学的；社会学上的)；sociologist(*n.* 社会学家)

vault

[vɔːlt]

n. 拱顶；金库，保险库；撑杆跳 *v.* (用手支撑或撑杆)跳过

例 Previously the poor quality of the iron had restricted its use in architecture to items such as *vaults* and walls. 以前铁的质量不好，限制了其自身在建筑中的拱顶和墙壁等方面的使用。

派 vaulted(*a.* 拱状的)

efficiency

[ɪˈfɪʃnsi]

n. 效率，功效(effectiveness)

记 词根记忆：ef(出) + fic(做) + iency → 做出来的成绩 → 功效

例 Since the developing of scientific technology, there has been a great improvement in energy *efficiency* at the factory. 科学技术的发展让工厂的能源利用率得到了大幅提高。

mime

[maɪm]

v. 模拟，模仿(simulate) *n.* 喜剧(comedy)；哑剧；哑剧演员；模拟表演

记 词根记忆：mim(模仿) + e → 模拟

例 He *mimed* and copied all her actions. 他模仿她的一举一动。

派 mimetic(*a.* 模仿的，好模仿的)

stratigraphy

[strəˈtɪgrəfi]

n. 地层学；地层中的岩石组成

记 词根记忆：strat(散布) + i + graph(写；图) + y → 有关(岩石的)分布情况 → 地层学

例 Scientists can identify the living age of some species by studying *stratigraphy*. 科学家们可以通过研究岩石组成来确定一些物种的生存年代。

advance

[ədˈvæns]

v. 前进，向前移动；发展，进步；促进；预付 *n.* 前进；进展；预付(款) *a.* 预先的；先头的

搭 in advance 预先

例 This research has done much to *advance* our understanding of language learning. 这项研究大大提高了我们对语言学习的认识。

派 advanced(*a.* 高级的；先进的；前进的)

estimate

[ˈestɪmeɪt] *v.* 评估，估计(*judge, *reckon)；估价(value)

[ˈestɪmət] *n.* 估计；估价；评价，看法

记 联想记忆：评估(estimate)地产(estate)

例 One of these migrating swarms was *estimated* to contain 124 billion locusts. 据估计，这些迁徙的蝗虫中的一批有 1240 亿只。

派 underestimate(*v./n.* 低估)

□ sociology   □ vault   □ efficiency   □ mime   □ stratigraphy   □ advance

□ estimate

impetus [ˈɪmpɪtəs]	*n.* 促进，推动(impulse)；刺激；推动力 记 词根记忆：im(内) + pet(追求) + us → 内心追求 → 促进；刺激 例 The danger of the fire gave an *impetus* to the use of more durable material. 火灾的危险推动了耐火力更好的材料的使用。
attend [əˈtend]	*v.* 出席，参加(present)；照料，看管；专心，注意；陪同 记 词根记忆：at + tend(伸展) → 伸长脖子看 → 专心 搭 attend the tournament 出席比赛；attend the conference 出席会议 例 Some of the representatives hadn't planned to *attend* the international conference. 一些代表没打算参加这次国际会议。 参 tend(*v.* 趋向；照顾)
solar [ˈsəʊlər]	*a.* 太阳的，日光的；(利用)太阳能的 记 词根记忆：sol(太阳) + ar → 太阳的 搭 solar year 阳历年；solar cell 太阳能电池 例 The problem with *solar* energy is that it works only when the sun is shining. 太阳能的问题在于其只在阳光照耀下才工作。
lodge [lɑːdʒ]	*n.* (海狸等的)巢穴；旅社；乡间小屋 *v.* 正式提出；租住，借宿；为…提供住宿；寄存 记 发音记忆："落脚" → 落脚的地方 → 巢穴 例 The beaver's penchant for building *lodges* and canals has got it into a lot of hot water lately. 最近，海狸搭巢和筑坝的嗜好使其陷入了困境。
commentary [ˈkɑːmənteri]	*n.* 评论，注释；(尤指电视台或电台所作的)实况报道，现场解说 搭 political commentary 政治评论 例 I prefer non-fiction: history, social *commentary* and stuff like that. 我喜欢纪实性读物：历史、社会评论等诸如此类。 参 commentator(*n.* 评论员；现场解说员) 你不是一个人在战斗！ commentary
instruct [ɪnˈstrʌkt]	*vt.* 指示(direct)；教授(teach) 记 词根记忆：in + struct(建筑) → 教人如何建筑 → 教授 例 His work is to *instruct* newcomers about bicycle maintenance. 他的工作是指导新来者如何维修自行车。 派 instructive(*a.* 有益的；知识丰富的)；instructor(*n.* 教练)
gorilla [gəˈrɪlə]	*n.* 大猩猩 记 联想记忆：go(去) + rill(小河) + a → 到小河边去看大猩猩 → 大猩猩 例 They launched a program to protect the *gorilla*. 他们启动了大猩猩保护项目。
logical [ˈlɑːdʒɪkl]	*a.* 逻辑的；符合逻辑的，合理的(reasonable)；有逻辑头脑的 记 来自logic(*n.* 逻辑；逻辑学)；log(言语) + ic → 言语正确 → 逻辑 例 The apartment's room arrangement was not *logical*. 公寓房间的格局不合理。

□ impetus　　　□ attend　　　□ solar　　　□ lodge　　　□ commentary　　□ instruct
□ gorilla　　　□ logical

incubate [ˈɪŋkjubeɪt]	*v.* 孵化(hatch)；培育(细菌等)；(疾病)潜伏 词根记忆：in(在…里面) + cub(躺) + ate → 躺在里面 → 孵化 The researchers remove eggs from the nests of parrots and *incubate* them under laboratory conditions. 研究人员从鹦鹉巢里取走鸟蛋，并在实验室环境下将其孵化。 incubation(*n.* 孵卵；潜伏期；繁殖)；incubator(*n.* 孵化器)
monster [ˈmɑːnstər]	*n.* 怪物；庞然大物；恶魔 *a.* 巨大的，庞大的 联想记忆：mon(音似：猛) + ster → 凶猛可怕的 → 怪物 The dog is an absolute *monster*! 那条狗好大啊！
intriguing [ɪnˈtriːgɪŋ]	*a.* 引起兴趣(或好奇心)的，吸引人的(*fascinating, *attractive) The urban life seemed particularly *intriguing* to those raised in rural isolation. 对在农村偏远地区长大的人来说，城市生活似乎特别有吸引力。
sedimentary [ˌsedɪˈmentri]	*a.* 沉积的，沉淀性的(precipitable) Stratigraphy is the description of strata in *sedimentary* rock. 地层学描述了沉积岩层。
participate [pɑːrˈtɪsɪpeɪt]	*vi.* (in)参与，参加(take part in) 词根记忆：part(部分) + i + cip(拿，取) + ate(动词后缀) → 拿住部分 → 参与 They *participated* in the last three races. 他们参加了最后三项比赛。 participation(*n.* 参与)；participator(*n.* 参与者)
resemble [rɪˈzembl]	*vt.* 与…相似，像(*look like) 词根记忆：re(再，又) + sembl(一样，相同) + e → 与…相似，像 Giant pandas *resemble* bears in shape. 大熊猫和熊在体形上相似。 resemblance(*n.* 相似，相像)
mason [ˈmeɪsn]	*n.* 石匠，泥瓦匠 联想记忆：ma(音似：妈) + son(儿子) → 妈妈不希望儿子成为泥瓦匠 → 泥瓦匠 The *mason* worked hard but earned little. 那个泥瓦匠工作很辛苦，赚得却很少。 masonry(*n.* 石建筑；石工)
nationalism [ˈnæʃnəlɪzəm]	*n.* 国家主义；民族主义，民族优越感 *Nationalism* unites people of different classes and ideologies. 国家主义将来自不同阶级、具有不同意识形态的人联系在了一起。
heading [ˈhedɪŋ]	*n.* 标题；主题 The *heading* should be catching. 标题必须引人入胜。

unpredictable
[ˌʌnprɪˈdɪktəbl]

a. 不可预知的；无法预言的

记 联想记忆：un(不) + predict(预言) + able(能…的) → 不可预知的；无法预言的

例 Their major discovery illustrated how *unpredictable* consequences could come from rather modest beginnings. 他们的重要发现表明了看似极其平常的初始是如何产生了预想不到的结果的。

派 unpredictability(*n.* 不可预知性)

preoccupation
[priˌɑːkjuˈpeɪʃn]

n. 主要考虑因素；全神贯注(concern, involvement)

记 来自 preoccup(y)(*vt.* 使忧心忡忡)

例 The beggar's main *preoccupation* at this time is getting some money and food. 乞讨者此时满脑子想着的是弄到一些钱和食物。

Every day I remind myself that my inner and outer life are based on the labors of other men, living and dead, and that I must exert myself in order to give in the same measure as I have received and am still receiving.

每天我都提醒着自己：我的精神生活和物质生活都是以别人的劳动为基础的，我必须尽力以同样的分量来报偿我所获得的和至今仍在接受着的东西。

——美国科学家 爱因斯坦(Albert Einstein, American scientist)

音频

词根、词缀预习表

frag	打碎	fragile *a.* 易碎的	mot	动	promote *vt.* 促进
ag	做	agile *a.* 敏捷的	rid	笑	ridiculous *a.* 荒唐的，可笑的
vac	空	vacant *a.* 空的	fract	折断	refraction *n.* 折射
portion	部分	apportion *vt.* 分配	mut	变化	mutual *a.* 相互的；共有的
juven	年轻的	juvenile *a.* 幼稚的	cracy	统治	bureaucracy *n.* 官僚机构

---

communal
[kəˈmjuːnl]

a. 公共的，共享的；社区的
记 词根记忆：com(共同) + mun(服务) + al → 为大家服务的 → 公共的
例 His paintings depict the *communal* cultural experience of Mexican descended people in the US. 他的绘画描写了在美墨西哥后裔的社区文化体验。

fragile
[ˈfrædʒl]

a. 易碎的(brittle)；脆弱的(delicate, frail)；纤巧的；虚弱的
记 词根记忆：frag(打碎) + ile → 容易被打碎的 → 易碎的
例 His muscle fibers were short and *fragile*. 他的肌肉纤维短而脆弱。// The old woman is now 90 and in *fragile* health. 那个老妇人现已90高龄，身体虚弱。
派 fragility(*n.* 脆弱；虚弱)

agile
[ˈædʒl]

a. 敏捷的，灵活的(nimble, brisk)
记 词根记忆：ag(做) + ile(能…的) → 做事灵活的 → 敏捷的
搭 an agile brain 灵活的头脑
例 The leader of a country needs an *agile* mind to solve sophisticated problems. 国家领导人需要敏捷的头脑来解决复杂的问题。
派 agility(*n.* 敏捷，灵活)

competence
[ˈkɑːmpɪtəns]

n. 能力，胜任；权限；技能
记 来自compete(*vi.* 竞争)
例 By the age of three the babies will be well on their way to communicative *competence*. 孩子们到了三岁时就能很好地进行交流了。

lettuce
[ˈletɪs]

n. 生菜；莴苣
例 Please buy a *lettuce* and some tomatoes for me. 请帮我买一棵生菜和一些西红柿。

---

vacant ['veɪkənt]	*a.* 空的(empty);闲置的(unused);(神情等)茫然的,(心灵)空虚的 记 词根记忆:vac(空) + ant(形容词后缀) → 空的 例 There are still *vacant* rooms. 现在仍有空房间。 派 vacancy(*n.* 空处;空缺) 有人不?　vacant
apportion [ə'pɔːrʃn]	*vt.* 分配(distribute, allot);分派 记 词根记忆:ap + portion(部分) → 分成部分 → 分配 例 The man's property was *apportioned* among his children after his death. 那个男人过世后,财产为其子女所分。
emotional [ɪ'moʊʃənl]	*a.* 感情(上)的, 情绪(上)的;引起情感的;易动感情的 例 Very soon, these differences in adult stress and intonation can influence babies' *emotional* states and behaviors. 很快,成人话语中的重音和语调的不同会影响婴儿的情绪和行为。 派 emotionally(*ad.* 在情绪上) 参 emotive(*a.* 激起感情的,有感染力的) emotional
juvenile ['dʒuːvənl]	*n.* 幼体;未成年人, 少年 *a.* 幼稚的, 不成熟的;少年的, 未成年的 记 词根记忆:juven(年轻的) + ile → 幼体的 例 The successful prevention of *juvenile* delinquency requires efforts on the part of the entire society. 要想成功预防青少年犯罪,需要整个社会共同努力。
status ['steɪtəs]	*n.* 身份, 地位(rank, position);情况(condition) 记 联想记忆:stat(看做 state, 声明) + us → 声明我们是谁 → 身份 例 A woman's *status* was changed by marriage. 女人的地位因婚姻而发生改变。
promote [prə'moʊt]	*vt.* 促进(boost, advance);提升;宣传, 推销(advertise) 记 词根记忆:pro(向前) + mot(动) + e → 向前动 → 促进 例 In the early decades of the United States, the agrarian movement *promoted* the farmer as society's hero. 美国建国初几十年里,农业运动把农民提升为社会的英雄。 派 promotion(*n.* 晋升;提升;宣传)
academic [ˌækə'demɪk]	*a.* 学术的(scholarly);学校的, 学院的;纯理论的(theoretical) *n.* 大学教师 记 来自 academy(*n.* 学会,研究院) 搭 academic status 学术地位;a purely academic question 一个纯理论问题;academic conference 学术会议 例 Recently, universities have become involved with students' emotional lives and their *academic* lives. 最近,大学已开始关注学生的情感生活和学术活动。 派 academician(*n.* 学者;学会会员)

rigor [ˈrɪɡər]	*n.* 严格(strictness)；(气候、条件等的)严酷 例 Everyone has to understand the utmost *rigor* of the law. 每个人都必须理解法律至高无上的严格性。 派 rigorous(*a.* 严格的)
complex	[kəmˈpleks] *a.* 合成的，综合的；复杂的，错综的，难以理解的(*intricate, complicated) [ˈkɑːmpleks] *n.* 建筑群；综合体，集合体；情结 记 词根记忆：com(共同) + plex(重叠) → 重叠交叉的 → 错综的 例 The decision involves a large number of variables with *complex* relationships. 这个决定涉及很多关系复杂的变量。// Have you inquired at the apartment *complex* down the street? 你询问过街道那边的公寓综合楼吗？ 派 complexity(*n.* 复杂性)
X-ray [ˈeks reɪ]	*n.* X 射线，X 光；X 光照片 例 The doctor studied the *X-rays* of her lungs. 医生研究了她肺部的 X 光照片。
franchise [ˈfræntʃaɪz]	*n.* 特权，特许(privilege)；特许经销权；(公民)选举权 *vt.* 赋予特权；赋予选举权 搭 a franchise company 特约代销公司 例 That restaurant is expanding through the sale of *franchise*. 那家餐厅正通过销售特许权扩展业务。
item [ˈaɪtəm]	*n.* 项目，条款(clause)；一件商品(或物品)；(新闻等的)一条，一则 搭 item on the agenda 议程条款；news item 新闻要点 例 The computer was his largest single *item* of expenditure. 电脑是他花钱最多的一样东西。
grip [ɡrɪp]	*v.* 控制(control, command)；紧握；吸引住…的注意 *n.* 控制，影响力；紧握；理解 记 联想记忆：和 trip(*n.* 旅行)一起记 搭 in the grip of 在…的掌控下，受制于… 例 The kids were totally *gripped* by the story. 孩子们完全被这个故事吸引住了。// I couldn't get a *grip* on what was going on. 我不知道正在发生什么。
ridiculous [rɪˈdɪkjələs]	*a.* 荒唐的，可笑的(absurd) 记 词根记忆：rid(笑) + icul + ous(形容词后缀) → 被人嘲笑的 → 荒唐的，可笑的 例 Never have I heard such a *ridiculous* excuse. 我从没听过如此荒唐的借口。 ridiculous
mode [moʊd]	*n.* 方式，形式(manner)；风格(style)；时尚(fashion) 例 Heat is a *mode* of motion. 热是运动的一种形式。

8

cactus [ˈkæktəs]	*n.* [*pl.* cacti] 仙人掌 例 *Cacti* are unusual plants, which are adapted to extremely arid and hot environments. 仙人掌是极不寻常的植物，能适应极其干旱炎热的环境。
silica [ˈsɪlɪkə]	*n.* 硅石，硅土；二氧化硅 参 silicate(*n.* 硅酸盐)；siliceous(*a.* 硅酸的，硅土的)
willful [ˈwɪlfl]	*a.* 成心的，有意的；任性的(unruly) 例 He was a *willful* child. 他是个任性的孩子。
refraction [rɪˈfrækʃn]	*n.* 折射(deflection) 记 词根记忆：re(向后) + fract(折断) + ion → 向后折断 → 折射 例 *Refraction* in the atmosphere is complicated by the continuous change in density of the air. 空气中的折射因空气密度的持续变化而被复杂化。
fortuitous [fɔːrˈtuːɪtəs]	*a.* 偶然的，意外的(*lucky, sudden, casual) 例 They fell in love with each other in a *fortuitous* meeting. 他们偶然相遇后就双双坠入了爱河。 派 fortuitously(*ad.* 偶然地)
insight [ˈɪnsaɪt]	*n.* 洞察力；领悟(perception) 记 联想记忆：in(进入) + sight(眼光) → 眼光深入 → 洞察力 例 Lillian Hellman's plays are marked by *insight* and finesse. 莉莲·赫尔曼的剧作以富有洞察力和写作技巧著称。 派 insightful(*a.* 富有洞察力的，有深刻见解的)
discard [dɪsˈkɑːrd]	*vt.* 丢弃(reject) 记 联想记忆：dis(分离) + card(纸牌) → 出牌，把牌扔出去 → 丢弃 例 I've *discarded* all thought of promotion. 我已经打消了晋升的念头。
concept [ˈkɑːnsept]	*n.* 概念，观念(notion, thought)；设想 记 词根记忆：con(共同) + cept(拿，取) → 共同拿取 → 观念 例 I'll give a lecture on the different *concepts* of political thought. 我会就政治思想的不同概念做一次讲座。 派 conceptual(*a.* 概念上的)；conception(*n.* 观念)；misconception(*n.* 误解) 参 precept(*n.* 规则)
swift [swɪft]	*a.* 敏捷的，速度快的(rapid) *n.* 雨燕 记 联想记忆：电梯(lift)速度很快(swift) 例 The current was too *swift* for boats to cross easily. 水流太急，船很难渡过。 派 swiftly(*ad.* 很快地)；swiftness(*n.* 迅速)
noted [ˈnoʊtɪd]	*a.* 著名的(famous) 例 These journals contain essays by several *noted* historians. 这些杂志刊登有几位著名历史学家的文章。

离我远点

cactus

release [rɪ'liːs]	*n./vt.* 释放; 发布, 公开(issue); 发泄 例 The government has been working hard to secure the *release* of the hostages. 政府一直在努力争取使人质获释。// Police have *released* no further details about the accident. 关于这起事故, 警方并未透露更多细节。
propensity [prə'pensəti]	*n.* 倾向, 癖好(inclination, tendency, disposition) 记 词根记忆: pro(向前) + pens(悬挂) + ity → 预先挂好 → 癖好 搭 have a propensity for 有…的倾向; a propensity to do sth. 喜欢做某事, 有做某事的倾向 例 He showed a *propensity* for violence. 他表现出暴力倾向。
fable ['feɪbl]	*n.* 寓言; 谎言 记 词根记忆: fa(说) + (a)ble(能…的) → 能说的 → 传说的 → 寓言 例 That's a mere *fable*. 那纯属无稽之谈。
diplomat ['dɪpləmæt]	*n.* 外交官; 有手腕的人 例 The *diplomat* solved the international problem by negotiating. 那名外交官通过谈判解决了那个国际问题。
mutual ['mjuːtʃuəl]	*a.* 相互的; 共有的(joint, common) 记 词根记忆: mut(变化) + ual(形容词后缀) → 改变是相互作用的结果 → 相互; 共有的 例 It is this intense *mutual* engagement that elicits the display of skill and shapes the emerging performance. 正是这种强烈的互动, 才使技能展现出来, 并塑造出逐渐成形的表演。 派 mutually(*ad.* 互相地)
odd [ɑːd]	*a.* 单数的(singular); 奇数的; 奇异的, 古怪的(bizarre); 偶尔发生的 记 联想记忆: 奇奇(odd)相加(add)为偶 例 He makes the *odd* mistake — nothing too serious. 他偶尔会犯错误, 但不怎么严重。
confidant ['kɑːnfɪdænt]	*n.* 知己, 密友 记 词根记忆: con(完全) + fid(相信) + ant(表人, 名词后缀) → 完全相信的人 → 知己, 密友 例 You keep telling yourself that she is only your *confidant*. 你一直告诉自己, 她只是你的知己而已。
bureaucracy [bjʊ'rɑːkrəsi]	*n.* 官僚主义, 官僚作风; 政府机构, 官僚机构 记 词根记忆: bureau(桌子, 引申为"政府的局") + cracy(统治) → 官僚机构 例 When our focus is on action instead of *bureaucracy*, things will get done quickly and easily. 当我们将注意力集中于行动而不是官僚作风上时, 事情就能很快且很容易地办妥。
abate [ə'beɪt]	*v.* (使)减少, 减轻 记 联想记忆: a + bate(减少) → (使)减少, 减轻 例 To *abate* the noise in big cities is a tough job. 消除大城市中的噪音是件棘手的事。

□ release □ propensity □ fable □ diplomat □ mutual □ odd
□ confidant □ bureaucracy □ abate

dignify [ˈdɪgnɪfaɪ]	*vt.* 使有尊严，使高贵；美化 记 词根记忆：dign（价值）+ ify（使…）→ 使有价值 → 使有尊严 例 The ambassador was there to *dignify* the celebrations. 大使的光临为庆祝活动增辉。
feign [feɪn]	*vt.* 装作，假装；伪造 记 联想记忆：设计（design）伪造（feign）品 例 I think you're right that sense of humor is born in nature which could not be *feigned*. 我想你是对的，幽默是天生的，装不出来。
melodious [məˈloʊdiəs]	*a.* 旋律优美的，悦耳的 例 I heard *melodious* music come from the room. 我听到屋里传出优美的音乐。
disastrous [dɪˈzæstrəs]	*a.* 灾难性的 记 来自 disaster（*n.* 灾难） 例 The war was *disastrous*, and many people lost their homes and families. 这场战争极具灾难性，很多人失去了家园和亲人。
complaint [kəmˈpleɪnt]	*n.* 诉苦，抱怨；投诉；控告 例 The customer has made a *complaint* to the manager. 那位顾客向经理投诉了。
negligent [ˈneglɪdʒənt]	*a.* 忽略的；疏忽的；粗心大意的 记 词根记忆：neg（不）+ lig（选择）+ ent → 不选择的 → 忽略的；疏忽的 例 We learned an important lesson from this incident: One should not be *negligent* of traffic regulations. 我们从这个事件中学到了宝贵的一课：对交通规则不可掉以轻心。
frail [freɪl]	*a.* （指人）体弱的，虚弱的；易碎的 记 联想记忆：她身体太弱（frail），未能通过（fail）体育考试 例 Grandma is old and *frail*, so I don't think she can travel to Paris with you. 奶奶年老体弱，我认为她不能跟你一起去巴黎。
blaze [bleɪz]	*n.* 火焰；光辉，强烈（或眩目）的光；（感情的）迸发 *vi.* 燃烧，着火；发光，放光彩；怒视 记 联想记忆：上釉（glaze）靠火焰（blaze） 搭 blaze a trail 开拓道路，领先 例 Luckily, the firefighters were able to control the *blaze* within a short period of time. 幸运的是，消防员在短时间内就控制了火势。
cherish [ˈtʃerɪʃ]	*vt.* 爱护，珍爱；怀有，抱有（希望等） 记 联想记忆：要珍爱（cherish），不要毁坏（perish） 例 I will *cherish* each study opportunity I can get in this company. 我会珍惜在公司得到的每一个学习机会。
snide [snaɪd]	*a.* 伪造的；不诚实的；讽刺的，挖苦的，含沙射影的 记 联想记忆：把 n 藏在一边（side）→ 伪造的；不诚实的 搭 snide remarks 挖苦的话语 例 I suddenly realized I was deceived by a *snide* businessman. 我忽然意识到我上了一个卑鄙商人的当。

empiricism [ɪmˈpɪrɪsɪzəm]	*n.* 经验论，经验主义 记 词根记忆：em(在…里面) + pir(实验) + ic + ism(表主义，名词后缀) → 在内部进行实验 → 经验论，经验主义 例 Logical *empiricism* was not widely embraced in Britain or the United States. 逻辑经验主义在英国和美国都没有被广泛接受。
falter [ˈfɔːltər]	*v.* 衰退，衰落；(声音)发抖，结巴地说；蹒跚 记 联想记忆：f + alter(改变) → 忽然改变立场，不再理直气壮 → (声音)发抖，结巴地说 例 Trembling with shock, she *faltered* out a few words of thanks. 她惊讶得直发抖，结结巴巴地说出了几句表示感谢的话。
mismanage [ˌmɪsˈmænɪdʒ]	*vt.* 对…管理不当，处理不当(mishandle) 记 联想记忆：mis(不) + manage(管理，处理) → 对…管理不当，处理不当 例 The manager *mismanaged* intrinsic conflicts, which had serious consequences for the company. 那名经理对内部矛盾处理不当，给公司造成了严重后果。
lust [lʌst]	*n.* 性欲；强烈的欲望 *v.* 对…有强烈的欲望 搭 lust after/for 极度渴望 例 It's difficult to satisfy his *lust* for power. 很难满足他对权力的强烈欲望。
stampede [stæmˈpiːd]	*v.* (使)狂奔，涌向；使仓促行事 *n.* 逃窜，狂奔；热潮，风尚 记 联想记忆：为买张邮票(stamp)到处狂奔(stampede) 例 I don't want to be *stampeded* into making any hasty decisions. 我不愿仓促行事，草草做决定。// The new policy has led to a *stampede* to buy property. 新政策引发了一场购房热。
overnight	[ˈoʊvərnaɪt] *a.* 通宵的，一整夜的；一夜之间的 [ˌoʊvərˈnaɪt] *ad.* 整夜；一夜之间 记 组合词：over(越过) + night(夜) → 跨越一整夜 → 通宵的 例 The movie was an *overnight* success. 这部电影一夜成名。
torpor [ˈtɔːrpər]	*n.* 迟钝；死气沉沉(lethargy, inertia) 例 In the heat they sank into a state of *torpor*. 炎热的天气使得他们萎靡不振。
shed [ʃed]	*vt.* 抛弃，摆脱(*discard, slough)；流出；散发；发出(光等)；脱落 *n.* 小屋(hut, shanty) 记 联想记忆：she(她) + d → 女孩子容易流眼泪 → 流出 例 The huge impact created a vapor that *shed* out into space and eventually condensed as the Moon. 巨大的冲击产生了蒸汽，蒸汽喷入太空并最终冷凝成了月球。

8

hierarchy [ˈhaɪərɑːrki]	*n.* 统治集团；等级制度；阶层(rank) 记 词根记忆：hier(神圣) + archy(统治) → 僧侣统治 → 等级制度 搭 social hierarchy 社会阶层 例 The author puts honesty first in her *hierarchy* of values. 作者把诚实置于她的价值观体系中的首位。
aluminum [ˌæljəˈmɪniəm]	*n.* 铝 搭 aluminium foil 铝箔；an aluminum saucepan 铝锅
deplete [dɪˈpliːt]	*vt.* 使枯竭，耗尽(use up, exhaust) 记 词根记忆：de + plet(满) + e → 不满 → 倒空 → 使枯竭 例 Food supplies are quickly *depleted*. 食物储备快耗尽了。 派 depletion(*n.* 消耗；用尽)
pattern [ˈpætərn]	*n.* 模式，方式；样式，图案；样品，样本 *vt.* 仿制(imitate)；使形成，促成 例 World trade *patterns* are indicative of the important economic issues that confront the world today. 世界贸易模式影射了当今世界面临的重要经济议题。 派 patterned(*a.* 有图案的，带花样的)
shirk [ʃɜːrk]	*v.* 逃避，规避 记 联想记忆：通过假笑(smirk)来逃避(shirk)责任 例 I will not *shirk* my share of the responsibility. 我不会逃避我所应担负的责任。
dormant [ˈdɔːrmənt]	*a.* 静止的(inactive)；休眠的(resting)；隐匿的 记 词根记忆：dorm(睡眠) + ant → 休眠的 搭 a dormant volcano 休眠火山 例 When water is scarce, lichens may become *dormant*. 苔藓缺水时可能会停止生长。
quasar [ˈkweɪzɑːr]	*n.* 类星体 例 *Quasars* are the most luminous objects in the universe. 类星体是宇宙中最亮的天体。
humorous [ˈhjuːmərəs]	*a.* 幽默的，滑稽的，诙谐的 记 来自 humor(*n.* 幽默) 例 There are two sons and one daughter of Joe's marriage in the story: the daughter married a *humorous* artist and led a happy life in the end. 故事中乔婚后有两个儿子和一个女儿：女儿嫁给了一个幽默的艺术家，最后过着幸福的生活。
bolster [ˈboʊlstər]	*vt.* 支持(support)；改善(improve) *n.* 垫子，枕垫 搭 bolster up 改善；激活 例 The miners *bolstered* their morale by shouting slogans. 矿工们通过喊口号来提高士气。
cite [saɪt]	*vt.* 引用，引证(quote)；传唤，传讯；表彰，嘉奖 例 Where in the passage does the author *cite* the goal of the Academy Institute? 作者在这篇文章的什么地方引用了研究院的目标？

offensive [əˈfensɪv]	*a.* 攻击性的(aggressive); 冒犯的，使人不快的; 攻方的 *n.* 进攻，攻击; 攻势 记 词根记忆：of + fens(打) + ive → 打击别人 → 攻击性的 搭 take the offensive 先发制人 例 The *offensive* team carried the ball closer to the goal. 进攻的球队把球带到了离球门更近的地方。// The government has launched a new *offensive* against crime. 政府发动了打击犯罪的新攻势。 派 inoffensive(*a.* 无害的)
emerge [iˈmɜːrdʒ]	*vi.* 显露，暴露(*appear); (从水中)出来，现出 记 词根记忆：e(出) + merg(浸没) + e → 从浸没之中出来 → 显露，暴露 例 Several outstanding musicians *emerged* as leading jazz artists in Chicago. 几位出色的音乐家脱颖而出成为芝加哥引领风骚的爵士乐艺术家。 派 emergence(*n.* 形成; 出现); emergency(*n.* 紧急情况，突发事件)
tactic [ˈtæktɪk]	*n.* 手段，策略(means, strategy); [*pl.*]战术 记 词根记忆：tact(接触) + ic → 通过手段来接触 → 手段 例 The manager discussed *tactics* with his colleagues. 经理和他的同事们讨论了策略问题。
awareness [əˈwernəs]	*n.* 知道，意识，察觉(*realization) 记 来自aware(*a.* 知道的，意识到的) 搭 self awareness 自我意识; public awareness 公共意识 例 We should increase public *awareness* of the importance of eating a healthy diet. 我们应该增强公众对健康饮食重要性的认识。
distract [dɪˈstrækt]	*vt.* 分散注意力，使分心 记 词根记忆：dis(分开) + tract(拉) → (注意力)被拉开 → 分散注意力，使分心 例 The thunderstorm *distracted* the little boy from his homework. 雷雨使得小男孩无法专心写作业。 派 distracted(*a.* 心烦意乱的); distracting(*a.* 令人分心的); distraction (*n.* 分散注意力的事)
rehabilitate [ˌriːəˈbɪlɪteɪt]	*vt.* 使恢复原状，修复 (restore); 改造 (罪犯等)，使恢复正常生活; 恢复…的名誉 记 词根记忆：re(再，又) + hab(拥有) + ilit + ate → 重新拥有 → 使恢复原状，修复 例 San Antonio's leaders *rehabilitated* existing structures. 圣安东尼奥市的领导人修复了现存的建筑。 派 rehabilitation(*n.* 恢复，复原)
blizzard [ˈblɪzərd]	*n.* 暴风雪，大风雪 例 Because of the raging *blizzard* all flights have been cancelled. 由于猛烈的暴风雪，所有的航班都被取消了。 参 bazaar(*n.* 集市); bizarre(*a.* 古怪的)

mold [moʊld]	*n.* 霉菌(fungus); 模型(type) *vt.* 塑造(shape, figure) 例 The higher the clay content in a sample, the more refined and durable the shapes into which it can be *molded*. 样品中黏土含量越高，其所能塑成的形状就越精细和持久。
ease [iːz]	*n.* 不费力，容易; 悠闲，自在 *v.* 缓和，减轻 例 The *ease* of solving a jigsaw puzzle depends on the design of the picture. 解决智力拼图的难易程度取决于图画的设计。
roe [roʊ]	*n.* 鱼卵 记 发音记忆: "肉" → 鱼卵也是鱼妈妈身上的一块肉 → 鱼卵 例 Sturgeons are prized for their blackish *roe*. 鲟鱼因其黑色鱼卵而受到珍视。
fin [fɪn]	*n.* 鳍; 鳍状物; (飞机等的)翼 搭 dorsal fin 背鳍 例 A *fin* helps fish to keep balance. 鳍帮助鱼保持平衡。
mythology [mɪˈθɑːlədʒi]	*n.* 神话; 神话学; 虚幻的想法 例 Indian *mythology* is one of the richest elements of Indian culture, which enriches it further and makes it a unique one in the world. 印度神话是印度文化中最丰富的元素之一，其进一步丰富了印度文化，并使它在世界文化之林中独树一帜。 派 mythological(*a.* 神话的; 虚构的)
drastic [ˈdræstɪk]	*a.* 剧烈的，猛烈的，激烈的(fierce, intense) 记 词根记忆: dra(驱动) + stic → 剧烈的 例 What forms of life are able to make such a *drastic* change in lifestyle? 哪种生命能在生活方式上作出如此剧烈的改变? 派 drastically(*ad.* 激烈地; 彻底地)
healing [ˈhiːlɪŋ]	*a.* 有治疗功用的(*curative) *n.* 康复，治疗; 复原 记 来自 heal(*v.* 治疗，治愈) 例 Honey also contains a variety of minerals and vitamins and has a long history as a *healing* food. 蜂蜜还富含各种矿物质和维生素，在历史上很长一段时间都被用做保健品。
blush [blʌʃ]	*vi.* 脸红; 羞愧(flush) *n.* (因羞愧等)脸上泛起的红晕 记 联想记忆: 果园里一片繁茂(lush)，苹果红了脸(blush) 例 She *blushed* furiously at the memory of the conversation. 她一想起那次谈话就气得满脸通红。 // The kid turned away to hide her *blushes*. 那个小孩转过身去，不让人看见她脸红。
melodic [məˈlɑːdɪk]	*a.* 旋律的，曲调的; 音调优美的(tuneful) 记 来自 melody(*n.* 旋律) 例 Emotional health is evidenced in the voice by free and *melodic* sounds of the happy. 快乐者自由且音调优美的声音证明其情绪健康。 // In jazz music, a riff is a simple *melodic* figure. 在爵士乐中，重复段是一个简单的曲调音型。

□ mold　　□ ease　　□ roe　　□ fin　　■ mythology　　□ drastic
□ healing　　□ blush　　□ melodic

cubism
[ˈkjuːbɪzəm]

n. 立体派；立体主义

例 *Cubism* was one of the most influential visual art styles of the early twentieth century. 立体主义是 20 世纪初最有影响力的一种视觉艺术。

magnet
[ˈmæɡnət]

n. 磁铁，磁体；有吸引力的人(或事物)

例 Both nickel and iron are whitish metals that are attracted by *magnets*. 镍和铁都是能被磁铁吸引的白色金属。

派 magnetism(*n.* 磁力；磁性); magnetize(*vt.* 磁化，吸引)

magnet

8

pensive
[ˈpensɪv]

a. 沉思的 (meditative)；忧虑的

记 词根记忆：pens(悬挂) + ive → 悬挂于心的 → 沉思的；忧虑的

例 There was a *pensive* look on her face. 她神情忧伤。

pensive

signify
[ˈsɪɡnɪfaɪ]

v. 意味 (mean)；表示，预示；要紧，有重要性

记 词根记忆: sign(标记) + ify → 加上标记 → 意味

例 Dark clouds *signify* that it will rain soon. 乌云意味着很快会下雨。

派 significant (*a.* 意义重大的；显著的；意味深长的)；significance(*n.* 意义，重要性；意思)

aware
[əˈwer]

a. 知道的；意识到的 (perceptible)

搭 be aware of 意识到

例 People are becoming increasingly *aware* of national and international issues. 人们越来越关注国内外事务了。

派 unaware(*a.* 未意识到的)

informant
[ɪnˈfɔːrmənt]

n. 提供消息或情报的人，线人；(为研究)提供资料的人；合作者

例 His *informants* were mid-class professional women. 他的合作者是中产阶级职业女性。

dubious
[ˈduːbiəs]

a. 怀疑的，拿不准的；可疑的，靠不住的 (questionable)

记 词根记忆: dub(二，双) + ious → 前后两种态度的 → 可疑的

例 I am *dubious* that a new stove will improve my cooking. 我对新炉子能提高我的烹饪技术持怀疑态度。

dubious

proponent
[prə'pounənt]

n. 支持者(*supporter); 倡导者(advocate)

记 词根记忆: pro(在···前面) + pon(放) + ent(表人, 名词后缀) → 处在前面的人 → 倡导者

例 *Proponents* of the worksheet procedure believe that it will yield optimal, that is, the best decisions. 工作表程序的支持者认为，这一程序会得出最佳的决定。

参 component(*n.* 成分)

narrate
[nə'reɪt]

v. 讲述, 叙述(relate)

例 The passage is organized by *narrating* a story about excellent teachers. 本段叙述了一个关于优秀教师的故事。

派 narration(*n.* 叙述); narrator(*n.* 叙述者)

former
['fɔːmər]

a. 从前的(previous) *n.* 前者

记 联想记忆: form(形成) + er → 已形成的东西 → 前者

例 I saw my *former* roommate a year ago. 我一年前见过以前的室友。// The *former* are called endotherms, and the latter are called ectotherms. 前者叫温血动物，后者叫冷血动物。

accredit
[ə'kredɪt]

vt. 委任, 授权(authorize, commission); 把···归于; 正式认可

记 词根记忆: ac + cred(相信) + it → 授权

例 The dean in our department will *accredit* you as his assistant soon. 我们的系主任将很快委任你为他的助理。

puddle
['pʌdl]

n. 水坑, 水洼(sump)

记 注意不要和 peddle(*v.* 沿街叫卖)相混

例 You can't tell how deep a *puddle* is until you step into it. 在涉足水洼前，你根本不知道它有多深。

puddle

tragic
['trædʒɪk]

a. 悲惨的(miserable); 悲剧的

记 联想记忆: t + rag(破旧衣服) + ic → 穿着破旧衣服过着悲惨的日子 → 悲惨的

例 Arthur Miller's play *Death of a Salesman* is a *tragic* story. 阿瑟·米勒的剧作《推销员之死》是一个悲剧故事。

assert
[ə'sɜːt]

v. 断言, 声称(affirm, declare)

记 词根记忆: as(表加强) + sert(放置) → 强行插入观点 → 断言, 声称

例 The new generation *asserts* its own style as the representative of American art. 新一代声称自己的风格代表着美国艺术。

concomitant
[kən'kɑːmɪtənt]

a. 伴随的 *n.* 伴随物

记 联想记忆: con(共同) + com(看做 come, 来) + itant → 一起来 → 伴随的; 伴随物

例 However, little is known about the occurrence and prevalence of *concomitant* infections of the two diseases in mosquito and human populations in these areas. 然而在这些区域，很少听到关于这两种疾病在蚊子和人群中爆发或流行伴随性感染。

词根、词缀预习表

terr	使惊吓	terrific *a.* 非常的；可怕的	aud	听	audio *a.* 声音的
pict	描写，画	depict *vt.* 描写，描绘	peal	驱使	appeal *vi.* 吸引
ten	支撑	sustenance *n.* 维持	mod	样式	modify *vt.* 修改
tend	伸展	tend *v.* 趋于	prehend	抓住	comprehend *v.* 理解，领会
femin	女性	feminist *n.* 女权主义者	lumin	光	luminous *a.* 发光的

---

oversleep
[ˌoʊvərˈsliːp]

v. (使)睡过头；(使)睡得过久
例 I *overslept* this morning, so I ran out of the house without listening to the forecast. 我今天早晨睡过头了，没听天气预报就跑出了门。

---

terrific
[təˈrɪfɪk]

a. 极好的(wonderful)；非常的，极度的；可怕的
记 词根记忆：terr(使惊吓) + ific(做) → 做得吓人 → 非常的；可怕的
例 I feel absolutely *terrific* today! 我今天感觉真是好极了! //
A: Good news. I'm not going to need surgery after all. The doctor says I can start working out again soon. And maybe play soccer again in a few weeks.
B: That's *terrific*. It would be great if you could get back in shape in time for the state tournament.
A: 好消息。我不需要动手术了。医生说我很快就能开始训练。或许几周之后就能踢足球了。
B: 太棒了。如果你能及时恢复参加州锦标赛就好了。

---

motif
[moʊˈtiːf]

n. 主题，主旨(subject, theme, mythos)；(装饰)图形(*design)
记 词根记忆：mot(移动) + if → 移动的动力 → 主旨
例 The sky seen from an airplane became one of her favorite *motifs* and the subject of her largest work. 在飞机上看到的天空成为她最喜欢的主题之一，也是她巨著的主题。

---

parachute
[ˈpærəʃuːt]

n. 降落伞 *v.* 跳伞；空投
例 Planes dropped supplies by *parachute*. 飞机用降落伞空投补给。

---

shore
[ʃɔːr]

n. (江、河、湖、海等的)滨，岸(coast, beach) *vt.* (up)支撑，支持
搭 on the shore of 在⋯畔
例 The ship was anchored off *shore*. 船停泊在离岸不远的地方。

☐ oversleep　　☐ terrific　　☐ motif　　☐ parachute　　☐ shore

chapel [ˈtʃæpl]	*n.* (小)教堂；祈祷室 记 联想记忆：c + hap(运气) + el → 祈祷自己好运 → 祈祷室 例 We always go to *chapel* on Sundays. 我们总在星期天去教堂(做礼拜)。 参 cathedral(*n.* 大教堂)
pollinate [ˈpɑːləneɪt]	*vt.* 给…授粉 记 联想记忆：pollin(=pollen 花粉) + ate → 给…授粉 例 These moths continue to *pollinate* the flowers until well into September. 这些飞蛾继续给花朵授粉，直至 9 月才停止。 派 pollination(*n.* 授粉)；pollinator(*n.* 传粉媒介，传粉昆虫) 参 cross-pollinate(*v.* 异花授粉)
depict [dɪˈpɪkt]	*vt.* 描写，描述，描绘(*present, *describe, portray) 记 词根记忆：de(表加强) + pict(描写，画) → 描写，描绘 例 The Impressionists want to *depict* what they see in nature. 印象派画家 想描绘他们眼中的自然。 派 depiction(*n.* 描写，叙述)
courageous [kəˈreɪdʒəs]	*a.* 勇敢的，有胆量的(brave) 记 来自 courage(*n.* 勇气) 例 We hope people will be *courageous* enough to speak out against this injustice. 我们希望人们能大胆说出来，反对这种不公。 参 righteous(*a.* 正直的)
twig [twɪg]	*n.* 嫩枝，小枝 例 Large mammals also have their own tactics for browsing among food- rich *twigs*. 大型哺乳动物在吃富含食料的嫩枝时也有自己的一套策略。
ablaze [əˈbleɪz]	*a.* 着火的，燃烧的；闪耀的(burning; bright)；情绪激动的 记 联想记忆：a + blaze(火焰) → 火焰般的 → 燃烧的 例 The whole building was soon *ablaze*. 整幢大楼很快就燃烧了起来。
vacate [vəˈkeɪt]	*vt.* 腾出，空出；离(职)，退(位) 记 词根记忆：vac(空的) + ate → 腾出，空出 例 You must *vacate* your room by June 3rd. 你必须在 6 月 3 日前腾出你的 房间。
explosion [ɪkˈsploʊʒn]	*n.* 爆炸(blast)；爆发；激增 记 来自 explode〔*v.* (使)爆炸；激增〕 例 Planets are a billion times dimmer than their parent stars. It would be like trying to see the light of a candle next to a huge *explosion*. 行星的亮 度比母恒星暗十亿倍，就如同大爆炸旁边的一抹烛光。
virtue [ˈvɜːrtʃuː]	*n.* 美德(excellence)；优点(merit) 搭 by/in virtue of 依靠；由于 例 I'll be focusing on the *virtues* of his designs. 我将关注他设计上的优点。

course [kɔːrs]	*n.* 课程，教程；过程，进程（process）；路线（route）；一道菜（dish） 搭 required course 必修课；in the course of 在…期间，在…的过程中；in the course of time 最后，终于 例 The college runs specialist language *courses*. 这所学院开设有专门语言课程。// A: I already know what I want to take next semester. So why do I have to make an appointment to see my advisor? All I need is her signature on my *course* sheet. B: I'm afraid it doesn't work that way. She has to talk with you to make sure everything is on the right track. A: 我已经知道下学期想上什么课了。所以我为何还要约见我的指导教师呢？我只需要她在我的课程单上签字就可以了。 B: 恐怕不能这样。她要和你谈谈，确保一切正常。
feudal ['fjuːdl]	*a.* 封建（制度）的 记 来自 feud（*n.* 世仇） 例 The *feudal* system lasted for more than two thousand years in China. 封建制度在中国持续了两千多年。
sustenance ['sʌstənəns]	*n.* 食物（food）；生计（living）；维持（maintenance） 记 词根记忆：sus(在…下面) + ten(支撑) + ance → 在下面支撑 → 维持 例 During the Neolithic period, some hunters and gatherers began to rely chiefly on agriculture for their *sustenance*. 在新石器时代，一些猎人和采集者开始主要依靠农业来维生。
tend [tend]	*v.* 趋于，易于（incline）；照料，看护 记 本身为词根，意为"伸展" → 趋于 搭 tend to do 趋向做… 例 Children *tend* to be influenced by their parents' behaviors and habits. 孩子们往往会受到父母的行为和习惯的影响。 派 tendency（*n.* 趋向，趋势） 参 tent（*n.* 帐篷）
charcoal ['tʃɑːrkoʊl]	*n.* 木炭 记 组合词：char(烧焦) + coal(煤) → 像烧焦的煤 → 木炭 例 We use *charcoal* to grill the steaks. 我们用木炭烤牛排。
varied ['verid]	*a.* 各式各样的（*different, diverse） 记 词根记忆：vari(改变，变化) + ed → 各式各样的 例 There are several levels, dotted with kiosks and fountains, which offer *varied* prospects of San Francisco Bay. 这里有好多楼层，其间星罗棋布地点缀着大大小小的亭子和喷泉。在那里可以欣赏旧金山湾的各种风光。

9

offer [ˈɔːfər]	**v.** 提供(provide, supply)；自愿给予；提出，提议 **n.** 提议；报价，出价；特价 **搭** offer sth. to sb. 向某人提供某物；on offer 可买到；可使用；特价出售 **例** It's so thoughtful of you to *offer* to drop me off at the train station. 你真体贴人，要把我送到火车站。// Thank you for your kind *offer* of help. 谢谢你的好心帮助。// They've decided to accept our original *offer*. 他们已决定接受我们最初的报价。
axis [ˈæksɪs]	**n.** 轴(shaft)；轴线，中心线 **例** Mars takes longer to revolve on its *axis* than the Earth. 火星自转一周的时间比地球的长。 **参** ax(n. 斧头)
feminist [ˈfemənɪst]	**n.** 女权主义者 **记** 词根记忆：femin(女性) + ist(表人，名词后缀) → 女权主义者 **例** Certain *feminists* showed a keen sense of history by keeping records of activities in which women were engaged. 一些女权主义者通过坚持记录女性参与的各项活动展示出了敏锐的历史感。
identification [aɪˌdentɪfɪˈkeɪʃn]	**n.** 身份证明；辨认，鉴定 **记** 来自identify(v. 识别；鉴定) **例** In the modern world, fingerprinting as a means of *identification* has been widely used in many fields. 在当代社会，指纹作为一种身份鉴定手段广泛应用于很多领域。
audio [ˈɔːdioʊ]	**a.** 音频的(acoustic)；声音的(vocal) **记** 词根记忆：aud(听) + io → 声音的 **例** She bought some *audio* equipment. 她购买了一些音频设备。
caterpillar [ˈkætərpɪlər]	**n.** 毛毛虫 **例** *Caterpillars* are voracious feeders and many of them are considered pests in agriculture. 毛毛虫很贪婪，在农业上许多毛毛虫都被视为害虫。
rash [ræʃ]	**a.** 鲁莽的，轻率的 **n.** 疹，皮疹；(短时期内出现的)一连串令人不快的事物 **记** 联想记忆：r + ash(灰) → 民间秘方，可以用草木灰治疹子 → 皮疹 **例** Think twice before doing anything *rash*. 切忌草率行事。
appeal [əˈpiːl]	**vi.** 上诉，起诉；呼吁，恳求；吸引 **n.** 上诉，申诉；呼吁，恳求；感染力，吸引力(*attraction) **记** 词根记忆：ap(向) + peal(=pel 驱使) → 驱使过去 → 吸引 **搭** appeal court 上诉法院；take appeal to/against 对…提出上诉 **例** This modern wildlife art *appeals* to large numbers of nature lovers. 这一现代野生动物艺术吸引着大量热爱自然的人。 **派** appealing(a. 吸引人的；打动人心的)

modify [ˈmɑːdɪfaɪ]	*vt.* 修改，更改(*change, alter)；缓和；【语】修饰 记 词根记忆：mod(样式) + ify(动词后缀) → 改变样式 → 修改 例 Water precipitates many chemical compounds and is constantly *modifying* the face of the Earth. 水使很多化合物沉淀，并不断改变着地球的表面。 派 modified(*a.* 改良的，修正的)；modification(*n.* 改变；修正)
diversity [dɪˈvɜːrsəti]	*n.* 多样性(variety) 记 词根记忆：di(分离) + vers(转) + ity → 可向多个方向转 → 多样性 搭 biological diversity 生物差异；species diversity 物种多样性 例 The author argues that there is more *diversity* of life in the sea than in the rain forests. 作者辩称，海洋里的生物比雨林里的更加多样化。
comprehend [ˌkɑːmprɪˈhend]	*v.* 理解，领会(understand, grasp)；包括，由…组成 记 词根记忆：com(全部) + prehend(抓住) → 全部抓住要领 → 理解，领会 例 He needed to look up some words in the dictionary in order to *comprehend* the novel. 他需要用字典查一些词才能理解这部小说。 派 comprehensible(*a.* 可理解的)；comprehensive(*a.* 全面的；综合的)
timber [ˈtɪmbər]	*n.* 木材，木料(wood, lumber) 记 联想记忆：timb(看做 time，时间) + er → 小树苗变成木材需要时间 → 木材 例 The old couple lived in a small house built of *timber*. 那对老夫妇住在一间小木屋里。
astute [əˈstuːt]	*a.* 机敏的，精明的(shrewd, judicious) 搭 an astute politician 机敏的政治家；an astute investor 精明的投资者 例 It is *astute* to sell out the stocks just before prices go down. 股价下跌之前清仓是明智的。 派 astuteness(*n.* 机敏，精明)
uniform [ˈjuːnɪfɔːrm]	*n.* 制服(costume) *a.* 统一的(unitive)；均匀的(homogeneous) 记 词根记忆：uni(单一的) + form(形式) → 单一的形式 → 统一的 例 Textile mills turn to wool for blankets and *uniforms*. 纺织厂需要用羊毛来做毯子和制服。 派 uniformly(*ad.* 一律地；均一地)；uniformity(*n.* 同样；一致)
luminous [ˈluːmɪnəs]	*a.* 发光的，明亮的(light) 记 词根记忆：lumin(光) + ous → 发光的 例 The most distant *luminous* objects seen by telescopes are very far. 通过望远镜看到的最远的发光体离我们非常遥远。
tavern [ˈtævərn]	*n.* 小旅馆，客栈(inn)；小酒店 例 The news spread in homes, workshops and *taverns*. 这个消息传遍了家家户户、车间和小酒馆。

□ modify   □ diversity   □ comprehend   □ timber   □ astute   □ uniform
□ luminous   □ tavern

conciliate [kən'sɪlieɪt]	*vt.* 安抚，抚慰(reconcile, pacify)；调和 记 联想记忆：concil(看做 council, 委员会) + iate → 开委员会协商解决问题的方法 → 安抚 例 It will be hard to *conciliate* the views of labor and management regarding health benefits. 要调和劳资双方在健康福利政策方面的观点并不容易。
devout [dɪ'vaʊt]	*a.* 虔敬的；诚恳的 记 联想记忆：那个虔诚的(devout)人津津有味地读着(devour)佛经 例 He is a *devout* Christian. 他是一名虔诚的基督徒。
gait [geɪt]	*n.* 步法，步态 记 联想记忆：等(wait)没人注意到自己的步法(gait)时才敢走 例 Kids walk with a rolling *gait*. 小孩走起路来摇摇摆摆的。
gouge [gaʊdʒ]	*vt.* 挖出；敲竹杠 *n.* 凿子 记 联想记忆：挖出(gouge)一条大峡谷(gorge) 例 The tyrant *gouged* the dissenter's eyes out. 那个暴君挖出了他的反对者的双眼。
candid ['kændɪd]	*a.* 坦白的，直率的，直言不讳的 记 词根记忆：cand(白色) + id → 坦白的 例 I must be *candid* with you that this plan will not work out. 我必须坦白告诉你，这个计划无法实施。
terrorism ['terərɪzəm]	*n.* 恐怖主义 记 词根记忆：terr(恐吓) + or + ism(主义) → 恐怖主义 搭 an act of terrorism 恐怖主义行动 例 *Terrorism* is a serious concern by many countries around the world now. 目前恐怖主义是一个备受全球很多国家关注的严重问题。
subjugate ['sʌbdʒugeɪt]	*vt.* 征服，制伏，使服从 记 词根记忆：sub(在…下面) + jug(捆绑) + ate → 在下面捆绑 → 征服 例 Her personal ambitions had been *subjugated* to the needs of her family. 她个人的雄心壮志让位给了家庭的需要。
throng [θrɔːŋ]	*n.* 一大群人 *v.* 群集，拥向 记 发音记忆："死拥" → 一大群人死命拥挤 → 一大群人；群集 例 We pushed our way through the *throng*. 我们挤过人群。// People are *thronging* to see her new play. 人们成群结队去看她的新戏。
corporeal [kɔːr'pɔːriəl]	*a.* 肉体的，身体的；物质的；实体的 记 词根记忆：corp(身体) + or + eal → 身体的 例 Many states have outlawed *corporeal* punishment in schools. 许多州宣布在学校里进行体罚是非法的。
invasive [ɪn'veɪsɪv]	*a.* 侵入的，侵略的；开刀的 记 词根记忆：in(进入) + vas(走) + ive → 未经许可进入的 → 侵入的 例 The *invasive* surgery made me feel fearful. 开刀手术让我感到恐惧。

□ conciliate   □ devout   □ gait   □ gouge   □ candid   □ terrorism
□ subjugate   □ throng   □ corporeal   □ invasive

stray [streɪ]	*vi.* 迷路；分心，走神；离题 *a.* 迷路的；孤立的 *n.* 走失的家畜；离群者 记 联想记忆：要待在(stay)这里，不然很容易迷路(stray) 例 We seem to be *straying* from the main theme of the debate. 我们似乎偏离了辩论的主题。
practicable [ˈpræktɪkəbl]	*a.* 能实行的，可行的，适用的 记 来自 practice(*v./n.* 实践) 例 The only *practicable* way is to ask her for help. 唯一可行的方法是向她求助。
modernity [məˈdɜːrnəti]	*n.* 现代性 例 He was impressed by the architecture's *modernity*. 这个建筑的现代性给他留下了深刻的印象。
contempt [kənˈtempt]	*n.* 轻视，鄙视，轻蔑 记 词根记忆：con(表加强) + tempt(小看) → 轻视，轻蔑 搭 hold in contempt 轻视，对…不屑一顾 例 Mary speaks in *contempt* of the others. 玛丽以轻蔑的口吻谈论他人。 参 attempt(*n./v.* 尝试)
antonym [ˈæntənɪm]	*n.* 反义词 记 词根记忆：ant(=anti 反) + onym(字，词) → 意思相反的字词 → 反义词 例 The word has two possible *antonyms*. 这个单词可能有两个反义词。
tuition [tuˈɪʃn]	*n.* 学费(schooling)；(某一学科的)教学，讲授 例 She can't afford to pay her *tuition*. 她负担不起学费。
emergent [iˈmɜːrdʒənt]	*a.* 突现的；新兴的；紧急的 记 词根记忆：e(出) + merg(浸没) + ent(形容词后缀) → 从浸没的水中现出来 → 突现的 例 It's so *emergent* that you have to help me. 事情太紧急了，你得帮帮我。
outrageous [aʊtˈreɪdʒəs]	*a.* 残暴的；骇人的；反常的，过度的 记 联想记忆：out(出) + rage(愤怒) + ous(形容词后缀) → 出离愤怒的 → 骇人的 例 The housing price has gone up in an *outrageous* way. 房价涨得太离谱了。
vain [veɪn]	*a.* 徒然的，无效的；自负的，虚荣的 记 联想记忆：自负(vain)没有收获(gain) 搭 in vain 白费力气；be vain of/about 为…自负 例 After hearing what he said, I tried to keep back my tears, but in *vain*. 听到他那么说，我怎么也忍不住我的眼泪。
advantage [ədˈvæntɪdʒ]	*n.* 优点；优势，有利条件 *vt.* 有益于 搭 take advantage of 利用；to advantage 有利，使优点突出 例 Many men think that is an *advantage* for being a woman. 许多男人认为那就是作为女人的一种优势。 参 disadvantage(*n.* 不利条件)

9

decisive [dɪ'saɪsɪv]	*a.* 决定性的(definitive)；果断的 例 Excellent communication skill is one of the *decisive* factors in work. 出色的沟通能力是工作中的决定因素之一。
corona [kə'roʊnə]	*n.* 日冕，日华(sunglow)；光环(aura) 记 词根记忆：coron(冠状物) + a → 日冕；光环 例 The *corona* is not always evenly distributed across the surface of the Sun. 日冕并不总是平均分布于太阳表面。
neglect [nɪ'glekt]	*vt./n.* 忽略，忽视(omit)；疏忽 记 词根记忆：neg(不) + lect(选择) → 不选它 → 忽视 例 What I *neglected* to mention was the controversy around Peary's pioneering accomplishment. 我忘记提皮尔里开创性成就所带来的争议了。
deciduous [dɪ'sɪdʒuəs]	*a.* (树木等)落叶的；非永久的，短暂的 记 词根记忆：de(向下) + cid(落下) + uous → 落叶的 例 *Deciduous* trees shed their leaves in autumn. 落叶木在秋天落叶。
utilitarian [ˌjuːtɪlɪ'teriən]	*a.* 实用的(*functional)；功利主义的 *n.* 功利主义者 记 词根记忆：ut(用) + ilitar + ian → 实用的；功利主义的 例 Stoneware used to be simple, *utilitarian* kitchenware. 粗陶器过去是简单实用的厨房用品。// By our narrow standards, scrub doesn't meet our selfish *utilitarian* needs. 根据我们狭隘的标准，灌木丛不能满足我们自私的功利性需求。
subtract [səb'trækt]	*vt.* 减去 记 词根记忆：sub(在…下面) + tract(拉) → 拉下去 → 减去 例 Most photographic filters work by *subtracting* portions of visible light from the subject. 大多数摄影滤光器的作用是把部分可见光从摄影对象中滤掉。
perceptive [pər'septɪv]	*a.* 感知的，知觉的；有洞察力的，理解力强的 例 A *perceptive* scholar questioned the professor's theory. 一位有洞察力的学者质疑这个教授的理论。 参 perception(*n.* 见解；感知)；perceptual(*a.* 感知的，知觉的)
commission [kə'mɪʃn]	*n.* 授权，委任(charge)；委员会；佣金，回扣 *vt.* 委托，授权(appoint, assign) 记 词根记忆：com(共同) + miss(送) + ion → 送交给某人 → 委任；委托 搭 in/out of commission 可/不可使用 例 Artists are taking the distinction between public and private spaces into account when executing their public *commissions*. 艺术家在执行公众委任的事务时，会考虑到公共场合与私人空间的区别。 派 commissioner(*n.* 委员，专员)

breakthrough [ˈbreɪkθruː]	*n.* 突破，重大进展(improving)
	记 来自词组 break through(突破)
	例 In fact important *breakthroughs* in the field of astronmy can come from students' work. 事实上，天文学领域的很多重要突破都可能来自学生们的工作。
inspire [ɪnˈspaɪər]	*vt.* 鼓舞，激励(stimulate)；给…以灵感
	记 词根记忆：in(使…) + spir(呼吸) + e → 使呼吸澎湃 → 鼓舞
	例 His stories are *inspired* by his travels. 他写小说的灵感来自他的游历。
	派 inspiration(*n.* 灵感；激励)；inspiring(*a.* 使人振奋的，鼓舞人心的)
cognition [kɑːɡˈnɪʃn]	*n.* 感知，认知，认识(perception)
	记 词根记忆：cogn(知道) + ition → 认知，认识
	例 Tool use may indicate that animals have some *cognition*. 对工具的使用或许表明动物具有一定的认知能力。
	参 cognitive(*a.* 认知的，感知的)
penicillin [ˌpenɪˈsɪlɪn]	*n.* 青霉素，盘尼西林
	例 *Penicillin* is still one of the most widely used antibiotic agents. 青霉素仍是最为广泛使用的抗生素之一。
ethnology [eθˈnɑːlədʒi]	*n.* 民族学，文化人类学
	记 词根记忆：ethn(民族，种族) + ology(…学) → 民族学
	例 *Ethnology* is a branch of anthropology that deals with how various cultures developed. 民族学是人类学的一个分支，研究各种文化的发展历程。
volcano [vɑːlˈkeɪnoʊ]	*n.* 火山
	记 源于古罗马的火神 Vulnus
	例 How often is a *volcano* likely to erupt? 火山可能多长时间爆发一次？
	派 volcanic(*a.* 火山的)；volcanism(*n.* 火山作用)
	参 iceberg(*n.* 冰山)
cellist [ˈtʃelɪst]	*n.* 大提琴演奏家
	例 He is considered the greatest *cellist* of his time. 他被认为是他所处时代最伟大的大提琴家。
	参 fiddler(*n.* 拉小提琴的人，小提琴家)
uniformity [ˌjuːnɪˈfɔːrməti]	*n.* 同样，一致；一致性
	记 来自 uniform(*a.* 统一的)
	例 Students should avoid a lack of *uniformity* in evidence when writing their papers. 学生在写论文时应该避免论据不一致。
neutron [ˈnjuːtrɑːn]	*n.* 中子
	记 词根记忆：ne(不，没有) + utr(=uter 两者之间) + on(名词后缀) → 不偏向任何一方 → 中子

9

BOOM

volcano

informed [ɪnˈfɔːrmd]	*a.* 有学识的(learned); 见多识广的, 有见识的 记 来自 inform(*vt.* 通知) 例 We are not fully *informed* about the developments. 我们不完全清楚进展情况。
rate [reɪt]	*n.* 率, 比率; 速度; 价格; 等级 *v.* 估价; 评级, 评价; 把…列为 记 词根记忆: rat(清点) + e → 清点的结果 → 率, 比率 搭 at any rate 无论如何, 至少; at the rate of 以…速度 例 Freight trains have an accident *rate* that is only 1/3 that of the trucking industry. 货运火车的事故率只是卡车的三分之一。// A: Another one of the letters I mailed last week has been returned! B: Didn't you realize the airmail *rates* went up a month ago? A: 我上周寄的一封信又被退回来了! B: 难道你不知道航空邮件的资费上个月就涨了吗?
underneath [ˌʌndərˈniːθ]	*prep.* 在…下面(beneath) *ad.* 在下面(below) 例 The paper is *underneath* the book. 论文在书下面。
maneuver [məˈnuːvər]	*v.* 操纵, 控制(manipulate); 耍花招 *n.* 策略(strategy); 花招(trick) 记 词根记忆: man(手) + eu + ver(工作) → 用手来做 → 操纵 例 She *maneuvered* her way to the top of the company. 她施展手腕使自己进入了公司最高领导层。
journalism [ˈdʒɜːrnəlɪzəm]	*n.* 新闻业, 新闻工作 例 *Journalism* is a fulfilling career that combines the excitement of covering the news with the satisfaction of a life of public service. 新闻工作是一个令人感觉充实的职业, 既能感受到报道新闻时的刺激兴奋, 又能收获为公众服务所带来的满足感。
terrain [təˈreɪn]	*n.* 地势, 地形(landform); 地带 记 词根记忆: terr(地) + ain → 地势, 地形 例 The Moon may be divided into two major *terrains*. 月球也许可分为两种主要地形。
excursion [ɪkˈskɜːrʒn]	*n.* 远足, 短途旅游(hike) 记 词根记忆: ex(出, 外) + curs(跑) + ion → 跑出去 → 远足 例 The society's activities also included organized sketching *excursions* along the Hudson River. 这个社团的活动也包括沿着哈德逊河进行的有组织的写生远足活动。
saturation [ˌsætʃəˈreɪʃn]	*n.* 饱和(状态)(satiety); 饱和度 记 词根记忆: sat(充足) + ur + ation → 充足 → 饱和(状态) 搭 saturation point 饱和点, 极限 例 The company was beset by price wars and market *saturation*. 那家公司深受价格战和市场饱和的困扰。

abundant [əˈbʌndənt]	*a.* 大量的，充足的，丰富的(*rich, *plentiful) 记 词根记忆：ab(表加强) + und(波浪；荡漾) + ant → 用力荡漾 → 大量的，充足的 例 Feldspar is the most *abundant* mineral on the Earth's surface. 长石是地球表面最丰富的矿物质。 派 abundantly(*ad.* 丰富地，充裕地); abundance(*n.* 大量，充足，丰富)
rehearse [rɪˈhɜːrs]	*v.* 预演，排练；默诵；照搬，重复 记 联想记忆：re(再，又) + hear(听) + se → 导演在一旁一遍遍听、看她们排练 → 排练 例 We *rehearse* only one night a week. 我们一周只排练一晚上。 派 rehearsal(*n.* 排练，排演；复述，重复)
subsist [səbˈsɪst]	*vi.* 存活，生存(exist) 记 词根记忆：sub(在…下面) + sist(站立) → 站在下面 → 生存 例 Many prehistoric people *subsisted* as hunters and gatherers. 很多史前人类靠狩猎和采集维生。 派 subsistence(*n.* 生存，生计；存活)
cascara [kæsˈkɑːrə]	*n.* 缓泻剂 例 *Cascara* is added to many popular natural weight-loss supplements. 缓泻剂被添加于许多广受欢迎的自然减肥药中。

9

A man is not old as long as he is seeking something. A man is not old until regrets take the place of dreams.

只要一个人还有所追求，他就没有老。直到后悔取代了梦想，一个人才算老。

——美国演员 巴里穆尔(J. Barrymore, American actor)

Word List 10

音频

glue
[glu:]

vt. 胶合，黏合（cement）；紧附于（attach）*n.* 胶，胶水（gumwater）
记 联想记忆：警方终于从一瓶蓝色（blue）胶水（glue）中找到了线索（clue）
例 Her eyes were *glued* to the screen. 她目不转睛地盯着屏幕。

inflation
[ɪnˈfleɪʃn]

n. 通货膨胀，物价上涨；（充气而引起的）膨胀
例 The governments in some countries have taken measures to control the *inflation* rate. 一些国家的政府已经采取了措施来控制通货膨胀率。

certificate
[sərˈtɪfɪkət]

n. 证书，证明书；文凭，结业证书
记 词根记忆：cert(确认) + (i)fic(做) + ate → 确认有做某事的资格 → 证书
例 The Birth *Certificate* is issued by the provincial or territorial government and is required as identification to apply for other important personal documents. 出生证明由省或地区政府开具，在申请其他重要的个人文件时必须出具出生证明。

certificate

summit
[ˈsʌmɪt]

n. （山等的）最高点，峰顶，极点（peak）；峰会
例 Scientists need to put a special receiver on the *summit* to receive signals from the satellites. 科学家们需要在山顶放置一个特殊的接收器来接收卫星发出的信号。

nucleus
[ˈnjuːkliəs]

n. [*pl.* nuclei]核，核子，原子核；细胞核；核心（core）
例 At the core of every ice crystal is a minuscule *nucleus*. 每个冰晶体的核心是一个极小的核子。

attribute	[ˈætrɪbjuːt] *n.* 属性，特征(*characteristic, trait)
[ˈætrɪbjuːt]	[əˈtrɪbjuːt] *vt.* 把…归于(ascribe)
	记 词根记忆：at + tribut(给予) + e → 把…归于
	例 John has many good *attributes* that make him eligible for the job. 约翰有很多优点，这使得他能胜任这份工作。// Jane *attributed* her lateness to the heavy traffic. 简把迟到归咎于交通拥挤。
	派 attribution(*n.* 归因)
	参 tribute(*n.* 颂词；贡物)；distribute(*vt.* 分发)；contribute(*v.* 捐助)
planetary	*a.* 行星的
[ˈplænətəri]	搭 planetary motions 行星运动；a planetary system 行星系
	例 Many *planetary* orbits are not circles. 很多行星轨道都不是圆形的。
lash	*v.* 将(物品)系牢，捆绑(fasten)；(风、雨等)猛烈打击；鞭打；猛烈抨击，严厉斥责 *n.* 鞭打；睫毛
[læʃ]	记 联想记忆：l + ash(灰) → 对敌人的鞭打似有挫骨扬灰之势 → 猛烈打击
	例 There are other drums that have skins *lashed* onto both sides. 有的鼓两面都绑有皮面。// Freak rainstorms once *lashed* in the central and southern sections of the state. 不寻常的暴风雨曾在这个州的中南部肆虐。
delicate	*a.* 易损的(fragile)；微妙的(subtle)；精巧的(exquisite)；娇弱的，纤细的
[ˈdelɪkət]	例 The tiny, *delicate* skeletons are usually destroyed by weathering before they can be fossilized. 小的易碎骨骼通常在能变成化石之前就已经风化了。
	派 delicately(*ad.* 微妙地)
	参 dedicate〔*vt.* (使)致力于，奉献给〕
proficient	*a.* 熟练的，精通的(skilled, expert)
[prəˈfɪʃnt]	记 词根记忆：pro(在…前面) + fic(做) + ient → 提前做了，更熟练 → 熟练的，精通的
	例 The scrolls were written in a language that is really rare today. Only a few people are *proficient* at it. 卷轴上的语言现在非常罕见，只有很少的人精通于此。
	参 efficient(*a.* 生效的)；sufficient(*a.* 充分的)
repertory	*n.* 保留剧目(repertoire)；保留剧目轮演；库存，储备；仓库
[ˈrepərtɔːri]	例 The *repertory* of a concert band includes marches, and other forms of music. 管乐团的保留曲目包括进行曲和其他形式的音乐。
enormous	*a.* 巨大的，极大的(*remarkable, massive)
[ɪˈnɔːrməs]	记 联想记忆：e(出) + norm(规范) + ous(形容词后缀) → 超出常规的 → 巨大的
	例 The problems facing the manager are *enormous*. 经理面临的问题是巨大的。
unify	*vt.* 统一，联合(unite)
[ˈjuːnɪfaɪ]	记 词根记忆：uni(单一) + fy(动词后缀) → 统一
	例 The area was economically *unified*. 这个地区在经济上实现了统一。

10

relief [rɪ'liːf]	*n.* 缓解，减轻，轻松；援救，救济；宽慰；浮雕(法或作品) 例 We should have some *relief* by the end of the week. 这个周末我们应该轻松一下。// Molds are used to create particular effects for some products, such as *relief*-decorated vessels and figurines. 模子用来为一些产品制造特殊效果，例如有浮雕装饰的器皿和小雕像。 relief
deceptive [dɪ'septɪv]	*a.* 欺骗性的，导致误解的(fraudulent) 记 来自 deceive(*v.* 欺骗) 例 Its simplicity of appearance is *deceptive*. 它简单的外表具有欺骗性。 deceptive
miracle ['mɪrəkl]	*n.* 奇事，奇迹(wonder) 记 词根记忆：mir(惊奇) + acle(表物) → 奇事 搭 work/perform miracle 创造奇迹；有奇效 例 It's a *miracle* that nobody was hurt in the traffic accident. 这次交通事故中无一人受伤，真是个奇迹。 派 miraculous(*a.* 奇迹的；不可思议的)
simultaneous [ˌsaɪml'teɪnɪəs]	*a.* 同时的，同步的(synchronous) 记 词根记忆：simul(相同) + taneous → 时间相同的 → 同时的 例 These ponderous machines reaped the grain, threshed it, and bagged it, all in one *simultaneous* operation. 这些笨重的机器收割谷子，脱粒，然后打包，所有这些都在同一个操作流程里完成。 派 simultaneously(*ad.* 同时地)
paradigm ['pærədaɪm]	*n.* 范例，典范 记 词根记忆：para(在旁边) + digm(显示) → 在旁边显示给人看 → 范例，典范 例 The war was *paradigm* of the destructive side of human nature. 那场战争尽显人性中具有破坏性的一面。
foliage ['fəʊlɪɪdʒ]	*n.* (植物的)叶(leaf) 记 词根记忆：foli(叶) + age → (植物的)叶 例 The insect is active at night and rests motionless amid *foliage* during the day. 这种昆虫夜间活跃，白天却在树叶间一动不动地休息。
spontaneous [spɒn'teɪnɪəs]	*a.* 自发的，自然产生的(instinctive, unplanned)；自然的，无雕饰的 搭 spontaneous generation 自然发生；spontaneous combustion 自燃 例 The audience burst into *spontaneous* applause. 观众自发地鼓起掌来。 派 spontaneously(*ad.* 自然地，自发地；情不自禁地)
quarry ['kwɔːri]	*n.* 采石场，石矿；猎物，追捕的对象(prey) *v.* 采石；采集 记 联想记忆：运送(carry)物资到采石场(quarry) 例 The police lost their *quarry* in the crowd. 警察在人群中找不到他们要追捕的人了。

improvise [ˈɪmprəvaɪz]	*v.* 即兴创作；临时准备 记 词根记忆：im(不) + pro(在…前面) + vis(看) + e → 没有预先看过 → 即兴创作；临时准备 例 The musical arrangement was normally *improvised* in the greatest hurry. 乐曲通常都是在极其匆忙的情况下即席创作出来的。 派 improvisation(*n.* 即席创作；即兴作品)
tragedy [ˈtrædʒədi]	*n.* 惨事，灾难(disaster)；悲剧(作品) 搭 Greek tragedy 希腊悲剧 例 It's a *tragedy* that the famous writer died so young. 那位著名作家如此英年早逝真是一大惨事。
outbreak [ˈaʊtbreɪk]	*n.* 发作；爆发(eruption, explosion, out-burst) 记 来自词组 break out(突发，爆发) 搭 the outbreak of war 战争爆发 例 With the *outbreak* of natural disaster, there has been a massive epidemic sweeping over the region. 随着自然灾害的爆发，一场大规模的流行病横扫了这个地区。
plateau [plæˈtoʊ]	*n.* 高原(tableland)；(上升后的)稳定期，停滞期 *vi.* 保持稳定水平 记 联想记忆：plat(平的) + eau → 高出平地的地 → 高原 例 Inflation has reached a *plateau*. 通货膨胀停了下来。
novel [ˈnɑːvl]	*a.* 新颖的(innovative, new) *n.* (长篇)小说(fiction) 记 词根记忆：nov(新的) + el → 新颖的 例 The engine that became standard on Western steamboats was of a *novel* design. 成为西方蒸汽船标准的引擎拥有一个新颖的设计。 派 novelty(*n.* 新奇的事物；新鲜感)
decay [dɪˈkeɪ]	*v./n.* 腐烂(*rot)，腐朽；衰退，衰落(decline) 记 联想记忆：骗(decoy)人变坏(decay) 例 The rest of the organism has *decayed*. 生物体的其余部分已经腐烂。// The San Antonio project was designed to combat urban *decay*. 圣安东尼奥项目旨在防止城市衰落。
avenue [ˈævənjuː]	*n.* 途径，手段(approach)；大街 例 They will explore every *avenue* until they find an answer. 他们会探索一切途径，直到找到答案为止。
potency [ˈpoʊtnsi]	*n.* 影响力，支配力；效力 记 词根记忆：pot(有力的) + ency → 影响力，支配力 例 A medicine may lose its *potency* if you keep it too long. 药物存放太久，可能会失去效力。
benevolent [bəˈnevələnt]	*a.* 慈善的；善心的 记 词根记忆：bene(善，好) + vol(意志) + ent → 好意的 → 慈善的；善心的 例 The club has received *benevolent* donations nationwide. 俱乐部收到了来自全国的慈善捐款。 派 benevolence(*n.* 善心，仁心)

10

causal [ˈkɔːzl]	*a.* 原因的，因果关系的
	记 来自 cause(*n.* 原因)
	例 A *causal* ceremony will be held to mark this occasion. 为了纪念这个日子，我们将举行一个典礼。

acquisition [ˌækwɪˈzɪʃn]	*n.* 习得(物)，获得(物)；收购，购置
	记 词根记忆：ac(表加强) + quis(追求) + ition → 为了获得而不断追求 → 习得(物)，获得(物)
	例 If other *acquisition* opportunities come up, we would certainly consider them. 如果有其他的收购机会，我们肯定会考虑的。

unanimous [juˈnænɪməs]	*a.* 全体一致的，一致同意的
	记 词根记忆：un(一个) + anim(精神) + ous → 大家都秉持同一种精神的 → 全体一致的，一致同意的
	例 This plan got an *unanimous* consent at the weekly meeting. 这个计划在周例会上获得了一致通过。

unanimous

ornamental [ˌɔːrnəˈmentl]	*a.* 装饰性的，装饰用的(decorative) *n.* 装饰物
	记 词根记忆：orn(装饰) + a + ment(名词后缀) + al(形容词后缀) → 装饰性的
	例 If you are a weekend gardener and don't have an abundance of time to maintain your landscape — *ornamental* grasses are the perfect choice. 如果你只有在周末才有时间进行园艺工作，没有太多时间用于景观美化，那观赏草类会是最佳选择。

blunt [blʌnt]	*a.* 钝的；不敏感的；直率的 *vt.* 使迟钝，使减弱
	记 发音记忆："不拦的" → 口无遮拦的 → 直率的
	例 Don't drink too much alcohol, or it will make all your senses *blunt*. 不要喝太多的酒，酒精会使你感觉迟钝。

credence [ˈkriːdns]	*n.* 可信性，真实性；信任；信念
	记 词根记忆：cred(相信) + ence(名词后缀) → 可信性
	例 They gave no *credence* to the findings of the survey. 他们不相信这次调查的结果。

fictitious [fɪkˈtɪʃəs]	*a.* 虚构的；假的；假装的，虚伪的
	记 词根记忆：fict(做) + itious → 做出来的 → 虚构的
	例 All the characters and places in this novel are *fictitious*. 这篇小说中所有的人物和地点都是虚构的。

somber [ˈsɑːmbər]	*a.* 昏暗的；忧郁的
	记 联想记忆：冷静的(sober)和忧郁的(somber)有时只差一点点(m)
	例 She has a *somber* expression on her face and I wonder what's the matter with her. 她的脸上有一种忧郁的神情。我在想她发生什么事了。

doodle [ˈduːdl]	*vi.* 乱涂，胡画
	记 联想记忆：一边吃面条(noodle)一边随手乱涂乱画(doodle)
	例 I often *doodle* when I'm on the phone. 我打电话时常常信手乱画。

□ causal □ acquisition □ unanimous □ ornamental □ blunt □ credence
□ fictitious □ somber □ doodle

allocate ['æləkeɪt]	*vt.* 分配，分派，把…拨给 记 词根记忆：al(=ad 向) + loc(地方) + ate → 给予不同的地方 → 分配 例 Can you tell me what budget you are prepared to *allocate* for our department? 你能告诉我你准备给我们部门拨多少预算吗? 派 allocation(*n.* 配给，分配)
blurt [blɜːrt]	*vt.* 脱口而出 记 联想记忆：脱口而出(blurt)的话往往容易伤人(hurt) 例 You must repeat to yourself many times before *blurting* out the sentences. 一个句子必须重复很多遍，你才可能脱口而出。
cradle ['kreɪdl]	*n.* 摇篮；发源地 记 联想记忆：烛(candle)光摇曳，摇篮(cradle)里的婴儿正睡得香 搭 from the cradle to the grave 一生，从生到死 例 The mother puts her baby in a *cradle* and rocks it to and from. 母亲把婴儿放在摇篮里，然后来回摇晃。
deceitful [dɪ'siːtfl]	*a.* 欺诈的，惯于欺骗的，不诚实的 记 联想记忆：deceit(欺骗) + ful(=full 满的) → 惯于欺骗的 例 Don't make this *deceitful* excuse again; I won't trust you any more. 不要再编这种骗人的借口了，我不会再相信你了。
aftermath ['æftərmæθ]	*n.* 后果，余波 记 联想记忆：after(在…之后) + math(数学) → 考完数学后，发现考得一塌糊涂 → 后果 例 In the *aftermath* of the financial crisis, everything changed dramatically. 在金融危机之后，所有的一切都发生了巨变。
bleak [bliːk]	*a.* 阴冷的(dismal, gloomy)；无望的，令人沮丧的；乏味的；荒凉的 记 联想记忆：核泄露(leak)令人沮丧(bleak) 例 As *bleak* as this situation is, we still have reasons to be hopeful. 虽然情况如此令人沮丧，我们仍有理由抱有希望。
diminution [ˌdɪmɪ'nuːʃn]	*n.* 减少(量)，缩减(量) 记 词根记忆：di(=dis 分离) + min(小的，少的) + ution → 减少(量) 例 The country experienced a *diminution* of population growth during the 1980s. 20 世纪 80 年代，该国人口增长幅度下降。
metaphor ['metəfər]	*n.* 隐喻，暗喻 记 词根记忆：meta(变化) + phor(带来) → 给意义带来变化 → 隐喻，暗喻 例 Here he uses a *metaphor* to illustrate his arguments. 这里他用了一个隐喻来阐述自己的观点。
committee [kə'mɪti]	*n.* 委员会(council) 记 词根记忆：com(共同) + mitt(送) + ee(表人) → 共同发送命令等的人 → 委员会 搭 curriculum committee 课程编制委员会; advisory committee 咨询委员会 例 The *committee* meets once a year. 委员会委员每年碰面一次。

□ allocate　　□ blurt　　□ cradle　　□ deceitful　　□ aftermath　　□ bleak
□ diminution　　□ metaphor　　□ committee

tropic [ˈtrɑːpɪk]	*n.* 回归线；热带地区 *a.* 热带的 词 词根记忆：trop(转) + ic → 太阳每年在回归线来回转 → 回归线 例 Heat is transported from the *tropics* to the middle and high latitudes. 热量被从热带传输到中高纬度地区。 派 tropical(*a.* 热带的)；subtropical(*a.* 亚热带的)
disrupt [dɪsˈrʌpt]	*vt.* 使中断(interrupt)；扰乱(disturb)；使分裂，使瓦解 词 词根记忆：dis(分开) + rupt(打破，断裂) → 使断裂 → 使中断 例 An accident has *disrupted* railway services into and out of the city. 一场事故使得进出这个城市的铁路交通陷入混乱。
exalted [ɪɡˈzɔːltɪd]	*a.* 崇高的，高贵的，显赫的(*superior) 词 词根记忆：ex + alt(高的) + ed → 崇高的 搭 an exalted position 显赫的地位 例 Their products, primarily silver plates and bowls, reflected their *exalted* status and testified to their customers' prominence. 他们的产品——主要是银盘和银碗——既反映了他们高贵的地位，也证明了他们的客人的尊贵身份。
octopus [ˈɑːktəpəs]	*n.* 章鱼 词 词根记忆：octo(八) + pus(脚) → 长八只脚的鱼 → 章鱼 例 Scientists believe that *octopuses* began to evolve more than 400 million years ago. 科学家们认为章鱼是在四亿多年前开始进化的。
ambience [ˈæmbiəns]	*n.* 周围环境，气氛 词 词根记忆：ambi(周围) + ence(名词后缀) → 存在于四周的东西 → 周围环境，气氛 例 The manager tries to create a pleasant *ambience* in the office. 经理努力在办公室营造一种愉快的氛围。
spectacle [ˈspektəkl]	*n.* 精彩的表演；壮观的场面；奇观；壮丽的景象；[*pl.*]眼镜(glasses) 词 词根记忆：spect(看) + acle → 引人驻足观看 → 精彩的表演；奇观 例 The carnival parade was a magnificent *spectacle*. 狂欢节游行场面热烈，蔚为大观。
voyage [ˈvɔɪɪdʒ]	*n.* 旅行(travel)；航程(journey, sail) 词 词根记忆：voy(路) + age → 旅行；航程 例 According to the original records of the flight, the *voyage* lasted 46 minutes. 根据飞行的原始记录，航程持续了 46 分钟。 派 voyager(*n.* 航行者，航海者)

revitalize [ˌriːˈvaɪtəlaɪz]	*vt.* 使恢复生机，使再生(*bring new life to)；使更强壮 记 联想记忆：re(再，又) + vital(有活力的) + ize → 使恢复生机 例 In numerous cities, art is being raised as a symbol of the commitment to *revitalize* urban areas. 在很多城市，人们把艺术提升为使城区恢复生机的行为的象征。 复活吧 revitalize
onslaught [ˈɑːnslɔːt]	*n.* 冲击(impact)；攻击，猛攻 例 In the face of this *onslaught*, living things have evolved a variety of defense mechanisms. 面对这次冲击，生物演化出了各种防卫机制。 参 slaughter(*n./v.* 屠杀)
arid [ˈærɪd]	*a.* 干旱的(dry)；贫瘠的(barren)；无趣的 例 *Arid* soils are typically alkaline. 贫瘠的土壤往往是碱性的。
demolish [dɪˈmɑːlɪʃ]	*vt.* 拆除(dismantle)；破坏(destroy)；驳倒，推翻(论点等) 记 词根记忆：de(表加强) + mol(磨) + ish → 完全磨成粉 → 破坏 例 The human species is altering the physical and chemical world and *demolishing* the environment. 人类正在改变着物理和化学世界，并破坏着环境。
clam [klæm]	*n.* 蛤，蛤肉；〈口〉守口如瓶的人，寡言的人 记 联想记忆：和 claim(*v./n.* 声称；要求)一起记 例 The little boy was as happy as a *clam* in high water. 那个小男孩非常高兴。 参 oyster(*n.* 牡蛎)；crab(*n.* 螃蟹)；abalone(*n.* 鲍鱼)；sponge(*n.* 海绵)；coral(*n.* 珊瑚)
nicotine [ˈnɪkətiːn]	*n.* 尼古丁 记 来自人名 Nicot，1560 年将烟草引入法国 搭 nicotine patch 尼古丁贴剂 例 *Nicotine* is a bitter-tasting compound that occurs in large amounts in the leaves of tobacco plants. 尼古丁是一种味道苦涩的复合物，大量存在于烟叶中。
guideline [ˈɡaɪdlaɪn]	*n.* [常 *pl.*]指导方针，准则，行动纲领 记 组合词：guide(指导) + line(路线) → 指导方针，准则 例 The government has drawn up *guidelines* on the treatment of the mentally ill. 政府制订了治疗精神病的指导方针。
signal [ˈsɪɡnəl]	*n.* 信号，暗号；标志(sign, indication) *v.* 发信号，示意；标志 *a.* 显要的，重大的 记 联想记忆：sign(签名) + al → 用签名作为自己的标志 → 标志 例 Pheromones *signal* the ants that the nest has been invaded and must be abandoned. 信息素向蚂蚁发出信号，表示巢穴遭到入侵，必须放弃。

junction [ˈdʒʌŋkʃn]	*n.* 交叉点，汇合处(intersection)；连接，接合 记 词根记忆：junct(连接) + ion(名词后缀) → 交叉点，汇合处 例 A major railroad *junction* in Decatur Illinois has become an important commercial hub for the region's farm products and livestock. 迪凯特伊利诺伊州的一个主要铁路枢纽，现在已成为该地区农产品和牲畜交易的重要商业中心。
abnormal [æbˈnɔːrml]	*a.* 反常的，变态的(unusual, exceptional) 记 词根记忆：ab(反) + norm(规则) + al → 违反规则的 → 反常的 搭 abnormal behavior 变态行为 例 The warm December weather in northern Canada was *abnormal*. 加拿大北部12月份的温暖天气是不正常的。
sympathy [ˈsɪmpəθi]	*n.* 同情，同情心(pity)；赞同，支持 记 词根记忆：sym(相同) + path(感觉) + y → 怀有相同的感觉 → 同情 例 Expressive leaders often offer *sympathy* when someone experiences difficulties. 富于感情的领导者经常对身处困境的人给予支持。 派 sympathize(*vi.* 同情；共鸣)
intellect [ˈɪntəlekt]	*n.* 智力，理解力；知识分子 记 词根记忆：intel(在…之间) + lect(选择) → 能在很多事物中作出选择 → 智力，理解力 例 As a child, sculptor Anne Whitney showed a high level of *intellect* and artistic talent. 雕塑家安妮·惠特尼小时候就表现出了极强的理解力和艺术天赋。 派 intellectual(*a.* 智力的 *n.* 知识分子)
thrifty [ˈθrɪfti]	*a.* 节省的，节俭的(saving, sparing) 记 来自 thrift(*n.* 节约) 例 The *thrifty* housewife only buys grocery items that are on sale. 那个节俭的家庭妇女只买减价的杂货。
drought [draʊt]	*n.* 干旱(期)，旱灾 记 联想记忆：dr(看做 dry，干的) + ought(应该) → 处于干旱期到处都应该很干 → 干旱(期) 例 The businessman stored large quantities of grain during periods of *drought*. 这个商人在旱灾期间囤积了大量粮食。 参 draught(*n.* 气流；拖，拉)
abandon [əˈbændən]	*vt.* 离弃，放弃(desert) *n.* 放纵，放任 记 联想记忆：a + band(乐队) + on → 乐队解散，放弃演出 → 放弃 例 She and her tribe had to *abandon* their lands and retreat to Canada. 她和她的部落不得不放弃他们的土地，撤退到加拿大。 派 abandoned(*a.* 被抛弃的；废弃的); abandonment(*n.* 放弃，抛弃)
trivial [ˈtrɪviəl]	*a.* 琐碎的，微不足道的(unimportant, trifling) 记 词根记忆：tri(三) + vi(路) + al → 三条路的会合点(古罗马妇女喜欢停在十字路口闲聊些无关紧要的事) → 琐碎的，微不足道的 例 Don't bother him with *trivial* things. 别拿琐碎事烦他了。

damp [dæmp]	*a.* 潮湿的(moist) *n.* 潮湿；湿气 *vt.* 弄湿；减弱，抑制 〔记〕联想记忆：dam(水坝) + p → 水坝上总是很潮湿 → 潮湿的 〔例〕Farmers often squeeze the *damp* soil into three basic shapes. 农民们经常把潮湿的土捏成三种基本形状。 〔派〕dampen(*vt.* 弄湿，使潮湿；抑制)
staggering [ˈstægərɪŋ]	*a.* 巨大的，势不可挡的(*overwhelming)；惊人的，令人吃惊的(astounding) 〔例〕We need a *staggering* amount of money in the initial investment. 在投资初期，我们需要巨额钱款。
ignorant [ˈɪɡnərənt]	*a.* 无知的，愚昧的(*naive)；无知觉的(unaware) 〔记〕词根记忆：i(不) + gno(r)(知道) + ant(形容词后缀) → 不知道的 → 无知的 〔例〕The scholar argues that without formal education people would remain *ignorant*. 这个学者辩称没有受过正规教育的人会一直无知下去。 〔派〕ignorance(*n.* 无知，不了解)
emission [iˈmɪʃn]	*n.* 散发物，排放物；发射，排放 〔记〕词根记忆：e(出，外) + miss(放) + ion(名词后缀) → 放出来的东西 → 散发物；发射 〔搭〕emission control 排放控制 〔例〕The government has pledged to clean up industrial *emissions*. 政府已保证要清除工业排放物。
vertebrate [ˈvɜːrtɪbrət]	*n.* 脊椎动物 *a.* 有脊椎的 〔记〕来自 vertebra(*n.* 脊椎骨) 〔搭〕vertebrate animals 脊椎动物 〔例〕The nervous system of *vertebrates* is characterized by a nerve cord. 脊椎动物神经系统的特点是具有神经索。
range [reɪndʒ]	*n.* 范围(extent)；山脉(mountain)；一系列；射程，距离 *v.* (在某范围内)变动；散布；漫游 〔搭〕in/within range of 在可及的范围内；range from 延伸；(在一定范围内)变化 〔例〕This was outside the *range* of her experience. 这超出了她的阅历。// He no longer believes short-*range* forecasts. 他不再相信短期预测。 〔派〕ranger(*n.* 护林员)
emotion [ɪˈmoʊʃn]	*n.* 感情，激情，情绪(sentiment, feeling) 〔记〕词根记忆：e(出) + mot(动) + ion → 心里释放出的东西 → 感情，情绪 〔例〕He lost control of his *emotions*. 他的情绪失去了控制。

10

ignorant

stiff [stɪf]	*a.* 硬的，僵直的(rigid)；呆板的；拘谨的；艰难的，费劲的；(风等)强烈的 *ad.* 极其，非常；僵硬地 记 联想记忆：长时间不动(still)就变得僵硬(stiff) 搭 stiff paste 浓膏；a stiff wind 强风 例 Her hands had become too *stiff* to sew. 她的手变得太僵硬，以至于无法缝纫。// The new proposal has met with *stiff* opposition. 新提案遭到了强烈的反对。 派 stiffen(*v.* (使)变僵硬)
boost [buːst]	*vt.* 提高，推进(*raise, push)；替…做广告，宣扬 *n.* 增加，帮助 记 联想记忆：boo(看做 boot，靴子) + st → 穿上靴子往高处走 → 提高 例 These innovations in manufacturing *boosted* output and living standards to an unprecedented extent. 这些生产创新将产量和生活水平提高到了前所未有的程度。 参 boast(*n./v.* 自夸)
microprocessor [ˌmaɪkrou'prousesər]	*n.* 微处理器 记 联想记忆：micro(微小的) + processor(处理器) → 微处理器
oceanographer [ˌouʃə'nɑːɡrəfər]	*n.* 海洋学者 记 联想记忆：ocean(海洋) + o + graph(用图表示) + er(表人，名词后缀) → 通过图表示海洋情况的人 → 海洋学者 例 *Oceanographers* use their knowledge of biology, chemistry, physics and geology to study the seas and oceans. 海洋学者运用生物、化学、物理和地理方面的知识来研究海洋。
insanity [ɪn'sænəti]	*n.* 精神错乱，疯狂(madness) 记 来自 insane(*a.* 精神失常的，疯狂的)；in(不) + san(健全的) + e → 精神不健全的 → 精神失常的 例 Hers is a world of violence, *insanity*, fractured love, and hopeless loneliness. 她的世界充满了暴力、疯狂、破裂的爱情和无望的孤独。 insanity
successive [sək'sesɪv]	*a.* 接替的，继承的；接连的，连续的(consecutive, subsequent) 记 词根记忆：suc(在…之下) + cess(走) + ive → 跟在后面走的 → 接替的 搭 successive generation 连续世代 例 The team has won five *successive* games. 这个队已经连续赢了五场比赛。 参 succession(*n.* 连续；一系列)
alternate	[ˈɔːltərneɪt] *v.* (使)轮流，(使)交替 [ˈɔːltərnət] *a.* 交替的，轮流的(*rotate, in turn)；间隔的 记 词根记忆：altern(其他人或物) + ate → 其他的 → 交替的，轮流的 搭 alternate between...and... 在…与…间交替 例 Dark stripes *alternate* with pale ones. 深浅条纹相间。 派 alternately(*ad.* 交替地；间隔地)；alternation(*n.* 交替，轮流)

burgeon [ˈbɜːrdʒən]	*vi.* 迅速成长，发展（bloom, flourish） 词 词根记忆：burg(=bud 花蕾) + eon → 像花蕾一样成长 → 迅速成长 例 As the number of wage earners in manufacturing rose, the number of huge plants in Philadelphia *burgeoned*. 随着制造业雇佣劳动者数量的增加，费城的大型工厂的数量也在迅速增长。
dull [dʌl]	*a.* 乏味的，单调的（*drab）；迟钝的（slow）；（色彩等）无光泽的；萧条的；阴沉的，昏暗的 例 The game was pretty *dull*. 那场比赛打得十分沉闷。// It was a *dull*, grey day. 那是一个阴沉昏暗的日子。
stanza [ˈstænzə]	*n.* (诗)节，段（verse） 例 It so impressed Stevens that he was inspired to write a thirty-two-*stanza* poem entitled *The Man with the Blue Guitar*. 这给史蒂文斯留下了如此深刻的印象，并给了他灵感写出《弹蓝吉他的人》这首 32 行诗。

10

You have to believe in yourself. That's the secret of success.
人必须相信自己，这是成功的秘诀。
——美国演员 卓别林（Charles Chaplin, American actor）

Word List 11

音频

词根、词缀预习表

gust	味道	disgust *vt.* 厌恶	fut	倾泻	refute *vt.* 反驳
metic	害怕	meticulous *a.* 细心的	lit	选择	elite *a.* 卓越的
di	放	condiment *n.* 调味品	dol	伤心	condole *vi.* 慰问
dign	价值	indignant *a.* 愤慨的	lyz	分开	paralyze *vt.* 使瘫痪
tort	扭曲	tortuous *a.* 折磨人的	pass	感情	passion *n.* 激情，热情

cowhand [ˈkaʊhænd]	*n.* 牛仔，牧牛工 例 He rides a horse like a *cowhand*. 他像个牛仔那样骑着马。
spacecraft [ˈspeɪskræft]	*n.* 航天器，宇宙飞船 记 组合词：space(太空) + craft(技术) → 太空技术造出的机器 → 宇宙飞船 搭 a manned spacecraft 载人宇宙飞船 例 *Spacecraft* are used for a variety of purposes, including communications, earth observation, planetary exploration, etc. 宇宙飞船用途广泛，可用于通信、地球观测、行星探测等。
disgust [dɪsˈɡʌst]	*vt.* 厌恶，嫌恶(detest, loathe) 记 词根记忆：dis(不) + gust(味道) → 不喜欢这个味道 → 厌恶 例 The raw fish *disgusted* me, so I left the table. 生鱼让我感到恶心，所以我离开了餐桌。 派 disgusted(*a.* 厌烦的，厌恶的) 参 gusto(*n.* 爱好，嗜好); degust(*vt.* 品尝)
lore [lɔːr]	*n.* 学问，学识；传说，传统 记 联想记忆：好学(lore)的人难以抵挡书的诱惑(lure) 例 She lived alone in the forest, relying on her knowledge of herb *lore* to survive. 她独自一人住在森林里，靠自己的草药知识生存了下来。
meticulous [məˈtɪkjələs]	*a.* 细心的，小心翼翼的(*careful) 记 词根记忆：metic(害怕) + ul + ous(多…的) → 非常害怕的 → 细心的 例 George is a *meticulous* man. 乔治是个细心的人。 派 meticulously(*ad.* 小心翼翼地)

dawn [dɔːn]	*n.* 破晓，黎明；开始，发端（outset） 例 They arrived in Paris as *dawn* broke. 他们在黎明时分到达巴黎。// Peace marked a new *dawn* in the country's history. 和平使这个国家的历史翻开了新的一页。 派 dawning（*n.* 拂晓，黎明）
bruise [bruːz]	*v.* (使)出现伤痕；挫伤 *n.* 伤痕，擦痕，青肿 记 发音记忆："不如死" → 对她来说，脸上有伤痕还不如死 → 伤痕 例 It looks like you've just *bruised* the bone on your foot. 你好像伤到脚骨头了。
abut [əˈbʌt]	*v.* 邻接，毗邻（adjoin, border on） 记 联想记忆：a(无) + but(但是) → 没有转折 → 不需要绕弯就能直接到达 → 邻接，毗邻 搭 abut against 紧靠；abut on 接连，邻接 例 His land *abuts* onto a road. 他的土地紧靠公路。
condiment [ˈkɑːndɪmənt]	*n.* 调味品（dressing, flavoring） 记 词根记忆：con(一起) + di(放) + ment(名词后缀) → 放在一起 → 调味品 例 This kind of substance is recognized as a very precious *condiment* and food preservative. 这种物质被认为是非常珍贵的调味品和食物防腐剂。
discourage [dɪsˈkɜːrɪdʒ]	*vt.* 使泄气，使灰心；阻止，劝阻 记 词根记忆：dis(不) + cour(精神) + age → 使没有精神 → 使泄气 例 This rule is likely to *discourage* people from buying cars. 这个规定很可能会阻止人们购买汽车。
glitter [ˈɡlɪtər]	*vi.* 闪烁，闪耀 *n.* 灿烂的光辉；诱惑力，魅力 记 联想记忆：g + litter(看做 little，小的) → 一闪一闪小星星 → 闪烁 例 An old saying goes like this: all that *glitters* is not gold. 俗话说得好，闪闪发光的不一定都是金子。
indignant [ɪnˈdɪɡnənt]	*a.* 愤慨的，恼怒的 记 词根记忆：in(不) + dign(价值) + ant → 不值得的 → 愤慨的 例 I'm *indignant* over the treatment I received at this restaurant. 我对自己在这家饭馆所受到的待遇感到愤慨。
amalgamation [əˌmælɡəˈmeɪʃn]	*n.* 融合，合并；联合，结合 记 来自 amalgamate〔*v.* (使)合并，联合〕 例 The new company was formed by the *amalgamation* of two small businesses. 这家新公司是由两个小企业合并而成的。
tortuous [ˈtɔːrtʃuəs]	*a.* 折磨人的，令人痛苦的；曲折的，蜿蜒的；含混不清的，拐弯抹角的 记 词根记忆：tort(扭曲) + u + ous(形容词后缀) → 令人身心扭曲的 → 折磨人的 例 As the saying goes: while the road ahead is *tortuous*, the future is bright. 俗话说得好，道路是曲折的，前途是光明的。

11

noteworthy [ˈnoʊtwɜːrði]	*a.* 显著的，值得注目的 例 The sales in the past year has seen no *noteworthy* growth. 过去一年，销售量没有显著的增长。
dateline [ˈdeɪtlaɪn]	*n.* 日期栏；国际日期变更线 记 组合词：date(日期) + line(字句) → 用于标明日期等的字句 → 日期栏
refute [rɪˈfjuːt]	*vt.* 反驳，驳斥 记 词根记忆：re(向后) + fut(倾泻) + e → 向后倾泻 → 反驳 例 One of the best ways to *refute* a point is to cite examples from your own experiences. 驳斥论点的最好办法之一是用自己的亲身经历举例。
antecede [ˌæntɪˈsiːd]	*vt.* 居先(antedate, precede)；(地位上)高于 记 词根记忆：ante(在…前面) + ced(走) + e → 走在前面 → 居先 例 She *anteceded* me in the job. 她是我这份工作的前任。
conducive [kənˈduːsɪv]	*a.* 有助于…的，有益于…的 记 来自 conduce(v. 导致；有益于) 例 Doing regular exercise is *conducive* to good health. 定期做运动有益健康。
deem [diːm]	*vt.* 认为，相信 记 联想记忆：别以为事情表面似乎(seem)是这样，就认为(deem)八九不离十了 例 Do you *deem* this proposal plausible? 你认为这个提案可行吗？
ripple [ˈrɪpl]	*n.* 细浪，涟漪 *v.* 起涟漪；扩散 记 联想记忆：谜语(riddle)变 dd 为 pp → 细浪(ripple) 搭 ripple effect 连锁反应 例 The air was so still that there was hardly a *ripple* on the pond's surface. 没有风，池塘的水面上几乎看不到波纹。
urbanization [ˌɜːrbənaɪˈzeɪʃn]	*n.* 都市化 记 来自 urbanize(*vt.* 使都市化；使文雅) 例 With economic development around the world, *urbanization* has become a global trend. 随着世界经济的发展，都市化已成为一个全球性趋势。
slash [slæʃ]	*v.* 砍；大幅削减 *n.* 砍痕，伤痕；斜线号 记 联想记忆：sl + ash(灰尘) → 举着斧子乱砍，弄得到处是灰 → 砍 搭 slash costs 大幅降低成本 例 Many families have to *slash* spending to cope with inflation. 很多家庭不得不削减开支以应对通货膨胀。
elite [ɪˈliːt]	*a.* 卓越的，精锐的 *n.* 精英 记 词根记忆：e(出) + lit(选择) + e → 精心选出来的 → 卓越的 例 Mark argues that an *elite* education will cease to be so if it is provided to everyone. 马克辩解道，精英教育如果对每个人开放，便不再是精英教育了。

abolish [əˈbɑːlɪʃ]	*vt.* 废止，废除（annual） 记 联想记忆：ab(相反) + (p)olish(抛光) → 通过抛光把不好的东西去掉 → 废止，废除 例 The proposal suggests *abolishing* the national holiday system. 提案建议取消全国性的长假制度。
breach [briːtʃ]	*n.* 违背；破裂；缺口 *vt.* 打破；违反 记 联想记忆：brea(k)(打破；违反) + ch → 打破；违反 例 It is said that he has *breached* the American Privacy Laws. 据说他违反了美国的隐私法。
derive [dɪˈraɪv]	*v.* (from)取得；起源（originate） 记 联想记忆：de + rive(r) → 黄河是中华文明的发源地 → 起源 例 The subject of a sculpture should be *derived* from classical stories. 雕塑的主题可能源自古典故事。
pupil [ˈpjuːpl]	*n.* 小学生（schoolchild）；瞳孔 例 How many *pupils* does this school have? 这所小学有多少学生？
condole [kənˈdoʊl]	*vi.* 向…吊唁；慰问 记 词根记忆：con + dol(伤心) + e → 表达伤心 → 慰问 例 Mary wrote to *condole* with her friend on the death of his father. 玛丽写信慰问朋友的丧父之痛。 派 condolence(*n.* 吊唁，哀悼)
altruistic [ˌæltruˈɪstɪk]	*a.* 利他的，无私心的，为他人着想的 搭 altruistic act 无私行为 例 *Altruistic* behavior is common throughout the animal kingdom, particularly in species with complex social structures. 无私行为在动物界很普遍，尤其是在那些有着复杂社会结构的种群中。
grill [grɪl]	*vt.* 烧烤；拷问，盘问 *n.* 烤架 记 联想记忆：在小河(rill)边烧烤(grill)
saddle [ˈsædl]	*n.* 马鞍；(自行车的)车座 *vt.* 给…备鞍 记 联想记忆：骑马上鞍(saddle)，划船用桨(paddle) 搭 in the saddle 掌权；saddle...with 使…肩负重任 例 I've been *saddled* with organizing the conference. 我被派担负组织会议的重任。
paralyze [ˈpærəlaɪz]	*vt.* 使瘫痪，使麻痹；使无效 记 词根记忆：para(半) + lyz(分开) + e → 身体的一边像是分开了 → 使瘫痪，使麻痹 例 Those tiny poison threads can *paralyze* small sea animals. 这些细细的毒针能麻痹小型海洋动物。 派 paralysis(*n.* 瘫痪)

11

disintegrate
[dɪsˈɪntɪɡreɪt]

v. (使)瓦解(collapse); (使)碎裂(smash)

记 联想记忆: dis(不) + integrate(一体化, 使完整) → (使)瓦解

例 The books printed less than one hundred years ago are beginning to *disintegrate*. 这些印刷还不到 100 年的书开始散了。

tenuous
[ˈtenjuəs]

a. 纤细的(slender); 稀薄的; 脆弱的

记 词根记忆: ten(伸展) + uous → 无限伸展的 → 纤细的

例 The cord tying the boat to the rock is *tenuous*. 把船绑在岩石上的绳子很细。

activate
[ˈæktɪveɪt]

vt. 刺激, 使活动(stimulate)

记 联想记忆: activ(e)(活跃的) + ate(使…) → 使活跃 → 使活动

例 If you press the red button near the bottom it will *activate* the washing machine. 按靠近底部的红色按钮, 就会启动洗衣机。

occasional
[əˈkeɪʒənl]

a. 偶然的, 不经常的(infrequent); 临时的

记 来自 occasion(n. 时机)

例 Auctions were another popular form of *occasional* trade. 拍卖是临时交易的另一种流行形式。

court
[kɔːrt]

n. 法院, 法庭; 宫廷, 朝廷; 球场(playground, field) vt. 献殷勤, 讨好; 招致; 求爱

搭 the Supreme Court 最高法院

例 There wasn't enough evidence to bring the case to the *court*. 没有足够的证据可以把此案提交法庭。// As a politician he has often *courted* controversy. 作为政治人物, 他常常招致非议。

派 courtship(n. 求爱; 求爱期)

scene
[siːn]

n. 地点, 现场(location, spot); 景色(setting, spectacle); (戏剧的)一场, (电影、电视的)一个镜头; 场面; 活动领域, 圈子

例 Hundreds of police in riot gear were on the *scene* immediately. 数百名身带防爆装备的警察立刻赶到了现场。// She witnessed some very distressing *scenes*. 她目睹过一些令人非常痛苦的场面。

派 scenic(a. 风景如画的); scenery(n. 风景, 景色)

inconvenient
[ˌɪnkənˈviːniənt]

a. 不便的(inappropriate); 让人不舒服的(uncomfortable)

记 联想记忆: in(不) + convenient(方便的) → 不便的

例 The campus bus runs at really *inconvenient* time. 校园巴士运行的时间真是不方便。

passion
[ˈpæʃn]

n. 激情, 热情(emotion, enthusiasm)

记 词根记忆: pass(感情) + ion → 激情, 热情

例 It's been my *passion* since I collected my first Lincoln dime in 1971. 自从我 1971 年收藏第一枚林肯十分钱硬币以来, 这就成了我的嗜好。

incompatible [ˌɪnkəmˈpætəbl]	*a.* 不兼容的；不协调的，合不来的 记 词根记忆：in(不) + com(共同) + pat(感情) + ible(能…的) → 感情不一致的 → 不协调的 例 After a week together on a field trip, it is obvious that the partners are totally *incompatible*. 共同进行野外考察一周后(发现)同组伙伴们之间完全合不来。
metropolis [məˈtrɑːpəlɪs]	*n.* 首府(capital)；大都市 记 词根记忆：metro(大的) + polis(城市) → 大都市 派 metropolitan(*a.* 大都市的)
expose [ɪkˈspoʊz]	*vt.* 暴露，显露；揭露，揭穿；使接触，使面临 记 词根记忆：ex(出) + pos(放) + e → 放出来 → 暴露，显露；揭露 搭 be exposed to 暴露于 例 She did not want to *expose* her fears and insecurity to anyone. 她不想向任何人显露她的恐惧与不安。// A group of mice was placed in a brightly lit open box with no hiding places. Some of the mice wandered around the box and didn't appear to be bothered about being so *exposed*. 一群老鼠被放在了照亮的无盖的盒子里，里面没有躲藏的地方。有些老鼠在盒子里转来转去，好像并不介意暴露在灯光之下。
register [ˈredʒɪstər]	*v./n.* 登记，注册(enroll) 记 词根记忆：re(回) + gist(=gest 带来) + er → 带回来 → 登记 例 There are two more days to *register* for the class. 注册这门课的时间还有两天。 派 registrar(*n.* 登记员)；registration(*n.* 登记，注册)
deter [dɪˈtɜːr]	*v.* 威慑，阻止(prevent) 记 词根记忆：de + ter(=terr 吓唬) → 威慑，阻止 例 The cost of construction and the very high risk *deterred* private investment in this town. 建筑成本和高风险使私人不敢在这个镇上投资。 参 defer(*v.* 推迟)
occur [əˈkɜːr]	*vi.* 发生，出现(happen, appear)；存在于 记 词根记忆：oc(向) + cur(跑) → 跑向 → 发生，出现 搭 occur to sb. 被想到，出现在头脑中 例 Most manufacturing *occurred* in relatively small plants. 大多数生产活动在相对较小的工厂里进行。 派 occurrence(*n.* 事件；发生) 参 recur(*vi.* 重现)
enterprise [ˈentərpraɪz]	*n.* 企业，公司(corporation)；事业 记 词根记忆：enter(进入) + pris(握住) + e → 进入市场，把握先机 → 公司 搭 a joint enterprise 合办事业；state-owned/public enterprise 国有企业 例 He works in a private *enterprise*. 他在一家私人企业工作。 参 entrepreneur(*n.* 企业家，创业人)

11

chaos [ˈkeɪɑːs]	*n.* 混乱（muddle, disorder） 记 发音记忆："吵死" → 混乱 例 Unprecedented change in the nation's economy would bring social *chaos*. 这个国家前所未有的经济变化将导致社会动乱。 派 chaotic(*a.* 混乱的，无秩序的); chaotically(*ad.* 混乱地）
violent [ˈvaɪələnt]	*a.* 暴力的(forcible)；感情强烈的，激情的；强烈的，激烈的 例 The American Revolution was not a sudden and *violent* overturning of the political and social framework. 美国革命不是以暴力的方式突然推翻政治和社会框架的。 派 violence(*n.* 暴力行为); nonviolence(*n.* 非暴力） 参 violin(*n.* 小提琴); violet(*n.* 紫罗兰); violate(*vt.* 违背；亵渎；侵犯）
homogeneous [ˌhoʊməˈdʒiːniəs]	*a.* 同类的，相似的，同质的(*uniform) 记 联想记忆：homo(同类的) + gene(基因) + ous → 基因相同的 → 同类的，相似的 例 In a small community, behavioral norms are more likely to be *homogeneous* than in a large city. 在小社区，行为规范可能比在大城市更趋于统一。
boundary [ˈbaʊndri]	*n.* 分界线；边界(bound, border) 记 联想记忆：bound(被束缚的) + ary(表场所) → 加以束缚的界限 → 分界线；边界 例 The neighbors had a long-standing disagreement over the *boundary*. 邻居们就分界线存在着长期的分歧。
male [meɪl]	*a.* 雄的，公的；男性的 *n.* 男子；雄性动(或植)物 例 All the attackers were *male*, aged between 25 and 30. 所有的攻击者都是男性，年龄在25到30岁之间。 参 female[*n./a.* 雌性(的)]
sheath [ʃiːθ]	*n.* 鞘，外壳（holder, scabbard）；（工具的）套；（电线等的)护皮；紧身连衣裙 派 sheathe(*vt.* 把…插入鞘中，给…加护套）
appointment [əˈpɔɪntmənt]	*n.* 约会，约定(date)；任命，委派；职位 例 I've made an *appointment* to see my dentist. 我和我的牙医约好了。
exhilarating [ɪɡˈzɪləreɪtɪŋ]	*a.* 令人高兴的，使人兴奋的(exciting) 记 来自 exhilarate(*vt.* 使高兴，使愉快; ex(表加强) + hilar(欢快的) + ate(使…) → 使非常欢快 → 使高兴，使愉快 例 The children screamed with delight on the *exhilarating* carnival ride. 在令人兴奋的狂欢旅程上，孩子们开心地喊叫着。
fabricate [ˈfæbrɪkeɪt]	*vt.* 编造(create)；制造(*construct, manufacture) 记 词根记忆：fabric(构造) + ate → 构造出来 → 编造；制造 例 She thought that writers should tell the truth about human affairs, not *fabricate* romance. 她认为，对于人类事务，作家应讲真话，而不应编造传奇故事。

□ chaos   □ violent   □ homogeneous □ boundary   □ male   □ sheath
□ appointment □ exhilarating □ fabricate

artistic [ɑːrˈtɪstɪk]	*a.* 艺术(家)的(aesthetical)；富有艺术性的，精美的；有艺术天赋的 例 We'll see many *artistic* works depicting the major events of her life. 我们将看到描写她一生主要事件的许多艺术作品。 派 artistically(*ad.* 艺术地，艺术上) 参 artistry(*n.* 艺术技巧)
keen [kiːn]	*a.* 灵敏的，敏锐的(sharp)；热心的，渴望的；激烈的；锋利的 例 Their *keen* senses of hearing and smell have made some types of dogs valuable in hunting and tracking and as security guards. 某些种类的狗因听觉和嗅觉灵敏而在狩猎、追踪和保卫方面很有价值。 派 keenly(*ad.* 敏锐地；热心地；激烈地)
seismology [saɪzˈmɑːlədʒi]	*n.* 地震学 记 词根记忆：seism(震动) + ology(…学) → 地震学 例 This event marks the beginning of the modern era of *seismology*. 这一事件标志着地震学研究新时代的开始。
welfare [ˈwelfer]	*n.* 福利(well-being)；安宁，幸福 记 联想记忆：wel(l)(健康的) + fare(费用) → 让人们保持健康的费用 → 福利 搭 welfare state 福利国家 例 The company's *welfare* officer deals with employees' personal problems. 公司负责福利的工作人员负责处理雇员的个人问题。
gross [ɡroʊs]	*vt.* 总收入为 *a.* 总的，毛的；粗俗的，粗野的；令人不快的 *n.* 一罗(为 12 打，144 个)；[常 *pl.*]毛收入，总收入 搭 gross weight 毛重 例 The company *grossed* 4 million. 该公司获得了 400 万美元毛利。
edge [edʒ]	*n.* 边，边缘(border)；刀口，刃；优势 *v.* (使)徐徐移动；略为增加；给…加边 搭 on the edge of 在…的边缘；on edge 紧张；激动 例 He stood on the *edge* of the cliff. 他站在悬崖边。// The company needs to improve its competitive *edge*. 该公司必须提高其竞争力。// I have to give a presentation in class this afternoon, and I am a little on *edge*. 我下午要在班上做个报告，感觉有点紧张。
revert [rɪˈvɜːrt]	*v.* 恢复(原状)；(财产、权利等)归还，归属 记 词根记忆：re(反) + vert(转) → 反转 → 恢复 搭 revert to 恢复；重提；归还 例 A glacier can *revert* to a fluffy mass. 冰川能够重新变回蓬松的一团。
appliance [əˈplaɪəns]	*n.* 用具，器具；装置 记 来自 apply(*v.* 应用) 例 The *appliances* in the kitchen are all made of stainless steel. 厨房用具都是不锈钢做的。

11

slender [ˈslendər]	*a.* 细长的(thin)；苗条的，纤细的(slim)；微薄的，不足的 记 联想记忆：温柔(tender)和纤弱(slender)都是用来形容女孩子的 例 Our team won the game by a *slender* margin. 我们队以微弱的优势赢得了比赛。 派 slenderness(*n.* 苗条，纤细)
noxious [ˈnɑːkʃəs]	*a.* 有害的(*harmful)；有毒的(poisonous) 记 词根记忆：nox(毒) + ious → 有毒的 例 The result is an increased concentration of *noxious* chemicals in the air. 结果是空气中有毒化学品的浓度增加。
calendar [ˈkælɪndər]	*n.* 日历，挂历，月历；日程表 记 联想记忆：cal(看作 call，叫) + end(尽头) + ar → 一年到头对日子的叫法 → 日历，月历 搭 calendar year 日历年 例 It's an exhibition of wildlife art *calendar* from about a hundred years ago. 这是一个关于大约 100 年前的野生动物艺术日历的展览。
quiz [kwɪz]	*n.* 小测验；智力竞赛 *vt.* 测验；盘问，查问，询问 记 联想记忆：他最终放弃(quit)了口语测试(quiz) 例 We are *quizzed* on our views about education. 我们被征询对教育的看法。
universe [ˈjuːnɪvɜːrs]	*n.* 宇宙(cosmos)；世界(world) 记 词根记忆：uni(单一) + vers(转) + e → 一个旋转着的整体空间 → 宇宙 例 The *universe* is filled with puzzling materials. 宇宙中充满了令人不解的物质。 派 universal(*a.* 普遍的，全体的)；universally(*ad.* 普遍地，全体地)
agreeable [əˈɡriːəbl]	*a.* 使人愉快的(pleasant)；欣然同意的(willing) 记 来自 agree(*v.* 同意，赞成) 例 We find Bob *agreeable* most of the time. 我们发现鲍勃大部分时间都比较随和。// They were most *agreeable* on the subject of voting rights. 他们非常愿意谈论选举权这个话题。
grant [ɡrænt]	*v.* 给予，授予(award)；允许，同意(approve)；承认(admit) *n.* 拨款；津贴；授予物 记 联想记忆：授予(grant)显赫的(grand)贵族爵位 搭 take...for granted 认为…理所当然 例 The bank *granted* her a loan to cover her school expenses. 银行为她提供贷款来支付上学费用。// Mary seems surprised that she got a research *grant*. 玛丽对得到研究经费好像很惊讶。
perception [pərˈsepʃn]	*n.* 感知，感觉；认识，观念；洞察力 记 词根记忆：per(全部) + cept(抓住) + ion → 全部抓住 → 感知，感觉 例 All the statues along the road seem perfectly designed for the grand religious *perception* the local people often had there. 路旁所有的雕像似乎完全是为迎合当地人拥有的宏大宗教观念而设计的。 参 exception(*n.* 例外)

□ slender　　□ noxious　　□ calendar　　□ quiz　　□ universe　　□ agreeable
□ grant　　□ perception

ethic [ˈeθɪk]	*n.* [常 *pl.*]道德规范，道德准则；伦理学 记 词根记忆：eth(习俗) + ic → 道德规范；伦理学 例 He began to question the *ethics* of his position. 他开始对他的立场是否符合道德准则提出了质疑。 派 ethical(*a.* 道德的，伦理的；合乎道德的)；unethical(*a.* 不道德的)；ethically(*ad.* 伦理上)
maglev [ˈmæɡlev]	*n.* 磁力悬浮火车 例 *Maglev* will not actually ride on the tracks but will fly above tracks that are magnetically activated. 磁悬浮火车实际上并不在轨道上行驶，而是漂浮在磁力驱动的轨道上快速行驶。
cosmic [ˈkɑːzmɪk]	*a.* 宇宙的；无限的 记 词根记忆：cosm(宇宙) + ic → 宇宙的 搭 cosmic dust 宇宙尘埃；cosmic ray 宇宙光 例 The extinction of the dinosaurs was caused by some physical event, either climatic or *cosmic*. 恐龙灭绝是由某个气候或宇宙的物理事件造成的。
anchor [ˈæŋkər]	*v.* 抛锚；使固定(fix)；(使)扎根，(使)基于；主持(电视、广播节目等) *n.* 锚；给人安全感的物(或人)，精神支柱 例 Her novels are *anchored* in everyday experience. 她的小说取材自日常生活经验。
engineering [ˌendʒɪˈnɪrɪŋ]	*n.* 工程；工程学 记 来自 engineer(*n.* 工程师) 搭 electronics engineering 电子工程学 例 The bridge is a triumph of modern *engineering*. 这座桥是现代工程的一大成就。// Could you give me a ride to the *engineering* building? 你能开车送我去工程系大楼吗？
crew [kruː]	*n.* 全体船员；全体工作人员 记 发音记忆："可入" → 仅限工作人员进入，闲人免进 → 全体工作人员 例 None of the passengers and *crew* were injured in the accident. 在这次事故中，没有一名乘客和工作人员受伤。
delay [dɪˈleɪ]	*v.* 耽搁，延迟(defer, postpone) *n.* 耽搁，延迟 记 联想记忆：de + lay(放下) → 放下不管 → 耽搁 例 He *delayed* telling her the truth, waiting for the right moment. 他没有马上把真相告诉她，而是在等待合适的时机。// Report it to the police without *delay*. 赶快将此事报告给警方。
halt [hɔːlt]	*n.* 停止，阻止；暂停 *v.* (使)停住，停下 记 联想记忆：h + alt(高) → 高处不胜寒，该停住了 → 停止 例 Work has to come to a *halt* when the machine goes wrong. 机器出故障时必须停止工作。

都过了合同期限啦！

再宽限几天啦～

delay

staple [ˈsteɪpl]	*n.* 主要产品；原材料(*basic element)；主食；订书钉 *a.* 主要的(*important) *vt.* 把…订起来(fasten) 记 联想记忆：主要产品(staple)收成好，国家稳定(stable) 搭 staple cotton 原棉 例 Rubber became the *staple* of the Malayan economy. 橡胶成了马来西亚经济的支柱产品。// In southern China the *staple* crop is rice. 在中国南部，水稻是主要农作物。
vibrate [ˈvaɪbreɪt]	*v.* (使)颤动，(使)振动(swing) 记 词根记忆：vibr(摆动) + ate → (使)颤动，(使)振动 例 The quartz crystal in a heater *vibrates* at a particular frequency. 加热器中的水晶振子按照某个特定频率振动。
champion [ˈtʃæmpiən]	*n.* 冠军（winner, victor）；拥护者（defender, protector）*vt.* 声援 记 发音记忆："产品" → 冠军是付出无数汗水后的"产品" → 冠军 例 One popular candidate *champions* tax reform. 一位受欢迎的候选人支持税收改革。
stimulus [ˈstɪmjələs]	*n.* [*pl.* stimuli]刺激(物)，激励，促进因素 记 词根记忆：stimul(刺) + us → 刺激 搭 sensory stimulus 感官刺激；stimulus to 对…的刺激 例 The invention of the steam engine acted as a *stimulus* to industrial development. 蒸汽机的发明促进了工业发展。
attempt [əˈtempt]	*n./vi.* 尝试(try)；努力(strive) 记 词根记忆：at(表加强) + tempt(诱惑) → 尝试；努力 例 The bird flaps one wing in an apparent *attempt* to take to the air. 这只鸟扇动着一只翅膀，明显是想飞起来。 参 contemplate(*v.* 凝视；考虑)；contemporary(*n.* 同时代的人)；tempting(*a.* 吸引人的)
mercury [ˈmɜːrkjəri]	*n.* [M-]水星；水银，汞 记 联想记忆：mer(音似：没) + cury(看做 cure, 治愈) → 水银中毒没治了 → 水银
fragrant [ˈfreɪɡrənt]	*a.* 芬芳的，香的(aromatic, spicy) 记 联想记忆：和 flagrant(*a.* 恶名昭著的)一起记，fragrant 中的两个 r 像两朵花，所以是"芳香的" 例 The flowers emit a *fragrant* odor. 花朵散发出芳香。 派 fragrance(*n.* 芬芳，香气)

champion

□ staple   □ vibrate   □ champion   □ stimulus   □ attempt   □ mercury
□ fragrant

scar [skɑːr]	*vt.* 给…留下疤痕（blemish）；给…留下精神创伤；损害…的外观 *n.* 疤痕（seam）；创伤 记 联想记忆：s + car（汽车）→ 被汽车撞了一下，留下伤痕 → 疤痕 搭 scar tissue 疤痕组织 例 Thousands of mine disposal sites *scarred* the coal-rich regions. 成千上万的矿井处理场破坏了煤含量丰富的地区的景观。
log [lɔːg]	*n.* 原木，木材（timber, wood）；日志，（尤指）航海日志，飞行日志 *vt.* 记录；伐木 搭 log in/on 登录，进入（计算机系统）；log off/out 注销，退出（计算机系统） 例 The captain keeps a *log*. 那位船长记航海日志。// The police *log* all phone calls. 警方对所有电话都做记录。
stir [stɜːr]	*v.* 搅拌；煽动（provoke）；激发，打动；（使）行动，活动 *n.* 搅拌，搅动；激动，震动 记 本身是词根，意为"刺激" 搭 stir up 激起，鼓动，煽动 例 She was *stirred* by his sad story. 她被他悲惨的故事打动了。// Would you please give the tea a *stir*? 请把茶搅一搅好吗？
refer [rɪˈfɜːr]	*v.* 提到，谈及（relate to）；查阅，参考（consult） 记 词根记忆：re（又）+ fer（带来，拿来）→ 提到，谈及 例 She never *referred* to her daughter again. 她再也没有提起过她女儿。// You may *refer* to your notes if you want. 如果需要，可以查阅笔记。
enthusiasm [ɪnˈθuːziæzəm]	*n.* 热情（passion）；积极性（positivity）；热衷的事物 例 I have a real *enthusiasm* for the work. 我的确热衷于这项工作。 参 enthusiastic（*a.* 热情的）；enthusiastically（*ad.* 狂热地）；enthusiast（*n.* 爱好者；热烈支持者）

11

scar

Word List 12

音频

词根、词缀预习表

ciner	灰	incinerate *vt.* 焚化，焚毁	frain	笼头	refrain *v.* 抑制
trud	刺	intrude *vi.* 闯入	tract	拉	retract *v.* 收回；缩回
quaint	知道	acquaint *vt.* 使熟悉	lur	吸引	allure *n./v.* 诱惑
merg	浸没	submerge *v.* 浸没	ann	年	biannual *a.* 一年两次的
bl	扔	emblem *n.* 徽章	lig	捆绑	obligate *vt.* 使负义务

---

yeast
[jiːst]

n. 酵母，发酵粉
记 联想记忆：y + east(东方) → 据说酵母最早是由东方人发明的 → 酵母
派 yeasty(*a.* 发酵的)

---

wreck
[rek]

vt. 使失事；破坏(destroy) *n.* 沉船；失事
例 The scandal *wrecked* the politician's chances of being elected. 丑闻使这个政客失去了当选的可能。
参 shipwreck(*n.* 船只失事)

---

incinerate
[ɪnˈsɪnəreɪt]

vt. 焚化，焚毁(cremate)
记 词根记忆：in + ciner(灰) + ate(使…) → 使成灰 → 焚化，焚毁
例 The waste is *incinerated* in a large furnace. 垃圾在一个巨大的炉子里焚化。
派 incinerator(*n.* 焚化炉)

---

scope
[skoʊp]

n. 范围，界限(*extent, range)；眼界，见识；(发挥能力等的)余地，机会
记 联想记忆：事情处理(cope)得多了，眼界(scope)自然就会开阔起来
例 This issue is outside the *scope* of the article. 这个问题不在本文的论述范围之内。// Our powers are limited in *scope*. 我们的权限不大。
参 telescope(*n.* 望远镜)；microscope(*n.* 显微镜)

---

intrude
[ɪnˈtruːd]

vi. 侵入，闯入；打扰，侵扰
记 词根记忆：in(进入) + trud(刺) + e → 刺入 → 闯入
例 The sound of the telephone *intruded* into his dreams. 电话铃声把他从梦中惊醒了。
派 intrusion(*n.* 入侵)；intruder(*n.* 入侵者)
参 extrude(*v.* 逐出)；detrude(*vt.* 推倒，扔掉)

---

bronze [brɑːnz]	*n.* 青铜；青铜色；青铜制品；铜牌 *a.* 青铜色的 搭 Bronze Age 青铜器时代 例 She won a *bronze* in skiing. 她在滑雪中获得了一块铜牌。
topsoil ['tɑːpsɔɪl]	*n.* 表层土 记 组合词：top(顶上的) + soil(土地) → 表层土 例 The fieldstones remain in a frozen layer of *topsoil*. 大卵石仍然在表层的冻土里。
acquaint [ə'kweɪnt]	*vt.* 使认识(inform)；使熟悉(familiarize) 记 词根记忆：ac + quaint(知道) → 使熟悉 例 She's well *acquainted* with the subject. 她对这个主题非常熟悉。 派 acquaintance(*n.* 了解；熟人)
bake [beɪk]	*v.* 烘，烤，焙 例 The cake was over *baked*. 蛋糕烤过头了。 参 sunbaked(*a.* 晒裂的)
submerge [səb'mɜːrdʒ]	*v.* 浸没，淹没(immerge) 记 词根记忆：sub(在…下面) + merg(浸没) + e → 被吞没下去 → 浸没，淹没 例 The rest of the peninsula was *submerged*. 剩下的半岛被水淹没了。 派 submerged(*a.* 淹没的；在水中的)
emblem ['embləm]	*n.* 徽章(badge)；标记，象征 记 词根记忆：em(内) + bl(=bol 扔) + em → 向内扔 → 徽章 例 The dove is an *emblem* of peace. 鸽子是和平的象征。
breed [briːd]	*n.* 品种 *v.* 饲养(raise)；繁殖(reproduce)；养育；酿成，导致 记 联想记忆：专用面包(bread)来饲养(breed)动物，成本真够高的啊 例 Our dog is a rare *breed*. 我们的狗是稀有品种。// The songbirds have finished *breeding*. 鸣禽完成了繁殖。 参 inbreeding(*n.* 同系繁殖，近亲交配)
tributary ['trɪbjəteri]	*n.* 支流(branch)；进贡者 *a.* 支流的；进贡的；辅助的 记 词根记忆：tribut(给予) + ary → 进贡者 例 This stream is a *tributary* of the Yellow River. 这条小河是黄河的一条支流。
sound [saʊnd]	*a.* 可靠的(secure)；健康的，完好无损的 (healthy)；合理的(reasonable) *v.* 似乎(seem)；测量…的深度 例 My father gave me some very *sound* advice. 我父亲给了我一些非常合理的建议。 派 soundly(*ad.* 可靠地；不错地)
malicious [mə'lɪʃəs]	*a.* 怀有恶意的，恶毒的 记 来自 malice(*n.* 恶意) 例 That girl's reputation was ruined by the *malicious* gossip. 那个女孩的名誉被恶毒的流言给毁了。

12

submerge

equal ['iːkwəl]	*vt.* 等于(amount)；相当于 *a.* 相同的(same) *n.* 同等的人；相等的事物 例 The pressure of the gases being breathed must *equal* the external pressure applied to the body. 吸进的气体压力必须等于施加在身体上的外部压力。 派 equality(*n.* 平等)；equally(*ad.* 相等地；平等地)
inevitably [ɪn'evɪtəbli]	*ad.* 不可避免地，必然地(*unavoidably, necessarily) 记 来自 inevitable(*a.* 不可避免的) 例 The focus of educators and of laymen interested in education *inevitably* turned toward the lower grades. 教育家和对教育感兴趣的门外汉不可避免地将关注点转向了更低的年级。
pulp [pʌlp]	*vt.* 使成浆状 *n.* 纸浆；浆状物 记 发音记忆："啪扑" → 纸被砸成纸浆时发出的声音 → 纸浆 例 Unsold copies of the magazine had to be *pulped*. 没卖出去的杂志只好被打成纸浆。
naked ['neɪkɪd]	*a.* 裸露的，无遮盖的(bare)；直白的，露骨的，不加掩饰的 搭 a naked body 赤裸的身体；the naked truth 明摆着的事实 例 The planet should be visible to the *naked* eye. 这颗行星肉眼就能看见。
refrain [rɪ'freɪn]	*n.* 反复句，副歌 *v.* 抑制；戒除 记 词根记忆：re(向后) + frain(笼头) → 笼头向后 → 抑制 搭 refrain from 抑制，克制 例 *Refrain* from using informal languages in your essay. 请不要在论文里使用非正式语言。
disclose [dɪs'kloʊz]	*vt.* 泄露，透露；揭发 记 词根记忆：dis(不) + clos(关闭) + e → 不关闭 → 泄露，透露 例 Many actresses are not willing to *disclose* their true ages. 很多女演员不愿透露其真实年龄。
retract [rɪ'trækt]	*v.* 收回，撤销；缩回 记 词根记忆：re(往后) + tract(拉) → 往后拉 → 收回；缩回 例 I don't want to rush into any statements now in case I'll have to *retract* them later. 我不想现在轻率地下结论，以防之后还要收回自己说过的话。
indolent ['ɪndələnt]	*a.* 懒惰的，懒散的；不活跃的 记 词根记忆：in(不) + dol(悲痛) + ent → 无大悲大喜 → 懒惰的 例 The *indolent* girl resisted doing her homework. 那个懒惰的女孩不愿做家庭作业。
allure [ə'lʊr]	*n./v.* 诱惑，吸引 记 词根记忆：al(向) + lur(吸引) + e → 诱惑 例 The beautiful beaches of Hawaii *allure* many tourists from all over the world. 夏威夷美丽的海滨吸引了许多来自世界各地的游客。

□ equal □ inevitably □ pulp □ naked □ refrain □ disclose
□ retract □ indolent □ allure

widespread
[ˈwaɪdspred]

a. 分布广泛的，普遍的

记 组合词：wide(广的) + spread(传播，分布) → 分布广泛的，普遍的

例 It is reported that child abuse is *widespread* in that country. 据报道，那个国家虐待孩子的情况很普遍。

dissolute
[ˈdɪsəluːt]

a. 放荡的，放纵的，道德沦丧的

记 词根记忆：dis(分离) + solu(解开) + te → 完全解开 → 放荡的

例 That young girl led a *dissolute* life. 那个年轻女孩过着放纵的生活。

interpret
[ɪnˈtɜːrprɪt]

v. 解释，说明(explain)；理解(comprehend)；翻译

记 词根记忆：inter (在…之间) + pret → 在两种语言之间沟通 → 翻译

例 It is difficult for babies to *interpret* emotions. 让婴儿理解情感很难。

派 interpretation(*n.* 解释，说明；演绎)；interpretive (*a.* 解释的；理解的；演绎的)

> Hello!
> 他说你好
>
> interpret

slacken
[ˈslækən]

v. (使)松弛，(使)放松；(使)减缓，放慢

记 联想记忆：slack(松弛的，放松的) + en → (使)松弛，(使)放松

例 We've been really busy, but things are starting to *slacken* off now. 近来我们的确很忙，不过现在情况开始有所缓解了。

biannual
[baɪˈænjuəl]

a. 一年两次的

记 词根记忆：bi(两) + ann(年) + ual → 一年两次的

例 The committee holds *biannual* meetings in March and November. 这个委员会一年开两次会，分别在3月和11月。

prophet
[ˈprɑːfɪt]

n. 先知；预言者；拥护者，鼓吹者

记 词根记忆：pro(在…前面) + phe(说) + t → 提前说出 → 先知；预言者

例 The famous writer was also one of the early *prophets* of socialism. 那位著名作家也是社会主义的早期拥护者之一。

mainstream
[ˈmeɪnstriːm]

n. 主流，主要倾向；主流思想

记 组合词：main(主要的) + stream(溪，流) → 主流

例 Its simple design made it become *mainstream*. 其简约的设计使其成为主流。

obligate
[ˈɑːblɪɡeɪt]

vt. 使负义务，强迫

记 词根记忆：ob(表加强) + lig(捆绑) + ate → 用力捆绑 → 使负义务

例 The contract *obligates* the firm to complete the work in six weeks. 根据合同，该公司必须在六个星期内完成工作。

rip
[rɪp]

v. 扯破，撕坏 *n.* 裂口，裂缝

例 You'd better *rip* the seal off the box first. 你最好先把盒子上的封条撕开。

code
[koʊd]

vt. 编纂(法典等)；把…编码 *n.* 法典，法规(law, rule)；密码，代码

搭 code of laws 法典；bar code 条形码；instruction code 指令(代)码

例 They are specially *coded*. 它们是经过特别编码的。

派 codify(*vt.* 编成法典)

12

scoff [skɔːf]	*vi.* (at)嘲笑，讥笑(mock) 记 联想记忆：s + coff(看做 coffee，咖啡) → 人们总喜欢在喝咖啡时议论、嘲笑他人 → 嘲笑，讥笑 例 They all *scoffed* when I told them that I planned to become a writer. 当我告诉他们我想成为一名作家时，他们都嗤之以鼻。
oppressive [əˈpresɪv]	*a.* 压迫的，压制的；令人焦虑的 记 词根记忆：op + press(压) + ive → 压迫的，压制的 例 The air is stale and *oppressive*, and I feel it hard to breathe. 空气混浊不堪、令人窒息，我感到呼吸困难。
impede [ɪmˈpiːd]	*vt.* 妨碍，阻碍，阻止 记 词根记忆：im(在…中) + ped(脚) + e → 在…中插一脚 → 妨碍，阻碍 例 Will working overtime *impede* you from choosing a job? 加班会成为你不选择一份工作的理由吗？
endanger [ɪnˈdeɪndʒər]	*vt.* 危及，危害 记 联想记忆：en(使) + danger(危险) → 使遭到危险 → 危及 例 You will *endanger* your health by eating such unhealthy food. 吃这种不健康的食物会危害你的健康。
intermediate [ˌɪntərˈmiːdiət]	*a.* 中间的；中级的 *n.* 中间体，媒介 记 词根记忆：inter(在…之间) + medi(中间) + ate → 中间的 例 This country is still at an *intermediate* stage of economic development. 这个国家仍然处于经济发展的中间阶段。
scornful [ˈskɔːrnfl]	*a.* 轻蔑的，鄙视的 记 联想记忆：scorn(藐视) + ful → 轻蔑的 例 He was *scornful* of anyone who disagreed with his political beliefs. 他看不起所有与他持不同政见的人。
chip [tʃɪp]	*v.* 削(或凿)下(break off) *n.* 碎片(piece, bit)；芯片(integrated circuit) 搭 silicon chip 硅片 例 Early settlers used to *chip* out blocks of ice to melt for drinking water. 早期移民常常凿下冰块，把它们融化成饮用水。
imbibe [ɪmˈbaɪb]	*v.* 喝(drink)；吸收，接受(信息等) 记 词根记忆：im(里，内) + bib(喝) + e → 喝进去 → 喝；接受(信息等) 例 Camels can *imbibe* over 100 liters in a few minutes. 骆驼在几分钟之内可以喝 100 多升水。
prospect [ˈprɑːspekt]	*n.* 前景，前途(outlook)；可能性(*possibility)；景象；期望(expectation) *v.* 勘探，勘察(explore) 记 词根记忆：pro(向前) + spect(看) → 向前看 → 前景，前途 例 In Nevada, Twain *prospected* for sister and gold without much luck, but did succeed as a writer. 在内华达州，吐温在寻找姐姐和金子上面运气都不太好，不过作为作家他的确成功了。 派 prospector(*n.* 勘探者；采矿者)；prospective(*a.* 可能的，预期的)

□ scoff　　□ oppressive　　□ impede　　□ endanger　　□ intermediate　　□ scornful
□ chip　　□ imbibe　　□ prospect

mass [mæs]	*n.* 质量；块，团(block)；众多；群众，平民百姓 *a.* 大量的(large-scale) 搭 mass communication 大众传播 例 The sky was full of dark *masses* of clouds. 天空中乌云密布。// I've got *masses* of work to do. 我有一大堆的工作要做。 派 massive(*a.* 巨大的，大而重的；非常严重的)
alkali ['ælkəlaɪ]	*n.* 碱 派 alkaline(*a.* 含碱的，碱性的)
unearth [ʌn'ɜːrθ]	*vt.* 掘出，发掘(dig out)；揭露 记 联想记忆：un(解开) + earth(地) → 使从地里出来 → 掘出，发掘 例 They did *unearth* the bones of a 45-foot-long dinosaur. 他们的确挖掘出了有着45英尺长的恐龙的骨骼。
suffragist ['sʌfrədʒɪst]	*n.* 妇女政权论者 例 In 1916, United States *suffragist* Alice Paul founded the National Women's Party dedicated to establishing equal rights for women. 1916年，美国妇女政权论者爱丽丝·保罗建立了全美女性党，致力于为女性争取平等的权利。
amusement [ə'mjuːzmənt]	*n.* 可笑；娱乐，消遣(*entertainment, recreation) 例 She could not hide her *amusement* at the way he was dancing. 她看见他跳舞的姿势，忍俊不禁。
pharmacy ['fɑːrməsi]	*n.* 药店(drugstore)；药剂学 记 词根记忆：pharmac(药) + y → 药店；药剂学 例 She's studying *pharmacy* at the university. 她在大学里学药剂学。 参 pharmacology(*n.* 药理学，药物学)；pharmacopeia(*n.* 药典)
shallow ['ʃæloʊ]	*a.* 浅的(superficial)；浅薄的 *n.* 浅滩，浅水处 例 The beautifully preserved fossil fish lived in a vast *shallow* lake. 保存得完好的化石鱼曾生活在一片广阔的浅水湖中。
casual ['kæʒuəl]	*a.* 非正式的，随便的；漫不经心的(informal, purposeless)；漠不关心的，冷淡的；偶然的，碰巧的；临时的 记 联想记忆：平常(usual)可以穿非正式的(casual)服装 搭 casual clothes 便装；a casual remark 漫不经心的话语 例 Nowadays, more and more young students prefer *casual* clothes to school uniforms. 如今越来越多的青年学生喜欢便装而非校服。 参 causal(*a.* 原因的)
irresistible [ˌɪrɪ'zɪstəbl]	*a.* 无法抗拒的，诱人的；不能自已的 记 联想记忆：ir(不) + resistible(可抵抗的) → 不可抵抗的 → 无法抗拒的 例 I felt an *irresistible* urge to laugh. 我忍不住要笑出来。
sprawl [sprɔːl]	*vi.* 伸开四肢坐(或躺)；扩展，蔓延(expand, overspread) *n.* 扩展，蔓延；蔓延物 记 联想记忆：伸展手脚趴(sprawl)在地上潦草地写(scrawl) 例 The town *sprawled* along the side of the lake. 小镇沿着湖边扩展。

□ mass   □ alkali   □ unearth   □ suffragist   □ amusement   □ pharmacy
□ shallow   □ casual   □ irresistible   □ sprawl

rival [ˈraɪvl]	*vt.* 与…相匹敌，比得上（match）*n.* 竞争对手 *a.* 竞争的，对抗的 记 联想记忆：对手（rival）隔河（river）相望，分外眼红 例 Ships cannot *rival* aircraft for speed. 船在速度上无法同飞机相比。// This latest design has no *rivals*. 这种最新款式独领风骚。
monarch [ˈmɑːnərk]	*n.* 君主，帝王（ruler, emperor） 记 词根记忆：mon（单个）+ arch（统治）→ 个人统治 → 君主 搭 monarch butterfly 黑脉金斑蝶 派 monarchy（*n.* 君主政体；君主国）
faint [feɪnt]	*a.* 模糊的，不清楚的；无力的，虚弱的；眩晕的 *vi.* 昏厥，晕倒 *n.* 昏厥 例 Astronomers use sighting telescopes to study the motions of many of the *faint* stars. 天文学家使用瞄准望远镜来研究很多暗星的运动。 参 feint（*vi.* 佯攻）
criterion [kraɪˈtɪriən]	*n.* [*pl.* criteria]标准，准则（standard） 记 词根记忆：cri（判断）+ ter + ion → 根据一定标准做判断 → 标准，准则 例 What *criteria* are used for assessing a student's ability? 用什么标准来评定一个学生的能力？
epidemic [ˌepɪˈdemɪk]	*n.* 流行（popularity）；流行病 *a.* 流行性的，传染性的 记 词根记忆：epi（在…之间）+ dem（人民）+ ic → 在一群人之间 → 流行 例 The terrible *epidemic* killed most of the people it infected. 可怕的流行病使大部分受感染的人丧生。
joint [dʒɔɪnt]	*n.* 关节，骨节；接头，接合处 *a.* 连接的；共同的，共有的，联合的 记 词根记忆：join（结合，连接）+ t → 关节 例 They can cause severe pains, particularly around the *joints*. 它们能导致严重的疼痛，尤其在关节部位。
convict [kənˈvɪkt]	*vt.* 定罪，宣告…有罪（criminate）*n.* 服刑囚犯 记 词根记忆：con（表加强）+ vict（征服）→ 完全征服 → 定罪 例 The jury *convicted* the man, and he was sentenced to twenty years in prison. 陪审团宣告此人有罪，他被判入狱 20 年。 派 conviction（*n.* 确信） 参 evict（*vt.* 驱逐）；victorious（*a.* 胜利的）
debris [dəˈbriː]	*n.* 岩屑；残骸（ruin, remains）；碎屑（fragment） 记 发音记忆："堆玻璃" → 一堆碎玻璃 → 碎屑 例 Emergency teams are still clearing the *debris* from the plane crash. 各抢救小组仍在清理失事飞机的残骸。

permanent [ˈpɜːrmənənt]	*a.* 持久的，永久的(long-lasting)；固定不变的(stable) 记 词根记忆：per(贯穿) + man(停留) + ent(形容词后缀) → 始终停留着的 → 持久的 搭 permanent residence 固定住处 例 Some of the baskets have been placed on *permanent* display at the Philadelphia museum of art. 在费城艺术博物馆，一些篮子已经成为永久性的展览品。 派 permanency(*n.* 永存；持久性)；permanently(*ad.* 永久地)
annex [ˈæneks]	*vt.* 兼并；附加(append, add) 记 词根记忆：an(近) + nex(捆绑) → 绑在一起 → 兼并；附加 例 Money and reputation are not always *annexed* to happy life. 金钱和名气并非总是与幸福生活相关。
draft [dræft]	*n.* 草图，草稿(sketch)；汇票；气流 *vt.* 起草；征募，选派 *a.* 供役使的 记 发音记忆："抓夫" → 征募，选派 例 I've made a first *draft* of my speech for Friday, but it still needs a lot of work. 我已经写出了星期五演讲的初稿，可是还需要进行大量加工。 派 redraft(*vt.* 改写)；updraft(*n.* 上升气流)
soccer [ˈsɑːkər]	*n.* 足球 搭 a soccer match 足球比赛
prominent [ˈprɑːmɪnənt]	*a.* 卓著的，杰出的(*distinguished, *famous)；突起的，凸出的(protuberant) 记 词根记忆：pro(向前) + min(突出) + ent → 向前突出的 → 突起的；卓著的 例 Mercy Otis was born into a *prominent* family in Barnstable. 默西·奥蒂斯生于巴恩斯特布尔的一个显赫之家。
ore [ɔːr]	*n.* 矿；矿物，矿石(mineral) 记 联想记忆：矿主们总想要开采到更多的(more)矿石(ore) 参 roe(*n.* 鱼卵)
accommodate [əˈkɑːmədeɪt]	*v.* 提供(住宿、座位等)(supply)；容纳；(使)适应，顺应(conform, adjust to) 记 联想记忆：ac + commo(看做 common，普通的) + date(日子) → 人要适应过普通的日子 → (使)适应 例 His house can *accommodate* a meeting of the entire committee. 他的房子可以容纳整个委员会开会。 派 accommodation(*n.* 住宿，膳宿)
display [dɪˈspleɪ]	*vt./n.* 陈列(*exhibit)；展示(demonstrate)；显示(show) 记 联想记忆：dis(分开) + play(播放，表演) → 分别播放 → 陈列；展示 搭 on display 正在展览中 例 Her artwork is *displayed* in a museum. 她的艺术品正在博物馆展出。// Birds also *display* remarkable behavior in collecting building materials. 鸟类在搜集筑巢材料方面也表现出了不同寻常的行为。

12

refine [rɪˈfaɪn]	*vt.* 精炼，精制；使完善(improve)；净化，提纯 记 联想记忆：re(一再) + fine(好的) → 使变好 → 精炼 例 They do their best to *refine* their interviewing techniques. 他们尽全力完善自己的采访技巧。 派 refinement(*n.* 改进；精炼)；refiner(*n.* 精炼者)；refining(*n.* 精炼)
cumbersome [ˈkʌmbərsəm]	*a.* 笨重的(awkward)；麻烦的(troublesome)；累赘的，冗长的 记 联想记忆：cumber(阻碍) + some → 受到阻碍的 → 笨重的 例 The company changed its *cumbersome* title to something easier to remember. 这家公司把它那复杂累赘的名称改得好记一些了。
gentility [dʒenˈtɪləti]	*n.* 有教养，文雅 记 联想记忆：gent(le)(温和的，文雅的) + ility → 有教养，文雅 例 Many people think fine clothes are a mark of *gentility*. 很多人认为精致的服饰是文雅的标志。
stagecoach [ˈsteɪdʒkoʊtʃ]	*n.* 公共马车，驿站马车 记 组合词：stage(驿站) + coach(马车) → 驿站马车，公共马车
despoil [dɪˈspɔɪl]	*vt.* 夺取，掠夺(pillage)；蹂躏 记 联想记忆：de(表加强) + spoil(损坏) → 完全损坏 → 蹂躏 搭 despoil sb. of rights 剥夺某人的权利 例 The foreign soldiers *despoiled* the small town of all its treasures. 外国士兵掠夺了小镇所有的财宝。 派 despoiler(*n.* 掠夺者)
folklore [ˈfoʊklɔːr]	*n.* 民间传说；民俗学 记 组合词：folk(乡民) + lore(学问，学识) → 民间传说 例 Nancy Ward, a Cherokee leader of the 1700s, became a legendary figure in Tennessee *folklore*. 18世纪切罗基人的领袖南希·沃德成为田纳西民间故事中的传奇人物。
glacial [ˈgleɪʃl]	*a.* 冰川期的，冰河时代的；寒冷的，冰冷的；冷若冰霜的 记 词根记忆：glaci(冰) + al → 冰川期的；冰冷的 例 A glacier maintains the same shape throughout the *glacial* process. 冰川在整个冰河期都保持同样的形状。
microscope [ˈmaɪkrəskoʊp]	*n.* 显微镜 记 词根记忆：micro(微小的) + scop(看) + e → 用来看小东西 → 显微镜 例 In the play, love and marriage are put under the *microscope*. 这部话剧对爱情和婚姻进行了细致入微的探讨。 派 microscopic(*a.* 用显微镜可见的；极小的)
beat [biːt]	*v.* 打拍子，指挥；敲打；打败，胜过；(心脏等)跳动 *n.* (心脏等的)跳动(声)；节拍，节奏；有规律的敲击(声) *a.* 疲惫的 例 They want to *beat* the speed record. 他们想打破这一速度记录。// The music had a steady *beat* that people could dance to. 音乐有稳定的节奏，人们可以随之起舞。// We were just *beat* after raking all the leaves. 我们用耙子耙完所有树叶后都累坏了。

disorder [dɪsˈɔːrdər]	*n.* 混乱，凌乱(chaos)；动乱，骚乱；失调，紊乱(maladjustment) 记 联想记忆：dis(不) + order(顺序) → 无序 → 混乱；失调 例 We have nothing to help us distinguish mental health from mental *disorder*. 没有任何东西能帮助我们区分精神健康和精神失常。
spinet [ˈspɪnət]	*n.* 小型立式钢琴 参 spine(*n.* 脊椎，脊柱)
consume [kənˈsuːm]	*vt.* 消耗，损耗(spend, use up)；消费；吃，喝；使充满；烧毁，毁灭 记 词根记忆：con (表加强) + sum (拿，取) + e → 全部拿出来(花掉) → 消费 例 How much of a day's total calories should be *consumed* at breakfast? 早餐应该摄入一天所需总热量的多少？ 派 consumer(*n.* 消费者，用户)
besides [bɪˈsaɪdz]	*prep.* 除…之外 *ad.* 而且，还有 例 I don't really want to go. *Besides*, it's too late now. 我并不真的想去。而且现在太晚了。
affect [əˈfekt]	*vt.* 影响(influence)；感染 记 词根记忆：af(表加强) + fect(做) → 反复做就会有影响 → 影响 例 Let's take a look at Parry's research and how it *affects* what modern scholars think about Homer. 我们来看看帕里的研究，看它如何影响当代学者对荷马的认识。 派 unaffected(*a.* 未受影响的) 参 effect(*n.* 作用；影响)；infect(*vt.* 传染；感染)
libel [ˈlaɪbl]	*vt.* 诽谤(malign) *n.* (文字)诽谤；诽谤性文字 记 词根记忆：lib(文字) + el → 以文字损害名誉 → (文字)诽谤 例 She claimed she had been *libeled* in an article the magazine had published. 她声称她遭到了在那家杂志上发表的一篇文章的诽谤。 派 libellant(*n.* 诽谤者)；libelous(*a.* 含有诽谤性文字的) 参 label(*n.* 标签)
ethnic [ˈeθnɪk]	*a.* 种族的(racial)；民族的(national) 记 词根记忆：ethn(种族；民族) + ic → 种族的；民族的 例 Massive waves of immigration brought new *ethnic* groups into the country. 大规模移民潮给这个国家带来了新的种族群体。 参 ethic(*n.* 道德规范)
fitness [ˈfɪtnəs]	*n.* 健康，健壮；适合(某事物或做某事) 例 You should convince us of your *fitness* for the task. 你应该让我们相信你适合做这项工作。

12

consume

lax [læks]	*a.* 懒散的; 不严格的, 马虎的(slack) 记 本身为词根, 意为"松的" 例 The company's *lax* attitude towards intellectual property violations has angered the professor. 那家公司对侵犯知识产权的马虎态度激怒了那名教授。
evacuation [ɪˌvækjuˈeɪʃn]	*n.* 撤离(withdrawal) 记 词根记忆: e(出) + vacu(空的) + ation → 空出来 → 撤离 例 The radio mentioned possible *evacuation* routes. 广播提到了可能的撤退路线。
quaint [kweɪnt]	*a.* 古色古香的(old-timey); 离奇有趣的 例 The museum displayed *quaint* advertisements from the 1920s. 博物馆展出了20世纪20年代以来古色古香的广告。
pamphlet [ˈpæmflət]	*n.* 小册子(booklet, brochure) 记 来自拉丁文 *pamphilus*, 是一首爱情名诗; pam(=pan 全部) + phil(爱) + us → 表达爱情 例 *Pamphlets* are very useful especially in areas where there is no easy access to newspapers and radio. 在报纸和广播没有普及的地区, 小册子尤其有用。 参 chapbook (*n.* 小本诗歌集或故事书)
predominant [prɪˈdɑːmɪnənt]	*a.* 占优势的, 主导的, 支配的(dominant, principal); 显著的, 盛行的 记 联想记忆: pre(在…前面) + dominant(统治的) → 在前面统治的 → 占优势的, 支配的 例 Dark blue is the *predominant* color in the prince's room. 深蓝色是王子房间里的主要颜色。 派 predominantly(*ad.* 主要地; 多数情况下); predominance(*n.* 优势; 支配地位)
concentrate [ˈkɑːnsntreɪt]	*v.* 集中(注意力), 专心(focus); (使)浓缩 *n.* 浓缩物 记 词根记忆: con(共同) + centr(中心) + ate → 聚集在一个中心 → 集中 搭 concentrate on 集中, 全神贯注于 例 The beat's so strong that I can't *concentrate* on my work. 节奏太强了, 我都无法专心做功课。 // We should *concentrate* resources on the most run-down areas. 我们应该把资源集中用于最枯竭的地区。

音频

词根、词缀预习表

fin	最后	finance n. 财政，金融	spect	看	retrospect n. 回顾，反顾
vis	看	supervise vt. 监督	vacu	空的	evacuate v. 疏散，撤离
sanct	神圣的	sanction vt./n. 同意，许可	lingu	语言	bilingualism n. 双语现象
hanc	高的	enhance vt. 提高；增强	tent	测试	tentative a. 试验性的
pend	悬挂	append vt. 附加	agon	挣扎	agonize vi. 苦苦思索

---

systematic
[ˌsɪstə'mætɪk]

a. 系统的，体系的(methodic)
记 来自 system(*n.* 系统)
例 While Edison's approach to invention was often cut-and-try, it was highly *systematic*. 虽然爱迪生用于发明的方法经常是试验性的，但这个方法却极具系统性。
派 systematize(*vt.* 使系统化，使制度化)

client
['klaɪənt]

n. 委托人，当事人；顾客(customer)
例 Social workers must always consider the best interests of their *clients*. 社会工作者必须时刻考虑其当事人的最佳利益。

把猫干掉

client

dye
[daɪ]

n. 颜料，染料 *v.* 染色
记 联想记忆：劣质染料(dye)会致人死亡(die)
例 I want to *dye* my hair blonde. 我想把头发染成金黄色。

turtle
['tɜːrtl]

n. 龟，海龟
记 发音记忆："特逗" → 龟(turtle)的样子特逗 → 龟

finance
['faɪnæns]

vt. 给…提供资金(*subsidize) *n.* 财政，金融；[常 *pl.*]财务情况
记 词根记忆：fin(最后) + ance → 最后起作用的东西 → 财政，金融
例 The troupe is *financed* by the elders. 剧团由老年人提供资金。
派 financing(*n.* 融资，财务); financial(*a.* 财政的，金融的); financier(*n.* 金融家)

---

supervise [ˈsuːpərvaɪz]	*vt.* 监督(oversee)；指导 記 词根记忆：super(在…上面) + vis(看) + e → 在上面看 → 监督 例 The National Academy of Design for the painters *supervised* the incorporation of new artistic techniques. 为画家而开设的国家设计研究院指导新艺术技巧的融合。 派 supervision(*n.* 监督)；supervisor(*n.* 主管；监督员)
tariff [ˈtærɪf]	*n.* 关税(tax, duty)；(旅馆、饭店等的)价目表，收费表 例 The regulations keep *tariffs* high. 这些规定使关税一直居高不下。
copious [ˈkoʊpiəs]	*a.* 丰富的，富饶的 記 联想记忆：copi(看做 copy, 复制) + ous → 能不断复制的 → 丰富的 例 Scientists support the theory of relativity with *copious* evidence. 科学家们用大量证据支持相对论。
exposure [ɪkˈspoʊʒər]	*n.* 暴露，显露；揭露；曝光；面临，遭受(危险或不快) 記 来自 expose(*vt.* 暴露，显露；揭露；使面临，使遭受) 例 Vaccines for some rare diseases are given only to persons who risk *exposure* to the diseases. 某些罕见疾病的疫苗只供有可能接触这些疾病的人使用。 参 extension(*n.* 延长)；expansion(*n.* 扩充)
substance [ˈsʌbstəns]	*n.* 物质；主旨，实质(matter)；根据；重要性(significance) 記 词根记忆：sub(在…下面) + st(站) + ance → 站在下面的东西 → 实质 例 The Moon isn't much like the Earth in terms of *substance*. 从物质方面来看，月亮不太像地球。// Nothing of any *substance* was achieved in the meeting. 会议没有取得任何实质性成果。
neoclassical [ˌniːoʊˈklæsɪkl]	*a.* 新古典主义的 例 The *neoclassical* sculptors seldom held a mallet or chisel in their own hands. 新古典主义雕塑家很少亲自手持槌棒或凿子。 派 neoclassicism(*n.* 新古典主义)
array [əˈreɪ]	*n.* 一系列(series)；阵列 *vt.* 布置，排列；部署 記 联想记忆：ar + ray(光线) → 像光线一样 → 一系列 例 Glasses of all shapes and sizes were *arrayed* on the shelves. 架子上整齐地排列着大大小小各式各样的玻璃杯。
counselor [ˈkaʊnsələr]	*n.* (尤指针对私人问题的)顾问(advisor)；律师 例 She worked as a marriage guidance *counselor*. 她是一名婚姻指导顾问。
sanction [ˈsæŋkʃn]	*vt.* 同意，许可；惩罚，实施制裁 *n.* 同意，许可；约束；制裁 記 词根记忆：sanct(神圣的) + ion → 神圣之物，原指教会的法令，后引申为"同意，许可" → 同意，许可 搭 sanction against 制裁，处罚 例 Based on previous experience, the government will not *sanction* such a bill. 根据之前的经验，政府不会批准这种法案的。

enhance [ɪnˈhæns]	*vt.* 提高(*increase, improve); 增强(enrich) 记 词根记忆: en(使…) + hanc(高的) + e → 提高; 增强 搭 enhance one's reputation 提高声誉 例 Many poets *enhance* their work by creating a contrast between realism and symbolism in a given poem. 很多诗人通过在一首诗中制造现实主义与象征主义间的反差, 来提升他们的作品。 派 enhancement(*n.* 增加); enhanced(*a.* 增强的; 提高的)
overact [ˌoʊvərˈækt]	*v.* 把(角色)表演得过火; 表现做作 记 组合词: over(过度, 过分) + act(表演) → 把(角色)表演得过火 例 We must *overact* our part in some measure, in order to produce any effect. 为了产生效果, 我们在表演角色时必须夸张一点。
append [əˈpend]	*vt.* 附加, 增补 记 词根记忆: ap(在…之上) + pend(悬挂) → 悬挂在某物之上 → 附加 例 I *append* a list of those organizations from which you can get useful information. 我附上一张机构名单, 从中你可以得到有用的信息。
chilly [ˈtʃɪli]	*a.* 寒冷的; 冷淡的, 不友好的 记 来自 chill(*n.* 寒意) 例 I feel *chilly*; I may be catching a cold. 我感觉有点冷, 可能感冒了。
retrospect [ˈretrəspekt]	*n.* 回顾, 反顾 记 词根记忆: retro(向后) + spect(看) → 向后看 → 回顾, 反顾 搭 in retrospect 回想起来, 事后看来 例 But in *retrospect*, what Jack has said might have a point. 但现在回想起来, 杰克说的话可能有道理。
havoc [ˈhævək]	*n.* 混乱, 大破坏 搭 play havoc with 毁坏, 扰乱 例 This new rule is causing *havoc* in the office. 这条新规定使得办公室混乱一片。
apprehend [ˌæprɪˈhend]	*vt.* 逮捕; 领会, 理解 记 词根记忆: ap + prehend(抓住) → 逮捕 例 I cannot *apprehend* the underlying meaning of this sentence. 我无法理解这句话的深层意思。 派 apprehension(*n.* 焦虑, 担忧; 逮捕)
sacrifice [ˈsækrɪfaɪs]	*v.* 牺牲, 献出; 以…做祭献 *n.* 牺牲, 献身; 献祭, 祭品 记 词根记忆: sacri(神圣的) + fic(做) + e → 为了神圣的事情而去做 → 牺牲 搭 sacrifice for 为…做牺牲 例 The official says, people don't have to *sacrifice* the environment to promote economic growth. 那名官员称, 人们不必为了促进经济增长而牺牲环境。

sacrifice

evacuate [ɪˈvækjueɪt]	*v.* 疏散，撤离；排空
	记 词根记忆：e(出) + vacu(空的) + ate → 往外搬空 → 疏散，撤离
	例 You'd better prepare a family emergency kit, in case you need to *evacuate* the house. 你最好准备一个家庭应急工具箱，以备撤离所需。
bilingualism [ˌbaɪˈlɪŋɡwəlɪzəm]	*n.* 双语现象
	记 词根记忆：bi(双，两) + lingu(语言) + al + ism(抽象名词后缀) → (说)两种语言 → 双语现象
	例 However, in some communities *bilingualism* may be viewed negatively. 然而一些社会可能视双语现象为负面现象。
tentative [ˈtentətɪv]	*a.* 试验性的(experimental)；不确定的，暂定的；犹豫的(hesitant)
	记 词根记忆：tent(测试) + ative → 试验性的；不确定的
	例 The manager attempted a *tentative* reform last month, but it didn't succeed. 经理上个月尝试进行试验性的改革，但是没有成功。
zest [zest]	*n.* 趣味；热情，狂热
	搭 zest for... 对…的热情
	例 All staff took part in the company's annual party with *zest*. 全体员工积极地参加了公司年会。
agonize [ˈæɡənaɪz]	*vi.* 苦苦思索；焦虑不已
	记 词根记忆：agon(挣扎) + ize → 苦苦挣扎 → 苦苦思索
	例 There's no reason to *agonize* over something that has already happened. 对于已经发生的事，没有理由再为它感到焦虑。
etiquette [ˈetɪket]	*n.* 礼节，礼仪
	记 联想记忆：e + tiquette(=ticket 票) → 凭票出入 → 礼节，礼仪
	搭 medical etiquette 医学界的行业规矩
	例 *Etiquette* is considered the most important aspect in business between the two companies. 在这两个公司的贸易往来中，礼仪被视为是最重要的方面。
disinterest [dɪsˈɪntrəst]	*n.* 无兴趣，冷漠；客观，公正
	记 联想记忆：dis(不) + interest(兴趣，关心) → 无兴趣，冷漠
	例 Some children act naughty in order to attract the parents' attention and change their *disinterest*. 一些孩子淘气是为了吸引家长的注意并改变他们对自己的不关心。
stipulate [ˈstɪpjuleɪt]	*v.* 规定，明确要求；(以…为条件)约定
	记 词根记忆：stip(压) + ul + ate(使…) → 使一起按压 → 规定
	例 This company *stipulates* that all of its employees work eight hours a day, five days a week. 公司明文规定员工一天工作八小时，一周工作五天。
oratorio [ˌɔːrəˈtɔːriəʊ]	*n.* 清唱剧，宗教剧
	记 词根记忆：or(说) + at + orio(表音乐类) → 配以说话的音乐 → 清唱剧
	参 oratory(*n.* 讲演术，雄辩术)

adamant [ˈædəmənt]	*a.* 坚定不移的，坚决的(unyielding)；固执的(inflexible) 记 词根记忆：a(不) + dam(征服，驯服) + ant(形容词后缀) → 不被征服的 → 坚定不移的；固执的 例 Mary was *adamant* that she would not come. 玛丽坚决不来。
discredit [dɪsˈkredɪt]	*vt.* 使丧失声誉；使怀疑 *n.* 名誉丧失 记 词根记忆：dis(不) + cred(相信) + it → 不信 → 使怀疑 例 Such behavior will *discredit* you among your boss and colleagues. 这样的行为会让你在老板和同事面前丧失名誉。
morgue [mɔːrg]	*n.* 停尸房，太平间 记 词根记忆：mor(死) + gue → 停放死人的地方 → 停尸房，太平间 例 The police went to the *morgue* and examined the body, but they didn't find anything suspicious. 警察去停尸房检查了死尸，但是没有发现任何可疑之处。
democracy [dɪˈmɑːkrəsi]	*n.* 民主政体，民主制度；民主国家；民主精神 记 词根记忆：demo(人民) + cracy(统治) → 人民统治 → 民主政体 例 We always stick to the principles of *democracy* and serve the public. 我们向来坚持民主的原则并服务于大众。
coral [ˈkɔːrəl]	*n.* 珊瑚(虫) *a.* 珊瑚色的，红色的 记 联想记忆：cor(看做 core，核心) + al → 大海的核心之处有珊瑚 → 珊瑚(虫) 搭 coral reefs 珊瑚礁
pheromone [ˈferəmoʊn]	*n.* 信息素 例 *Pheromones* play numerous roles in the activities of insects. 信息素在昆虫的活动中有着各种各样的作用。
ornament	[ˈɔːrnəmənt] *n.* 装饰(品)(decoration, adornment) [ˈɔːrnəment] *vt.* 装饰，点缀 记 词根记忆：orn(装饰) + ament → 装饰(品) 例 The *ornaments* on the Christmas tree shined and sparkled. 圣诞树上的装饰品闪闪发光。 派 ornamental(*a.* 装饰性的，装饰用的)
deport [dɪˈpɔːrt]	*vt.* 驱逐出境 记 联想记忆：de(离开) + port(港口) → 驱逐出境 例 Even if they didn't put him in jail, they would possibly *deport* him. 即使他们不把他关起来，也很可能把他驱逐出境。
outgas [ˌaʊtˈɡæs]	*vt.* 除去(固体中的)气 记 联想记忆：out(外面) + gas(气体) → 使气体到外面去 → 除去(固体中的)气
chaste [tʃeɪst]	*a.* 贞洁的；简朴的，朴实的 记 联想记忆：贞洁的(chaste)姑娘被追逐(chase) 例 They lived a *chaste* life. 他们过着简朴的生活。

13

tract [trækt]	*n.* 地域(area)；领域(field)；传单，小册子；大片(土地或森林) 例 Despite the intent of the law, speculators often manage to obtain large *tracts*. 尽管法律有意禁止，但投机者还是常常能设法获得大片土地。 派 traction(*n.* 牵引)；tractor(*n.* 拖拉机)
cipher ['saɪfər]	*n.* 密码，暗号(code) 例 The army uses a special *cipher* so that military messages are kept secret. 军队使用一种特殊密码，军事电讯因此得以保密。
soloist ['souloʊɪst]	*n.* 独奏者，独唱者，单独表演者 例 After the concert, all those people were crowding around the back stage to see Jackson and the *soloist*. 音乐会结束后，那些人都拥挤在后台，想一睹杰克逊和独奏者的风采。
purity ['pjʊrəti]	*n.* 纯度；纯洁，纯净，纯粹 记 词根记忆：pur(干净的) + ity(名词后缀) → 纯度；纯洁 例 The *purity* of the water is tested regularly. 水的纯度会定期检测。
notwithstanding [ˌnɑːtwɪθ'stændɪŋ]	*ad./prep.* 虽然，尽管如此(despite) 例 The team played on, *notwithstanding* the rain. 尽管下着雨，比赛仍继续。
seem [siːm]	*v.* 好像，似乎(appear) 例 Do whatever *seems* best to you. 你觉得什么最好，就做什么。// I was going to get something to eat at the cafeteria, but it *seemed* to be closed. 我本来打算在餐厅弄点吃的，但是好像关门了。
protagonist [prə'tægənɪst]	*n.* (戏剧、故事、小说中的)主角，主人公；领导者，倡导者 记 词根记忆：prot(在…前面) + agon(打；行动) + ist → 首先行动者 → 领导者 例 He is a leading *protagonist* of the conservation movement. 他是资源保护运动的急先锋。 参 stooge(*n.* 配角，陪衬)
recruit [rɪ'kruːt]	*v.* 招募(新兵)，征募(enlist) *n.* 新兵；新成员 记 词根记忆：re + cruit(=cres 成长) → 使部队成长壮大 → 招募(新兵) 例 The Argentine ants can quickly *recruit* a huge army from their network of nests. 阿根廷蚂蚁可以从相互联系的巢穴中迅速募集一大批蚁群。 派 recruitment(*n.* 招聘；吸收新成员) 下一个 小不点 征兵处 recruit
supplant [sə'plænt]	*vt.* 取代，代替(*replace) 记 联想记忆：sup(在…下面) + plant(种植) → 在下面种植 → 取代，代替 例 Within a short time the trading company had *supplanted* the individual promoter of colonization. 在很短的时间内，这个贸易公司已经取代了殖民化的个体推动者。

□ tract　　　□ cipher　　　□ soloist　　　□ purity　　　□ notwithstanding □ seem
□ protagonist　□ recruit　　　□ supplant

prolonged [prə'lɔːŋd]	*a.* 长期的，持久的(*extended) 记 来自 prolong(*vt.* 延长) 例 Poverty is increasing as *prolonged* drought is destroying ways to make a living in the country. 长期干旱使得谋生方式遭到破坏，从而加剧了该国的贫困。
bet [bet]	*n.* 打赌；赌注 *v.* 打赌；敢说，确信 搭 I bet that... 我敢肯定；you bet 的确，当然 例 He *bet* $3,000 on the final score of the game. 他下 3000 美元赌比赛的最后比分。// A: Hey, congratulations on winning the essay contest. That thousand-dollar prize money should really come in handy. B: You *bet*! I've already put it aside to cover the increase my landlord just announced for next year. A: 嗨，祝贺你论文比赛获胜。那 1000 元的奖金早晚派得上用场。 B: 你说对了。我的房东刚宣布明年要涨租金，我已经留着它用来支付这部分费用了。 参 bat(*n.* 蝙蝠；球棒)
physical ['fɪzɪkl]	*a.* 物理(学)的；物质的，有形的(substantial)；身体的，肉体的(corporal) *n.* 体检 记 词根记忆：physi(自然) + cal → 物质的 搭 physical attribute 物理特性；身体素质 例 The ordeal has affected both her mental and *physical* health. 痛苦的经历损害了她的身心健康。 派 physically(*ad.* 身体上；根本上)
incursion [ɪn'kɜːrʒn]	*n.* 袭击，突然入侵(raid)；介入 例 The enemy troops have made an *incursion* into the country. 敌军突然入侵该国。 参 incurious(*a.* 不感兴趣的；漫不经心的)
metric ['metrɪk]	*a.* 米制的；公制的 记 词根记忆：metr(测量) + ic(形容词后缀) → 米制的；公制的 搭 metric measurements 公制尺寸 例 The woman could use his *metric* ruler. 这个女子可以使用他的米尺。
transplant	[træns'plænt] *vt.* 移植(器官等)；使迁移，使移居；移栽，移种(植物等) ['trænsplænt] *n.* (器官等的)移植(transfer) 记 词根记忆：trans(转移) + plant(种植) → 移植 例 The farmers gathered the baby oysters and *transplanted* them in waters to speed up their growth. 养殖户把牡蛎幼体集中起来，然后移植到水中以加速其生长。// The scientists might *transplant* specific genes to increase the release of the chemical signals. 科学家们可以通过移植特异基因来增强化学信号的释放。

13

incursion

fresco
['freskoʊ]

n. 湿壁画(mural)；湿壁画技法 *v.* 绘湿壁画于

记 联想记忆：fres(看做 fresh，新鲜的) + co(看做 cool，凉爽的) → 壁画的清新画面让人仿佛感受到了迎面而来的凉爽新鲜的气息 → 湿壁画

例 A 19th century *fresco* was damaged beyond repair. 一幅 19 世纪的湿壁画遭到了破坏，再也无法修复。

mission
['mɪʃn]

n. 代表团，使团(delegation)；任务，使命(task)

记 词根记忆：miss(发送) + ion → 代表团；任务

例 The homing pigeon can be trained to carry out the *missions* that people demand. 通过训练，信鸽可以执行人们所要求的任务。

expansion
[ɪk'spænʃn]

n. 扩张；膨胀

记 来自 expand(*v.* 扩张；膨胀)

例 The graph on the wall shows the *expansion* of international business in the company. 墙上的图表显示了公司国际业务的增长。

参 extent(*n.* 广度；限度)

spray
[spreɪ]

n. 浪花；飞沫；喷雾 *v.* 喷射(sprinkle, splash)；(使)溅散

记 联想记忆：sp(音似：四泼) + ray(光线) → 光线向四面射去 → 喷射

例 An insulating material was *sprayed* on the engine parts. 引擎喷上了绝缘材料。

tectonics
[tek'tɑːnɪks]

n. 构造地质学

记 词根记忆：tect(构造) + on + ics(…学) → 有关地球表面构造的学科 → 构造地质学

搭 the theory of plate tectonics 板块构造学说

例 The theory of plate *tectonics* was developed in the 1960s. 板块构造学说于 20 世纪 60 年代提出。

assign
[ə'saɪn]

vt. 指派(*prescribe)；指定(时间、地点等)；分配(apportion)；布置(作业)

记 联想记忆：as + sign(签名) → 找那个大牌明星签名的任务指派给你了 → 指派

例 That novel she *assigned* us is so boring. 她指定我们读的小说特别无聊。

派 assignment(*n.* 分派的任务；作业)

assign

swell
[swel]

v. (使)增加，扩大；膨胀，肿胀 *n.* 波浪的涌动；隆起(处)；增强，增加

记 联想记忆：s + well(井) → 像井水一样冒出来 → (使)增加；膨胀

例 The group of onlookers soon *swelled* to a crowd. 旁观者很快变成了一大群人。

派 swelling(*n.* 肿胀，肿块)

outlying [ˈaʊtlaɪɪŋ]	*a.* 边远的，偏僻的(remote, distant)；无关的，题外的 记 联想记忆：out(外) + lying(躺着的) → 躺在外面的 → 边远的 搭 outlying areas 边远地区 例 In the nearby town, at least 2,000 people are trapped under the debris and huge rocks have buried roads to *outlying* villages. 在附近的镇子里，至少有 2000 人被困在废墟之下，大石块已经掩埋了通往偏僻村庄的道路。
blink [blɪŋk]	*v.* 眨眼睛；闪亮，闪烁 *n.* 眨眼睛 记 联想记忆：b + link(连接) → 用眨眼睛来联络感情 → 眨眼睛 搭 in the blink of an eye 一瞬间，很快 例 When I told her the news she didn't even *blink*. 我把那个消息告诉她时，她连眼都没眨一下。
dialect [ˈdaɪəlekt]	*n.* 方言，土话(idiom) 记 词根记忆：dia(在…之间) + lect(讲) → 一群人中所讲的语言 → 方言 例 The novel was written in Wu *dialect*. 那部小说是用吴语写的。
shortly [ˈʃɔːrtli]	*ad.* 不久(soon)；简要地(briefly)；不耐烦地 例 He caught a cold *shortly* after the tournament. 锦标赛之后不久他就感冒了。
applaud [əˈplɔːd]	*v.* 鼓掌，喝彩(cheer)；称赞(acclaim) 记 词根记忆：ap(表加强) + plaud(击，打) → 双手用力击打 → 鼓掌，喝彩 例 The audience stood up and *applauded*. 观众们起立鼓掌。
larva [ˈlɑːrvə]	*n.* [*pl.* larvae] 幼虫，幼体 记 发音记忆："lover" → 幼虫是两条虫子爱情的结晶 → 幼虫 例 These eggs develop into *larvae*, which can swim freely. 这些卵发育成可以自由游动的幼虫。
monastery [ˈmɑːnəsteri]	*n.* 男修道院，寺院 记 词根记忆：mon(孤独的) + as + tery(处所) → 孤独者所在之处 → 寺院 例 The *monastery* is open to the general public. 那所寺院向公众开放。
bluff [blʌf]	*n.* 悬崖，峭壁；虚张声势，唬人 *v.* 虚张声势，吓唬 *a.* 直率的，坦率的 记 联想记忆：虚张声势(bluff)的北美野牛(buffalo) 搭 bluff sb. into doing sth. 哄某人做某事 例 It was just a game of *bluff*. 那只不过是唬人的把戏。
facet [ˈfæsɪt]	*n.* (宝石的)小平面；(问题等的)方面 记 词根记忆：fac(脸，面) + et → 方面 例 Now we should look at another *facet* of the problem. 现在我们应该看看问题的另一面。
primal [ˈpraɪml]	*a.* 最初的(original)；主要的，首要的(chief) 记 词根记忆：prim(第一) + al → 最初的；主要的 例 The Sun is far less radiant today than the *primal* Sun. 现在的太阳远远没有最初的太阳那么亮。

applaud

13

□ outlying   □ blink   □ dialect   □ shortly   □ applaud   □ larva
□ monastery   □ bluff   □ facet   □ primal

accomplishment [əˈkɑːmplɪʃmənt]	*n.* 成就；完成；才艺，技艺 例 It was one of the President's greatest *accomplishments*. 那是总统最伟大的成就之一。// A: Let me tell you, I'm really happy I got that scholarship, but I wish my parents would stop bragging to everybody. B: What, that's quite an *accomplishment*. If you ask me, I think you deserve a little bit recognition. A: 我告诉你吧，得到奖学金真让我开心，但是我希望父母别再向每个人炫耀这件事了。 B: 这的确了不起。如果你问我的话，我觉得你应该得到一些赞誉。
longevity [lɔːnˈdʒevəti]	*n.* 长寿 (long life)；寿命 记 词根记忆：long(长的) + ev(时间) + ity → 活得时间长 → 长寿 搭 longevity of …的寿命 例 A balanced diet, enough sleep as well as a positive attitude towards everything contribute to *longevity*. 均衡的饮食、充足的睡眠以及对万事持积极的态度有助于长寿。 派 longevous(*a.* 长寿的) longevity
revolt [rɪˈvoʊlt]	*v.* 反叛，反抗 (rebel)；违抗；(使)厌恶，(使)反感 *n.* 起义，叛乱，反抗 (uprise) 记 词根记忆：re(反) + volt(转) → 反转 → 反叛，反抗 例 The Imagists *revolted* against earlier poets' emphasis on the classics. 意象派诗人抵制早期诗人过于注重古典文学的做法。// It caused a prison *revolt*. 这导致了监狱暴乱。
subsistence [səbˈsɪstəns]	*n.* 生存，生计 记 联想记忆：subsist(生存) + ence → 生存，生计 搭 below the subsistence level 在基本生活水平线以下 例 *Subsistence* is impossible in such extreme conditions. 在这种极端的条件下生存是不可能的。
ceremonial [ˌserɪˈmoʊniəl]	*a.* 礼仪的，礼节的 (formal) *n.* 礼仪，礼节 (ritual, ceremony) 例 The visit was conducted with *ceremonial* pride. 这次访问极为隆重。
seasoning [ˈsiːzənɪŋ]	*n.* 调味品，调料 (flavoring, spice) 例 The fruit of this kind of plant can be used for *seasoning*, such as in chili powders. 这种植物的果实可以用做调料，比如加入辣椒粉中。 seasoning
abreast [əˈbrest]	*ad.* 并列地，并排地 (side by side) 记 联想记忆：a + breast (胸) → 胸和胸并排 → 并列地，并排地 例 Edison kept *abreast* of recent scientific developments. 爱迪生了解科学的最新发展。

pioneer [ˌpaɪəˈnɪr]	*vt.* 开拓，开创(exploit) *n.* 开拓者，创始人(settler, trailblazer) 例 Local music store owners *pioneered* their own recording industry. 当地音乐商店的店主们开创了他们自己的录制行业。
division [dɪˈvɪʒn]	*n.* 除，除法；分开，分隔；分配；(分出来的)部分；分歧，分裂；部门 记 来自 divide(*v.* 划分；除以)；di(分离) + vid(看) + e → 分别看 → 划分 例 All meteorites are assigned to three broad *divisions* on the basis of two kinds of material. 所有的陨星都根据两种材料划分为三大类。
horn [hɔːrn]	*n.* (牛、羊、鹿等的)角；号角，喇叭(speaker, trumpet) 记 联想记忆：牛、羊、鹿等天生(born)就有角(horn) 搭 on the horns of a dilemma 进退两难
fix [fɪks]	*v.* 修理；使固定，安装；安排；找到，确定 *n.* 解决方法；困境，窘境 搭 fix the problem 解决问题；fix up 修理；装饰 例 The prices are *fixed* until the end of the year. 价格一直到年底都固定不变。// They've *fixed* on Greece for their honeymoon. 他们已决定到希腊度蜜月。
ecological [ˌiːkəˈlɑːdʒɪkl]	*a.* 生态(学)的 搭 ecological balance 生态平衡；ecological disaster 生态灾难 例 By enhancing this natural response in plants, researchers might reduce, some day even eliminate, the need for chemical pesticide, which can cause *ecological* damage. 通过增强植物的这一自然反应，研究人员可以减少，甚至在某一天消除对破坏生态的化学杀虫剂的需要。
label [ˈleɪbl]	*vt.* 标记(mark) *n.* 标签(tag)；称号 记 联想记忆：lab(实验室) + el → 实验室里的试剂瓶上贴有标签 → 标签 例 Other chimpanzees have learned to use numerals to *label* quantities of items and do simple sums. 其他黑猩猩已经学会了使用数字来标记物品的数量，并做简单的加法运算。
displace [dɪsˈpleɪs]	*vt.* 取代(replace)；撤职；迫使…离开家园 记 联想记忆：dis(分离) + place(位置) → 使从原位置上离开 → 取代 例 Many feared that radio would *displace* the newspaper industry altogether. 很多人担心广播会完全取代报纸业。 派 displacement(*n.* 取代，停职；置换)
appropriate	[əˈproʊprieɪt] *vt.* 拨款；占用，挪用(engross) [əˈproʊpriət] *a.* 适当的(suitable, becoming) 记 词根记忆：ap(向) + propr(自身的，固有的) + iate → 变为自己的 → 占用，挪用 例 The United States Congress *appropriates* some four million dollars a year for the upkeep of the White House. 美国国会每年为白宫的维修拨款大约 400 万美元。 派 appropriately(*ad.* 适当地)；inappropriate(*a.* 不适合的)

13

scientific [ˌsaɪən'tɪfɪk]	*a.* 科学(上)的；细致严谨的 记 来自 science(*n.* 科学) 搭 scientific study 科学研究 例 This morning I want to tell you about a recent *scientific* discovery dealing with the relation between plants and animals. 今天上午我想告诉你们一项有关动植物关系新近科学发现。
wear [wer]	*v.* 穿，戴；留（须、发等）；面露，面带；磨损，用旧 *n.* 穿戴，衣着；服装，穿戴物；磨损，损坏 例 I'm thinking about *wearing* a suit to the party tonight. 我打算穿西装参加今晚的派对。// His shoes were beginning to show signs of *wear*. 他那双鞋看样子快穿坏了。 参 fear(*n./v.* 恐惧)

Trouble is only opportunity in work clothes.
困难只是穿上工作服的机遇。

——美国实业家 凯泽（H. J. Kaiser, American businessman）

Word List 14

词根、词缀预习表

myria	许多的	myriad *n.* 无数；大量	**plor**	流泪	implore *v.* 哀求
portion	部分	apportionment *n.* 分派	**vulg**	人们，大众	vulgar *a.* 通俗的
trud	伸出	protrude *v.* (使)突出	**crim**	罪行	crime *n.* 犯罪；罪行
trans-	穿过	transient *a.* 短暂的	**tain**	拿住	pertain *vi.* 存在；适用
man	手	emancipate *vt.* 解放	**calcul**	计算	calculate *v.* 计算；推测

---

myriad [ˈmɪriəd]	*n.* 无数(innumerability)；大量(multitude) *a.* 无数的(numerous)；大量的 (*many) 记 词根记忆：myria(许多的) + d → 无数；大量 例 A snowfall consists of *myriads* of minute ice crystals. 雪是由无数细小 的冰晶体构成的。// In all its *myriad* forms, glass represents a major achievement in the history of technological developments. 玻璃有着多种 形态，是技术发展史上的一项重大成就。
apportionment [əˈpɔːrʃnmənt]	*n.* 分派，分摊，分配 记 词根记忆：ap + portion(部分) + ment → 分成部分 → 分派，分摊 例 The *apportionment* of seats in the House of Representatives is based on the population of each state. 众议院的席位是根据各州的人口分配的。
increment [ˈɪŋkrəmənt]	*n.* 增加；增量；定期的加薪 记 词根记忆：in(在…里面) + cre(生长) + ment → 在里面增长 → 增加； 增量 例 It is estimated that the annual *increment* will be achieved by 20% in the following years. 预计今后每年将以20%的年增长率逐年增加。
stiffen [ˈstɪfn]	*v.* (使)变僵硬；(使)变坚定，变强硬 记 联想记忆：stiff(硬的，僵硬的) + en → (使)变僵硬 例 The threat of punishment has only *stiffened* their resolve. 惩罚的威胁愈 发坚定了他们的决心。
protrude [proʊˈtruːd]	*v.* (使)突出，伸出 记 词根记忆：pro(向前) + trud(伸出) + e → 向前伸出 → (使)突出，伸出 例 He hung his coat on a nail *protruding* from the wall. 他把上衣挂在突出 墙面的一根钉子上。 派 protrusive(*a.* 突出的，伸出的)

□ myriad   □ apportionment □ increment   □ stiffen   □ protrude   153

audition [ɔːˈdɪʃn]	*n.* 旁听；试演(rehearsal) 例 You won't need a text for the *audition*. 旁听不需要课本。
sexism [ˈseksɪzəm]	*n.* 性别歧视 例 Her works focus on the subjects of *sexism* and racism. 她的作品关注性别歧视和种族歧视这样的话题。
attentive [əˈtentɪv]	*a.* 注意的，专心的；关心的 记 词根记忆：at(一再) + tent(伸展) + ive → 一再伸长脖子听 → 注意的，专心的 例 This is the last French class this year, so I want to be *attentive* to what the teacher says. 这是今年最后一堂法语课，所以我要专心听讲。
graze [greɪz]	*v.* (牛、羊等)吃草；放牧；擦伤(皮肤等) *n.* 擦伤(处) 记 联想记忆：牧童注视着(gaze)牛羊吃草(graze) 例 There is a vast land suitable for livestock to wander and *graze* on. 那有一片广阔的土地，适合放牧牲畜。
transient [ˈtrænziənt]	*a.* 短暂的，转瞬即逝的；临时的 记 词根记忆：trans(穿过) + ient → 时光穿梭 → 短暂的 例 Motels mainly cater to tourists and other *transient* guests. 汽车旅馆主要接待旅游者和其他临时的客人。
anguish [ˈæŋgwɪʃ]	*n.* 极度痛苦(torment) *v.* (使)极度痛苦(torment) 记 词根记忆：angu(痛苦) + ish → 极度痛苦 例 The injured soldier cried in *anguish* until the doctor gave him an anesthetic. 这名受伤的士兵痛苦地哭泣，直到医生给他打了麻醉剂为止。
emancipate [ɪˈmænsɪpeɪt]	*vt.* 解放，解除 记 词根记忆：e(外) + man(手) + cip(抓) + ate → 抓着他人的手往外 → 解放 例 This new machine will *emancipate* workers from doing all the work by hand they used to do. 这种新机器将会把工人们从过去的手工劳动中解放出来。
squander [ˈskwɑːndər]	*vt.* 浪费，挥霍(时间、金钱等) 记 联想记忆：squand(看做 squad，军队) + er → 军队杜绝浪费 → 浪费 例 Don't *squander* your time and money in reading those science fictions. 不要把你的时间和金钱浪费在看那些科幻小说上。
implore [ɪmˈplɔːr]	*v.* 哀求，恳求(supplicate) 记 词根记忆：im(表加强) + plor(流泪) + e → 伤心地流泪 → 哀求 例 We *implore* the international community to interfere in this incident. 我们呼吁国际社会干预这一事件。

sage [seɪdʒ]	*a.* 贤明的；审慎的 *n.* 智者，圣人 记 联想记忆：s + age(年龄) → 智慧需要一年年的积累 → 智者，圣人 例 I am extremely grateful for your *sage* advice. 我非常感谢你贤明的忠告。
ambiguous [æmˈbɪɡjuəs]	*a.* 不明确的，模棱两可的 记 词根记忆：amb(周围) + ig(走，驱动) + uous → 在(中心意思)周围走动的 → 模棱两可的 例 When you write your essay, please use precise language and avoid *ambiguous* words. 当你写论文时，注意语言要准确，避免使用有歧义的词汇。
quell [kwel]	*vt.* 制止，镇压；缓解，减轻(smother) 例 It doesn't *quell* my remorse; I shouldn't have told her about that. 这并不能消除我的悔恨之心，我不该告诉她那件事的。
vocalize [ˈvoʊkəlaɪz]	*v.* 用言语表达(articulate, express)；说(话)，唱(歌)，发声 记 词根记忆：voc(叫，喊) + al + ize(动词后缀) → 用言语表达 例 Showing kids pictures can help them to *vocalize* their ideas. 让儿童看图画有助于他们用言语表达思想。
corollary [ˈkɔːrəleri]	*n.* 必然的结果；推断 例 Good health is a *corollary* of having healthy diet and regular exercises. 良好的身体状况是健康的饮食和定期做运动的必然结果。
vulgar [ˈvʌlɡər]	*a.* 下流的，粗俗的；普通的，通俗的 记 词根记忆：vulg(人们，大众) + ar → 通俗的 例 The speaker attracted audiences by telling *vulgar* jokes. 为了吸引听众，那位演讲者讲起了粗俗的笑话。 派 vulgarity(*n.* 粗俗，下流)；vulgarian(*n.* 粗俗的人)
swirl [swɜːrl]	*n.* 漩涡；螺旋形(物体) *v.* (使)打旋，旋转 例 The movie shows that the hurricane begins to *swirl* in a clockwise motion. 电影中飓风开始顺时针打旋。
crime [kraɪm]	*n.* 犯罪；罪行 记 词根记忆：crim(罪行) + e → 犯罪；罪行 例 The study compares the *crime* rate in 20 districts established after 2000 with that in recent two years. 这项研究将 2000 年以后建立的 20 个地区与近两年建立的地区的犯罪率进行了比较。
warp [wɔːrp]	*v.* (使)扭曲，弯曲，变形；使不合情理 *n.* (织物的)经线 记 联想记忆：战争(war)扭曲(warp)了人们的心灵 例 The window frames had begun to *warp*. 窗框已经开始变形。// The *warp* is always made of willow. 经线一般是用柳木做的。
swear [swer]	*v.* 诅咒(curse)；宣誓，发誓(vow) 搭 swear sb. in/into 使某人宣誓就职 例 He *swore* revenge on the man who had killed his wife. 他发誓要对那个杀死他妻子的人进行报复。// Remember, you have *swore* to tell the truth. 别忘了，你宣誓过要讲实话的。

14

typical [ˈtɪpɪkl]	*a.* 典型的，有代表性的（representative） 记 来自 type（*n.* 典型） 例 Hard work was so *typical* of immigrants and pioneers who settled the American Midwest. 勤劳是在美国中西部定居的移民和拓荒者的典型特征。// A: What's keeping Kevin? He said last night he'd meet us here by 2 o'clock and it's already 2:30. B: It's so *typical* of him, isn't it? Just watch, he's going to show up in 5 minutes with some wild excuses. A: 凯文怎么还不到？他昨晚说两点在这里和我们见面，现在已经两点半了。 B: 他就是这个样子，不是吗？你看着吧，五分钟后他露面时准会给出一些荒唐的借口。 派 typically（*ad.* 典型地，有代表性地）
confirm [kənˈfɜːrm]	*vt.* 证实（validate, verify）；使巩固（strengthen）；批准（approve） 记 词根记忆：con（表加强）+ firm（坚固的）→ 使巩固 例 They *confirmed* earlier theories about the Moon's surface. 他们证实了早期关于月球表面的理论。// Has tomorrow's meeting been *confirmed*? 明天的会议得到批准了吗？ 派 confirmation（*n.* 确认；证明） 参 conform [*v.* （使）符合，一致]
descent [dɪˈsent]	*n.* 血统，世系（ancestry）；下降（drop） 记 来自 descend（*v.* 遗传；下降） 例 We watched the airplane's graceful *descent*. 我们看到飞机优雅地降落了。 参 decent（*a.* 正派的） descent
gallop [ˈɡæləp]	*v.* 飞奔，疾驰（spur） 记 联想记忆：汽车加了一加仑（gallon）油，于是疾驰（gallop）而去 例 She came *galloping* down the street. 她沿街飞奔而来。
erosion [ɪˈroʊʒn]	*n.* 腐蚀，侵蚀（corrosion）；削弱，减少 记 来自 erode（*v.* 腐蚀，侵蚀） 搭 swale erosion 洼地侵蚀；soil erosion 土壤侵蚀 例 Your professor has asked me to talk to you today about the topic that should be of real concern to civil engineers: the *erosion* of the US beaches. 你们的教授让我今天和你们谈谈土木工程师真正应该关心的问题：美国海岸的侵蚀。
scuba [ˈskuːbə]	*n.* 水中呼吸器，水肺 记 联想记忆：s + cuba（音似：哭吧）→ 潜水时丢了水中呼吸器只有哭的份 → 水中呼吸器 例 *Scuba*-diving has become one of the greatest recreational sports all around the world. 佩戴水肺潜水已成为全球最流行的娱乐运动之一。

pertain [pər'teɪn]	*vi.* 存在；适用 记 词根记忆：per(始终) + tain(拿住) → 始终拿着 → 存在；适用 搭 pertain to 与…相关，关于 例 Almanacs provided the perfect steady seller because their information *pertains* to the locale in which they would be used. 年鉴的销量非常稳定，因为其信息与所使用的地区相关。
bandanna [bæn'dænə]	*n.* 色彩鲜艳的围巾(或头巾) 例 She uses her *bandanna* to keep the hair out of her eyes. 她扎上头巾，以免头发挡住眼睛。
technological [ˌteknə'lɑːdʒɪkl]	*a.* 技术的，工艺的(technical) 记 来自 technology(*n.* 技术) 搭 scientific and technological advances 科技进步 例 The country has made a major *technological* breakthrough in cancer research. 这个国家在癌症研究方面取得了一项重大技术突破。
chant [tʃænt]	*n.* 圣歌；单调的吟唱；反复呼喊的话语 *v.* 唱圣歌；反复呼喊 记 联想记忆：形似拼音"chang"(唱) → 咏唱 → 圣歌 例 We've been studying Zulu *chants* of South Africa. 我们一直在研究南非祖鲁人的圣歌。
firm [fɜːrm]	*n.* 公司(corporation) *a.* 结实的(*hard, fixed)；坚定的，坚决的(steadfast) 例 Children with parents whose guidance is *firm*, consistent, and rational are inclined to possess high levels of self-confidence. 从父母那能得到坚定、明确和理性的指导的孩子往往有着极强的自信心。 派 firmly(*ad.* 稳固地)
overview ['oʊvərvjuː]	*n.* 梗概，概述 例 Let me give you just an *overview* of Plato's ethical theory. 我来给你们概述一下柏拉图的道德理论。 参 viewpoint(*n.* 观点)
calculate ['kælkjuleɪt]	*v.* 计算，核算(count, figure)；估计，推测(speculate)；计划，打算(*determine) 记 词根记忆：calcul(计算) + ate(动词后缀) → 计算；推测 例 They *calculated* the length of triangle sides. 他们计算了三角形各边的长度。 派 calculation(*n.* 计算)；calculator(*n.* 计算器)；miscalculate(*v.* 误算)
experimental [ɪkˌsperɪ'mentl]	*a.* 实验(性)的，用于实验的 记 来自 experiment(*n.* 实验) 搭 experimental station 实验站 例 The *experimental* course which I registered for yesterday is Child Psychology. 我昨天注册的实验课是儿童心理学。

14

□ pertain   □ bandanna   □ technological   □ chant   □ firm   □ overview
□ calculate   □ experimental

shift [ʃɪft]	*v.* 转移(transfer); 改变(change) *n.* 转移(transfer); 改变(change); 轮班 记 联想记忆: 电脑键盘上的切换键即 Shift 键 搭 shift one's ground 改变立场 例 Builders of tunnels was beginning to *shift* from Europe to the United States. 隧道建造者开始从欧洲转向美国。
gland [glænd]	*n.* 腺 记 联想记忆: g + land(地带, 地区) → 体内的特殊地带 → 腺 例 Examples of exocrine *glands* are the tear *glands* and the sweat *glands*. 外分泌腺有泪腺和汗腺。 派 glandular(*a.* 腺的)
landmark [ˈlændmɑːrk]	*n.* 路标, 地标;〈喻〉里程碑 记 组合词: land(土地) + mark(标志) → 地上的标志 → 路标 搭 a landmark decision 具有里程碑意义的决定 例 You should really keep the map with you for the first couple of weeks, at least until you become familiar with the buildings and *landmarks*. 最初几周你确实应该带着这张地图, 至少等到你熟悉了建筑物和地标。
season [ˈsiːzn]	*n.* 季节; 时节; 时期(period) 例 The hotels are always full during the peak *season*. 在旺季, 这些旅馆总是客满。 派 seasonal(*a.* 季节的; 季节性的)
arboreal [ɑːrˈbɔːriəl]	*a.* 树栖的(tree-dwelling); 树木的(treelike) 记 词根记忆: arbor(树) + eal → 树木的 例 Plant-ants, like most other *arboreal* ants, protect their host plants from defoliators. 与其他大多数树栖蚂蚁一样, 生活于植物上的蚂蚁也保护着它们的寄主植物免受食叶害虫的侵袭。
topography [təˈpɑːɡrəfi]	*n.* 地形学; 地形, 地貌 记 词根记忆: top(地方) + o + graph(写; 图) + y → 地形学 例 The parks should be adapted to the local *topography*. 公园应该顺应当地的地貌特征。
proposal [prəˈpoʊzl]	*n.* 提议, 建议(suggestion); 求婚 记 来自 propose(*v.* 提议, 建议; 求婚) 搭 proposal for sth./doing sth. …的提议; a proposal to do sth. …的提议 例 Scientists have put forward a *proposal* to reduce the emission of greenhouse gases since the 1980s. 自 20 世纪 80 年代起, 科学家们就提出了一项减少温室气体排放的建议。// Bill Smith has volunteered to write a summary of the *proposals* we've agreed on. 比尔·史密斯主动提出就我们达成一致的提议写一份总结。 proposal

□ shift   □ gland   □ landmark   □ season   □ arboreal   □ topography
□ proposal

genial [ˈdʒiːniəl]	*a.* 亲切的，和蔼的(amiable, kindly)；(指气候)温和的，温暖的 记 联想记忆：做个和蔼的(genial)天才(genius)；注意不要和 genital(*a.* 生殖的)混淆 例 His *genial* character and good-natured way of explaining things made him a favourite in the school. 和蔼的性格以及解释事物时娓娓道来的方式使得他成为学校最受欢迎的老师之一。 参 congenial(*a.* 性格相似的；适宜的)
represent [ˌreprɪˈzent]	*vt.* 代表；表现(manifest)；描绘(portray)；象征 记 联想记忆：re + present(出席) → 代表出席 → 代表 例 The picture below *represents* the addition of the red, green, and blue light. 下面的图画代表增加了红色、绿色和蓝色光。 派 representation(*n.* 表现；代表)；representational(*a.* 具象派的；代表性的)；representative(*n.* 代表 *a.* 有代表性的)
apparent [əˈpærənt]	*a.* 显然的，明显的(*obvious, *evident, *detectable)；表面上的，貌似(真实)的 记 联想记忆：ap + parent(父母) → 父母对儿女的爱是显而易见的 → 显然的 例 They noticed an *apparent* change in the position of the North Star. 他们注意到了北极星位置的明显变化。 派 apparently(*ad.* 显然地)
effective [ɪˈfektɪv]	*a.* 有效的，生效的；显著的；实际的，事实上的 记 来自 effect(*n.* 影响，效果) 搭 effective measures 有效措施；an effective remedy 有效药物 例 He has now taken *effective* control of the country. 他目前已经有效地控制了这个国家。// A: I am going to tell that neighbor of mine to turn down that music once and for all. B: I see why you are angry. But I've always found that the polite route is the most *effective*. A: 我要告诉我的邻居，把那个音乐声彻底关小。 B: 我明白你为什么发火了。但是我一直认为礼貌的处理办法最有效。 派 ineffective(*a.* 无效的)；effectively(*ad.* 有效地；实际上)；effectiveness(*n.* 效力)
summarize [ˈsʌməraɪz]	*v.* 概括，总结(generalize) 记 来自 summary(*n.* 摘要，概要) 例 The authors, as a rule, *summarize* their views at the beginning of each passage. 一般来说，作者们会在每个段落的开头概述他们的观点。
aquatic [əˈkwætɪk]	*a.* 水生的；水上的(marine) 记 词根记忆：aqua(水) + tic → 水生的；水上的 例 Most *aquatic* animals breathe by means of gills. 大多数水生动物都用鳃呼吸。

14

verify [ˈverɪfaɪ]	*v.* 检验，核实（check） 记 词根记忆：ver(真实的) + ify(使…) → 使…真实 → 核实 例 While a person could describe his thoughts, no one else can see or hear them to *verify* the accuracy of his report. 一个人可以描述他的想法，但是其他人都不能看到或听到这些想法，从而无法验证这一描述的精确性。
notch [nɑːtʃ]	*n.* 等级，档次；(边缘或表面的)圆形切口 *vt.* 在…上刻下切口；获得 例 The quality of the food in this restaurant has dropped a *notch* recently. 这家饭店的饭菜质量最近下降了一个档次。

notch

vulnerable [ˈvʌlnərəbl]	*a.* 易受攻击的，易受伤的(*unprotected) 记 词根记忆：vuln(伤害) + er + able → 易受伤的 例 Amphibians are especially *vulnerable* to pesticides dissolved in the water. 两栖类动物尤其容易受到溶解在水中的杀虫剂的伤害。
intentionally [ɪnˈtenʃənli]	*ad.* 有意地，故意地 例 She would never *intentionally* hurt anyone. 她从来不会故意伤害任何人。
admiration [ˌædməˈreɪʃn]	*n.* 钦佩，赞赏，羡慕 例 I have great *admiration* for the writer. 我十分钦佩这位作家。
eviscerate [ɪˈvɪsəreɪt]	*vt.* 取出内脏；除去主要部分(disembowel) 记 联想记忆：e(出) + viscera(内脏) + te → 取出内脏 例 The censors *eviscerated* the book to make it inoffensive to the leaders of the party. 审查员删减了书的精华部分，使其不冒犯政党领导人。
plunge [plʌndʒ]	*v.* 掉入(*drop, fall)；暴跌，突降 *n.* 跳水；猛跌，骤降；卷入 记 发音记忆："扑浪急" → 掉入海里，着急地扑打着浪花 → 掉入 例 With the continued rise in sea level, more ice would *plunge* into the ocean. 随着海平面的继续上升，更多的冰会掉入海里。

plunge

roost [ruːst]	*vi.* 栖息(alight, perch) *n.* (鸟类的)栖息处，鸟巢 记 联想记忆：鸟巢(roost)是鸟落脚(root)的地方 搭 rule the roost 当家 例 Curses come home to *roost*. 诅咒他人，应验自身。 派 rooster(*n.* 公鸡)
wane [weɪn]	*vi.* 衰退，减弱(decline)；减少；(指月亮)亏，缺 *n.* 月亏；衰落 记 联想记忆：天鹅(swan)的数量在减少(wane) 搭 on the wane 衰弱，减弱 例 Not only had household production *waned*, but technological improvements were rapidly changing the rest of domestic work. 不仅家庭作坊的数量减少了，而且技术进步也在迅速改变其他的家庭工作。

160
□ verify　　　□ notch　　　□ vulnerable　　□ intentionally　□ admiration　□ eviscerate
□ plunge　　　□ roost　　　□ wane

nutrient [ˈnuːtriənt]	*n.* 滋养物，营养品(nourishment) *a.* 滋养的，有营养的 记 词根记忆：nutri(营养) + ent → 滋养物，营养品 例 The soil loses its *nutrients*, so it needs to be fertilized. 土壤失去了养分，需要施肥。
motor [ˈmoʊtər]	*a.* 机动的；肌肉运动的 *n.* 发动机，电动机(engine) 例 Both *motor* and sensory functions are affected. 运动功能和感觉功能都受到了影响。
ribbon [ˈrɪbən]	*n.* 带状物；丝带，缎带；绶带；(打印机等的)色带 记 联想记忆：rib(肋骨) + bon(看做 bone，骨头) → 像肋骨一样狭长 → 带状物 搭 ribbon development 带状开发区；ribbon lake 带状湖 例 I went through a whole box of paper and a printer *ribbon* just trying to get my résumé right. 为了让简历好看一些，我用了整整一箱纸和一条打印色带。 派 ribbonlike(*a.* 带状的)
insist [ɪnˈsɪst]	*v.* 坚持要求(demand)；坚决主张 记 词根记忆：in(在…里面) + sist(站立) → 一直站在里面 → 坚持要求；坚决主张 搭 insist on/upon 坚持 例 She *insisted* on her innocence. 她坚持说自己是无辜的。// Jane *insists* she's coming to my graduation. 简坚持要来参加我的毕业典礼。 派 insistence(*n.* 坚持，坚决要求) 参 consist(*vi.* 由…组成)；persist(*vi.* 坚持)
basic [ˈbeɪsɪk]	*a.* 基本的，基础的(fundamental)；初步的，初级的 搭 basic rights 基本权利 例 Drums are *basic* to African music. 鼓是非洲音乐的基本乐器。
glossy [ˈɡlɑːsi]	*a.* 光滑的(slick)；光彩夺目的；浮华的 记 来自 gloss(*n.* 光泽，光亮) 例 The *glossy* magazine has lots of pictures of fashionable clothes. 那本用亮光纸印刷的杂志上登有许多时装照片。
separate 	[ˈsepəreɪt] *v.* 分离(*split, *unravel)；划分；区别(*sort out)；分居 [ˈseprət] *a.* 分离的；个别的(*discrete, *distinct) 记 词根记忆：se(分开) + par(相等) + ate → (使)分成相等的部分 → 分离；划分 例 Horse-powered threshing machines to *separate* the seeds from the plants were already in general use. 把种子与植株分离的马力脱粒机已经得到了广泛的应用。 派 separable(*a.* 可分离的)
reception [rɪˈsepʃn]	*n.* 招待会；反响；接纳，接待；(无线电、电视等的)接收(效果) 搭 reception desk (旅馆、饭店等的)接待处，服务台 例 We arranged to meet in *reception* at 6. 我们约定六点钟在接待处会面。// His latest novel has met with a mixed *reception* from public. 他的最新小说在公众之间反响不一。

14

hygiene [ˈhaɪdʒiːn]	*n.* 卫生(sanitation); 卫生学 记 在希腊神话中有一个女神叫 Hygeia，被人奉为健康女神，她的名字所基于的希腊词根 hygi 含有"健康的"之意。现在 hygiene 这个词作为医学术语，表示"卫生，卫生学，保健(法)" 搭 personal hygiene 个人卫生 例 In the interests of *hygiene*, please wash your hands. 为了卫生，请洗手。
metabolic [ˌmetəˈbɑːlɪk]	*a.* 新陈代谢的 记 词根记忆：meta(越过) + bol(扔) + ic → 往别的地方扔 → 改变身体内的机制 → 新陈代谢的 例 Sea cucumbers have the capacity to become quiescent and live at a low *metabolic* rate. 海参能够保持静止状态，并以很低的新陈代谢率生存。 派 metabolism(*n.* 新陈代谢)
cashier [kæˈʃɪr]	*n.* 收银员，出纳员 例 A petrol station *cashier* was threatened by the armed robbers at midnight. 加油站的一名收银员在午夜时分受到了持械抢劫犯的威胁。
definitive [dɪˈfɪnətɪv]	*a.* 确定的，最后的，决定性的；最完整可靠的 *n.* 限定词 例 The *definitive* version of the text will be published. 文本的最终版本将被发布。 派 definitively(*ad.* 决定性地，最后地)
furnish [ˈfɜːrnɪʃ]	*vt.* 提供，供应(*provide, supply)；布置，为…配备家具 记 联想记忆：fur(皮毛) + nish → 用皮毛布置房间 → 布置 例 Perhaps the dean's office can *furnish* the report. 或许系主任办公室可以提供这份报告。 派 furnishings(*n.* 室内陈设)
librarian [laɪˈbreriən]	*n.* 图书馆馆长；图书管理员 记 来自 library(*n.* 图书馆) 例 Her mother is the *librarian* of our school library. 她母亲是我们学校的图书馆馆长。
prototype [ˈproʊtətaɪp]	*n.* 原型，雏形(archetype) 记 词根记忆：proto(首先) + typ(形状) + e → 首先的形状 → 原型 例 The water of the early oceans might thus have become the chemical *prototype* for the fluids of all animal life. 早期的海水可能就成了所有动物体液的化学原型。
wipe [waɪp]	*v./n.* 擦，揩，抹 搭 wipe out 抹掉，擦去；彻底消灭 例 She *wiped* her hands on a clean towel. 她用一块干净的毛巾擦了擦手。 // Last night when I was putting the finishing touches on my paper, that electrical storm completely *wiped* out my computer files. 昨天晚上我在给论文做最后润色时，那场雷暴使我电脑里的文件全部丢失了。

allude
[əˈluːd]

vi. 暗指，影射，间接提到（imply, refer to）

记 词根记忆：al + lud（玩）+ e → 玩笑着提及 → 暗指，影射

搭 allude to sb./sth. 暗指…

例 Some people say that the movie may *allude* to racism. 有些人说这部电影可能暗指种族主义。

challenge
[ˈtʃælɪndʒ]

n. 挑战（书）；艰巨任务，难题；质疑，质问 *vt.* 向…挑战；公然反抗；对…质疑

搭 accept/take up challenge 接受挑战

例 The role will be the biggest *challenge* of his acting career. 扮演这个角色将是他演艺生涯中最大的挑战。// The old man doesn't like anyone *challenging* his authority. 那个老人不喜欢任何人挑战他的权威。

派 unchallenged（*a.* 未起争议的；未受过挑战的）；challenging（*a.* 具有挑战性的）

frank
[fræŋk]

a. 坦白的，直率的

记 联想记忆：弗兰克（Frank）是个很坦率的（frank）人

例 To be *frank* with you, I think you have little chance of passing the exam. 坦诚相告，我认为你不大可能通过考试。

您真胖

frank

sweep
[swiːp]

v. 打扫（clean）；席卷，横扫；挥动，舞动；迅速传播；扫视 *n.* 打扫；广度；（手臂等的）挥动

例 The students in the laboratory helped *sweep* up the glass. 实验室里的学生帮着把玻璃擦干净了。// Rumors of his resignation *swept* through the company. 他辞职的传言在全公司传开了。

backup
[ˈbækʌp]

n. 后援，增援；（文件等的）备份 *a.* 候补的，替补的

例 The police had *backup* from the army. 警方得到了军人的增援。//
A: I know I promised to drive you to the airport next Tuesday. But I am afraid that something has come up. And they've called a special meeting.
B: No big deal. Jenny said she was available as a *backup*.
A: 我知道我答应你下周二开车送你去机场。不过我恐怕有事去不了了。我们要召开一个特别会议。
B: 没关系。珍妮说她可以作为后备。

Word List 15

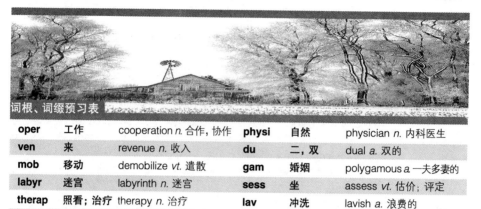

词根、词缀预习表

oper	工作	cooperation *n.* 合作，协作	physi	自然	physician *n.* 内科医生
ven	来	revenue *n.* 收入	du	二，双	dual *a.* 双的
mob	移动	demobilize *vt.* 遣散	gam	婚姻	polygamous *a.* 一夫多妻的
labyr	迷宫	labyrinth *n.* 迷宫	sess	坐	assess *vt.* 估价；评定
therap	照看；治疗	therapy *n.* 治疗	lav	冲洗	lavish *a.* 浪费的

cooperation [kouˌɑːpə'reɪʃn]	*n.* 合作，协作 记 词根记忆：co(共同，一起) + oper(工作) + ation → 一起工作 → 合作，协作 搭 in cooperation with 与…合作 例 There is an urgent need to strengthen international *cooperation* during the financial crisis. 在经济危机期间迫切需要加强国际合作。
ledge [ledʒ]	*n.* (建筑物或岩石的)突出部分；暗礁 记 联想记忆：l + edge(边缘) → 位于边缘处的东西 → 突出部分 例 McAdoo's men were forced to blast when they ran into a *ledge* of rock. 麦卡杜的士兵被一块石头的突出部分挡住了去路，不得不把它炸掉。
analyze ['ænəlaɪz]	*vt.* 分析，研究 记 词根记忆：ana(贯穿) + lyz(分开) + e → 整个分开 → 分析 例 Experts *analyze* spider webs using a computer program. 专家们用电脑程序分析蜘蛛网。
sufficient [sə'fɪʃnt]	*a.* 足够的，充分的(*adequate) 例 It takes only 10 to 20 minutes of exposure to sunlight a day to ensure *sufficient* Vitamin D production. 每天只需 10 到 20 分钟的日晒就能确保产生足够的维生素 D。 派 sufficiency(*n.* 充足); sufficiently(*ad.* 充分地，十分地)
nest [nest]	*v.* 做窝，筑巢 *n.* 巢，窝 记 联想记忆：在巢(nest)里休息(rest) 例 As many of you probably know, south beach is an important *nesting* site for the green turtle. 你们中很多人可能都知道，南海滩是绿海龟一个重要的筑窝地。 参 west(*n.* 西方); east(*n.* 东方)

revenue [ˈrevənjuː]	*n.* (尤指大宗的)收入(income); 税收 记 词根记忆: re(回) + ven(来) + ue → 回来的东西 → 收入 搭 financial revenue 财政收入 例 The tourist attraction does not generate any *revenue* for the town. 这个旅游景点没有给镇上带来任何收入。
demobilize [diːˈmoʊbəlaɪz]	*vt.* 遣散; 使复员 记 词根记忆: de(分离) + mob(移动) + ilize → 向不同的方向移动 → 遣散 例 The child soldiers in the country have been *demobilized* recently. 该国的娃娃兵最近被遣散了。
enrollment [ɪnˈroʊlmənt]	*n.* 登记(人数), 注册(人数); 入学 例 School *enrollments* are currently falling. 目前学校的注册人数在减少。// A: I read that the *enrollment* in the School of Business is on the rise! B: Well, that's been a trend for several years now. A: 我获悉商学院的招生人数在增加! B: 这个趋势已经持续好几年了。
statesman [ˈsteɪtsmən]	*n.* 政治家(politician) 记 组合词: states(国家, 政府) + man(人) → 管理国家事务的人 → 政治家
accustom [əˈkʌstəm]	*vt.* 使习惯于(familiarize) 记 联想记忆: ac + custom(习惯) → 使习惯于 例 It took me a long time to *accustom* myself to the idea. 我花了很长一段时间才习惯这个想法。 派 accustomed(*a.* 惯常的, 通常的; 习惯的)
contour [ˈkɑːntʊr]	*n.* 等高线; 轮廓(outline) 例 Ground plans and *contour* maps of the Earth can be drawn from aerial photographs. 可以用空中拍摄的相片来绘制地球的平面图和等高线地形图。
labyrinth [ˈlæbərɪnθ]	*n.* 迷宫; 错综复杂的事件 记 词根记忆: labyr(迷宫) + inth → 迷宫 例 In reality, the old castle itself is a *labyrinth* with dark corridors. 实际上, 这座古老的城堡本身就是一座由黑暗走廊构成的迷宫。
irregular [ɪˈreɡjələr]	*a.* 不规则的, 无规律的; 不整齐的; 不合常规的 搭 an irregular coast line 曲折的海岸线 例 He visited his grandparents at *irregular* intervals. 他不定期地去看望祖父母。 派 irregularity(*n.* 不规则性, 无规律性; 不合常规的行为)
therapy [ˈθerəpi]	*n.* 治疗, 疗法(treatment) 记 词根记忆: therap(照看; 治疗) + y → 治疗, 疗法 例 In the third era of nutritional history, vitamin *therapy* began to fall into disrepute. 在营养史的第三个阶段, 维生素疗法的名声开始变坏。

15

artesian [ɑːrˈtiːʒn]	*a.* 自流水的，喷水的 **搭** artesian spring 自流泉；artesian well 自流井 **例** Some geographers are interested in *artesian* spring. 一些地理学家对自流泉很感兴趣。
gear [gɪr]	*n.* 齿轮，传动装置；（排）挡；设备(equipment) *vt.* 调节，使适应 **记** 联想记忆：耳朵(ear)是身上用于听(hear)的设备(gear) **例** It must have several *gears*. 它肯定有好几个齿轮。// The course had been *geared* towards the specific needs of its members. 课程已做调整，以满足学员的具体需要。 gear
physician [fɪˈzɪʃn]	*n.* 内科医生 **记** 词根记忆：physi(自然) + c + ian(表人，名词后缀) → 内科医生 **例** The *physician* prescribed him some medicine. 内科医生给他开了一些药。
conductivity [ˌkɑːndʌkˈtɪvəti]	*n.* 传导性；传导率 **例** The nerve cells exhibit to a great degree the phenomenon of *conductivity*. 神经细胞在很大程度上体现了传导现象。
dual [ˈduːəl]	*a.* 双的，二重的 **记** 词根记忆：du(二，双) + al → 双的 **例** It has a *dual* function. 它有着双重功能。
Paleolithic [ˌpæliəˈlɪθɪk]	*a.* 旧石器时代的 *n.* 旧石器时代 **记** 词根记忆：paleo(旧的) + lith(石头) + ic → 旧石器的 → 旧石器时代的 **例** The *Paleolithic* Age covered an immense time span, and during this period major climatic changes occurred. 旧石器时代的时间跨度很大，在此期间，气候发生了重大的变化。
dupe [duːp]	*n.* 上当者 *vt.* 欺骗，愚弄 **记** 发音记忆："丢谱" → 乱摆谱，结果上了当 → 上当者 **例** They soon realized they had been *duped*. 他们很快便意识到自己上当了。
campus [ˈkæmpəs]	*n.* (大学)校园 **记** 联想记忆：camp(营地) + us(我们) → 校园是我们学生学习的营地 → (大学)校园 **搭** live on campus 住校 **例** The *campus* was so great and I loved it. 校园真大，我很喜欢。
polygamous [pəˈlɪgəməs]	*a.* 一夫多妻的，一妻多夫的 **记** 词根记忆：poly(多) + gam(婚姻) + ous → 一夫多妻的，一妻多夫的 **例** Although polygamy was criminalized by the leader, it is estimated that 3,000 individuals continue to be involved in *polygamous* relationships in the area. 尽管一夫多妻制遭到领导人的批判，但据估计那个地区仍有3000个人卷入一夫多妻的关系中。

flick [flɪk]	*v.* 轻拍；(快速地)移动 *n.* 轻拍；浏览 记 联想记忆：fli(看做 fly，飞) + ck → 轻拍翅膀，展翅高飞 → 轻拍 搭 flick through 浏览，草草翻阅 例 Let me show you how to operate this machine: put your clothes in and *flick* the switch, and it's done. 我来教你怎么使用这台机器：把衣服放进去，然后轻轻一按开关就可以了。
universal [ˌjuːnɪ'vɜːrsl]	*a.* 普遍的，全体的；通用的，万能的；宇宙的，全世界的 记 词根记忆：uni(单一) + vers(转) + al → 全部转为单一的 → 普遍的 例 One explanation to why this kind of thing happened is the lack of *universal* health insurance. 对于之所以发生这种事情的一种解释是全民医疗保险不健全。
assess [ə'ses]	*vt.* 估价；评定 记 词根记忆：as(靠近) + sess(坐) → 坐在旁边 → 估价；评定 例 Testing students by examinations has been considered an effective way to *assess* students' abilities. 通过考试来测试学生已经被认为是评估学生能力的有效方法。
officious [ə'fɪʃəs]	*a.* 爱发号施令的，爱指手画脚的 记 词根记忆：of(在路上) + fic(做) + ious → 挡在路上 → 爱指手画脚的 例 You need to speak out and stop being pushed around by the *officious* guy. 你应该说出自己的心声，不要被那个爱发号施令的家伙支来支去。
prone [proʊn]	*a.* 平卧的，俯卧的；易于做…的，倾向于…的 记 联想记忆：pr(看做 pro，向前) + on(在…上) + e → 向前卧倒在地上 → 平卧的 搭 be prone to 易于…，倾向于… 例 If you know the geography well, you must know China has numerous quake *prone* areas. 如果你具有丰富的地理知识，就一定知道中国有许多地震易发区。
afoul [ə'faʊl]	*ad.* 相抵触，有冲突 记 联想记忆：a(向) + foul(缠结) → 纠缠着 → 相抵触，有冲突 例 Your act ran *afoul* of the law. 你的行为触犯了法律。
bewilder [bɪ'wɪldər]	*vt.* 使迷惑，使不知所措 记 联想记忆：be + wild(荒野的) + er → 迷失荒野中 → 使迷惑 例 Mike doesn't like parties, for he is *bewildered* by the noise and the crowd. 迈克不喜欢参加派对，因为喧闹声和人群会把他弄得晕头转向的。 喵喵 bewilder
pinch [pɪntʃ]	*v.* 捏，掐；夹痛；偷窃；逮捕 *n.* 捏，掐；一撮，微量 记 联想记忆：p + inch(英寸) → 只把肉提起一英寸 → 捏，掐 搭 at/in a pinch 必要时，在紧急关头；take...with a pinch of salt 对…有保留，对…半信半疑；pinch off/out 摘掉，掐掉 例 I'd like a cup of coffee, with cream and just a *pinch* of sugar, please. 我想要杯咖啡，加奶和少量的糖。

□ flick   □ universal   □ assess   □ officious   □ prone   □ afoul
□ bewilder   □ pinch

malleable [ˈmæliəbl]	*a.* 有延展性的，易成型的；易受影响的，可塑的 记 词根记忆：malle(锤子) + able(能…的) → 能捶打的 → 可塑的 例 When dropped on the floor, *malleable* glass would bend rather than shatter into bits. 韧性玻璃掉到地上后，会弯曲，而不会破碎。
interweave [ˌɪntərˈwiːv]	*v.* 交织，编结 记 联想记忆：inter(在中间) + weave(编织) → 交织，编结 例 Do as I told you and *interweave* these two pieces of cloth together. 按我说的做，把这两块布编在一起。
lavish [ˈlævɪʃ]	*vt.* 慷慨给予，滥用；浪费，挥霍 *a.* 大方的，慷慨的；大量的；浪费的 记 词根记忆：lav(冲洗) + ish → 花钱如流水 → 浪费的 例 The grandparents *lavish* too much care on their only grandson. 祖父母对他们唯一的孙子过于溺爱。
prohibitive [prəˈhɪbətɪv]	*a.* 禁止的，抑制的；(价格等)高得令人难以承受的 记 词根记忆：pro(在…前面) + hibit(拿住) + ive → 提前拿住的 → 禁止的 例 The cost of travelling to Fiji Island is *prohibitive*. 到斐济岛旅游的费用高得令人不敢问津。
Mesolithic [ˌmesəˈliθik]	*a.* 中石器时代的 *n.* 中石器时代 例 The *Mesolithic* period dates from the end of the last Ice Age and was a period of rising temperatures and rising sea levels caused by melting glaciers. 中石器时代起源于上一个冰河时代末期。在中石器时代，气温升高，冰川融化使得海平面上升。
gamble [ˈgæmbl]	*n./v.* 投机，冒险；赌博，打赌 记 联想记忆：赌博（gamble）可不是小游戏（game） 搭 gamble away 赌掉，输光；take a gamble 冒风险；gamble on 赌博，打赌 例 Drive carefully and don't *gamble* with your life. 小心驾驶，别拿你的生命冒险。 gamble
understate [ˌʌndərˈsteɪt]	*vt.* 轻描淡写，避重就轻地说 记 联想记忆：under(在…下面) + state(声明) → 轻描淡写 例 I can't *understate* the importance of being concerned about safety issues. 我必须充分强调注意安全问题的重要性。
outweigh [ˌaʊtˈweɪ]	*vt.* (在重量、价值、影响等上)超过 例 Clearly, the advantages of the plan *outweigh* the disadvantages. 很明显，该计划的优点胜过缺点。 outweigh
sterile [ˈsterəl]	*a.* 不育的(infertile)；贫瘠的(barren)；无菌的(germfree)；无结果的，没有实际价值的；刻板的 例 He felt creatively and emotionally *sterile*. 他觉得自己既缺乏创造力又没有充沛的感情。 派 sterility(*n.* 不育；乏味)；sterilize(*vt.* 杀菌；使绝育)

component	*n.* 成分，组成部分(*part, element) *a.* 组成的，构成的(*constituent)
[kəmˈpoʊnənt]	记 词根记忆：com(共同) + pon(放) + ent → 放到一起(的东西) → 成分
	例 Community service is an important *component* of education here at our university. 社区服务是我们这所大学教育体系中的重要组成部分。
	参 opponent(*a.* 对立的)
ammonia	*n.* 氨，氨水
[əˈmoʊniə]	例 *Ammonia* is a colorless gas with a strong smell. 氨是种无色并有强烈气味的气体。
photosynthesis	*n.* 光合作用
[ˌfoʊtoʊˈsɪnθəsɪs]	记 组合词：photo(光) + synthesis(合成) → 光合作用
	例 *Photosynthesis* in plants and a few bacteria is responsible for feeding nearly all life on Earth. 植物和一些细菌的光合作用给地球上几乎所有生命提供了养分。
mar	*vt./n.* 损坏，损毁
[mɑːr]	记 发音记忆："骂" → 弄坏了东西，所以挨骂 → 损坏
	例 You have to pay extra attention to the mistake, because it would *mar* your career. 你要格外注意这个错误，因为它会毁掉你的事业。
consist	*vi.* 在于，存在于；由…组成，由…构成(compose)
[kənˈsɪst]	记 词根记忆：con(共同) + sist(站) → 站在一起 → 由…组成，由…构成
	搭 consist of 由…组成；consist in 在于，存在于
	例 Ancient Greek philosophers thought the Earth *consisted* of five elements. 古希腊哲学家认为地球由五种元素构成。// A balanced meal *consists* of five key elements: proteins, carbo-hydrates, fats, vitamins and minerals. 平衡的膳食包括五个关键要素：蛋白质、碳水化合物、脂肪、维生素和矿物质。
	参 insist(*v.* 坚持); persist(*vi.* 坚持)
flair	*n.* 才能，本领；天资
[fler]	记 联想记忆：才能(flair)无法在集市(fair)上买到
	例 She has a *flair* for languages. 她有学语言的天赋。
selective	*a.* 选择的，选择性的；精挑细选的
[sɪˈlektɪv]	记 词根记忆：se + lect(选择) + ive → 选择的
	例 I wouldn't mind going to that university. It has an excellent reputation for commercial art, but I have a feeling that it's very *selective*. 我不介意去那所大学。它在商业美术方面享有盛誉，但我觉得它非常挑剔。
pin	*vt.* 钉住；固定 *n.* 大头针；钢钉；胸针；徽章
[pɪn]	搭 pin sb. down 使某人动弹不得；使说清楚
	例 She *pinned* the badge onto her jacket. 她把徽章别到外衣上。// A: It sounds like Karen isn't happy at all with her new roommate. Did she say why? B: Believe me, I tried to find out. But I simply couldn't *pin* her down. A: 听起来卡伦对室友很不满意。她说原因了吗？B: 相信我，我努力问过了，但她就是没有明白地告诉我。

15

□ component　　□ ammonia　　□ photosynthesis　□ mar　　　□ consist　　　□ flair
□ selective　　□ pin

concrete [ˈkɑːŋkriːt]	*a.* 混凝土制的；具体的(material)；确凿的 *n.* 混凝土(cement) 记 词根记忆：con(共同) + cret(增长) + e → 一起增长 → 坚固的 → 具体的 例 It is easier to think in *concrete* terms rather than in the abstract. 结合具体的事物进行思考要比抽象思考容易些。
battery [ˈbætri]	*n.* 电池；排炮；一系列，一批 记 联想记忆：batt(看做 bat，蝙蝠) + ery → 给蝙蝠飞行提供能量 → 电池 例 The calculator needs a new *battery*. 计算器需要一块新电池。// We faced a *battery* of questions. 我们面临一连串的问题。
painstaking [ˈpeɪnzteɪkɪŋ]	*a.* 煞费苦心的，勤勉的(diligent, industrious) 记 组合词：pains(痛苦) + taking(花费…的) → 煞费苦心的 例 Panel painting involved a *painstaking*, laborious process. 镶板绘画是个费心费力的过程。
continuation [kənˌtɪnjuˈeɪʃn]	*n.* 延长，延续，持续(prolongation)；延长物，扩建物；延续部分 例 Which topic will most probably be included in the *continuation* of today's lecture? 今天这堂课接下来的部分最有可能包含哪个话题？
humanity [hjuːˈmænəti]	*n.* 人类(mankind)；人性；人道，仁慈 记 词根记忆：hum(人) + an + ity(表性质，名词后缀) → 人类 例 The soldiers devote their lives to unselfish service of *humanity*. 战士们把自己的一生献给了无私地服务于人类的事业。
access [ˈækses]	*n.* 通道(approach)；接近，进入；(接近或享用的)机会(opportunity) *vt.* 进入；使用；存取(计算机文件) 记 词根记忆：ac(向，往) + cess(走) → 走向 → 进入 例 Finding a water route across the continent was to gain easy *access* to the gold and other riches of the Northwest. 找到横穿大陆的水路就能轻松获得西北地区的黄金和其他财富。
shade [ʃeɪd]	*n.* 阴凉处，遮光物(shelter)；阴暗(shadow)；色度；差别 *vt.* 遮蔽，遮光 搭 shades of …的痕迹，遗风；put...in the shade 使…黯然失色，相形见绌 例 These plants don't like the direct sunlight and little *shade* could help them immensely. 这些植物不喜欢阳光直晒，一点阴凉对它们大有裨益。
manual [ˈmænjuəl]	*a.* 手工的(by hand)；体力的 *n.* 手册，指南(guidebook, handbook) 记 词根记忆：manu(手) + al(形容词后缀) → 手工的 例 I am good at *manual* tasks, but I don't do math well. 我擅长手工，但是数学不好。
bush [bʊʃ]	*n.* 灌木(丛)(shrub)；荒野 搭 beat about the bush 旁敲侧击 例 There is an abundance of wildlife in the *bushes*, such as snakes and mushrooms. 灌木丛中有很多野生动植物，例如蛇和蘑菇。

hardware [ˈhɑːrdwer]	*n.* 五金制品，金属制品；硬件 记 组合词：hard(硬的，坚固的) + ware(器皿) → 五金制品；硬件 例 Relatively little *hardware* was used during this period. 这个时期金属制品使用得相对较少。 参 kitchenware(*n.* 厨房用具)；stoneware(*n.* 粗陶器)
proprietor [prəˈpraɪətər]	*n.* 所有者，业主(owner) 例 My uncle is the *proprietor* of a chain of supermarkets. 我叔叔是一家连锁超市的业主。
terrestrial [təˈrestriəl]	*a.* 陆地的，陆生的，陆栖的；地球的 记 词根记忆：terr(地) + estr + ial → 陆地的，陆生的 例 The highest *terrestrial* mountain is Mount Everest. 陆地上最高的山是珠穆朗玛峰。// Ichthyosaurs had a higher chance of being preserved than *terrestrial* creatures did. 鱼龙被保存下来的几率比陆生生物要高。
flask [flɑːsk]	*n.* 细颈瓶；烧瓶 记 联想记忆：水在烧瓶(flask)里闪闪发光(flash) 例 The shop sells all sorts of vacuum *flasks*. 那家商店出售各种保温瓶。
crawl [krɔːl]	*v.* 缓慢行进；爬行(creep) *n.* 缓慢的速度 记 联想记忆：c + raw(生疏的) + l → 对地形生疏，车开慢点 → 缓慢行进 例 I'm so out of shape. I might have to *crawl* the rest of the way. 我不行了，剩下的路可能要爬着回去了。// This ordinary backyard dirt is *crawling* with microbes. 这种寻常的后院泥土上爬满了微生物。
locomotive [ˌloʊkəˈmoʊtɪv]	*n.* 机车，火车头 *a.* 运动的(kinetic)；移动的 记 词根记忆：loc(某地) + o + mot(移动) + ive(形容词后缀) → 从一地移到另一地 → 运动的；移动的 例 In the 19th century, North American *locomotives* ran on hardwood fuel. 在19世纪，北美的机车依靠硬木燃料运行。// The "railroad novel" offers the ambience of station yards and *locomotive* cabs. 这部"铁路小说"再现了站台和机车驾驶室里的氛围。
pound [paʊnd]	*v.* 猛击(strike)；捣碎(mash)；(心)怦怦跳 *n.* 磅；英镑 记 发音记忆："胖的" → 重达几百磅 → 磅 例 After drying the fish, the women *pounded* some of them into fish meal. 这些女人把鱼晾干之后，捣碎了其中一些鱼干做成鱼肉饭。
cereal [ˈsɪriəl]	*n.* 谷物(grain)；谷类食物 记 联想记忆：ce + real(真正的) → 真正的健康食品 → 谷类食物 例 The most healthful *cereals* are made with whole grains and not much else. 最健康的谷类食物完全由谷物制作而成，而且不含什么其他物质。
lunar [ˈluːnər]	*a.* 月亮的 搭 lunar day 太阴日，月球日

precipitate	[prɪˈsɪpɪteɪt] *v.* 使…突然降临；加速；降水；使突然陷入；(使)沉淀 *n.* 沉淀物 [prɪˈsɪpɪtət] *a.* 仓促的，鲁莽的 记 词根记忆：pre(在…前面) + cip(落下) + it + ate → 提前落下 → 使…突然降临 例 Water dissolves, transports, and *precipitates* many chemical compounds. 水溶解、运送许多化合物并使之沉淀。 派 precipitation(*n.* 降水；降水量)
manufacture [ˌmænjuˈfæktʃər]	*vt.* 大量制造，成批生产(mass-produce)；捏造 *n.* 大量制造；[*pl.*]制造品，产品(product) 记 词根记忆：manu(手) + fact(制作，做) + ure → 用手制作 → 大量制造 例 Those companies rely on high accuracy scales to *manufacture* and package medicine. 那些公司依靠高精度秤来生产和包装药品。 派 manufacturing(*n.* 制造业)；manufacturer(*n.* 生产者，制造商)
seismograph [ˈsaɪzməɡræf]	*n.* 地震仪，测震仪 记 词根记忆：seism(震动) + o + graph(写；图) → 能描绘地震情况的(仪器) → 地震仪 例 The modern *seismograph* was invented in the late 1800s. 现代地震仪发明于 19 世纪晚期。
concise [kənˈsaɪs]	*a.* 简明的，简练的(terse) 记 词根记忆：con(全部) + cis(切) + e → 把(多余的)全部切掉 → 简明的，简练的 例 Worksheets require defining the problem in a clear and *concise* way. 工作表要求清晰、简要地阐述问题。
prey [preɪ]	*vi.* 捕食，捕获 *n.* 猎物；受害者，牺牲品 记 联想记忆：心中暗自祈祷(pray)不要成为受害者(prey) 搭 prey on sb.'s mind 萦绕心头，使某人耿耿于怀 例 Some human hunters *prey* on animals of all ages, but gray wolves concentrate their efforts on young animals. 一些猎人捕捉各个年龄段的动物，但是灰狼专门捕食年幼的动物。
fluctuate [ˈflʌktʃueɪt]	*v.* (使)波动(undulate)；(使)变化 记 词根记忆：flu(流) + ctu + ate → 水流动 → (使)波动；(使)变化 例 The temperature often *fluctuates* dramatically. 温度经常剧烈变化。// The level of carbon dioxide in the atmosphere *fluctuated* between 190 and 280 parts per million. 大气中二氧化碳的含量在每百万 190–280 之间波动。 派 fluctuation(*n.* 波动，起伏)

adaptable [əˈdæptəbl]	*a.* 能适应的(adaptive, flexible, revisable); 可改编的 记 词根记忆: ad + apt(适合的) + able(能…的) → 能适应的 例 The twins are always *adaptable* to fit new conditions. 这对双胞胎总能适应新的环境。
solder [ˈsɑːdər]	*vt.* 焊接(weld) *n.* 焊料, 焊锡 记 联想记忆: 我们的战士(soldier)是钢铁焊接(solder)而成的 例 This guide explains how you can *solder* a variety of components using a few different techniques. 这个指南解释了如何通过使用一些不同的技术来焊接各种各样的零件。
outstanding [aʊtˈstændɪŋ]	*a.* 优秀的, 杰出的, 出色的(remarkable); 未解决的; 未偿付的 记 联想记忆: out(出) + standing(站立的) → 站出来的 → 鹤立鸡群的 → 杰出的 例 If you are interested in gymnastics, the university has an *outstanding* team. 如果你对体操感兴趣, 这所大学有一支非常不错的体操队。
cargo [ˈkɑːrɡoʊ]	*n.* (船或飞机装载的)货物(freight) 记 联想记忆: car(汽车) + go(走) → 汽车运走的东西 → 货物 例 The tanker began to spill its *cargo* of oil. 油轮开始漏油。
administer [ədˈmɪnɪstər]	*vt.* 管理(*manage); 执行(execute); 给予, 提供 记 联想记忆: ad + minister(大臣) → 大臣要精于管理 → 管理 例 Professor Andrews has agreed to *administer* the exam. 安德鲁斯教授已同意进行考试。 派 administration(*n.* 管理, 行政); administrative(*a.* 管理的, 行政的); administrator(*n.* 管理者, 行政官)
inferior [ɪnˈfɪriər]	*a.* 劣等的, 较差的; 次要的; 级别低的 *n.* 下级, 下属, 晚辈 记 联想记忆: infer(推断) + ior → 推断的东西是次要的, 事实才是依据 → 次要的 例 Vase painters sometimes produce *inferior* wares. 花瓶的绘画者有时会做出次品。 派 inferiority(*n.* 低等; 劣势; 自卑感)
quiescent [kwiˈesnt]	*a.* 静止的, 寂静的; 静态的 记 词根记忆: qui(平静的) + esc + ent → 平静的状态 → 静止的 例 It is unlikely that such an extremist organization will remain *quiescent* for long. 这种激进组织是不太可能长期保持沉默的。
coherent [koʊˈhɪrənt]	*a.* 条理清楚的, 连贯的(consistent); 有表达能力的 记 词根记忆: co + her(黏附) + ent → 黏附在一起 → 连贯的 搭 a coherent narrative 条理清楚的叙述 例 Ethics is the branch of philosophy that deals with the values of life in a *coherent*, systematic, and scientific manner. 伦理学是哲学的一个分支, 以连贯、系统和科学的方式研究人生的价值。 派 coherence(*n.* 连贯性, 条理性); incoherence(*n.* 不连贯)

□ adaptable　　□ solder　　□ outstanding　　□ cargo　　□ administer　　□ inferior
□ quiescent　　□ coherent

removal [rɪ'muːvl]	*n.* 除去(elimination)；移动，搬迁 例 The field of "sanitary science" is concerned with waste *removal*, water purification and so on. 卫生科学领域研究废物处理，以及水净化等问题。
insufficient [ˌɪnsə'fɪʃnt]	*a.* 不足的，不够的(deficient) 记 联想记忆：in(不) + sufficient(充分的) → 不足的，不够的 例 Funds for research were *insufficient*. 研究经费不足。
tenement ['tenəmənt]	*n.* 廉租公寓 记 联想记忆：ten(十) + e + men(人) + t → 十个人住一间屋子 → 廉租公寓 例 The *tenements* lacked both running water and central heating. 廉租公寓既没有自来水，也没有集中供暖。
impermeable [ɪm'pɜːrmiəbl]	*a.* 不可渗透的，不透水的 记 词根记忆：im(不) + per(穿过) + mea(流过) + (a)ble(能…的) → 不能流过的 → 不可渗透的 例 The objects are covered with *impermeable* decorative coatings of glasslike material. 这些物体上覆盖着不透水的玻璃状装饰涂层。
astronomy [ə'strɑːnəmi]	*n.* 天文学 记 词根记忆：astro(星星) + nomy(法则；学科) → 研究星星的学科 → 天文学 例 The ancient Egyptians had a limited knowledge of *astronomy*. 古埃及人的天文学知识非常有限。 派 astronomical(*a.* 天文学的；庞大的)；astronomer(*n.* 天文学家)
temple ['templ]	*n.* 寺庙，教堂(church)；太阳穴 记 发音记忆："淡泊" → 神殿中人淡泊名利 → 寺庙，教堂 例 He had black hair, graying at the *temples*. 他的头发是黑色的，但两鬓已见斑白。
intrusion [ɪn'truːʒn]	*n.* 侵扰，干扰；侵犯；侵入，闯入 搭 intrusion into/on/upon 侵入，干涉 例 They claim the noise from the new airport is an *intrusion* on their lives. 他们声称新机场的噪音干扰了他们的生活。
spectator ['spekteɪtər]	*n.* 观众(audience)；旁观者 记 词根记忆：spect (看) + at + or (表人) → 观众；旁观者 例 Horse racing is a leading *spectator* sport in many countries. 赛马在许多国家是一项主要的观赏运动。

temple

妖猴哪去了

孙悟空

spectator

词根、词缀预习表

grad	步，级	grading *n.* 评分；等级	cess	走	excess *a.* 过量的
muni	服务	municipal *a.* 市政的	soci	结交；同伴	associative *a.* 联想的
radic	根	radical *a.* 根本的	gn	知道	cognitive *a.* 认知的
plic	重叠	implication *n.* 含义；暗示	nost	回家	nostalgic *a.* 思乡的
ex-	出	extend *v.* 延长；舒展	wor	价值	worship *n./v.* 崇拜

---

adolescence
[ˌædəˈlesns]

n. 青春(期)(youthhood)

记 联想记忆：ado（看做 adult，成年人）+ lescence（看做 licence，许可证）→ 青少年即将拿到成年的许可证 → 青春(期)

例 *Adolescence* is the life stage that bridges childhood and adulthood. 青春期是从儿童到成人的人生过渡阶段。

派 adolescent(*n.* 青少年)

我长胡子了

我长喉结了

adolescence

---

snowflake
[ˈsnəʊfleɪk]

n. 雪花，雪片

记 组合词：snow(雪) + flake(薄片) → 雪花，雪片

例 *Snowflakes* come in a variety of sizes and shapes. 雪片大小不一，形状多变。

---

audit
[ˈɔːdɪt]

vt. 旁听；审计

记 词根记忆：aud(听) + it → 旁听

例 If you *audit* a course, you don't have to take the tests. 如果你仅是旁听，就不需要参加考试。

---

grading
[ˈɡreɪdɪŋ]

n. 评分；等级(rank)

记 词根记忆：grad(步，级) + ing → 评分；等级

例 He doesn't know if Dr. Wilson has finished the *grading* of the midterm exams. 他不知道威尔逊博士是否已经批改完期中考试的试卷。

---

exception
[ɪkˈsepʃn]

n. 除外，例外

搭 without exception 无例外地；with the exception of 除…之外

例 We've now discussed how most snakes move, but there are some notable *exceptions*. 我们已经讨论了大多数蛇是如何移动的，但是有一些例外情况值得注意。

---

shell [ʃel]	*n.* 壳，外壳(crust)；壳状物；骨架，框架；外表；炮弹 *vt.* 给…去壳；炮击 记 联想记忆：坏蛋被一炮弹(shell)轰进地狱(hell) 例 The house was now a *shell* gutted by flames. 房子被火烧得只剩个空骨架了。 参 shellfish(*n.* 水生有壳动物)
inhibit [ɪnˈhɪbɪt]	*vt.* 阻碍，抑制(*hinder) 记 词根记忆：in(不) + hib(拥有) + it → 使不能拥有 → 阻碍，抑制 例 They may discipline group members who *inhibit* attainment of the group's goals. 他们可以处罚那些阻碍实现团队目标的成员。 派 inhibition(*n.* 阻止，禁止)
argue [ˈɑːrgjuː]	*v.* 争论，辩论(debate)；主张，论证；说服，劝说 记 发音记忆："阿Q" → 阿Q喜欢和人争论 → 争论 例 Idealists *argue* that the representatives needed to control a series of problems in order for the United States to survive. 理想主义者认为，代表们需要对一系列问题进行调控以使美国渡过难关。 派 argument(*n.* 争论，辩论；论据，论点)
municipal [mjuːˈnɪsɪpl]	*a.* 市政的；内政的；地方性的(local) 记 词根记忆：muni(服务) + cip(拿) + al → 提供城市公共服务的 → 市政的 例 The *municipal* government ordered landlords to roll back their rents to the levels charged in 1978. 市政府下令让房东们把房租降到1978年的收取水平。
configuration [kənˌfɪgjəˈreɪʃn]	*n.* 布局，格局；结构，构造，形状(structure, shape)；配置 记 来自configure(*vt.* 安置；设定) 例 The awkward *configuration* of the kitchen is very inefficient. 厨房的布局别扭，很不实用。
lawn [lɔːn]	*n.* 草地，草坪(grassplot)；操场 记 联想记忆：law(法律) + n(形似一道门) → 很多人乱踏草坪，所以要运用法律制造一道保护的门 → 草坪 例 In summer we have to mow the *lawn* twice a week. 夏天我们每周得修剪草坪两次。
radical [ˈrædɪkl]	*a.* 根本的(fundamental)；激进的，极端的(drastic)；全新的，不同凡响的 *n.* 激进分子；游离基，自由基 记 词根记忆：radic(根) + al → 根本的 搭 free radical 自由基，游离基 例 Cities had undergone *radical* social change. 城市经历了根本性的社会变革。 派 radically(*ad.* 根本上)
wither [ˈwɪðər]	*v.* (使)枯萎，凋谢(fade, perish)；衰退(decline)；萎缩；破灭 记 联想记忆：慢慢变冷的天气(weather)使花都枯萎(wither)了 例 Some of the elm's leaves have *withered* and turned yellow. 一些榆树叶已经枯萎变黄了。

□ shell   □ inhibit   □ argue   □ municipal   □ configuration   □ lawn
□ radical   □ wither

seashore [ˈsiːʃɔːr]	*n.* 海岸, 海滨(coast, beach, shore) 例 Every day the old man goes to the *seashore* before daybreak. 这个老人每天天亮前都去海滩。
interest [ˈɪntrəst]	*n.* 兴趣, 关注; 业余爱好; 利息; 利害关系 [常 *pl.*]权益(benefit) *vt.* 使感兴趣, 引起…关注 例 Chisholm was known for advocating the *interests* of the urban poor. 齐泽姆因维护城市贫民的利益而闻名。// Politics doesn't *interest* me. 我对政治不感兴趣。
fantastic [fænˈtæstɪk]	*a.* 荒诞的, 奇异的; 极好的(terrific); 极大的 记 来自 fantasy(*n.* 幻想) 例 My new neighbor has a *fantastic* collection of classical music. 我的新邻居有一系列极好的古典音乐收藏品。
championship [ˈtʃæmpiənʃɪp]	*n.* [常 *pl.*]锦标赛; 冠军地位 例 The soccer *championship* is run right now on Channel 8. 足球锦标赛正在第八频道播出。
implication [ˌɪmplɪˈkeɪʃn]	*n.* 含义(*significance); 暗示, 暗指(suggestion); 卷入, 牵连 记 词根记忆: im(里面) + plic(重叠) + ation → 有多重含义 → 含义; 暗示 例 What are the social *implications* of meat-eating? 食肉有什么社会含义?
extend [ɪkˈstend]	*v.* 延长, 延伸(*stretch, *increase); 扩大…的范围(或影响); 舒展(肢体) 记 词根记忆: ex(出) + tend(伸展) → 延长; 舒展 例 Careful maintenance can *extend* the life of your car. 精心保养可延长你的汽车的寿命。// The company plans to *extend* its operation into Japan. 公司打算将业务扩展到日本。
meager [ˈmiːgər]	*a.* 不足的, 贫乏的(deficient, scanty); 消瘦的 记 联想记忆: m + eager(热心的) → 光靠热心是不够的 → 不足的 例 Prior to this report, Seattle's park development was very limited and funding *meager*. 在这个报告之前, 西雅图的公园发展非常有限, 而且缺乏资金。
dump [dʌmp]	*vt.* 丢弃, 倾倒; 抛弃; 推卸; 倾销 *n.* 垃圾场 记 发音记忆: "当铺" → 到当铺去倾销 → 倾销 例 He has got no right to keep *dumping* his problems on me. 他没有权利总是把他的问题推到我身上。// The freighter was caught in a big storm and thousands of pairs of sneakers got *dumped* into the Pacific Ocean. 这艘货船遇到了大风暴, 上千双运动鞋被卷进了太平洋。 派 dumping(*n.* 倾倒)

□ seashore □ interest □ fantastic □ championship □ implication □ extend
□ meager □ dump

177

recognition
[ˌrekəɡˈnɪʃn]

n. 承认，认同（admission）；认出，识别，辨认；赏识

记 来自 recognize（*vt.* 认出；承认）

搭 social recognition 社会认同

例 There is a growing *recognition* of the urgent need for reform. 越来越多的人认识到迫切需要改革。// He received the award in *recognition* of his success over the past year. 他受到了奖励，这是对他过去一年的成绩的肯定。

already
[ɔːlˈredi]

ad. 已，已经

例 There are far too many people *already*. We can't take any more. 已经有太多的人，我们再也接待不了。

preeminent
[priˈemɪnənt]

a. 卓越的，杰出的

记 联想记忆：pre（在…前面）+ eminent（著名的）→ 比著名的人还著名 → 卓越的，杰出的

例 The TV show invited some *preeminent* experts to take part in today's topic. 这档电视节目邀请了一些著名的专家参与今天的话题讨论。

suction
[ˈsʌkʃn]

n. 吸，抽吸；吸力

搭 suction pump 真空泵

例 Neither the water pumps nor the vacuum cleaners could work without *suction*. 水泵和真空吸尘器没有吸力都是无法工作的。

excess

[ɪkˈses] *n.* 过度，超过（superfluity）[ˈekses] *a.* 过量的；额外的（extra）

记 词根记忆：ex（出）+ cess（走）→ 走出界限 → 过量的

例 Are you suffering from an *excess* of stress in your life? 你生活中的压力是否太大了？

派 excessive（*a.* 过多的，过度的）

associative
[əˈsəʊʃiətɪv]

a. 联想的；结合的；关联的

记 词根记忆：as（表加强）+ soci（结交；同伴）+ ative → 联想的；结合的

例 It is said that *associative* memory is the basic function of the human brain. 据说联想记忆是人脑的一项基本功能。

cognitive
[ˈkɑːɡnətɪv]

a. 认识的；认知的，有感知的

记 词根记忆：co（共同）+ gn（知道）+ itive → 认知的

例 The study showed that *cognitive* behavioral therapy has clinical value. 研究表明，认知行为疗法具有临床价值。

trek
[trek]

n./v. 艰苦跋涉

记 联想记忆：tr（看做 try，努力）+ ek（看做 nek，山峡）→ 努力翻越山峡 → 艰苦跋涉

例 My boots were worn out after our long *trek* in the mountains. 因为我们在山中漫长的艰苦跋涉，我的靴子都磨破了。

nostalgic
[nəˈstældʒɪk]

a. 思乡的；怀旧的

记 词根记忆：nost（回家）+ alg（痛）+ ic → 想回家想到心痛 → 思乡的

例 I feel quite *nostalgic* for the place where I grew up. 我很怀念我长大的地方。

□ recognition　　□ already　　□ preeminent　　□ suction　　□ excess　　□ associative
□ cognitive　　□ trek　　□ nostalgic

delineate [dɪˈlɪnieɪt]	*vt.* 描绘，描述；解释 记 联想记忆：描绘（delineate）家族兴衰（decline） 例 You should *delineate* your objectives precisely. 你应该解释清楚你的目标。
baffle [ˈbæfl]	*vt.* 使困惑，难住 记 联想记忆：战役（battle）开始，一向忠诚的 tt 反戈，让人困惑（baffle）→ 使困惑 例 The explanations of these concepts *baffle* a lot of beginners. 对这些概念的阐述令很多初学者感到困惑。
corpus [ˈkɔːrpəs]	*n.* 文集，文献，汇编；语料库 记 词根记忆：corp（身体）+ us → 知识体 → 文集，文献 例 The use of *corpus* can supplement the deficiencies of conventional teaching. 语料库的使用可以弥补传统教学的不足。
worship [ˈwɜːrʃɪp]	*n./v.* 祭拜；崇拜，崇敬（adoration） 记 词根记忆：wor（价值）+ ship（名词后缀）→ 给予高度评价 → 崇拜 搭 a place of worship 礼拜场所 例 Susan looked at the famous designer with *worship* in her eyes. 苏珊以敬慕的目光注视着这位著名设计师。
monotony [məˈnɑːtəni]	*n.* 单调，千篇一律 记 词根记忆：mono（单个）+ ton（声音）+ y → 一个声音 → 单调，千篇一律 例 Listening to the music relieves the *monotony* of daily life. 音乐使得日常生活不再那么单调。
dissuade [dɪˈsweɪd]	*vt.* 劝阻，阻止 记 词根记忆：dis（分离）+ suad（说服）+ e → 说服某人以使其脱离 → 劝阻，阻止 例 I tried to *dissuade* her from giving up her job. 我努力劝她不要放弃自己的工作。
tremulous [ˈtremjələs]	*a.* 发抖的，颤抖的；害怕的 记 词根记忆：trem（发抖）+ ul + ous → 发抖的；害怕的 例 The little girl answered the teacher's question in a *tremulous* voice. 那个小女孩颤抖着声音回答了老师的问题。
slough	[slʌf] *vt.* 使脱落 [sluː] *n.* 泥坑，沼泽；绝境 记 联想记忆：s（音似：四）+ lough（湖）→ 湖四周有很多泥坑 → 泥坑 例 Responsibilities are not *sloughed* off so easily. 责任可不是那么容易推卸的。
conscientious [ˌkɑːnʃiˈenʃəs]	*a.* 凭良心的；认真谨慎的，一丝不苟的 记 词根记忆：con（共同）+ sci（知道）+ ent + ious（多…的）→ 大家都应该知道的 → 凭良心的 例 The boss told me I had to be more *conscientious* about my work. 老板告诉我工作时必须更加谨慎。

16

beneficent [bɪ'nefɪsnt]	*a.* 有益的；行善的，慈善的 词根记忆：bene(善，好) + fic(做) + ent → 有益的；行善的，慈善的 例 The former singer now has a life filled with *beneficent* activities. 这个之前的歌手，目前积极投身于各种慈善活动。
appease [ə'piːz]	*vt.* 平息；安抚，抚慰；绥靖 联想记忆：ap + pease(看做 peace，平静) → 使得到平静 → 平息；安抚 例 There is a way to *appease* the hostility between you and her. 有一个办法能平息你与她之间的敌意。
discord ['dɪskɔːrd]	*n.* 不一致；不和，纷争；(音调的)不和谐 词根记忆：dis(分开) + cord(心) → 不同心 → 不一致 例 I would rather not see any *discord* in our society nowadays. 我不愿意看到当今社会中存在任何不和谐。
extort [ɪk'stɔːrt]	*vt.* 勒索，敲诈，强夺 词根记忆：ex(出) + tort(扭曲) → 扭曲使出来 → 强夺 例 The police used every means to *extort* confession from the suspect. 警察想尽办法逼迫嫌疑犯招供。
bluster ['blʌstər]	*v.* 虚张声势地恫吓；(风)猛刮 联想记忆：风猛刮(bluster)，刮掉了雕塑的光泽(luster) 例 When quarreling, Mike tends to *bluster* at first, but he soon will drop. 每当争吵时，迈克起初总爱吵闹一阵，但一会儿就不做声了。
iceberg ['aɪsbɜːrg]	*n.* 冰山；冷冰冰的人 组合词：ice(冰) + berg(大冰块) → 冰山 例 A massive *iceberg* — more than twice the size of New York's Manhattan island — is drifting slowly toward the country. 一座巨大的冰山，面积是纽约曼哈顿岛的两倍多，正慢慢地向该国漂移。
energetic [ˌenər'dʒetɪk]	*a.* 精力充沛的，积极的(active, vigorous) 来自 energy(*n.* 精神，活力) 例 The interviewers are usually willing to offer posts to job applicants who are *energetic*, hardworking and responsible. 面试官一般愿意把职位提供给那些充满活力、工作勤奋和有责任心的求职人员。
colonial [kə'loʊniəl]	*a.* 殖民的；殖民国家的 来自 colony(*n.* 殖民地) 例 The country achieved independence from French *colonial* rule in 1956. 该国于 1956 年从法国的殖民统治下获得独立。
exorbitant [ɪg'zɔːrbɪtənt]	*a.* (价格、索价等)过高的，不合理的 词根记忆：ex(出) + orbit(轨道，常规) + ant → 走出常规的 → 不合理的 例 It's a nice car, but they are charging an *exorbitant* price for it. 车是不错，但他们的要价高得离谱。

□ beneficent   □ appease   □ discord   □ extort   □ bluster   □ iceberg
□ energetic   □ colonial   □ exorbitant

slope [sloup]	*n.* 斜坡，斜面(slant, inclination)；斜度 *v.* (使)倾斜 记 联想记忆：在斜坡(slope)上大步跑(lope) 例 The house is built on a *slope*. 这座房子建在斜坡上。 派 sloping(*a.* 倾斜的，有坡度的)
match [mætʃ]	*n.* 比赛(contest)；对手(opponent) *v.* 匹配(suit) 例 The man's socks *match* his shirt well. 那个人的袜子与他的衬衫很配。 派 matching(*a.* 匹配的)；unmatched(*a.* 无可匹敌的)
deal [di:l]	*n.* 交易，买卖；协议 *v.* 处理，对付(handle)；给予；做买卖，经营 搭 a good deal (of) 许多；deal with 处理；deal in 经营，买卖 例 They were hoping for a better pay *deal.* 他们希望就提高工资达成协议。// A: I just got this car and already it's falling apart. First, one of the door handles fell off and now the inside light won't go on when you open the door. B: Hey, what's the big *deal*? Falling apart is when your car needs a new engine, like mine does. A: 我这辆车刚买就快散架了。先是一个门把手掉了，现在打开车门时里面的灯也不亮了。 B: 这有什么大不了的？车需要换发动机的时候才算散架，比如我的车。 派 dealer(*n.* 经销商)；dealing(*n.* 行为；交易)
archaeology [ˌɑːrkiˈɑːlədʒi]	*n.* 考古学 记 词根记忆：arch(古老的) + ae + ology(…学) → 考古学 例 The purpose of *archaeology* is to learn more about past societies and the development of the human race. 考古学旨在进一步了解过去社会以及人类的演化。 派 archaeological(*a.* 考古学上的)；archaeologist(*n.* 考古学家)
legend ['ledʒənd]	*n.* 传奇故事，传说(tale)；传奇文学 记 词根记忆：leg(读) + end → 一直传读下来的 → 传奇故事，传说 例 Cultures from the myths and *legends* are passed down from one generation to another. 神话传奇的文化世代相传。 派 legendary(*a.* 传奇的；有名的)
inanity [ɪˈnænəti]	*n.* 空虚，空洞(emptiness)；无意义的事物 例 Their statement was a downright *inanity.* 他们的声明是彻头彻尾的废话。
airborne ['erbɔːrn]	*a.* 空气传播的；空运的 记 联想记忆：air(空气) + borne(bear 的过去分词，传播) → 空气传播的 例 You increase your exposure to *airborne* viruses just when your body's resistance is already low from all the running-around you do. 你跑来跑去，使身体抵抗力下降，这使得你更加容易感染通过空气传播的病毒。

slope

blues [bluːz]	*n.* 布鲁斯音乐，蓝调 例 The history of Chicago *blues* since the 1960s has been a contradictory one, combining periods of recession and renewal. 自 20 世纪 60 年代起，芝加哥的蓝调音乐史开始互相矛盾，有衰退期，也有复兴期。
crest [krest]	*n.* 顶峰，顶点（peak）；浪尖；羽冠 *v.* 达到顶点 记 联想记忆：c + rest（休息）→ 爬到顶峰再休息吧 → 顶峰 例 The level of debt *crested* at a massive $300 billion in 2000. 2000 年的债务高达 3000 亿美元。
primitive [ˈprɪmətɪv]	*a.* 原始的，远古的（original, ancient）；简单的，粗糙的 *n.* 原始人；原始事物 记 词根记忆：prim（第一）+ it + ive（具…性质的）→ 第一的 → 原始的 例 The origins of *primitive* sea life were explained. 远古海洋生物的起源得到了解释。
extract	[ɪkˈstrækt] *vt.* 取出（*remove）；提取，榨取（distill） [ˈekstrækt] *n.* 提出物（selection）；摘录，选段；精，汁（juice） 记 词根记忆：ex（出）+ tract（拉）→ 拉出 → 取出；提取；提出物 例 Some fossils can be *extracted* from these sediments by putting the rocks in an acid bath. 把石头放到酸性溶液中，就可以将一些化石从这些沉淀物中提取出来。
comic [ˈkɑːmɪk]	*a.* 可笑的，滑稽的（funny, laughable）；喜剧的 *n.* 喜剧演员 例 There are many *comic* characters in this play. 这出戏剧中有很多喜剧人物。
buckle [ˈbʌkl]	*n.* 皮带扣环 *v.* 扣紧（fasten）；（使）变形，弯曲 例 Two plates continued to float and therefore *buckled* to form a mountain chain. 两个板块继续漂移，碰撞后形成了山脉。
deform [dɪˈfɔːrm]	*v.* （使）变形（distort） 记 词根记忆：de（离去）+ form（形式）→（使）没有形式 →（使）变形 例 The intense heat from the fire *deformed* the metal chair. 火产生的高温使金属椅子变形了。 派 deformation（*n.* 变形）；deformed（*a.* 不成形的）
ceremony [ˈserəmoʊni]	*n.* 典礼，仪式；礼节 记 联想记忆：cere（蜡）+ mony（看做 money，钱）→ 为办典礼花钱买蜡烛 → 典礼 搭 graduation ceremony 毕业典礼；without ceremony 不拘礼节；粗鲁无礼；stand on ceremony 讲究客套，拘于礼节 例 The opening *ceremony* will last approximately two and a half hours. 开幕仪式将持续约两个半小时。 派 ceremonial（*a.* 礼节的，礼仪的 *n.* 礼节，礼仪）
informative [ɪnˈfɔːrmətɪv]	*a.* 提供消息的，给予知识的；见闻广博的 例 The talk was both *informative* and entertaining. 这次谈话既让人长见识又饶富趣味。

mention [ˈmenʃn]	*v.* 提及，说起（remark） 搭 not to mention 且不说 例 Today I want to *mention* an even earlier form of transportation. 今天我想谈一谈更早期的一种运输方式。
immunity [ɪˈmjuːnəti]	*n.* 免疫力；保护（*protection）；免除，豁免（exemption） 例 The advantage of nesting on cliffs is the *immunity* seabirds give from foxes. 在悬崖上筑巢的优势是能使海鸟免于遭受狐狸的侵害。
origin [ˈɔːrɪdʒɪn]	*n.* 起源，由来；[常 *pl.*]出身，血统 记 词根记忆：ori(产生) + gin → 开始 → 起源，由来 搭 the origin of civilization 文明的起源；have origins in 源于 例 To weather broadcasters, the *origin* of winds is more important than its destination. 对天气广播员而言，风的起源比其目的地更加重要。// The *origin* of Earth's moon, the largest moon in the solar system, is still something of a mystery. 地球的卫星月亮，也是太阳系最大的卫星，其起源仍然是个谜。
arthritis [ɑːrˈθraɪtɪs]	*n.* 关节炎 记 词根记忆：arthr(连接；关节) + itis(炎症) → 关节炎 例 Some forms of *arthritis* and rheumatic diseases are known to occur more frequently in women than in men. 女性比男性更经常得某些关节炎和风湿性疾病。
commemorate [kəˈmeməreɪt]	*vt.* 庆祝，纪念（celebrate, honor） 记 词根记忆：com(共同) + memor(记住) + ate → 共同记住 → 纪念 例 Thank you for coming here this morning to *commemorate* the first balloon voyage in the United States. 感谢大家今天上午前来庆祝美国首次热气球旅行。
poisonous [ˈpɔɪzənəs]	*a.* 有毒的，有害的；恶毒的 记 来自 poison(*n.* 毒药) 例 This recent scientific discovery is about a desert shrub whose leaves can shoot up a stream of *poisonous* resin a distance of six feet. 这一最近的科学发现是关于一种沙漠灌木，其叶子能往六英尺外的地方喷射出有毒树脂。
humid [ˈhjuːmɪd]	*a.* 湿的，潮湿的（damp）；湿润的（wettish） 记 联想记忆：hum(嗡嗡声) + id → 蚊虫发出嗡嗡声，潮湿的地方多蚊虫 → 潮湿的 例 The southwestern coastal region has a *humid* mild marine climate. 西南沿海地区有着湿润的温带海洋气候。 派 humidity(*n.* 湿度)

16

□ mention □ immunity □ origin □ arthritis □ commemorate □ poisonous
□ humid

ecology [ɪˈkɑːlədʒi]	*n.* 生态；生态学；生态环境 记 词根记忆：eco（家庭）+ logy（…学）→ 研究地球这个大家庭的学科 → 生态学 例 Oil pollution could damage the fragile *ecology* of the coral reefs. 石油污染可能破坏珊瑚礁脆弱的生态环境。 派 ecological(*a.* 生态的；生态学的)；ecologist(*n.* 生态学家)
falcon [ˈfælkən]	*n.* 猎鹰，隼 例 The peregrine *falcon* feeds almost exclusively on medium-sized birds. 游隼几乎只以中等体型的鸟为食。 派 falconer(*n.* 养猎鹰者)
acting [ˈæktɪŋ]	*a.* 代理的（representative） *n.* 演戏，表演 例 She will play the *acting* coach. 她将担任代理教练一职。
deficiency [dɪˈfɪʃnsi]	*n.* 不足，缺乏（lack） 记 来自 deficient(*a.* 不足的，缺乏的) 搭 deficiency symptom 营养缺乏症状 例 Vitamin D *deficiency* can lead to serious bone diseases. 缺乏维生素 D 会导致严重的骨骼疾病。 参 sufficiency(*n.* 充足)
exchange [ɪksˈtʃeɪndʒ]	*vt.* 兑换（change）；交易（trade）；调换，交换；交流 *n.* 交易(所)；兑换；交换；交流 记 联想记忆：ex + change（更换）→ 双方相互交换 → 交易 搭 New York Stock Exchange 纽约证券交易所 例 I shook hands and *exchanged* a few words with the manager. 我与经理握了握手，交谈了几句。// We need to promote an open *exchange* of ideas and information. 我们需要促进思想和信息的公开交流。
complementary [ˌkɑːmplɪˈmentri]	*a.* 补充的；互补的 搭 complementary colors 互补色 例 The school's approach must be *complementary* to that of the parents. 学校与家长的教育方法必须相辅相成。
grudge [grʌdʒ]	*n.* 怨恨，积怨（malice） *v.* 勉强做；不情愿地给 记 联想记忆：无缘无故让人去做苦工（drudge），肯定让人心存怨恨（grudge） 搭 hold grudges 心存怨恨 例 The old man has a *grudge* against the world. 这位老人对社会心存不满。 grudge
decode [ˌdiːˈkoʊd]	*vt.* 译(码)，解(码)，破译 例 The Rosetta Stone was found by scholars trying to *decode* ancient languages. 罗塞塔石碑是由试图破译古代语言的学者们发现的。
bagel [ˈbeɪɡl]	*n.* 硬面包圈 例 There'll be *bagels*, pastries and fruit at the party. 派对上会有硬面包圈、糕点和水果。

eager [ˈiːɡər]	*a.* 渴望的，热切的（keen） 搭 eager to do 渴望做…；eager for 渴望… 例 A crowd of *eager* shareholders are waiting outside the big company. 一群焦急的股东正在这家大公司外面等待。 参 eagle（*n.* 鹰）
preserve [prɪˈzɜːrv]	*vt.* 保护，维护（*protect）；保存，保养 记 联想记忆：pre(在…前面) + serve(服务) → 提前提供服务 → 保护；保存 例 Welcome to the Forewinds Historical Farm where traditions of the past are *preserved* for visitors like you. 欢迎来到前风历史农庄，这里为你们这样的游客保留了过去的传统。 派 preservation（*n.* 保护；保存）；preservationist（*n.* 环境保护者）
indicate [ˈɪndɪkeɪt]	*v.* 表明，显示（*evidence）；指出，指示（point）；象征，预示；暗示，间接提及 记 词根记忆：in + dic（说） + ate → 说出 → 指出；象征 例 When speaking before a group, a person's tone may *indicate* unsureness or fright, confidence or calm. 在一群人面前说话时，一个人的语气可能显示其是犹疑、恐惧、自信或者镇静。 派 indication（*n.* 表明；迹象；象征）；indicative（*a.* 指示的）；indicator（*n.* 指示信号；迹象；指示器）
blossom [ˈblɑːsəm]	*n.* 花 *vi.* 开花（bloom）；长成 记 联想记忆：bloom 中间开出两朵 s 形的花 例 The trees are in *blossom*. 树上繁花似锦。// You may have noticed trees in your area *blossoming*. 你或许已经注意到，你所在地区的树木正鲜花盛开。
watercourse [ˈwɔːtərkɔːrs]	*n.* 水道，河道 记 组合词：water(水) + course(路线) → 水道 例 Pesticides are sometimes responsible for contamination of *watercourses*. 有时，杀虫剂是造成水道污染的原因。
statue [ˈstætʃuː]	*n.* 雕像（sculpture） 记 词根记忆：stat(站，立) + ue → 总是站着的 → 雕像 例 The inspiration for the *Statue* of Liberty arose from his dream of international friendship, peace, and progress. 他对全世界友谊、和平与发展的梦想是他创作自由女神像的灵感所在。 派 statuette（*n.* 小雕像） 参 status（*n.* 身份，地位）；statute（*n.* 法令）；stature（*n.* 身材）
destined [ˈdestɪnd]	*a.* 注定的（doomed）；以…为目的地的 例 They were *destined* never to meet again. 他们注定再也无法见面了。 参 destination（*n.* 目的地）

In the *indicate* entry illustration:

Meeting Room →

indicate

16

□ eager   □ preserve   □ indicate   □ blossom   □ watercourse   □ statue
□ destined

assure

[əˈʃʊr]

vt. 确保(guarantee)；使确信(convince)

记 联想记忆：as + sure(确定的) → 确保；使确信

例 People who're dieting need a variety of foods to ***assure*** a constant supply of nutrients their bodies need. 节食的人需要各种食物，以确保身体所需的营养能得到持续供应。// She ***assured*** him that the chapter was finished. 她向他保证这一章写完了。

参 ensure(*vt.* 保证)；insure(*vt.* 给…保险)；secure(*a.* 安全的)

If you would go up high, then use your own legs! Do not let yourselves carried aloft; do not seat yourselves on other people's backs and heads.

如果你想要走到高处，就要使用自己的两条腿！不要让别人把你抬到高处；不要坐在别人的背上和头上。

——德国哲学家 尼采(F. W. Nietzsche, German philosopher)

词根、词缀预习表

val	力量	prevalent *a.* 流行的	**jur**	诅咒	conjure *v.* (念咒)召唤
miser	同情	miserable *a.* 可怜的	**secu**	跟随	secular *a.* 世俗的
circum-	周围	circumstance *n.* 环境	**chrom**	颜色	chromosome *n.* 染色体
tain	拿住	contain *vt.* 包含，容纳	**mel**	蜂蜜	mellow *a.* 醇香的
nounc	讲话	announce *vt.* 宣布；通知	**mater**	母亲	maternal *a.* 母亲的

---

prevalent
[ˈprevələnt]

a. 流行的，普遍的(*common, universal)
记 词根记忆：pre(在…前面) + val(力量) + ent
→ 有走在前面的力量的 → 流行的
例 Colds are particularly *prevalent* in winter in this area. 在该地区，感冒在冬天尤其流行。

prevalent

---

exclude
[ɪkˈskluːd]

vt. 把…排除在外
记 词根记忆：ex (出，外) + clud (关闭) + e →
关出去 → 把…排除在外
例 Please don't *exclude* grains from your diet. 请不要把谷物排除在你的膳食之外。
派 exclusion(*n.* 排斥)；exclusive(*a.* 排他的)
参 conclude(*v.* 结束；作结论)

---

miserable
[ˈmɪzrəbl]

a. 痛苦的(tearing)；可怜的(wretched)；令人不快的
记 词根记忆：miser(同情) + able(能…的) → 能令人同情的 → 可怜的
例 I spent a *miserable* weekend alone at home. 我独自一人在家度过了一个惨兮兮的周末。

---

algebra
[ˈældʒɪbrə]

n. 代数
派 algebraic(*a.* 代数的)
例 It is here that *algebra* was further developed. 正是在这里代数得到了进一步发展。

---

destructive
[dɪˈstrʌktɪv]

a. 破坏性的，毁灭性的(ruinous)
搭 destructive effects 破坏性影响
例 The *destructive* power of fungi is impressive. 真菌的破坏力令人惊叹。

---

projector
[prəˈdʒektər]

n. 放映机, 幻灯机, 投影仪

例 *Projectors* have been widely used in class in developed countries. 在发达国家, 投影仪已在课堂上得到广泛使用。//
A: This *projector* is out of order and I need it for my presentation.
B: There's a spare in the storeroom.
A: 这台投影仪出问题了, 我做报告要用。
B: 仓库有一台备用的。

circumstance
[ˈsɜːrkəmstæns]

n. 环境, 条件(environment); 境况, (尤指)经济状况(condition, situation)
记 词根记忆: circum(周围) + st(站立) + ance → 存在于周围的 → 环境
例 I know I can trust him in any *circumstance*. 我知道我在任何情况下都能相信他。// Grants are awarded according to your financial *circumstances*. 补助金根据经济状况发放。

efficient
[ɪˈfɪʃnt]

a. 有效的, 有效率的(effective); 有能力的, 能胜任的
记 词根记忆: ef(出) + fic(做) + ient → 能做出来的 → 有能力的
例 Comparing the new car to a moderately fuel-*efficient* conventional car, it can go 400~700km on a tank of gas. 把这辆新车与燃油效率适中的传统车相比, 它用一箱油就能跑 400~700 公里。
派 inefficient(*a.* 效率低的)
参 effective(*a.* 有效的)

replicate
[ˈreplɪkeɪt]

v. 复制(duplicate); 再制, 再生
记 词根记忆: re(再, 又) + plic(重叠) + ate → 一再重叠 → 复制
例 The virus *replicates* by attaching to a cell and injecting its nucleic acid. 病毒通过附着在细胞上, 并往其中输入核酸来实现复制。

hazel
[ˈheɪzl]

n. 榛树 *a.* 浅赤褐色的
例 *Hazel* is widely distributed throughout much of Europe. 榛树广泛分布于欧洲。

reward
[rɪˈwɔːrd]

n. 报答, 奖赏, 报酬(prize, pay) *vt.* 奖赏, 奖励, 给以报酬
例 My flight was done with no expectation of *reward*. 我飞行不是为了得到奖赏。// The winner will be *rewarded*. 优胜者将会获奖。
派 rewarding(*a.* 报酬高的; 值得做的, 有益的)
参 award(*vt.* 授予)

sewerage
[ˈsuːərɪdʒ]

n. 排水系统(drainage); 污水处理; 污水(waste)
例 About 4 billion tonnes of untreated *sewerage* flows daily into the river. 每天约有 40 亿公吨未经处理的污水流入这条河。

even
[ˈiːvn]

a. 平滑的, 平坦的; 平稳的, 均匀的; 均衡的; 平均的; 偶数的 *ad.* 甚至, 连; 甚至可以说 *v.* (使)平坦; (使)相等
例 The two teams were pretty *even*. 两队不分上下。// House prices keep rising and falling but they should eventually *even* out. 房价一直时涨时落, 但最终应该会趋于稳定。
派 evenly(*ad.* 平坦地; 均匀地); evenness(*n.* 平均)

intense [ɪnˈtens]	*a.* 强烈的(*extreme)；热切的(*acute)；激烈的
	例 The metal burned with an *intense* flash. 金属燃烧时发出了强光。// It was a period of *intense* activity. 那是活动剧烈的时期。
	派 intensity(*n.* 强烈，强度，烈度)；intensive(*a.* 密集的；彻底的；集约的)

beam [biːm]	*v.* 面露喜色；发射(无线电信号等)，播送；照射 *n.* (粒子的)束，波束，光线；梁(timber, bar)；笑容，喜色
	记 联想记忆：be + am → 做我自己，成为国家的栋梁 → 梁
	搭 a laser beam 激光束；a beam of sunlight 一束阳光；off beam 不正确，错误
	例 Live pictures of the ceremony were *beamed* around the world. 典礼经实况转播传到世界各地。

crossing [ˈkrɔːsɪŋ]	*n.* 十字路口，人行横道；过境处；交叉点；穿越，横渡
	搭 grade crossing 铁路轨道；平面交叉
	例 He was arrested by guards at the border *crossing*. 他在边境过境处被卫兵逮捕了。
	参 crossroad(*n.* 十字路口)；intersection(*n.* 十字路口，交叉口)

dedication [ˌdedɪˈkeɪʃn]	*n.* 献身，奉献；献词；奉献仪式
	例 Abraham Lincoln delivered his most famous address at the *dedication* of the soldiers' cemetery in Gettysburg. 亚伯拉罕·林肯在葛底斯堡士兵墓地揭幕礼上发表了他最著名的演说。

rim [rɪm]	*n.* (圆形物体的)边，轮缘；边界 *vt.* 给…镶边
	记 联想记忆：打靶(aim)不能打边(rim)
	例 Unluckily, his shot hit the *rim* of the hoop and bounced out. 不走运的是，他投篮砸到了篮筐边沿，弹了出来。

jelly [ˈdʒeli]	*n.* 果冻，胶状物
	记 联想记忆：果冻(jelly)吃多了胃(belly)会胀
	参 jellyfish(*n.* 海蜇)

contain [kənˈteɪn]	*vt.* 包含，容纳(include)；控制(control)；防止…蔓延(或恶化)
	记 词根记忆：con(共同) + tain(拿住) → 全部拿住 → 包含，容纳
	例 The committee's report *contains* mistakes. 委员会的报告有错误。// Starting in the late 18th century, the United States *contained* increasing numbers of such people. 从 18 世纪末开始，这种人在美国越来越多。
	派 container(*n.* 容器；集装箱)；containment(*n.* 控制；遏制)

stunt [stʌnt]	*vt.* 阻碍生长；遏制 *n.* 特技表演；噱头；愚蠢行为
	记 联想记忆：stun(震惊) + t → 电影里的特技表演让人震惊 → 特技表演
	例 His illness had not *stunted* his creativity. 疾病没有扼杀他的创造力。// She did all her own *stunts*. 所有特技都是她自己完成的。

17

frame [freɪm]	*n.* 框架；总的思想，体系 *vt.* 设计，构成(*pose)；给…镶框；表达 记 联想记忆：很有名望(fame)，所以将照片镶在框(frame)里以示尊敬 搭 frame of minds 心态，心绪 例 In this course we hope to look at literature in the *frame* of its social and historical context. 在这门课程中，我们希望从社会和历史背景的整体结构来看文学。 参 framework(*n.* 构架，框架；机制)
vast [væst]	*a.* 巨大的；大量的；范围广的(large, broad, extensive) 记 联想记忆：古老的东方(east)地大(vast)物博 搭 in vast numbers 大量的；the vast majority 绝大多数 例 In the *vast* majority of cases, this should not be a problem. 在绝大多数情况下，这应该不成问题。 派 vastness(*n.* 巨大)；vastly(*ad.* 广大地)
characteristic [ˌkærəktəˈrɪstɪk]	*n.* 特性，特征(property) *a.* 特有的；典型的(typical) 例 Different types of matter have different *characteristics*. 不同类型的物质有着不同的特性。 派 characteristically(*ad.* 独特地)
squash [skwɑːʃ]	*v.* 压碎，挤压；(使)挤进，塞入；制止 *n.* 软式墙网球，壁球；果汁汽水 记 联想记忆：s + quash(取消) → 壁球比赛取消了，大家很失望 → 壁球 例 The statement was an attempt to *squash* the rumors. 这份声明旨在辟谣。
announce [əˈnaʊns]	*vt.* 宣布(*herald, proclaim)；通知(notify)；声称，宣称；广播，播音 记 词根记忆：an(=ad 向) + nounc(讲话) + e → 向他人讲话 → 宣布；通知；广播 例 It was *announced* that new speed restrictions would be introduced. 据宣布，将出台新的限速规定。// They *announced* that the flight would be delayed. 广播通知，该航班将误点。 派 announcement(*n.* 宣告；发表)；announcer(*n.* 广播员，播音员)
dedicate [ˈdedɪkeɪt]	*vt.* (to)致力于，奉献给(*devote)；题献词于(著作等)上 记 词根记忆：de(表加强) + dic(分配，分派) + ate → 为…分派 → 致力于 例 The man *dedicated* his life to fighting crime in the city. 那个人致力于和城市中的犯罪行为作斗争。
personal [ˈpɜːrsənl]	*a.* 个人的，私人的(private, individual)；亲自的 例 He doesn't like to ask *personal* questions. 他不喜欢提私人问题。 派 personalize(*vt.* 使人性化，使人格化)；personally(*ad.* 就本人而言；亲自；个别地)
simmer [ˈsɪmər]	*vi.* 充满(难以控制的感情，尤指怒火)；煨，炖 *n.* 煨，炖 记 联想记忆：在夏天(summer)，人比较容易充满难以控制的怒火(simmer) 例 You are not going to like your new neighbors when you do meet them if you keep on *simmering*. 如果你一肚子气，那么当你见到新邻居时就不会喜欢他们。

mate [meɪt]	*n.* 配偶(spouse); 朋友, 伙伴; 同事; (商船的)大副 *v.* (使)交配(copulate) 例 They've been best *mates* since school. 他们从上学起就是最要好的朋友。 派 mating(*n.* 鸟兽等的交配, 交尾) 参 classmate(*n.* 同学); workmate(*n.* 同事); roommate(*n.* 室友)
entrench [ɪnˈtrentʃ]	*vt.* 使(观念等)根深蒂固, 牢固确立(establish, root) 例 Sexism is deeply *entrenched* in our society. 性别歧视在我们这个社会根深蒂固。
acquiesce [ˌækwiˈes]	*vi.* 默许, 默认 记 词根记忆: ac(表加强) + qui(安静的) + esce → 变得非常安静 → 默许, 默认 例 I have to *acquiesce* to his decision even though I have a different opinion. 尽管我有不同的看法, 但我不得不默认他的决定。 派 acquiescent(*a.* 默认的, 顺从的); acquiescence(*n.* 默许)
ensconce [ɪnˈskɑːns]	*vt.* 使安顿, 安置, 使安坐 记 联想记忆: en(进入) + sconce(小堡垒) → 进入小堡垒 → 使安顿, 安置, 使安坐 例 She *ensconced* herself in a comfortable armchair. 她安坐在一把舒适的扶手椅上。
conjure [ˈkʌndʒər]	*v.* 变魔术, 变戏法; (念咒)召唤 记 词根记忆: con(共同) + jur(诅咒) + e → 共同诅咒 → (念咒)召唤 例 My mother can *conjure* up a fantastic meal in an hour. 我妈妈能在一个小时内变戏法般地做出一顿美味的饭菜。
middleman [ˈmɪdlmæn]	*n.* 中间人, 调解人; 经纪人 例 I decided to contact the retailers directly, without any *middleman*. 我打算直接联系零售商, 不经过任何中间人。
secular [ˈsekjələr]	*a.* 现世的; 世俗的; 非宗教的 记 词根记忆: secu(跟随) + lar → 做事总是跟随别人, 随波逐流 → 世俗的 搭 secular music 世俗音乐 例 Lisa believes in eternal love in this *secular* world. 莉萨相信这个世俗的世界有着永恒的爱情。
chromosome [ˈkroʊməsoʊm]	*n.* 染色体 记 词根记忆: chrom(颜色) + o + som(体) + e → 染色体 例 *Chromosomes* also determine the sex of animals. 染色体也决定着动物的性别。
righteous [ˈraɪtʃəs]	*a.* 正直的, 公正的; 正义的, 正当的 记 联想记忆: right(正直, 公正) + eous → 正直的, 公正的 例 The judgment of the court is true and *righteous*. 法院的裁判是完全真实且公道的。

audible
[ˈɔːdəbl]

a. 听得见的

记 词根记忆：aud(听) + ible(能…的) → 听得见的

例 I was sitting in the back row of the theater, and the music was barely *audible*. 我坐在剧院的后排，勉强能听见音乐声。

mellow
[ˈmeloʊ]

a. 醇香的；柔和的；成熟的 *v.* (使)醇香；(使)柔和；(使)成熟

记 词根记忆：mel(蜂蜜) + low → 散发蜂蜜般的醇香 → 醇香的

搭 mellow out 怡然自得

例 The *mellow* wine is as inviting as freshly served desserts. 醇香的酒和刚端上来的甜点一样诱人。

deplore
[dɪˈplɔːr]

vt. 悲叹，哀叹，公开谴责

记 词根记忆：de(表加强) + plor(流泪，哭泣) + e → 非常伤心地哭泣 → 悲叹

例 What *deplored* Jack greatly was his wife left him. 最令杰克心痛的是他妻子离开了他。

laborious
[ləˈbɔːriəs]

a. (工作等)艰苦的，费力的，艰难的；(人)勤劳的

记 联想记忆：labor(劳动) + ious → 需要劳动的 → 艰苦的

例 It looks like a long and *laborious* task. 看起来这将是一项长期且艰巨的任务。

dispel
[dɪˈspel]

vt. 驱散，驱逐；消除

记 词根记忆：dis(分离) + pel(推) → 往不同的方向推 → 驱散

例 This experiment would *dispel* some doubts which students might have about this theory. 这一实验会消除学生们对这个理论可能持有的一些疑虑。

esteem
[ɪˈstiːm]

n./vt. 尊重，敬重

记 联想记忆：e(音似：一) + stee(看做 steel，钢铁) + m(看做 man，人) → 一个有着钢铁般意志的人值得尊敬 → 尊重，敬重

搭 have great esteem for 对…大为敬佩

例 In this situation, too much self-*esteem* can be very dangerous. 在这种情况下，太多的自尊可能会很危险。

singular
[ˈsɪŋɡjələr]

a. 单数的；突出的，卓越的(outstanding)；异常的(eccentric, peculiar)

搭 singular form 单数形式

例 People say excellence is not a *singular* act, but a habit. 人们认为优秀不是单一的行为，而是一种习惯。

maternal
[məˈtɜːrnl]

a. 母亲的，母系的

记 词根记忆：mater(母亲) + nal → 母亲的

例 The sight of those orphans kindled the woman's *maternal* instinct. 看到那些孤儿们，那位妇女的母性本能被激发了。

enthusiastic
[ɪnˌθuːziˈæstɪk]

a. 热情的，热心的

例 The wonderful speech by the President drew *enthusiastic* applause. 总统精彩的演讲博得了热烈的掌声。

□ audible   □ mellow   □ deplore   □ laborious   □ dispel   □ esteem
□ singular   □ maternal   □ enthusiastic

alienate	*vt.* 使疏远，使不友好；转让，让渡(财产等)
[ˈeɪliəneɪt]	记 词根记忆：ali(其他的) + en + ate(使…) → 使变成他者 → 使疏远
	例 You'd better not *alienate* yourself from your colleagues and friends. 你最好不要与同事和朋友疏远开来。

fabulous	*a.* 寓言式的；难以置信的；极好的
[ˈfæbjələs]	记 词根记忆：fa(说) + bul + ous → 代代相传，变成寓言 → 寓言式的
	例 His descriptions about the things he met during his travels were *fabulous*. 他对旅途中所见所闻的描述太令人难以置信了。

rectify	*vt.* 矫正，纠正；整顿
[ˈrektɪfaɪ]	记 词根记忆：rect(直的) + ify(使…) → 使变直 → 矫正，纠正；整顿
	例 Now we have a chance to *rectify* it, and we must take action. 现在，我们有机会改正它，必须行动起来。

circuit	*n.* 电路；线路(circular line)；巡回；环行；环行路线
[ˈsɜːrkɪt]	记 词根记忆：circ(圆，环形) + uit → 巡回
	搭 short circuit 短路；closed circuit 闭合电路
	例 The Earth takes a year to make a *circuit* of the Sun. 地球绕太阳运行一周需要一年的时间。

| **mathematics** | *n.* 数学(math) |
| [ˌmæθəˈmætɪks] | 例 She had no formal education in *mathematics*. 她没有受过有关数学的正规教育。 |

scuffle	*n./vi.* 扭打，混战
[ˈskʌfl]	记 联想记忆：scu(看做 scar，伤疤) + ffle → 伤疤是参加混战的结果 → 扭打，混战
	例 It is said that a *scuffle* broke out between the two teams the night after the match. 据说在比赛后的那晚，两队之间爆发了混战。

opposed	*a.* 反对的(opposite)；截然不同的
[əˈpoʊzd]	例 They are bitterly *opposed* to abortion. 他们强烈反对堕胎。// The have *opposed* views on the question. 在这个问题上他们的观点大相径庭。
	派 opposing(*a.* 相反的；对立的)；opposition(*n.* 反对；对手)

construct	[kənˈstrʌkt] *vt.* 建造(build)；创立(found) [ˈkɑːnstrʌkt] *n.* 构想，观念
	记 词根记忆：con(表加强) + struct(建筑) → 建造；创立
	例 The Anasazi lived in houses *constructed* of adobe and wood. 阿那萨奇人居住在泥砖和木头建造的房子里。
	派 reconstruct(*vt.* 重建，改造)

visible	*a.* 看得见的，明显的(observable, noticeable)
[ˈvɪzəb]	记 词根记忆：vis(看) + ible(能…的) → 看得见的，明显的
	例 The impact caused an explosion clearly *visible* from the Earth. 碰撞造成了爆炸，在地球上清晰可见。
	派 visibility(*n.* 可见性；可见度)；visibly(*ad.* 明显地)；invisible(*a.* 看不见的，无形的)

visible

invisible

juice [dʒuːs]	*vt.* 榨出(水果或蔬菜的)汁液 *n.* 汁，液 例 *Juice* two lemons. 榨两个柠檬的汁。
rainfall [ˈreɪnfɔːl]	*n.* 降雨；降雨量 记 组合词：rain(雨) + fall(下降) → 降雨 例 There has been below average *rainfall* this month. 这个月的降雨低于平均降雨量。
mundane [mʌnˈdeɪn]	*a.* 世俗的(earthly)；平凡的(*ordinary) 记 词根记忆：mund(世界) + ane → 关于全世界的 → 世俗的；平凡的 例 The thinker or philosopher stood apart from this *mundane* world. 思想家或哲学家与世俗世界格格不入。
granite [ˈgrænɪt]	*n.* 花岗岩，花岗石 记 词根记忆：gran(=grain 颗粒) + ite → 颗粒状石头 → 花岗岩 例 This building is made of white *granite* and marble. 这座建筑是由白花岗岩和大理石建造而成的。
prescribe [prɪˈskraɪb]	*v.* 开处方；规定；指示(assign) 记 词根记忆：pre(在…前面) + scrib(写) + e → 内科 prescribe 预先写好 → 规定 例 The pills you *prescribed* are giving me a headache. 服完你开的药，我觉得头疼。 派 prescribed(*a.* 规定的，指定的) 参 ascribe(*vt.* 归因于)；inscribe(*vt.* 铭刻)
rare [rer]	*a.* 稀有的，罕见的(*infrequent)；(肉类)半熟的 记 联想记忆：稀有的(rare)东西要小心(care)对待 例 They are a *rare* breed. 它们是稀有品种。// I prefer my meat *rare*. 我要半熟的肉。 派 rarely(*ad.* 稀有地，罕见地)；rarity(*n.* 稀有，罕见)
abound [əˈbaʊnd]	*vi.* 富于(flourish)；大量存在(teem)；充满(overflow) 记 联想记忆：a + bound(边界) → 没有边界 → 大量存在；充满 例 The state *abounds* in colonial architecture. 这个州有很多殖民时期的建筑。
pure [pjʊr]	*a.* 纯洁的(virgin)；纯净的；完全的(absolute)；纯理论的，抽象的 例 Is the cup made of *pure* gold? 这只杯子是纯金的吗？ 派 purely(*ad.* 纯粹地，完全地)
criticize [ˈkrɪtɪsaɪz]	*v.* 批评；吹毛求疵，非难；评论 记 词根记忆：crit(判断) + ic + ize → 作出判断 → 评论 例 The decision to build permanent settlements on the beach was *criticized* by environmental groups. 环保组织批评了在海滩上建立永久居住区的决定。
behave [bɪˈheɪv]	*v.* 行为，表现(conduct)；表现得体，有礼貌；(事物)作出反应 记 联想记忆：be + have(有) → 所拥有的 → 行为，表现 例 He *behaved* like a true gentleman. 他表现得像位真正的绅士。

194
□ juice　　　□ rainfall　　　□ mundane　　　□ granite　　　□ prescribe　　　□ rare
□ abound　　　□ pure　　　□ criticize　　　□ behave

alumnus [əˈlʌmnəs]	*n.* [*pl.* alumni] 男校友 例 We got the *alumni* to make donations. 我们让男校友进行捐赠。
customs [ˈkʌstəmz]	*n.* 关税，进口税(duties, tax)；海关 搭 customs duties 进口税；customs union 关税同盟 例 The *Customs* have seized large quantities of smuggled heroin. 海关查获了大量走私的海洛因。
memo [ˈmemoʊ]	*n.* 备忘录 例 Please write a *memo* to be attached to the notice board when inviting your colleagues to join in the training program. 邀请你的同事参加培训项目时，请写一份备忘录贴在公告板上。
ascend [əˈsend]	*v.* 上升，升高；攀登(*climb) 例 The air became colder as we *ascended*. 随着我们往上攀登，空气就更加寒冷了。// He *ascended* to the peak of sporting achievement. 他达到了运动成就的顶峰。
press [pres]	*n.* 报刊；新闻界，新闻工作者；报道，评论；出版社；印刷厂；压，按，挤 *v.* 压，按，挤；压榨，压迫；催促，逼迫 搭 press conference 新闻发布会，记者招待会 例 The event is bound to attract wide *press* coverage. 这个事件一定会在各报刊广泛报道。// I'll be really *pressed* to get it done. 办这件事情我会顶着很大的压力。
fiction [ˈfɪkʃn]	*n.* 小说；虚构，编造 记 发音记忆："费口舌" → 费口舌瞎编 → 小说 例 Such claims make it difficult for the general public to separate fact from *fiction*. 这种声明使一般公众很难分辨虚实。 派 fictional(*a.* 虚构的；小说式的)
absorb [əbˈsɔːrb]	*vt.* 吸收(take in, engage)；理解，掌握；吸引…的注意，使全神贯注；使并入，同化 记 词根记忆：ab(离去) + sorb(吸) → 吸收 例 This gamma radiation is *absorbed* by atoms inside the Sun. 这种伽马射线被太阳内部的原子吸收。// Mary is so smart that she just *absorbs* any book she reads. 玛丽真聪明，读什么书都能领会。 派 absorbent(*a.* 能吸收的)；absorbed(*a.* 全神贯注的)
framework [ˈfreɪmwɜːrk]	*n.* 框架，构架(skeleton, structure)；原则，准则；机制，结构 例 This law will provide a *framework* for employers and employees to sign a contract. 这部法律将给雇主和雇员提供一个签订合同的准则。
install [ɪnˈstɔːl]	*vt.* 安置，安装(fix) 记 词根记忆：in(进入) + stall(放) → 放进 → 安置，安装 例 This morning the carpenters *installed* the new kitchen cabinets. 今天上午木匠安装了新的餐具柜。 派 installation(*n.* 安装)

17

来投资吧~
好处多多哦

外资

absorb

plaque [plæk]	*n.* 匾额；牙斑 例 There is a rock behind the bushes with a rusty *plaque* riveted it. 灌木丛后面有一块石头，上面钉有一块锈迹斑斑的匾额。
hypothesize [haɪˈpɑːθəsaɪz]	*v.* 假定，假设(*speculate, suppose) 记 词根记忆：hypo(在…下面) + thes(放) + ize → 放在下面，还不作为正式的 → 假定，假设 例 One researcher *hypothesized* that there were two parts to the explanation. 一位研究人员假设这个解释包含两个部分。 参 hypothetical(*a.* 假定的，假设的)
tedium [ˈtiːdiəm]	*n.* 单调，乏味(boredom) 例 Their ancestors had traditionally relieved the *tedium* of life. 他们的祖先以传统方式缓解了生活的乏味。 参 tedious(*a.* 单调乏味的，沉闷的)
layer [ˈler]	*n.* 层，层次 记 来自 lay(*n.* 层面) 例 The filling was a soft *layer* of wool which had been cleaned and separated. 填充物是一层经过清洗并分拣好了的柔软的羊毛。
deliver [dɪˈlɪvər]	*v.* 传送，传递(transmit, pass)；发表，宣布(state)；履行诺言；移交，交出；接生 记 词根记忆：de(离开) + liver(=liber 自由) → 使离开，得到自由 → 传送；移交 例 They'll *deliver* a bucket at no charge. 他们将免费递送一桶。// The jury finally *delivered* its verdict. 陪审团终于宣布了裁决。 派 delivery(*n.* 投递；送交)
versatile [ˈvɜːrsətl]	*a.* 多才多艺的(talented, competent)；多用途的(all-purpose) 记 词根记忆：vers(转) + atile → 玩得转的 → 多才多艺的 例 Her unique background made her an unusually interesting and *versatile* human being. 独特的背景使她成为非常有趣和多才多艺的人。 派 versatility(*n.* 多才多艺；多功能性)
thrive [θraɪv]	*vi.* 茂盛(flourish)；茁壮成长(grow vigorously)；兴旺，繁荣 记 联想记忆：th + rive(看做 river，河) → 古时大河都是文明的发源地 → 茂盛 例 Fungi *thrive* in a wide variety of environments. 真菌在多种环境中繁衍。// Why have ants been able to *thrive* for such a long time? 为什么蚂蚁能茁壮成长这么久？
plate [pleɪt]	*n.* 盘子；(金属)板条，板材；号码牌 *vt.* 镀，电镀；(用金属板)覆盖 例 The tanks were mainly constructed of steel *plates*. 这些坦克车主要是用钢板制造的。

anthropology [ˌænθrəˈpɑːlədʒi]	*n.* 人类学 🔠 词根记忆: anthrop(人，人类) + ology(…学) → 人类学 🔠 The science of *anthropology* is divided into two major disciplines, physical *anthropology* and cultural *anthropology*. 人类学被分为体质人类学和文化人类学两大学科。 🔠 anthropological(*a.* 人类学的); anthropologist(*n.* 人类学家)
regardless [rɪˈɡɑːrdləs]	*ad.* (of 不顾，不管(no matter what) 🔠 联想记忆: regard(关心) + less(无) → 不关心的 → 不顾，不管 🔠 Chicago would become a great city *regardless* of the disadvantageous characteristics of the available site. 尽管其可用位置具有不利因素，芝加哥仍将成为一座伟大的城市。 🔠 disregard(*vt.* 不理会)
domestic [dəˈmestɪk]	*a.* 国内的(internal); 家庭的(household); 驯养的 🔠 词根记忆: dom(家) + estic → 家庭的; 驯养的 🔠 domestic market 国内市场 🔠 At twelve she left home and was in *domestic* service until twenty-seven. 她自 12 岁离开家后就从事家政服务，一直做到 27 岁。 🔠 domestically (*ad.* 国内地); domesticate (*vt.* 驯养，驯化); domestication(*n.* 驯养，驯化) 好粗野 domestic
fume [fjuːm]	*vi.* 冒烟; (对…)大为恼火 🔠 词根记忆: fum(烟) + e → 冒烟 🔠 He sat in the car, silently *fuming* at the traffic jam. 他坐在车里，对交通堵塞大为恼火。
pit [pɪt]	*vt.* 使有坑，使…表面有斑点 *n.* 大坑，深坑(*hole, cavity); 矿井(mine); 陷阱(trap) 🔠 联想记忆: 猪(pig)拱了个大坑(pit) 🔠 pit...against... 使竞争; 使经受考验 🔠 The champion was *pitted* against the young contender. 冠军与年轻的竞争者对垒。
quota [ˈkwoʊtə]	*n.* 配额，限额，定额(ration) 🔠 发音记忆: "阔的" → 出手阔绰，没有限额 → 限额 🔠 The club president announced that each member had a *quota* of ten tickets to sell for the talent show. 俱乐部主席宣布每个成员都得销售十张才艺表演会的票。 我要钓鲨鱼
barb [bɑːrb]	*n.* 鱼钩，倒钩; 挖苦的话 🔠 联想记忆: barb 原也指倒翘的胡子，后来胡子一词变为 beard barb

17

harness [ˈhɑːrnɪs]	*vt.* 利用…产生动力；给(马等)上挽具 *n.* 马具 记 联想记忆：har(看做 hard，结实的) + ness → 马具必须结实 → 马具 例 The waterwheel is a mechanism designed to *harness* energy from a source instead of animals. 水车是利用能源而非动物来产生动力的机械装置。
opportunity [ˌɑːpərˈtuːnəti]	*n.* 机会，时机(chance, occasion) 例 There was no *opportunity* for further discussion. 没有机会深入讨论了。// I'd like to take this *opportunity* to thank my classmates for their support. 我谨借此机会感谢同学们的支持。
initial [ɪˈnɪʃl]	*a.* 开始的，最初的 *n.* 词首大写字母 记 词根记忆：in(向内) + it(走) + ial → 开始的，最初的 例 The bank manager changed the date of the *initial* interview. 银行经理变更了第一轮面试的日期。
pebble [ˈpebl]	*n.* 小圆石，鹅卵石 例 You are not the only *pebble* on the beach. 你并非必不可少的人。
devoid [dɪˈvɔɪd]	*a.* 全无的(empty) 记 联想记忆：de(表加强) + void(空的) → 全无的 例 The hot air is *devoid* of even the slightest amount of moisture. 热空气中没有一点水汽。 参 void(*a.* 空的)；voidance(*n.* 排出，放出；取消)；avoid(*vt.* 避免)

When an end is lawful and obligatory, the indispensable means to it are also lawful and obligatory.

如果一个目的是正当而必须要达到的，则达到这个目的的必要手段也是正当而必须采取的。

——美国政治家 林肯(Abraham Lincoln, American statesman)

词根、词缀预习表

ambl	走	amble vi. 缓行	linqu	离开	delinquency n. 失职
dorm	睡眠	dormancy n. 休眠；催眠状态	cur	跑	concur v. 同时发生
vi	道路	viable a. 可行的	radic	根	eradicate vt. 根除
auc	提高	auction n./v. 拍卖	patr	父亲	patron n. 赞助人
chron	时间	chronicle n. 编年史	ferm	热	ferment v. (使)发酵

amble
[ˈæmbl]

vi. 缓行，漫步(stroll, wander)

记 词根记忆：ambl(=ambul 走) + e → 缓行

例 We *ambled* down to the beach. 我们漫步向海滩走去。

sharpen
[ˈʃɑːrpən]

v. 削尖，磨锐；使敏锐；(使)变得清晰

记 联想记忆：sharp(锋利的) + en(使…) → 使锋利的 → 削尖，磨快

例 I haven't gotten around to *sharpening* the knife yet. 我一直没空磨那把刀。// The outline of the trees *sharpened* as it grew lighter. 随着天色转亮，树的轮廓变得清晰了。

参 shorten(*v.* 缩短，变短)；strengthen(*vt.* 加强，巩固)；lengthen(*v.* 延长)

dormancy
[ˈdɔːrmənsi]

n. 休眠；催眠状态；隐匿

记 词根记忆：dorm(睡眠) + ancy → 休眠；催眠状态

例 That huge volcano erupted after twenty years of *dormancy*. 那座巨大的火山在休眠了 20 年后再次爆发。

dormancy

urge
[ɜːrdʒ]

v. 促进，力劝(impel)；驱赶，驱策 *n.* 强烈的欲望，冲动

例 Do you think we should *urge* Bob to study Spanish? 你觉得我们应该劝鲍勃学习西班牙语吗？

派 urgent(*a.* 紧急的，迫切的；催促的)；urgency(*n.* 紧急，紧急情况)

viable
[ˈvaɪəbl]

a. 可行的，可实施的(feasible)；可生长发育的

记 词根记忆：vi(道路) + able(能…的) → 有路的 → 可行的

例 Bessemer's process for converting iron into steel made the material more commercially *viable*. 贝西默把铁转化成钢的方法使这种原料在商业上更为可行。

派 viability(*n.* 可行性；生存能力)

bland [blænd]	*a.* 平淡的，乏味的；清淡的；沉稳的 记 发音记忆："布蓝的" → 布是清淡的蓝色 → 清淡的；注意不要和 blend（*n./v.* 混合）相混 例 This pizza tastes *bland*. There is not enough sauce. 这个比萨饼吃起来没味道，调味汁不够。
contribute [kən'trɪbjuːt]	*v.* 贡献，捐赠（donate）；有助于（*promote）；投稿（submit articles to） 记 词根记忆：con(完全) + tribut(给予) + e → 完全给予 → 贡献，捐赠 例 I believe the social elements *contributed* to the development of bebop music. 我认为社会因素促进了比博普爵士音乐的发展。// She often *contributes* to the fashionable journal. 她经常给时尚杂志投稿。 派 contribution(*n.* 贡献；捐献物；稿件) 参 attribute(*n.* 属性); distribute(*vt.* 分发)
trilogy ['trɪlədʒi]	*n.* (书籍、电影等的)三部剧，三部曲 例 He was best known for his *trilogy* "Jiliu", which was written between 1931 and 1940, and included three semi-autobiographical novels. 他因"激流"三部曲而最富盛名，这个三部曲写于1931-1940年间，包括三部半自传的小说。
embed [ɪm'bed]	*vt.* 把…嵌入(或插入)；使深留脑中 记 联想记忆：em(里面) + bed(床) → 把…嵌入床中 → 把…嵌入 搭 be embedded in 植根于 例 Some companies *embedded* wireless modules into laptops, making it easier to work. 有些公司把无线模块嵌入笔记本电脑内，使工作更加便捷。
auction ['ɔːkʃn]	*n./v.* 拍卖 记 词根记忆：auc (提高) + tion → 提高价格 → 拍卖 例 *Auctions* are another popular form of occasional trade. 拍卖是临时交易的另一种流行形式。
feedback ['fiːdbæk]	*n.* 反馈；反馈信息 记 组合词：feed(喂养；提供) + back(反) → 反馈 搭 information feedback 信息反馈 例 I'm waiting for your *feedback* on the proposal I handed in last week. 我等着你对我上周提交的提案的反馈意见。
chronicle ['krɑːnɪkl]	*vt.* 把…载入编年史 *n.* 编年史，年代记 记 词根记忆：chron(时间) + ic + le → 按时间编排 → 编年史 例 His achievements are *chronicled* in a new biography out this week. 他的成就已载入本周将出版的一本新传记。

sober [ˈsoʊbər]	*a.* 清醒的，未醉的；持重的，冷静的；(颜色)素净的 *v.* (使)清醒；(使)变得冷静 搭 sober up (使)清醒 例 On *sober* reflection, I don't think I really need a car after all. 冷静地想了一下，我觉得我其实并不需要车。
taboo [təˈbuː]	*n.* (文化或宗教习俗方面的)禁忌，忌讳；禁止，避讳 *a.* 忌讳的 记 发音记忆："特不" → 特不准干的事 → 禁忌，忌讳 搭 taboo word 禁忌词 例 In every culture, there are topics that are *taboos* to talk about. 每种文化中都有一些不能谈论的禁忌话题。
prioritize [praɪˈɔːrətaɪz]	*v.* 划分优先顺序；优先处理 记 来自 priority(*n.* 优先事项；优先，重点) 例 You should learn to *prioritize* your work when you are given several tasks at the same time. 当你在同一时间被分配了几项工作时，得学会划分优先顺序。
impel [ɪmˈpel]	*vt.* 驱使，促使 记 词根记忆：im(在…里面) + pel(推) → 在里面推 → 驱使 例 Inflation *impels* families to cut back on spending. 通货膨胀迫使家庭削减开支。
delinquency [dɪˈlɪŋkwənsi]	*n.* 行为不良；过失，失职 记 词根记忆：de(分开) + linqu(离开) + ency(名词后缀) → 离开自己的岗位 → 失职 例 Juvenile *delinquency* becomes a serious social problem in this region now. 如今，青少年犯罪成为该地区一个严重的社会问题。
entourage [ˈɑːntʊrɑːʒ]	*n.* 〈总称〉随从，随行人员 记 联想记忆：en(进入) + tour(游行) + age(集体名词后缀) → 一起游行的人 → 随从 例 The prince and his entire *entourage* were allowed to go into the palace. 王子以及他的所有随从可以进出宫殿。
concur [kənˈkɜːr]	*v.* 同时发生；意见一致 记 词根记忆：con(共同) + cur(跑) → 一起跑 → 同时发生 例 Some people run after wealth in order to be happy, but wealth and happiness do not always *concur*. 有些人为了幸福而追逐财富，但财富与幸福并非总是并存的。
ridicule [ˈrɪdɪkjuːl]	*vt.* 嘲笑，奚落(make fun of) *n.* 嘲笑，奚落(mockery) 记 词根记忆：rid(笑) + icule → 嘲笑，奚落 例 You can argue with reason but not with *ridicule*. 你可以用理性与他们抗辩，而不是嘲弄。
mischievous [ˈmɪstʃɪvəs]	*a.* 恶作剧的，顽皮的，淘气的；恶意的 记 来自 mischief(*n.* 恶作剧，淘气；恶意) 例 I remember Mark was pretty *mischievous* when he was a kid. 我记得马克小的时候很顽皮。

18

ensue [ɪnˈsuː]	*vi.* 继而发生，接着发生 记 联想记忆：确保(ensure)了的事情就会接着发生(ensue) 例 If the fire wasn't put out, a disaster would *ensue*. 如果火没能扑灭，一场灾难就会接踵而至。
consensus [kənˈsensəs]	*n.* 共识，一致同意；舆论 记 词根记忆：con(共同) + sens(感觉) + us → 感觉相同 → 共识 例 It seems we have reached a *consensus*: the commodity price must be controlled by the end of this month. 看来我们已经达成了共识：必须在这个月底前控制住物价。
kindle [ˈkɪndl]	*v.* 点燃，开始燃烧；激起(兴趣等) 记 联想记忆：点燃(kindle)蜡烛(candle) 例 Our team tried to *kindle* the boss's interest with the new idea. 我们团队想用这个新想法引起老板的兴趣。
lateral [ˈlætərəl]	*a.* 侧面的，旁边的；横向的 记 词根记忆：later(侧面，边) + al → 侧面的，旁边的 例 On the Internet there is much misleading and erroneous information about *lateral* thinking. 网上有很多关于横向思考的错误信息。
eradicate [ɪˈrædɪkeɪt]	*vt.* 根除，灭绝 记 词根记忆：e(出) + radic(根) + ate(使…) → 使连根拔出 → 根除 例 The campaign aims to *eradicate* illiteracy, which was also a part of basic education. 这个活动旨在消除文盲，这也是基础教育工作的一部分。
recede [rɪˈsiːd]	*vi.* 退，后退；渐渐远去；逐渐减弱 记 词根记忆：re(向后) + ced(走) + e → 向后走 → 后退 例 Streets were overwhelmed by the flood, but fortunately the water began to *recede*. 街道已经被洪水淹没，但幸运的是洪水正在消退。
operant [ˈɑːpərænt]	*a.* 运转中的；生效的；操作性的 *n.* 起作用的人 记 词根记忆：oper(工作；运转) + ant → 运转中的；起作用的人 例 *Operant* conditioning has been widely applied in clinical settings as well as teaching. 操作性条件反射广泛应用于临床环境以及教学中。
aspire [əˈspaɪər]	*v.* 有志于；热望，向往 记 联想记忆：a + spire(塔尖，尖顶) → 向塔尖看 → 热望，向往 例 There are many students that *aspire* to be business leaders one day. 有许多学生向往有一天成为商业领袖。
canoe [kəˈnuː]	*vi.* 乘独木舟，划独木舟 *n.* 独木舟 例 We will go *canoeing* this Sunday. 我们这个周日要去划独木舟。
patron [ˈpeɪtrən]	*n.* 资助人，赞助人(benefactor)；老主顾，顾客(client) 记 词根记忆：patr(父亲) + on → 像父亲一样进行帮助 → 赞助人 例 The old man was the *patron* of many artists. 这个老人是许多艺术家的赞助人。 派 patronage(*n.* 资助，赞助；惠顾，光顾)

larynx [ˈlærɪŋks]	*n.* 喉 参 laryngeal(*a.* 喉的；喉音的)；laryngitis(*n.* 喉炎)
novelty [ˈnɑːvlti]	*n.* 新奇，新颖；新奇的事物 记 词根记忆：nov(新的) + elty → 新奇，新颖 例 There's no doubt that radio broadcasting was quite a *novelty* in those days. 毫无疑问，在那些岁月里无线电广播是个新鲜玩意儿。
ferment	[fərˈment] *v.* (使)发酵；骚动 [ˈfɜːrment] *n.* 发酵；动乱，骚动 记 词根记忆：ferm(=ferv 热) + ent → (使)发酵 例 Yogurt contains a higher percentage of lactic acid than other *fermented* milks. 酸奶比其他发酵的奶制品含有更多的乳酸。 // The area is in *ferment*. 该地区动荡不安。 派 fermenter(*n.* 发酵物)；fermentation(*n.* 发酵)
severe [sɪˈvɪr]	*a.* 严重的(serious)；严厉的(strict, harsh)；剧烈的(drastic)；严峻的，艰巨的；朴素的，不加装饰的 记 联想记忆：曾经(ever)艰难的(severe)日子，一去不复返了 例 The party suffered *severe* losses during the last election. 该党在上次选举中遭到惨败。 // The marathon is a *severe* test of stamina. 马拉松是对耐力的严峻考验。 参 sever(*v.* 切断)
breeze [briːz]	*n.* 微风，和风 *vi.* 飘然移动 记 联想记忆：春天到了，和风(breeze)阵阵，结冰(freeze)的河流解冻了 搭 breeze through 轻易通过，轻松完成 例 The flowers were gently swaying in the *breeze*. 花儿在微风中轻轻舞动。
potential [pəˈtenʃl]	*n.* 潜能，潜力 *a.* 潜在的；可能的(*possible) 记 词根记忆：po + tent(伸展) + ial → 无限伸展的 → 潜在的；可能的 例 The agricultural *potential* of the area was enormous if water for irrigation could be found. 如果能找到灌溉用水，该地区的农业潜力会很大。 派 potentially(*ad.* 潜在地) 参 patent(*n.* 专利)
anxious [ˈæŋkʃəs]	*a.* 渴望的；担忧的(eager, keen; worried)；令人焦虑的 例 Workers were a bit *anxious* about the safety of the machines bought abroad at first. 工人们起初有点儿担忧那些从国外买来的机器的安全性。
spinning [ˈspɪnɪŋ]	*a.* 旋转的(revolving) *n.* 纺纱 记 来自 spin(*v.* 旋转；纺纱)
fasten [ˈfæsn]	*v.* 使固定(fix)；系牢，扎牢(tie)；握住，抓牢 搭 fasten on... 对…锲而不舍；坚决跟随 例 The lighthouses in the Northeast are *fastened* to the surrounding rock. 东北部的灯塔都固定在周边岩石上。

breeze

18

playwright [ˈpleɪraɪt]	*n.* 剧作家(dramatist) 记 组合词：play(戏剧) + wright(制造者) → 剧作家 例 As a *playwright* he wrote tragedies, comedies and historical plays. 作为一名剧作家，他著有悲剧、喜剧以及历史剧。
contaminate [kənˈtæmɪneɪt]	*vt.* 污染(pollute) 记 词根记忆：con(共同) + tamin(触摸) + ate → 共同触摸脏东西 → 污染 例 They are so *contaminated* with lead that they shouldn't be used. 它们受到了严重的铅污染，不能再用了。 派 contamination(*n.* 污染)
bicameral [ˌbaɪˈkæmərəl]	*a.* 两院制的，有两个议院的 搭 bicameral legislature 两院立法
pigment [ˈpɪɡmənt]	*n.* 颜料(paint)；色素 例 The company mainly produces organic *pigment*. 那家公司主要生产有机颜料。 派 pigmented(*a.* 天然色的，本色的)；pigmentation(*n.* 染色，上色)
salmon [ˈsæmən]	*n.* 鲑鱼，大马哈鱼 记 词根记忆：sal(跳跃) + mon → 在水中欢快跳跃 → 鲑鱼，大马哈鱼
major [ˈmeɪdʒər]	*a.* 较大的；主要的(principal)；主修的 *n.* 专业 *vi.* 主修，专攻 记 词根记忆：maj(大的) + or → 较大的 搭 major category 主要范畴；major course 主修课 例 At that time Quebec was a *major* market for livestock, crops and fish. 当时魁北克是牲畜、谷物和鱼类的主要市场。 派 majority(*n.* 大多数，大半；多数票)
elegant [ˈelɪɡənt]	*a.* 优美的，高雅的；雅致的，精美的；简练的，简洁的 记 词根记忆：e(出) + leg(选择) + ant(形容词后缀) → 精心选出来的 → 优美的，高雅的 例 The glass objects of this style are *elegant* in outline. 这种风格的玻璃制品轮廓雅致。 派 elegance(*n.* 典雅，雅致)
stardom [ˈstɑːrdəm]	*n.* 明星的身份(或地位) 例 He is being groomed for *stardom*. 为成为明星，他正在接受培训。
carnivore [ˈkɑːrnɪvɔːr]	*n.* 食肉动物 记 词根记忆：carn(肉) + i + vor(吃) + e → 食肉动物 例 Wolves are classified as *carnivores*. 狼被列为食肉动物。 派 carnivorous(*a.* 食肉的)
expedition [ˌekspəˈdɪʃn]	*n.* 远征(队)；探险(队)(exploration) 记 词根记忆：ex(出) + ped(脚) + ition → 出行 → 远征(队)；探险(队) 例 His initial *expedition*, which sailed in 1578 with a patent granted by Queen Elizabeth, was defeated by the Spanish. 他在 1578 年的首次远征获得了伊丽莎白女王的批准，但是被西班牙人击败了。

metropolitan [ˌmetrəˈpɑːlɪtən]	*a.* 大都市的；本土的 例 While every *metropolitan* area has experienced some negative economic consequences from the Great Recession, not all areas have suffered equally. 虽然每个都会区在经济上都受到了大衰退的负面影响，但受损程度参差不齐。
wit [wɪt]	*n.* 智力，才智（intellect, cleverness）；风趣；机智幽默的人 记 联想记忆：运用才智（wit）取胜（win） 搭 at one's wits' end 一筹莫展，不知所措 例 The game was a long battle of *wits*. 这场游戏是长时间的斗智。
beverage [ˈbevərɪdʒ]	*n.* 饮料 例 We don't sell any alcoholic *beverages*. 我们不出售任何含酒精的饮料。
sediment [ˈsedɪmənt]	*n.* 沉淀物，沉积物（deposit） 记 词根记忆：sed（坐）+ iment → 长久坐下来的东西 → 沉淀物 例 The *sediments* that rivers transport actually play quite an important role in shaping the environment and even in our own lives. 实际上，河流带来的沉积物对环境的塑造甚至我们人类的生活都有着相当重要的作用。 派 sedimentation（*n.* 沉淀，沉积）；sedimentary（*a.* 沉积的）
marble [ˈmɑːrbl]	*n.* 大理石；（用玻璃、石头等制成的）子弹 记 联想记忆：mar（三月）+ ble → 大理三月好风光 → 大理石 例 The Minnesota State Capitol building is made of white granite and *marble*. 明尼苏达州的州议会大楼是由白色花岗岩和大理石建成的。
frivolity [frɪˈvɑːləti]	*n.* 轻浮（flippancy, levity）；愚蠢的行为 例 It was just a piece of harmless *frivolity*. 这仅仅是无恶意的愚蠢行为。
seclusion [sɪˈkluːʒn]	*n.* 独处，隐居；隔离；与世隔绝，归隐 例 He keeps himself in *seclusion* during his off hours. 他在工作之余过着深居简出的生活。
edifice [ˈedɪfɪs]	*n.* 大厦，宏伟的建筑物 记 词根记忆：edi（建筑）+ fic（做）+ e → 费力做出来的建筑物 → 大厦 例 The White House is the oldest public *edifice* in Washington D.C. 白宫是华盛顿特区最古老的公共建筑。 seclusion
constricted [kənˈstrɪktɪd]	*a.* 狭窄的（confined）；收缩的（contractive）；抑制的，约束的 记 来自 constrict（*v.* 紧缩，压缩） 例 When an asthmatic suffers an attack, the airway path was *constricted*, making it difficult for the person from breathing normally. 哮喘症患者发病时，呼吸道会收缩，使患者难以正常呼吸。
sidewalk [ˈsaɪdwɔːk]	*n.* 人行道（sideway, pavement） 例 It's so hot out today. You could fry an egg on the *sidewalk*. 今天外面太热了，都可以在人行道上煎鸡蛋了。

18

absence [ˈæbsəns]	*n.* 缺席；缺乏(lack) 记 词根记忆：ab(离去) + sen(t)(送) + ce → 送走 → 缺席 例 I know your course has no *absence* policy. 我知道您的课不允许缺席。 absence
commerce [ˈkɑːmɜːrs]	*n.* 贸易，商业(trade, business)；交往，交流 记 词根记忆：com(共同) + merc(交易) + e → 双方进行交易 → 贸易，商业 例 The leaders of industry and *commerce* attended the meeting. 工商界领导人参加了这次会议。 派 commercial(*a.* 商业的；商业性的)；commercialize(*vt.* 使商业化) 参 commence(*v.* 开始，着手)
tundra [ˈtʌndrə]	*n.* 苔原，冻原，冻土地带 记 联想记忆：t + undra(看做 under，在…之下) → 在冰雪覆盖之下 → 冻土地带 例 In the Arctic *tundra*, ice fog may form under clear skies in winter. 在北极的冻土地带，冬季晴天时会形成冰雾。
bubble [ˈbʌbl]	*n.* (气、水)泡；泡沫 *vi.* 冒泡，起泡；洋溢着 记 发音记忆：拟声词，指水冒泡的声音 例 When the *bubble* finally burst, thousands of people lost their jobs and became homeless. 当泡沫最终破灭时，成千上万人丢了饭碗，无家可归。
abolition [ˌæbəˈlɪʃn]	*n.* 废除，废止；废奴运动 记 来自 abolish(*vt.* 废除，废止) 例 During the 1850s, reform movements advocating temperance and the *abolition* of slavery gained strength in the United States. 在 19 世纪 50 年代，提倡禁酒和废除奴隶制的改革运动在美国得到了发展。 派 abolitionist(*n.* 废奴主义者)
reliable [rɪˈlaɪəbl]	*a.* 可靠的，可信赖的(dependable, trustworthy) 记 来自 rely(*v.* 信赖) 例 The majority of companies are willing to look for employees who are *reliable* and hard-working. 大部分公司愿意雇用可靠勤劳的员工。 派 reliability(*n.* 可靠性)
perishable [ˈperɪʃəbl]	*a.* 易腐的，易变质的 记 联想记忆：perish(毁灭；腐烂) + able(能…的) → 易腐的 例 Most organic materials are *perishable*. 大多数有机材料都容易腐坏。
warehouse [ˈwerhaʊs]	*n.* 仓库，货栈(storehouse) 记 组合词：ware(器皿) + house(房屋) → 放器皿的房子 → 仓库 例 I've called the *warehouse* and they are shipping copies to us. We should have them Monday morning. 我已经给库房打电话了，他们正在给我们发货。周一早上应该就能到书店。

remote [rɪˈmoʊt]	*a.* 偏僻的，偏远的(*faraway)；久远的；远程的；关系远的；微乎其微的；冷漠的 搭 in the remote future 在遥远的将来 例 He's confused by the *remote* controls. 他被遥控器弄糊涂了。
inception [ɪnˈsepʃn]	*n.* 开端，开始(*beginning, start) 记 词根记忆：in(进入) + cept(拿) + ion → 拿进来 → 开端，开始 例 From their *inception*, most rural neighborhoods in colonial North America included at least one carpenter, joiner, and sawyer. 在初创时期，北美殖民地的大多数农村地区都至少有一个木匠、工匠和锯工。
approximate 	[əˈprɑːksɪmət] *a.* 大约的，近似的(about) [əˈprɑːksɪmeɪt] *vt.* 接近，近似(close to) 记 词根记忆：ap(向) + prox(近) + im + ate → 向…靠近 → 近似；大约的 例 The Greeks first calculated the *approximate* distance around the circumference of the Earth. 希腊人首先计算出了地球圆周的大概距离。 派 approximately(*ad.* 近似地，大约) 参 proximity(*n.* 接近，邻近)
mature [məˈtʃʊr]	*a.* 成熟的(ripe)；技艺精湛的 *v.* (使)成熟(ripen) 记 联想记忆：自然(nature)中的 n 更换成 m 就是成熟的(mature) 搭 on mature consideration/reflection 经过深思熟虑 例 The best gardeners are very *mature*. 最优秀的园丁技艺精湛。// Orchid seeds take up eighteen months to *mature* before they sprout. 兰花籽在发芽之前需要 18 个月才会成熟。
authentic [ɔːˈθentɪk]	*a.* 真正的，真实的(real, genuine)；逼真的；可靠的 例 The novel is an *authentic* account of life in the desert. 这部小说是对沙漠生活的真实描述。// A: I really enjoy the play. The students did a great job with the scenery. It looks so *authentic*. I felt like I was back in the 19th century. B: I wish you could say the same thing about the costumes. A: 我很喜欢这部戏。学生们做的布景很棒，相当逼真，感觉像回到了 19 世纪。 B: 我希望你对服装有同样的评价。
meridian [məˈrɪdiən]	*n.* 子午线，经线 记 词根记忆：meridi(南、北) + an → 连接南北极之间的线 → 经线
combustible [kəmˈbʌstəbl]	*a.* 可燃的，易燃的(flammable) 记 词根记忆：combus(燃烧) + t + ible(能…的) → 可燃的 例 Burning would also stop when the *combustible* substance was emptied of all its phlogiston. 把易燃物里的燃素全部提取出来，燃烧也会停止。 参 blockbuster(*n.* 巨型炸弹)

18

leap [li:p]	*n.* 跳跃；骤变；激增 *vi.* 跳跃(jump)；急速行动；骤变；激增 搭 by leaps and bounds 飞跃地；大量地 例 A number of insects rely on *leaping* or jumping as a way of escaping from enemies. 很多昆虫依靠跳跃来逃避敌人。
malnutrition [ˌmælnuːˈtrɪʃn]	*n.* 营养不良 记 联想记忆：mal(坏) + nutrition(营养) → 营养不好 → 营养不良 例 Various diseases often follow *malnutrition*. 营养不良经常会引发多种疾病。
trash [træʃ]	*n.* 无价值之物，废物(rubbish)；拙劣的文学(或艺术)作品；没用的人 *vt.* 捣毁，破坏 记 联想记忆：tr + ash(灰) → 像灰尘一样微不足道 → 废物 搭 trash can 垃圾桶 例 Most people don't like to take the time to separate their *trash*. 大多数人都不喜欢花时间给垃圾分类。
cookout [ˈkʊkaʊt]	*n.* 野外烧烤宴会 例 Tom will bring food for the Friday night *cookout* for everyone. 汤姆将给每个人带周五晚上的野外烧烤宴会的食物。
scruffy [ˈskrʌfi]	*a.* 不整洁的，邋遢的(shabby, unkempt) 例 She looked a little *scruffy*. 她看上去有点儿邋遢。
threat [θret]	*n.* 恐吓，威胁；坏兆头，危险迹象(hazard) 搭 pose a major threat to 对…构成重大威胁 例 These ancient woodlands are under *threat* from new road developments. 新道路开发可能对这些古老的林地造成破坏。
craft [kræft]	*n.* 手艺，工艺(art) *v.* 手工制作 例 It is wonderful to see this disappearing *craft* return to popularity. 很高兴看到这种消失的工艺重新流行起来。 // The men wove textile and *crafted* tortoise jewelry. 这些人编织物品，手工制作玳瑁首饰。
adverse [ˈædvɜːrs]	*a.* 负面的(negative, contrary)；不利的(unfavorable)；逆的 记 词根记忆：ad(向) + vers(转) + e → 转向另一方 → 负面的；不利的 搭 adverse effect 反作用 例 The Group of Seven welcomed *adverse* criticism because it would help them to improve as artists. 七人组欢迎负面的批评，因为这能帮助他们提高艺术素养。 // They could grow crops despite *adverse* weather. 尽管天气不利，他们也能种植作物。 派 adversely(*ad.* 不利地，有害地)；adversity(*n.* 逆境) 参 averse(*a.* 不愿意的，反对的)
layout [ˈleɪaʊt]	*n.* (书刊等的)编排，版面设计；规划，布局(arrangement) 记 来自词组 lay out (布置，安排) 例 Municipal planners deal chiefly with the physical *layout* of communities. 城市规划者主要负责社区的实体布局。

cousin [ˈkʌzn]	*n.* 堂(或表)兄弟, 堂(或表)姐妹 例 My *cousin*, who is a geography teacher, helped us plan our trip. 我的堂兄是地理老师, 他帮助我们筹划了旅行。
porcelain [ˈpɔːrsəlɪn]	*n.* 瓷器, 瓷(china) 记 发音记忆: "跑四邻" → 卖瓷器需要跑四邻八方 → 瓷器 例 The small shop around the corner sells various *porcelain* ware. 拐角处的那家小店出售各种瓷器。
solitary [ˈsɑːləteri]	*a.* 孤独的(lonely); 单独的, 独自的(single, individual); 单个的; 唯一的, 仅有的 记 词根记忆: sol(单独) + it + ary → 孤独的 例 She enjoys long *solitary* walks. 她喜欢独自一人长距离地散步。
trait [treɪt]	*n.* 特性, 特点(characteristic, feature) 记 联想记忆: 要根据每位队员的特点(trait)进行训练(train) 例 They share similar physical *traits*. 它们外形特征相似。
decimal [ˈdesɪml]	*a.* 十进位的, 小数的 *n.* 小数 记 词根记忆: deci(十分之一) + mal → 十进位的 搭 the decimal system 十进制 例 You should treat *decimals* as the whole number to solve the mathematical problem. 解这道数学题时, 你应该把小数当做整数来处理。
transit [ˈtrænzɪt]	*n.* 运输, 运送(transport); 中转; 转变; 交通运输系统 记 词根记忆: trans(穿过) + it(走) → 在两地间穿行 → 运输 搭 mass transit 公共交通 例 The city encourages everyone to take full advantage of the public *transit* system. 该市鼓励每个人充分利用公共交通运输系统。
germ [dʒɜːrm]	*n.* 微生物, 细菌(bacteria, microorganism); 萌芽 记 本身是词根, 意为"芽" → 微生物, 细菌; 萌芽 例 Some diseases are caused by *germ*-carrying insects. 一些疾病是由携带细菌的昆虫引起的。
perfume [pərˈfjuːm]	*n.* 香味; 香水 *vt.* 使充满香气; 洒香水于 记 联想记忆: per(贯穿) + fume(气体) → 缭绕在身上的气体 → 香味 例 We stock a wide range of *perfumes*. 我们备有各种各样的香水。// The room was *perfumed* with the smell of rose. 房间里弥漫着玫瑰的芳香。
radius [ˈreɪdiəs]	*n.* 半径; 周围, 范围 记 词根记忆: rad(光线) + ius → 半径就像是从同一点发散出来的许多光线 → 半径 例 The roads reached out to more than 80 satellite villages within a 60-kilometer *radius*. 这些道路通向方圆 60 公里内的 80 多个卫星村。

18

compress [kəm'pres]	v. 压缩(condense); 缩短(shorten); 浓缩
	记 词根记忆: com(表加强) + press(压) → 压缩; 缩短
	例 Some geologists think that the Earth's interior contains a highly *compressed* ball of incandescent gas. 一些地质学家认为, 地球内部包含着高度压缩的白炽气团。// She *compressed* two days' work into one. 她把两天的工作时间缩短成了一天。
	派 compression(n. 压缩; 浓缩); compressible(a. 可压缩的)
incongruity [ˌɪnkɑːn'gruːəti]	n. 不一致, 不和谐(incompatibility, disharmony)
	记 联想记忆: in(不) + congruity(一致, 和谐) → 不一致, 不和谐
	例 We were struck by the *incongruity* of the situation. 这一局面煞是怪异, 让我们惊愕不已。

If you put out your hands, you are a laborer; if you put out your hands and mind, you are a craftsperson; if you put out your hands, mind, heart and soul, you are an artist.

如果你用双手工作, 你是一个劳力; 如果你用双手和头脑工作, 你是一个工匠; 如果你用双手和头脑工作, 并且全身心投入, 你就是一个艺术家。

——美国电影 *American Heart and Soul*

词根、词缀预习表

cumb	躺	succumb *vi.* (因…)死亡	greg	人群	segregate *vt.* 隔离
gam	婚姻	monogamous *a.* 一夫一妻制的	mat	想	automatic *a.* 自动的
optim	最好的	optimize *vt.* 使最优化	orb	轨道	orbit *n.* 轨道
quant	数量	quantum *n.* 量子；定量	arithm	数字	arithmetic *n.* 算术
insul	岛屿	insulate *vt.* 使隔离，使隔绝	doc	教授	doctrine *n.* 教条

innovate [ˈɪnəveɪt]	*v.* 革新，创新 记 词根记忆：in(进入) + nov(新的) + ate(使…) → 使进入新的状态 → 革新，创新 例 We should constantly *innovate* to ensure success in an increasingly competitive market. 我们应该不断创新，以确保在竞争日益激烈的市场中取得成功。 参 renovate(*vt.* 修复)
reliever [rɪˈliːvər]	*n.* 救济者；缓解物 例 You still don't look too good. Didn't you take the pain *reliever* I gave you? 你看上去气色还是不太好。你没有服用我给你的止痛药吗？
extremity [ɪkˈstreməti]	*n.* 末端；极端，极度 例 The poor man was in an *extremity* of pain after being driven out of his home. 这个穷人在被赶出家门后处于极度痛苦之中。
load [ləʊd]	*n.* 负荷(量)，负担(*weight)；装载(量) *vt.* 装载，使负担(burden) 例 Leslie has a heavier course *load* than usual this term. 莱斯利这个学期的课业负担比往常重。// They *loaded* my suitcases on the last plane. 他们把我的行李箱装上了最后一架飞机。
narrative [ˈnærətɪv]	*n.* 叙述(depiction)；记叙体，叙述技巧 *a.* 叙述性的 例 Oral *narratives* are a valid form of literature. 口述是文学的一种有效形式。
prosperity [prɑːˈsperəti]	*n.* 繁荣，兴旺(flourish, blossom) 例 The *prosperity* of the Erie encouraged the state to enlarge its canal system by building several branches. 伊利湖的繁荣促使这个州通过挖掘数条支流来扩大运河系统。

reapply [ˌriːəˈplaɪ]	*v.* 再申请；再利用 搭 reapply for 再申请 例 Students are taught a number of skills that can be *reapplied* throughout their studies. 教给学生们一些方法，让他们在整个学习过程中可以反复使用。
succumb [səˈkʌm]	*vi.* 屈服，屈从；(因…)死亡 记 词根记忆：suc (在…下面) + cumb (躺) → 躺在下面，不再起来 → (因…)死亡 例 There were more than 10 people who died in the accident, including 7 people who *succumbed* to their injuries. 事故造成十多人死亡，其中包括受伤不治而死的七个人。
monogamous [məˈnɑːgəməs]	*a.* 一夫一妻制的；单配的 记 词根记忆：mono(单个) + gam(婚姻) + ous → 单一婚姻的 → 一夫一妻制的 例 Most birds are *monogamous*. 大多数飞禽都是单配性的。
hypocritical [ˌhɪpəˈkrɪtɪkl]	*a.* 伪善的，虚伪的 例 I found the whole thing *hypocritical* after the incident was exposed last month. 自上个月这个事件被曝光后，我就觉得整件事情很虚伪。
grid [grɪd]	*n.* 格子，栅格；地图上的坐标方格，网格；输电网，煤气输送网 搭 power grid 电力网 例 The new invention allows power from different generators to be distributed through the *grid*. 这项新发明使不同发电机产生的电能可以通过电网来分送。
hypertext [ˈhaɪpərtekst]	*n.* 超文本 记 联想记忆：hyper(高于) + text(文本) → 超文本 例 *Hypertext* has been used as an essential feature of the World Wide Web. 超文本已经作为一个基本特征应用于互联网。
indecipherable [ˌɪndɪˈsaɪfrəbl]	*a.* 无法破译的；难以领悟的 记 联想记忆：in(不) + decipher(破解，破译) + able(能…的) → 无法破译的 例 Usually, computer language is *indecipherable* to the average people. 通常，电脑语言是一般人无法解读的。
optimize [ˈɑːptɪmaɪz]	*vt.* 使最优化；充分利用 记 词根记忆：optim(最好的) + ize → 使最好 → 使最优化 例 To organize and *optimize* the material resources and human resources during the production is the core and essential work. 组织并优化生产过程中所需的原料资源和人力资源是核心工作，也是基础工作。
perceptual [pərˈseptʃuəl]	*a.* 感知的，知觉的 例 The study shows that people's *perceptual* and filtering processes will create misunderstandings. 研究显示，人们的感知过程和过滤过程会产生误解。

| **alienable** [ˈeɪliənəbl] | *a.* 可转让的 |
| | 例 Land is *alienable* according to the laws of the state. 根据州法律，土地是可转让的。 |

quantum [ˈkwɑːntəm]	*n.* [*pl.* quanta] 量子；定量
	记 词根记忆：quant(数量) + um → 量子；定量
	搭 quantum theory 量子理论
	例 He says conceitedly that no one understands *quantum* theory like he does. 他自大地说没有人比他更了解量子理论。

| **retrieval** [rɪˈtriːvl] | *n.* 数据检索；取回，索回 |
| | 例 As a reader, you can find any book you want by using the *retrieval* system. 作为一个读者，你可以通过使用检索系统找到自己想要的书。 |

virtual [ˈvɜːrtʃuəl]	*a.* (通过计算机软件)模拟的，虚拟的；实际上的，事实上的
	搭 virtual memory 虚拟内存；virtual reality 虚拟现实；virtual library 虚拟图书馆
	例 Customers can design and order clothes directly from the *virtual* shops now. 现在，顾客可以直接通过虚拟商店来设计和定制服装。

sequential [sɪˈkwenʃl]	*a.* 序列的；连续的；随之而来的
	记 词根记忆：sequ(跟随) + ent + ial → 一个跟着一个的 → 序列的；连续的；随之而来的
	搭 sequential data processing 顺序数据处理
	例 Though our thinking tends to be less creative, it is more logical and *sequential*. 尽管我们的想法比较缺乏创意，却更有逻辑性和连贯性。

interface [ˈɪntərfeɪs]	*n.* 界面，分界面；接口
	记 联想记忆：inter(在…之间) + face(面) → 两者之间的面 → 界面
	例 We have a computer editing device that allows everyone to have a different *interface*. 我们有一个计算机编辑装置，可以使每个人都拥有不同的界面。

template [ˈtempleɪt]	*n.* 模板，样板(templet)
	搭 set up a template 设一个模板
	例 If you want to upload the *template*, you have to be in the table layout instead of reports. 要想上传模板，你不能用报告的形式，必须用表格的形式。

synchronizer [ˈsɪŋkrənaɪzər]	*n.* 同步装置
	记 词根记忆：syn(相同) + chron(时间) + izer → 使时间相同 → 同步装置
	例 The *synchronizer* can help you to synchronize the folders and disks on the computer. 同步器可让计算机上的文件夹和磁盘保持同步。

| **telecommunication** [ˌtelikəˌmjuːnɪˈkeɪʃn] | *n.* 电信 |
| | 例 The *telecommunication* system was established after the successful trial in other countries. 该电信系统是在别国试验成功之后建立起来的。 |

19

ventilation [ˌventɪˈleɪʃn]	*n.* 通风设备；空气流通 记 联想记忆：ventilate(*vt.* 使通风)；vent(来) + il + ate(使…) → 使风进来 → 使通风 例 The office has been renovated recently and the *ventilation* system has been improved. 这间办公室最近重新装修过，通风系统也得到了改善。
advisory [ədˈvaɪzəri]	*a.* 顾问的，咨询的；劝告的 *n.* 警报 搭 an advisory body 咨询机构 例 Mark was appointed to the *advisory* committee last month. 马克上个月被任命为顾问委员会委员。
magnetic [mægˈnetɪk]	*a.* 磁的，磁石的；有磁性的；有吸引力的 搭 magnetic field 磁场；magnetic compass 磁盘指南针 例 The block becomes *magnetic* when the current is switched on. 一通上电，这块板就会有磁性。
static [ˈstætɪk]	*n.* 静电噪音；静电；[-s]静力学 *a.* 静态的，静止的(stationary)；静电的；静力的 记 词根记忆：stat(站立) + ic → 静止的 搭 static pressure 静压 例 There was so much *static* that I couldn't make out what he was saying. 静电噪音太大，以致于我听不清他在说什么。
count [kaʊnt]	*v.* 数，计算(calculate)；算入；看做，认为；值得考虑，有重要意义 *n.* 计数，计算；总数；(被指控的)罪状 搭 count on 算上；lose count (of) 数不清，不知道 例 I'm *counting* on you to make notes from the history lecture. 我正指望着你记历史课的笔记呢。// A: I got an invitation to a financial planning seminar. And I don't want to go alone. B: *Count* me in. I need all the help to manage my money. A: 我收到邀请去参加一个财务规划研讨会。我不想自己一个人去。 B: 把我算上。我需要理财方面的各种帮助。 参 mount(*n.* 山 *v.* 攀登；上马) 成本越算越高？ count
tinker [ˈtɪŋkər]	*vi.* 做焊锅匠；做拙劣修补 *n.* 补锅匠 记 联想记忆：认真考虑考虑(think)，你真的要做补锅匠(tinker)吗 例 In the past, only a few people who *tinkered* with wireless telegraphs as a hobby owned receivers. 过去，只有少数以捣鼓无线电报为嗜好的人拥有接收器。 参 thinker(*n.* 思想家)
jumble [ˈdʒʌmbl]	*vt.* 混杂，掺杂(mix) *n.* 杂乱的一堆，混乱的一团 记 联想记忆：jum(看做 jump，跳) + ble → 上蹿下跳，群魔乱舞 → 混杂 例 Swift currents and waves *jumble* and carry away small bones of the dead animals. 湍急的水流和波浪裹挟着动物尸体的小块骨头。

brittle ['brɪtl]	*a.* 易碎的(*easily broken, fragile); 脆弱的; (声音)尖利的 例 A lot of pages are turning brown and becoming *brittle*. 很多书页都发黄、变脆了。
insulate ['ɪnsəleɪt]	*vt.* 使隔离, 使隔绝(isolate) 记 词根记忆: insul(岛屿) + ate(使…) → 使成为孤岛 → 使隔离, 使隔绝 例 The ice shelves currently *insulate* the Antarctic Continent from wind. 眼下, 冰架使南极洲免受风的侵袭。 派 insulation(*n.* 绝缘; 隔绝, 孤立); insulator(*n.* 绝缘体)
favor ['feɪvər]	*n.* 帮助; 赞同, 支持; 偏爱 搭 do sb. a favor 帮某人忙; owe sb. a favor 欠某人的情; in favor of 支持, 赞同 例 I was wondering if you could do me a *favor*. 我在想你能否帮我一个忙。// The new program has lost *favor* with audience recently. 近来这个新节目已不受观众欢迎。 参 flavor(*n.* 风味)
segregate ['segrɪgeɪt]	*vt.* 隔离, 使分开(separate) 记 词根记忆: se(分离) + greg(人群) + ate → 使脱离人群 → 隔离 例 They are easily *segregated* from sand and silt. 它们可以轻易地从沙子和淤泥中分离出来。
dimension [dɪ'menʃn]	*n.* 维, 元; 尺寸(measure); 方面(aspect); 特点; [常 *pl.*]大小, 规模 记 词根记忆: di + mens(测量) + ion → 尺寸 例 The *dimensions* of the cosmos are so large that using familiar units of distance would make little sense. 宇宙太大了, 使用常用的距离单位没有什么意义。// Another *dimension* of relationship banking is the development of highly personalized relationships between employee and client. 关系银行业务的另一个方面就是要在雇员和客户之间培养高度个人化的关系。 派 dimensional(*a.* 空间的) 参 three-dimensional(*a.* 三维的)
nonverbal ['nɑːnvɜːrbl]	*a.* 非语言的 搭 nonverbal communication 非语言交际 例 Body language such as a gesture is the most important *nonverbal* expression. 像手势这种肢体语言是最重要的非语言表达。
barrier ['bæriər]	*n.* 屏障, 障碍物(obstruction); 检票口; 障碍, 阻力; 隔阂 记 联想记忆: bar(栅栏) + rier → 屏障 例 The Earth's magnetosphere is a *barrier* to the solar winds. 地球的磁气圈阻挡了太阳风。

19

隔离区　segregate

throw [θroʊ]	*v.* 投，掷，抛(fling)；丢，扔；使陷入，使处于；使困惑，使吃惊 *n.* 投，掷，抛；投掷的距离 **搭** throw up 扬起，猛地举起或抬起；使显眼 **例** They were *thrown* into confusion by the news. 他们被那消息弄得惊慌失措。// A: Should I help clean up by *throwing* away these newspapers? B: I want to clip a couple of articles first. A: 我帮你清理一下，把这些报纸扔了吧？ B: 我想先剪几篇文章。
shipwright [ˈʃɪpraɪt]	*n.* 造船者，造船工人；修船工 **记** 组合词：ship(船) + wright(建造人，制作者) → 造船者
automatic [ˌɔːtəˈmætɪk]	*a.* 自动的(self-acting)；无意识的(instinctive)；必然的，自然的 *n.* 自动手枪(或步枪)；自动换挡汽车 **记** 词根记忆：auto(自己) + mat(想) + ic → 自己就能想的 → 自动的 **例** My new camera is supposed to be completely *automatic*. 我的新照相机应该是全自动的。 **参** automation(*n.* 自动化)
naturalist [ˈnætʃrəlɪst]	*n.* 自然主义者；博物学家 **例** *Naturalists* brought to their writing a passion for direct and honest experience. 博物学家让他们的写作对一种直接客观的经验产生了激情。 **派** naturalistic(*a.* 自然主义的；写实的)
simplicity [sɪmˈplɪsəti]	*n.* 简单(性)，容易(性)；朴素，质朴(easiness, plainness) **记** 联想记忆：simpl(e)(简单的) + ic + ity(表性质、状态，名词后缀) → 简单(性) **例** The *simplicity* of this cartoon book makes it suitable for small children. 这本卡通书简单易懂，适合小孩子阅读。 **派** simplification(*n.* 简化)；simplify(*vt.* 使简化) **参** explicitly(*ad.* 明确地，明白地)
orbit [ˈɔːrbɪt]	*n.* 轨道(track)；势力范围 *v.* (绕…)作轨道运行 **记** 词根记忆：orb(轨道) + it → 轨道 **例** The Earth takes a year to *orbit* the Sun. 地球绕太阳一周需要一年的时间。 **派** orbital(*a.* 轨道的)
kiln [kɪln]	*n.* (砖、石灰等的)窑，炉(furnace) **记** 联想记忆：煤窑(kiln)倒塌杀死(kill)了许多人 **例** More and more large *kilns* were built to create the high-fired stoneware. 为了制造高温焙烧的陶器，建造了越来越多的大型窑炉。
proofread [ˈpruːfriːd]	*v.* 校对，校正(revise) **记** 组合词：proof(验证) + read(读) → 校对，校正 **例** Beth missed several errors while *proofreading* her paper. 贝丝校对论文时漏掉了几处错误。
arithmetic [əˈrɪθmətɪk]	*n.* 算术 **记** 词根记忆：arithm(数字) + etic(表学问、学科，名词后缀) → 算术

landscape [ˈlændskeɪp]	*n.* 风景，景色；地貌，地形(landform)；风景画 *vt.* 美化…的环境 记 组合词：land(陆地) + scape(景色) → 风景 例 In her versions the figures become more stylized and the *landscapes* less naturalistic. 在她的版本里，人物更加脸谱化，风景也不再那么写实。
doctrine [ˈdɑ:ktrɪn]	*n.* 教条，教义(dogma, teachings)；学说(theory) 记 词根记忆：doc(教授) + tr + ine → 用于教导的 → 教条 例 For a while in the United States, laisser faire was a popular *doctrine*. 曾几何时，自由主义在美国是风靡一时的学说。
suppose [səˈpoʊz]	*v.* 假设，推测(presume)；认为，料想；要不 记 词根记忆：sup(在…下面) + pos(放) + e → 放在下面 → 将某种想法放在心底 → 假设，推测 例 This theory *supposes* the existence of life on other planets. 这个理论假设其他行星存在生命。// Now, *suppose* you got a bag and you put a bunch of locks in it. 现在假设你有一个袋子，往里面放了一串锁。 派 supposed(*a.* 假定的；所谓的)；supposedly(*ad.* 按照推测，据说)；supposition(*n.* 推测，推断) 参 purpose(*n.* 目的)；propose(*vt.* 建议)
matrimony [ˈmætrɪmoʊni]	*n.* 婚姻，婚配 记 词根记忆：matri(母亲) + mony(表行为、状态，名词后缀) → 成为母亲 → 婚姻 例 Being so young she did not think herself fit to bear the burden of *matrimony*. 她如此年轻，认为自己还担不起婚姻的重任。
adapt [əˈdæpt]	*v.* (使)适合(adjust)；(使)适应；调整(alter)；改编，改写 记 词根记忆：ad + apt(适合的) → 使适合 例 When we moved to France, the children *adapted* to the change very well. 我们家搬到法国之后，孩子们很快便适应了这个变化。 派 adaptation(*n.* 适应；改写本)；adaptable(*a.* 能适应的)；adaptive(*a.* 适应的；有适应能力的) 参 adopt(*v.* 采用；收养)；adept(*a.* 熟练的)
span [spæn]	*n.* 跨度；持续时间(period) *vt.* 跨越；持续，贯穿；包括 搭 life span 寿命 例 The project must be completed with a specific time *span*. 这项工程必须在特定期限内完成。
veto [ˈvi:toʊ]	*n.* 否决权；禁止(ban, prohibition) *vt.* 否决；禁止 记 在拉丁文中，veto 的意思是"我不准"(I forbid)，在英语中则表示"否决"或"否决权" 搭 pocket veto 搁置否决权；veto message 否决通知书 例 The government used its *veto* to block the proposal. 政府行使其否决权阻止了这项提案。// Often, lawmakers simply revised the *vetoed* bill and passed it again. 立法者往往修改被否决的议案，然后再次通过。

19

□ landscape □ doctrine □ suppose ■ matrimony □ adapt □ span
□ veto

mechanic
[mə'kænɪk]

n. 技工，机修工(machinist, technician)

记 词根记忆：mechan(机械) + ic(表人，名词后缀) → 机修工

例 She knows a *mechanic* who can help her fix her car. 她认识一个机修工，能帮忙修理她的车。

派 mechanical(*a.* 机动的，机械的)

---

glimpse
[ɡlɪmps]

n. 一看，一瞥(glance) *vt.* 瞥见(spot, catch sight of)

记 联想记忆：glim(灯光) + pse → 像灯光一闪 → 一瞥

搭 catch a glimpse of 瞥见

例 I caught a *glimpse* of him in the crowd. 我一眼在人群里瞥见他。

---

claim
[kleɪm]

v./n. 声称，断言(assert)；要求(request)；索赔

记 本身为词根，意为"大声叫喊" → 声称，断言

例 The farmers *claimed* that the iron poisoned the soil and made the weeds grow wildly. 农民们声称铁污染了土壤，而且使得野草疯长。// Peary's *claim* was surrounded by controversy. 皮尔里的要求饱受争议。

---

plausible
['plɔːzəbl]

a. 似有道理的，似乎正确的(specious)

记 词根记忆：plaus(鼓掌) + ible(能…的) → 值得鼓掌的 → 似有道理的

例 Well, as *plausible* as it sounds, it's only a theory. 这听起来似乎有道理，不过还只是个理论。

---

restore
[rɪ'stɔːr]

vt. 恢复；修复(renovate)；归还，交还

记 联想记忆：re(重新) + store(储存) → 身体重新储存能量 → 恢复；修复

例 The factory was *restored* to full working order. 工厂完全恢复了工作秩序。

派 restoration(*n.* 恢复；修复)

---

arouse
[ə'raʊz]

vt. 唤醒，唤起(awake)；激起，引起(evoke)

记 联想记忆：a + rouse(唤醒；激起) → 唤醒；激起

搭 arouse one's anxiety/curiosity/interest 引起某人的不安/好奇/兴趣

例 Mary is *aroused* by her clock's alarm at 9 o'clock every morning. 玛丽每天早上 9 点被闹钟叫醒。// The strange behavior of the neighbor *aroused* Mike's curiosity. 邻居奇怪的举止引起了迈克的好奇。

参 arise(*v.* 出现，发生)

---

landmass
['lændmæs]

n. 大片陆地

记 组合词：land(陆地) + mass(大量) → 大片陆地

例 *Landmasses* occupy only one-third of the Earth's surface. 陆地只占地球表面的三分之一。

---

treadmill
['tredmɪl]

n. 踏车；枯燥乏味的工作(或生活方式)

记 联想记忆：tread(踩踏) + mill(磨坊) → 在磨坊里踩踏车 → 枯燥乏味的工作

例 I hope to escape the office *treadmill*. 我想摆脱枯燥乏味的办公室工作。

treadmill

ecosystem
[ˈiːkoʊsɪstəm]

n. 生态系统
记 词根记忆：eco(家庭的) + system(系统) → 有关地球这个大家庭的系统 → 生态系统
搭 balanced ecosystem 平衡的生态系统
例 An *ecosystem* includes all of the living organisms in a specific area. 一地的生态系统涵盖了该特定地域上所有活着的有机体。

opal
[ˈoʊpl]

n. 蛋白石
搭 an opal ring 蛋白石戒指

centric
[ˈsentrɪk]

a. 以…为中心的
例 Anyone who wants to make friends with others should not be ego *centric*. 任何想和他人交朋友的人都不应该以自我为中心。
参 ethnocentric(*a.* 种族中心主义的)

scent
[sent]

n. 香味，香气(odor, fragrance)；气味(smell)；踪迹，线索；香水 *vt.* 闻出；察觉
搭 on the scent of 已获得线索
例 The air was filled with the *scent* of wild flowers. 空气中弥漫着野花的芬芳。// The press could *scent* a scandal. 记者觉察出有桩丑闻。

attorney
[əˈtɜːrni]

n. 辩护律师；代理人
记 词根记忆：at(向) + torn(转) + ey → 转向他人 → (在法庭上)为他人代言的人 → 辩护律师
例 When I was six years old, my father was selected as the district *attorney*. 我六岁时，父亲被选为区检察官。

confession
[kənˈfeʃn]

n. 供认，招供，坦白；供词；承认(admission)
记 词根记忆：con(全部) + fess(说) + ion → 全部说出 → 供认，招供
例 My *confession* won't solve anything. 我坦白了也解决不了任何问题。

idiom
[ˈɪdiəm]

n. 习惯用语；术语；(在艺术上所表现的)风格，特色(style)
例 Martha Graham's debut dance concert in her new *idiom* occurred on April 18, 1926. 1926 年 4 月 18 日，玛莎·格雷厄姆首次举办了体现她新特色的舞蹈音乐会。

fort
[fɔːrt]

n. 要塞，堡垒(stronghold)；营地
记 联想记忆：在重要港口(port)建筑堡垒(fort)
搭 hold down the fort 代为照看，代为负责
例 *Fort* Drum has been used as a military training site since 1908. 自1908年起，德拉姆堡就被用做军事训练场所。
参 fortress(*n.* 要塞；堡垒)

immune
[ɪˈmjuːn]

a. 免疫的，有免疫力的；不受影响的；免除的，豁免的
记 词根记忆：im(没有) + mun(作用) + e → 没有作用 → 免疫的
搭 immune system 免疫系统
例 They were *immune* to drought. 他们未受旱灾的影响。// No one should be *immune* from prosecution. 任何人都不应被免予起诉。
派 immunity(*n.* 免疫力；免除，豁免)
参 immure(*vt.* 监禁；使闭门不出)

immune

19

quilt [kwɪlt]	*v.* 缝被；缝制 *n.* 被褥 记 联想记忆：他辞职(quit)后就天天躺在被窝(quilt)里度日 例 The bedcover was *quilted* in a flower design. 床罩上缝有花的图案。 派 quilted(*a.* 絮棉的，加衬芯的)
coincide [ˌkoʊɪn'saɪd]	*vi.* 同时发生；一致，相符(agree, accord)；重合 记 词根记忆：co(共同) + in + cid(切) + e → 共同切分 → 一致 例 The interests of employers and employees do not always *coincide*. 雇主和雇员的利益并不总是一致的。 派 coincidence(*n.* 巧合；并存；相符，一致)；coincident(*a.* 巧合的)
carve [kɑːrv]	*v.* 雕刻(*incise)；切(cut, slice) 搭 be carved in stone (决定、计划等)不可更改 例 The flutes are *carved* from a length of soft, straight-grained wood. 笛子 是由一根直纹软木刻制而成的。 派 carving(*n.* 雕刻；雕刻品)；carver(*n.* 雕刻匠)
solid ['sɑːlɪd]	*a.* 固体的；实心的；结实的，稳固的(*substantial, firm)；可靠的；连续的 *n.* 固体(substance) 搭 solid mass 实体；solid particle 固体微粒 例 As yet, they have no *solid* evidence. 他们至今还没有任何可靠的证据。 派 solidarity(*n.* 团结)；solidify(*v.* 凝固)；solidly(*ad.* 牢固地)
ranch [ræntʃ]	*n.* 大牧场，饲养场 记 联想记忆：牛马在大牧场(ranch)里驰骋(ran) 搭 ranch hands 牧场工人 例 He works on a sheep *ranch*. 他在一个牧羊场工作。 派 rancher(*n.* 牧场主)
consort	[kən'sɔːrt] *vi.* 结交(associate)；鬼混 ['kɑːnsɔːrt] *n.* (尤指统治者的)配偶；团伙 记 联想记忆：con(共同) + sort(类型) → 同类相聚 → 结交 例 Some colonial urban portraitists *consorted* with affluent patrons. 殖民时 期的一些城市肖像画家与富有的赞助人结交。 派 consortium(*n.* 财团，联营企业) 参 assorted(*a.* 各式各样的)；resort(*n.* 度假胜地 *vi.* 诉诸；经常去)
sociable ['soʊʃəbl]	*a.* 好交际的，合群的；友善的，友好的(outgoing) 记 词根记忆：soci(同伴，结交) + able → 好交际的 例 A good *sociable* ability is good for one's growth. 出色的交际能力有助 于个人的发展。
across [ə'krɔːs]	*ad.* 横过；到对面，向对面 *prep.* 穿过，越过；在对面 搭 go/walk/run across 穿过 例 I happened to be looking through some of my roommate's science magazines and I came *across* an article on phrenology. 我碰巧在翻阅室 友的科学杂志，看到一篇关于颅相学的文章。

observe [əbˈzɜːrv]	*v.* 遵守，奉行；观察；察觉，看到(notice)；评说，评论 记 词根记忆：ob(表加强) + serv(维持) + e → 遵守，奉行 例 Like other behaviorists, John believes that psychologists should study only the behaviors they can *observe* and measure. 与其他行为主义者一样，约翰也认为心理学家应该只研究那些他们能观察和测量的行为。 派 observable(*a.* 应遵守的；看得见的)；observer(*n.* 遵守者；观察者) 参 preserve(*vt.* 保护，保存)；reserve(*vt.* 储备；预订)
symmetry [ˈsɪmətri]	*n.* 对称(性)；相似，相仿 记 词根记忆：sym(共同) + metr(测量) + y → 测量结果相同 → 对称(性) 搭 radial symmetry 径向对称，放射对称 例 You will be shown a shape and you have to tell the computer how many lines of *symmetry* it has. 你将看到一个图形，然后得告诉计算机这个图形有多少条对称线。
rugged [ˈrʌɡɪd]	*a.* 崎岖的，凹凸不平的(uneven)；(生活)艰难的(tough)；粗犷的；结实的，耐用的；粗野的，不文雅的 例 Most of British Columbia is mountainous, with long, *rugged* ranges running north and south. 英属哥伦比亚大部分地区是山区，有着从北向南延伸的绵延不绝的崎岖山脉。
commute [kəˈmjuːt]	*v.* (乘公交车)上下班往返，经常往返；代偿；减刑 记 词根记忆：com(=with 以) + mut(改变) + e → 坐车换车 → (乘公交车)上下班往返 例 More and more people live far from the old city center and still *commute* there for work. 越来越多的人住在远离老市中心的地方，不过他们仍然乘公交车去那里上班。 派 commuter(*n.* 经常往返者，通勤者)

19

Word List 20

音频

词根、词缀预习表

mpt	拿	prompt *vt.* 促进，推动	pris	拿，带	apprise *vt.* 通知，告诉
phas	说	emphasize *vt.* 强调，着重	decor	装饰	decorative *a.* 装饰性的
son	声音	resonance *n.* 共振，共鸣	dexter	右手	dexterous *a.* 惯用右手的
front	额头，脸	confront *vt.* 使面临；对抗	dom	家	domicile *n.* 住处，住所
ami	爱	amiable *a.* 可爱的	brilli	发光	brilliant *a.* 闪耀的

---

episode
[ˈepɪsəʊd]

n. 一段时期(period)；片段，插曲(incident)；(电视剧等的)一集
搭 glacial episode 冰河时期
例 I missed the first *episode* of the new TV show, but I hope to watch a later one. 我错过了新电视节目的第一集，不过我希望能看到下一集。

---

caribou
[ˈkærɪbuː]

n. 北美驯鹿
例 Although *caribou* look like deer, they are different from other members of their family in many ways. 虽然北美驯鹿看上去像鹿，但它们与家族里的其他成员之间存在诸多不同之处。

---

prompt
[prɑːmpt]

vt. 促进，推动(accelerate, incite)；提示；鼓励(encourage) *a.* 敏捷的；及时的，迅速的 *n.* 提词，提示
记 词根记忆：pro(向前) + mpt(=empt 拿) → 向前拿 → 促进，推动
例 Bob's dislike for hot weather *prompted* him to move north. 鲍勃不喜欢炎热的天气，这促使他迁往北方。
派 promptly(*ad.* 迅速地，立即)

---

source
[sɔːrs]

n. 源，源泉；来源，出处(origin)；信息来源
搭 at source 在源头；从一开始；energy source 能源
例 Historians use a wide range of primary and secondary *sources* for their research. 历史学家在研究中使用大量的原始资料和二手资料。//
A: Excuse me, does this library have anything on the international arts festival coming this summer or should I go to the art library for that?
B: If you give a minute, I think we have a few *sources* for that kind of information.
A: 打扰一下，这个图书馆有关于今年夏天国际艺术节的信息吗？还是我该去艺术图书馆问问？
B: 请稍等，我想我们有一些这方面的信息。
参 resource(*n.* 资源)

---

campaign [kæmˈpeɪn]	*vi.* 竞选；参加战斗 *n.* 竞选活动；(政治或商业性)活动；战役 🔑 联想记忆：camp(营地) + aign → 军队在野外扎营 → 参加战斗 🔲 Mary shouldn't have *campaigned* against Steve. 玛丽本不该开展反对史蒂夫的运动。
musical [ˈmjuːzɪkl]	*a.* 音乐的；悦耳的(melodious, tuneful)；有音乐天赋的，爱好音乐的 *n.* 音乐剧 🔲 Ella is the perfect *musical* partner for her friend. 埃拉是她朋友的完美音乐搭档。 📶 musicality(*n.* 乐感，音乐性)；musically(*ad.* 音乐上)
emphasize [ˈemfəsaɪz]	*vt.* 强调，着重(*stress) 🔑 词根记忆：em(表加强) + phas(说) + ize → 强调，着重 🔲 The story *emphasized* the courage of a man made him a hero. 这个故事强调了勇气能使一个人成为英雄。 📖 emphasis(*n.* 强调，重点)
cater [ˈkeɪtər]	*v.* 迎合；提供饮食 🔑 联想记忆：cat(猫) + er → 猫饿了，喂点猫粮 → 提供饮食 📦 cater for 迎合；cater to 供应伙食 🔲 Some websites are popular among some young people, because they *cater* to their low taste. 有些网站因为迎合了一些年轻人的低级趣味而大受欢迎。
fuse [fjuːz]	*v.* (使)融合；熔接(mix, melt)；(使)熔化；因保险丝烧断而断电；合并(combine) *n.* 保险丝；引信；导火线 🔲 The resulting mass was further heated to *fuse* the mass into what was called potash. 生成的物质被进一步加热，熔合成所谓的碳酸钾。 📶 fusion(*n.* 熔解；核聚变)
resonance [ˈrezənəns]	*n.* 共振，共鸣；回声，反响 🔑 词根记忆：re(再，又) + son(声音) + ance → 声音再次响起 → 共振，共鸣 🔲 The musical tone of an electric guitar is created not by the *resonance* of the body of the guitar but electronical amplification. 电吉他的乐音不是靠吉他本身的共振产生的，而是靠电子扩音器。
involve [ɪnˈvɑːlv]	*vt.* 包含(include)；牵涉，牵连；使参加 🔑 词根记忆：in(进入) + volv(卷) + e → 卷入 → 牵涉，牵连 🔲 Your main responsibilities will *involve* ensuring the safety of everyone who skis here. 你主要的责任将是确保所有在这里滑雪的人的安全。 // I want to be *involved* from start to finish. 我想自始至终参与其中。

20

□ campaign □ musical □ emphasize □ cater □ fuse □ resonance
□ involve

223

brew [bruː]	*v.* 酿造；冲泡；酝酿，行将发生 *n.* 冲泡（或酿造）的饮料；（尤指某地酿造的)啤酒 记 联想记忆：喝下自酿(brew)的苦酒，他紧皱起眉头(brow) 例 This store provides good service including *brewing* tea for the waiting customers. 这家商店为顾客提供优质的服务，包括为等待的顾客沏茶。
cast [kæst]	*vt.* 浇铸(mold)；投掷(throw)；投射(光、视线等)；蜕(皮) *n.* 铸件；演员表，全体演员；投，抛 例 They had invented bronze, an alloy that could be *cast* in molds, out of which they made tools and weapons. 他们已经发明了青铜，这种合金可以在模子里浇铸，做成工具和武器。
surrender [səˈrendər]	*v.* 投降；(被迫)放弃，交出 *n.* 投降；屈服，屈从；放弃 记 联想记忆：sur(在…下面) + render(递交) → 把放在下面的东西交上去 → 投降；放弃 搭 surrender (oneself) to sth. 听任(感情、习惯等)的摆布 例 The murderer finally *surrendered* to the police. 凶犯最终向警方投降。
foremost [ˈfɔːrməʊst]	*a.* 最先的；最著名的，最重要的(*leading, chief) 记 组合词：fore(前面) + most(最) → 站在最前面的 → 最先的；最著名的 例 He is one of the *foremost* pianists of our day. 他是我们这个时代最著名的钢琴家之一。
drill [drɪl]	*v.* 钻(孔)，打眼(bore)；训练(practice) *n.* 钻(孔)；训练 记 联想记忆：dr(看做 dry，干燥的) + ill(生病的) → 生病了还坚持训练 → 训练 例 The first oil well was *drilled* by E. L. Drake, a retired railroad conductor. 第一口油井是 E.L.德雷克开凿的，此人是一名退休的铁路列车长。
confront [kənˈfrʌnt]	*vt.* 使面临，使遭遇(face, encounter)；对抗(oppose) 记 词根记忆：con(共同) + front(额头，脸) → 对顶额头 → 使面临；对抗 例 Staggering tasks *confronted* the people of the United States, North and South, when the Civil War ended. 内战结束后，美国南北方的人民都面临着艰巨的任务。
era [ˈɪrə]	*n.* 纪元，年代，时代(*period of time, epoch)；代 记 联想记忆：反过来拼写是 are 搭 Neolithic era 新石器时代；silent film era 无声电影时代，默片时代 例 This is an end of an *era*. 这是一个时代的终结。

glamorous [ˈglæmərəs]	*a.* 富有魅力的，迷人的（attractive, charming） 记 来自 glamor（*n.* 魅力） 例 The shore of the Italian Riviera is considered to be the most *glamorous* and picturesque in Europe. 意大利里维埃拉海岸被认为是欧洲最迷人、最风景如画的海滨地区。
amiable [ˈeɪmɪəbl]	*a.* 可爱的；友好的，和蔼的，亲切的 记 词根记忆：ami（爱）+ able（能…的）→ 可爱的 例 The hostess greeted her customers with an *amiable* smile. 女主人带着亲切的微笑迎接客人们的到来。
stark [stɑːrk]	*a.* 赤裸的（barren, bare）；严酷的，严峻的；（指区别）明显的，鲜明的（clear）；十足的，极端的（utter, sheer）*ad.* 十足 记 联想记忆：鲨鱼（shark）是十足（stark）危险的动物 例 The dark stones stand out in *stark* contrast to the white snow and ice. 深色的石头与洁白的冰雪形成鲜明的对比。
apprise [əˈpraɪz]	*vt.* 通知，告诉；评价 记 词根记忆：ap（向，往）+ pris（拿，带）+ e → 把某物带给某人 → 通知，告诉 例 My friend was eager to tell me that my thesis was *appraised* as worthless. 我的朋友焦急地告诉我，我的论文被评价为一无是处。
intuitive [ɪnˈtuːɪtɪv]	*a.* 直觉的 例 What does make them good is having an *intuitive* feeling for how the music works. 他们之所以优秀，是因为对音乐如何发挥作用拥有一种直觉。
bait [beɪt]	*n.* 鱼饵，诱饵 *vt.* 下诱饵；激怒 记 联想记忆：等（wait）鱼吃饵（bait） 例 It was a tempting *bait* indeed, and I won't let it slide. 这确实是一个绝好的机会，我不会让它溜走的。
decorative [ˈdekəreɪtɪv]	*a.* 装饰性的，做装饰用的 记 词根记忆：decor（装饰）+ at + ive（形容词后缀）→ 装饰性的 例 That color doesn't match the rest of your *decorative* scheme. 那个颜色与你装饰设计的其他部分不搭调。
stylish [ˈstaɪlɪʃ]	*a.* 漂亮的，时髦的（fashionable）；高雅的，有格调的 例 It was a *stylish* performance by both artists. 这是由两位艺术家共同演出的一场高雅的节目。
brisk [brɪsk]	*a.* （天气）清新的；敏捷的，活泼的 记 联想记忆：b + risk（冒险）→ 喜欢冒险的人 → 敏捷的，活泼的 例 It's lucky that the weather is good with light *brisk* winds. 真幸运我们碰上了好天气，清风徐徐。

intact [ɪnˈtækt]	*a.* 无损伤的，完整的(undamaged) 记 词根记忆：in(不) + tact(触碰) → 未被触碰过的 → 无损伤的，完整的 例 The ice shelf had remained *intact* for centuries despite the weather. 尽管天气变化，历经了数个世纪，冰架依然完好无损。 参 contact(*v.* 接触；联系)
clasp [klæsp]	*n.* 搭扣，扣环；紧抱；紧握 *vt.* 握紧；抱紧；扣住，扣牢 记 联想记忆：毕业时，同班(class)同学紧抱(clasp)在一起 例 Mary's necklace fell off because the *clasp* was loose. 玛丽的项链掉了下来，因为钩环松了。
soda [ˈsoʊdə]	*n.* 苏打，纯碱 搭 soda lime 碱石灰
clip [klɪp]	*v.* 夹住，扣住；修剪；(从报纸上)剪下 *n.* 夹子，回形针，别针；弹夹，弹仓；电影片段，剪报 搭 clip off 缩短，削减；clip sb.'s wings 限制某人的自由(或权力) 例 My mother *clipped* out all the reports about my performances. 我妈妈剪下所有有关我演出的报道。
prevail [prɪˈveɪl]	*vi.* 盛行，流行(predominate, fashion)；(over, against)战胜，压倒；(on, upon)劝说 记 词根记忆：pre(在…前面) + vail(=val 力量) → 在力量上领先，居主导地位 → 战胜，压倒 例 Most goods are handmade, and a subsistence economy *prevails*. 大多数商品都是手工制作的，自给经济占主导地位。
dexterous [ˈdekstrəs]	*a.* 惯用右手的；灵巧的，熟练的 记 词根记忆：dexter(右手) + ous(形容词后缀) → 惯用右手的 例 I was secretly envious of her when I saw her so *dexterous*. 看到她那股灵巧劲儿，我心里暗生嫉妒。
bountiful [ˈbaʊntɪfl]	*a.* 慷慨的(generous)；大量的，充足的 记 来自bounty(*n.* 慷慨之举) 例 We found a *bountiful* supply of sea food on the island. 我们发现岛上的海鲜产品供应充足。
cramp [kræmp]	*n.* 痉挛，抽筋；[*pl.*](腹部)绞痛 *vt.* 阻碍，阻止(restrict) 记 联想记忆：出去露营(camp)居然腿抽筋(cramp) 例 I was seized with the *cramp* in the cold water when I was swimming. 我游泳的时候，忽然在冷水中抽筋了。
expenditure [ekˈspendɪtʃər]	*n.* 花费，支出 记 词根记忆：ex(出，外) + pend(支付) + it + ure → 花费，支出 例 In the face of the inflation, local government is also reducing *expenditure*. 面对通货膨胀，地方政府也在减少支出。

226
□ intact □ clasp □ soda □ clip □ prevail □ dexterous
□ bountiful □ cramp □ expenditure

reflection [rɪˈflekʃn]	n. 反映(expression); 映像; 深思, 考虑; 回忆; 记录, 描述 搭 without reflection 轻率; on reflection 经过再三思考 例 After a few days of *reflection* the little girl decided to leave the city with her mother. 经过几天的思考, 小女孩决定跟母亲离开这座城市。 派 reflectionism(n. 反映论); reflectional(a. 反射的; 反映的)
famish [ˈfæmɪʃ]	v. (使)饥饿(starve) 例 They are all resolved rather to die than to *famish*. 他们已下定决心, 宁愿死也不愿挨饿。
cuisine [kwɪˈziːn]	n. 烹饪; 烹调法, 烹调风格 记 发音记忆: "口味新" → 烹饪出新口味 → 烹饪 例 We're going to a restaurant which is famous for its fine French *cuisine*. 我们要去一家以精致的法式菜肴闻名的餐厅。
domicile [ˈdɑːmɪsaɪl]	n. 住处, 住所 记 词根记忆: dom(家) + icile → 住处, 住所 例 The applicant must be willing and able to take *domicile* in Beijing. 申请者必须愿意并能常驻北京。
loose [luːs]	a. 松散的, 宽松的; 不精确的, 不严密的; 不牢固的(unstable); 自由的, 散漫的 记 联想记忆: 带子太松(loose)了, 东西很容易丢(lose)的 例 I'm going to fix some *loose* shutters on my house. 我打算修理下家里一些不牢固的百叶窗。 派 loosen(v. 解开, 松开; 放松) loose
dwindle [ˈdwɪndl]	v. (使)减少; (使)缩小 记 联想记忆: d + wind(风) + le → 随风而去, 越来越小 → (使)缩小 例 Your invitations will *dwindle* and your circle of friends will definitely shrink. 你接到的邀请会减少, 朋友圈也会缩小。
embark [ɪmˈbɑːrk]	v. 上船(或飞机、汽车等) 记 联想记忆: em + bark(犬吠声) → 狗在后面边吠边追, 不得不上船 → 上船(或飞机、汽车等) 搭 embark on/upon 从事, 着手 例 When you *embark* on a difficult task, it is important that you're well-prepared. 当你开始一项艰难的任务时, 做好准备工作很重要。 embark
slog [slɑːg]	v. 艰难行进(tramp); 埋头苦干; 猛击 记 联想记忆: 扛着木头(log)艰难行进(slog) 例 She started to *slog* her way through the undergrowth. 她踏上了穿越林莽的艰难征程。

20

translucent [træns'luːsnt]	*a.* 半透明的 记 词根记忆：trans(穿过) + luc(光) + ent → 光线能穿过的 → 半透明的 例 Glass can be colored or colorless, transparent, *translucent*, or opaque. 玻璃可以是有色或无色的，透明、半透明或不透明的。 参 limpid(*a.* 清澈的；透明的)
imaginary [ɪ'mædʒɪneri]	*a.* 想象中的，虚构的，假想的 搭 an imaginary world 虚构的世界 例 The so-called equator, which we often mention, is actually an *imaginary* line around the middle of the Earth. 我们经常提到的所谓的赤道，其实是环绕地球中部的一条假想的线。 参 imaginative(*a.* 富有想象力的；创新的)
brilliant ['brɪliənt]	*a.* 给人印象深刻的；闪耀的(bright)；杰出的，卓越的(outstanding) 记 词根记忆：brilli(发光) + ant → 发光的 → 闪耀的 例 Scientists predicted the comet would be a *brilliant* spectacle. 科学家预言彗星将成为奇观。// Tiffany is a *brilliant* designer. 蒂法尼是个杰出的设计师。 派 brilliance(*n.* 闪耀；杰出)
cohesion [koʊ'hiːʒn]	*n.* 内聚力；凝聚力；团结，结合(*unity) 记 词根记忆：co(共同) + hes(黏附) + ion → 黏在一起 → 团结，结合 例 Social *cohesion* is the capacity of a society to ensure the well-being of all its members, minimizing disparities and avoiding marginalization. 社会凝聚力是指一个社会有能力保证所有成员的健康幸福，能使不平等最小化，并避免出现排斥现象。
Pueblo ['pweblou]	*n.* 普韦布洛印第安人村落；普韦布洛人 记 联想记忆：pue(看做 pure，纯洁的) + blo(音似：部落) → 纯洁的部落 → 普韦布洛印第安人村落 例 The largest *Pueblos* had five stories and more than 800 rooms. 最大的普韦布洛印第安人村落有五层建筑物，共 800 多个房间。
belt [belt]	*n.* 地带，地区(area)；腰带，皮带；带状物 例 The southern states are sometimes referred to be the *Bible Belt*. 南方各州有时被称为《圣经》地带。
council ['kaʊnsl]	*n.* 委员会；地方议会 搭 Security Council 联合国安理会 例 She's on the local *council*. 她是地方议会的议员。
license ['laɪsns]	*n.* 许可证，执照(permit) *vt.* 批准，许可(permit) 记 词根记忆：lic(允许) + ense → 许可 搭 a driver's license 驾驶执照 例 You need a *license* to fish in this lake. 从这个湖里钓鱼要有许可证。 license 我可不是无照行乞
silicon ['sɪlɪkən]	*n.* 硅 搭 silicon chip 硅片；silicon resin 硅树脂

formal	*a.* 正规的，正式的（normal）；形式的
[ˈfɔːrml]	例 Everyone was wearing *formal* suits or gowns. 所有人都身穿西装或礼服。// I'd rather not make the gardening club something *formal* and structured. 我不想把园艺俱乐部办得那么正式和结构分明。
	派 formally(*ad.* 正式地)
humidity	*n.* 湿度；潮湿
[hjuːˈmɪdəti]	记 来自 humid(*a.* 潮湿的)
	搭 relative humidity 相对湿度
	例 People living in this area have to endure the relatively high *humidity* in summer. 在夏天，生活在这个地区的人不得不忍受极重的湿气。
journal	*n.* 期刊，杂志；日记，日志
[ˈdʒɜːrnl]	记 词根记忆：journ(日) + al → 每天都进行记录 → 日记，日志
	例 By 1892, for example, the circulation of the *Ladies' Home Journal* had reached an astounding 700,000. 例如，到 1892 年，《女士居家杂志》的发行量令人吃惊，已达到了 70 万份。
	派 journalism(*n.* 新闻业，新闻工作)；journalist(*n.* 新闻工作者)
territory	*n.* 领土，版图；(个人、群体、动物等占据的)领域，地盘(domain)
[ˈterətɔːri]	记 词根记忆：terr(地) + it + ory(表地点) → 领土；领域
	搭 come/go with the territory 成为必然的结果(或部分)
	例 How did spiders defend their *territory*？蜘蛛如何捍卫地盘？
sneaker	*n.* 鬼鬼祟祟的人，卑鄙者；运动鞋
[ˈsniːkər]	例 Those are great *sneakers*. Were they very expensive? 这双运动鞋真不错。很贵吧？
commonplace	*n.* 平凡的事；老生常谈(platitude) *a.* 普通的，平凡的(ordinary)
[ˈkɑːmənpleɪs]	记 联想记忆：common(公共的) + place(地方) → 在公共的地方都能见到的 → 平凡的事
	例 Compared to 10 years ago, traveling by air is a *commonplace* now. 与十年前相比，现在坐飞机旅行是家常便饭。
retire	*v.* (使)退休，引退，退役；退出；撤退；就寝
[rɪˈtaɪər]	记 联想记忆：re(再，又) + tire(劳累) → 不再劳累 → (使)退休
	例 My grandfather was a consultant in the company before he *retired*. 我祖父退休前是公司的顾问。
	派 retirement(*n.* 退休)；retiree(*n.* 退休人员)
bustle	*n.* 忙乱嘈杂，喧嚣 *vi.* 奔忙，匆匆忙忙
[ˈbʌsl]	例 Many people are tired of the hustle and *bustle* of city life. 很多人厌倦都市生活的喧嚣。
	参 hustle(*n.* 忙碌)

20

civil ['sɪvl]	*a.* 市民的，公民的，平民的(civic)；民事的；国家的，政府的；文明的，有教养的 记 词根记忆：civ(市民，公民) + il → 市民的，公民的 搭 civil rights 公民权；civil war 内战；civil defense 民防 例 The American *Civil* War was one of the most violent times in the history of the United States. 美国内战是美国历史上最混乱的时期之一。 派 civilian(*n.* 平民 *a.* 平民的)；civility(*n.* 礼貌，客气)
mannerism ['mænərɪzəm]	*n.* 怪癖，癖性(idiosyncrasy, peculiarity, habit)；(绘画、写作等中)过分的独特风格 记 联想记忆：manner(风格，方式) + ism(抽象名词后缀) → 个人独有的风格 → 怪癖 例 She has an annoying *mannerism* of biting her nails. 她咬指甲的怪癖令人讨厌。
bark [bɑːrk]	*n.* 树皮；犬吠声 *v.* 吠叫；厉声质问 例 The dog suddenly started *barking* at us. 那条狗忽然开始对我们汪汪叫。
spice [spaɪs]	*n.* 香料，调味品(season, flavor)；趣味，情趣 *vt.* 加香料于；给…增添趣味 例 We need an exciting trip to add some *spice* to our life. 我们需要一次振奋人心的旅行来调剂一下生活。 派 spicy(*a.* 加香料的；刺激的，粗俗的)
crown [kraʊn]	*n.* 王冠；花冠 *v.* 加冕；使圆满，使完美 记 联想记忆：crow(乌鸦) + n → 给乌鸦戴帽子 → 王冠 例 Their efforts were finally *crowned* with success. 他们的努力终于取得了圆满成功。
shelter ['ʃeltər]	*n.* 掩蔽处，庇护所(harbor, shield)；居所，住所；掩蔽，保护 *vt.* 保护，掩蔽(protect)；躲避 记 联想记忆：shel(看做 shell，壳) + ter → 像壳一样的地方 → 庇护所 例 They use the canopy of the trees for *shelter* from heat and cold. 他们将树冠用做庇护所，来避暑防寒。 派 sheltered(*a.* 遮蔽的；受庇护的)
aspect ['æspekt]	*n.* 方面(*facet)；(建筑物的)朝向，方向；外表，外观 例 We should look at the problem from all *aspects*. 我们应该全面考虑这个问题。
incense ['ɪnsens]	*n.* 熏香 *vt.* 激怒，使愤怒 记 词根记忆：in + cens(=cand 光亮的) + e → 能发出亮光 → 熏香 例 The law *incensed* the workforce. 这条法律激怒了劳工大众。
augment [ɔːg'ment]	*vt.* 增加，提高(increase) 记 词根记忆：aug(增加) + ment → 增加，提高 例 While searching for a way to *augment* the family income, she began making dolls. 她开始做玩偶，作为增加家庭收入的一种方式。

230　□ civil　　□ mannerism　　□ bark　　□ spice　　□ crown　　□ shelter
　　　□ aspect　　□ incense　　□ augment

sow [soʊ]	*v.* 播种，种；灌输；煽动 例 The fields had been *sown* with wheat. 地里种上了小麦。 派 sowing(*n.* 播种)；sower(*n.* 播种者；播种机)
reside [rɪˈzaɪd]	*vi.* 居住于，定居(dwell, live)；(性质等)存在，在于 记 词根记忆：re(再) + sid(坐) + e → 久坐于(某地) → 居住于 例 Two species of these finches *reside* in the evergreen forests of North America. 这些雀中的两个种类居住在北美的常绿树林里。 派 residence(*n.* 住处；居住)
amplify [ˈæmplɪfaɪ]	*vt.* 放大(声音等)；增强(strengthen)；详述，充实(陈述等) 记 词根记忆：ampl(大的) + ify(使…) → 放大；增强 例 Can you *amplify* the sound so we can hear it better? 你能大声点让我们听得更清楚吗？ // Seeing the ballet *amplified* Jane's desire to learn to dance. 看了芭蕾舞剧，简学习跳舞的欲望更强了。 派 amplification(*n.* 扩大；充实)；amplifier(*n.* 放大器；扩音器) amplify
obscure [əbˈskjʊr]	*a.* 暗的，模糊的，朦胧的(dim)；费解的，晦涩的；不著名的，不重要的 *vt.* 使变模糊；使费解 记 词根记忆：ob(在…上面) + scur(遮盖) + e → 在上面遮盖 → 晦涩的 例 The path we had taken became more *obscure* in the heavy rain. 我们走的那条路在大雨中变得更难以辨认了。
cosmos [ˈkɑːzmoʊs]	*n.* 宇宙(universe) 记 词根记忆：cosm(宇宙) + os → 宇宙
wary [ˈweri]	*a.* 小心翼翼的，留神的，警惕的(*cautious, alert) 例 Be *wary* of strangers who offer you a ride. 要提防那些主动让你搭车的陌生人。 // The farmers keep a *wary* eye on the weather. 农民们密切关注着天气变化。 派 unwary(*a.* 粗心的)
laureate [ˈlɔːriət]	*n.* 桂冠诗人；荣誉获得者 *a.* 享有殊荣的 搭 a poet laureate 桂冠诗人 例 The old man was a Nobel *laureate* in physics. 那位老人是诺贝尔物理学奖获得者。
conscious [ˈkɑːnʃəs]	*a.* 自觉的，意识到的；有知觉的，有意识的(perceptual)；有意的，刻意的 记 词根记忆：con(共同) + sci(知道) + ous → 共同知道的 → 自觉的 例 Humans should be more *conscious* of the influence they have on ecosystems. 人类应更清楚地认识到自己对生态系统的影响。 派 consciousness(*n.* 知觉；意识)；unconscious(*a.* 无意识的) 参 conscientious(*a.* 尽责的)

20

unaided [ʌnˈeɪdɪd]	*a.* 未受协助的，独立的(independent) 搭 unaided eye 肉眼 例 Eventually, the metal will crumple and uncrumple, totally *unaided*. 最后，在没有任何辅助的情况下，金属会变皱，然后恢复平整状态。
optional [ˈɑːpʃnəl]	*a.* 可以任选的，非强制的(voluntary) 记 来自 option(*n.* 选择) 例 In place of the usual Wednesday class, I've arranged an *optional* review session. Since it is *optional*, attendance will not be taken. 周三的课换了，我已经安排了可任选的复习课。既然是选修的，就不会记考勤。
admission [ədˈmɪʃn]	*n.* 准许进入；入场费；承认(acknowledgement) 记 来自 admit(*v.* 承认；准许进入) 例 It was the first rodeo to charge *admission*. 这是第一次收入场费的牛仔竞技表演。
dolphin [ˈdɑːlfɪn]	*n.* 海豚 搭 a school of dolphins 一群海豚
spill [spɪl]	*v.* (使)溢出，溅出(overflow)；蜂拥而出 *n.* 溢出(的东西)，泄漏(的东西) 记 联想记忆：s + pill(药丸) → 药丸太满了，洒了一地 → 溢出 例 Thousands of gallons of crude oil were *spilled* into the ocean. 数千加仑原油泄漏，流入了海洋。// She's not upset about the *spill*. 溢出的东西并没有令她不安。
phenomenon [fəˈnɑːmɪnən]	*n.* 现象，迹象；非凡的人(或事物) 记 词根记忆：phen(出现) + omen(预兆) + on → 出现的预兆 → 现象，迹象 例 A similar *phenomenon* has also occurred in other parts of the animal kingdom. 在动物世界的其他地方也出现了类似现象。
counseling [ˈkaʊnsəlɪŋ]	*n.* 咨询；辅导 例 Vocational education and *counseling* extended the influence of public schools. 职业教育和咨询扩大了公立学校的影响。
nickel [ˈnɪkl]	*n.* 镍；五分镍币 记 发音记忆："你抠" → 连五分镍币都舍不得给 → 五分镍币
disrepute [ˌdɪsrɪˈpjuːt]	*n.* 坏名声，不光彩(discredit, dishonor) 记 联想记忆：dis(不) + repute(名声) → 不好的名声 → 坏名声 例 The player's bad behavior on the field is likely to bring the team into *disrepute*. 这名球员在赛场上的恶劣表现很可能会使这支球队臭名远扬。 派 disreputable(*a.* 声名狼藉的)
mine [maɪn]	*v.* 开矿，采矿；在…布雷 *pron.* 我的 *n.* 矿，矿井；地雷，水雷 例 This area has been *mined* for gold for centuries. 这个地区已有数世纪开采黄金的历史。 派 miner(*n.* 矿工)

nauseous

['nɔːʃəs]

a. 恶心的；令人作呕的，令人厌恶的

例 This prescription is supposed to be effective from paining, but it's maybe too strong for me. I took it when I woke up in pain in the middle of the night, and now I feel *nauseous*. 这个处方应该能缓解疼痛，但对我来说可能药效太强了。我半夜疼醒吃了一片，现在觉得恶心。

Jovons saw the kettle boil and cried out with the delighted voice of a child; Marshal too had seen the kettle boil and sat down silently to build an engine.

杰文斯看见水壶开了，高兴得像孩子似的叫了起来；马歇尔也看见水壶开了，却悄悄地坐下来造了一部蒸汽机。

——英国经济学家 凯恩斯（John Maynard Keynes, British economist）

20

Word List 21

音频

词根、词缀预习表

all	其他的	parallel a. 平行的；相似的	prag	做	pragmatic a. 务实的
fut	流	futile a. 无效的	dig	需要；不足	indigent a. 贫困的，贫穷的
sign	记号	significant a. 有重大意义的	ped	脚	pedestrian n. 步行者
aero	空气	aerobics n. 有氧运动	cav	洞	excavate vt. 挖掘；掘出
fil	线	filament n. 细丝	nutri	营养	nutrition n. 营养；营养学

---

hoard
[hɔːd]

v. 贮藏，囤积 n. 储藏(物)，贮存(物)
记 联想记忆：把东西藏(hoard)在木板(board)后
搭 hoard up 囤积
例 It is better to *hoard* money in the bank for tomorrow than spend it today. 我认为把钱存入银行以备将来之用比现在就把钱花掉要好。

---

parallel
[ˈpærəlel]

a. 平行的；相似的(*similar) n. 相似处；纬线 vt. 与…平行；与…相似；比得上
记 词根记忆：par(并列) + all(其他的) + el → 把不同的东西并列放置 → 平行的；相似的
例 It is possible to draw a *parallel* between their experience and ours. 在他们的经历和我们的经历中找到相似之处是可能的。
派 unparalleled(a. 空前的)

---

litter
[ˈlɪtər]

n. 废弃物，垃圾(rubbish)；一窝幼崽 v. 乱扔；使凌乱
记 联想记忆：把 little 的"l"丢掉，错拿了"r" → 乱扔；注意不要和 glitter(vi. 闪光)相混
例 We'll be putting the *litter* in these plastic trash bags. 我们要把这些垃圾扔到塑料垃圾袋里。// The ground under towering oaks is often *littered* with thousands of half-eaten acorns. 参天的橡树下经常是成千上万被啃了一半的橡子。

---

underlying
[ˌʌndərˈlaɪɪŋ]

a. 潜在的(latent)；基础的(basal)
记 联想记忆：under(在…下) + lying(躺着的) → 在下面躺着的 → 潜在的
例 An interviewer can go beyond written questions and probe for a subject's *underlying* feelings and reasons. 面试官可以不局限于书面问题，了解接受面试者潜在的情感和理智。

---

symbol
[ˈsɪmbl]

n. 符号，标志(sign)；象征
例 The common meal served at a common hearth is a powerful *symbol*, a mark of social unity. 在公共壁炉旁共同就餐是社会团结的一个有力象征。
派 symbolism(n. 象征主义); symbolize(vt. 象征); symbology(n. 象征学)

---

futile	*a.* 无效的，无用的，无意义的；琐细的；（人）没出息的
[ˈfjuːtl]	记 词根记忆：fut(=fus 流) + ile → 恰似东流水 → 无效的
	例 If something does not belong to you, it's going to be *futile* no matter how hard you try. 某些东西如果不属于你，你再怎么努力也是徒劳。

diet	*n.* 饮食，食物；规定饮食 *vi.* 节食
[ˈdaɪət]	搭 on a diet 节食
	例 People who're *dieting* need a variety of foods to assure a constant supply of nutrients their bodies need. 节食者需要各种食物，以确保身体所需的营养能得到持续的供应。
	派 dietary(*a.* 饮食的); dieter(*n.* 节食者); dietitian(*n.* 营养学家)

significant	*a.* 有重大意义的，重要的，显著的(noteworthy, important)；意味深长的
[sɪɡˈnɪfɪkənt]	记 词根记忆：sign(记号) + i + fic(做) + ant → 值得做记号的 → 有重大意义的
	搭 significant change 重大转变; a significant smile 意味深长的微笑
	例 The experimental result shows that there are no *significant* differences between the two groups of students. 实验结果显示，这两组学生之间没有显著的差异。
	派 significantly(*ad.* 有重大意义地，显著地；意味深长地)

positive	*a.* 肯定的(affirmative)；积极的(active)；确凿的(conclusive)；自信的，乐观的；正电的
[ˈpɑːzətɪv]	记 词根记忆：pos(放) + it + ive → 放心的 → 肯定的；积极的
	搭 positive charge 正电荷
	例 He believed writers should emphasize the *positive* aspects of life. 他认为作家应该强调生活的光明面。
	派 positively(*ad.* 肯定地；积极地；带正电地)

lumber	*v.* 笨拙地移动；迫使担负(责任等) *n.* 木材，木料(timber)；杂物
[ˈlʌmbər]	例 A family of elephants *lumbered* by. 一群大象迈着缓慢而沉重的步伐从旁边经过。
	派 lumbering(*n.* 伐木业，采伐林木 *a.* 缓慢吃力的)

roam	*vi.* 漫游，漫步，闲逛(wander) *n.* 漫步，漫游
[roʊm]	记 联想记忆：他的思绪漫游(roam)在广阔的空间(room)里
	搭 roam over/around/about 闲逛，徘徊
	例 Four male chimpanzees often *roam* together over a certain period. 四只雄猩猩在某个时间段经常一起漫游。

fervor	*n.* 热情，热烈(passion)
[ˈfɜːrvər]	例 The political leaders are always speaking with great *fervor*. 政治领导人演说时总是满腔热情。
	参 apathy(*n.* 冷漠)

affection	*n.* 喜爱，钟爱(fondness)；[常 *pl.*]爱情
[əˈfekʃn]	记 来自 affect(*v.* 影响；深深打动)
	例 Children need lots of love and *affection*. 孩子们需要多多疼爱和关怀。
	派 affectionate(*a.* 爱的，挚爱的)

21

□ futile　　　□ diet　　　□ significant　　　□ positive　　　□ lumber　　　□ roam
□ fervor　　　□ affection　　　□ attention

upheaval [ʌpˈhiːvl]	*n.* 剧变，动乱，大变动 记 来自 upheave(*v.* 举起，鼓起) 例 As the Indo-Europeans encroached on Old Europe from the east, the Continent underwent *upheavals*. 随着印欧人侵占了古欧洲，欧洲大陆经历了剧变。
simplify [ˈsɪmplɪfaɪ]	*vt.* 简化，使简单，使单纯 记 来自 simpl(e)(*a.* 简单的) 例 This technology can *simplify* network operations, significantly reducing recurring costs. 这项技术能够简化网络操作，大大降低重复的成本。 参 simplicity(*n.* 简单，简易；朴素；直率；单纯)
dozen [ˈdʌzn]	*n.* 一打，十二个 搭 dozens of 许多的 例 There were *dozens* of people waiting in the hall for autographs. 大厅里有许多人等着要签名。// A: Have you guys decided whether you are going to get an apartment off campus next year or are you staying in the dorm? B: We are still talking about the pros and cons. To me it seems like six of one and half of *dozen* of the other. A: 你们决定了明年是在校外租公寓还是住在宿舍了吗？ B: 我们仍然在讨论利弊。对我来说，都可以。
realtor [ˈriːəltər]	*n.* 房地产经纪人 记 联想记忆：real(不动产的) + tor → 房地产经纪人 例 The *realtor* has assured us that it will be no problem to sell the house. 房地产经纪人向我们保证说卖掉这房子不会有问题的。
bacteria [bækˈtɪriə]	*n.* 细菌 记 联想记忆：bac(看做 back，背后) + ter + ia(表病) → 总是偷偷让人得病的东西 → 细菌 搭 bacteria infection 细菌感染 例 Like the other microbes, *bacteria* are single-cells. 跟其他微生物一样，细菌是单细胞生物。// A: Now we have lots of antibiotics that kill *bacteria*. B: Well, penicillin kills *bacteria*, but not all antibiotics do. A: 现在我们有很多杀死细菌的抗生素。 B: 是啊，盘尼西林能杀菌，但不是所有的抗生素都能做到这一点。
aerobics [eˈroʊbɪks]	*n.* 有氧运动 记 词根记忆：aero(空气) + b + ics(…活动) → 有氧运动 例 I have to take an *aerobics* class now. 现在我得上有氧运动课程了。
filament [ˈfɪləmənt]	*n.* 灯丝；细丝 记 词根记忆：fil(线) + ament → 细丝 例 I can see that the *filament* in the bulb is already broken. 我看到灯泡里的灯丝已经断了。

□ upheaval □ simplify □ dozen □ realtor □ bacteria □ aerobics
□ filament

gossip [ˈɡɑːsɪp]	*n.* 闲话，流言飞语；爱说长道短的人 *vi.* 传播流言飞语，说长道短 记 联想记忆：美国电视剧 *Gossip Girl*《绯闻女孩》 例 Regarding the *gossips*, you can either face them or ignore them. 对于流言飞语，你可以勇敢面对，也可以无视它们。
hitch [hɪtʃ]	*v.* 搭便车；提起，拉起；（用绳、钩等）拴住 *n.* 故障，障碍 记 联想记忆：hit(撞) + ch → 车子撞坏后，渴望能搭便车 → 搭便车 搭 hitch up 提起，拉起 例 I stopped the car to pick up a young man who wanted to *hitch* a ride. 我停下车来搭载一个想搭车的小伙子。
pragmatic [præɡˈmætɪk]	*a.* 务实的，注重实效的，实用的(realistic) 记 词根记忆：prag(做) + matic → 用实际行动表示的 → 务实的，注重实效的 例 It's said that American people are *pragmatic* by nature. 据说美国人天生注重实效。
grump [ɡrʌmp]	*vi.* 发脾气，发牢骚 *n.* 脾气不好的人 例 The once obedient kid has turned into a teenage *grump*. 那个曾经听话的小孩已变成暴躁的少年。
indigent [ˈɪndɪdʒənt]	*a.* 贫困的，贫穷的 记 词根记忆：in(里，内) + dig(需要；不足) + ent → 内部缺乏的 → 贫困的，贫穷的 例 Mike's persistence was forged in an *indigent* childhood. 童年的贫苦生活造就了迈克的坚持不懈。
knack [næk]	*n.* 诀窍；技能，本领；习惯，癖好 记 联想记忆：敲(knock)开脑袋，获得诀窍(knack) 例 It's said that humans have the *knack* of changing the natural environment. 据说人类有改变自然环境的本领。
lighthearted [ˌlaɪtˈhɑːrtɪd]	*a.* 无忧无虑的；愉快的 记 组合词：light(轻的) + hearted(有…心情的) → 心情轻松的 → 无忧无虑的 例 It was a *lighthearted* card with a cartoon inside. 这是一张令人愉快的卡片，里面有一幅卡通画。
necessitate [nəˈsesɪteɪt]	*vt.* 需要，使成为必要 记 词根记忆：ne(不) + cess(走开) + it + ate(使…) → 使不走开 → 使成为必要 例 Your mistakes *necessitate* doing this task once again. 因为你犯的这些错误，这项工作得重做一遍。
pedestrian [pəˈdestriən]	*n.* 步行者，行人 *a.* 徒步的；缺乏想象力的 记 词根记忆：ped(脚) + estrian → 用脚走的人 → 步行者 例 The car knocked into a *pedestrian*, and drove away. 那辆车撞倒了一个行人后开走了。

21

ramble
[ˈræmbl]

vi. 漫游；漫谈，闲聊 *n.* 漫步

记 词根记忆：r + ambl(走) + e → 随意地走 → 漫游

例 The mother told her boy not to *ramble* on the street after school. 母亲告诉儿子放学后不要在街上闲逛。

---

setback
[ˈsetbæk]

n. 挫折，阻碍；倒退

记 来自词组 set back(使推迟，耽误)

例 The breakdown in talks represents a temporary *setback* in the peace process. 谈判破裂意味着和平进程暂时受挫。// Susan seemed better after illness but then she had a sudden *setback*. 苏珊病后看起来好些了，但后来病情又突然恶化。

---

hull
[hʌl]

n. (果实等的)外壳；船身，船体 *vt.* 给…去外壳

记 联想记忆：空有外壳(hull)，毫无价值(null)

搭 a wooden hull 木质船体

例 The popcorn, with its special *hull*, doesn't always pop. 爆米花拥有特殊外壳，有的不能爆开。

---

taut
[tɔːt]

a. 绷紧的；肌肉结实的；结构严谨的，紧凑的

记 联想记忆：t + au + t → au 被两个 t 夹着，绷得紧紧的 → 绷紧的

例 Tom pulled hard at the *taut* tow-rope to bring the boat alongside. 汤姆用力拉住那根绷紧的缆绳，想把小船拉回来。

---

sleigh
[sleɪ]

n. (尤指马拉的)雪橇

例 Santa Claus will come to my house riding a *sleigh* pulled by the reindeer. 圣诞老人会坐着驯鹿拉的雪橇来到我家。

---

excavate
[ˈekskəveɪt]

vt. 挖掘(dig)；掘出(unearth)

记 词根记忆：ex(出) + cav(洞) + ate(动词后缀) → 挖出洞 → 挖掘；掘出

excavate

例 The deepest bone-bearing deposit was *excavated* in 1914. 最深的含有骨头的矿床于 1914 年被挖掘出来。

派 excavation[*n.* 挖掘，发掘；(常 *pl.*)发掘现场]

---

transport

[ˈtrænspɔːrt] *n.* 运输；运输系统，运载工具

[trænˈspɔːrt] *vt.* 运输；传播

记 词根记忆：trans(穿过) + port(搬运) → 在两地间搬运 → 运输；传播

例 In China, more than 70% of coal *transport* is still by rail. 在中国，70% 以上的煤炭仍通过铁路进行运输。

attention [ə'tenʃn]	*n.* 注意(力)，留心；立正 记 词根记忆：at + tent(伸展) + ion(名词后缀) → 听得伸长了脖子 → 注意(力) 搭 pay attention to 注意 例 The article in the magazine caught her *attention*. 杂志上的这篇文章引起了她的注意。// *Attention*, please, ladies and gentlemen. Our bus is approaching Cambridge, Massachusetts, where we'll be stopping to eat. 女士们，先生们，请注意，我们的公交车很快将到达马萨诸塞州的剑桥市，我们要在那里停下来就餐。
nutrition [nu'trɪʃn]	*n.* 营养；营养学 记 词根记忆：nutri(营养) + tion → 营养；营养学 例 Vitamin D is important to human *nutrition* because it helps the body to absorb Calcium. 维生素 D 帮助人体吸收钙，对人的营养很重要。 派 nutritional(*a.* 营养的)；nutritionist(*n.* 营养学家)；malnutrition(*n.* 营养不良)
daylight ['deɪlaɪt]	*n.* 日光(sunlight)；白昼 记 组合词：day(白天) + light(光) → 白天的光 → 日光 搭 daylight robbery 漫天要价，敲竹杠 例 The African grass mouse is active during *daylight* hours. 非洲草鼠在白天很活跃。
gilding ['gɪldɪŋ]	*n.* 镀金；贴金层，镀金层；金色涂层 例 *Gilding* has long signified an ostentatious display of wealth. 在很长一段时间里，人们用镀金来炫耀财富。
intoxication [ɪnˌtɑːksɪ'keɪʃn]	*n.* 醉，醉酒；极度兴奋 记 来自 intoxicate(*vt.* 使醉)；in(里) + tox(毒) + ic + ate(使…) → 使毒进入身体 → 使醉 搭 water intoxication 水中毒 例 At a depth of 5 atmospheres nitrogen causes symptoms resembling alcohol *intoxication*. 在五个大气压的深度，氮会导致类似醉酒的症状。

intoxication

rotate ['rəʊteɪt]	*v.* (使)转动，旋转(revolve)；(使)轮流(*alternate) 记 词根记忆：rot(旋转) + ate(使…) → (使)转动，旋转 例 It was difficult to move or *rotate*. 这很难移动或转动。 派 rotation(*n.* 转动，旋转)
spike [spaɪk]	*n.* 长钉，大钉；猛增，急升 例 This year has seen a sudden *spike* in the price of agricultural products. 今年农产品价格急剧上涨。

21

locality
[loʊˈkæləti]

n. 地点(site); 位置(position)

记 词根记忆: loc(地点) + al + ity → 地点; 位置

例 There are *localities* that have specific restrictions with regard to noise pollution. 有些地区对噪音污染有明确的限制。

参 location(*n.* 位置, 场所)

---

undergo
[ˌʌndərˈɡoʊ]

vt. 经历(*experience); 遭受(suffer)

例 All forms of art were *undergoing* a revolution at that time. 当时, 所有的艺术形式都经历着革新。

---

colony
[ˈkɑːləni]

n. (生物)群, 群体(community); 殖民地(settlement); (侨民等的)聚居地

记 词根记忆: col(耕种) + on + y(表场所, 名词后缀) → 在某处耕种 → 殖民地

例 The MacDowell *Colony*, founded in 1907, is the oldest artists' *colony* in the United States. 建于 1907 年的麦克道尔艺术区是美国最古老的艺术区。

派 colonist(*n.* 殖民者); colonial(*a.* 殖民的; 殖民国家的)

---

mottled
[ˈmɑːtld]

a. 有杂色的, 斑驳的(spotted)

记 发音记忆: "毛头的" → 头发颜色多的 → 有杂色的

例 Drinking water containing excessive amounts of fluorides may leave a *mottled* effect on the enamel of teeth. 含有过量氟化物的饮用水会在牙齿的珐琅质上留下斑点。

---

suite
[swiːt]

n. 套, 组; 套房

记 联想记忆: 这套(suite)家具很适合(suit)这间套房(suite)

搭 a suite of rooms 一套房间

例 All of our one-bedroom *suites* have been recently redecorated with plush furnishings. 我们所有的单卧室套房最近都重新进行了装修, 配上了丝绒装饰品。

派 suited(*a.* 适合的, 适当的; 般配的)

---

military
[ˈmɪləteri]

a. 军事的(martial) *n.* [the ~] 军队, 军方(army, troops)

记 词根记忆: milit(打架) + ary → 军事的

例 The *military* stationed at the various forts. 军队驻扎在各个堡垒。

---

enclose
[ɪnˈkloʊz]

vt. 围住; 把…装入(信封、包裹等)

记 词根记忆: en(进入) + clos(关闭) + e → 关在里面 → 围住

例 The application instructions say you should *enclose* a check or money order for twenty dollars. 申请指示说要往信封里装一张 20 美元的支票或汇票。

派 enclosed(*a.* 被围住的); enclosure(*n.* 围栏)

enclose

---

stature
[ˈstætʃər]

n. 身材, 身高(natural height); 地位, 声望, 名望(status)

记 词根记忆: stat(站立) + ure(表状态、名词后缀) → 站的状态 → 身材, 身高

例 She is small in *stature*. 她个头小。

□ locality   □ undergo   □ colony   □ mottled   □ suite   □ military
□ enclose   □ stature

livelihood [ˈlaɪvlihʊd]	*n.* 生计，谋生手段(living) 例 The experts guard their knowledge to prevent others from stealing their *livelihood*. 专家们守护着自己的知识，以防其他人偷走他们谋生的手段。
sole [soʊl]	*a.* 单独的(*single)；唯一的(*only, individual) *n.* 鞋底，脚底 记 词根记忆：sol(单独) + e → 单独的；唯一的 例 The rich investor is the *sole* owner of the office building. 这位富有的投资商是这幢写字楼唯一的所有人。 派 solely(*ad.* 只，仅)
mountainous [ˈmaʊntənəs]	*a.* 多山的；巨大的 搭 a mountainous terrain 多山的地形 例 We traveled through wild *mountainous* country. 我们的旅行途经了一个荒凉多山的地区。
sample [ˈsæmpl]	*n.* 样品，标本(specimen) *vt.* 抽样调查；品尝，体验 记 联想记忆：简单的(simple)样品(sample) 例 Fossils provide a limited *sample* of ancient organisms. 化石提供了有关古代生物的有限的样品。 派 sampling(*n.* 取样)
flux [flʌks]	*n.* 变迁，不断的变动(change) 记 词根记忆：flu(流动) + x → 变动 → 变迁 例 Life on Earth has continually been in *flux* as slow physical and chemical changes have occurred on Earth. 随着地球上缓慢发生的物理和化学变化，生命也一直处于变化之中。 派 influx(*n.* 流入)
assume [əˈsuːm]	*vt.* 假定(premise, suppose)；承担(bear) 记 词根记忆：as + sum(拿，取) + e → 假定；承担 例 I *assume* everyone here is a sophomore, since this is the Nursing Department second-year physiology course. 我假定在座的各位都是二年级学生，因为这是护理系二年级的生理学课程。 派 assumption(*n.* 假定；担任) 参 presume(*v.* 假定；认为)；consume(*vt.* 消耗；消费)；resume(*v.* 重新开始；恢复)
complain [kəmˈpleɪn]	*v.* 诉苦，抱怨；诉讼；控告 记 联想记忆：com + plain（平淡的）→ 太过平淡的生活让人抱怨 → 抱怨 搭 complain of 诉说；complain to 向…抱怨 例 My mother always *complains* that her knee hurts just before a storm. 我母亲总是抱怨每次暴风雨前她的膝盖都会疼。// One day, a customer came into a drugstore *complaining* of a headache and asked for a bottle of cola syrup. 一天，一名顾客走进药店，说自己头疼，想买一瓶可乐糖浆。 complain

veil [veɪl]	*n.* 面纱(cover, hide); 遮蔽物 *vt.* 以面纱掩盖; 掩饰 记 联想记忆: 邪恶的(evil)人总是试图掩饰(veil)自己的意图 搭 draw a veil over sth. 遮住某物 例 Even nowadays, most women in this region wear *veils* in public places. 时至今日, 该地区的大多数女性在公众场合仍蒙着面纱。 派 veiled(*a.* 蒙着面纱的; 含蓄的, 掩饰的)
infest [ɪnˈfest]	*vt.* 大批滋生, 大批出没于 记 联想记忆: in(进入) + fest(集会) → 拥挤着参加集会 → 大批滋生 搭 be infested with 多得成灾 例 The waters are *infested* with sharks. 这片水域到处都是鲨鱼。 派 infestation(*n.* 滋生, 大批出没)
tolerant [ˈtɑːlərənt]	*a.* 宽容的; 容忍的 记 词根记忆: tol(支撑) + er + ant → 能自我支撑的 → 宽容的; 容忍的 例 The prejudiced man is not at all *tolerant*. 这个怀有偏见的男子一点都不宽容。 派 tolerance(*n.* 忍耐, 忍受)
forecast [ˈfɔːrkæst]	*vt./n.* 预报(predict); 预测, 预料 记 联想记忆: fore(前面) + cast(扔) → 预先扔下 → 预测, 预料 搭 weather forecast 天气预报 例 Severe weather conditions have been *forecasted* following these mild days. 这几天风和日丽, 不过预报说过后天气就会变得恶劣。
alter [ˈɔːltər]	*vt.* 改变(*change, vary) 记 本身是词根, 意为"改变状态" 例 The effect of super saturation is simply to *alter* the growth rate. 过饱和的效果仅仅是为了改变生长速度。 派 alteration(*n.* 改变, 更改); unaltered(*a.* 未被改变的; 不变的) 参 altar(*n.* 祭坛) alter
mobile [ˈmoʊbl]	*n.* 动的雕塑 *a.* 可移动的(movable); 多变的(changeable) 记 词根记忆: mob(动) + ile → 可移动的; 多变的 例 One of the sculptures is a *mobile* that is made of pieces of aluminum. 其中一个雕塑是用铝片做的, 可以移动。 派 mobility(*n.* 流动性; 移动的能力); immobilize(*vt.* 使不动)
linear [ˈlɪniər]	*a.* 线的, 直线的; 线性的; 长度的 记 来自 line(*n.* 直线) 搭 linear algebra 线性代数; linear equations 线性方程 例 In her art she broke the laws of scientific *linear* perspective. 她在自己的绘画艺术中打破了科学的直线透视法则。

confidence [ˈkɑːnfɪdəns]	*n.* 信任；信心(faith, belief) 记 词根记忆：con(表加强) + fid(相信) + ence → 信心 例 The teacher has every *confidence* in her students' abilities. 那个老师完全相信她学生的能力。// She answered the questions with *confidence*. 她信心满满地回答了那些问题。 参 self-confidence(*n.* 自信)；overconfident(*a.* 过于自信的)
stash [stæʃ]	*vt.* 隐藏，藏匿(conceal) *n.* 贮藏物 记 联想记忆：st + ash(灰) → 躲在灰里 → 隐藏，藏匿 例 Garbage has been *stashed* in the building's basement despite sanitation laws to the contrary. 垃圾被藏到了这座建筑的地下室，尽管卫生法规定不允许这么做。
inflate [ɪnˈfleɪt]	*v.* (使)充气，膨胀(expand)；鼓吹，吹捧；(使)涨价 记 词根记忆：in(进入) + flat(吹) + e → 往里面吹气 → 使充气；鼓吹 例 The yellow balloon is *inflated* with helium. 黄气球里充的是氦气。 派 inflation(*n.* 通货膨胀)
amid [əˈmɪd]	*prep.* 在…中，被…围绕 记 词根记忆：a + mid(中间) → 在…中 例 The katydid, a type of grasshopper, is active at night and rests *amid* foliage during the day. 纺织娘是一种蚱蜢，夜里活跃，白天停在树叶间休息。
paddle [ˈpædl]	*n.* 桨；桡足 *v.* 用桨划船；涉水，戏水 记 联想记忆：pad(动物的肉趾，如鸭蹼) + dle → 鳍状肢 → 桡足 例 John accidentally dropped his *paddle* in the lake. 约翰不小心把桨掉进了湖里。 派 paddler(*n.* 划桨者；涉水者)
cornerstone [ˈkɔːrnərstoʊn]	*n.* 墙角石，奠基石；基础 记 组合词：corner(墙角) + stone(石) → 墙角石 例 Homer was the poet that laid down the *cornerstone* of Western literature. 诗人荷马奠定了西方文学的基础。
fund [fʌnd]	*n.* 基金，专款；储备，蕴藏；[常 *pl.*]现款，资金(capital) *vt.* 为…提供资金 记 发音记忆："放的" → 发放资金 → 专款 例 The project has been cancelled because of lack of *funds*. 这个项目因缺乏资金已被撤销。

21

venture [ˈventʃər]	*n.* 冒险，投机(gamble)；投机活动，(商业等的)风险项目 *v.* 敢于去；冒险(risk) 记 发音记忆："玩车" → 玩车一族追求的就是冒险 → 冒险 例 The whole *venture* seemed so impractical and foolish. 整个冒险活动看上去特别不切实际，而且还很愚蠢。// The monarch butterfly produces as many as four generations a year, each one of which *ventures* a little farther north. 黑脉金斑蝶一年产下四批后代，每一代都朝着北方挺进一段距离。 派 venturesome(*a.* 好冒险的)
unequal [ʌnˈiːkwəl]	*a.* (在规模、数量等方面)不同的，不相等的(disproportionate)；(力量、能力等)不平等的，不相称的；不胜任的 例 It's generally admitted that people with *unequal* talents should be paid *unequal* amounts. 人们普遍认为才智不同的人应该得到不同的报酬。
chorus [ˈkɔːrəs]	*n.* 合唱曲；合唱队；副歌，叠句；齐声，齐声说的话 *v.* 齐声说；随声附和 搭 chorus master 合唱队指挥；in chorus 一起，同时 例 Her proposal received a *chorus* of praise. 她的提议获得一片好评。
nonsense [ˈnɑːnsens]	*n.* 胡说，废话(rubbish)；冒失(或轻浮)的行为 记 联想记忆：non(不) + sense(意义) → 无意义的话 → 废话 搭 make (a) nonsense of 使…的价值大打折扣；使…显得荒诞 例 They are talking *nonsense*! 他们在胡说八道！
purple [ˈpɜːrpl]	*a.* 紫色的 *n.* 紫色 记 联想记忆：很多人(people)喜欢紫色(purple) 例 On hearing this, her face was *purple* with anger. 听到这个消息，她气得脸色发紫。
ration [ˈræʃn]	*n.* 配给量，定量(quota)；给养，口粮 *vt.* 配给，定量供应 记 词根记忆：rat(清点) + ion → 清点财物，进行分配 → 配给量，定量；配给 例 Once these latest *rations* run out, the country will again face hunger and starvation. 最后这批口粮一旦用完，该国又将面临饥荒。
mat [mæt]	*n.* 垫子(rug, cushion) 记 联想记忆：戴着帽子(hat)坐在垫子(mat)上 例 Please wipe your feet on the *mat* before you come in. 请在垫子上擦擦脚再进来。
profound [prəˈfaʊnd]	*a.* 巨大的，深远的(deep-seated)；知识渊博的；深奥的(difficult to understand) 记 联想记忆：pro(在…前面) + found(创立) → 有超前的创见性 → 深远的 例 Globalization effects very *profound* changes in modern lifestyles. 全球化使现代人的生活方式发生了巨大的变化。 派 profoundly(*ad.* 深刻地)；profundity(*n.* 深刻性；巨大，严重)

attire [ə'taɪər]	*n.* 穿着，服饰（clothing, dress） *vt.* 给…穿衣，打扮 记 联想记忆：at + tire(疲劳) → 穿得太多，累 → 穿着，服饰 例 We will *attire* him in fine clothing so he can make a good impression. 我们将给他穿上精美的服饰，好让他给人留下一个好印象。 参 attic(*n.* 阁楼，顶楼)
ornithology [ˌɔːrnɪ'θɑːlədʒi]	*n.* 鸟类学 记 词根记忆：ornith(鸟) + ology(…学) → 鸟类学 例 I wish I'd seen it since that's what we're studying in my *ornithology* class. 我真希望自己看到了，因为那是我们正在鸟类学课上学习的内容。
palatable ['pælətəbl]	*a.* 美味的，可口的（delicious）；合意的，认可的 记 联想记忆：palat(看做 plate, 盘子) + able(能…的) → 端上来没多久就被消灭光的一盘子食物 → 美味的 例 This soup isn't excellent, but it's *palatable*. 这个汤不算太好，不过还算可口。 派 unpalatable(*a.* 不好吃的)

palatable

The supreme happiness of life is the conviction that we are loved.
生活中最大的幸福是坚信有人爱我们。
——法国小说家 雨果（Victor Hugo, French novelist）

Word List 22

词根、词缀预习表

count	数	account n. 账目	ord	顺序	primordial a. 最初的
proper	固有的	property n. 财产，所有物	**techn**	技艺	technical a. 技术的，工艺的
part	离开	depart vi. 离开；背离	**nav**	船	naval a. 海军的
pand	张开	expand v. 扩张；膨胀	**graph**	写	biography n. 传记
fest	打	manifest vt. 显示	**ana-**	类似	analogy n. 类比，类推

account [əˈkaʊnt]	v. 说明，解释；（在数量上）占 n. 解释，描述，叙述(interpretation)；账目；账户(record) 记 词根记忆：ac(表加强) + count(数) → 账目需要一数再数 → 账目 搭 take...into account 考虑，重视；account for 说明；占 例 The three main television networks in the United States *account* for more advertising dollars than any other medium. 美国三大电视网络占有的广告费比其他任何媒体都要多。 派 accounting(n. 会计学); accountant(n. 会计师); accountable(a. 应作解释的；应负责的)
cease [siːs]	v./n. 结束，终止，停止(*stop, end) 记 联想记忆：c + ease(安逸) → 生于忧患，死于安乐 → 停止 例 It *ceased* snowing. 雪停了。 派 ceaseless(a. 不停的，无休止的)
turkey [ˈtɜːrki]	n. 火鸡(肉)；失败 记 联想记忆：据说土耳其(Turkey)出产的火鸡(turkey)最好吃 例 Her latest novel is a real *turkey*. 她最近的那部小说真是一大败笔。
impulse [ˈɪmpʌls]	n. 冲动，一时的念头(urge)；刺激，推动力；脉冲(pulse) 记 词根记忆：im(使…) + puls(推) + e → 冲动 例 Fish also use such ability to produce and detect electrical *impulses* to communicate. 鱼类也通过它们产生和探测电脉冲的能力来进行交流。 参 propulsion(n. 推进力)

normally
['nɔːrməli]

ad. 通常地(usually); 正常地

例 It *normally* takes me half an hour to get there by bike. 我骑自行车去那儿一般要花半个小时。//
A: Those were such funny stories Tom told last night. He was like a totally different guy.
B: Yeah, really. He is *normally* so serious.
A: 汤姆昨晚讲的故事太逗了。他简直像换了个人。
B: 没错，他平常很严肃的。

property
['prɑːpərti]

n. 财产，所有物(possession); 所有权(ownership); 房产，地产(real estate); 特性(characteristic)

记 词根记忆：proper(固有的) + ty(表物，名词后缀) → 固有物 → 财产，所有物

例 Silver's most distinguishing *property* is its electrical conductivity. 导电性是银最显著的特性。

absolute
['æbsəluːt]

a. 完全的，绝对的; 地道的; 无疑的，确凿的; 不受限制，不受约束的

记 词根记忆：ab(表加强) + solu(松开) + te → 完全松开 → 完全的

搭 absolute zero 绝对零度; with absolute certainty 绝对肯定地

例 Beauty cannot be measured by any *absolute* standard. 美没有绝对的衡量标准。

switch
[swɪtʃ]

n. 开关，电闸; 转换，改变; 枝条，鞭子 *v.* (使)转变，改变(transform); 交换，掉换

搭 switch off 切断; switch on 打开; switch to 转到，转变成

例 I couldn't make myself *switch* off the TV. 让我关电视，我做不到。

intelligent
[ɪn'telɪdʒənt]

a. 有才智的，聪明的(clever)

记 词根记忆：intel(在…之间) + lig(选择) + ent(形容词后缀) → 能在很多事物中作出选择的 → 有才智的，聪明的

例 He didn't realize how *intelligent* Mary really was. 他没有意识到玛丽有多聪明。

派 intelligence(*n.* 智力)

depart
[dɪ'pɑːrt]

vi. 离开(leave, exit); (from)背离(deviate)

记 词根记忆：de(去掉，离开) + part(离开) → 离开; 背离

例 Some musicians consciously *depart* from strict meter to create a relaxed sense of phrasing that also emphasizes the underlying rhythms. 一些音乐家有意摆脱严格的韵律，试图在强调基本旋律的同时创造一种松散的编排方式。

派 departure(*n.* 离开，出发)

expand
[ɪk'spænd]

v. 扩张(outspread); 膨胀(swell); 伸展，伸开

记 词根记忆：ex(向外) + pand(张开) → 向外张开 → 扩张; 膨胀

例 The new university greatly *expanded* in size and course offerings, breaking completely out of the old. 那所新的大学在规模和课程选择上都有了大幅增加，完全摆脱了旧的模式。

派 expanding(*a.* 扩大的); expansion(*n.* 扩张; 扩展的部分)

22

□ normally　　□ property　　□ absolute　　□ switch　　□ intelligent　　□ depart
□ expand

rite [raɪt]	*n.* (宗教的)仪式，典礼(ritual) 例 In this area there are certain things one should not do in everyday life because they are linked to funeral *rites*. 在该地区，有些与丧葬仪式相关的事在日常生活中是不应该做的。
curriculum [kəˈrɪkjələm]	*n.* [*pl.* curricula]全部课程(course) 例 French is in the *curriculum*. 法语已纳入课程内容。
manifest [ˈmænɪfest]	*vt.* 表明，显示(indicate, show) *n.* 货物清单 *a.* 明显的(apparent) 记 词根记忆：mani(手) + fest(打) → 用手打开 → 显示 例 The contradiction *manifested* itself in the employment situation. 这个矛盾在就业形势中显现了出来。 派 manifestation(*n.* 显示，表明)
strategic [strəˈtiːdʒɪk]	*a.* 对全局有重要意义的，关键的；战略性的(tactical) 例 The bridge is one of the most *strategic* card games. 桥牌是最具有战略性的纸牌游戏之一。
inject [ɪnˈdʒekt]	*vt.* 注射(药液等)；注入，灌输；投入 记 词根记忆：in(进入) + ject(投，掷) → 投进去 → 注射(药物等) 例 Snakes frequently subdue their prey without *injecting* poison. 蛇经常无需注射毒液就能制服猎物。
puzzle [ˈpʌzl]	*n.* 难题，谜(riddle) *vt.* 迷惑，使困惑 搭 jigsaw puzzle 七巧板，拼图；puzzle over/about 苦苦思索 例 For a while, the zookeepers were *puzzled* by the accident, but they finally discovered what happened. 动物园管理员一度被这件事所困惑，但他们最终发现了事情的来龙去脉。 派 puzzlement(*n.* 困惑)
stick [stɪk]	*v.* 刺，戳，插；粘住，粘贴(attach)；放置(put)；卡住 *n.* 棍，棒；手杖(wand) 搭 stick with 紧跟；持续，坚持 例 *Stick* a message in a bottle and throw it in the sea. 在瓶子里放一张纸条，然后把它扔进大海。 派 sticker(*n.* 贴纸，不干胶标签)；sticky(*a.* 有黏性的；棘手的)
primordial [praɪˈmɔːrdiəl]	*a.* 原始的，最初的(primeval, primitive)；基本的(fundamental) 记 词根记忆：prim(第一) + ord(顺序) + ial → 在顺序上处于第一的 → 最初的 例 It must be some *primordial* impulse that drives me to play electric keyboard instruments. 一定是某种本能冲动驱使着我去弹奏电子键盘乐器。
raft [ræft]	*n.* 筏，木排；充气船 *v.* 用筏运送；乘筏渡河 记 联想记忆：坐木筏(raft)漂流(drift) 搭 a raft of 大量，许多 例 Traditional *rafts* are usually constructed of wood or reeds. 传统的筏子经常用木头或芦苇做成。

periodic [ˌpɪriˈɑːdɪk]	*a.* 周期的，定期的（regular） 记 来自 period（*n.* 周期） 搭 periodic table 元素周期表 例 This *periodic* extinction might be due to intersection of the Earth's orbit with a cloud of comets. 造成这种周期性灭绝的原因可能是地球轨道和彗星云的交叉。 派 periodical（*n.* 期刊，杂志）；periodically（*ad.* 定期地，周期地）
sledding [ˈsledɪŋ]	*n.* 进展 例 This bill faces tough *sledding* in the legislature. 这项法案在立法过程中面临着重重阻挠。
comprehensive [ˌkɑːmprɪˈhensɪv]	*a.* 全面的；综合的 记 词根记忆：com（共同）+ prehens（抓住）+ ive → 全部抓住 → 全面的；综合的 例 Our customers are supplied with a *comprehensive* range of services. 我们给顾客提供一系列全方位的服务。
forage [ˈfɔːrɪdʒ]	*vi.* 觅食（*search for food）；搜寻（rummage）*n.* 草料，饲料（*feed, fodder） 记 联想记忆：for（为了）+ age（年龄）→ 为了成长寻找草料 → 草料；觅食 例 Many ants *forage* across the countryside in large numbers. 蚂蚁成群结队地在田里觅食。
forward [ˈfɔːrwərd]	*vt.* 发送；转交，转递 *ad.* 向前；向将来 *a.* 向前的，前部的，前面的；鲁莽的，冒昧的 搭 look forward to（doing）sth. 期盼… 例 We will be *forwarding* you our new catalog next Monday. 我们将于下周一给您寄送新的商品目录。
technical [ˈteknɪkl]	*a.* 技术的，工艺的；专业的 记 词根记忆：techn（技艺）+ ical → 技术的，工艺的 搭 technical innovation 技术革新；technical hitch 技术故障 例 I have to admit the word "ethnography" scared me a little at first. It seems so *technical*. 我得承认"人种学"这个词一开始有点吓着我了。它显得如此专业。 派 technically（*ad.* 在技术上；在专业上）
hook [hʊk]	*v.* 连接到无线电设备；勾住 *n.* 钩，吊钩（clasp, hanger）；钩状物 例 She *hooks* the computer up to the printer. 她将计算机连上打印机。
random [ˈrændəm]	*a.* 随机的，任意的（*unpredictable, arbitrary）*n.* 随机，随意 记 联想记忆：ran（跑）+ dom（领域）→ 可以在各个领域跑 → 任意的 搭 at random 随意地，任意地 例 The effect of gravity at high altitude is *random*. 在高海拔的地方重力的影响是不确定的。 派 randomly（*ad.* 随便地）

22

向前向前向前～
我们的队伍向太阳～

♪ ♫

forward

lounge [laʊndʒ]	*n.* 等候室, 休息室(lobby) *vi.* 懒洋洋地站(或倚、躺) 记 联想记忆: loung(看做 long, 长的) + e → 等候室一般都放有长椅子 → 等候室 例 Several students were *lounging* around, reading newspapers. 有几个学生懒洋洋地坐着看报纸。
flora [ˈflɔːrə]	*n.* 植物群 记 来自 Flora(弗洛拉, 希腊神话中的花神) 例 Plants are grouped into *floras* based on region, period, special environment, or climate. 植物根据其所处的区域、时期、特定环境以及地带而被分为各种植物群。 派 floral(*a.* 植物的; 绘有花的)
staggered [ˈstægərd]	*a.* 交错的, 错开的(interlaced); 震惊的 例 I was *staggered* at the foreigner's knowledge of Chinese literature. 那个外国人的中国文学知识之丰富程度着实令我吃惊。
pine [paɪn]	*n.* 松树 *vi.* (因疾病等)憔悴; 难过, 悲伤 例 He was *pining* for the mountains of his motherland. 他对祖国的青山思念不已。 参 pineapple(*n.* 菠萝)
naval [ˈneɪvl]	*a.* 海军的 记 词根记忆: nav(船) + al → 船的 → 在海上的 → 海军的 搭 naval academy 海军军官学校 例 England emerged as a major *naval* power in the mid-17th century. 17 世纪中叶, 英格兰成为一个主要的海军强国。
avoid [əˈvɔɪd]	*vt.* 避免, 规避(*shy away from, *prevent) 记 联想记忆: a + void(空旷; 空虚) → 使空旷 → 避免 例 You should listen to radio reports to *avoid* traffic jams. 你应该听听广播报道, 以免碰上交通堵塞。 派 avoidable(*a.* 可避免的); avoidance(*n.* 避免); unavoidably(*ad.* 不得已, 无可奈何地)
biography [baɪˈɑːgrəfi]	*n.* 传记 记 词根记忆: bio(生活) + graph(写) + y → 记录生活 → 传记 例 *Biography* began to flower thanks to new publishing technologies and an expanding reading public. 得益于新的出版技术和越来越多的公众开始阅读, 传记文学开始得到发展与成熟。 派 biographical(*a.* 传记的); biographer(*n.* 传记作者)
elm [elm]	*n.* 榆树 例 The hedgerows were planted with *elm*. 这一排树篱是用榆树植成的。
implicit [ɪmˈplɪsɪt]	*a.* 含蓄的(implied); 绝对的(absolute); 内含的 记 词根记忆: im(在…里面) + plic(重叠) + it → (意义)叠在里面 → 含蓄的 例 The doctor gave an *implicit* answer. 医生给出了一个含蓄的回答。 参 explicit(*a.* 清楚的; 外在的)

hardly ['hɑːrdli]	*ad.* 几乎不，简直不；刚刚，仅仅(barely, scarcely) 例 It was *hardly* worth the price of admission. 花钱买那张电影票都不值。// I *hardly* ever use the dictionary anyway. 反正我几乎不用字典。 参 rarely(*ad.* 很少地，罕见地)；nearly(*ad.* 几乎)
centigrade ['sentɪɡreɪd]	*a.* 百分度的；摄氏温度的 记 联想记忆：centi(百) + grade(等级) → 百分度的；摄氏温度的 例 This substance has relatively high ignition temperature of 180 degrees *centigrade*. 这种物质的燃点相对较高，能达到 180 摄氏度。
barbecue ['bɑːrbɪkjuː]	*n.* 烧烤野餐；金属烤架 *v.* 在烤架上烧烤 例 He put another steak on the *barbecue*. 他在烤架上又放了一块肉排。
element ['elɪmənt]	*n.* 元素，要素，组成部分(component)；[常 *pl.*] 基本原理，基础 (foundation) 例 Customer relations is an important *element* of the job. 客户关系是这个 工作的重要组成部分。 派 elemental(*a.* 基本的，主要的)
sensory ['sensəri]	*a.* 感觉的，感官的(esthetic) 记 词根记忆：sens(感觉) + ory → 感觉的 例 In Europe, interest in *sensory* science has grown and will continue to play an essential role in understanding the European consumer's perception of food quality. 在欧洲，人们对感官科学的兴趣日益浓厚，在人 们理解欧洲消费者对食品安全的感知上，这一兴趣将继续发挥着重要的作用。
yarn [jɑːrn]	*n.* 纱，纱线(thread, wool)；(尤指夸张的或编造的)故事 记 联想记忆：那家商店的纱线(yarn)论码(yard)出售 例 The little boy spun *yarns* about his time on the Greek island of Kos. 那个小男孩编造了一些有关他在希腊科斯岛时的离奇故事。
analogy [ə'nælədʒi]	*n.* 类比，类推 记 词根记忆：ana(类似) + log(说话) + y → 放在一起说 → 类比，类推 例 The teacher made an *analogy* between the lens of a camera and the lens of an eye. 老师把相机的镜头比做眼球的晶体。 派 analogous(*a.* 类似的)
convenience [kən'viːniəns]	*n.* 便利(fitness or suitability)；便利设施 记 词根记忆：con(共同) + ven(来) + i + ence → 共同行动来维护便利设 施 → 便利设施 例 For me the *convenience* of having a laundromat so close to where I live is worth the extra dollar. 对我而言，住处附近的自助洗衣店所带来的便 利抵得上多花了的钱。 派 inconvenience(*n.* 麻烦，不方便之处)

22

publication [ˌpʌblɪˈkeɪʃn]	*n.* 出版，发行；出版物；公布，发表 例 When she was eighty years old, some twenty-five volumes were awaiting *publication*. 时至80高龄，她仍有约25卷书等待出版。
compulsory [kəmˈpʌlsəri]	*a.* 必须做的，义务的；强制性的；（课程）必修的 记 词根记忆：com(共同) + puls(推) + ory → 共同推进的 → 义务的 搭 compulsory education 义务教育 例 These subjects are *compulsory* in our department. 这些科目是我们系的必修课。
pointed [ˈpɔɪntɪd]	*a.* 尖的，尖角的(sharp-angled)；尖锐的，尖刻的 记 来自point(*n.* 尖头) 例 Some of the comments he heard were *pointed*, especially concerning problems of inner cities. 他所听到的评论中有一些很尖锐，尤其是关于内城问题的那些。
spread [spred]	*v.* 展开(unfold, extend)；蔓延，扩散；散布(distribute)；涂，敷 *n.* 传播，蔓延；涉及幅度，活动范围 记 联想记忆：散布(spread)传单给人们看(read) 搭 spread like wildfire 像野火般蔓延，迅速传开 例 The fire rapidly *spread* to adjoining buildings. 大火迅速蔓延到了邻近的建筑物。
assemble [əˈsembl]	*v.* 集合(gather)；装配(fit together) 记 词根记忆：as(接近) + sembl(一样，相等) + e → 使接近一样 → 集合 例 When a nest intruder is too large for one individual to handle, nestmates can be quickly *assembled* by alarm signals. 当鸟巢侵犯者太大，一只鸟无法应付时，报警信号可以迅速聚集巢里的其他成员。 参 resemble(*vt.* 像，与…相似)
clone [kloʊn]	*n.* 克隆动物(或植物)，无性繁殖动物(或植物)；复制品，翻版 *vt.* 克隆，以无性繁殖技术复制 记 联想记忆：他怕自己的小狗太孤单(alone)，就克隆(clone)了另一只来与它做伴 例 A team from the UK were the first to successfully *clone* an animal. 英国的一个小组率先成功克隆了一只动物。
discourse [ˈdɪskɔːrs]	[ˈdɪskɔːrs] *n.* 演讲；论文；话语 [dɪsˈkɔːrs] *vi.* 讲述，论述 记 联想记忆：dis + course(课程) → 讲课 → 演讲；讲述 搭 discourse on/upon 讲述，论述 例 We listened to the president's *discourse* on the importance of education. 我们听了校长有关教育重要性的演讲。
aquifer [ˈækwɪfər]	*n.* 含水土层 记 词根记忆：aqui(=aqua 水) + fer(带来) → 带来水的地方 → 含水土层 例 An *aquifer* is an underground layer of rock or sediment that has pores or holes in it. 含水土层处于地下，是多孔洞的岩石或沉积物层。

reverse [rɪˈvɜːrs]	*v.* (使)反转；彻底转变，颠倒；撤销，废除；交换(位置或功能)；倒车 *n.* 相反的情况；反面，背面；倒退 *a.* 相反的(opposite) 记 词根记忆：re(反) + vers(转) + e → 使反转；彻底转变 例 The government has failed to *reverse* the economic decline. 政府未能扭转经济滑坡的趋势。// You are the *reverse* of polite. 你真没礼貌。 派 reversal(*n.* 颠倒，倒转)；reversible(*a.* 可翻转的；可逆的)
conversion [kənˈvɜːrʒn]	*n.* 转变，变换；改变信仰，皈依 记 词根记忆：con(完全) + vers(转) + ion → 转变 例 The *conversion* of steam-powered engines into battery-powered ones can improve energy efficiency. 把蒸汽引擎换成电池驱动的引擎能提高能源的利用率。
summary [ˈsʌməri]	*n.* 摘要，概要(abstract) *a.* 概括的，概要的；即刻的，立即的 记 词根记忆：summ(=sum 总的) + ary → 得出一个总的东西 → 摘要 例 In *summary*, this was a disappointing performance. 总的来说，这场演出令人失望。 派 summarize(*v.* 概括，总结)；summarization(*n.* 摘要，概要)
carbon [ˈkɑːrbən]	*n.* 碳 搭 carbon dioxide 二氧化碳；carbon monoxide 一氧化碳 例 All forms of *carbon* are highly stable, requiring high temperature to react even with oxygen. 所有的碳都很稳定，就算与氧产生反应也需要高温。 参 carbonate(*n.* 碳酸盐)
petroleum [pəˈtroʊliəm]	*n.* 石油 记 词根记忆：petr(石) + oleum(油) → 石油 例 *Petroleum* is also the raw material for many chemical products. 石油也是许多化学产品的原材料。 参 petrifaction(*n.* 石化作用)
accessory [əkˈsesəri]	*n.* 附件，零件(adjunct)；配饰；从犯，同谋 *a.* 辅助的 记 词根记忆：ac(附近) + cess(走) + ory → 在主体部件附近起辅助作用的 → 附件 例 He was charged with being an *accessory* to murder. 他被控为谋杀罪的从犯。
planet [ˈplænɪt]	*n.* 行星 例 The *planet's* discoverers were optimistic about the prospects for finding life there. 这颗行星的发现者对在其上找到生命充满信心。 派 planetary(*a.* 行星的)
appreciation [əˌpriːʃiˈeɪʃn]	*n.* 欣赏(recognition)；理解，体谅；感激；鉴定，评价 例 European ladies once showed great *appreciation* of hats decorated with ostrich feathers. 欧洲女士曾经十分热衷于有鸵鸟毛装饰的帽子。

22

□ reverse □ conversion □ summary □ carbon □ petroleum □ accessory
□ planet □ appreciation

elongate [ɪˈlɔːŋgeɪt]	v. 延长，伸长（lengthen, extend）
	记 词根记忆：e(外，出) + long(长的) + ate(使…) → 使向外变长 → 延长，伸长
	例 The singer's face is too *elongated* in the photos. 在照片中歌手的脸被拉得太长了。
	派 elongation(n. 延长)
oblivious [əˈblɪvɪəs]	a. 遗忘的（forgetful）；未注意的，不知不觉的
	记 词根记忆：ob(反，逆) + liv(活) + ious → 不再活的 → 不再活着的东西渐渐被人遗忘 → 遗忘的
	例 The lad standing beside the mast seems *oblivious* to the spray of the bow waves. 站在桅杆旁的小伙子似乎没有察觉到舷波。
therefore [ˈðerfɔːr]	ad. 因此，从而（consequently）*conj.* 因此
	例 The transplanted bone may not be compatible with the patient's body, and *therefore* runs the risk of rejection. 移植的骨头可能与病人的身体不匹配，因此存在被排斥的风险。
imagist [ˈɪmɪdʒɪst]	a. 意象派的 n. 意象派诗人
	例 The *imagist* movement in poetry arose during the second decade of the twentieth century. 诗歌领域的意象主义运动兴起于20世纪20年代。
path [pæθ]	n. 道路（pathway）；路线（route）；小路，小径
	例 He threw himself into the *path* of an oncoming vehicle. 他冲到迎面有汽车驶来的路上。
	参 pathway(n. 路)
yoke [joʊk]	n. 裤腰；牛轭；奴役，束缚 vt. (强行)使结合，连接
	记 联想记忆：他把烟斗(toke)挂在裤腰(yoke)上
	例 Before the Civil War, slaves were under the *yoke* of their masters. 美国内战前，奴隶们受尽主人的奴役。
	参 yolk(n. 蛋黄)
abridge [əˈbrɪdʒ]	vt. 缩短，删节，节略，精简（abbreviate, curtail）
	记 联想记忆：a + bridge(桥) → 桥缩短了两地之间的距离 → 缩短，删节
	例 A book publisher may alter or *abridge* the author's work with the permission of the writer. 经作者许可，图书出版商可对作品进行修改或删节。
collaborate [kəˈlæbəreɪt]	v. 协作，合作；勾结，通敌
	记 词根记忆：col(一起，共同) + labor(工作) + ate → 协作，合作
	例 I hope your department could *collaborate* with me on the new project. 我希望你们部门能够在新项目上配合我工作。
adept [əˈdept]	a. 熟练的，精通的，内行的 n. 行家，熟手
	记 词根记忆：ad + ept(适合) → 正好适合于某物，合适的 → 精通的
	例 Jack was *adept* at horse riding and enjoyed other outdoor activities. 杰克擅长骑马，而且也喜欢其他户外运动。
	参 adapt(v. 使适合；调整)；adopt(v. 采取；收养，领养)

□ elongate　　□ oblivious　　□ therefore　　□ imagist　　□ path　　□ yoke
□ abridge　　□ collaborate　　□ adept

controversial [ˌkɑːntrəˈvɜːrʃl]	*a.* 引起争论的，有争议的 记 词根记忆：contro(相反) + vers(转) + ial → 反着转 → 引起争论的 例 Organ transplant is still a *controversial* issue in many countries. 在很多国家，器官移植仍是一个有争议的话题。
agenda [əˈdʒendə]	*n.* 议程，议程表 记 词根记忆：ag(做，行动) + enda(表名词复数) → 要做的事情 → 议程 例 Controlling the price hike is now on the *agenda* of the government. 现在，政府已将控制涨价提上了工作日程。
latitude [ˈlætɪtjuːd]	*n.* 纬度；[常 *pl.*]纬度地区 记 词根记忆：lat(宽的) + it + ude → 纬度 例 Each aurora hangs like a curtain of light stretching over the polar regions and into the higher *latitudes*. 每束极光像窗帘一样挂在极地地区，并延伸至高纬度地区。 参 longitude(*n.* 经度)；altitude(*n.* 高度)；gratitude(*n.* 感激)
appraise [əˈpreɪz]	*vt.* 估价；估量；评价，评定 记 词根记忆：ap(给，向) + prais(价格) + e → 给定价 → 估价；评价 例 Before you decide to buy the house, you should find an expert to *appraise* it. 在决定买房之前，你应该找一名专家对房子进行估价。
session [ˈseʃn]	*n.* (议会等的)会议；开庭(sitting)；开庭期；一节 例 The committee met in closed *session*. 委员会召开了秘密会议。
hail [heɪl]	*n.* 冰雹；一阵 *v.* 招呼；高呼；赞扬，称颂；下冰雹 记 联想记忆：冰雹(hail)让航行(sail)计划流产(fail)了 例 Telecommuting has been *hailed* as a solution to all kinds of problems related to office work. 远程办公被誉为能解决所有与办公相关的问题的方法。
aptitude [ˈæptɪtjuːd]	*n.* 适合，恰当；天资，才能，资质 记 词根记忆：apt(适合) + it + ude(名词后缀) → 适合，恰当；天资 例 Ted has an *aptitude* for languages, for he can speak six languages. 特德有语言天赋，他能说六国语言。 参 attitude(*n.* 态度)
trifle [ˈtraɪfl]	*n.* 少许；琐事，小事；无价值的东西 *vi.* 不认真对待，怠慢 记 词根记忆：tri(三) + fle → 完整的东西被分成三份后，变得琐碎 → 少许；琐事 搭 a trifle 有点儿，稍微；trifle with 小看，怠慢 例 Do not *trifle* away your time on such meaningless things. 不要把时间浪费在这些毫无意义的事情上。
dismiss [dɪsˈmɪs]	*v.* 不再考虑，不接受(wave aside)；消除，摒除；免职，解雇(fire)；解散，遣散；驳回，不受理 记 词根记忆：dis(分开) + miss(送) → 解散，遣散 例 This is the second time John was *dismissed*. 这是约翰第二次被解雇。// The case was *dismissed*. 此案已被驳回。

22

session

□ controversial □ agenda   □ latitude   □ appraise   □ session   □ hail
□ aptitude   □ trifle   □ dismiss

archive [ˈɑːrkaɪv]	*n.* 档案室 *vt.* 存档 例 This letter has been found accidentally in the *archive*. 这封信是在档案室里偶然发现的。	archive
browse [braʊz]	*v.* 吃嫩叶或草；浏览 *n.* 嫩叶；浏览 记 联想记忆：brow(眉毛) + se → 眉毛般纤细的叶子 → 嫩叶 例 Customers are welcomed to *browse* our website and come to our store. 欢迎顾客登录我们的网站浏览信息，也欢迎顾客惠顾我们的商店。	
collaborative [kəˈlæbəreɪtɪv]	*a.* 合作的，协作的 记 来自 collaborate(*v.* 合作，协作) 例 Sue will be assigned to a group of five for *collaborative* work. 苏将被分配到五人小组协作完成工作。	
defer [dɪˈfɜːr]	*v.* 推迟，延期 记 词根记忆：de(向下) + fer(搬运) → 向下搬运 → 推迟，延期 例 Many women *defer* children-bearing in response to career development. 很多女性为了事业发展而推迟生育。	
prefer [prɪˈfɜːr]	*v.* 更喜欢，宁愿 例 I almost always *prefer* fresh air, if possible. 如果可能，我想一直都能呼吸到新鲜空气。// The donor *prefers* to remain anonymous. 捐赠者不希望披露姓名。	
comprehensible [ˌkɑːmprɪˈhensəbl]	*a.* 可理解的，能懂的，能充分理解的 例 The theory is *comprehensible* only to scientists. 这个理论只有科学家才能充分理解。	
diligent [ˈdɪlɪdʒənt]	*a.* 勤奋的，刻苦的，勤勉的 记 词根记忆：di(=dis 分开) + lig(选择) + ent → 一个个地进行选择 → 勤奋的 搭 be diligent in 勤于… 例 Mary is the most intelligent and *diligent* student in her class. 玛丽是全班最聪明、最努力的学生。	
enlighten [ɪnˈlaɪtn]	*vt.* 启发，启迪；开导；阐明 记 联想记忆：en + light(点亮) + en → 点亮心灵 → 启发，启迪 例 I suggest you choose the courses that will *enlighten* you. 我建议你报些对你有启发性的课程。	
frenzy [ˈfrenzi]	*n.* 狂暴，狂热，疯狂(fury) 记 词根记忆：fren(=phren 心灵) + zy → 心里发狂的 → 狂暴 例 Adams lamented the role that the new *frenzy* for business was playing in eroding traditional values. 新的商业狂热侵蚀了传统价值观，这让亚当斯痛惜不已。 参 frenetic(*a.* 发狂的，狂乱的)	frenzy

remarkable [rɪˈmɑːrkəbl]	*a.* 显著的，值得注意的；非凡的(*extraordinary, incredible) 例 The newer ones experienced *remarkable* growth, which reflected basic changes in the economy. 新生事物经历了显著的增长，这反映了经济的根本变化。 派 remarkably(*ad.* 显著地，非常地)
dispatch [dɪˈspætʃ]	*vt./n.* 分派，派遣；发送 记 词根记忆：dis(分开) + patch(=ped 脚) → 使脚分开走 → 分派，派遣 例 The post office will *dispatch* these letters tomorrow. 明天邮局将把这些信件发送出去。

And gladly would learn, and gladly teach.
勤于学习的人才能乐于施教。

——英国诗人 乔叟(Chaucer, British poet)

Word List 23

音频

词根、词缀预习表

capac	握住	incapacitate *vt.* 使无资格	bat	打	batter *v.* 连续猛击
corp	身体	incorporate *vt.* 纳入；吸收	lab	拿	syllabus *n.* 教学大纲
spic	看，看到	perspicuous *a.* 明了的	turb	搅动	disturb *vt.* 搅乱
rig	直的	rigorous *a.* 缜密的；严格的	mon	忠告	monitor *vt.* 监控
pod	脚	podium *n.* 讲坛	tempt	尝试	tempt *vt.* 引诱，诱惑

radioactive [ˈreɪdɪoʊˈæktɪv]	*a.* 放射性的，有辐射的 记 词根记忆：radi(光线) + o + act(行动) + ive → 光线行动活跃的 → 放射性的 例 *Radioactive* waste disposal practices have changed substantially over the last twenty years. 在过去 20 年里，放射性废物的处理方法有着重大的变化。 派 radioactivity(*n.* 放射性，辐射)
incapacitate [ˌɪnkəˈpæsɪteɪt]	*vt.* 使无资格；使失去能力；使不胜任 记 词根记忆：in(无) + capac(=cap 握住) + it + ate(使…) → 使无力握住 → 使无资格；使失去能力 搭 be incapacitated for 不能胜任…；be incapacitated from 使失去…资格 例 Helen's poor sight *incapacitates* her for working as a taxi driver. 海伦视力不佳，不能胜任出租车司机的工作。 派 incapacitation(*n.* 无能；不胜任)
potassium [pəˈtæsiəm]	*n.* 钾 搭 potassium carbonate 碳酸钾
incorporate [ɪnˈkɔːrpəreɪt]	*vt.* 纳入，合并(combine)；包含；吸收；注册成立 记 词根记忆：in(进入) + corp(身体) + or + ate → 进入身体成为一部分 → 纳入；吸收 例 When hypotheses are confirmed, they are *incorporated* into theories. 假设被证实后，就可以纳入理论了。 派 incorporation(*n.* 结合，合并；吸收)
crippling [ˈkrɪplɪŋ]	*a.* 令人震惊的(surprising)；严重损害身体的；极其有害的 记 来自 cripple(*vt.* 使残废；严重毁坏) 例 Despite the advances in the medical sciences, there are still many *crippling* diseases that affect people. 尽管医学取得了进步，但仍有很多严重损害健康的疾病威胁着人类。

slip [slɪp]	*v.* 滑倒，失足；滑落；悄悄疾行，溜；摆脱；下降，跌落；陷入 *n.* 差错，纰漏；滑倒；纸片 记 联想记忆：s + lip(嘴唇) → 从唇边滑落 → 滑落 例 His hat had *slipped* over one eye. 他的帽子滑下来遮住了一只眼睛。// The little boy recited the whole poem without making a single *slip*. 那个小男孩一字不差地背出了整首诗。 派 slipper(*n.* 拖鞋)；slippery(*a.* 光滑的；滑头滑脑的)
impending [ɪmˈpendɪŋ]	*a.* 即将发生的，迫近的 记 来自 impend(*vi.* 即将发生) 例 Some members of the flock warn others of *impending* dangers. 鸟群中的一些成员警告其他成员危险即将来临。
decline [dɪˈklaɪn]	*n./v.* 下降(descend)；衰退(decay)；拒绝，谢绝 记 词根记忆：de(向下) + clin(倾斜) + e → 向下倾斜 → 下降；衰退 例 Her mother's health was *declining* rapidly. 她母亲的健康状况迅速恶化。 参 recline(*v.* 向后倚靠，斜倚)；incline[*v.* (使)倾斜]
pepper [ˈpepər]	*n.* 胡椒(粉)；辣椒 *vt.* (在食物上)撒胡椒粉；大量给予 记 发音记忆："拍拍" → 拿着小罐拍点胡椒粉 → 胡椒(粉) 例 Many people like adding white *pepper* to their dishes. 很多人喜欢往菜里加白胡椒。
bison [ˈbaɪsn]	*n.* 美洲(或欧洲)野牛 记 发音记忆："拜神" → 印度人视牛为神物，美洲野牛去印度肯定也被当成神来拜 → 美洲野牛 搭 a herd of bison 一群野牛 例 Due to commercial hunting and slaughter in the 19th century, the *bison* nearly went extinct. 19 世纪，北美野牛因商业捕猎和屠宰几近灭绝。
gist [dʒɪst]	*n.* 主旨，要点，大意 记 联想记忆：——列出(list)要点(gist) 例 I cannot understand the *gist* of this complicated reading material. 我没能理解这篇复杂的阅读材料的主旨。
hypothetical [ˌhaɪpəˈθetɪkl]	*a.* 假设的 记 词根记忆：hypo(在…下面) + thet(放) + ical → 放在下面的 → 假设的 例 I must emphasize that this is only a *hypothetical* case. 我必须强调，这只是个假设的例子。
illustrative [ɪˈləstrətɪv]	*a.* 作为例证的；用做说明的；解释性的 记 词根记忆：il(向内) + lus(光) + trative → 向心灵投入光的 → 解释性的 例 This example is *illustrative* of the issue we are discussing. 这个例子正好说明了我们正在讨论的问题。

pepper

perspicuous [ˌpɜːr ˈspɪkjʊəs]	*a.* (文章等)明白易懂的；明了的 记 词根记忆：per(完全) + spic(看，看到) + uous → 完全看到的 → 明了的 例 Such solutions were more manageable, more *perspicuous*, and can be applied. 这样的方法更易于掌握，也更明白，可被采用。
intern 	[ˈɪntɜːrn] *n.* 实习生 [ɪn ˈtɜːrn] *vt.* 拘禁，软禁 记 联想记忆：internal(*a.* 内部的)去掉 al → 关在内部 → 拘禁 例 The days as an *intern* made me feel the hardship of working. 实习的日子让我体会到了工作的艰辛。
rigorous [ˈrɪɡərəs]	*a.* 缜密的，谨慎的；严格的，严厉的 记 词根记忆：rig(直的) + or + ous → 使一直保持直的状态 → 缜密的；严格的 例 You could be more *rigorous* when you take the test. 做测试时你应该更加谨慎。
skim [skɪm]	*v.* 撇去；掠过，擦过；浏览，略读 记 联想记忆：一眼掠过(skim)，只见皮(skin)毛 例 You must *skim* through the play quickly, for you have forgotten the plot. 你已经忘了剧中的情节，必须快速浏览一下剧本。
podium [ˈpoʊdiəm]	*n.* 讲坛，讲台；指挥台 记 词根记忆：pod(=ped 脚) + ium → 立足之处 → 讲坛 例 Upon hearing my name, I nervously inched my way to the *podium*. 一听到我的名字，我就紧张地一步一步挪向讲台。
subordinate 	[sə ˈbɔːrdɪneɪt] *vt.* 使处于次要地位，使从属于 [sə ˈbɔːrdɪnət] *a.* 次要的；下级的 *n.* 部属，下属(inferior) 记 词根记忆：sub (在…下面) + ordin (顺序) + ate → 顺序在下 → 次要的 搭 subordinate to 次要的，从属的 例 From primary school, we learned that we should *subordinate* personal interests to that of the collective. 从小学起，我们就学会了应该将集体利益置于个人利益之上。
swap [swɑːp]	*v.* 交换，掉换 *n.* 交换，掉换；交换物，被调换者 例 This comic book was a *swap* that I got from my friend Tom. 这本漫画书是我从朋友汤姆手里换来的。
transcribe [træn ˈskraɪb]	*vt.* 记录，抄录；转录；改编 记 词根记忆：tran(=trans 穿过) + scrib(写) + e → 用另一种方式来写 → 抄写 例 Clerks *transcribe* everything that is said in court. 书记员把法庭上所有的话都记录在案。

abbey [ˈæbi]	*n.* 修道院；大教堂 记 联想记忆：ab + bey(看做 obey，遵守) → 需要遵守很多清规戒律的地方 → 修道院 例 The stone *abbey* was built around 1045~1050 by the King as part of his palace. 国王于 1045–1050 年间建了座石头教堂，作为宫殿的一部分。
batter [ˈbætər]	*v.* 连续猛击 *n.* (棒球等的)击球手；面糊 记 词根记忆：bat(打) + ter → 连续猛击 搭 batter down (连续重击以致)砸毁 例 Severe winds have been *battering* the east coast. 狂风一直在东海岸肆虐。
landing [ˈlændɪŋ]	*n.* 登陆；着陆，降落 例 The voyage lasted 46 minutes, from its departure in Philadelphia to its *landing* across the Delaware River. 那趟旅程从费城出发，跨越特拉华河在对面着陆，共持续了 46 分钟。
syllabus [ˈsɪləbəs]	*n.* 教学大纲，课程提纲 记 词根记忆：syl(一起) + lab(拿) + us → 把(不同的课程)拿到一起 → 教学大纲 例 The *syllabus* aims at arousing curiosities and interests in children to share their ideas and experiences. 这个教学大纲旨在激发孩子们与他人分享自己的想法和经历的好奇心和兴趣。
brag [bræg]	*v.* 吹嘘，自夸，自吹自擂 记 联想记忆：bag(口袋)中间加个 r，"r"像一个嘴巴在吹 → 吹嘘 例 The captain said after winning the match:"I don't want to *brag* about myself, and this victory belongs to everyone. " 在赢得比赛后，队长说："我不想自夸，球队的胜利属于每个人。"
curtsy [ˈkɜːrtsi]	*n.* 屈膝礼 *vi.* 行屈膝礼 记 联想记忆：curt(简略的) + sy → 一种简略的礼节 → 屈膝礼 例 The ballerina *curtsied* to the audience before leaving the stage. 那名芭蕾舞女演员在离开舞台前向观众行了个屈膝礼。
feast [fiːst]	*n.* 节日；盛宴，宴会 *v.* 尽情享用 记 联想记忆：太阳刚从东方(east)跳出，盛宴(feast)就开始了 搭 feast on 尽情地吃；feast one's eyes (on sth./sb.) 大饱眼福，尽情欣赏 例 Mark thinks this movie is a good one, because there are many pretty girls that he can *feast* his eyes on. 马克认为这部电影不错，因为影片里有很多美女，可以大饱眼福。
gorge [ɡɔːrdʒ]	*v.* 狼吞虎咽 *n.* 山峡，峡谷 记 发音记忆："过急" → 吃东西过急，狼吞虎咽 → 狼吞虎咽 搭 the Three Gorges 三峡 例 After a long journey, she started to *gorge* herself on chocolate biscuits. 长途跋涉后，她开始猛吃巧克力饼干。

23

□ abbey　　□ batter　　□ landing　　□ syllabus　　□ brag　　□ curtsy
□ feast　　□ gorge

lope [loʊp]	*vi.* 轻松地大步跑 *n.* 轻快的步伐 记 注意不要和 lobe(*n.* 耳垂)相混 例 The dog *loped* along beside the old man. 那条狗在老人身边轻快地奔跑着。
systematize ['sɪstəmətaɪz]	*vt.* 使系统化, 使条理化, 使成体系(organize) 记 词根记忆: sy(=syn 一起) + st(站立) + emat + ize(使…) → 使站在一起 → 使系统化 例 The aim of science is to amass and *systematize* knowledge. 科学的目的在于积累知识, 并使知识系统化。
disturb [dɪ'stɜːrb]	*vt.* 打扰(upset, bother); 搅乱, 弄乱; 使烦恼, 使不安 记 词根记忆: dis(分开) + turb(搅动) → 搅开了 → 搅乱 例 If you get up early, please do not *disturb* everyone else. 如果你起得早, 请不要打扰别人。 派 disturbance(*n.* 打扰; 骚乱, 骚动; 紊乱, 失调)
envelope ['envəloʊp]	*n.* 信封 例 A: Look, I got a letter from my cousin Jeff in Alaska. B: Can I get the return address from the *envelope*? A: 你瞧, 我收到了在阿拉斯加的堂兄杰夫的一封信。 B: 能给我信封上的寄信人地址吗? 参 develop(*v.* 发展)
monitor ['mɑːnɪtər]	*vt.* 监控(track, watch); 调节(regulate) *n.* 显示器; 监视器; 班长 记 词根记忆: mon(忠告) + itor → 给出忠告 → 监控 例 The students' progress is closely *monitored*. 学生们的进展情况受到密切的关注。
submit [səb'mɪt]	*v.* 提交, 呈递; 屈从; 主张, 建议 记 词根记忆: sub(在…下面) + mit(放) → 放在下面 → 提交, 呈递; 屈从 例 The application must be *submitted* by 20 May. 申请必须在 5 月 20 日前提交上来。
palate ['pælət]	*n.* 上腭; 味觉, 品尝力 搭 hard palate 硬腭 例 He has no *palate* for red wine. 他不懂得品红葡萄酒。
manage ['mænɪdʒ]	*v.* 勉力完成; 应付; 操纵, 控制; 管理(*preside over, *administer) 记 词根记忆: man(手) + age → 用手做 → 操纵, 控制 例 She wasn't able to *manage* the project well. 她没能力管理好这个项目。 派 manageable(*a.* 易管理的; 可操纵的); management(*n.* 管理; 管理部门)

squabble	*vi.* 发生口角，争吵 *n.* 口角，争吵（quarrel）
[ˈskwɑːbl]	例 The girls were *squabbling* over what to watch on TV. 女孩子们正为看哪个电视节目争吵。//

squabble

A: It's not fun being around Debbie and Mike these days. All they do is quarrel.

B: I've noticed it too. I wish they would keep their *squabbles* to themselves.

A: 这些日子跟德比和迈克在一起不好玩，他们老吵架。

B: 我也注意到了。希望他们的争吵不要影响到别人。

recommend	*vt.* 推荐（nominate）；建议（suggest）
[ˌrekəˈmend]	记 联想记忆：re（一再）+ com（共同）+ mend（修改）→ 这本书是大家一再修改的成果，强力推荐 → 推荐
	例 He doesn't *recommend* going to Central Mountain. 他不推荐去中部山区。
	派 recommendation（*n.* 推荐；介绍信）

compatible	*a.* 协调的，一致的（harmonious, coherent）；兼容的；能和睦相处的
[kəmˈpætəbl]	记 词根记忆：com（共同）+ pat（=path 感觉）+ ible → 有共同感觉的 → 协调的
	例 This project is not *compatible* with the company's long-term plans. 这个方案与公司的长远计划不一致。
	派 incompatible（*a.* 不协调的；合不来的；不兼容的）

23

unity	*n.* 团结一致，统一，联合（unification, combination）；协调；统一体
[ˈjuːnəti]	记 词根记忆：uni（单一）+ ty → 统一，联合
	例 Monet and his 29 fellow artists in the exhibit adopted the same name as a badge of their *unity*. 莫奈和参加展览的 29 位艺术家同行采用了同样的名字，以示团结。

parliament	*n.* 国会，议会（congress）
[ˈpɑːrləmənt]	记 联想记忆：parlia（看做 parle，谈话）+ ment → 谈论政务的地方 → 议会
	例 *Parliament* is open to all members of the UK public and overseas visitors. 国会向所有的英国民众和海外游客开放。
	派 parliamentary（*a.* 国会的，议会的）

mere	*a.* 仅仅的，纯粹的（pure, absolute）
[mɪr]	记 联想记忆：要想抓住爱情，仅仅（mere）在这儿（here）徘徊是不行的
	例 From *mere* spectators, they became willing passengers and finally pilots in their own right. 他们开始只是旁观者，后来心甘情愿地成为乘客，并最终凭自身的努力成为飞行员。
	派 merely（*ad.* 仅仅，只不过）

hive	*v.* （使）入蜂箱；群居 *n.* 蜂箱，蜂房（cell）；闹市，忙碌之地
[haɪv]	记 联想记忆：蜜蜂们生活（live）忙，建蜂房（hive）
	搭 hive off 把一部分分离出来
	例 The IT Department is being *hived* off into a new company. 信息技术部将被分离出来，成立一个新公司。

□ squabble　　□ recommend　　□ compatible　　□ unity　　□ parliament　　□ mere

□ hive

tempt [tempt]	*vt.* 引诱，诱惑(entice, allure)；吸引 记 本身为词根，意为"尝试" → 受到诱惑，要尝试 → 引诱，诱惑 例 The government designs a new program to *tempt* young people into teaching in poor areas. 政府规划了一个新项目，旨在吸引年轻人去贫困地区支教。 派 temptation(*n.* 引诱，诱惑) 参 attempt(*n./vt.* 尝试，企图)
resort [rɪˈzɔːrt]	*vi.* 求助(*use) *n.* 度假胜地；手段 记 联想记忆：向上级打报告(report)求助(resort) 例 A woodworker can join a chest together without *resorting* to nails or glue. 木工无需钉子或胶水就能拼好一个箱子。
ravine [rəˈviːn]	*n.* 沟壑，溪谷(gorge) 例 A *ravine* is narrower than a canyon. 沟壑比峡谷更窄。

ravine

meteorologist [ˌmiːtiəˈrɑːlədʒɪst]	*n.* 气象学者 例 Many radio and television weather forecasters are professional *meteorologists*, while others are merely reporters with no formal meteorological training. 很多电台和电视天气预报员都是专业的气象学者，其他一些则是没有接受过正规气象学训练的播音员。
vocation [voʊˈkeɪʃn]	*n.* 职业(occupation, profession)；使命感；圣召 例 The guidance counselor helps the student choose a *vocation*. 指导老师帮助学生选择职业。// He is a teacher with a strong sense of *vocation*. 他是一位具有强烈使命感的教师。 派 vocational(*a.* 职业的，业务知识的) 参 avocation(*n.* 消遣，业余爱好)
crevice [ˈkrevɪs]	*n.* 缺口，裂缝(gap) 记 词根记忆：crev(裂开) + ice → 裂缝 例 *Crevice* corrosion usually occurs at narrow openings or spaces between two metal surfaces. 缝隙腐蚀经常发生于两个金属表面之间狭小的缺口或空间处。
trial [ˈtraɪəl]	*n.* 审讯；试验，试用(test)；令人伤脑筋的人(或事) 记 联想记忆：加紧审讯(trial)，追查踪迹(trail) 搭 a trial period 试验期，试用期；bring sb. to trial 审判某人；clinical trials 临床试验；medical trials 医学试验；trial and error 反复试验，不断摸索 例 The man will stand *trial* for murder. 那个男人因涉嫌谋杀罪将受到审判。// The system was introduced on a *trial* basis for two months. 这个制度已引进试行了两个月。

contest	［kən'test］ *vt.* 竞争；争辩，就…提出异议
	［'kɑːntest］ *n.* 竞赛(game)；辩论(debate)；争夺
	记 联想记忆：con(共同) + test(测试) → 大家汇聚到一起参加测试 → 竞争
	例 Four candidates *contested* the leadership. 有四位候选人角逐领导权。
	派 contestant(*n.* 比赛者，竞争者)；uncontested(*a.* 无竞争的；无异议的)
recognize ［'rekəgnaɪz］	*vt.* 认出，识别(identify)；认可(acknowledge)
	记 词根记忆：re(再，又) + co(=com 共同) + gn (知道) + ize → 再次让大家都知道 → 认出；认可
	例 She didn't *recognize* the man because of his haircut. 她没有认出这个男子，因为他理发了。
	派 recognizable(*a.* 可辨认的)；recognized(*a.* 公认的)；recognition(*n.* 认出；承认；表彰)
	recognize
split ［splɪt］	*v.* 分开，分裂(divide, separate)；撕裂；分担，分享；断绝关系，分手 *n.* 裂口；分化，分裂
	记 发音记忆："死劈了它" → 劈开 → 分开
	搭 split away/off (from sth.) (使)脱离，分裂出去；split up (with sb.) (和某人)断绝关系
	例 A bolt *split* the sky. 一道闪电划破长空。// The couple *split* up last month. 那对夫妇上个月离婚了。
counteract ［ˌkaʊntər'ækt］	*vt.* 消除(clear up)；抵消(neutralize)
	记 联想记忆：counter(反) + act(动作) → 做相反的动作 → 消除；抵消
	例 Antacid will *counteract* the excess acid in your stomach. 解酸剂会消除胃里过多的酸。
validity ［və'lɪdəti］	*n.* 合法性；符合逻辑
	记 来自 valid(*a.* 有效的)
	搭 period of validity 有效期
	例 Employees must confirm the *validity* of a contract when signing it with employers. 雇员与雇主签订合同时必须确认合同的合法性。
receiver ［rɪ'siːvər］	*n.* 接收器；(电话)听筒；接收者；官方接管人
	例 He's more of a giver than a *receiver*. 他更乐于给予而不是接受。
facility ［fə'sɪləti］	*n.* [常 *pl.*]设备，工具(instrument, equipment)
	记 词根记忆：fac(做) + ility → 辅助人们做事的东西 → 设备
	例 The dormitories have limited cooking *facilities*. 宿舍里的烹饪设备很有限。
infection ［ɪn'fekʃn］	*n.* 传染，感染；传染病
	记 来自 infect(*vt.* 传染，感染)
	搭 respiratory infection 呼吸道感染
	例 Many individuals develop a variety of *infections* in their lifetime, but quickly overcome them. 很多人一生中会感染各种疾病，但都能很快征服它们。// He had an ear *infection*. 他耳部感染了。

23

crater
[ˈkreɪtər]

n. 火山口；坑

例 After the volcano erupted, lava domes formed inside the new *crater*. 火山爆发后，新生成的火山口的内部会形成熔岩穹丘。

参 curator(*n.* 馆长，监护人)

balcony
[ˈbælkəni]

n. 阳台；(电影院等的)楼厅，楼座

记 发音记忆："白给你" → 这个价位的戏票，整个包厢都相当于"白给你" → 包厢

例 Please keep the *balcony* door shut. 请不要打开阳台门。

balcony

strike
[straɪk]

v. 碰，撞，撞击(hit, smack)；侵袭(attack)；突然想到；给…以深刻印象；罢工；(钟等)敲响 *n.* 罢工(walkout)；袭击

例 The small village was *struck* by an outbreak of cholera. 那个小村庄爆发了霍乱。// Volatile substances usually *strike* the bloodhound's nose as an entire constellation of distinctive scents. 大猎犬的鼻子遇到易挥发性物质时通常能辨别出那是完全不同的一组气味。// The taxi drivers are threatening to come out on *strike*. 出租车司机威胁说要举行罢工。

派 striking(*a.* 惹人注目的，惊人的)；strikingly(*ad.* 引人注目地)

chunk
[tʃʌŋk]

n. 厚片，大块(lump)；相当大的部分(或数量)；矮胖的人(或物)

记 发音记忆："常客" → 饭馆的常客占客人的很大一部分 → 相当大的部分

搭 a chunk of 一大块

例 The impact caused the cores of the two planets to melt together and *chunks* of Earth's crust to be thrown out into space. 这一碰撞使两颗行星的核融化在一起，大量的地球碎片飞入太空。

sac
[sæk]

n. 囊，液囊

记 联想记忆：sacred(神圣的)中去了 red(红色)，只剩下实质的囊(sac)

scratch
[skrætʃ]

vt. 刮擦，划(scrape)；抓，搔 *n.* 划痕(mark, nick)；挠痒

搭 scratch out 删除；from scratch 从头开始，从零开始；up to scratch 达到要求

例 Mind you don't *scratch* the table with those scissors! 小心剪刀划坏桌面！// They escaped without a *scratch*. 他们毫发未损地逃了出去。

vaccine
[vækˈsiːn]

n. 疫苗(bacterin)

记 词根记忆：vacc(牛) + ine → 牛痘苗 → 疫苗

例 She was criticized for developing the risky *vaccine*. 她因开发有危险的疫苗而受到了批评。

派 vaccinate(*v.* 预防接种)；vaccination(*n.* 接种疫苗)

paramount
[ˈpærəmaʊnt]

a. 至为重要的(foremost)；最高权力的，至尊的

记 联想记忆：par + amount(数量) → 在量上超过别的 → 至为重要的

例 Tradition is *paramount*, and change comes infrequently and slowly. 传统是至高无上的，变化出现得并不频繁，也很缓慢。

version [ˈvɜːrʒn]	*n.* 译文，译本(translation)；版本(edition)
	记 词根记忆：vers(转) + ion → 从原文转化而来 → 译文，译本
	例 That rather romantic *version* of the story is not what actually happened. 那个相当浪漫的故事版本不符合实际情况。
	参 vision(*n.* 视力；视觉；洞察力)
aesthetic [esˈθetɪk]	*a.* 审美的，美学的；美的，艺术的(artistic)
	记 词根记忆：(a)esthet(感觉) + ic(形容词后缀) → 美感的 → 审美的，美学的
	例 One of the oldest types of *aesthetic* theory is that of formalism. 最古老的美学理论类型之一就是形式主义。// The new furniture was more *aesthetic* than functional. 这些新家具是美观多于实用。
	派 aesthetically(*ad.* 审美地)
provincialism [prəˈvɪnʃlɪzəm]	*n.* 地方主义，乡土性(regionalism, localism)
	搭 narrow-minded provincialism 狭隘的地方主义
	例 While reflecting on *provincialism*, it is also important to re-think about the citizenship in a multi-ethnic, multi-cultural context. 在探究地方主义时，站在一个多种族、多文化的背景下重新思索何谓公民同样重要。
sharply [ˈʃɑːrpli]	*ad.* 急剧地；猛烈地；尖刻地；鲜明地
	例 Profits fell *sharply* following the takeover. 接管后，利润突然大幅下降。
colonize [ˈkɑːlənaɪz]	*vt.* 聚居于，大批生长于；开拓(或建立)殖民地，移居于(settle)
	记 来自colony(*n.* 殖民地；群体)
	例 The area is *colonized* by flowering plants. 这个地区长满了开花植物。
	派 colonization(*n.* 殖民；殖民地化)
extrinsic [eksˈtrɪnsɪk]	*a.* 外来的，外在的，非本质的
	搭 extrinsic factors 外在因素
	例 Today the professor will introduce a couple of technical terms: *extrinsic* value and intrinsic value. 今天教授将介绍两个专业词汇：外在价值和内在价值。
	参 intrinsic(*a.* 固有的，内在的)
authorize [ˈɔːθəraɪz]	*vt.* 授权(empower)；批准，许可(permit, sanction)
	例 I'm not *authorized* to give out this kind of information. 我无权发布此类信息。// It should be *authorized* by the source. 这应该由资料提供者授权。
	派 authorization(*n.* 授权；认可)；unauthorized(*a.* 未经授权的)
margin [ˈmɑːrdʒən]	*n.* 边缘(*edge, rim)；页边空白；差数，差额；余地，余裕
	例 Predators find it easier to catch small birds perching at the *margins* of the roost. 捕食者发现捕捉在栖息处边缘休息的小鸟更加容易。
disadvantage [ˌdɪsədˈvæntɪdʒ]	*n.* 缺点，障碍，不利之处(drawback, handicap)
	记 联想记忆：dis(不) + advantage(优点) → 缺点，障碍，不利之处
	例 There are many *disadvantages* to his plan. 他的计划有诸多缺陷。// The fact that she cannot speak English put her at a distinct *disadvantage*. 她不会讲英语，这使她处于明显不利的地位。
	派 disadvantageous(*a.* 不利的)

23

surplus [ˈsɜːrpləs]	*n.* 过剩(量)，剩余(额)(excess)；盈余，顺差 *a.* 过剩的，多余的 记 联想记忆：sur(在…之上；超过) + plus(加) → 过剩(量) 例 *Surpluses* of food could also be bartered for other commodities. 剩余的食品也能用来交换其他商品。
harmonic [hɑːrˈmɑːnɪk]	*n.* 泛音；和声 *a.* 和声的，谐音的 记 词根记忆：harm(关节；连接) + onic → 把不同的连在一起的 → 和声的 例 The untrained human ear typically does not perceive *harmonics* as separate notes. 一般而言，人类耳朵未经训练，无法将和声作为单独音符区分开来。
Saturn [ˈsætɜːrn]	*n.* 土星 例 Though there is no direct information about *Saturn's* internal structure, it is thought that its interior is similar to that of Jupiter. 虽然没有关于土星内部结构的直接资料，但人们认为土星的内部结构与木星的相似。
acoustic [əˈkuːstɪk]	*a.* 非电声乐器的，原声的；听觉的，声音的 记 词根记忆：acou(听) + stic → 听觉的 例 I don't think the most ardent supporters of electronic instruments expect them to completely replace *acoustic* instruments. 我认为就算最支持电子乐器的人也不希望它们完全取代原声乐器。
disprove [ˌdɪsˈpruːv]	*vt.* 证明…不成立，证明…是错误的 记 联想记忆：dis(不) + prove(证明) → 证明…不成立 例 The theory has now been *disproved*. 这一理论现已证明是错误的。
mosaic [moʊˈzeɪɪk]	*n.* 马赛克；镶嵌工艺 记 发音记忆："马赛克" 例 *Mosaic* is the art of closely setting small, colored pieces, such as stone or glass, into a surface to create a decorative design. 马赛克是指把小块彩色石头或玻璃片紧密嵌入一个平面，从而形成装饰图案的一种艺术。
insert [ɪnˈsɜːrt]	*vt.* 插入 记 词根记忆：in(在…里面) + sert(放置) → 放在里面 → 插入 例 Now use your hands to *insert* the keys in the locks. 现在用手把钥匙插到锁里。 insert
aloof [əˈluːf]	*a.* 远离的；冷淡的，冷漠的(remote, indifferent) 搭 keep/hold oneself aloof 无动于衷；漠不关心 例 You should not keep yourself *aloof* from the poor. 你不应该对穷人漠不关心。
simulate [ˈsɪmjuleɪt]	*vt.* 模仿，模拟(imitate)；假装，伪装 记 词根记忆：simul(相同) + ate(使…) → 使相同 → 模仿 例 The computer program *simulated* the effects of aging. 电脑程序模拟了变老的效果。 simulate

funding [ˈfʌndɪŋ]	*n.* 基金，资金；提供资金 例 I think I'd like to bring up government *funding* for state universities. 我想我宁愿政府为州立大学提供资助。
persuasive [pərˈsweɪsɪv]	*a.* 有说服力的，让人信服的 记 来自 persuade(*v.* 劝说) 例 You'll have to be a lot more *persuasive* if you want to convince the committee to accept your proposal. 如果想说服委员会接受你的提议，你就得大大增加说服力。
render [ˈrendər]	*vt.* 给予，提供(give)；致使(cause)；递交，呈献；表达；翻译 记 词根记忆：ren(=re 回) + der(给) → 还给 → 给予，提供 例 Rapid ecological changes may *render* serious damage to a species. 生态的快速变化会对物种造成严重破坏。 派 rendering(*n.* 表现，描写)
influenza [ˌɪnfluˈenzə]	*n.* 流行性感冒 记 联想记忆：流行性感冒(influenza)会影响(influence)很多人的生活 例 Three *influenza* pandemics occurred in the 20th century and killed tens of millions of people. 20 世纪爆发了三大流感，夺去了几千万人的性命。
advanced [ədˈvænst]	*a.* 先进的(progressive)；高级的，高等的(exclusive)；晚期的，后期的 例 They were an *advanced* agricultural people who used irrigation to help grow their crops. 他们这个民族拥有先进的农业，利用灌溉促进作物的生长。 参 advancement(*n.* 进步)
destruction [dɪˈstrʌkʃn]	*n.* 毁坏，毁灭(destroy) 例 Some citizens in New York seek to rescue historic buildings from *destruction*. 一些纽约市民试图抢救历史建筑使其免于毁灭。

23

Word List 24

词根、词缀预习表

just	正确的	justice n. 正义，公正	ment	想法；思考	comment v./n. 评论
pact	系紧	impact v. 影响	cur	注意；关心	accurate a. 正确无误的
ob-	表加强	obtain v. 获得	sumpt	用	sumptuous a. 奢华的
arti	技巧	artifact n. 人工制品	cuss	打	percussion n. 打击乐器
pan-	全	panorama n. 全景	popul	人	populate vt. (大批地)居住于

---

depot
[ˈdiːpoʊ]

n. 库房，仓库（depository, storehouse）；公共汽车站，火车站
例 The building was used as an arms *depot*. 该楼曾被用做军械库。

---

romantic
[roʊˈmæntɪk]

a. 爱情的；浪漫的，富有情调的；多情的；不切实际的，幻想的；[R-]浪漫主义(风格)的
例 Keats is one of the greatest *Romantic* poets.
济慈是最伟大的浪漫主义诗人之一。
派 romanticism (*n.* 浪漫主义；浪漫精神)；
romanticize(*v.* 浪漫化；传奇化)

---

tycoon
[taɪˈkuːn]

n. (商界)巨头，大亨（magnate）
记 发音记忆："太酷"→ 那些商界巨头真酷→
(商界)巨头
例 For every crooked *tycoon* there are thousands of ordinary citizens living on fixed incomes. 每个奸诈的商界巨头身后都有成千上万靠固定收入为生的普通人。

---

justice
[ˈdʒʌstɪs]

n. 法官；司法；正义，公正（equity）
记 词根记忆：just(正确的) + ice → 正义，公正
例 Martin Luther King Jr.'s magnificent speaking ability enabled him to effectively express the demands for social *justice* for Black Americans.
伟大的演说才能使马丁•路德•金有效地表达了美国黑人对社会公平的要求。

---

panel
[ˈpænl]

n. 面板，镶板；仪表盘；专门小组 *vt.* 镶板
记 词根记忆：pan(布) + el(小) → 一小块布 → 面板
例 The walls were made of plaster or wood, sometimes elaborately *paneled*. 墙由灰泥或木板做成，有时镶嵌得很精美。

---

guilty ['gɪlti]	*a.* 有罪的，犯罪的；内疚的 例 You are washing your car even on vacation. It makes me feel *guilty*. 你假期都洗车，这让我感到内疚。
decipher [dɪ'saɪfər]	*vt.* 破译(decode) 记 联想记忆：de(去掉) + cipher(密码) → 解开密码 → 破译 例 Ancient Egyptian hieroglyphic script was finally *deciphered*. 古埃及象形文字最终得到了破译。
cushion ['kʊʃn]	*vt.* 起缓冲作用 *n.* 垫子(pillow) 记 发音记忆："苦行" → 苦行僧盘腿坐在垫子上 → 垫子 搭 air-cushion vehicle 气垫运载工具 例 The carpet *cushioned* the fall of the vase. 地毯缓冲了花瓶的坠落。
microorganism [ˌmaɪkroʊ'ɔːrgənɪzəm]	*n.* 微生物 记 联想记忆：micro(微小的) + organism(生物) → 微生物 例 Some types of *microorganisms* have adapted to the extreme conditions. 一些类型的微生物已适应了极其恶劣的环境。
awful ['ɔːfl]	*a.* (感到)不舒服的(unwell)；糟糕的(terrible)；可怕的(awesome)；非常的 记 来自awe(*n.* 敬畏，惧怕) 例 I feel *awful*. I think I'm coming down with that flu. 我感觉特难受，觉得自己得了流感。// The cafeteria food was *awful*. 自助餐厅的饭糟透了。 派 awfully(*ad.* 非常，很)
surgery ['sɜːrdʒəri]	*n.* 外科手术；外科学；手术室，诊疗室 记 联想记忆：sur(e)(对…有把握的) + gery → 医生对这个外科手术很有把握 → 外科手术 搭 heart bypass surgery 心脏搭桥手术 例 As a rule, doctors hold *surgeries* between 9 and 11:30 every day. 一般来说，医生每天9点到11点半做手术。
impact	[ɪm'pækt] *v.* 影响(affect)；冲击，撞击 ['ɪmpækt] *n.* 影响(力)(effect)；冲击，撞击(collision) 记 词根记忆：im(表加强) + pact(系紧) → 用力系紧 → 影响 搭 impact on/upon 对…有影响 例 How did the agricultural societies *impact* people's family relationships? 农业社会如何影响着人们的家庭关系？
crustacean [krʌ'steɪʃn]	*n.* 甲壳类动物 *a.* 甲壳类的 记 联想记忆：crust(外壳) + acean(看做 ocean，海洋) → 海洋中的有壳动物 → 甲壳类动物 例 Every year more than one million tons of *crustaceans* are produced by fishery for human consumption in the country. 在该国，水产业每年都要出产100多万吨甲壳类动物供人们食用。

24

□ guilty   □ decipher   □ cushion   ■ microorganism   □ awful   □ surgery
□ impact   □ crustacean

obtain [əbˈteɪn]	*v.* 获得(*acquire, procure); 通用, 流行 记 词根记忆: ob(表加强) + tain(拿住) → 用力拿住 → 获得 例 Desalination of water is the best way to *obtain* drinking water. 给水脱盐是获取饮用水的最佳方法。 参 attain(*vt.* 达到; 获得); abstain(*vi.* 弃权; 戒除; 放弃)
respondent [rɪˈspɑːndənt]	*n.* 回答者, 响应者; 调查对象; 被告 *a.* 回答的 例 Only 20% of the *respondents* agreed with the suggestion. 只有 20%的调查对象同意这项建议。
particular [pərˈtɪkjələr]	*a.* 特定的(selected); 独特的(*unique); 详细的; 挑剔的 *n.* 详情, 细目 记 词根记忆: part(部分) + icular(属于…的) → 只属于部分的 → 特定的 例 Each person is responsible for a *particular* part of the process. 每个人负责这个过程的特定部分。// Bill is very *particular* about his clothing. 比尔穿衣服很挑剔。 派 particularly(*ad.* 特别, 尤其) 参 peculiar(*a.* 奇特的)
newsprint [ˈnjuːzprɪnt]	*n.* 新闻纸 例 *Newsprint* is used in the printing of newspapers, flyers, and other printed materials intended for mass distribution. 新闻纸用于印刷报纸、广告传单以及其他旨在向大众发放的印刷品。
gregarious [grɪˈgeriəs]	*a.* 群居的; 合群的, 爱社交的(sociable) 记 词根记忆: greg(群体) + ari + ous → 群居的 例 Man is a *gregarious* animal. 人是一种群居动物。
chafe [tʃeɪf]	*v.* 擦破, 擦痛(abrade, rub); (因受限制而)恼怒, 焦躁 例 She soon *chafed* at the restrictions of her situation. 她很快因处处受到限制而感到恼火。
lizard [ˈlɪzərd]	*n.* 蜥蜴 记 联想记忆: 巫师(wizard)像蜥蜴(lizard)一样恶毒 例 Many *lizards* can detach their tails to escape from predators. 许多蜥蜴能自断尾巴来逃脱捕食者。
manner [ˈmænər]	*n.* 方式, 风格(way, style); [*pl.*]礼貌(courtesy); 习惯(habit) 例 It was the *manner* of expressing, the satiric method that made them interesting and entertaining. 正是表现方式, 即嘲讽的风格使其有趣并令人愉悦。 派 mannerism(*n.* 特殊习惯, 怪癖)
artifact [ˈɑːrtɪfækt]	*n.* 人工制品, 手工艺品 记 词根记忆: arti(技巧) + fact(制作) → 用技巧制作的东西 → 人工制品 例 *Artifacts* are contrasted to natural objects; they are products of human actions. 人工制品是与自然物体相对而言的, 是人类活动的产物。

crystal
['krɪstl]

n. 水晶；晶体，结晶体 *a.* 透明的，清澈的（clear）；结晶状的

记 联想记忆：cry（哭泣）+ stal（看做 star，星星）→ 水晶犹如星星哭泣时掉下的泪 → 水晶

例 Glass has an interlocking *crystal* network. 玻璃有一个连锁的晶体网络。

派 crystalline（*a.* 结晶的；水晶制的；透明的）；crystallize〔*v.*（使）结晶；（使）明确〕；crystallization（*n.* 结晶）

crystal

gravel
['grævl]

n. 沙砾，砾石

记 词根记忆：grav（重的）+ el（表小玩意、小东西，名词后缀）→ 重的小东西 → 沙砾

例 There is a *gravel* path from my home to school. 从我家去学校有一条沙砾小路。

参 engrave（*vt.* 雕刻）

string
[strɪŋ]

n. 细绳，带子；一串；一系列；弦 *v.* 用线串；悬挂

记 联想记忆：st + ring（铃）→ 系铃的小绳 → 细绳

搭 string out 延长，拖长时间

例 Flags were *strung* out along the route. 沿途悬挂着旗子。

派 stringed（*a.* 有弦的）

panorama
[ˌpænəˈrɑːmə]

n. 全景，全貌；概观，综述

记 词根记忆：pan（全）+ orama（景色）→ 全景

例 There is a superb *panorama* of the mountains from the hotel. 从旅馆可饱览群山的壮丽景色。

unparalleled
[ʌnˈpærəleld]

a. 空前的，无比的（unequaled, matchless）

记 联想记忆：un（无）+ parallel（平行）+ ed → 没有东西可与之平行的 → 无比的

例 Chicago possesses an almost *unparalleled* situation in economy development. 芝加哥在经济发展方面具有几乎无与伦比的环境。

suspend
[səˈspend]

vt. 吊，悬挂（*hang）；暂缓，暂停，中止

记 词根记忆：sus（在…下面）+ pend（悬挂）→ 悬挂在下面 → 悬挂；暂缓

例 Grain Exchange's trading was *suspended*, and farmers sold at prices fixed by the board. 谷物交易所的交易被中止了，农民们按照委员会确定的价格出售谷物。

派 suspended（*a.* 暂停的，缓期的）

afflict
[əˈflɪkt]

vt. 使苦恼，折磨（torment, torture）

记 词根记忆：af（向）+ flict（打，击）→ 向某人发出攻击 → 使苦恼，折磨

例 Financial difficulties *afflicted* the Smiths. 经济困难困扰着史密斯一家。

stripe
[straɪp]

n. 条纹，斑纹

记 联想记忆：和 strip（*n.* 条）一起记

例 This skirt has a red *stripe* around the edge. 这条裙子的边上有一圈红色条纹。

24

clay [kleɪ]	*n.* 泥土，黏土(earth, mud) 记 联想记忆：c + lay(层) → 泥土成一层一层分布 → 泥土 例 Because of these properties, *clay* is used for making pottery items. 正因为这些特性，黏土被用于制作陶瓷器。
comment [ˈkɑːment]	*v./n.* 评论(review)；注释(remark, note) 记 词根记忆：com(共同) + ment(想法；思考) → 共同进行思考 → 评论 例 The teacher *comments* on his musical training at the Juilliard School. 老师评价了他在朱利亚德学校所接受的音乐培训。
scholarship [ˈskɑːlərʃɪp]	*n.* 奖学金；学问，学识 搭 full scholarship 全额奖学金 例 His brother won a *scholarship* to study at Harvard. 他哥哥获得了奖学金，得以在哈佛求学。
patch [pætʃ]	*vt.* 修补，打补丁 *n.* 小片，小块(scrap)；补丁；小块土地 记 联想记忆：要想抓住(catch)这么小片(patch)的东西，可不容易啊 搭 patch up 修理，临时修补；言归于好；勉强同意 例 They have managed to *patch* up their differences. 他们终于弥合了分歧。
restrict [rɪˈstrɪkt]	*vt.* 限制，约束(limit, restrain) 记 联想记忆：re(再，又) + strict(严格的) → 一再对人严格 → 限制，约束 例 The girl's parents were blamed for *restricting* her activities. 女孩的父母因限制其活动受到了指责。 派 restriction(*n.* 限制，约束)；restrictive(*a.* 限制性的)
accurate [ˈækjərət]	*a.* 正确无误的，精确的(*precise, exact) 记 词根记忆：ac(表加强) + cur(注意；关心) + ate → 不断关心，使之正确无误的 → 正确无误的 例 Most scientists believe the theory to be *accurate*. 大多数科学家认为这个理论是正确的。 派 accurately(*ad.* 正确地，精确地)；inaccurate(*a.* 错误的，不准确的)
comprise [kəmˈpraɪz]	*vt.* 包含(include)；由…组成(*consist of) 记 词根记忆：com(共同) + pris(抓住) + e → 抓在一起 → 包含 例 The Earth *comprises* three principal layers. 地球主要由三层构成。 参 compromise(*n./v.* 妥协)
enzyme [ˈenzaɪm]	*n.* 酶，酵素 记 词根记忆：en(在…里) + zym(酵母) + e → 在里面放入酵母 → 酵素 例 Some *enzymes* are used commercially, for example, in the synthesis of antibiotics. 一些酶具有商业用途，比如，用于抗生素的合成。

patch

□ clay   □ comment   □ scholarship   □ patch   □ restrict   □ accurate
□ comprise   □ enzyme

sumptuous [ˈsʌmptʃuəs]	*a.* 奢华的，豪华的(luxurious, magnificent, splendid) 词根记忆：sumpt(用) + uous(多…的) → 用得太多的 → 奢华的 例 We dined in *sumptuous* surroundings. 我们在富丽堂皇的环境中用餐。
allegiance [əˈliːdʒəns]	*n.* 忠诚，效忠，拥戴(loyalty, devotion) 词根记忆：al(向) + leg(法律) + iance → 朝向法律 → 忠诚，效忠 例 Some chants showed people's *allegiance* to religious leaders or symbols. 一些赞美歌表现了人们对宗教领袖或宗教信条的忠诚。 allegiance
invasion [ɪnˈveɪʒn]	*n.* 侵入，侵略，侵犯 词根记忆：in(进入) + vas(走) + ion → 未经允许走进来 → 侵入，侵略 例 An *invasion* of the introduced species had threatened the development of agriculture. 引入物种的入侵威胁了农业的发展。
cabinet [ˈkæbɪnət]	*n.* 内阁；储藏柜，陈列柜 搭 a cabinet meeting 内阁会议 例 The china was displayed in a glass *cabinet*. 瓷器陈列在玻璃柜里。
hover [ˈhʌvər]	*vi.* 徘徊，彷徨(wander)；(鸟等)翱翔，盘旋 联想记忆：在爱人(lover)身边徘徊(hover) 例 The criminal is *hovering* between life and death. 这个罪犯在生死之间徘徊。 参 hovercraft(*n.* 气垫船) hover
accuracy [ˈækjərəsi]	*n.* 准确(性)，精确(性)(nicety, precision) 来自 accurate(*a.* 正确无误的，精确的) 例 Those companies rely on high *accuracy* scales to manufacture and package medicine. 那些公司依靠高精度标准来生产和包装药品。
expire [ɪkˈspaɪər]	*vi.* (协议等)到期，期满，失效；断气，去世 词根记忆：ex(出) + pir(呼吸) + e → 停住了呼吸 → 到期；去世 例 Ronald has to renew his passport because it has *expired*. 罗纳德的护照过期了，他不得不去续签。 参 aspire(*v.* 有志于；热望，向往)；perspire(*vi.* 出汗，流汗)
gasoline [ˈgæsəliːn]	*n.* 汽油(petrol) 联想记忆：gas(气体) + o + line(排队) → 人们排着队去加油 → 汽油 例 When *gasoline* burns, nothing visible remains. 汽油燃烧后，没有什么可见剩余物。
diminish [dɪˈmɪnɪʃ]	*v.* 降低，贬低(debase, devalue)；(使)减少，减弱(decrease) 词根记忆：di + mini(小) + sh → (使)变少 例 I don't mean to *diminish* Revere's role. 我并不打算降低里维尔的职位。

angular [ˈæŋgjələr]	*a.* 有角的, 尖角的;（指人）消瘦的, 瘦骨嶙峋的 例 The man has an *angular* face. 那个男人长着一张瘦削的脸。
immense [ɪˈmens]	*a.* 巨大的, 极大的(vast, huge) 记 词根记忆：im(不) + mens(测量) + e → 不能测量的 → 巨大的, 极大的 例 Horsetail rushes in prehistoric times grew to *immense* size. 史前的木贼灯心草长得很大。
owl [aʊl]	*n.* 猫头鹰 记 发音记忆："嗷" → 像猫头鹰的叫声；注意不要和 awl(*n.* 尖钻)相混 例 Most *owls* are nocturnal. 大多数猫头鹰都是夜行性动物。 派 owlish(*a.* 似猫头鹰的；儒雅的)
percussion [pərˈkʌʃn]	*n.* 打击乐器 记 词根记忆：per(表加强) + cuss(打) + ion → 用力打的东西 → 打击乐器 例 The track features Joey Langton on *percussion*. 唱片的这段乐曲是乔伊·兰顿演奏的打击乐。
crooked [ˈkrʊkɪd]	*a.* 不诚实的；欺诈的；弯曲的 记 来自 crook(*vt.* 弯曲) 搭 a crooked businessman 不诚实的商人 例 Don't take *crooked* ways to solve the problem. 不要用歪门邪道来解决这个问题。
stratum [ˈstreɪtəm]	*n.* [*pl.* strata]岩层, 地层；社会阶层 例 People from all social *strata* attended this meeting. 来自不同社会阶层的人都参加了这次会议。
instead [ɪnˈsted]	*ad.* 代替, 顶替；反而, 却 例 This casserole really tastes good. I guess that's because the vegetables in it are fresh *instead* of canned. 这个砂锅味道真不错。我猜这是因为里面是新鲜蔬菜, 而不是罐装蔬菜。
populate [ˈpɑːpjuleɪt]	*vt.* (大批地)居住于(inhabit) 记 词根记忆：popul(人) + ate(使…) → 使人在某处安家 → (大批地)居住于 例 The town is heavily *populated* by immigrants. 该镇居住着很多外来移民。 派 population(*n.* 人口；人口密度)
ambitious [æmˈbɪʃəs]	*a.* 有雄心的, 有野心的(aspiring, enterprising) 记 来自 ambition(*n.* 雄心, 野心) 例 According to the survey, many *ambitious* college students want to be their own boss after graduation. 调查显示, 很多雄心勃勃的大学生想在毕业后自己当老板。

sentimental [ˌsentɪˈmentl]	*a.* 情感的；伤感的，多愁善感的(emotional) 记 来自 sentiment(*n.* 情感；伤感) 例 He kept the letters for *sentimental* reasons. 他出于情感上的原因保留了那些信件。 派 sentimentalism(*n.* 感伤主义); sentimentality (*n.* 感伤情调)
ultimate [ˈʌltɪmət]	*a.* 最后的，最终的；根本的(fundamental, essential) *n.* 最好的事物；最大的或最先进的事物 记 词根记忆: ultim(最后) + ate → 最后的，最终的 搭 in ultimate 到最后，结果 例 Her discovery may help to answer some of our questions about the *ultimate* of the universe. 她的发现可能有助于回答我们关于宇宙终极的一些问题。
evergreen [ˈevərgriːn]	*a.* 常绿的 *n.* 常绿树，常青树 搭 evergreen trees 常青树 例 In addition, the shelter provided by *evergreen* plants can make it easier for younger *evergreen* plants to survive cold and drought. 此外，常绿植物提供的庇护更有利于常绿植物幼苗熬过严寒和干旱。
plumage [ˈpluːmɪdʒ]	*n.* 鸟类羽毛(feather) 例 The bird's *plumage* has turned grey over one night. 这只鸟的羽毛在一夜之间变成了灰色。
decadent [ˈdekədənt]	*a.* 堕落的，颓废的(depraved) 记 词根记忆: de(向下) + cad(掉，落) + ent → 向下落的 → 堕落的 例 Due to arguments over the nature of morality, whether a society is *decadent* or not is a matter of debate. 鉴于何谓道德本质仍存有争议，一个社会是否堕落是个有待辩论的问题。
subspecies [sʌbˈspiːʃiːz]	*n.* 亚种(subgroup) 记 联想记忆: sub(在…下面) + species(物种) → 下一等的物种 → 亚种 例 Organisms that belong to different *subspecies* of the same species are capable of interbreeding. 同一物种下不同亚种间的生物可杂交。
hummingbird [ˈhʌmɪŋbɜːrd]	*n.* 蜂鸟 记 组合词: humming(嗡嗡叫) + bird(鸟) → 扇动翅膀发出嗡嗡声的鸟 → 蜂鸟 例 *Hummingbirds* are capable of slowing down their metabolism at night, or any other time food is not readily available. 蜂鸟能在夜间或任何食物难以获得的情况下减缓新陈代谢作用。

sentimental

无可奈何
花落去

24

你树老
珠黄咯

evergreen

estate [ɪˈsteɪt]	*n.* 地产(lands); (尤指)庄园; 个人财产, (尤指)遗产 **记** 词根记忆: e(出) + st(站立) + ate → 赖以生存的 → 地产 **搭** real estate 房地产 **例** The old woman left her *estate* to her granddaughter. 那个老妇人将她的遗产留给了孙女。
stylistic [staɪˈlɪstɪk]	*a.* 风格上的, 文体上的 **搭** stylistic features 风格特点 **例** The professor observes that, in practice, most *stylistic* analysis has attempted to deal with the complex and "valued" language within literature. 教授发现, 在实际运用中, 大多数文体分析试图处理文学作品中复杂且"有价值的"语言。
declare [dɪˈkler]	*v.* 表明(announce); 断言, 声称(assert); 申报 **记** 词根记忆: de(表加强) + clar(清楚) + e → 说清楚 → 表明; 声称 **例** "My flight was done with no expectation of reward," she *declared*, "just purely for the love of accomplishment." "我飞行并不是为了得奖," 她宣称, "纯粹是为了有所成就。"
varnish [ˈvɑːrnɪʃ]	*vt.* 上清漆 *n.* 清漆 **记** 联想记忆: 涂上清漆(varnish), 这个图案就不容易消失(vanish)了 **例** The main task of the painters was to *varnish* furniture. 油漆工的主要任务是给家具上清漆。 **派** varnished(*a.* 上过清漆的)
wonder [ˈwʌndər]	*v.* 诧异, 纳闷, 想知道 *n.* 惊奇, 惊异; 奇迹, 奇事 **搭** no wonder 难怪, 怪不得 **例** I've been running a mile every afternoon for the past month, but I still haven't been able to lose more than a pound or two. I *wonder* if it's worth it. 过去一个月里我一直坚持每天下午跑一英里, 但是体重也就减轻了一两磅。我不知道跑步到底值不值。// Tom and I are having a party next week. We *wonder* if you and Joe would be free to join us. 汤姆和我下周要开派对。不知道你和乔是否有空来参加。 **参** wander(*v.* 徘徊)
justify [ˈdʒʌstɪfaɪ]	*v.* 证明…是正当的; 为…辩护 **例** An important task for both of these Presidents was to *justify* to their citizens why the war was necessary. 这两位总统的一项重要任务是向他们的公民证明为何战争是必要的。
dissolve [dɪˈzɑːlv]	*v.* (使)溶解(melt, liquefy); 清除(eliminate); 解散, 结束 **记** 词根记忆: dis(分离) + solv(松开) + e → 松开, 分散 → (使)溶解 **例** His calm response *dissolved* her anger. 他冷静的回答化解了她的怒气。

superficial [ˌsuːpərˈfɪʃl]	*a.* 肤浅的，浅薄的；表面的，外表的，外层的（surface） 记 词根记忆：super(在…上面) + fic(做) + ial → 只在上面做 → 肤浅的 例 The book shows only a *superficial* understanding of the historical context. 这本书表现出对历史背景肤浅的理解。
peninsula [pəˈnɪnsələ]	*n.* 半岛 记 词根记忆：pen(几乎) + insula(岛) → 几乎是岛 → 半岛 例 Though the Cold War ended two decades ago, people on the Korean *Peninsula* are still living in its shadow. 尽管冷战 20 年前就结束了，但朝鲜半岛上的人们仍活在它的阴影下。
luxurious [lʌɡˈʒʊriəs]	*a.* 奢侈的，奢华的 记 来自 luxury(*n.* 奢侈品；奢华) 例 I wish I could own a *luxurious* sports car like this, but I can't afford it. 我希望能拥有一辆像这样的奢华跑车，但是我买不起。
ornate [ɔːrˈneɪt]	*a.* 华丽的，豪华的 记 词根记忆：orn(装饰) + ate → 用于装饰的 → 华丽的，豪华的 例 This music fountain is famous for its *ornate* and unique design. 这个音乐喷泉因其华丽独特的设计而闻名。
plaudit [ˈplɔːdɪt]	*n.* [常 *pl.*]鼓掌，喝彩；赞誉，称赞 记 词根记忆：plaud(鼓掌) + it → 鼓掌，喝彩 例 When the performance was over, all the performers got *plaudits* from the audience. 演出完毕，所有表演人员都得到了观众的喝彩。
quiver [ˈkwɪvər]	*n.* 颤抖；箭筒 *vi.* 颤动，抖动（tremble） 例 When I put the little bird in my palm, I can feel the *quiver* of it. 当我把小鸟放到我的手心时，我能感受到它在轻轻地颤抖。
saunter [ˈsɔːntər]	*vi./n.* 闲逛，漫步（stroll） 记 联想记忆：s(看做 see，看) + aunt(姑姑) + er → 看姑姑去 → 闲逛而去 → 闲逛 例 Many tourists *saunter* along the streets with shopping bags. 很多旅游者拿着购物袋在街上闲逛。
tackle [ˈtækl]	*v.* 对付，处理；阻截；抢球 *n.* 拦截；用具 记 联想记忆：tack(大头钉) + le → 大头钉也是一种用具 → 用具 例 The candidate claimed he would *tackle* the problem of climate change, an issue his rivals have neglected. 那个候选人声称他将处理气候变化问题，这正是他的竞争对手所忽略的。
usher [ˈʌʃər]	*n.* 领座员，招待员 *v.* 引领，引导 例 We followed the *usher* down the aisle and found our seats. 我们跟着领座员沿着通道走过去，找到了我们的座位。
vigor [ˈvɪɡər]	*n.* 活力，精力 记 词根记忆：vig(生活) + or → 活力，精力 例 Chinese traditional culture adds new *vigor* to the Olympic opening ceremony. 中国的传统文化为奥运开幕式增添了新的活力。

24

□ superficial □ peninsula □ luxurious □ ornate □ plaudit □ quiver
□ saunter □ tackle □ usher □ vigor

solitude [ˈsɑːlətjuːd]	*n.* 孤独，单独；独处，独居；隐居处 记 词根记忆：sol(独自的) + itude → 孤独，单独 例 I can't believe that man in the news passed 25 years in *solitude*. 我不敢相信新闻中的那个人在孤独中度过了 25 年。 solitude
whim [wɪm]	*n.* 一时的兴致，冲动；怪念头，奇想 搭 at whim 任性 例 Lisa had a sudden *whim* to go shopping today. 今天莉莎一时兴起，想去逛街。
apparatus [ˌæpəˈrætəs]	*n.* 器械，器具，设备，装置；机构，组织；器官 记 词根记忆：ap(靠近) + para(排列) + tus → 靠近排列(起作用) → 器械 例 That passage covers all kinds of heating *apparatus*. 那篇文章谈及各种取暖装置。
vogue [voʊg]	*n.* 时尚，风气，流行 *a.* 流行的，时髦的 记 联想记忆：对时尚(vogue)茫然(vague) 搭 in vogue 流行 例 Jogging is in *vogue* all over the world. 慢跑运动正风靡全世界。
brace [breɪs]	*vt.* 绷紧肌肉；使顶住；使防备；加强，加固 *n.* 支架，托架 记 联想记忆：b(音似：绷) + race(赛跑) → 赛跑时肌肉会绷紧 → 绷紧肌肉 例 You're a grown-up, and you must *brace* yourself and take the responsibility. 你已经是大人了，一定要鼓起勇气承担责任。
censor [ˈsensər]	*n.* 审查员 *vt.* 审查，检查(书报) 记 词根记忆：cens(评价) + or(表人，名词后缀) → 审查员 例 Some of the scenes were cut by the *censor*. 有几个镜头被审查员剪掉了。 派 censorship(*n.* 审查制度)
respire [rɪˈspaɪər]	*v.* 呼吸(breathe) 记 词根记忆：re(再，又) + spir(呼吸) + e → 呼吸 例 To my surprise, some aquatic animals living under the water *respire* through their skins. 令我惊奇的是，一些水生动物用皮肤呼吸。
morphology [mɔːrˈfɑːlədʒi]	*n.* 形态学，形态论 记 词根记忆：morph(形状) + ology(…学) → 形态学，形态论 例 In this way, *morphology* is the branch of linguistics that studies patterns of word formation within and across languages. 在这个意义上而言，形态学是语言学的一个分支，研究语言内部以及不同语言之间的单词的形式。
adroit [əˈdrɔɪt]	*a.* 精明的，干练的；熟练的，灵巧的(adept, dexterous) 记 词根记忆：a(向) + droit(正确的) → 总能向着正确的方向 → 精明的 例 Jack is a quick-learner, and soon he becomes *adroit* at driving. 杰克学东西很快，很快就熟练掌握了驾驶技术。

□ solitude □ whim □ apparatus □ vogue □ brace □ censor
□ respire □ morphology □ adroit

moss [mɔːs]	*n.* 苔藓 例 The little boy was asleep on a pile of leaves and *moss* when he was found. 当人们发现小男孩时，他正熟睡在一堆树叶和苔藓上。
perch [pɜːrtʃ]	*v.* (鸟)栖息，停留；把…置于较高处；(使)坐于 *n.* (鸟类的)栖息处，栖木；高处，较高的位置；鲈鱼 记 联想记忆：per(每个) + ch(音似：车) → 每人一车 → 居高位的人，每人都有车 → 较高的位置 例 The Greens live in a remote small village which is *perched* at the foot of a mountain. 格林一家住在山脚一个偏远的小村子里。
recipient [rɪˈsɪpiənt]	*n.* 接受者，收受者 记 词根记忆：re(反) + cip(拿，取) + ient → 不主动拿的人 → 接受者 例 The *recipients* of the awards of the best leading actor and actress will be announced at the film festival. 本届电影节将公布最佳男女主角获奖者。
fare [fer]	*vi.* 进展(evolve) *n.* (车、船、飞机等的)费用(charge) 例 How are you *faring* with your project? 你的项目进展如何？
neon [ˈniːɑːn]	*n.* 氖；霓虹灯 记 发音记忆："霓虹" 例 Two quite different kinds of *neon* lighting are in common use. 两种相当不同的霓虹灯得到广泛使用。
minimize [ˈmɪnɪmaɪz]	*vt.* 将…减到最少，使最小化；降低，贬低 记 词根记忆：min(小) + im + ize → 将…减到最少，使最小化 例 Good hygiene helps to *minimize* the risk of infection. 保持清洁有助于最大程度地减少感染的危险。
permeate [ˈpɜːrmieɪt]	*v.* 弥漫(*spread through)；渗透(*spread through, penetrate) 记 词根记忆：per(贯穿) + mea(经过，流过) + e → 全部流过 → 弥漫；渗透 例 Water will *permeate* blotting paper. 水能够渗透吸水纸。 参 permeable(*a.* 可渗透的)；impermeable(*a.* 不能渗透的)
midterm [ˌmɪdˈtɜːrm]	*a.* 中间的，期中的 *n.* 期中考试；(任期)中期；(学期的)期中 例 Next Friday, a week from today, is the *midterm* exam, marking the half way point in the semester. 一周之后，也就是下周五就要进行期中考试，这标志着学期已经过了一半。 // A: How about seeing the new movie at the North Park Theater tonight? B: Sounds great. But I got to go over my notes for tomorrow's *midterm*. A: 今天晚上去北公园剧院看新电影如何？ B: 好是好，但是我要为明天的期中考试复习笔记。

24

Word List 25

音频

词根、词缀预习表

gest	搬运	digest v. 消化	**bitr**	进发	arbitrary a. 专断的
creas	肉	pancreas n. 胰腺	**ess**	存在	essential a. 基本的，本质的
mony	声明	testimony n. 证词	**sooth**	真实的	soothe vt. 抚慰
noct	夜	nocturnal a. 夜行性的	**drench**	喝	drench vt. 使湿透
gon	角	polygon n. 多角形，多边形	**tig**	接触	contiguous a. 接壤的

stress [stres]	*n.* 压力(pressure)；强调(emphasis)；精神压力，紧张；重音，重读 *v.* 强调(*emphasize)；重读；(使)焦虑不安 搭 stress management 压力管理 例 *Stress* is often a factor in the development of long-term sickness. 心理压力常常是形成长期疾病的一个因素。 派 stressful(*a.* 充满压力的；紧张的)
digest	[daɪ'dʒest] *v.* 消化，吸收(absorb)；领悟 ['daɪdʒest] *n.* 摘要，概要 记 词根记忆：di(向下) + gest(搬运) → 运下去 → 消化 例 The sea cucumber has the ability to *digest* whatever nutrients are present. 无论什么营养物海参都能消化。 派 digestion(*n.* 消化，吸收)
pancreas ['pæŋkriəs]	*n.* 胰腺 记 词根记忆：pan(全部) + creas(肉) → 给身体生长提供营养的器官 → 胰腺 例 The *pancreas* is a storage depot for digestive enzymes. 胰腺是消化酶的储藏所。 派 pancreatic(*a.* 胰腺的)
Gothic ['gɑːθɪk]	*a.* 哥特式的，哥特风格的 *n.* 哥特式建筑 例 It was famous for its use of *Gothic* decorative detail. 它因使用哥特式装饰细节而著名。
undergraduate [ˌʌndər'grædʒət]	*n.* 大学肄业生；大学本科生 记 组合词：under(在…下面) + graduate(毕业生) → 还不是毕业生 → 大学肄业生 例 You might give a little more explanation about your unique *undergraduate* background. 你不妨再稍微解释一下你独特的本科背景。

conversation [ˌkɑːnvər'seɪʃn]	*n.* 交谈，会话 记 来自 converse(*vi.* 交谈，会话) 例 I will have a long *conversation* with my mother tomorrow. 明天我将和母亲作一次长谈。 派 conversational(*a.* 非正式的，用于交谈的，口语的；交谈的)
rust [rʌst]	*v.* (使)生锈(corrode) *n.* 锈，铁锈；锈病 记 联想记忆：铁不磨一定(must)会生锈(rust) 搭 rust away 锈坏 例 Water had got in and *rusted* the engine. 发动机进水生锈了。 派 rusty(*a.* 生锈的；衰退的)
testimony ['testɪmoʊni]	*n.* 证词；证据，证明 记 词根记忆：test(目击) + i + mony(声明) → 目击声明 → 证词 例 The pyramids are an eloquent *testimony* to the ancient Egyptians' engineering skills. 金字塔是古埃及人非凡工程技术的明鉴。
wick [wɪk]	*n.* 蜡烛芯，灯芯 参 wicker(*n.* 柳条，枝条)
perish ['perɪʃ]	*v.* 灭亡(die out)；湮灭，毁灭；(使橡胶、皮革等)老化 记 联想记忆：珍惜(cherish)生命，不应随意毁灭(perish) 例 When a species is no longer adapted to a changed environment, it may *perish*. 一个物种不能再适应环境的变化时就会灭亡。 派 perishable(*a.* 易腐烂的，易变质的)
nocturnal [nɑːk'tɜːrnl]	*a.* 夜行性的(active at night)；夜间发生的 记 词根记忆：noct(夜) + urnal → 夜行性的；夜间发生的 例 Most mice are *nocturnal*, but the African grass mouse is active during daylight hours. 大多数老鼠是夜行性的，但是非洲草鼠在白天活跃。
application [ˌæplɪ'keɪʃn]	*n.* 请求，申请(书、表)；应用，运用；敷用 记 来自 apply(*v.* 申请；应用) 搭 application for 申请…；the application of …的申请 例 Many overseas *applications* for full scholarships are turned down every year in the US. 在美国，每年都有很多海外学生的全额奖学金申请遭到拒绝。// A: Excuse me, I heard that there were a couple of jobs available in the library. So I'd like to apply for one of them. Can I fill out the *application* form at home and bring it back next week? B: Sure, but you should know that we're about to start looking at the *applications*, and we hope to make some job offers in a few days. A: 打扰一下，我听说图书馆有几个工作机会。我想申请一个。我能在家填写申请表，下周再带回来吗？ B: 当然可以，但是你应该知道我们就要开始看这些申请了，我们希望几天之内确定一些合适的人选。

25

distant
['dɪstənt]

a. 远离的，遥远的；疏远的，冷淡的(remote)；久远的；不同的
记 词根记忆：di(分开) + st(站) + ant → 分开站的 → 远离的，遥远的；疏远的
例 Peace was just a *distant* hope. 和平不过是遥不可及的希望。
派 distance(*n.* 距离，间距；远方，远处；差异)
参 instant(*a.* 立即的)

polygon
['pɑːlɪɡɑːn]

n. 多角形，多边形
记 词根记忆：poly(多的) + gon(角) → 多角形，多边形
搭 convex polygon 凸多边形
派 polygonal(*a.* 多角形的，多边形的)

arbitrary
['ɑːrbətreri]

a. 任意的(random)；专制的，专断的
记 词根记忆：ar(向着) + bitr(进发) + ary(形容词后缀) → 向着某物进发的 → 专断的
搭 an arbitrary character 反复无常的性格；an arbitrary decision 武断的决定
例 In the US, some people argue that a ban on some types of guns is *arbitrary*. 在美国，一些人认为禁止某些类型的枪支的决定是专断的。

membrane
['membreɪn]

n. 薄膜；细胞膜
记 词根记忆：membr(成分) + ane → 身体上起保护作用的部分 → 薄膜；细胞膜
搭 a waterproof *membrane* 防水薄膜
例 Synthetic *membrane* can be fabricated from a large number of different materials. 人工膜可通过大量不同的原材料制造而成。

essential
[ɪ'senʃl]

a. 基本的，本质的(fundamental, substaintial)；极其重要的，必不可少的
n. 要素，实质；必需品
记 词根记忆：ess(存在) + ential → 存在的 → 基本的，本质的
例 Calcium is *essential* for maintaining bones and teeth. 钙对保持骨骼和牙齿健康至关重要。
派 essentially(*ad.* 本质上，根本上)

soothe
[suːð]

vt. 缓和，减轻(relieve)；抚慰，安慰(calm)
记 词根记忆：sooth(真实的) + e → 通过证实他人的话属实使其得到安慰 → 抚慰
搭 soothe away 解除，消除
例 The music *soothed* the girl for a while. 音乐让那个女孩安静了一会儿。

robust
[roʊ'bʌst]

a. 健壮的，强壮的(*strong)
记 联想记忆："乐百氏"(Robust)矿泉水
例 The bird has a large, *robust* bill. 这只鸟的喙大而结实。

robust

venomous ['venəməs]	*a.* 有毒的，分泌毒液的(poisonous)；恶意的，狠毒的 记 来自 venom(*n.* 毒液) 例 The politician was accused of a *venomous* attack on his political opponents at the meeting. 这名政客被指控在会议上恶意攻击他的政治对手。
chamber ['tʃeɪmbər]	*n.* 会议厅；议院；洞穴(cavity)；(人体、植物或机器内的)腔，室；(作特定用途的)房间(room, compartment) 例 The archaeologists found themselves in a vast underground *chamber*. 考古学者发现他们置身于一个地下大洞穴。
reversible [rɪ'vɜːrsəbl]	*a.* 可逆的，可翻转的；正反两用的；可恢复原状的 记 词根记忆：re(反) + vers(转) + ible(能…的) → 能反转的 → 可逆的 例 Scientists say most of the damage to the cells caused by poisonous chemicals is *reversible*. 科学家称，大多数由有毒化学物导致的细胞损伤是可医治的。
sleek [sliːk]	*a.* (毛发等)光滑而有光泽的；线条流畅的；时髦的 *vt.* 使(头发等)平整光亮 记 联想记忆：一直想找到(seek)一辆线条流畅的(sleek)小汽车 例 Edward fell in love with a beautiful girl with *sleek* black hair and big eyes. 爱德华爱上了一个有着黑亮头发和大眼睛的漂亮女孩。
copilot ['koʊˌpaɪlət]	*n.* (飞机的)副驾驶员 记 联想记忆：co(共同) + pilot(飞行员) → (飞机的)副驾驶员
tactile ['tæktaɪl]	*a.* 触觉的；有触觉的；可感触的 记 词根记忆：tact(触摸) + ile → 触觉的；有触觉的 搭 tactile stimuli 触觉刺激 例 The poor boy not only had auditory difficulties but *tactile* ones. 这个可怜的男孩不仅患有听觉障碍，还有触觉障碍。
variant ['veriənt]	*n.* 变体，变形 *a.* 不同的，变异的 记 词根记忆：vari(改变) + ant → 变体；不同的 例 Some game players think this new game is just a *variant* of the previous famous game. 一些游戏玩家认为，这个新游戏只不过是之前那个著名游戏的变体。
choppy ['tʃɑːpi]	*a.* (海面等)波浪起伏的，不平静的；不连贯的，支离破碎的 例 The peaceful sea became *choppy* soon when the windstorm was coming. 当暴风来临时，平静的海面立刻变得波涛汹涌。
solvent ['sɑːlvənt]	*n.* 溶剂 *a.* 有溶解力的；有偿付能力的 记 词根记忆：solv(=solu 解开；溶解) + ent → 有溶解力的 例 The oil giant made many more efforts to scatter the industrial *solvents* for removing the oil from the polluted sea. 这家石油巨头加大力度给被污染的海域撒清除油污的工业溶剂。

25

viscous [ˈvɪskəs]	*a.* 黏滞的，黏性的 例 Studies show that this newly-found species in the tropical forest can create a kind of *viscous* substance. 研究表明，这种在热带雨林中新发现的物种可以分泌一种黏性物质。
yolk [joʊk]	*n.* 蛋黄，卵黄 记 联想记忆：民间(folk)有说法，蛋黄(yolk)是大补品 例 You'd better separate the egg white from the *yolk* to feed your baby. 你最好把蛋白和蛋黄分开来喂孩子。
cavern [ˈkævərn]	*n.* 大洞穴，大山洞 记 联想记忆：cave(洞) + rn → 大洞穴 例 The underground *cavern* is found by accident where boxes of treasure are hidden. 人们无意间发现了这个地下洞穴，里面藏有成箱的财宝。 cavern
drench [drentʃ]	*vt.* 使湿透(soak) 记 词根记忆：drench(=drink 喝) → 喝水 → 使湿透 例 The expedition was caught in the heavy rain halfway and got *drenched*. 探险队半路遇到大雨，被淋透了。
landslide [ˈlændslaɪd]	*n.* 山崩，塌方；压倒性胜利 记 组合词：land(地) + slide(滑行) → 地向下滑 → 山崩，塌方 例 The rescuers made great efforts to save the victims from the *landslide*. 营救人员尽力挽救山崩的受害者。
contiguous [kənˈtɪɡjuəs]	*a.* 接壤的，毗邻的(neighboring)；不间断的 记 词根记忆：con(和) + tig(=ting 接触) + uous → 相接触的 → 接壤的 例 The two countries are *contiguous* with each other, but the tradition and religion are quite different. 这两个国家彼此接壤，但是风俗和宗教却相去甚远。
moor [mʊr]	*n.* 沼泽；旷野，荒野 *v.* (使)停泊，系泊 记 联想记忆：月光(moon)下，那个可怜的(poor)老人走在旷野(moor)中 例 It was about half an hour's walk from Jim's house to the *moor*. 从吉姆家步行到那片荒野约需半小时。
crescent [ˈkresnt]	*a.* 新月形的；逐渐增强的 *n.* 新月；新月形，月牙形 记 联想记忆：cre + scent(香味) → 新月长到满月，月饼飘香 → 新月 例 A *crescent* moon hangs in the east, and then swims into the dim clouds. 一轮新月挂在东方，然后隐没在朦胧的云彩里了。
missile [ˈmɪsl]	*n.* 发射物；导弹，飞弹 记 词根记忆：miss(发送) + ile(表物，名词后缀) → 发送出去的物体 → 发射物 例 The experts tried to find out the reason why the *missile* exploded. 专家们尽力查明导弹爆炸的原因。

☐ viscous ☐ yolk ☐ cavern ☐ drench ☐ landslide ☐ contiguous
☐ moor ☐ crescent ☐ missile

shroud [ʃraʊd]	*vt.* 隐藏，遮蔽（conceal）*n.* 裹尸布，寿衣；遮蔽物 记 联想记忆：下大雨（pour）了，应该（should）找个地方避避（shroud） 例 The languages spoken by early Europeans are still *shrouded* in mystery. 早期欧洲人说的语言仍未为人所知。
mound [maʊnd]	*n.* 土墩，土丘；堆，垛 记 发音记忆："满的" → 堆起来才会满 → 堆，垛 例 There is a round *mound* among houses on which children can play. 房子之间有个圆形的土丘，可供孩子们玩耍。
creative [kriˈeɪtɪv]	*a.* 有创造力的，创造性的 例 He's very *creative* — he writes poetry and paints. 他极富创造力，既赋诗又作画。 派 creativity（*n.* 创造力，创造性）
eccentric [ɪkˈsentrɪk]	*n.* 古怪的人 *a.* 古怪的，反常的（odd, abnormal） 记 词根记忆：ec（出）+ centr（中心）+ ic → 偏离中心的 → 古怪的，反常的 例 She began to dress only in white — a habit that added to her reputation as an *eccentric*. 她开始只穿白衣服——这个习惯使人们越发觉得她古怪。 派 eccentricity（*n.* 古怪，反常）
solo [ˈsoʊloʊ]	*a.* 单独的（sole）；独唱的，独奏的 *ad.* 独自，单独地 *n.* 独唱，独奏（曲），独舞 记 词根记忆：sol（单独）+ o → 单独的；独唱的，独奏的 例 After five years with the band she decided to go *solo*. 跟那支乐队合作了五年后，她决定单飞。 派 soloist（*n.* 独奏者，独唱者；单独表演者）
conserve [kənˈsɜːrv]	*vt.* 保存，保藏（*retain, preserve） 记 词根记忆：con（表加强）+ serv（保持）+ e → 保存，保藏 例 We're trying to protect and *conserve* some of the open spaces on campus. 我们正在努力保护校园里的一些空地。 派 conservative（*a.* 保守的 *n.* 保守派）
volume [ˈvɑːljuːm]	*n.* 体积，容积，容量（amount, capacity）；音量；卷，册；书（book） 例 Joyce's first publication was a *volume* of short fiction. 乔伊斯最早出版的是一本短篇小说集。
temperate [ˈtempərət]	*a.* 气候温和的，温带的；温和的，自我克制的（benign） 记 词根记忆：temper（节制）+ ate → 有节制的 → 温和的 搭 temperate climate 温带气候 例 The early comparison of tropical and *temperate* butterfly's richness has been well confirmed. 有关热带蝴蝶和温带蝴蝶的种类多少的早期比较已得到充分证实。 参 tropical（*a.* 热带的；炎热的） 寒带　热带　温带 temperate

asset [ˈæset]	*n.* 资产，财产；有价值的人（或物）；长处，优点（advantage）
	记 词根记忆：as（靠近）+ set（充分）→ 在近处充分拥有 → 资产，财产
	例 Sometimes a sense of humor is a great *asset*. 有时幽默感是很大的一笔财富。

cliff [klɪf]	*n.* 悬崖，峭壁（precipice）
	例 The castle perched high on the *cliffs* above the river. 那个城堡高高耸立在临河的峭壁上。

cliff

mess [mes]	*n.* 肮脏，杂乱；混乱，困境 *vt.* 弄脏，弄乱；搞糟
	搭 make a mess 弄乱，搞糟；a mess of 很多；in a mess 混乱；陷入困境
	例 The room was in a *mess* after the party. 派对过后，房间里杂乱不堪。//
	A: Sue, would you like to be my lab partner with the next experiment?
	B: Sure. I just can't believe you still want to work with me after I *messed* up last time.
	A: 苏，你愿意在下一个实验中当我的实验伙伴吗？
	B: 当然愿意。我上次搞砸了，真不敢相信你还想跟我合作。

neutral [ˈnjuːtrəl]	*a.* 中性的；中立的（indifferent）
	记 词根记忆：ne（不）+ utr（两者之间）+ al → 不偏向两者的任何一方 → 中立的
	搭 neutral particle 中性粒子
	例 His attitude toward the claims made by advocates of health foods is *neutral*. 他对健康食品支持者的主张持中立态度。
	派 neutrality（*n.* 中性）；neutralize（*vt.* 中和）

abbreviate [əˈbriːvieɪt]	*vt.* 缩略，缩写（shorten）
	记 词根记忆：ab（表加强）+ brev（短的）+ i + ate（使…）→ 使变短 → 缩略，缩写
	例 The Jet Propulsion Laboratory is usually *abbreviated* to JPL. 喷气推进实验室通常缩写为 JPL。
	派 abbreviation（*n.* 缩写；缩写词，缩写形式）；abbreviated（*a.* 缩写的；简短的）

delight [dɪˈlaɪt]	*v.* （使）愉快，（使）高兴（please）*n.* 快乐，高兴；令人高兴的事，乐趣
	记 联想记忆：de（向下）+ light（日光）→ 沐浴在阳光下 → 快乐，高兴
	例 Their basic aim is to *delight* and instruct the students. 他们最基本的目的是使学生们感到愉悦，并给他们提供指导。
	派 delighted（*a.* 高兴的，愉快的）；delightful（*a.* 令人愉快的，宜人的）

plot [plɑːt]	*n.* 情节(plan); 阴谋, 密谋; 小块土地 *v.* 密谋, 暗中策划(conspire); 划分; (在地图上)画出, 标出; 绘制(图表等); 布局, 设计情节 例 The novel is well organized in terms of *plot*. 这部小说的故事布局非常严谨。// Over the same period, another 550,000 lots were *plotted* outside the city limits but within the metropolitan area. 在同一时期, 在市区之外大都会区以内的区域又划分出了 55 万块地。
crustal ['krʌstl]	*a.* 外壳的, (尤指)地壳的 例 In the end of June, 2000, intense *crustal* activity took place in the area. 2000 年 7 月末, 该地区发生了剧烈的地壳活动。
glow [gloʊ]	*vi.* 发光(*shine); 发红, 发热; (感情等)洋溢 *n.* 暗淡的光; 容光焕发; 喜悦 例 Her face *glowed* with embarrassment. 她窘得满脸通红。 派 glowing(*a.* 炽热的; 容光焕发的; 热情洋溢的)
upset	[ʌp'set] *vt.* 使心烦意乱(distress); 颠覆, 推翻; 搅乱(disturb, overturn) [ˌʌp'set] *a.* 心烦意乱的(concerned, worried); (肠胃等)不适的 ['ʌpset] *n.* 困扰, 麻烦; 出乎意料的结局; 苦恼 记 联想记忆: up(向上) + set(放置) → 底朝天放着 → 颠覆, 推翻 例 The new policy is likely to *upset* a lot of people engaged in retail industry. 新政策很可能会让很多从事零售业的人感到不安。
notate ['noʊteɪt]	*vt.* 以符号表示, 把…写成记号(或标志) 记 词根记忆: not(知道) + ate(使…) → (通过标识)使人知道 → 以符号表示 例 Composers of Western music used a system of *notating* their compositions so they could be performed by musicians. 西方音乐的作曲家使用了一套符号系统, 以便音乐家能够演奏他们的作品。 派 notation(*n.* 符号)
pose [poʊz]	*vt.* 摆姿势; 造成; 提出(*frame) *n.* 姿势 例 If this does *pose* a problem for you, you should contact me as soon as possible. 如果这对你确实是个问题, 你应该尽快联系我。
hurricane ['hɜːrəkən]	*n.* 飓风, 暴风(storm) 记 联想记忆: hurri(看做 hurry, 匆忙) + cane → 来得很匆忙的风 → 飓风 例 The storm surge and winds of *hurricanes* may be destructive to human-made structures. 飓风带来的风暴潮和风会破坏人造建筑。 参 cyclone(*n.* 气旋; 龙卷风); typhoon(*n.* 台风)
interact [ˌɪntər'ækt]	*vi.* 相互作用; 互相配合 记 词根记忆: inter(在…之间) + act(行动) → 互动 → 相互作用; 互相配合 例 The people in the office should *interact* with each other and with outside clients. 办公室人员应该互相交流, 也应该与外面的客户交流。 派 interaction(*n.* 相互作用, 相互影响); interactive(*a.* 交互式的; 相互合作的)

25

□ plot □ crustal □ glow □ upset □ notate □ pose
□ hurricane □ interact

pore [pɔːr]	*vi.* 仔细阅读，审阅；审视 *n.* 气孔，小孔（*hole） 搭 pore space 孔隙 例 He *pored* over the classified ads in search of a new job. 为找一份新工作，他仔细阅读了分类广告。
entertain [ˌentərˈteɪn]	*v.* 招待，款待；使快乐，娱乐（amuse） 记 词根记忆：enter（进入）+ tain（拿住）→ 拿着东西进入 → 招待，款待 例 Movie attendance dropped when audience members chose to stay at home and be *entertained*. 当观众选择待在家里娱乐时，去电影院的人就少了。 派 entertainer（*n.* 表演者，艺人）；entertainment（*n.* 娱乐活动；招待） entertain
granular [ˈɡrænjələr]	*a.* 粒状的；含颗粒的 记 词根记忆：gran（=grain 颗粒）+ ular → 粒状的；含颗粒的 例 Many phenomena observed in *granular* materials are still not yet fully understood. 在观察颗粒物质时发现的许多现象仍未被充分理解。
unique [juˈniːk]	*a.* 唯一的（sole, exclusive）；独特的，罕见的（*rare）；特有的 记 词根记忆：uni（单一）+ que（有…特点的）→ 唯一的；独特的 例 He considers each photograph to be *unique*. 他认为每张照片都是独一无二的。 派 uniquely（*ad.* 唯一地；独特地）；uniqueness（*n.* 独特，独一无二）
bead [biːd]	*n.* 珠子；（水、血、汗的）小滴 例 The Homestead Act of 1862 gave *beads* of families or individuals the right to own 160 acres of public land. 1862 年的《宅地法》保证了很多家庭和个人有权拥有 160 英亩公共土地。 bead
craftsman [ˈkræftsmən]	*n.* 能工巧匠，手艺人，工艺师 例 In the 15th century, Paris, as the capital of arts, attracted a vast number of *craftsmen*, architects and musicians. 在 15 世纪，巴黎作为艺术之都吸引了大量的工匠、建筑师和音乐家。
grasp [ɡræsp]	*vt./n.* 抓住（seize）；掌握，理解，领会 记 联想记忆：他紧紧抓住（grasp）她，把她当成救命稻草（grass） 例 Their hands and feet are designed for holding and *grasping* branches. 它们的手和脚天生是用来抓握树枝的。
bias [ˈbaɪəs]	*n.* 偏见，偏心（*prejudice）*vt.* 使有偏见，使偏心 记 词根记忆：bi（两）+ as → 两者只取其一 → 偏见，偏心 例 Throughout the 19th century and into the 20th, citizens of the United States maintained a *bias* against big cities. 整个 19 世纪，甚至到 20 世纪，美国公民对大城市一直持有偏见。 bias

predict
[prɪˈdɪkt]

v. 预言，预测（expect, foretell）

记 词根记忆：pre(在…前面) + dict(说) → 预言，预测

例 Experts *predict* that the gourmet coffee market in the United States is growing. 专家们预计美国的精品咖啡市场需求将会增长。

派 predictable(*a.* 可预言的，可预测的)；predictability(*n.* 可预言性，可预测性)；prediction(*n.* 预言，预测)

参 addict(*vt.* 使沉溺)；contradict(*v.* 同…矛盾)；indict(*vt.* 起诉)

---

triangle
[ˈtraɪæŋgl]

n. 三角形；三角形物体

记 词根记忆：tri(三) + angl(角) + e → 三角形

搭 equilateral triangle 等边三角形

例 They calculated the length of *triangle* sides. 他们计算出了三角形的边长。

---

outcome
[ˈaʊtkʌm]

n. 结果，成果（consequence, effect）

记 来自词组 come out(出来；长出)

例 We are waiting for the final *outcome* of the negotiations. 我们正在等谈判的最终结果。

---

decorate
[ˈdekəreɪt]

v. 装饰，布置（*adorn, ornament）

记 词根记忆：decor(装饰) + ate(动词后缀) → 装饰，布置

例 The stoneware is *decorated* with simple, abstract designs. 粗陶器装饰有简单且抽象的图案。

派 decoration(*n.* 装饰(品))；decorative(*a.* 装饰性的)；decorator(*n.* 装饰者)

25

---

unconsolidated
[ˌʌnkənˈsɑːlɪdeɪtɪd]

a. 松散的，疏松的（loose）

例 An *unconsolidated* aggregate of silt particles is also termed silt, whereas consolidated aggregate is called siltstone. 一团松散的粉砂颗粒仍称为淤泥，而一团固结的淤泥就叫做粉砂石。

---

citadel
[ˈsɪtədəl]

n. 堡垒，要塞（fort, fortress）

例 The place was once a *citadel* in the First World War. 此地曾是第一次世界大战中的一个要塞。

---

pinpoint
[ˈpɪnpɔɪnt]

vt. 精准定位；准确解释（或说明）*n.* 极小的范围；光点 *a.* 准确的，精确的

记 组合词：pin(钉，针) + point(点，尖端) → 针尖 → 精准定位

例 Radar can help *pinpoint* the location of an object within its range. 雷达能够帮助确定其监测范围内的物体的位置。

---

hatch
[hætʃ]

v. 孵化，孵出 *n.* (地面或天花板的)开口；(飞机等的)舱门

记 联想记忆：hat(帽子) + ch → 像扣上一顶帽子一样孵卵 → 孵化

例 The young spiders *hatch* in mid-spring or early summer. 年轻的蜘蛛在仲春或初夏孵卵。

approach [əˈprəʊtʃ]	*v.* 接近(near)；处理 *n.* 方法，手段(measure, way) 记 词根记忆：ap(向) + proach(接近) → 接近；处理 搭 approach to 接近；类似 例 Our bus is *approaching* the town where we'll be stopping to eat. 我们的公交车快到镇上了，我们要在那里停下来吃饭。// She took the wrong *approach* in her dealings with the little girl. 她和那个小女孩打交道的方法不对。
fossil [ˈfɑːsl]	*a.* 化石的；陈腐的 *n.* 化石；老顽固 例 Even scratches found on *fossil* human teeth offer clues. 就连人类牙齿化石上的划痕都能提供线索。 派 fossilize[*v.* (使)变成化石]
turnpike [ˈtɜːrnpaɪk]	*n.* 收费公路(toll road) 记 联想记忆：turn(转动) + pike(横杆) → 转动收费杆 → 收费公路 例 These *turnpike* roads were still very slow, and traveling on them was too costly for farmers. 在收费公路上行驶不仅速度慢，而且对农民来说成本太高。
detectable [dɪˈtekəbl]	*a.* 可发觉的，可察觉的(apparent) 例 The noise is barely *detectable* by the human ear. 这种噪音人的耳朵几乎无法察觉。
contrast 	[ˈkɑːntræst] *n.* 对比，对照 [kənˈtræst] *v.* 对比，对照(compare, balance) 搭 by contrast 对比之下；(与…)相对照 例 Because of these *contrasts*, "popular" may be viewed as clearly different from "folk". 由于这些对比，"流行"可能会被看成是与"民俗"明显不同的词。// The passage is organized by *contrasting* the meanings of two related words. 这段话是通过对比两个相关词的意思而组织起来的。
oasis [oʊˈeɪsɪs]	*n.* 绿洲；避风港(haven) 例 There is a green *oasis* in the heart of the city. 市中心有一片绿茵。
primary [ˈpraɪmeri]	*a.* 最初的；首要的(dominant, chief)；基本的(*fundamental) 记 词根记忆：prim(第一) + ary → 最初的；首要的；基本的 例 The phases of the Moon have served as *primary* divisions of time for thousands of years. 几千年来，月相都是区分时间的主要依据。 派 primarily(*ad.* 起初；主要地)

gulf [gʌlf]	*n.* 海湾 (bay); 分歧, 隔阂, 鸿沟 (branching, divergence)
	记 联想记忆：海湾 (gulf) 国家的富豪们喜欢玩高尔夫 (golf)
	例 Do you know that 90% of the coast is eroding in the *Gulf* of Mexico? 你知道墨西哥湾 90% 的海岸都正受到侵蚀吗？

pale [peɪl]	*a.* 苍白的；淡色的；暗淡的，微弱的 *vi.* 变得苍白，变得暗淡
	例 I think I'd really rather have some *pale* yellow paper for my correspondence. 我想我宁愿用一些浅黄色纸当信纸。

image ['ɪmɪdʒ]	*n.* 形象，印象；画像；影像，映像；意象，比喻
	记 联想记忆：image 可用于指网页上的"图片"
	搭 be the image of 酷似，和…非常相像
	例 The advertisements are intended to improve the company's *image*. 这些广告旨在提高公司的形象。//
	A: Which outfit should I wear to my job interview, the black dress or the navy blue suit?
	B: Well, Jane, you've got to consider the *image* you want to present, and I say the suit is more professional looking.
	A: 我应该穿什么衣服去参加面试？黑连衣裙还是藏青色套装？
	B: 简，你得考虑自己想展示的形象。我觉得套装看上去更职业。

beneficial [ˌbenɪ'fɪʃl]	*a.* 有益的，有利的 (advantageous, favorable)
	搭 be beneficial to 对…有益、有利
	例 A good diet is *beneficial* to health. 良好的饮食有益于健康。
	参 beneficiary (*n.* 受益者，受惠人)

25

spherical ['sferɪkl]	*a.* 球形的，球状的 (round)
	例 The Earth is a nearly *spherical* planet. 地球是一颗近似球体的行星。// The Greeks knew that during eclipses of the Moon, the Earth was between the Sun and the Moon, and they saw that during these eclipses, the Earth's shadow on the moon was always round. They realized that this could be true only if the earth was *spherical*. 希腊人知道发生月食时地球在太阳和月亮之间，他们发现这期间地球投在月亮上的影子总是圆的，于是他们意识到只有在地球是球形时才可能这样。

Word List 26

音频

词根、词缀预习表

gor	收集	category n. 种类	tegr	触摸	integrity n. 正直；完整
trait	拉	portrait n. 肖像	hum	人	posthumous a. 死后的
feas	做	feasible a. 可行的，行得通的	enn	年	centennial n. 百年纪念
fer	带来	fertile a. 肥沃的；能结果的	clar	清楚的	clarify vt. 澄清，阐明
cept	捕捉	susceptible a. 易受影响的	ori	升起	orient n. 东方

---

permit

［pərˈmɪt］v. 允许，许可(enable, allow)

［ˈpɜːrmɪt］n. 许可证，执照(license)

记 词根记忆：per(贯穿，自始至终) + mit(送) → 始终送出 → 允许，许可

例 She is not *permitted* to live off campus this year. 今年她没有获准住在校外。// His parking *permit* expired. 他的停车证到期了。

派 permission(n. 许可)

---

addition

［əˈdɪʃn］

n. 加，加法；添加(物)，增加(物)

记 联想记忆：add(加) + ition → 加，加法

搭 in addition 另外；in addition to 除…之外

例 In *addition* to exercising regularly, eating a good breakfast is considered by many health experts to be a significant part of a successful way of reduction plan. 除了坚持锻炼，很多健康专家认为一顿好的早餐也是减肥计划获得成功的重要部分。

派 additional(a. 附加的，额外的)

参 additive(a. 添加的 n. 添加剂，添加物)

---

divorce

［dɪˈvɔːrs］

n. 离婚；分离，脱离 v. 与…离婚；使分离，使脱离

记 联想记忆：di(分开) + vorce (看做 voice，声音) → 夫妻两个发出不同的声音 → 离婚

例 Nearly half of British marriages are likely to end in *divorce*, according to the bleak picture painted by a new statistical study. 最近一项统计研究得出一个令人沮丧的结果，在英国，近一半的婚姻很可能会以离婚告终。

divorce：

---

category	*n.* 种类(kind)；范畴
[ˈkætəgɔːri]	记 词根记忆：cate(在…下面) + gor(收集) + y → 在下面细细收集 → 种类
	例 The common broad leaf trees we have on campus fall into this *category*. 我们校园里常见的宽叶树均属于这个类别。
	派 categorize(*vt.* 分类)

figurative	*a.* 比喻的，借喻的，象征的；形象的
[ˈfɪgərətɪv]	记 来自 figure(*n.* 外形；象征)
	例 Before I go on to the biochemical specifics of how this works, let me provide a *figurative* example. 我先打一个比方，然后再具体解释这如何发生生化作用。

portrait	*n.* 肖像，画像(picture)；描写，描绘(depiction, description)
[ˈpɔːrtrət]	记 词根记忆：por(向前) + trait(拉) → 向前拉以便进行描绘 → 肖像
	搭 portrait painting 肖像画
	例 The writer gave a *portrait* of life at the French courts. 那个作家详细描绘了法国宫廷的生活。
	派 portraitist(*n.* 肖像画家)；portraiture(*n.* 画像，肖像；画像技法)

dioxide	*n.* 二氧化物
[daɪˈɑːksaɪd]	记 联想记忆：di(二) + oxide(氧化物) → 二氧化物
	搭 sulphur dioxide 二氧化硫
	例 Carbon *dioxide* is also generated as a by-product of combustion. 二氧化碳也是燃烧过程产生的一个副产品。

| **methanol** | *n.* 甲醇 |
| [ˈmeθənɔːl] | 例 The impurities are washed out with *methanol*, I think, before this gas is sent on to reactors where it's changed into oil. 我认为，该气体在被送往反应器转变为油之前，其杂质就已被甲醇清洗干净。 |

amass	*vt.* 积聚(accumulate)
[əˈmæs]	记 联想记忆：a + mass(团) → 变成一团 → 积聚
	例 The shellfish *amass* around the rocks in the shallow water. 贝类聚集在浅水区的岩石周围。

feasible	*a.* 可行的，行得通的(practicable, workable)
[ˈfiːzəbl]	记 词根记忆：feas(=fac 做) + ible(能…的) → 能做的 → 可行的，行得通的
	例 It is not *feasible* to build sea defenses to protect against erosion. 修建海防避免侵蚀是行不通的。
	派 feasibility(*n.* 可行性)

pleasing	*a.* 令人高兴的，愉快的(attractive, comfortable)
[ˈpliːzɪŋ]	搭 a pleasing performance 令人愉快的表演；pleasing to the eye 赏心悦目的
	例 The arrangement of the furniture and facilities formed a *pleasing* atmosphere in the mall. 家具和设备的布置为商场营造出一种愉快的氛围。

26

□ category　　□ figurative　　□ portrait　　□ dioxide　　□ methanol　　□ amass
□ feasible　　□ pleasing

score [skɔː]	*v.* 评分（grade）；划；获胜，成功 *n.* 得分，分数（mark）；乐谱（*musical composition*）；抓痕，划痕；二十
	记 联想记忆：分，分（score），考试的核心（core）
	例 The game was tied until John *scored* the winning point. 约翰得分赢得比赛，之前一直是平局。
simply ['sɪmpli]	*ad.* 简单地，简明地（clearly）；简直；仅仅，只（just）；朴素地，简朴地
	例 This vertical movement of the fieldstone is not *simply* an artifact of soil erosion. 卵石的垂直运动并非只是土壤侵蚀的结果。
	参 simplicity(*n.* 简单；朴素)；simplify(*vt.* 使简化)；simplistic(*a.* 过分简单化的)
fertile ['fɜːrtl]	*a.* 肥沃的，富饶的（rich）；能结果的，能繁殖的（productive）；想象力丰富的
	记 词根记忆：fer(带来) + tile → 可带来果实的 → 肥沃的；能结果的
	例 The soil near the forts is very *fertile*. 城堡附近的土壤非常肥沃。
	派 fertility(*n.* 肥沃，富饶；多产)；infertile(*a.* 贫瘠的；不生育的)
penmanship ['penmənʃɪp]	*n.* 书法（calligraphy）
	记 联想记忆：penman(书法家) + ship(名词后缀) → 书法
	例 *Penmanship* was often taught as a separate subject from the first grade. 书法通常从一年级开始就被作为一个独立的科目来教授。
imprecise [ˌɪmprɪ'saɪs]	*a.* 不精确的（inaccurate, inexact）；不严密的
	记 联想记忆：im(不) + precise(精确的) → 不精确的
	例 We have an old standard weight that we used to use. It had to be replaced because it was *imprecise*. 我们过去用一个旧标准的秤砣，但它因为不精确被换掉了。
wispy ['wɪspi]	*a.* 成束的；纤细的（slight）
	记 来自 wisp(*n.* 小把，小束)
	例 Objects in the universe show a variety of shapes: round planets (some with rings), tailed comets, *wispy* cosmic gas and dust clouds. 宇宙中的物体呈各种形状：圆的行星(有些带环状物)、带尾巴的彗星、束状的宇宙气体和灰尘云。
susceptible [sə'septəbl]	*a.* 易受感染的；易受影响的（*subject to*）；过敏的；感情丰富的；能经受…的，容许…的
	记 词根记忆：sus(表加强) + cept(捕捉) + ible(能…的) → 容易被捕捉的 → 易受影响的
	搭 susceptible to 对…过敏的；易受…影响的
	例 Wheat was *susceptible* to many parasites. 麦子容易受到很多寄生虫的侵袭。
respect [rɪ'spekt]	*vt.* 尊重，尊敬；遵守 *n.* 尊敬，尊重；重视；方面（aspect）
	记 词根记忆：re(再，又) + spect(看) → 一再注目 → 尊重，尊敬
	搭 in respect of 关于，就…而言；with respect to 关于，就…而言
	例 In this *respect*, the North American migratory locusts resemble their African relatives. 从这个方面讲，北美飞蝗类似于非洲的蝗虫。
	派 respectable(*a.* 值得尊敬的；相当好的)
	参 expect(*vt.* 期待，期望；要求)；aspect(*n.* 方面)；inspect(*v.* 检查，视察)；suspect(*v.* 怀疑；猜想)

effluent [ˈefluənt]	*n.* 流出物，废水，污水 记 词根记忆：ef(出) + flu(流) + ent → 流出来的 → 流出物，废水，污水 例 Dangerous *effluent* is poured into the river. 危险的污水正排入河里。 参 fluent(*a.* 流利的，流畅的)
integrity [ɪnˈtegrəti]	*n.* 正直(honesty)；完整 记 词根记忆：in(不) + tegr(触摸) + ity → 未被触摸 → 正直；完整 例 People greatly admired Washington's *integrity*. 人们十分敬仰华盛顿的正直。
thwart [θwɔːrt]	*vt.* 阻碍；使…受挫(baffle, frustrate) 例 The Rosetta Stone *thwarted* scholars' efforts for several decades until the early nineteenth century. 罗塞塔石碑使学者们的努力受挫几十年，直至 19 世纪初为止。
zone [zoʊn]	*vt.* 将…划做特殊区域；分区，划分地带 *n.* 地区，地域，地带(region, area)；气候带 例 The city center was *zoned* for office development. 市中心被划定为写字楼开发区。 派 zoning(*n.* 分区制)
jar [dʒɑːr]	*v.* (使)震动；冲突，抵触；(使)感到不快 *n.* 坛子；广口瓶 记 联想记忆：酒吧(bar)里摆满了酒坛子(jar) 例 Satire *jars* us out of complacence into a pleasantly shocked realization that many of the values we unquestioningly accept are false. 讽刺文学使我们受到震撼，摆脱自满，并且愉快地意识到我们不加怀疑就接受的很多价值观都是错的。 参 ajar〔*a.* (门、窗等)微开的〕
accordion [əˈkɔːrdiən]	*n.* 手风琴 记 来自 accord(*n./vi.* 一致，调和) 例 The size and weight of an *accordion* vary depending on its type, layout and playing range. 手风琴的大小轻重因类型、外形以及音域的不同而各不相同。
posthumous [ˈpɑːstʃəməs]	*a.* 死后的，身后的 记 词根记忆：post(在…之后) + hum(人) + ous → 在活着之后的 → 死后的 例 He received a *posthumous* award for his life of philanthropy. 他在死后，因一生贡献于慈善事业获得了奖项。
hamper [ˈhæmpər]	*vt.* 妨碍，阻挠(*hinder) *n.* (有盖的)大篮子 记 发音记忆："寒迫" → 饥寒交迫 → 妨碍 例 The development of a scientific approach to chemistry was *hampered* by several factors. 几个因素阻碍了化学研究的科学方法的发展。
sodium [ˈsoʊdiəm]	*n.* 钠 搭 sodium chloride 氯化钠，食盐 例 *Sodium's* relative rarity on land is due to its solubility in water. 钠在地球上相对稀缺，主要归因于其可溶于水的特性。

26

centennial [sen'teniəl]	*n.* 百年纪念 记 词根记忆：cent(百) + enn(年) + ial → 百年纪念 例 The country was celebrating the *centennial* of Lincoln's birth. 这个国家正在庆祝林肯100周年诞辰。
responsible [rɪ'spɑːnsəbl]	*a.* 有责任感的，负责的；需负责任的；责任重大的，重要的 记 词根记忆：re(再，又) + spons(承诺，约定) + ible(能…的) → 能一再遵守承诺的 → 有责任感的 例 Larry's roommate may be partly *responsible* for the problem. 拉里的室友可能对这个问题负有部分责任。 派 responsibility(*n.* 责任，职责) responsible 好汉做事 好汉当
series ['sɪriːz]	*n.* 系列，连续(succession)；连续剧 例 The incident sparked off a whole *series* of events that nobody had foreseen. 那一事件引发出一连串谁也未料到的事。
tendon ['tendən]	*n.* 腱 例 The *tendons* in the foot are highly complex and intricate. 脚上的腱极其错综复杂。
maturity [mə'tʊrəti]	*n.* 成熟；完备(full development) 搭 at maturity 成熟 例 The blue whale may grow to 100 feet and weigh 150 tons at *maturity*. 蓝鲸成熟时可以长到100英尺，重达150吨。
boulder ['boʊldər]	*n.* 巨石，巨砾 记 联想记忆：肩(shoulder)上扛着巨石(boulder) 例 A *boulder* is too large for a person to move. 巨石太大了，个人的力量无法移动。 boulder
careless ['kerləs]	*a.* 粗心的，疏忽的 (negligent)；无忧无虑的；不关心的，冷漠的 例 The police claimed that the serious traffic accident resulted from a *careless* driver. 警方声称一名粗心的司机导致了这起严重的交通事故。 派 carelessly(*ad.* 不注意地，粗心地；不关心地)
voracious [və'reɪʃəs]	*a.* 狼吞虎咽的，贪婪的(greedy, insatiable)；求知欲强的 记 词根记忆：vor(吃) + aci + ous(多…的) → 吃得多的 → 狼吞虎咽的 例 The boy has a *voracious* appetite for facts. 那个男孩如饥似渴地寻求事实。
clarify ['klærəfaɪ]	*vt.* 澄清，阐明(identify, explain) 记 词根记忆：clar(清楚的) + ify(…化) → 澄清，阐明 例 He tries to *clarify* his position. 他试图澄清自己的立场。

□ centennial   □ responsible   □ series   □ tendon   □ maturity   □ boulder
□ careless   □ voracious   □ clarify

relay	[rɪˈleɪ] *vt.* 转播(broadcast); 传达，转述(convey)
	[ˈriːleɪ] *n.* 接替人员，轮换者；接力赛；中继设备
	例 The pop festival was *relayed* all round the world. 这个流行音乐节目的盛况在全球转播。// Water is available at the *relay* station. 中继站有水供应。

molten	*a.* 熔化的，熔融的(melted)
[ˈməʊltən]	搭 molten glass 熔化玻璃，玻璃液; molten lava 熔岩
	例 Any rock that has cooled and solidified from a *molten* state is an igneous rock. 任何从熔化状态冷却并固化的岩石都是火成岩。

acute	*a.* 严重的；极度的，激烈的(*intense); 敏锐的(keen)
[əˈkjuːt]	记 联想记忆: a + cut(切) + e → 一刀切 → 极度的，激烈的
	例 It is urgent that the *acute* problem of air pollution in the city be solved. 该市空气污染这一严重问题亟待解决。

lethargy	*n.* 死气沉沉；无精打采，倦怠
[ˈleθərdʒi]	记 词根记忆: leth(死) + argy → 像死了一样 → 死气沉沉
	例 A surprise military attack roused the nation from its *lethargy*. 一场突然的军事袭击使这个国家从死气沉沉的状态中清醒了过来。

diverse	*a.* 不同的(*different); 多样的(*varied, various)
[daɪˈvɜːrs]	记 词根记忆: di (分离) + vers (转) + e → 转开 → 不同的
	例 The researcher observed babies and their mothers in six *diverse* cultures. 这名研究人员观察了来自六个不同文化背景的婴儿及其母亲。

diverse

acclaim	*n./vt.* 喝彩，称赞(*praise, applaud)
[əˈkleɪm]	记 词根记忆: ac(向) + claim(大声叫喊) → 向某人大声叫喊 → 喝彩，称赞
	例 These artists achieved widespread success and *acclaim*. 这些艺术家取得了广泛的成功，广受赞誉。
	派 acclaimed(*a.* 受赞誉的)
	参 exclaim(*v.* 呼喊); declaim(*v.* 巧辩); reclaim(*vt.* 要求归还; 开垦)

| **meteorite** | *n.* 陨石 |
| [ˈmiːtiəraɪt] | 例 As their name suggests, the iron *meteorites* consist almost entirely of metal. 正如其名称所示，铁陨石几乎全由金属构成。 |

meteorite

consumption	*n.* 消耗(量); 消费(量); 食用(*eating)
[kənˈsʌmpʃn]	搭 consumption pattern 消费模式
	例 All produce should be washed carefully before *consumption*. 所有农产品在食用之前都应该仔细清洗。

shrub	*n.* 灌木(丛)(bush)
[ʃrʌb]	记 联想记忆: sh + rub(摩擦) → 走过灌木丛，被擦伤了 → 灌木(丛)
	例 *Shrubs* can be either deciduous or evergreen. 灌木可以是落叶木，也可以是常绿木。

26

orient
[ˈɔːriənt]

n. [O-]东方 *vt.* 使适应；确定方向，定位

记 词根记忆：ori(升起) + ent → 太阳升起的地方 → 东方

搭 orient to/toward 以…为方向(或目标)；orient oneself 熟悉

例 Many young people from Western countries are crazy about paintings from the *Orient*. 许多来自西方的年轻人对东方的绘画很着迷。// The course focuses on preparing its graduates for work, so we're *oriented* very much towards employment. 这所大学的课程以职业为中心，注重毕业生工作之前的准备工作，因此将学生朝着就业方向培养。

---

pinnacle
[ˈpɪnəkl]

n. 山顶，顶峰；鼎盛时期；小尖塔

记 词根记忆：pinna(顶点) + cle → 山顶，顶峰

例 The professor spent more than thirty years to reach the *pinnacle* of his teaching career. 那名教授在 30 年后才迎来他教学生涯的顶峰。

---

endless
[ˈendləs]

a. 无止境的，无穷尽的(everlasting, eternal)

例 The possibilities are *endless*. 存在着无限的可能性。

---

frigid
[ˈfrɪdʒɪd]

a. 寒冷的(freezing, wintry)；冷淡的(cold, icy)

记 词根记忆：frig(冷的) + id → 寒冷的；冷淡的

例 The *frigid* ground in the far north acts as a remarkable preservative for animal fossils. 遥远的北方的寒冷地表成为动物化石极好的防腐剂。

---

fluid
[ˈfluːɪd]

n. 液体，流体 *a.* 液体的；流动的

记 词根记忆：flu(流) + id → 液体，流体；液体的；流动的

例 There's some kind of *fluid* with a strong smell on the balcony floor. 阳台的地板上有一种气味很重的液体。

---

crack
[kræk]

v. (使)破裂(break)，断裂；(使)发出爆裂声；重击，猛击；崩溃，瓦解 *n.* 裂缝，裂纹(split)

搭 crack down (on...) 镇压，严厉打击

例 The otter uses a stone to *crack* mussel shells. 海獭用石头敲碎贝壳。

参 crush(*vt.* 碾碎)；crash(*n.* 碰撞；撞击声)；craft(*n.* 工艺)

crack

---

tectonic
[tekˈtɑːnɪk]

a. 地壳构造的

记 词根记忆：tect(构造) + on + ic(形容词后缀) → 有关(地球表面)构造的 → 地壳构造的

例 *Tectonic* studies are also important to understanding erosion patterns in geomorphology. 地壳构造学对理解地貌学中的侵蚀模式也很重要。

---

democrat
[ˈdeməkræt]

n. 民主主义者；[D-]民主党人

记 词根记忆：demo(人民) + crat(统治) → 人民统治 → 民主主义者

例 The *Democrats* are also very strong in major cities. 民主党人在大城市中的势力也很强大。

派 democracy(*n.* 民主政体，民主主义)

boon [buːn]	*n.* 恩惠，恩赐(blessing, benefit)；益处 记 联想记忆：从月亮(moon)那得到恩惠(boon) 例 The invention will prove a *boon* to the public. 这项新发明将对公众大有益处。
photodissociation [ˌfoʊtoʊˈdɪˌsoʊʃiˈeɪʃn]	*n.* 光解(作用) 记 组合词：photo(光) + dissociation(离解，电解) → 光解(作用) 例 The sun split water vapor into hydrogen and oxygen during a process called *photodissociation*. 太阳在光解过程中把水蒸气分解为氢气和氧气。
soprano [səˈprɑːnoʊ]	*n.* 女高音 记 联想记忆：so(看做词根 son，声音) + prano(看做 piano，钢琴) → 声音高过钢琴 → 女高音
format [ˈfɔːrmæt]	*n.* 设计，安排；格式，样式 *vt.* 使格式化 记 联想记忆：form(形式) + at → 固定的形式 → 样式 例 Your presentation *format*, your grammar, all that stuff, they are looking at in your materials at the same time. 报告的版式、语法等所有你材料里的这些东西，他们都同时在研究。// The professor hopes to cover the entire process of writing a research paper, from selecting a topic to putting together the final *format* and presentation. 教授希望能讲授撰写研究型论文的整个过程，即从选题到组织最终的格式和作报告。
expressive [ɪkˈspresɪv]	*a.* 有表现力的，富有表情的；表示…的，表现…的 搭 expressive of 表示，表现 例 My own belief is that all music has an *expressive* power, some more and some less. 我个人相信，所有的音乐都有表现力，只是程度不同而已。 派 expressively(*ad.* 表现地)；expressiveness(*n.* 表现，表示)
acidity [əˈsɪdəti]	*n.* 酸度；酸性 记 联想记忆：acid(酸；酸的) + ity(名词后缀) → 酸度；酸性 例 The *acidity* of our bodies is important. 人体内的酸度很重要。 参 alkali(*n.* 碱)；alkaline(*a.* 碱性的)
focalize [ˈfoʊkəlaɪz]	*v.* 调节焦距；使聚焦；使集中 例 The director *focalized* the light on the leading man. 导演将灯光打在男主角身上。
observatory [əbˈzɜːrvətɔːri]	*n.* 天文台，天文观测站 记 联想记忆：observ(e)(观察) + at + ory(表地点，名词后缀) → 天文台，天文观测站 例 A group of students will pay a visit to the ancient *observatory* this week. 本周，一群学生将参观这座古老的天文台。
prospector [ˈprɑːspektər]	*n.* 勘探者，采矿者 记 词根记忆：pro(向前) + spect(看) + or(表人，名词后缀) → 向前看的人 → 负责向地下探测的人 → 勘探者 例 The public showed great concern for the *prospectors* trapped in the coal pit. 公众对困在煤矿下的矿工们表示深切的关心。

26

rotational [roʊˈteɪʃnl]	*a.* 旋转的；轮流的 记 词根记忆：rot(旋转) + ation + al → 旋转的；轮流的 例 The president is elected on a *rotational* basis in each of the united countries. 主席是从每个联盟国中轮流选举产生的。
swampy [ˈswɑːmpi]	*a.* 沼泽(多)的，湿地的；松软的 记 联想记忆：swamp(沼泽) + y(形容词后缀) → 沼泽(多)的，湿地的 例 You can find this kind of fierce animal on the *swampy* land all over the world. 你可以在全世界的沼泽地里发现这种凶猛的动物。
troposphere [ˈtroʊpəsfɪr]	*n.* 对流层 例 Rain and snow will fall in the *troposphere*, so planes can't fly on it. 雨雪会降在对流层，因此飞机不能在对流层飞行。
wintry [ˈwɪntri]	*a.* 冬天(似)的；寒冷的；冷淡的 记 联想记忆：wintr(看做 winter，冬天) + y → 冬天(似)的 例 The famous painter is good at drawing a picture of *wintry* scenes. 那位著名的画家擅长画冬景。
buoyant [ˈbɔɪənt]	*a.* 有浮力的，漂浮的；轻快的，快乐的；繁荣的；(价格等)看涨的 记 来自 buoy(*n.* 浮标) 例 Ships should be made of *buoyant* material, or it can't float on the water. 船应该用有浮力的材料来制造，否则不能漂浮在水面上。
cement [sɪˈment]	*n.* 水泥；胶合剂 *vt.* 巩固；使团结 记 联想记忆：ce + ment(看做 mend，修补) → 修补材料 → 水泥；胶合剂 例 The modern building is made of *cement* and steel rather than wood. 现代大楼是用水泥和钢铁建造的，而不是木材。
spatial [ˈspeɪʃl]	*a.* 空间的 记 联想记忆：spa(ce)(空间) + tial → 空间的 例 Scientists have studied the *spatial* distribution of population in this region for many years. 科学家已花了多年的时间研究该地区的人口空间分布。
dynamical [daɪˈnæmɪkl]	*a.* 动态的；动力的；充满活力的 记 词根记忆：dynam(力量) + ical → 力量的 → 动态的；动力的 例 The professor will give us a lecture on how the machine works with the *dynamical* system. 教授将给我们做一个关于机器如何利用其动力系统进行工作的讲座。
entity [ˈentəti]	*n.* 实体，独立存在物 记 词根记忆：ent(存在) + ity → 存在的东西 → 实体，独立存在物 例 As known to all, a corporation is considered as an *entity* in the law. 众所周知，法人在法律上被视为一个实体。
fusion [ˈfjuːʒn]	*n.* 熔化，熔解；熔合；核聚变；联合，合并 记 词根记忆：fus(流) + ion → 流到一起 → 熔化 例 The movie is a *fusion* of several famous styles of arts. 这部电影融合了几种著名的艺术形式。

hydraulic
[haɪˈdrɔːlɪk]

a. 水力的，液压的；液压驱动的；与水力(或液压)系统有关的
记 词根记忆：hydr(水) + aulic → 水力的，液压的
例 The government are going to build a new *hydraulic* power station to supply the western region with electricity. 政府将新建一座水电站以向西部地区供电。

condense
[kənˈdens]

v. (使)压缩(compress)；(使)凝结(contract)
记 联想记忆：con + dense(密集的) → 变得密集 → (使)压缩
例 Eventually, the water stored as vapor in the atmosphere will *condense* to liquid again. 最后，大气中储存的水蒸气将再次凝结为液体。
派 condenser(*n.* 冷凝器)

allergy
[ˈælədʒi]

n. 过敏性反应
记 词根记忆：all(异常的) + erg(起作用) + y → 异常的东西起作用 → 过敏性反应
例 I have an *allergy* to animal hair. 我对动物毛过敏。
派 allergic(*a.* 过敏的；对…讨厌的)

variable
[ˈveriəbl]

a. 易变的(fluctuating, inconstant)；可变的 *n.* 变数，变量
记 词根记忆：vari(改变) + able(能…的) → 能改变的 → 可变的
例 The weather has been *variable* the last three months. 最近三个月的天气变化无常。// The decision involves a large number of *variables* with complex relationships. 这个决定涉及很多关系复杂的变量。
派 invariably(*ad.* 不变地；总是)

evolution
[ˌiːvəˈluːʃn]

n. 发展 (development, progression)；演变，进化，进化论
记 来自evolve[*v.* (使)进化]
例 In the 19th century, the theory of *evolution*, put forward by Darwin was violently criticized by religious people. 19世纪，达尔文提出的进化论受到了宗教人士的激烈批判。

evolution

26

representative
[ˌreprɪˈzentətɪv]

n. 代表，代理人 *a.* 典型的，有代表性的(typical)
搭 sales representative 销售代表
例 You've all been selected as *representatives* to plan the graduation ceremonies. 你们都已被选为代表来筹划毕业典礼。

crystallize
[ˈkrɪstəlaɪz]

v. (使)结晶；(使)明确
记 联想记忆：crystal(结晶) + lize → (使)结晶
例 The solution begins to *crystallize* once it cools down at the low temperature. 这种溶液一在低温下冷却就会结晶。

gorgeous
[ˈɡɔːrdʒəs]

a. 漂亮的(beautiful)；令人愉快的；华丽的，灿烂的
记 联想记忆：gorge(峡谷) + ous → 春天到了，峡谷里开满花，很漂亮 → 漂亮的
例 What a *gorgeous* jacket! It must have cost a fortune. 多漂亮的夹克啊！肯定价格不菲。// I just love walking through this park. The trees are *gorgeous*. 我就喜欢在这个公园里散步，那里的树很漂亮。

angle [ˈæŋgl]	*n.* 角；角度，立场，观点(viewpoint) *v.* 把…放置成一角度；使(报道等)带上倾向性 记 词根记忆：angl(角) + e → 角；角度 例 We should look at the issue from a new *angle*. 我们应该从一个新的角度来看这个问题。 派 angular(*a.* 有角的；尖角的)
impose [imˈpouz]	*v.* 把…强加于(demand)；征(税等)(levy)；处以(罚款、监禁等) 记 词根记忆：im(使…) + pos(放) + e → 强行放置 → 把…强加于；征(税等) 搭 impose on sb. 占某人便宜（尤指施加不当的压力） 例 New regulations were *imposed* on non-traditional education. 新规定被强加于非传统教育。// The government *imposed* a new tax on public entertainment. 该政府对公共娱乐征收了一项新税。 派 imposing(*a.* 令人难忘的) impose

The man who has made up his mind to win will never say "impossible".
凡是决心取得胜利的人是从来不说"不可能的"。
——法国皇帝 拿破仑(Bonaparte Napoleon, French emperor)

Word List 27

音频

词根、词缀预习表

log	说话	apologize *vi.* 道歉	col	过滤	percolate *v.* 过滤
gress	行走	aggressive *a.* 侵略的	**sect**	切割	bisect *vt.* 把…二等分
mot	动	locomotion *n.* 移动	**quir**	追求	inquire *v.* 打听
ple	填满	complement *vt.* 补充	**leg**	法律	privilege *vt.* 给予特权
tain	拿	retain *vt.* 保持，保留	**furb**	装饰；整修	refurbish *vt.* 再装修

apologize [əˈpɑːlədʒaɪz]	*vi.* 道歉，认错；辩解 记 词根记忆：apo(远地) + log(说话) + ize → 觉得过意不去，远远地说 → 道歉 搭 apologize to sb. 向某人道歉；apologize for (doing) sth. 因(做)某事而道歉 例 Our sports center *apologizes* to every customer who makes a complaint about service. 我们的体育中心向每一位对服务投诉的客户道歉。 派 apology(*n.* 道歉，致歉)

colleague [ˈkɑːliːɡ]	*n.* 同事，同僚 记 词根记忆：col(一起，共同) + leag(=leg 聚集) + ue → 聚集在一起 → 同事 例 The Prime Minister and his Cabinet *colleagues* refused to accept the proposal. 首相及其内阁同僚拒绝接受这个提议。

colleague

pump [pʌmp]	*n.* 泵 *vt.* (用泵)抽 例 The sequoia tree can *pump* water to its very top, more than 100 meters above the ground. 美洲杉能把水抽到离地面 100 多米高的树顶。

exempt [ɪɡˈzempt]	*a.* 被免除的，被豁免的 *vt.* 免除，豁免 记 词根记忆：ex(出) + empt(拿) → 拿出去 → 免除，豁免 例 You are not *exempt* from the rules! 你必须遵守这些规定! 派 exemption(*n.* 免除，豁免)

marine [məˈriːn]	*a.* 海的；海生的；海上贸易的 *n.* 海军陆战队士兵 记 词根记忆：mar(海) + ine → 海的；海生的 例 The southwestern coastal region has a humid mild *marine* climate. 西南沿海地区是湿润的温带海洋气候。 派 mariner(*n.* 水手)；submarine(*n.* 潜水艇)
board [bɔːrd]	*n.* 膳食费用；委员会，董事会；板，木板 *v.* 登机，上船；搭伙，寄宿 搭 a bulletin board 公告牌；across the board 整体，全面 例 He has a seat on the *Board* of Education. 他是教育委员会成员。// Passengers are waiting to *board*. 乘客们正在候机。 派 boarder(*n.* 寄宿生；寄膳宿者)
immature [ˌiməˈtʃʊr]	*a.* 未成熟的，未充分发展的(unripe) 记 联想记忆：im(不) + mature(成熟的) → 未成熟的 例 This tomato plant is still *immature*. 这株西红柿仍未成熟。
orientation [ˌɔːriənˈteɪʃn]	*n.* 方向，方位(direction)；定位；(任职等前的)培训；情况介绍 例 My job is providing *orientation* for new campus staff. 我的工作是帮助新的校园员工熟悉环境。
aggressive [əˈgresɪv]	*a.* 侵略的，挑衅的(combative, offensive)；强有力的(strong)；敢作敢为的，有进取心的 记 词根记忆：ag(表加强) + gress(行走) + ive → 到处乱走的 → 侵略的，挑衅的 例 A successful businessman must be *aggressive*. 一个成功的实业家必定是有进取心的。 派 aggressively(*ad.* 强劲地；侵略地)；aggressiveness(*n.* 侵略；争斗)
cling [klɪŋ]	*vi.* 附着，黏住(adhere, stick)；紧紧抓住；挨近 搭 cling to 坚持，不放弃 例 The baby *clung* to its mother. 那个婴儿紧紧贴在母亲身上。
output [ˈaʊtpʊt]	*n.* 产量(yield)；输出(量)(export)；产生(production) 记 来自词组 put out(产生) 例 We must increase our *output* to meet the public's demand. 我们必须提高产量以满足公众的需求。
hostile [ˈhɑːstl]	*a.* 不友好的，敌意的(unamiable, unfriendly)；敌方的 记 联想记忆：host(主人) + ile → 鸿门宴的主人 → 不友好的，敌意的 例 The citizens were *hostile* to the report's conclusions. 公民们对报告的结论充满了敌意。 派 hostility(*n.* 敌意，敌对) hostile

resolve [rɪˈzɑːlv]	*v.* 解决(*find a solution for, solve); 决定, 决心(determine); 分解; 显现 *n.* 决心, 决议(resolution) 记 词根记忆: re(完全) + solv(解开) + e → 完全解开 → 解决 例 It took forever to *resolve* the problem with the account. 解决这个客户的问题用了很长时间。// Earth-based telescopes can *resolve* objects as small as a few hundred meters on the lunar surface. 放置在地球上的高倍望远镜能分辨出月球表面几百米大小的物体。 派 resolved(*a.* 坚定的, 下定决心的)
tile [taɪl]	*vt.* 铺瓦; 铺地砖 *n.* 瓦片; 地砖 搭 tile fish 方头鱼
undertaking [ˌʌndərˈteɪkɪŋ]	*n.* (重大或艰巨的)任务, 项目; 事业, 企业(enterprise); 承诺, 保证 例 Interviewing all the residents in town on their TV viewing habits is quite an *undertaking* for such a short-term project. 对这样的短期项目而言, 就看电视的习惯这一主题采访镇里的所有居民可是件大事。// The government gave an *undertaking* to spend more on education. 政府承诺增加教育经费。
transmit [trænsˈmɪt]	*v.* 传送, 传递, 输送(transfer); 传播, 传染(spread) 记 词根记忆: trans(穿过) + mit(送) → 从一地送到另一地 → 传送 例 Communications satellites can *transmit* data around the world. 通信卫星可以在全世界传输数据。// Liz insists that only female wasps *transmit* diseases. 利兹坚持认为只有母黄蜂才会传播疾病。 派 transmitter(*n.* 传播者; 发射机); transmission(*n.* 传送; 发射)
sloth [sloʊθ]	*n.* 树懒; 懒散, 怠惰 记 联想记忆: slo(看做 slow, 慢的) + th → 行动缓慢 → 树懒; 懒散 搭 ground sloth 地懒 派 slothful(*a.* 懒散的, 怠惰的)
popular [ˈpɑːpjələ]	*a.* 通俗的; 受欢迎的(*refreshing); 流行的(fashionable) 记 词根记忆: popul(人民) + ar → 受广大人民喜欢的 → 受欢迎的; 流行的 搭 popular tune 流行歌曲 例 Subsequently, the fashion industry largely returned to longer skirts such as the midi and the maxi. However, miniskirts remained *popular*. 随后时尚界在很大程度上又回到流行更长的裙子, 比如中长裙和长裙。然而迷你裙仍很流行。 派 popularize(*vt.* 普及); popularization(*n.* 普及)
furry [ˈfɜːri]	*a.* 毛皮似的; 盖着毛皮的; 生苔的 例 The African grass mouse's *furry* stripe is like a chipmunk's, which helps it blend in with its environment. 非洲草鼠毛茸茸的条纹就像花栗鼠的条纹, 这有助于它与周边环境很好地融合。

27

restraint [rɪˈstreɪnt]	*n.* 抑制，克制；限制(limitation)；约束力；管制措施 记 来自 restrain (*vt.* 克制；约束；管制) 例 The government has imposed import *restraints* on some products. 政府对一些产品实行了进口限制。 参 constraint (*n.* 约束，强制)
luminosity [ˌluːmɪˈnɑːsəti]	*n.* 亮度，发光度(light, radiance)；光明 记 词根记忆：lumin(光) + os + ity(名词后缀) → 亮度，发光度；光明 例 Scientists use this measurement when measuring the *luminosity* of other stars. 科学家用这种度量制度来测量其他星体的亮度。
outermost [ˈaʊtərmoʊst]	*a.* 最外面的，离中心最远的(farmost, utmost) 记 组合词：outer(外面的，远离中心的) + most(最) → 最外面的，离中心最远的 例 He fired and hit the *outermost* ring of the target. 他开枪射中了靶子的最外一环。 参 innermost (*a.* 最里面的，内心的)
slight [slaɪt]	*a.* 轻微的，微弱的 (subtle, tiny)；纤细的，瘦弱的；微不足道的 *vt./n.* 轻视，藐视 记 联想记忆：s + light(轻的) → 轻微的 例 Life resembles in only a *slight* degree to the popular image of it. 人生只在很低程度上与其通俗的表象相似。 派 slightly (*ad.* 稍微，稍稍)
butter [ˈbʌtər]	*n.* 黄油 *vt.* 涂黄油于 搭 butter sb. up 奉承，以甜言蜜语巴结某人
vegetative [ˈvedʒɪteɪtɪv]	*a.* 植物(性)的；有生长力的 例 For this kind of plant, botanists still depend on *vegetative* reproduction. 对于这种植物，植物学家仍然依靠营养培殖。
plasma [ˈplæzmə]	*n.* 血浆；等离子体 搭 plasma screen 等离子屏幕
swarm [swɔːrm]	*n.* 群，一大群(crowd) *vi.* 云集 *v.* 密集，云集；成群地飞行(或来回移动) 记 联想记忆：s + warm (暖和的) → 大家挤成一群比较暖和 → 一大群 例 One of these migrating *swarms* was estimated to contain 124 billion locusts. 估计这些迁徙的蝗虫一批就有1240亿只。
locomotion [ˌloʊkəˈmoʊʃn]	*n.* 移动(remotion)；运动(movement) 记 词根记忆：loco (地方) + mot (动) + ion → 从一地移动到另一地 → 移动；运动 例 The pterosaurs rely on wind power for their *locomotion*. 翼龙依靠风力来移动。// A great deal can be learned from the actual traces of ancient human *locomotion*. 从古人迁徙的实际路线上可以了解到很多信息。

utmost [ˈʌtmoʊst]	*a.* 最大限度的(extreme) *n.* 最大限度；最大量 记 联想记忆：ut(看做 at) + most(最多) → 到达最多 → 最大限度的 例 The clay used in prehistoric pot-making was invariably selected with the *utmost* care. 史前制造锅罐等所用的黏土往往都是精挑细选的。
dignity [ˈdɪɡnəti]	*n.* 尊严，庄严；高贵，尊贵(nobleness)；自尊，自重 记 词根记忆：dign(有价值的) + ity → 高贵 例 Many poor people struggle to maintain their *dignity*. 很多穷人努力地维持他们自己的尊严。 参 indignant(*a.* 愤慨的)；dignify(*vt.* 使有尊严；使高贵)
spot [spɑːt]	*v.* 认出，发现(*identify, recognize) *n.* 地点(position)；斑点(dot)；少量 搭 on the spot 当场，在现场 例 Chick Webb *spotted* her in an amateur competition when she was sixteen. 16 岁参加一次业余竞赛时，奇克·韦伯发现了她。 派 spotless(*a.* 没有污点的，非常洁净的)；spotted(*a.* 有斑点的) 参 spotlight(*n.* 聚光灯)
rudimentary [ˌruːdɪˈmentri]	*a.* 未充分发展的，原始的 (*undeveloped)；基本的，基础的(basic, fundamental) 记 词根记忆：rud(天然的) + iment + ary → 天然的状态 → 未充分发展的 例 Many animals are capable of using objects in the natural environment as *rudimentary* tools. 很多动物能把自然界的物体当做基本工具使用。
bud [bʌd]	*n.* 芽；蓓蕾 *vi.* 发芽，萌芽 记 联想记忆：泥土(mud)中发出的芽(bud) 例 The tree is in *bud* already. 这棵树已经发芽了。
remainder [rɪˈmeɪndər]	*n.* 剩余物，残余(remains)；其他的人；差数，余数 记 来自 remain(*v.* 保留) 例 My son ate part of his cake and I ate the *remainder*. 我儿子吃了他那部分蛋糕，我吃了剩下的。
depend [dɪˈpend]	*v.* (on)依靠，依赖(rely)；取决于(lie on) 记 词根记忆：de(在…下面) + pend(悬挂) → 悬挂于之下 → 依靠，依赖 例 He was the sort of person you could *depend* on. 他是那种可以让人依赖的人。 派 dependable (*a.* 可信赖的，可靠的)；dependence (*n.* 依靠，依赖)；dependent(*a.* 依赖的；取决于…的)
slumber [ˈslʌmbər]	*n.* [常 *pl.*]睡眠，安睡(sleep, doze) *vi.* 睡眠，安睡 记 联想记忆：s + lumber(木材) → 睡得很沉，像根木头 → 安睡 例 The baby fell into a deep and peaceful *slumber*. 那个婴儿睡着了，睡得又沉又香。

27

complement	[ˈkɑːmplɪmənt] *vt.* 补充，补足，使完善（*supplement, complete）；与…相配（match）[ˈkɑːmplɪmənt] *n.* 补充物，补足物；足数，足额；补语
	记 词根记忆：com(表加强) + ple(填满) + ment → 补充，补足，使完善
	例 The myths and songs *complemented* our historical knowledge of the lives of animals and of people here. 神话和歌曲完善了关于此地动物和人类生活的历史知识。// I think his new haircut really *complements* his beard. 我觉得他的新发型与胡子真的很配。
	参 compliment (*n./vt.* 称赞)；supplement (*n.* 补遗 *vt.* 增补)；implement (*n.* 工具)
strive [straɪv]	*vi.* 奋斗，努力（struggle）；力求
	记 联想记忆：s + trive(看做 drive，动力) → 奋斗需要动力 → 奋斗
	搭 strive for 为…奋斗，争取
	例 Like all artists, jazz musicians *strive* for an individual style. 爵士音乐家如同所有艺术家一样，都力求体现个人风格。
	参 stride (*v.* 大步走)
figure [ˈfɪɡjər]	*n.* 身材，体形（shape）；轮廓；数字（number）；图形，图表；人物，人士 *v.* 算出，估算（calculate, estimate）；是重要部分（feature）
	记 发音记忆："菲戈"(著名球星) → 人物
	搭 figure out 弄清楚，弄明白；计算
	例 These *figures* still don't add up right. Let's do the calculations over again. 这些数字加起来还是不对。我们再算一遍吧。// First I want to go over some basics about hearing, then we can take a look at our school's environment and see if we can *figure* out some ways to protect hearing. 首先，我想介绍一下关于听力的基本知识，然后我们可以看看学校的环境，看看能否想出些办法来保护听力。
credit [ˈkredɪt]	*vt.* 把…归于 *n.* 荣誉；学分；信用；贷款
	例 Watt should be *credited* with inventing the steam engine. 蒸汽机的发明应归功于瓦特。
	参 accredit(*vt.* 授权)；credence(*n.* 相信，信任)；credibility(*n.* 可信性，可靠性)
spaghetti [spəˈɡeti]	*n.* 意大利式细面条
	搭 spaghetti western 意大利式西部片
outcry [ˈaʊtkraɪ]	*n.* 大声疾呼，强烈的抗议（protest, shout）
	记 来自词组 cry out(大声呼喊，强烈抗议)
	搭 outcry against/about/over 反对
	例 If the government continues to build a large parking lot in this area, there'll be a great *outcry* among the local people. 如果政府继续在这个地区建造大型停车场，就会引发当地人的强烈抗议。

retain

[rɪˈteɪn]

vt. 保持，保留（keep）

记 词根记忆：re(再，又) + tain(拿) → 一再拿住 → 保持，保留

例 If suddenly cooled, the object *retains* the shape achieved at that point. 如果突然冷却，这个物体会保持当时的形状。

inertia

[ɪˈnɜːrʃə]

n. 惯性；惰性

记 词根记忆：in(不) + ert(动) + ia → 不活动 → 惰性

例 The car made use of *inertia* to move several meters on the pavement. 汽车利用惯性在人行道上移动了几米。

liquefy

[ˈlɪkwɪfaɪ]

v. (使)溶解，(使)液化

记 词根记忆：liqu(液体) + efy(=ify …化) → (使)液化

例 The researchers find it very hard to *liquefy* this substance at a relatively low temperature. 研究人员发现很难在相对较低的温度下液化这种物质。

shrimp

[ʃrɪmp]

n. 小虾

记 联想记忆：sh(看做 shui，水) + rim(边) + p → 生活在水边的小虾 → 小虾

派 shrimping(*n.* 捕小虾)

editorial

[ˌedɪˈtɔːriəl]

n. (报刊的)社论，重要评论 *a.* 社论的；编辑的

记 来自 edit(*vt.* 编辑)

例 Did you read the *editorial* in the paper about the mayor's speech? 你读报纸上关于市长演讲的社论了吗？

assimilate

[əˈsɪməleɪt]

v. 透彻理解，吸收，消化；(使)同化

记 词根记忆：as + simil (相同) + ate (使…) → 使相同 → (使)同化

例 Such kinds of foods are *assimilated* much more easily than others. 这种食物比其他食物更容易吸收。

派 assimilation(*n.* 消化，吸收；融合，同化)

assimilate

focus

[ˈfoʊkəs]

n. 焦点，焦距；(活动、兴趣等的)中心 *v.* 集中(注意力、精力等于)；(使)聚焦

记 联想记忆：foc(看做 for，为了) + us(我们) → 焦点访谈的口号是为我们人民大众服务 → 焦点

搭 focus on/upon 集中；be out of focus 模糊，不聚焦

例 We shall maintain our *focus* on the needs of the customer. 我们将继续重点关注顾客的需要。

focus

soybean

[ˈsɔɪbiːn]

n. 大豆（legume, soy）

记 组合词：soy(大豆) + bean(豆) → 大豆

例 Many farmers prefer not to sell their *soybeans* due to the low price. 很多农民因大豆价格过低而宁愿不出售大豆。

annoyed [ə'nɔɪd]	*a.* 生气的(angry) 例 She's *annoyed* with the man. 她在生这个男人的气。 参 annoying(*a.* 恼人的，讨厌的)
banner ['bænər]	*n.* 横幅 记 联想记忆：ban(禁止) + ner → 此处禁止悬挂横幅 → 横幅 例 *Banners* are used in many business ventures, marketing to their potential customers. 横幅被用于很多商业活动中，向潜在的顾客推销他们的商品。 参 ban(*n.* 禁令)
factor ['fæktər]	*n.* 要素，因素(element, ingredient)；因数；系数 例 I believe the first key *factor* to success is confidence. 我认为成功的首要关键因素是信心。
infiltrate ['ɪnfɪltreɪt]	*v.* 渗入，渗透；(使)悄悄进入，潜入 记 联想记忆：in(进入) + filtrate(滤液) → 进入滤液 → 渗入，渗透 例 The thick smoke has *infiltrated* through the window into the bedroom. 浓烟透过窗户进入了卧室。 派 infiltrator(*n.* 潜入者，渗入者)
leach [liːtʃ]	*v.* 过滤；溶解 *n.* 过滤器；过滤剂 例 Farmers scattered the fertilizer over the farmland, which was *leached* into the ground after rain. 农民把化肥撒在农田里，这些化肥在雨后会渗入地下。
momentum [moʊ'mentəm]	*n.* 动量；动力，冲力；势头 记 联想记忆：moment(瞬间) + um → 在瞬间爆发，需要动力 → 动力 例 The red team began to gain *momentum* in the first half of the game. 红队在前半场的比赛中势头强劲。 参 momentous(*a.* 重要的，重大的)
odorous ['oʊdərəs]	*a.* 有气味的，难闻的；香的，芬芳的 例 *Odorous* smells hang about a group of homeless children. 这群无家可归的孩子身上散发出臭味。
percolate ['pɜːrkəleɪt]	*v.* 过滤；渗入，渗透；逐渐流传，传开 *n.* 滤液 记 词根记忆：per(贯穿) + col(过滤) + ate → 过滤；渗入，渗透 例 The news that the general manager will resign is *percolating* through the firm. 总经理要辞职的消息在整个公司流传开来。
supersonic [ˌsuːpər'sɑːnɪk]	*a.* 超音速的，超音波的 *n.* 超音速，超声波 记 组合词：super(超级的) + sonic(音速的) → 超音速的 例 It is reported that the country is developing *supersonic* aircraft in secret. 据报道，该国正在秘密研制超音速飞机。
thermal ['θɜːrml]	*a.* 热的，热量的；保暖的，防寒的 *n.* 上升的热气流 记 词根记忆：therm(=thermo 热) + al → 热的，热量的 例 Jane's mother bought her a suit of *thermal* underwear as her birthday present. 简的妈妈给她买了一套保暖内衣作为生日礼物。

coefficient
[ˌkəʊɪˈfɪʃnt]

n. 系数

记 词根记忆：co(共同) + ef(出) + fic(做) + ient → 共同做出来 → 系数

例 This kind of liquid is considered having a variable *coefficient* of expansion. 人们认为这种液体的膨胀系数是可变的。

differential
[ˌdɪfəˈrenʃl]

a. 差别的，有区别的；微分的 *n.* 差别，差异；微分

记 来自different(*a.* 不同的)

例 Most of the students in our class don't know how to solve the *differential* equation. 我们班的大多数同学都不知道怎么解这个微分方程。

vaporize
[ˈveɪpəraɪz]

v. (使)蒸发，(使)汽化

例 When water is heated above 100 degrees Celsius, molecules of water begin to *vaporize*. 水加热到100摄氏度以上时，水分子会开始蒸发。

waggle
[ˈwægl]

v./n. 摆动

记 来自wag(*v.* 摇摆，摇动)

例 When a dog meets its owner, it often greets him by *waggling* its tail. 狗看到它的主人时，常常摇尾表示欢迎。

approximation
[əˌprɑːksɪˈmeɪʃn]

n. 接近；近似值

记 来自approximate(*vt.* 接近)；ap(向) + prox(接近) + imate → 向…接近 → 接近

例 I think what the professor said in class is an *approximation* of my idea. 我觉得教授在课堂上讲的和我的想法很接近。

bisect
[baɪˈsekt]

vt. 把…二等分，对半分

记 词根记忆：bi(二) + sect(切割) → 一切为二 → 把…二等分，对半分

例 Jim *bisected* a big red apple and gave them to two children. 吉姆把一个大红苹果切成两个等份，分给两个小孩。

27

calculable
[ˈkælkjələbl]

a. 可计算的；能预测的；可信的

记 词根记忆：calcul(计算) + able(能…的) → 可计算的；能预测的

例 The loss caused by the serious earthquake is not *calculable* each year. 每年，大地震造成的损失难以计算。

ellipse
[ɪˈlɪps]

n. 椭圆，椭圆形

记 联想记忆：el + lip(嘴唇) + se → 嘴张开呈椭圆形 → 椭圆形

参 ellipsis(*n.* 省略；省略号)

dividend
[ˈdɪvɪdend]

n. 红利，股息；回报，效益；被除数

搭 dividend payment 股息支付；an annual dividend 年度股息

例 The boss of our company declared to give every employee a large *dividend* at the annual meeting this year. 我们公司老板宣布会在今年年会上给每个员工一个大红包。

formula
[ˈfɔːrmjələ]

n. 公式，方程式；分子式；配方

记 词根记忆：form(形式) + ula → 使具有形式的方式 → 公式

例 Several students are trying to understand this difficult mathematical *formula*. 几个学生正在试图理解这个很难的数学公式。

□ coefficient　　□ differential　　□ vaporize　　□ waggle　　□ approximation □ bisect
□ calculable　　□ ellipse　　□ dividend　　□ formula

weathering [ˈweðərɪŋ]	*n.* (岩石的)侵蚀, 风化(corrasion) 例 Most of the fossils exposed on Earth's surface are destroyed by *weathering* processes. 大多数暴露在地球表面的化石都被风化作用毁坏了。
tarnish [ˈtɑːrnɪʃ]	*v.* (使)失去光泽; 玷污, 败坏(名声等) *n.* 污点; 瑕疵 记 词根记忆: tarn(隐藏) + ish → 隐藏光泽 → (使)失去光泽 例 Exposure to the open air *tarnished* the silver bowl. 暴露在空气中使这只银碗失去了光泽。// The news in the local newspaper has *tarnished* his image. 地方报纸上的这则消息损害了他的形象。
inquire [ɪnˈkwaɪər]	*v.* 打听, 询问(ask) 记 词根记忆: in(在…里面) + quir(追求) + e → 打听, 询问 例 The applicant *inquired* about meeting the other manager. 申请人询问了一下与另一位经理会面的事宜。 派 inquiry(*n.* 询问; 调查)
extrapolate [ɪkˈstræpəleɪt]	*v.* 外推; 推断, 推知 记 词根记忆: extra(外面) + pol(放) + ate → 放出想法 → 外推, 推断, 推知 例 A good leader can *extrapolate* future development direction of the company from present conditions. 一个出色的领导能够根据当前的形势推断公司未来的发展方向。
remains [rɪˈmeɪnz]	*n.* 剩余物, 残留物; 古代遗物, 遗迹, 遗址; 遗骸 搭 the remains of a Roman fort 罗马要塞的遗址 例 She fed the *remains* of her lunch to the dog. 她把剩下的午饭喂狗了。
flexibility [ˌfleksəˈbɪləti]	*n.* 灵活性; 弹性, 韧性; 适应性 记 来自 flexible(*a.* 易弯曲的; 柔韧的; 灵活的); flex(弯曲) + ible(能…的) → 易弯曲的; 柔韧的; 灵活的 例 Computers provide employees with a great degree of *flexibility* in the way work is organized. 计算机在组织工作方面给予雇员很大的灵活性。
mural [ˈmjʊrəl]	*n.* 壁画, 壁饰(fresco) *a.* 墙壁的; 在墙上的 记 词根记忆: mur(墙) + al → 墙壁的
balance [ˈbæləns]	*vt.* 使平衡, 使均衡(equilibrate) *n.* 天平, 秤; 平衡(equilibrium); 差额; 余款 记 联想记忆: bal(看做 ball, 球) + ance → 球操选手需要很好的平衡力 → 平衡 搭 lose one's balance 失去平衡; maintain balance 保持平衡; balance oneself 保持自身平衡; a balance of nature 自然平衡; on balance 总的来说 例 Winds are the natural way of *balancing* uneven distribution of air pressure over the Earth. 风是平衡地球气压分配不均的自然方式。 派 counterbalance(*n.* 平衡力 *vt.* 使平衡; 抵消); well-balanced(*a.* 营养均衡的)

mural

telegraph [ˈtelɪɡræf]	*n.* 电报；电报机 *v.* 打电报，发电报 记 词根记忆：tele(远的) + graph(写) → 以书写的方式带来远处的东西 → 电报 例 They tinkered with the wireless *telegraph*, hoping to find out the problem. 他们摆弄着那台无线电报机，希望找出问题所在。
privilege [ˈprɪvəlɪdʒ]	*vt.* 给予特权，特别优待 *n.* 特权，特殊待遇；特殊利益，优惠；荣耀，荣幸 记 词根记忆：priv(单个) + i + leg(法律) + e → 在法律上独享 → 给予特权 例 The Aliens and Hamiltons of Philadelphia introduced European art traditions to those colonists *privileged* to visit their galleries. 费城的外国人和汉密尔顿人向那些有权访问他们画廊的殖民者介绍了欧洲艺术传统。
chart [tʃɑːrt]	*vt.* 用图说明；制图；记录，跟踪（进展等）；计划 *n.* 图表(map, graph)；航海图 搭 flow chart 流程图 例 We can *chart* the history of innovation in musical notation. 我们可以用图来说明五线谱的改革史。 派 uncharted(*a.* 地图上未标明的；不明的)
scan [skæn]	*vt.* 细察，审视(*examine, scrutinize)；扫描；粗略地看，浏览 *n.* 扫描检查；浏览 记 发音记忆："四看" → 四处看 → 扫描 例 The patients' brains are *scanned* so that researchers can monitor the progress of the disease. 研究人员对病人的大脑进行扫描，以检测病情的发展。// He *scanned* through the report over lunch. 他边吃午饭边浏览报告。
congress [ˈkɑːŋɡrəs]	*n.* [C-] 议会，国会(parliament)；（代表）大会(convention) 记 词根记忆：con(共同) + gress(行走) → 走到一起去开会 → 大会 例 *Congress* will vote on the proposals tomorrow. 明天，国会将对提案进行投票表决。 派 congressional(*a.* 代表大会的；国会的) 参 digress(*vi.* 离题)；transgress(*v.* 越界；违法，犯罪)
amenity [əˈmenəti]	*n.* [pl.] 生活福利设施，便利设施；适意，愉快 记 联想记忆：a + men(人) + ity → 为人民服务 → 生活福利设施 搭 public amenities 公共设施 例 The little dog immediately found the *amenity* of its new surroundings. 很快，小狗就在新环境中找到了快乐。
pretension [prɪˈtenʃn]	*n.* 要求，主张(claim)；自命不凡；虚饰 记 联想记忆：pre(预先) + tension(紧张) → 预先感到紧张，要求放松下来 → 要求，主张 例 The movie mocks the *pretensions* of the upper class. 这部电影讽刺了上层社会的虚饰。

27

sensual [ˈsenʃuəl]	*a.* 感觉的，感官的；肉欲的；耽于感官享受的 记 词根记忆：sens(感觉) + ual → 感觉的，感官的 搭 sensual pleasure 感官之乐 例 The purpose of a poem need not inform the reader of anything, but rather to evoke feelings, to create a *sensual* pleasing experience. 诗歌的目的不是要让读者了解什么，而是要激发情感，让读者产生感官上的愉悦体验。
grimly [ˈgrɪmli]	*ad.* 冷酷地(ruthlessly)；严肃地；坚定地 记 来自 grim(*a.* 严肃的；坚定的；阴冷的) 例 It was a long way but he trudged along *grimly*. 这段路程很长，但他还是坚强地艰难赶路。
mechanics [məˈkænɪk]	*n.* 机械学，力学；技巧，方法 例 We've been talking about *mechanics* and then we still have a few minutes. 我们一直在讨论力学，之后我们还有几分钟时间。
presentation [ˌpriːzenˈteɪʃn]	*n.* 提供，显示；介绍，陈述；赠送；表演 记 来自 present(*vt.* 介绍；赠送；上演) 例 I need to get in touch with Bill about tomorrow's *presentation*. 我需要和比尔联系一下来谈谈明天的陈述。
refurbish [ˌriːˈfɜːrbɪʃ]	*vt.* 再装修，重新装饰(redecorate) 记 词根记忆：re(重新) + furb(装饰；整修) + ish → 再装修，重新装饰 例 Once the hotel's *refurbished*, it could start to attract people to our town again. 酒店重新装饰之后，就可以开始吸引人们再次来我们镇。
ancient [ˈeɪnʃənt]	*a.* 古代的(archaic)；古老的(*old) 记 发音记忆："安神" → 那古老的旋律让人心神安宁 → 古老的 例 What does the professor say about *ancient* Greeks who traveled south? 关于去南方旅游的古希腊人，教授讲了什么？

词根、词缀预习表

hib	拿住，拥有	exhibit v. 陈列，展览	curt	短的	curtail vt. 缩减
urb	城市	urban a. 城市的	fic	做	deficit n. 不足额
ann	年	annual a. 每年的	ject	扔	reject vt. 拒绝
numer	数字	numeric a. 数字的	frig	冷的	refrigerate vt. 冷冻
pens	支付	compensation n. 补偿	liber	自由的	liberate vt. 解放

---

portable

[ˈpɔːrtəbl]

a. 轻便的，便携的，手提式的

记 词根记忆：port(拿，运) + able(能…的) → 能拿的 → 轻便的

例 He designed a *portable* camera. 他设计了一种便携式照相机。

派 portability(*n.* 可携带，轻便)

portable

---

disciple

[dɪˈsaɪpl]

n. 门徒，弟子，追随者(follower, adherent)

记 联想记忆：门徒(disciple)必须遵守纪律(discipline)

例 Martin Luther King regarded himself as a real *disciple* of Gandhi. 马丁·路德·金自认为是甘地的真正门徒。

---

exhibit

[ɪɡˈzɪbɪt]

v. 陈列，展览(*display)；显示，表现(show) *n.* 展览(品)，陈列(品)

记 词根记忆：ex(出) + hib(拿住；拥有) + it → 把有的拿出来 → 陈列，展览

例 She will *exhibit* her new paintings in a local art gallery. 她将在当地画廊举行最新作品展。// I'm trying to find someone to come with me to the new sculpture *exhibit* in the art museum on Saturday. 我正试图找个人周六陪我去艺术博物馆看新的雕塑展览。

派 exhibition(*n.* 展览品；展览会；表现)

---

rekindle

[ˌriːˈkɪndl]

vt. 重新点燃；使振作

记 联想记忆：re(再，又) + kindle(点燃) → 重新点燃

例 Nothing can *rekindle* the old singer's fading passion. 什么都无法重新燃起老歌手淡去的激情。

---

meteor

[ˈmiːtiər]

n. 流星

例 Wind motion can be observed in the mesosphere by watching the trails of *meteors* passing through it. 通过观察流星经过中间层时留下的痕迹，可以观测到风在中间层的运动。

派 meteoric(*a.* 流星的；疾速的)

---

strap [stræp]	*n.* 带(strip) *vt.* 用带捆扎，束牢；用绷带包扎 记 联想记忆：用皮带(strap)拍打(rap) 例 This *strap* on my briefcase is broken. 我公事包的带子断了。// The drum skin was tightly *strapped* over the circle with rawhide laces. 用生牛皮带将鼓皮紧紧勒了一圈。 参 stripe(*n.* 条纹，斑纹)
urban ['ɜːrbən]	*a.* 城市的，市内的 记 词根记忆：urb(城市) + an → 城市的 例 The *urban* population decreased rapidly. 城市人口迅速减少。 派 urbanism(*n.* 城市化；城市主义)；urbanized(*a.* 城市化的；生活于城市的)；urbanization(*n.* 都市化)
deteriorate [dɪ'tɪriəreɪt]	*v.* 变坏，恶化；变质(erode) 记 词根记忆：de(向下) + ter(地) + ior + ate → 朝向地面下降 → 变糟糕 → 变坏，恶化 例 Relations between the two countries *deteriorated* rapidly. 两国关系急剧恶化。// Paper made from rags *deteriorated* quickly. 用破布做的纸很快就变质了。 派 deterioration(*n.* 恶化)
salamander ['sæləmændər]	*n.* 火蜥蜴；(神话中的)火蛇
bond [bɑːnd]	*n.* 联结，黏结；债券；黏合剂；契约，合同 *v.* (使)黏合，(使)结合 记 发音记忆："绑得" → 绑在一起 → 联结，黏结 搭 bond trader 证券交易员 例 For any adhesive to make a really strong *bond*, the surfaces to be glued must be absolutely clean and free from moisture or grease. 要想让黏合剂真正牢靠，需涂胶的表面必须非常干净，不能有任何湿气或油脂。
handy ['hændi]	*a.* 可用的(available)；易使用的，便利的；手巧的 搭 come in handy 有用处 例 I really need to keep the book *handy* just in case. 这本书我真的要放在手边，以备不时之需。
gauge [geɪdʒ]	*n.* 标准，规格；测量仪表，计量器 *vt.* 测量，度量 记 发音记忆："规矩" → 规格；测量仪表 例 I was surprised to find that some workers didn't know how to read the rain *gauge*. 我很惊奇地发现一些工作人员不知道怎么读测雨器。
embryo ['embriou]	*n.* 胚，胚胎；雏形 记 词根记忆：em + bryo(变大) → 种子等变大 → 胚胎 例 The plan, as yet, exists in *embryo*. 这个计划迄今为止仍在酝酿中。 派 embryonic(*a.* 胚胎的；胚胎期的，萌芽期的)

quadruple [kwɑːˈdruːpl]	*v.* (使)成四倍 *a.* 四部分组成的；四倍的 *n.* 四倍 记 词根记忆：quadr(四) + u + ple(折叠) → 折叠四次 → 四倍的 例 The population of this country has *quadrupled* in the past decade. 这个国家的人口在过去的十年里增长了三倍。
integral [ˈɪntɪɡrəl]	*a.* 构成整体所必需的，不可或缺的(*fundamental)；完整的 记 词根记忆：in(不) + tegr(触摸) + al → 未被触摸的 → 完整的 例 Martha developed a powerful, expressive style that was *integral* to the foundations of modern dance. 玛莎形成了一种有力且富有表现力的风格，这是构成现代舞蹈不可或缺的一部分。
urgent [ˈɜːrdʒənt]	*a.* 急迫的，紧迫的 记 词根记忆：urg(驱使) + ent(形容词后缀) → 不断驱使的 → 急迫的 例 The law is in *urgent* need of reform. 这项法律亟待修订。// A: I need these articles photocopied and stapled for my 4 o'clock meeting. Do you think you could have it done by then? B: There are several letters I need to type. They are not very *urgent* though. So I can make this top priority. A: 我需要把这些文章复印装订，四点开会要用，你觉得你到时能弄完吗？ B: 我需要录入几封信，不过这些信不太着急。所以，我可以先给你处理这件事。
quotient [ˈkwoʊʃnt]	*n.* 商；份额 记 词根记忆：quot(多少) + ient → 有多少 → 商；份额 例 Henry got a big *quotient* of his mother's property. 亨利得到了他母亲的大部分财产。
annual [ˈænjuəl]	*a.* 每年的，一年一度的(yearly) *n.* 年报，年刊，年鉴；一年生植物 记 词根记忆：ann(年) + ual → 每年的，一年一度的 例 Earth Day has become an *annual* international event. 地球日已经成为年度国际大事。 派 annually(*ad.* 一年一次地)
multiplicative [ˌmʌltɪplɪˈkeɪtɪv]	*a.* 倍增的；乘法的 参 multiplication(*n.* 相乘；增加)
studio [ˈstjuːdioʊ]	*n.* 工作室，画室；摄影室，演播室，录音室；练习室；电影公司 搭 a studio audience 演播室现场观众 例 In educational *studios*, students learn to develop skills related to design. 学生们在教育工作室里学习如何发展与设计相关的各种技能。
geometric [ˌdʒiːəˈmetrɪk]	*a.* 几何的，几何学的 记 来自 geometry(*n.* 几何学) 例 The book mainly talks about the solutions to numerous *geometric* progressions. 这本书主要讲述解决多种几何数列的方法。
minus [ˈmaɪnəs]	*a.* 减的，负的 *n.* 负数；减号；不足 *prep.* 减(去) 记 词根记忆：min(小) + us → 把东西变小 → 减(去)；减的 例 It is estimated that the temperature in this region is *minus* forty degrees Celsius today. 据估计，该地区今天的气温在零下 40 度。

28

ordinate [ˈɔːrdɪnət]	*n.* 纵坐标 记 词根记忆：ordin(顺序) + ate → 使数字按纵向顺序排列 → 纵坐标 例 Students should know what *ordinate* stands for when answering this question. 学生在回答这道题时应该知道纵坐标代表什么。
numeric [njuːˈmerɪk]	*a.* 数字的 记 词根记忆：numer(数字) + ic(形容词后缀) → 数字的 搭 numeric order 数字顺序 例 Mary majored in English, and she found it very difficult to understand the *numeric* data in the field of computers. 玛丽是学英语专业的，她觉得计算机领域的数字数据很难理解。
oblong [ˈɑːblɔːŋ]	*a.* 矩形的，长方形的；椭圆形的 *n.* 矩形，长方形；椭圆形 记 词根记忆：ob(向) + long(长的) → 向一边变长 → 矩形；椭圆形 例 The plain was of *oblong* shape. 这个平原呈长方形。
quantitative [ˈkwɑːntəteɪtɪv]	*a.* 数量的，定量的 记 来自 quantity(*n.* 数量，数目) 例 The boss said *quantitative* difference didn't play a crucial role in the profit increase. 老板说量的差异在利润增长中不起关键作用。
reciprocal [rɪˈsɪprəkl]	*a.* 相互的；互惠的；相应的；倒数的 *n.* 倒数 记 词根记忆：re(向后) + ci + pro(向前) + cal → 一前一后的 → 相互的；互惠的 例 The two major countries have established an important *reciprocal* relationship since 1980. 自 1980 年以来，这两个大国就已经建立了重要的互惠关系。
tangent [ˈtændʒənt]	*n.* 切线；正切 *a.* 切线的，相切的 记 词根记忆：tang(接触) + ent → 和圆相接触 → 切线 搭 go off on a tangent 突然转换话题；突然改变行动 例 Most of the students have difficulty in solving the problems related to *tangent*. 大多数学生在解决与正切相关的问题时都有困难。 派 tangential(*a.* 正切的；切线的；稍微沾边的，不相干的)
allot [əˈlɑːt]	*vt.* 分配，配给，拨给 记 联想记忆：all(所有的) + ot → 所有人都有份 → 分配，配给，拨给 例 The government has already made policies to *allot* the houses in that area. 政府已经制定政策在那个地区分配房子。
boycott [ˈbɔɪkɑːt]	*vt.* 联合抵制，拒绝购买(或使用、参加) 记 联想记忆：boy(男孩) + cott(看做 cut，剪) → 男孩们剪头以示抗议 → 联合抵制 例 The patriot called for all citizens to *boycott* foreign goods and support domestic ones. 这名爱国人士号召全体公民抵制洋货，支持国货。

□ ordinate　　□ numeric　　□ oblong　　□ quantitative　　□ reciprocal　　□ tangent
□ allot　　□ boycott

compensation [ˌkɑːmpenˈseɪʃn]	*n.* 补偿，赔偿；赔偿金 记 词根记忆：com（以）+ pens（支付）+ ation → 用某物来支付 → 补偿，赔偿 例 Linda was fired last week, but the *compensation* is very reasonable. 琳达上周被解雇了，但是赔偿金很合理。
ordinal [ˈɔːrdənl]	*a.* 序数的；顺序的 *n.* 序数词 记 词根记忆：ordin(顺序) + al → 顺序的；序数词 例 The English teacher asked three students to write the special *ordinal* numbers in English. 英语老师要求三个学生用英语写出特殊的序数词。
perimeter [pəˈrɪmɪtər]	*n.* 周长；外缘，边缘 记 词根记忆：peri(周围) + meter(测量) → 周边的长度 → 周长 例 Tom tried to work out how long the *perimeter* of his courtyard was. 汤姆试图计算出他家院子的周长。
triple [ˈtrɪpl]	*v.* (使)增至三倍 *a.* 三部分的；三方的；三倍的 记 词根记忆：tri(三) + ple → 三部分的，三倍的 例 According to the recent data, our company's net profits *tripled* compared with last year. 最新数据显示，我们公司今年的净利润是去年的三倍。
curtail [kɜːrˈteɪl]	*vt.* 缩短，缩减，削减(经费等) 记 词根记忆：curt(短的) + ail → 变短 → 缩短，缩减，削减(经费等) 例 The government decided to *curtail* its spending on education and agriculture. 政府决定削减教育和农业开支。
deficit [ˈdefɪsɪt]	*n.* 不足额；赤字，逆差 记 词根记忆：de(向下) + fic(做) + it → 经济走下坡路 → 不足额；赤字 搭 financial deficit 财政赤字；budget deficit 预算赤字 例 The survey showed that most of the people complained about current trade *deficit*. 调查显示，大多数人都抱怨当前的贸易赤字。
motto [ˈmɑːtoʊ]	*n.* 座右铭；箴言，格言(proverb) 记 词根记忆：mot(动) + to → 给动作以指示 → 座右铭；箴言，格言 例 The economists' *motto* was laisser faire at that time. 当时，经济学家们的座右铭是自由主义。
reject	[rɪˈdʒekt] *vt.* 拒绝，抵制(exclude)；抛弃，摈弃，排斥 [ˈriːdʒekt] *n.* 被拒货品，不合格产品 记 词根记忆：re(反) + ject(扔) → 被扔回来 → 拒绝 例 It reflects poetic techniques that were *rejected* by modern poets. 它反映了遭到现代诗人摒弃的诗歌技巧。 派 rejection(*n.* 拒绝)

28

reject

包装破损！拒收！

tension [ˈtenʃn]	n. 紧张(stress)；拉紧(tightness)；张力 记 词根记忆：tens(伸展) + ion → 伸展出的状态 → 拉紧 搭 tension spring 拉伸弹簧 例 The expressive leaders are attempting to minimize the *tension* and conflict. 富有表达能力的领导人正在试图最大限度地减少紧张和冲突。 参 tensile(a. 可拉长的，可伸长的)；tense(a. 紧张的；拉紧的)
flame [fleɪm]	n. 火舌，火焰（blaze）；光芒，光辉（brilliance）；强烈的感情 v. 燃烧(*burn)；闪耀(shine) 记 词根记忆：flam(燃烧) + e → 火舌，火焰 例 The house was in *flames*. 房子着火了。// The candles *flamed* brighter. 蜡烛燃烧得更亮了。 派 flaming(a. 燃烧的，满腔怒火的) flame
vent [vent]	n. 通风口（intake）；出口（outlet）vt. 表达，发泄（情感等） 记 本身是词根，意为"来" 搭 air vents 通气孔；give full vent to 充分表达；淋漓尽致地发泄 例 All along the *vents* there are these unusual microorganisms. 沿着整个通风口都是这些罕见的微生物。 派 ventilate(vt. 使通风；公开表达)；ventilation(n. 通风)；ventilator(n. 通风设备)
jog [dʒɑːɡ]	vi. 慢跑；(偶然地)轻轻触碰 记 联想记忆：一边慢跑(jog)一边遛狗(dog) 搭 jog sb.'s memory 唤起某人的记忆；提醒某人 例 Let's *jog* for another mile. 我们再慢跑一英里吧。 jog
mimic [ˈmɪmɪk]	vt. 模仿(imitate)；像 n. 模仿者；小丑 a. 模仿的，模拟的 记 联想记忆：mimi(音似：秘密) + c → 偷偷摸摸地模仿 → 模仿 例 People have always been fascinated by the parrot's ability to *mimic* human speech. 人们向来对鹦鹉模仿人类说话的能力惊叹不已。 派 mimicry(n. 模仿；模仿的技巧)
laboratory [ˈlæbrətɔːri]	n. 实验室，研究室 记 联想记忆：labor(工作) + at(在) + ory(表地点，名词后缀) → 工作的地方 → 实验室 例 Training is critical to the safe operation of the *laboratory* facility. 为确保安全操作实验室设备，(对实验设备使用者进行)培训很重要。
criss-cross [ˈkrɪsˌkrɔːs]	v. 构成十字形图案；交叉往来 a. 纵横交错的 例 The city is *criss-crossed* with canals. 这座城市里运河纵横交错。

□ tension   □ flame   □ vent   □ jog   □ mimic   □ laboratory
□ criss-cross

sour [ˈsaʊər]	*v.* (使)变酸；(使)变馊；(使)变坏，恶化 *a.* 酸(味)的(acid)；馊的；乖戾的，尖酸刻薄的；酸痛的 记 发音记忆："馊啊" → 酸的；馊的 例 The atmosphere in the room *soured*. 房间里的气氛不对了。
critique [krɪˈtiːk]	*n.* 批评，评论(criticism, comment) *vt.* 写评论 记 词根记忆：crit(判断) + ique → 作出判断 → 批评，评论 搭 film critique 影评 例 We'll talk more about the requirements of the *critique* later in the semester. 我们会在这学期晚些时候进一步讨论评论的要求。
viral [ˈvaɪrəl]	*a.* 病毒(性)的，病毒引起的 记 联想记忆：对抗(rival)病毒引起的(viral)疾病 例 The cell begins to manufacture *viral* proteins rather than its own. 细胞开始制造病毒的蛋白质，而不是自己的蛋白质。
fault [fɔːlt]	*n.* 过错，过失(error, defect)；缺点，弱点；断层 搭 fault plane 断层面；fault zone 断层带 例 *Faults* in the Earth's crust are most evident in sedimentary formations, where they interrupt previously continuous layers. 地壳的断层在沉积层中最明显，在那儿它们中断了之前一直连续的地层。 派 faultless(*a.* 没有错误的；完美的)；faulty(*a.* 错误的；不完美的) 参 layer/stratum(*n.* 地层)；plate(*n.* 板块)
schedule [ˈskedʒuːl]	*vt.* 安排，预定(assign, appoint) *n.* 时刻表，日程表(timetable, agenda)；清单，明细表 记 源自拉丁语 scheda(纸莎草的叶子)，后与法语 cedule 融合进入英语，词义也转变为"时刻表、日程表" 搭 ahead of schedule 提前；on schedule 如期；behind schedule 晚于预定日期 例 The meeting is *scheduled* for Monday. 会议安排在周一。// I am *scheduled* to meet for Thursday to go over your inventory report. 我预定周四开会审查你的库存报告。 派 scheduled(*a.* 预定的)；reschedule(*vt.* 重新安排，重新计划)
latter [ˈlætər]	*a.* 后面的，后半期的；后者的 *n.* 后者 例 This *latter* form is what is generally meant when one uses the term "satellite city". 后面这种形式就是人们使用"卫星城"这个词时一般所指的意思。
minimal [ˈmɪnɪməl]	*a.* 最小的(minimum)；最低限度的(the least possible) 记 词根记忆：min(小) + imal → 最小的 例 Are you aware that you can go to that school at a *minimal* cost? 你意识到你能以最低的花费去那所学校上学吗？ 派 minimalist(*n.* 极简抽象派艺术家；简约主义者)；minimalism(*n.* 极简抽象主义)

refrigerate [rɪˈfrɪdʒəreɪt]	*vt.* 冷冻, 冷藏; 使冷却, 使变冷 记 词根记忆: re + frig(冷的) + er + ate(使…) → 冷冻, 冷藏; 使变冷 例 Ice was used to *refrigerate* the meat products. 冰被用来冷藏肉制品。 派 refrigerator(*n.* 冰箱; 冷藏库)
fountain [ˈfaʊntn]	*n.* (人工)喷泉; 丰富来源, 源泉 记 联想记忆: 山(mountain)里有喷泉(fountain) 例 Tourism is a *fountain* of wealth for this country. 旅游业是该国财富的 源泉。
horizontal [ˌhɔːrɪˈzɑːntl]	*a.* 水平的(level); 与地面平行的 记 来自 horizon(*n.* 地平线) 搭 horizontal movement 水平运动 例 There are two worm gears, one vertical and one *horizontal*. 有两种涡 轮, 一种是垂直的, 另一种是水平的。
appetite [ˈæpɪtaɪt]	*n.* 胃口, 食欲(savor); 欲望 记 词根记忆: ap (向, 往) + pet (寻找) + ite → 到处寻找 → 食欲 例 I don't have an *appetite*. 我没有胃口。 派 appetizer(*n.* 开胃品); appetizing(*a.* 开胃的, 美味可口的) appetite
perpendicular [ˌpɜːrpənˈdɪkjələr]	*a.* 成直角的, 垂直的(vertical, upright) *n.* 垂直线 记 词根记忆: per(自始至终) + pend(挂) + icular → 自始至终挂着 → 垂 直的 例 It will take extreme courage to climb up the *perpendicular* mountain. 爬上垂直山峰需要极大的勇气。 参 horizontal(*a.* 水平的)
impressive [ɪmˈpresɪv]	*a.* 给人深刻印象的(*stunning); 感人的 记 来自 impress(*vt.* 给…以深刻印象; 使感动) 例 The destructive power of fungi is *impressive*. 真菌的破坏力令人惊叹。
generous [ˈdʒenərəs]	*a.* 慷慨的, 大方的(unselfish); 大量的, 丰富的(plentiful); 宽厚的, 宽宏大 量的 记 词根记忆: gen(产生) + er + ous(多…的) → 产生很多的 → 大量的, 丰 富的 例 After the Civil War, politicians rarely opposed the government's *generous* support to business owners. 内战之后, 政客们很少反对政府对 企业家的慷慨支持。 派 generosity(*n.* 慷慨, 大方; 宽宏大量)
liberate [ˈlɪbəreɪt]	*vt.* 解放; 释放(*discharge, release) 记 词根记忆: liber(自由的) + ate(使…) → 使自由 → 解放; 释放 例 This energy is *liberated* at the center of the Sun. 这一能量是从太阳的 中心释放出来的。

□ refrigerate   □ fountain   □ horizontal   □ appetite   □ perpendicular □ impressive
□ generous   □ liberate

completion [kəm'pliːʃn]	*n.* 完成，实现（accomplishment, realization）；结束 例 They do not need to carry each task to *completion* from start to finish. 他们不需要从头到尾完成每项任务。
synthesize ['sɪnθəsaɪz]	*vt.* 合成；综合 记 词根记忆：syn(共同) + thes(放) + ize → 放到一起 → 合成；综合 例 Vitamins are *synthesized* from foods. 维生素是利用食物合成的。 派 synthesizer(*n.* 音响合成器)；synthesis(*n.* 综合；综合体；合成)
inherent [ɪn'hɪrənt]	*a.* 固有的；内在的 记 词根记忆：in(向内) + her(黏附) + ent → 黏附在内的 → 固有的；内在的 例 Homing pigeons are not unique in this *inherent* skill. 并非只有信鸽才有这种先天的技能。 派 inherently(*ad.* 天性地；固有地)
disinterested [dɪs'ɪntrəstɪd]	*a.* 客观的，无私的，公正的（impartial, objective, unbiased）；无兴趣的，不关心的 例 The teacher gave me some *disinterested* advice. 老师给了我一些无私的忠告。
asthma ['æzmə]	*n.* 哮喘(症) 记 联想记忆：as + th(看做 the) + ma(拼音：妈) → 像大妈一样有哮喘病 → 哮喘(症) 搭 nasal asthma 鼻性哮喘；mild asthma 轻度哮喘 例 Now I want to answer a question one of you asked me yesterday about *asthma*. 现在，我来回答昨天你们有人提出的一个关于哮喘的问题。 asthma
mania ['meɪnɪə]	*n.* 躁狂；狂热（craze, madness）；癖好 记 词根记忆：man(狂热) + ia(表病，名词后缀) → 躁狂；狂热 例 The *mania* for architectural reconstruction had largely subsided by the 1950s and 1960s. 建筑改造的热潮在 20 世纪五六十年代就大幅消退了。
inspect [ɪn'spekt]	*vt.* 检查，视察（check） 记 词根记忆：in(向内) + spect(看) → 向内看 → 检查，视察 搭 inspect sth. for sth. 为…而检查… 例 Experts suggest car owners should have their cars *inspected* regularly. 专家建议车主应该定期检查车辆。 派 inspector(*n.* 检查员；巡视员) 参 aspect(*n.* 方面)；respect(*vt.* 尊重，尊敬)；prospect(*n.* 景色；前景)
scorch [skɔːtʃ]	*v.* 烧焦(*burn, sear)；(使)枯萎，枯黄 *n.* 焦痕 记 联想记忆：用火把(torch)烤焦(scorch) 例 The leaves will *scorch* if you water them in the sun. 在太阳底下浇水，叶子会枯黄。 派 scorcher(*n.* 大热天)；scorching(*a.* 酷热的；激烈的) scorch

28

aggregate ['ægrɪgət] *n.* 聚集物；总计 ['ægrɪgeɪt] *vt.* 聚集；总计
记 词根记忆：ag(往，靠近) + greg(群) + ate → 聚成一群 → 聚集物
例 Marine mammals have the misfortune to be swimming *aggregates* of commodities that humans want: fur, oil and meat. 海洋哺乳动物不幸成为人类需要的各种商品的游动集合体：皮毛、油脂和肉。
派 aggregation(*n.* 集合；集合体)

cylinder ['sɪlɪndər]
n. 圆筒，圆柱体；气缸
搭 work on all cylinders 竭尽全力，开足马力
派 cylindrical(*a.* 圆柱形的，圆筒状的)

impair [ɪm'per]
vt. 削弱(weaken)；损害(damage)
记 词根记忆：im(不) + pair(相等) → 使不相等 → 削弱；损害
例 Without regular supplies of some hormones, our capacity to behave would be seriously *impaired*. 如果荷尔蒙不能定期供应，我们的行为能力就会严重受损。

quality ['kwɑːləti]
n. 质，质量 (degree of excellence)；品德，品质 (*nature)；性质，特性 (property) *a.* 优良的，优质的
搭 be of good quality 质量好；quality of life 生活质量
例 Perhaps the most striking *quality* of satiric literature is its freshness, and its originality of perspective. 或许讽刺文学最显著的特点是其新颖性及其独特的视角。
派 qualitative(*a.* 质量的；定性的)

bureau ['bjʊroʊ]
n. 局，署；办公室；机构
记 本身为词根，意为"桌子"，引申为"政府的局" → 局
搭 an employment bureau 职业介绍所

excavation [ˌekskə'veɪʃn]
n. 挖掘，发掘；出土文物；挖掘现场
记 词根记忆：ex(出) + cav(洞) + ation(名词词尾) → 挖出洞 → 挖掘，发掘
例 The *excavations* are open to the public. 发掘现场对公众开放。

spin [spɪn]
v. (使)快速旋转(twirl, whirl)；纺纱(reel)；吐丝；(用洗衣机)甩干衣服 *n.* 旋转(twirl, whirl)
搭 in a flat spin 晕头转向，急得团团转
例 The plane was *spinning* out of control. 飞机失去控制，不停地旋转。

erode [ɪ'roʊd]
v. 侵蚀，腐蚀(corrode, rot)
记 词根记忆：e(去掉) + rod(咬) + e → 咬掉 → 侵蚀，腐蚀
例 Melting ice *erodes* the soil around it. 融化的冰侵蚀着周围的土壤。
派 erosion(*n.* 侵蚀，腐蚀)

settle
[ˈsetl]

v. 安定，安顿，定居；结束，解决；决定，确定；(使)平静下来；支付，结算；(鸟等)飞落，停留

记 联想记忆：set(放置) + tle → 安定，安顿

搭 settle down 平静下来；定居，过安定的生活；settle in/into 习惯于，适应

例 The man has agreed to *settle* out of court. 那个男人同意了庭外解决。//
A: I'm sort of upset with my brother. He hasn't answered either of my letters.
B: Well, just remember how hectic your freshman year was. Give him a chance to get *settled*.
A: 我有点担心我弟弟。我给他写了两封信，他都没有回复。
B: 想想你大学第一年有多忙吧。给他一个机会安顿下来。

virus
[ˈvaɪrəs]

n. 病毒；病毒性疾病

搭 a virus infection 病毒感染

例 The *virus* replicates by attaching to a cell and injecting its nucleic acid. 病毒通过附着在细胞上并向其中输入核酸来实现复制。

state
[steɪt]

n. 情况，状况 (condition)；国家 (nation)；州 *v.* 陈述，说明，声明 (express)；规定

例 The house is in a bad *state* of repair. 这幢房子年久失修。// The President was anxious about the *state* of the country's economy. 总统担心国家的经济状况。

派 statehood(*n.* 独立国家的地位；州的地位)；stately(*a.* 庄重的；宏伟的，壮观的)；statement(*n.* 陈述，声明；说法)

Fahrenheit
[ˈfærənhaɪt]

n. 华氏温度计 *a.* 华氏温度的

例 The temperature of the Sun is over 5,000 degrees *Fahrenheit* at the surface. 太阳表面的温度超过 5000 华氏度。

creep
[kriːp]

vi. 缓慢行进；爬行(crawl)；悄悄地移动

记 联想记忆：兔子偷懒睡觉(sleep)时乌龟缓慢地行进(creep)

搭 creep along 沿着…爬；creep into/over 爬进/过

例 I *crept* up the stairs in case I woke up my roommates. 我蹑手蹑脚地爬上楼梯，生怕吵醒我的室友。

派 creeper(*n.* 蔓生植物)；creeping(*a.* 逐渐发生的；缓慢行进的)；creepy(*a.* 爬行的；令人毛骨悚然的)

thorough
[ˈθɜːroʊ]

a. 彻底的(exhaustive)；详尽的(elaborate)；一丝不苟的(careful about detail)

例 The investigation of Peary's expedition wasn't *thorough*. 对皮尔里远征的调查是不彻底的。

派 thoroughly(*ad.* 十分地，彻底地)

spectrum
[ˈspektrəm]

n. 谱，光谱，频谱；范围，幅度(extension, range)

记 词根记忆：spect(看) + rum → 看到光的颜色 → 光谱

例 The representatives are constitutionally elected by a broad *spectrum* of the population. 代表由广泛的人群根据宪法选举产生。

28

overhaul	[ˈoʊvərhɔːl] *n.* 仔细检查(examination); 彻底检修 [ˌoʊvərˈhɔːl] *vt.* 仔细检查; 彻底检修 记 联想记忆: over(从头到尾) + haul(拉, 拖) → 全都拉上来进行修理 → 仔细检查 例 The citizens demanded an *overhaul* of the corrupt government. 公民要求全面治理腐败的政府。
innate [ɪˈneɪt]	*a.* 天生的, 固有的(inborn); 内在的, 直觉的 记 词根记忆: in(在内) + nat(出生) + e → 出生时就有的 → 天生的 例 Most researchers assume that the ability to perform and encode the dance is *innate*. 大多数研究者认为表演和编排舞蹈的能力是天生的。
picturesque [ˌpɪktʃəˈresk]	*a.* 如画的(scenic, beautiful); 别致的; (语言)生动的 搭 a picturesque village 风景如画的村庄 例 The place is remarkable for its *picturesque* scenery. 这个地区因风景如画而享有盛名。

We often hear of people breaking down from overwork, but in nine cases out of ten they are really suffering from worry or anxiety.

我们常常听人说，人们因工作过度而垮下来，但是实际上十有八九是因为饱受担忧或焦虑的折磨。

—— 英国银行家　卢伯克 .J.（John Lubbock, British banker）

音频

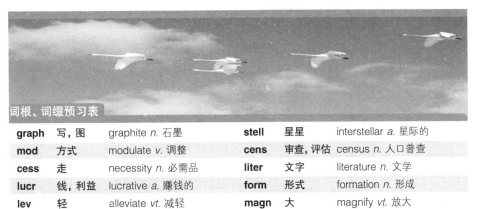

词根、词缀预习表

graph	写，图	graphite n. 石墨	stell	星星	interstellar a. 星际的
mod	方式	modulate v. 调整	cens	审查，评估	census n. 人口普查
cess	走	necessity n. 必需品	liter	文字	literature n. 文学
lucr	钱，利益	lucrative a. 赚钱的	form	形式	formation n. 形成
lev	轻	alleviate vt. 减轻	magn	大	magnify vt. 放大

---

graphite
['græfaɪt]

n. 石墨
记 词根记忆：graph(写；图) + ite → 用来写字、画画的东西 → 石墨

encourage
[ɪnˈkɜːrɪdʒ]

v. 鼓励，激励(*urge, stimulate)；促进，激发
记 联想记忆：en(使…) + courage(精神) → 使有精神 → 鼓励；促进
例 We *encourage* all students to volunteer for at least one community activity before they graduate. 我们鼓励所有学生在毕业之前至少要自愿参与一项社区活动。
派 encouragement(*n.* 鼓励，激励)

shuffle
[ˈʃʌfl]

v./n. 拖着脚走；洗(牌)；蒙混；搅乱
记 发音记忆："杀否" → 输了，再杀一盘可否 → 洗(牌)
搭 lose...in the shuffle 在混乱中没注意到，忽略；遗失
例 With sore throat and aching chest the patient *shuffled* over to the ward. 患者喉咙和胸口痛，拖着脚步走到了病房。
参 shuttle(*n.* 梭子；来往于两地之间的航班等 *v.* 频繁往来；往返运送)；muffle(*vt.* 压抑声音)

modulate
[ˈmɑːdʒəleɪt]

v. 调整，调节(声音等)(temper, adjust)；调制(声波等)
记 词根记忆：mod(方式，样式) + ul + ate → 改变样式 → 调整；调制
例 The ability to *modulate* a chemical signal is limited, compared with communication by visual or acoustic means. 与视觉或听觉交流相比，调节化学信号的能力是有限的。

rebate
[ˈriːbeɪt]

n. 回扣，折扣；退还款
记 词根记忆：re(再，又) + bate(减少) → 一再减少 → 回扣，折扣
例 The government promised that some companies could get a tax *rebate* on export at the end of the year. 政府承诺部分企业在年终能够得到出口退税。

□ graphite　　□ encourage　　□ shuffle　　■ modulate　　□ rebate

finch
[fɪntʃ]

n. 雀类

记 联想记忆：fin(鳍，鱼翅) + ch(音似：翅) → 雀类和鱼类都有翅 → 雀类

例 *Finches* are typically inhabitants of well-wooded areas, but some can be found in deserts. 雀类通常居住于树木繁茂的地区，但有些也出现于沙漠地区。

nostalgia
[nəˈstældʒə]

n. 思乡病，乡愁(homesickness)；怀旧之情，恋旧

记 词根记忆：nost(回家) + alg(痛) + ia(表病，名词后缀) → 想回家想到心痛 → 思乡病

例 The female novelist's work is pervaded by *nostalgia* for her hometown. 这位女性小说家的作品弥漫着思乡之情。

pants
[pænts]

n. 内裤，短裤(shorts)；裤子

搭 a pair of pants 一条裤子

例 My old pair of *pants* has worn thin at the knees. 我那条旧裤子的膝盖处已经磨薄了。

endorse
[ɪnˈdɔːrs]

vt. (在支票背面)签名；宣传，代言；签署；赞同，支持

记 词根记忆：en(在…里) + dors(背面) + e → 在(票据)背面写上名字 → (在支票背面)签名

例 Mary felt sorry that she couldn't *endorse* my advice about going out for dinner. 玛丽因不赞成我外出就餐的提议而感到很抱歉。

派 endorsement(*n.* 赞同，支持；宣传，代言)

fluctuation
[ˌflʌktʃuˈeɪʃn]

n. 波动，起伏

记 来自 fluctuate[*v.* (使)波动；(使)变化]

例 Gold prices in the international market are in a period of *fluctuation*. 国际市场上的黄金价格处于波动期。

subsidiary
[səbˈsɪdieri]

n. 子公司；附属机构；支流 *a.* 次要的；辅助的，附设的；附属的

记 词根记忆：sub(在…下面) + sid(坐) + iary → 坐在下面的 → 次要的；辅助的

搭 a subsidiary stream 支流；a subsidiary payment 补贴费

例 It is reported that group profit is mainly made by the *subsidiaries* in the East Asian countries. 据报道，集团的利润主要是由位于东亚国家的子公司创造的。

import

[ˈɪmpɔːrt] *n.* 进口(商品)，输入(额)；意义，要旨，重要性

[ɪmˈpɔːrt] *vt.* 进口，输入

记 联想记忆：im(进入) + port(港口) → 进入港口 → 进口(商品)

例 As was showed in the table, the *import* of iron ores went up sharply last year. 如图表所示，去年铁矿石的进口量急剧攀升。

参 export(*n.* 输出，出口；输出物)

perquisite
[ˈpɜːrkwɪzɪt]

n. 津贴，利益；特权

记 词根记忆：per(全部) + quisit(要求) + e → 要求全部得到 → 津贴，利益；特权

例 The *perquisites* of the executive management include the use of company cars. 行政管理层的特权包括使用公司的车。

mortgage [ˈmɔːrɡɪdʒ]	*n.* 抵押贷款，按揭(贷款)；抵押证书 *vt.* 用…作抵押 记 词根记忆：mort(死) + gage(誓言；抵押) → 以东西做抵押，以免交易失败 → 抵押贷款 例 The young couple worked very hard to pay their *mortgage* on the house. 这对年轻的夫妇努力工作来还房子的按揭贷款。
necessity [nəˈsesəti]	*n.* 必需品；必要，(迫切)需要；必然性 记 词根记忆：ne(不) + cess(走) + ity → 不能让它走的东西 → 必备之物 → 必需品 搭 of necessity 无法避免地，必定 例 As a famous saying goes, *necessity* is the mother of creation. 正如一句名言所说，需要是发明之母。
externality [ˌekstɜːrˈnæləti]	*n.* 外部性，外界效应 记 来自 external(*a.* 外部的) 例 The investigation aimed at studying the human beings' *externality* to a strange environment. 该调查旨在研究人类面对陌生环境时的外在反应。
insolvent [ɪnˈsɑːlvənt]	*a.* 财力不足的，破产的(bankrupt) 记 联想记忆：in + solvent(有偿付能力的) → 没有偿付能力的 → 财力不足的，破产的 例 With the advent of the financial crisis, some small companies in developing countries became *insolvent*. 由于金融危机的到来，一些发展中国家的小公司破产了。
lucrative [ˈluːkrətɪv]	*a.* 赚钱的，获利的，有利可图的 记 词根记忆：lucr(钱，利益) + ative → 赚钱的，获利的 例 Kate's husband is determined to look for a *lucrative* job this year. 凯特的丈夫决定今年找一份赚钱的工作。
negotiate [nɪˈɡoʊʃieɪt]	*v.* 谈判，商议；商定，达成；通过，越过 记 词根记忆：neg(否定) + oti + ate → (通过谈判)消除否定 → 谈判，商议 例 Most of the employees decided to *negotiate* with the employer about their salary increases. 大多数员工决定与老板协商加薪。
patronize [ˈpeɪtrənaɪz]	*v.* 以高人一等的态度对待；光顾；赞助，资助 记 词根记忆：patr(父亲) + on + ize → 扮演父亲的角色 → 赞助 例 The football club is often *patronized* by social celebrities such as politicians and movie stars. 这家足球俱乐部常常有社会名流光顾，比如政治家和电影明星。
recoup [rɪˈkuːp]	*vt.* 收回(成本)，弥补(亏损)(recover) 记 联想记忆：re(反) + coup(意外的行动) → 对意外行为的反馈 → 弥补(亏损) 例 Harry *recouped* himself for his economic losses by rectifying investments in time. 哈里通过及时调整投资挽回了经济损失。

29

monetary

[ˈmʌnɪteri]

a. 金钱的，货币的

记 联想记忆：monet(看做 money，钱) + ary → 金钱的

搭 monetary growth 货币增长

例 The central bank has made a new *monetary* policy to stimulate the economy. 央行制定了一项新的货币政策来刺激经济的发展。

redeem

[rɪˈdiːm]

vt. 赎回；偿清，付清；兑换；弥补，补偿 (compensate for)；履行，遵守（诺言）

记 词根记忆：red(=re 再，又) + eem(买) → 买回来 → 赎回

搭 redeem oneself 挽回声誉

例 The political party tried its best to *redeem* its reputation at a press conference. 该政党在新闻发布会上竭尽全力挽回声誉。

choir

[ˈkwaɪər]

n. 唱诗班，合唱队 *vi.* 合唱

记 联想记忆：坐在椅子(chair)上合唱(choir)一首歌

例 He sings in the school *choir*. 他是校合唱队的成员。

参 choral(*a.* 合唱队的)

stagnant

[ˈstægnənt]

a. 不景气的；停滞的；迟钝的；因不流动而污浊的

记 词根记忆：stagn(池塘) + ant(形容词后缀) → 犹如池塘里的死水 → 停滞的

例 Because of economic crisis, our company's sale has remained *stagnant*. 由于经济危机，我们公司的销售额停滞不前。

basin

[ˈbeɪsn]

n. 盆，脸盆；盆地；流域

例 The Amazon *Basin* has a tropical rainforest climate. 亚马孙河盆地属于热带雨林气候。

参 bison(*n.* 美洲野牛)

premise

[ˈpremɪs]

n. (企业、机构等使用的)房屋和地基，经营场址；前提，假设

记 词根记忆：pre(在…前面) + mis(放) + e → 放在前面的东西 → 前提，假设

例 We should cite some classic examples as *premises* for our argument. 我们应该引用一些经典的例子作为支持论点的前提。

surcharge

[ˈsɜːrtʃɑːrdʒ]

n. 额外费用，增收费，附加费 *vt.* 收取额外费用

记 联想记忆：sur(在…之上；超过) + charge(收费) → 收取额外费用

例 Tom asked the clerk about the *surcharge* on the express parcel in the post office. 汤姆向邮局的工作人员咨询快递包裹的额外邮资问题。

transact

[trænˈzækt]

v. 交易；执行，处理

记 词根记忆：trans(穿过) + act(做) → 在两者之间进行 → 交易

例 I don't know how to *transact* the procedure of going on board when travelling by air for the first time. 我第一次乘飞机旅行时都不知道怎么办理登机手续。

alleviate [əˈliːvieɪt]	*vt.* 减轻，缓解，缓和（relieve） 记 词根记忆：al(表加强) + lev(轻) + (i)ate(使…) → 使变轻 → 减轻，缓解，缓和 例 The drug *alleviated* the pain of Mary's broken leg. 这个药缓解了玛丽断腿带来的痛苦。
rodent [ˈroʊdnt]	*n.* 啮齿目动物(如松鼠或海狸等) *a.* 啮齿目的；咬的 记 词根记忆：rod(咬) + ent → 喜欢用牙咬的动物 → 啮齿目动物 例 Almost forty percent of mammal species are *rodents*, and they are found in vast numbers on all continents other than Antarctica. 几乎40%的哺乳动物都属啮齿目，它们数目众多，遍布除南极洲外的全球各大洲。 参 edentate(*n.* 贫齿目动物)
punctual [ˈpʌŋktʃuəl]	*a.* 守时的(being on time) 记 词根记忆：punct(刺) + ual → 像针刺那般准确 → 守时的 例 Fred is never *punctual*. 弗雷德从不守时。
dogged [ˈdɔːɡɪd]	*a.* 顽强的，坚持不懈的(persevering)；顽固的，固执的 记 联想记忆：dog(狗) + ged → 像狗一样顽强 → 顽强的 例 She is the recipient of a full scholarship from Harvard and her story is one of *dogged* determination and achievement. 她获得了哈佛大学的全额奖学金，她的故事就是一个通过顽强的决心取得成功的故事。
preliminary [prɪˈlɪmɪneri]	*a.* 预备的，初步的(*primary) *n.* 初步做法，起始行为 记 词根记忆：pre(预先) + limin(门槛；起点) + ary → 预先开始的 → 预备的 例 I'll expect a *preliminary* draft of each paper two weeks before the final due date. 我期望在截止日期前两周拿到每份论文的初稿。
transform [trænsˈfɔːrm]	*vt.* 使变形(transfigure)；改造，改革(reform)；转换(convert) 记 词根记忆：trans(穿过) + form(形状) → 使变形；改造；转换 例 The video equipment is capable of *transforming* raw weather data into words, symbols, and vivid graphic displays. 这个视频设备能把原始的气象数据转换成文字、符号和生动的图像显示。 派 transformation(*n.* 变形；转变)；transformer(*n.* 变压器)
aurora [ɔːˈrɔːrə]	*n.* 极光 记 注意和aurore(*a.* 朝霞色的)相区分 例 *Auroras* are associated with the solar wind, a flow of ions continuously flowing outward from the Sun. 极光与太阳风有关，太阳风是指太阳不断向外放射的离子组成的一条离子流。
interstellar [ˌɪntərˈstelər]	*a.* 星际的 记 词根记忆：inter(在…之间) + stell(星星) + ar(形容词后缀) → 星际的 例 Spiral galaxies are well supplied with the *interstellar* gas in which new stars form. 螺旋状星系由大量星际气体形成，而新的恒星在星际气体内形成。

29

realm [relm]	*n.* 王国，国度(kingdom)；界，范围，领域(region) 记 联想记忆：real(真正的) + m → 真正的好东西(如音乐、艺术等)无国界 → 王国 例 A successful outcome is not beyond the *realm* of possibility. 最后取得成功并非不可能。
consideration [kənˌsɪdəˈreɪʃn]	*n.* 考虑，思考；体谅，照顾；考虑因素，理由；报酬 搭 in consideration of 作为…的酬劳；take...into consideration 考虑到，顾及 例 The government should give careful *consideration* to issues of food safety. 政府应该仔细考虑食品安全的问题。
aviation [ˌeɪviˈeɪʃn]	*n.* 航空，航空学(navigation)；飞行(flying) 记 词根记忆：avi(鸟) + at + ion(名词后缀) → 像鸟一样飞 → 航空 例 Great progress was made in the field of *aviation* during the 1920s and 1930s. 20 世纪二三十年代，航空领域取得了重大进展。 参 aviator(*n.* 飞行家)
manipulate [məˈnɪpjuleɪt]	*vt.* 操作，处理(handle, use)；利用，操纵 记 词根记忆：mani(手) + pul(拉) + ate → 用手拉 → 操作，处理；利用，操纵 例 He accused the government of *manipulating* public opinion. 他谴责政府操纵公众舆论。 派 manipulation(*n.* 操作；操纵)
hammer [ˈhæmər]	*v.* 锤打(pound) *n.* 锤，槌(pestle)；锤子(mallet) 例 Silversmiths *hammer* these ingots to the appropriate thickness by hand. 银匠们用手工把这些铸锭锤打到合适的厚度。
synthetic [sɪnˈθetɪk]	*a.* 合成的，综合的；人造的(artificial) *n.* [常 *pl.*]合成物 记 词根记忆：syn(共同，相同) + thet(放) + ic → 放到一起的 → 合成的 搭 synthetic dye 合成染料；synthetic product 合成产品 例 *Synthetic* fibers account for about half of all fiber usage, with applications in every field of fiber and textile technology. 合成纤维约占所有纤维使用量的一半，应用于纤维和纺织技术的所有领域。
census [ˈsensəs]	*n.* 人口普查，人口统计 记 词根记忆：cens(审查，评估) + us → 评估数量 → 人口普查 搭 census bureau 人口普查局 例 The *census* provides a useful way of obtaining statistical information about a population. 人口普查是获得有关人口的统计学信息的有用途径。
sustain [səˈsteɪn]	*vt.* 保持，维持(生命)(*support, maintain)；支持，支撑(重量)；经受，承受(困难) 记 词根记忆：sus(在…下面) + tain(拿住) → 保持，维持 例 The hurricanes have *sustained* winds of 74mph and up. 飓风维持每小时 74 英里以上的风速。 派 self-sustaining(*a.* 自给自足的) 参 attain(*vt.* 达到)；retain(*vt.* 保持)

manipulate

clutch [klʌtʃ]	*n.* 一次所孵的卵(或蛋); (汽车、机器等的)离合器; 掌握, 控制; 把握, 抓紧 *v.* 企图抓住, 抓紧(take, clench) 记 联想记忆: clu(看做 clue, 线索) + tch → 抓住线索 → 抓紧 例 This species lays one and only one-*clutch* of forty eggs in a lifetime. 这个物种一生只孵一次蛋, 共有 40 个蛋。
sensible ['sensəbl]	*a.* 可察觉的, 可感知的 (perceptible); 明智的 (advisable); 切合实际的 (practical); 意识到的 记 词根记忆: sens(感觉) + ible(能…的) → 能感觉到的 → 可察觉的 例 The teacher was *sensible* of the fact that statistics is not a popular subject. 那位老师意识到统计学科不受欢迎。
target ['tɑːrgɪt]	*n.* 目标, 对象(aim); 靶子 *vt.* 把…作为目标 记 发音记忆: "他击的" → 是他击中目标的 → 目标 搭 target sth. at/on sb./sth. 把…作为…的目标 例 I thought your article on the school newspaper was right on *target*. 我觉得你在校报上发表的文章一语中的。// A: About this survey on the quality of life in the dorm I feel sort of awkward because, well, I'm not really comfortable here. Are you sure you want me to fill out this survey form? B: It's people like you who can help us *target* areas for improvement. A: 关于这个宿舍生活质量的调查, 我觉得有点尴尬, 因为我在这里住得不是很舒服。你肯定自己想让我填写这个调查表吗? B: 正是像你这样的人才能帮助我们找到改进之处。 派 targeted(*a.* 作为目标的, 作为对象的)
flamboyant [flæm'bɔɪənt]	*a.* 艳丽的, 绚丽夺目的; 炫耀的 记 联想记忆: flam(e)(火焰) + boy(男孩) + ant(蚂蚁) → 男孩高举着火把去捉蚂蚁 → 艳丽的 例 The President's *flamboyant* lifestyle was well known among the citizens. 总统炫耀的生活方式广为民众所知。
vein [veɪn]	*n.* 静脉; 叶脉; 纹理, 纹路; 方式, 风格 例 A number of other people commented in a similar *vein*. 其他一些人也以类似的方式进行评论。 派 veining(*n.* 脉络分布; 纹理)
jewelry ['dʒuːəlri]	*n.* 〈总称〉首饰(ornament); 珠宝(gem) 例 The old woman wears some lovely pieces of gold *jewelry*. 那个老妇人戴着几件漂亮的金首饰。
pack [pæk]	*v.* 收拾(行李), 打包; 捆扎; 塞满(stuff) *n.* 包, 包裹(parcel) 例 It is time to *pack* up my gloves and boots. 该把我的手套和靴子打包了。 派 packing(*n.* 包装); packer(*n.* 包装机)
satellite ['sætəlaɪt]	*n.* 卫星; 人造卫星 搭 weather satellite 气象卫星; satellite channel 卫星频道 例 The Moon is a *satellite* of the Earth. 月球是地球的卫星。

29

correspondent [ˌkɔːrəˈspɑːndənt]	*n.* 报道者，记者；通信者 搭 a war correspondent 战地记者 例 For example, a *correspondent* is expected to provide considerable context to the events being chronicled. 例如，记者应该对所记录的事件进行大量的背景介绍。
resilience [rɪˈzɪliəns]	*n.* 弹力，弹性；复原力；适应力 记 词根记忆：re(向后) + sil(跳) + ience → 向后跳的能力 → 弹力，弹性 例 Fostering *resilience* in children requires family environments that are caring and structured, hold high expectations for children's behavior, and encourage participation in the life of the family. 培养孩子的适应力需要一个充满关爱、井井有条的家庭环境，而且这个家庭要对孩子的行为抱有很高的期望，并鼓励参与家庭生活。
shower [ˈʃaʊər]	*n.* 阵雨，暴雨；淋浴(器)(bath)；一阵，一大批 *v.* (洗)淋浴；下阵雨；洒落，纷纷降落；抛撒 例 They were caught in a heavy *shower* halfway. 他们在半路遇上一阵大雨。// He got out of the *shower* to answer the phone. 他从淋浴里出来去接电话。
tedious [ˈtiːdiəs]	*a.* 单调乏味的，令人厌烦的(boring) 记 联想记忆：ted(看做 tea，茶) + i(我) + ous → 我一个人喝茶 → 单调乏味的 搭 a tedious debate 单调乏味的辩论；a tedious fellow 令人生厌的家伙 例 Professor Lee's lecture was so *tedious*. 李教授的讲座太乏味了。
charter [ˈtʃɑːrtər]	*vt.* 特许设立，给予特权(certify)；包租(车、船等) *n.* 纲领，宣言；宪章(constitution)；特许状 记 联想记忆：和 chart(*n.* 航图；图表)一起记 例 The states *chartered* manufacturing, baking, mining and transportation firms. 各州予以生产、烘烤、采矿和运输公司特许权。
forefront [ˈfɔːrfrʌnt]	*n.* 最前沿，最前线；中心(spotlight) 记 组合词：fore(前面) + front(前面) → 前面的前面 → 最前沿 例 I know many of you are already at the *forefront* of the workplace technology. 我知道你们很多人已经处于车间技术的最前沿。
spun [spʌn]	*a.* 拉成丝的 搭 spun glass 玻璃纤维
accessible [əkˈsesəbl]	*a.* 易接近的；可得到的(*available)；可进入的 例 Erosion on a hillside may make clay easily *accessible*. 山坡的腐蚀使人们可以轻易获得黏土。 派 inaccessible(*a.* 难到达的，不可及的)；accessibility(*n.* 可得到；易接近)
undertake [ˌʌndərˈteɪk]	*v.* 承担(take in hand)；进行，从事(engage) 例 The printer does not have the skills necessary to *undertake* large publishing projects. 这个印刷商不具备承接大规模印刷项目所需的技术。 派 undertaking(*n.* 事业；任务)

splash [splæʃ]	*n.* (报纸等旨在招徕读者的)重点文章；溅上的液体；(光、色等的)斑点 *v.* 溅，泼(dash) 例 Early advertisements were quite small and subtle, not the *splash* sheet whole page spreads of today. 早期的广告篇幅短小，也很精巧，不像如今整版的广告那样引人注目。 splash
weave [wiːv]	*v.* 迂回行进(swing)；编织(knit, interlace)；编造，编纂 *n.* 编法，织法 记 联想记忆：老板希望工人织(weave)好布赶快走(leave)人 搭 weave sth. together 将…结在一起 例 The history of baskets *woven* from strips of willow in the area can date back to the 18th century. 该地区用柳条编织篮子的历史可追溯到 18 世纪。 派 weaver(*n.* 织布者，织工)
gull [gʌl]	*n.* 鸥，海鸥 记 联想记忆：一只海鸥(gull)落在一只呆呆的(dull)公牛(bull)背上 例 Most *gulls* keep the nest area clear. 大多数海鸥保持鸟巢区域的清洁。
prose [proʊz]	*n.* 散文 记 联想记忆：p + rose(玫瑰) → 在散文中，玫瑰象征着美好的爱情 → 散文 例 Now Gertrude Stein is better known for her *prose* than for her poems. 现在格特鲁德•斯坦因的散文比她的诗歌更加有名。
flint [flɪnt]	*n.* 燧石，打火石 记 联想记忆：f + lint(看做 line，线) → 打火石产生的火光如同一条线 → 打火石 例 His eyes were as hard as *flint*. 他的眼神冷酷无情。
considerate [kənˈsɪdərət]	*a.* 考虑周到的，体贴的，体谅的(thoughtful) 例 What we need is a roommate who is neat and *considerate*. 我们需要一位爱整洁、为他人着想的室友。 派 consideration(*n.* 考虑；体贴)；inconsiderate(*a.* 不体贴的；未经考虑的)
subdue [səbˈduː]	*vt.* 制服，征服(conquer)；抑制，克制(感情) 记 联想记忆：sub(在…下面) + due(音似：丢) → 打得敌人丢盔弃甲 → 制服，征服 例 Snakes frequently *subdue* their prey by injecting poison. 蛇经常通过注射毒液来制服被捕食的动物。 派 subdued(*a.* 缓和的；被抑制的)
extension [ɪkˈstenʃn]	*n.* 延长(的期限)(postponement)；延伸(的部分)(*supplement)；电话分机，分机号码 例 The woman asked for an *extension* on the application deadline. 这个女子要求延长申请的截止期限。 参 extensive(*a.* 大量的，广泛的)

ceramic [sə'ræmɪk]	*n.* [常 *pl.*] 陶瓷器，陶瓷制品 *a.* 陶器的，瓷器的 记 联想记忆：c + era（时代，时期）+ mic → 古时中国以陶瓷而闻名 → 陶瓷器 例 Rockingham ware was one of the most important American *ceramics* of the nineteenth century. 罗金厄姆陶器是美国 19 世纪最重要的陶瓷制品之一。 参 metalwork(*n.* 金属制品); textile(*n.* 纺织品); handcraft(*n.* 手工)
reactor [ri'æktər]	*n.* 反应堆 记 联想记忆：react(反应) + or → 发生反应的东西 → 反应堆 搭 reactor pot 反应堆容器 例 After World War II, the US military sought other uses for nuclear *reactor* technology. 第二次世界大战后，美国军方探索核反应堆技术的其他用处。
adhere [əd'hɪr]	*vi.* 黏附，附着 (*stick); 坚持（cling); 遵守（observe） 记 词根记忆：ad(表加强) + her(黏附) + e → 黏附；坚持 搭 adhere to 坚持；遵守 例 Some of the sizable ice crystals *adhere* to each other to create a cluster of ice crystals or a snowflake. 一些大小相当的冰晶体黏附在一起，形成一簇冰晶体或一片雪花。 派 adhesion (*n.* 黏附；黏附力) adhere
token ['toʊkən]	*n.* 表示，标志，象征(symbol); 记号(mark); 信物; 代币; 礼券，代价券 *a.* 象征性的 记 联想记忆：拿走了(taken)代价券(token) 搭 token reward 象征性奖励 例 By the same *token*, the speech contest, I think, is a success. 出于同样的原因，我认为演讲比赛很成功。
startling ['stɑːrtlɪŋ]	*a.* 惊人的，令人吃惊的(astonishing) 记 来自 startle(*v.* 震惊) 例 Solar experts from around the world monitoring the Sun have made a *startling* discovery. 来自全球的太阳专家在观测太阳时有一个惊人的发现。
imperative [ɪm'perətɪv]	*a.* 迫切的，重要紧急的(urgent); 必要的(necessary); 命令的; 祈使的 *n.* 重要紧急的事，必要的事; 祈使语气(动词) 记 词根记忆：im(在…里面) + per(排列) + ative → 排列在里面的 → 迫切的; 必要的 例 With the gradual evolution of society, simple counting became *imperative*. 随着社会的逐渐演变，简单的计算变得必要了。

choreograph
[ˈkɔːriəɡræf]

v. 设计舞蹈动作，编舞

记 词根记忆：chor(跳舞) + eo + graph(写；图) → 画下跳舞的动作 → 设计舞蹈动作

例 She went back to her dance company to *choreograph* more dances. 她回到自己的舞蹈公司以编出更多的舞。

派 choreographic(*a.* 舞蹈术的，舞台舞蹈的)；choreography(*n.* 舞蹈编排)

---

applicable
[əˈplɪkəbl]

a. 可应用的，可实施的；适当的，合适的

记 来自 apply(*v.* 运用)

例 The new approach was widely *applicable* to all sorts of different problems. 这个新方法广泛应用于解决各种各样的难题。

---

prosper
[ˈprɑːspər]

vi. 繁荣，兴旺(flourish, thrive)；成功(succeed)

记 词根记忆：pro(在…前面) + sper(希望) → 希望就在前面 → 繁荣；成功

例 Over the next decades, the country will *prosper* and be strong. 再过几十年，这个国家会变得繁荣富强。

---

literature
[ˈlɪtrətʃər]

n. 文学；文学作品；文献

记 词根记忆：liter(文字) + ature → 文学；文学作品

搭 Nobel Prize for Literature 诺贝尔文学奖

例 Maria had the strongest influence on this period of American children's *literature*. 玛丽亚对这个时期的美国儿童文学影响力最大。

---

demanding
[dɪˈmændɪŋ]

a. 苛求的，难满足的(rigorous)；需要高的，费力的

记 来自 demand(*v.* 要求，需要)

例 His current schedule is also very *demanding*. 他当前的日程安排也非常紧张。

---

backhand
[ˈbækhænd]

n. 反手击球

例 After two weeks of tennis lessons, I think I finally managed to improve my *backhand*. 上了两周的网球课后，我觉得我的反手击球终于有进步了。

---

collapse
[kəˈlæps]

v./n. 崩溃，倒塌(crash)；虚脱

记 联想记忆：col + lapse(滑倒) → 一出门就滑倒，真让人崩溃 → 崩溃

例 Numerous houses *collapsed* as a result of the earthquake. 这次地震导致了无数房屋倒塌。

---

formation
[fɔːrˈmeɪʃn]

n. 形成，构成；形成物；(军队)编队

记 词根记忆：form(形式) + ation → 具有形式 → 形成，构成

例 I am reading an article about the *formation* of snowflakes. 我在读一篇关于雪花如何形成的文章。

29

radar [ˈreɪdɑːr]	*n.* 雷达 记 发音记忆: "雷达" 搭 on/off the radar screen 受/不受关注 例 The issue of terrorism is back on the *radar* screen. 恐怖主义这个问题重新受到人们的关注。
fascinating [ˈfæsɪneɪtɪŋ]	*a.* 迷人的, 醉人的(charming) 记 a fascinating shop window display 吸引人的商店橱窗陈列 例 Jane's novels provided a *fascinating* account of social life in seventeenth-century England. 简的小说生动地描绘了17世纪英国的社会生活。
catalyst [ˈkætəlɪst]	*n.* 催化剂, 触媒; 促使变化的人(或因素) 记 词根记忆: cata(在…下面) + lyst(分开) → 在下面起分解作用 → 催化剂, 触媒 例 He is dedicated to being a *catalyst* for innovation. 他致力于促进改革。 参 analyst(*n.* 分析家)
anomaly [əˈnɑːməli]	*n.* 反常, 异常; 异常的人(或物)(aberration, abnormality) 记 词根记忆: a(不) + nom(规则) + aly → 不合常规 → 反常, 异常 例 Weather *anomalies* in Indonesia caused a shorter dry season and damaged farm plants, threatening the supply of certain foods. 印度尼西亚的天气反常使得干旱期变短, 破坏了农作物, 从而威胁到某些食品的供应。
devour [dɪˈvaʊər]	*vt.* 狼吞虎咽地吃, 吞食(consume); 吞没, 吞噬(engulf); 如饥似渴地读 记 词根记忆: de(表加强) + vour(=vor 吃) → 狼吞虎咽地吃; 吞噬 例 It is not surprising that each whale *devours* more than one ton of krill daily. 每头鲸鱼一天要吞食一吨多磷虾, 这不足为奇。
sculpt [skʌlpt]	*vt.* 雕刻(carve) 例 The figures were *sculpted* from single blocks of marble. 这些雕像都是用整块大理石雕成的。 派 sculptor(*n.* 雕刻家); sculptural(*a.* 雕刻的, 雕刻般的)
magnify [ˈmæɡnɪfaɪ]	*vt.* 放大, 扩大(*increase); 夸大(exaggerate) 记 词根记忆: magn(大) + ify(使…) → 使…大 → 放大, 扩大 例 The dry summer has *magnified* the problem of water shortage. 干燥的夏季加剧了缺水的问题。 派 magnification(*n.* 扩大, 放大; 放大倍)

□ radar □ fascinating □ catalyst □ anomaly □ devour □ sculpt □ magnify

音频

词根、词缀预习表

gen	种属	genre *n.* 类型	vok	叫喊	provoke *vt.* 挑动，激怒
vor	吃	ivory *n.* 象牙	flex	弯曲	flexible *a.* 易弯曲的
son	声音	consonant *a.* 协调的	past	喂养	pasture *n.* 牧场
plac	平静的	placid *a.* 平静的	lat	搬运	relate *v.* (使)有关联
tang	触摸	tangible *a.* 可触摸的	caut	小心	cautious *a.* 小心的

---

melody
[ˈmelədi]

n. 旋律，曲调；(旋律简洁的)乐曲，歌曲
🔖 词根记忆：mel(快乐的) + ody(唱) → 快乐的歌声 → 旋律
📕 Ragtime is a kind of music that has a strongly syncopated *melody* and a regularly accented accompaniment. 拉格泰姆音乐有着强烈的切分旋律以及音调起伏均匀的伴奏。
📑 melodious(*a.* 声调优美的，悦耳的)

---

launch
[lɔːntʃ]

vt. 发动，发起(运动)；推出(产品)；使(船)下水；发射 *n.* 发射；(船)下水；(新产品)上市
🔖 联想记忆：边吃午餐(lunch)边谈论新产品的上市(launch)
📕 The United States government *launched* a series of weather satellites in 1966. 美国政府在 1966 年发射了一系列气象卫星。

---

formulate
[ˈfɔːrmjuleɪt]

vt. 阐明，确切表达(clarify, illuminate)；规划，构想；制定
🔖 词根记忆：form(形式) + ul + ate(使…) → 使具有形式 → 阐明
📕 Possible solutions to the problem are *formulated*. 解决这个问题的合理方案已经制定出来了。

---

genre
[ˈʒɑːnrə]

n. 类型(type)；流派(style)
🔖 词根记忆：gen(种属) + re → 类型；流派
📕 These writers can genuinely be said to have created a *genre*. 可以说这些作家真正创造了一个流派。

---

coarse
[kɔːrs]

a. 粗糙的(*rough)；粗俗的(vulgar)
🔖 联想记忆：coar(看做 coal，煤炭) + se → 煤炭是很粗糙的 → 粗糙的
📕 His *coarse* manners angered the teacher. 他粗鲁的举止让老师很生气。

---

pitch
[pɪtʃ]

n. 音高，音调；倾斜度；沥青，柏油；(板球、足球等的)球场 *v.* 定音高；投掷，扔；跟跄倒下；(船、飞机等)颠簸

例 A brass or woodwind player may hum while playing, to produce two *pitches* at once. 铜管或木管乐器演奏者可以在演奏时哼唱，同时产生两个音调。

参 pitcher (*n.* 大水罐)

millennium
[mɪˈleniəm]

n. [*pl.* millennia] 一千年，千禧年；(未来的)太平盛世

记 词根记忆：mill(千) + enn(年) + ium → 一千年

例 Over *millennia*, the sea has been getting saltier and saltier. 几千年来，海水变得越来越咸。

care
[ker]

n. 小心，谨慎(caution)；照看，照料；忧虑，焦虑 *v.* 关心，关怀；介意(mind)；担忧

搭 care for 喜欢；照顾

例 Many experts think that the government should take measures to improve medical *care*. 很多专家认为政府应该采取措施改善医疗状况。

参 fare(*n.* 费用)；mare(*n.* 母马)

ivory
[ˈaɪvəri]

n. 象牙；象牙制品；象牙色，乳白色

记 词根记忆：i + vor(吃) + y → 象牙

例 Today what little fossil *ivory* remains comes from Alaska! 如今出自阿拉斯加的象牙化石少之又少！

entail
[ɪnˈteɪl]

vt. 牵涉(involve)；使(某事物)必要，需要

记 联想记忆：en + tail (尾巴) → 被人抓住尾巴 → 牵涉

例 You should take a little while to think about what that would *entail* before making your final decision. 在做最后决定之前，你应该花点时间想想这会牵涉什么。

wrap
[ræp]

vt. 包，裹(make up, pack) *n.* 披肩，围巾；包装材料

搭 wrap up 顺利完成；be wrapped up in 专心致志于，完全沉浸于

例 I spent the whole weekend *wrapping* up the Christmas presents. 我花了一整个周末的时间来包圣诞礼物。// Are you ready to start studying for the test yet or to be *wrapped* up in that TV show? 你准备好开始复习考试了，还是要完全沉浸于那个电视节目？

ultraviolet
[ˌʌltrəˈvaɪələt]

a. 紫外(线)的

记 联想记忆：ultra(超出) + violet(紫罗兰，紫色) → 紫外(线)的

搭 an ultraviolet lamp 紫外线灯

例 Lichens are little affected by the strong *ultraviolet* rays in the mountains. 苔藓几乎不受山区强烈紫外线的影响。

league
[liːg]

n. 联盟，同盟(alliance)；等级，级别

记 联想记忆：那个联盟(league)里的成员都是同事(colleague)

例 When it comes to dancing, you are not in her *league*. 提到跳舞，你比她差远了。

consonant [ˈkɑːnsənənt]	*a.* 和谐的，协调的，符合的（harmonious）*n.* 辅音 记 词根记忆：con(共同) + son(声音) + ant → 同声的 → 协调的 例 The man is behaving with a dignity *consonant* with his rank. 此人举止得体，与其身份相符。
well-heeled [wel ˈhiːld]	*a.* 富有的，有钱的 记 联想记忆：well(好；很) + heeled(带着钱的) → 富有的，有钱的 例 It is well-known that *well-heeled* people might not be happy. 众所周知，有钱的人并不一定快乐。
binary [ˈbaɪnəri]	*a.* 二进制的；二元的；由两部分组成的 搭 binary arithmetic 二进制算术 例 As I know, most of the computers make use of the *binary* system. 据我所知，大多数电脑都使用二进制系统。
digitize [ˈdɪdʒɪtaɪz]	*vt.* 数字化 记 词根记忆：digit(手指，脚趾) + ize(动词后缀) → 用手指计数 → 数字化 例 Nowadays, *digitized* maps have been widely used among drivers. 如今，数字地图在司机中得到广泛应用。
subdivide [ˌsʌbdɪˈvaɪd]	*v.* 再分，细分 记 联想记忆：sub(在…下面) + divide(划分) → 再分，细分 例 Part of the classrooms in this building have been *subdivided* into students' dormitories. 这座大楼的一部分教室被隔开来做学生宿舍。
vibrant [ˈvaɪbrənt]	*a.* 振动的；活泼的，充满生气的 记 词根记忆：vibr(移动) + ant → 振动的 例 Please keep your cell phone in *vibrant* mode when the meeting is going on. 会议期间，请将手机调为振动模式。
pathetic [pəˈθetɪk]	*a.* 可怜的，引起怜悯的，令人怜惜的（pitiful） 记 词根记忆：path(感情) + etic → 让人产生感情的 → 可怜的，令人怜惜的 例 The little girl's miserable experience and her tears were *pathetic* to the audiences. 小女孩的悲惨经历和眼泪引起了观众的怜悯之情。
agitate [ˈædʒɪteɪt]	*v.* 鼓动，煽动（campaign）；激怒，使激动，使不安；搅动（液体等） 记 词根记忆：ag(开，驱动) + it + ate → 开走 → 鼓动，煽动 例 Nancy was *agitated* by her ex-boyfriend's appearance at the performance. 南希的前男友在表演中出现，这使她焦虑不安。 派 agitated(*a.* 焦虑不安的；激动的)；agitation(*n.* 焦虑不安；骚动)
generic [dʒəˈnerɪk]	*a.* 种类的，属的；一般的，普通的 记 词根记忆：gen(种类) + er + ic(形容词后缀) → 种类的，属的 例 Plastic Card is a *generic* term that is used to identify any of the various cards issued to cardholders. Plastic Card 是信用卡持有者拥有的任何信用卡的通称。

defiant [dɪˈfaɪənt]	*a.* 反叛的，挑衅的，公然违抗的 记 词根记忆：de(分离) + fi(=fid 相信) + ant(形容词后缀) → 不再相信的 → 反叛的 例 The local government received a *defiant* letter from the terrorists this morning. 今天早上，当地政府收到了一封来自恐怖分子的挑衅信。
placid [ˈplæsɪd]	*a.* 平静的，安静的；(指人、性情等)温和的，文静的 记 词根记忆：plac(平静的) + id → 平静的，安静的 例 After the heavy rain for the whole night, the lake restored its *placid* state as before. 在一整晚的大雨之后，湖水又恢复了往日的平静。
gloomy [ˈgluːmi]	*a.* 忧郁的，令人沮丧的；昏暗的，阴暗的，阴沉的 例 It was sunny ten minutes ago, but now it's *gloomy*. 十分钟前还是晴天，可现在天就阴沉沉的。
tangible [ˈtændʒəbl]	*a.* 可触摸的，可感知的；明确的，确凿的；有形的，实际的 记 词根记忆：tang(触摸) + ible(能…的) → 可触摸的 例 Any assumption cannot be included, and we can only accept *tangible* evidence. 任何假设都不能包括在内，我们只接受确凿的证据。
chronological [ˌkrɑːnəˈlɑːdʒɪkl]	*a.* 按年代顺序排列的，年代学的 记 词根记忆：chron(时间) + olog(y)(…学) + ical → 按年代顺序排列的，年代学的 例 Please arrange these books on the shelf in *chronological* order. 请按照年代顺序将书架上的书整理好。
extensive [ɪkˈstensɪv]	*a.* 广大的，广阔的；广泛的，大量的 记 词根记忆：ex(出) + tens(伸展) + ive → 伸展开的 → 广阔的 搭 extensive knowledge 广博的知识 例 The pavilion on the mountain top has an *extensive* view. 从山顶的凉亭可以看到大片景色。
provoke [prəˈvoʊk]	*vt.* 挑动，激怒，挑衅；引发，引起 记 词根记忆：pro(向前) + vok(叫喊) + e → 向前叫喊 → 挑动，激怒 例 Don't *provoke* the dog, or it will bite you. 你不要去招惹那条狗，否则它会咬你的。
diversify [daɪˈvɜːrsɪfaɪ]	*v.* (使)多样化，(使)不同 记 来自 diverse (*a.* 多样的，不同的) 例 I should try to *diversify* the hobbies to enrich my spare time. 我应该增加不同的兴趣爱好来丰富我的课余时间。

gloomy

tangible

□ defiant □ placid □ gloomy □ tangible □ chronological □ extensive
□ provoke □ diversify

overgraze [ˌoʊvərˈɡreɪz]	*v.* 过度放牧 例 In order to protect the grassland environment, it is not permitted to *overgraze*. 为了保护草地环境，不允许过度放牧。
ascertain [ˌæsərˈteɪn]	*vt.* 弄清，查明 记 词根记忆：as + cert(确定) + ain → 弄清，查明 例 The famous detective tries to *ascertain* every case. 那个知名侦探设法将每个案子都查个水落石出。
criteria [kraɪˈtɪriə]	*n.* [criterion 的复数形式]标准，准则(standard) 记 词根记忆：crit(判断) + eria → 根据一定标准做判断 → 标准，准则 例 The ability of making money is not the only *criteria* for success in life. 赚钱的能力不是衡量人生成功与否的唯一标准。
swoon [swuːn]	*vi./n.* 昏厥，昏倒(faint)；痴迷 例 Mary *swooned* into his arms when she knew her child had died in an accident. 当玛丽得知她的孩子在车祸中死去的消息时，便昏倒在他怀里。
monument [ˈmɑːnjumənt]	*n.* 纪念碑；历史遗迹 记 词根记忆：mon(提醒；警告) + u + ment(表物，名词后缀) → 提醒人们的东西 → 纪念碑 例 This is a *monument* to all those who died in the revolution war. 这座纪念碑是为所有在革命战争中献身的人而立的。
definite [ˈdefɪnət]	*a.* 清楚的，确切的(distinct, precise)；肯定的 记 来自 define(*v.* 下定义；限定) 例 He has no *definite* plans. 他没有明确的计划。 派 definitely (*ad.* 确切地；肯定地)；indefinitely (*ad.* 不定地，无穷地)；definition(*n.* 定义) 参 infinite(*a.* 无限的)
spring [sprɪŋ]	*v.* 跳跃(leap, jump)；涌现，突然出现；突然提出(或说出) *n.* 泉(stream)；弹簧，发条；春天；跳，跃 记 联想记忆：sp + ring(铃声) → 泉水叮咚似铃声 → 泉 搭 spring into action 突然行动起来；spring up 迅速出现；突然兴起 例 The dog *sprang* over the ditch. 狗跳过了沟渠。// Tears *sprang* to his eyes. 他眼里一下子涌出了泪水。
withdraw [wɪðˈdrɔː]	*v.* 取消(cancel)；撤销(retreat, recede)；提取(钱)；撤退，撤离 记 联想记忆：with(以，用) + draw(拉) → 用力拉 → 取消；撤销 例 Is it too late for me to *withdraw* from my music class? 我现在取消音乐课是不是太晚了？ 派 withdrawal(*n.* 收回；撤回；撤退)

30

patent	[ˈpætnt] *vt.* 取得专利权 *n.* 专利权(privilege) [ˈpeɪtnt] *a.* 有专利的；显而易见的
	例 He never tried to *patent* his discoveries or get wealth from them. 他从未试图为自己的发明申请专利或从中牟利。
	派 patentee(*n.* 专利获得者)
nourishment [ˈnɜːrɪʃmənt]	*n.* 营养，营养品
	例 Can plants obtain adequate *nourishment* from such poor soil? 土壤如此贫瘠，植物能获得足够的养分吗？
supplier [səˈplaɪər]	*n.* 供应者，供应商，供货方
	例 His company is a leading *supplier* of computers in this country. 他的公司是该国一家重要的电脑供应商。
congressional [kənˈɡreʃnl]	*a.* 立法机构的；代表大会的；国会的
	记 词根记忆：con(共同) + gress(行走) + ion + al → 走到一起去开会的 → 代表大会的；国会的
	搭 a congressional bill 国会议案；congressional representative 国会代表；a congressional committee 代表委员会；congressional record 国会报告
	例 William was given the *Congressional* Medal of Honor because of his great bravery during the war. 威廉因战争期间的英勇表现被授予国会荣誉勋章。
interfere [ˌɪntərˈfɪr]	*vi.* 干涉，干扰，妨碍(obstruct)
	记 词根记忆：inter(在…之间) + fer(搬运) + e → 在中间搬弄是非 → 干涉
	例 The government shouldn't *interfere* in private business. 政府不应该干预私营企业。// Skyscrapers also *interfere* with television reception. 摩天大楼也干扰电视信号的接收。
	派 interference(*n.* 干涉，干扰)
respective [rɪˈspektɪv]	*a.* 分别的，各自的
	记 词根记忆：re + spect(看) + ive → 从各个方向看 → 分别的，各自的
	例 Northerners and Southerners alike threw themselves into the task of supplying their *respective* armies. 北方人和南方人一样投身于各自军队的任务中去了。
	派 respectively(*ad.* 分别地，各自地)
monumental [ˌmɑːnjuˈmentl]	*a.* 纪念碑的；不朽的(enduring, imperishable)
	记 来自 monument(*n.* 纪念碑)
	例 The concert was a *monumental* tribute to the orchestra's first conductor. 这场音乐会是对管弦乐队首位指挥的不朽称颂。
remnant [ˈremnənt]	*n.* 残余物(remains)；布头；遗迹
	例 Most astronomers agree that comets are primordial *remnants* from the formation of the solar system. 大多数天文学家都认为彗星是太阳系形成时产生的原始残余物。

monumental

exotic [ɪɡˈzɑːtɪk]	*a.* 外来的，来自异国的(foreign)；奇异的(strange) 词 词根记忆：ex(出，外) + otic → 外来的 例 Leopold was to create a botanical garden where only *exotic* flowers grew. 利奥波德要造一个植物园，里面只种植异国花卉。
inherit [ɪnˈherɪt]	*v.* 继承，遗传而得 记 词根记忆：in + her(继承人) + it → 继承，遗传而得 例 She *inherited* all her mother's beauty. 她遗传了母亲所有的美丽之处。 派 inheritance(*n.* 遗传；继承物) inherit 财产继承人：小咪
rivalry [ˈraɪvlri]	*n.* 竞争(competition, contest)；敌对 记 来自 rival(*vt.* 竞争) 例 Due to the financial crisis, the *rivalry* between the two companies grew much more intense. 由于金融危机，两家公司之间的竞争更加激烈了。
protest	[prəˈtest] *v.* 抗议，反对(object) [ˈproʊtest] *n.* 抗议，反对 记 联想记忆：pro + test(测验) → 考试太多，遭到学生反对 → 抗议，反对 例 The students have been *protesting* against the increasing tuition. 学生们一直在抗议学费上涨。
flexible [ˈfleksəbl]	*a.* 易弯曲的；柔韧的(pliable)；灵活的，可变通的(elastic) 记 词根记忆：flex(弯曲) + ible(能…的) → 易弯曲的；柔韧的 例 Sea anemones have *flexible* bodies. 海葵的身体很柔软。// She can't offer the man a *flexible* schedule. 她无法给这个男子一个灵活的时间表。 派 flexibly(*ad.* 易曲地)；flexibility(*n.* 弹性；灵活性)；inflexible(*a.* 不易弯曲的；不屈的，顽固的)
sacrificial [ˌsækrɪˈfɪʃl]	*a.* 供奉(品)的，献祭(品)的，牺牲(品)的 记 词根记忆：sacri(神圣的) + fic(做) + ial → 为了神圣的事情而去做的 → 供奉(品)的，牺牲(品)的 搭 sacrificial ceremony 祭祀仪式 例 The temple located in the city is the largest surviving *sacrificial* temple in the world. 这座位于市里的庙宇是世界上现存最大的祭祀庙宇。 sacrificial
rebel	[ˈrebl] *n.* 叛逆者，起义者 [rɪˈbel] *vi.* 造反，起义，反抗 例 She insists she never started out to be a *rebel*. 她坚持认为自己并非一开始就是个叛逆者。 派 rebellion(*n.* 造反，叛乱)；rebellious(*a.* 造反的；反叛的，桀骜不驯的)
pendant [ˈpendənt]	*n.* 垂饰，下垂物 记 词根记忆：pend(悬挂) + ant → 悬挂着的东西 → 垂饰，下垂物 例 Some of the Pomo people's baskets were completely covered with shell *pendants*. 波莫人的一些篮子上挂满了贝壳垂饰。

30

tornado [tɔːr ˈneɪdoʊ]	*n.* 飓风，龙卷风（whirlwind, gale） 记 词根记忆：torn（转动）+ ado → 能转动万物的风 → 飓风，龙卷风 搭 tornado cellar 飓风避难地下室 例 The pressure at the center of a *tornado* is usually 13 pounds per square inch. 龙卷风中心的压力通常是每平方英寸 13 磅。
characterize [ˈkærəktəraɪz]	*vt.* 以…为特征；刻画（…的性格）（*distinguish, feature）；描述 例 The design elements have come to *characterize* the age of the skyscraper. 这些设计元素已成为摩天大楼时代的特征。
audience [ˈɔːdiəns]	*n.* 听众（listener）；观众（spectator）；读者（reader） 记 词根记忆：aud（听）+ ience → 听众 例 The target *audience* for this book was mainly women. 这本书的目标读者主要是女性。 参 inaudible（*a.* 听不见的）
pasture [ˈpæstʃər]	*n.* 牧场，草原（grassland, meadow）；[*pl.*] 生活状况；工作条件 *vt.* 放牧 记 词根记忆：past（喂养）+ ure → 喂养牛羊的地方 → 牧场，草原 搭 far-flung pasture 广袤的草原 例 The cattle were put out to *pasture*. 牛群放牧在牧场草地上。
delta [ˈdeltə]	*n.* （河流的）三角洲；希腊字母表的第四个字母 记 联想记忆：和 Delta Force（三角洲）一起记，著名 PC 射击游戏 搭 the Nile Delta 尼罗河三角洲 例 From north to south the *delta* is approximately 160km in length. 该三角洲从南到北约长 160 千米。
cram [kræm]	*v.* 填塞，塞满（pack）；匆忙准备，（为考试）临时死记硬背 例 The children all managed to *cram* into my car. 那些小孩好歹都挤进了我的车。
station [ˈsteɪʃn]	*n.* 所；站；台；岗位；身份，地位 *vt.* 安置；派驻，驻扎 记 relay station 中继站；space station 太空站 例 No one can leave his/her *station* without permission. 未经允许，任何人不得离开岗位。
precursor [priː ˈkɜːrsər]	*n.* 先驱；先兆，前兆；前身 记 词根记忆：pre（在…前面）+ curs（跑）+ or → 跑在前面的 → 先驱 例 Carbon compounds might have been the *precursors* of life on Earth. 碳化合物可能是地球上生命的最初形态。
teem [tiːm]	*vi.* 充满，到处都是（abound） 搭 teem with 富于，充满 例 The food was found to be *teeming* with bacteria. 发现食物满是细菌。

rank [ræŋk]	*n.* 等级(grade); 头衔(title) *v.* 属于某等级, 归类(class) 例 For a long time cotton *ranked* first among Alabama's crops, but today it accounts for only a fraction of the agricultural production. 长期以来, 棉花在亚拉巴马州的农作物中是最重要的, 但如今只占农业生产的一小部分。 派 ranking(*a.* 地位高的, 高级的 *n.* 排名)
alga [ˈælɡə]	*n.* [*pl.* algae] 藻类, 海藻(seaweed) 例 Today *algae* are used by humans in many ways; for example, as fertilizers, soil conditioners and livestock feed. 现在海藻被人类以多种方式使用, 比如, 用做肥料、土壤改良剂以及牲畜饲料。
devise [dɪˈvaɪz]	*vt.* 设计(contrive); 发明(invent); 想出(think out); 策划, 图谋 例 Every year the company *devises* a new plan. 公司每年都会提出一项新计划。
quit [kwɪt]	*v.* 停止; 放弃(abandon); 离开(depart); 辞(职)(abdicate) 例 She wants to *quit* her job in the chemistry lab. 她想辞去在化学实验室的工作。 派 quitter(*n.* 有始无终的人, 半途而废者)
hinterland [ˈhɪntərlænd]	*n.* 内地, 腹地(backland); 内地贸易区 记 组合词: hinter(=hinder 后面的) + land(土地) → 位于海岸后方的土地 → 内地, 腹地 例 Dunhuang is located in the *hinterland* of the great desert. 敦煌处于大漠腹地。
relate [rɪˈleɪt]	*v.* 叙述, 讲述; (使)有关联 记 词根记忆: re(又) + lat(搬运) + e → 又搬来 → (使)有关联 搭 relate to 与…有关; 涉及 例 The report seeks to *relate* the rise in crime to the increase in unemployment. 这份报告试图把犯罪上升与失业增加联系起来。 派 related(*a.* 有关的, 相联系的); unrelated(*a.* 无关的, 不相干的)
tutor [ˈtuːtər]	*n.* 导师; 家庭教师 *v.* 辅导(coach) 例 The man should hire a *tutor* before the midterm exam. 此人应该在期中考试前聘请一个家庭教师。 派 tutorial(*a.* 家庭教师的 *n.* 手册, 指南; 辅导课)
domain [doʊˈmeɪn]	*n.* 领土(territory); 领域(*field) 记 词根记忆: dom(统治) + ain → 领土; 领域 搭 public domain 公有土地 例 All these living things survived in the public *domain*. 这些生物在公有土地上存活了下来。

30

stellar [ˈstelər]	*a.* 星的，恒星的，星球的；精彩的；优秀的 例 She gave a *stellar* performance. 她进行了一场精彩的表演。
immutable [ɪˈmjuːtəbl]	*a.* 不可改变的，永恒不变的（*unchangeable） 记 词根记忆：im(不) + mut(变化) + able(能…的) → 不可改变的，永恒不变的 例 Adjustments in various places show that this standard is not *immutable*. 在不同地方所做的调整表明，这个标准并非是一成不变的。
marvel [ˈmɑːrvl]	*v.* 对…感到惊异，大为赞叹 *n.* 令人惊异的人（或事），奇迹（wonder）；不凡的成果 记 联想记忆：mar(毁坏) + vel(音似：well "好") → 遭到彻底的毁坏再重建好，真是奇迹 → 奇迹 例 We all *marveled* at his courage. 我们对他的勇气惊叹不已。 派 marvelous(*a.* 极好的，非凡的；不可思议的)
cannibalism [ˈkænɪbəlɪzəm]	*n.* 嗜食同类 记 来自 cannibal(*n.* 食人者，食同类的动物) 例 *Cannibalism* was widespread in the past among humans throughout the world, continuing into the 19th century in some isolated South Pacific cultures. 在过去，人类嗜食同类现象在全球都很常见，直到 19 世纪，南太平洋一些与世隔绝的文化里仍存在这一现象。
fraction [ˈfrækʃn]	*n.* 小部分，一点儿，少许（portion, segment） 记 词根记忆：fract(碎裂) + ion → 小部分 例 Only a small *fraction* of all the organisms that have ever lived are preserved as fossils. 所有曾经存活的生物中只有一小部分以化石的形式保存了下来。
syllable [ˈsɪləbl]	*n.* 音节 记 词根记忆：syl(=syn 一起) + lab(拿) + le → 把几个音拿到一起(构成一个音节) → 音节 例 Potato is stressed on the second *syllable*. Potato(土豆)一词的重音在第二个音节上。
grain [greɪn]	*n.* 谷物；颗粒(particle)；(木、织物等的)纹理；少量(a little) 记 联想记忆：食用谷物(grain)对大脑(brain)的发育十分有益 搭 go against the grain 违反常理；与…格格不入 例 There was at least a *grain* of truth in this. 这至少还有一点道理。 派 grainy(*a.* 颗粒状的)
diagram [ˈdaɪəɡræm]	*n.* 图表(graph, chart)；图解 记 词根记忆：dia(穿过) + gram(写；图) → 画带有交叉点的图 → 图表 例 The *diagram* indicates that there has been a sharp increase in unemployment rate for three months. 图表显示三个月来失业率急剧上升。 参 signal(*n.* 信号)；label(*n.* 标签)；mark(*n.* 标记)

scavenger ['skævɪndʒər]	*n.* 捡破烂的人，拾荒者(ashman)；食腐动物 记 来自 scavenge(*v.* 拾荒，捡破烂；以腐肉为食) 例 *Scavengers* play an important role in the ecosystem by contributing to the decomposition of dead animal and plant material. 食腐动物在生态系统中发挥着重要的作用，有助于动植物尸体的分解。 参 revenge(*vt.* 报仇)；avenge(*vt.* 为…报仇)
multitude ['mʌltɪtjuːd]	*n.* 大量，众多(a great number)；群众，民众；人群 记 词根记忆：multi(多)+ t + ude(表状态，名词后缀)→ 多的状态 → 大量，众多 搭 a multitude of 大量，许多 例 The man used to have a *multitude* of friends. 这个男人过去有很多朋友。// He preached to the assembled *multitude*. 他向聚集在那里的民众布道。
lost-and-found [ˌlɔːstənd'faʊnd]	*n.* 失物招领(处) 搭 lost-and-found case 失物招领箱 例 Is this the right way to the *lost-and-found* office? 去失物招领处是这样走吗？
statistic [stə'tɪstɪk]	*n.* 统计数字，统计资料；[*pl.*]统计学 记 联想记忆：stat(看做 state，国家)+ istic → 统计数字一般都由国家或政府部门完成并公之于众 → 统计数字 例 According to official *statistics* more than five thousand people were killed by the disease. 根据官方的统计数字，五千多人死于这种疾病。 派 statistician(*n.* 统计员，统计学家)
break [breɪk]	*v.* (使)破，裂，碎；使中止，打断，断绝；损坏，弄坏；违犯；打破(记录)；(天)破晓 *n.* 打断，中止；休息时间；破裂 搭 break away 突然挣脱；脱离，背叛；break...out into... 把…弄散组成… 例 He was *breaking* the speed limit. 他违章超速驾驶。// This is our last chance to take a *break* before finals. 这是决赛之前最后一次休息机会。
impart [ɪm'pɑːrt]	*vt.* 传授(initiate)；传达(convey)；给予(give) 记 词根记忆：im + part(部分)→ 把(知识等)分给某人 → 传授 例 Parents rarely encourage this instinctive attraction by *imparting* a knowledge of nature to their children. 父母很少通过给孩子传授自然知识来鼓励这种本能的吸引。
cautious ['kɔːʃəs]	*a.* 小心的，谨慎的(discreet) 记 词根记忆：caut(小心)+ ious → 小心的，谨慎的 例 Even the most *cautious* merchants became willing to risk shipping their goods over long distances. 甚至最谨慎的商人也愿意冒险长途运送他们的货物。 参 precaution(*n.* 预防措施；警惕)

30

substantiate [səb'stænʃieɪt]	*vt.* 证实，证明（*verify） 记 词根记忆：sub（在…下面）+ stant（站立）+ iate → 在下面给予支持，使屹立不倒 → 证实，证明 例 The hypothesis was *substantiated* soon afterward by the discovery. 这个假设后来很快就被这个发现证实了。 参 substantial（*a.* 可观的，大量的；实质的）；substantive（*a.* 实质性的，本质上的；重大的）
precious ['preʃəs]	*a.* 贵重的（valuable）；珍爱的（cherished） 记 词根记忆：prec（价值）+ ious → 有价值的 → 贵重的 例 I know this is *precious* to you, and I'll take good care of it. 我知道这对你来说很珍贵，我会好好保管的。 派 semiprecious（*a.* 半宝石的）
entrepreneur [ˌɑːntrəprə'nɜːr]	*n.* 企业家（businessperson）；承包人 记 词根记忆：enter（=inter 在…之间）+ pren（=prehend 拿）+ eur（表人，名词后缀）→ 在多人之间拿取的人 → 承包人 例 The owner of the company is an American *entrepreneur*. 这家公司的老板是一位美国企业家。 派 entrepreneurial（*a.* 创业的）

Victory won't come to me unless I go to it.
胜利是不会向我走来的，我必须自己走向胜利。

——美国女诗人 穆尔（M. Moore, American poetess）

词根、词缀预习表

fin	界限，范围	define *vt.* 定义	**vert**	转	divert *vt.* 使转向
vis	看	visualize *v.* 想象	**coil**	卷，盘绕	recoil *vi.* 弹回
voc	叫喊	vocal *a.* 声音的	**cor**	心	core *n.* 核心
pass	感情	passive *a.* 被动的	**vac**	空的	vacation *vi.* 度假
lus	光	illustrate *vt.* 阐明	**prim**	第一	prime *a.* 主要的

amount [ə'maʊnt]	*vi.* 总计（totalize）*n.* 总额（sum, quantity） 搭 amount to 总计… 例 By 1913 Seattle had 25 parks *amounting* to 1,400 acres. 到 1913 年，西雅图共有 25 个公园，总面积达 1400 英亩。
steer [stɪr]	*v.* 驾驶，为…操舵；引导（guide）*n.* 食用公牛 记 联想记忆：驾驶（steer）一艘钢铁（steel）打造的大船 例 Some of them *steer* by the position of the Sun. 他们中一些人通过观察太阳的位置来驾驶。 派 steering（*n.* 操纵，控制；转向装置）
violate ['vaɪəleɪt]	*vt.* 违反，违背；亵渎；侵犯，干扰 记 发音记忆："why late" → 违反制度迟到了 → 违反，违背 例 The advent of the troops *violated* the peace of the small village. 军队的到来打破了小村的平静。
interval ['ɪntərvl]	*n.* 间隔时间；间距（*distance）；幕间（或工间）休息 记 词根记忆：inter(在…之间) + val → 间距 搭 at intervals 不时；相隔一定距离 例 The earliest road markers were stones piled at *intervals*. 最早的路标是相隔一段距离摆放的石头。// Non-western music produces a greater number of distinct tones within the same *interval*. 非西方音乐会在同一个音程中产生数量更多的不同音调。
ponderous ['pɑːndərəs]	*a.* 笨重的（*heavy）；笨拙的（clumsy）；沉闷的（dull） 记 联想记忆：ponder(音似：胖的) + ous → 笨重的 例 These *ponderous* machines reaped the grain, and bagged it. 这些笨重的机器收割谷子，然后打包。

define [dɪˈfaɪn]	*vt.* 定义，解释(explain)；限定 记 词根记忆：de + fin(界限，范围) + e → 划定范围 → 定义，解释；限定 例 As the roles men and women played in society became more rigidly *defined*, so did the roles they played in the home. 随着男性和女性在社会中的角色限定越来越严格，他们在家庭中的角色也变得如此。 派 redefine(*vt.* 重新定义) 参 confine(*vt.* 限制)
visualize [ˈvɪʒuəlaɪz]	*v.* 想象，使形象化；构思 记 词根记忆：vis(看) + ual + ize → 使…看见 → 想象，使形象化 搭 visualize sb. doing sth. 设想某人做某事 例 An architect can take a look at a drawing and *visualize* the shape of the building. 建筑师看一眼设计图，就能想象出建筑物的形状。
frugal [ˈfruːgl]	*a.* 节约的，节俭的(thrifty)；少量的 记 发音记忆："腐乳过日" → 吃腐乳过日子 → 节俭的 例 *Frugal* people save cash in kitchen pots and jars. 节俭的人把现金存放在厨房的锅罐里。 派 frugality(*n.* 节省)
emerald [ˈemərəld]	*n.* 祖母绿，绿宝石；翡翠绿 例 She has an *emerald* ring. 她有枚绿宝石戒指。
reference [ˈrefrəns]	*n.* 提到，论及，涉及；引文，参考(书目)；介绍(人) 例 The interviewer said that my *references* were full of praise. 面试官说我的介绍信里满是赞誉之词。
vocal [ˈvoʊkl]	*a.* 声音的，嗓音的，发声的(phonic)；直言不讳的 *n.* [常 *pl.*] 歌唱部分，声乐部分 记 词根记忆：voc(叫喊) + al(形容词后缀) → 声音的，嗓音的 搭 vocal cords 声带 例 He has been very *vocal* in his criticism of the government's policy. 他对政府政策的批评一向直言不讳。 派 vocalize(*v.* 发声，说，唱；用言语表达)
passive [ˈpæsɪv]	*a.* 被动的，消极的(inactive)；被动语态的 记 词根记忆：pass(感情) + ive(形容词后缀) → 感情用事的 → 被动的，消极的 例 I urged my *passive* friend to be more assertive. 我鼓励消极的朋友要更加自信。
eschew [ɪsˈtʃuː]	*vt.* 避开，戒除，回避 记 联想记忆：es + chew(咀嚼) → 有意不咀嚼 → 回避 例 The movie star *eschewed* the personal questions during the interview. 这位电影明星在采访过程中回避了私人问题。

deductive [dɪˈdʌktɪv]	*a.* 演绎的，推论的 记 词根记忆：de(向下) + duct(拉) + ive → 向下拉的 → 一步步地向下推理的 → 演绎的，推论的 例 *Deductive* reasoning couldn't work all the time in debate. 在辩论中，演绎推理并不总是起作用的。 参 inductive(*a.* 归纳的)
illustrate [ˈɪləstreɪt]	*vt.* (用实例、图画等)说明，解释(clarify)；加插图于；显示…存在 记 词根记忆：il(向内) + lus(光) + trate → 向内投入光明 → 阐明 用图来表示… illustrate 例 These topics will be *illustrated* with computer animations to make explanations easy to follow. 这些话题将使用电脑动画来说明，这样解释起来比较容易理解。 派 illustration(*n.* 说明；例证；插图)
advisable [ədˈvaɪzəbl]	*a.* 可取的，适当的；明智的 记 联想记忆：advise(建议，劝告) + able(能…的) → 能听得进去的劝告 → 可取的 例 It's *advisable* to book the seat in advance. 提前订座是明智的。 派 advisability(*n.* 适当；明智)
hedge [hedʒ]	*n.* (矮树)树篱；防止损失的措施；防备 *v.* 用篱笆围；避免直接回答 记 联想记忆：草地边缘(edge)有一圈树篱(hedge)；h(看做 he，他) + edge(边缘) → 他站在边缘 → 防备 搭 hedge against 采取保护措施；hedge one's bets 两边下注；脚踩两船 例 Tony has invested some money overseas as a *hedge* against the rising inflation in the country. 托尼在海外投资了一些钱，以应对国内日益严重的通货膨胀造成的损失。
pyramid [ˈpɪrəmɪd]	*n.* 金字塔；锥体；金字塔形物；金字塔式的组织(或系统) pyramid 例 Plants are the basis of the food *pyramid* for all living things, even for other plants. 植物是所有生物，甚至其他植物的食物金字塔的基础。
liable [ˈlaɪəbl]	*a.* 有责任的，有义务的；易于…的 记 词根记忆：li(=lig 捆绑) + able(能…的) → 能被捆绑的 → 有责任的 搭 liable for 有法律责任的，有义务的；liable to 易于…的，有…倾向的 例 A wife is *liable* for her husband's debts, so the wife should and must take care of his money. 妻子对丈夫的债务是有法律责任的，所以妻子应该也必须看好他的钱。

31

exhort [ɪɡ'zɔːrt]	*vt.* 劝告，规劝，告诫 记 词根记忆：ex(表加强) + hort(催促) → 强烈地催促 → 劝告，规劝，告诫 例 No matter how his parents *exhort* John to study hard, he just doesn't like to go to school. 不管父母如何劝他要用功学习，约翰就是不喜欢上学。
disparate ['dɪspərət]	*a.* 迥然不同的 记 词根记忆：dis(不) + par(相等) + ate → 不相等的 → 迥然不同的 例 Her three evening dresses gave us quite *disparate* feelings. 她的三套晚礼服给了我们迥然不同的感觉。 派 disparately(*ad.* 迥然不同地)
homosexuality [ˌhoʊməˌsekʃuˈæləti]	*n.* 同性恋；同性恋行为 例 Don't despise *homosexuality*; it is allowed and legal in some countries. 不要歧视同性恋，在一些国家同性恋行为是被允许的，而且也是合法的。
vivify ['vɪvɪfaɪ]	*vt.* 赋予生气；使生动，使活跃 记 词根记忆：viv(生命) + ify(使…) → 赋予生气 例 Ivy's dubbing for the puppet *vivified* it. 艾薇为木偶配音，给它赋予了生气。
ignite [ɪɡ'naɪt]	*v.* 点燃，着火 记 词根记忆：ign(火) + ite → 点燃，着火 例 The little girl *ignited* the match, and she seemed to see her grandma. 小女孩点燃了火柴，在火光中她似乎看见了奶奶。
spurn [spɜːrn]	*vt./n.* 拒绝(refuse)；摈弃 记 联想记忆：那个人拒绝(spurn)给他的马用马刺(spur) 例 Mr. Smith *spurned* all the offers to travel around the world. 史密斯先生拒绝了所有的聘书，环游世界去了。
uproot [ˌʌp'ruːt]	*v.* 根除；(使)离开家园 记 联想记忆：up(向上) + root(根) → 使根向上，连根拔起 → 根除 例 The young girl *uprooted* herself from her hometown and went to Shanghai. 那个年轻的女孩离开家乡，去了上海。
retrieve [rɪ'triːv]	*vt.* 取回，索回；挽回，扭转颓势(regain)；检索 记 词根记忆：re(再，又) + triev(找到) + e → 再次找到原本丢失的东西 → 取回，索回 例 Don't forget to *retrieve* your card after you draw money from the ATM. 从自动柜员机上取完钱时，别忘了拿回你的银行卡。
tribute ['trɪbjuːt]	*n.* 贡品；颂词，称赞；悼念，致哀；(表示敬意的)礼物 记 词根记忆：tribut(给予) + e → 给予(皇室)的东西 → 贡品 例 All the people stood in silence and paid *tribute* to the people who died in the earthquake. 所有人都为地震中死去的人默立致哀。

expeditious [ˌekspəˈdɪʃəs]	*a.* 迅速而有效的，迅速完成的（efficient） 记 词根记忆：ex(出) + ped(脚) + itious → (很快)将脚迈出的 → 迅速而有效的 例 Let the children think by themselves; don't give them an *expeditious* response. 让孩子们自己去思考，不要很快就给他们答案。
repetition [ˌrepəˈtɪʃn]	*n.* 重复，反复；重复的事 记 来自 repeat(v. 重复) 例 We do not want to see a *repetition* of last month's tragic events. 我们不想看到上个月的悲剧重演。 参 repetitive(*a.* 重复的，反复性的)；repetitious(*a.* 重复的，反反复复的)
assail [əˈseɪl]	*vt.* 抨击，指责；猛攻；困扰 记 联想记忆：航行(sail)中一再遇到风浪的猛攻(assail) 例 It was too dark to recognize who *assailed* me last night. 昨天晚上天太黑了，我认不出攻击我的人。 派 assailant(*n.* 攻击者)
exemplify [ɪgˈzemplɪfaɪ]	*vt.* 是…的典型；例示，举例证明 记 联想记忆：ex(出) + empl(看做 empt，"取") + ify → 取出作为典型 → 是…的典型；例示 例 Tom's new album didn't *exemplify* his singing style. 汤姆的新专辑没有体现出他的演唱风格。
permanence [ˈpɜːrmənəns]	*n.* 永久，持久（durability） 记 词根记忆：per(始终) + man(拿住) + ence → 始终拿着 → 永久，持久 例 A child needs a family which keeps the sense of stability and *permanence*. 孩子需要一个稳定而持久的家。
recess [rɪˈses]	*n.* 休会期；休庭；暂停；凹室，壁龛 *v.* 宣布暂停，休庭 记 词根记忆：re(反) + cess(行走) → 反着走 → 暂停 例 One side of the baby's room has a *recess* designed to hold bookshelves. 婴儿房的一面有一个凹室，是用来放书架的。
gang [gæŋ]	*n.* 一帮，一伙；帮派 *vi.* 合伙(对付他人) 记 发音记忆："钢" → 大家团结成一伙才能铸就钢铁长城 → 一帮，一伙 搭 gang up 聚集，结成一伙；gang up on/against sb. 合伙对付某人 例 All the streetlights along this road were vandalized by a *gang* of youths. 这条路的所有街灯都被一帮年轻人故意弄坏了。
ingenious [ɪnˈdʒiːniəs]	*a.* (方法等)巧妙的；聪明的，机敏的（clever）；善于创造发明的；(物件等)设计独特的，别致的 记 词根记忆：in(里，内) + gen(产生) + ious(形容词后缀) → 头脑里产生很多点子的 → 聪明的；不要和 ingenuous(*a.* 坦率的，天真的)混淆 例 By such *ingenious* adaptations to specific pollinators, orchids have avoided the hazards of rampant crossbreeding in the wild. 通过这样巧妙地适应特定的传粉昆虫，兰花避免了在野外过度杂交的危险。 参 ingenuity(*n.* 独创力；聪明才智；心灵手巧)

31

elevate [ˈelɪveɪt]	*vt.* 举起，抬高(lift, raise)；提升(某人的)职位；使情绪高昂，使兴高采烈 记 词根记忆：e(出，外) + lev(举起) + ate(使…) → 举起，抬高 例 The birds began to *elevate* their nests in branches perhaps to avoid predators. 一些鸟把窝建在了高处的树枝上，可能是为了躲开捕食者。 派 elevation(*n.* 提高；海拔)；elevator(*n.* 电梯，升降机) 参 escalator(*n.* 自动扶梯)
replace [rɪˈpleɪs]	*vt.* 替换，取代(substitute)；归还，把…放回原处 记 联想记忆：re(重新) + place(位置) → 重新给个位置 → 替换，取代 例 The old one had to be *replaced* because it was imprecise. 原有的那个因为不精确只能被换掉。 // A: 200 to fix my computer? I thought you said you could do it for 50. B: I did, but it's not the keyboard after all. That's the major part inside the machine that will cost a lot more to *replace*. A: 修我的电脑要 200 美元？我以为你说的是 50 美元。 B: 我是这么说的，但是问题不在键盘。电脑内部的主要部分需要替换，这得花更多的钱。
twist [twɪst]	*v.* 缠绕，扭曲 (tangle, wind)；曲解，歪曲 *n.* 转折，突然变化；卷曲物 记 联想记忆：tw(看做 two，两个) + ist(表人) → 两个人扭打在一起 → 缠绕，扭曲 例 I heard Dan *twisted* his ankle during basketball practice yesterday. 听说丹昨天练篮球时把脚踝扭了。 // I think they *twisted* the meaning of what the mayor said. 我想他们曲解了市长的意思。 twist
extreme [ɪkˈstriːm]	*a.* 极度的(*intense)；极端的 *n.* 极端(uttermost) 搭 in the extreme 极其 例 I want to know how animals survive in *extreme* temperatures. 我想知道动物如何在极端温度下生存。 派 extremely(*ad.* 极端地，非常地)；extremity(*n.* 极端)
alphabet [ˈælfəbet]	*n.* 字母表 记 由希腊字母表中的头两个字母 alpha 和 beta 组合而成，列出从前到后所有的字母就成了字母表 例 There are dozens of *alphabets* in use today. 现在，人们使用的字母表有很多种。 派 alphabetical(*a.* 按字母顺序的；字母的)

contract	[ˈkɑːntrækt] *n.* 合同，契约（agreement, pact）
	[kənˈtrækt] *v.* 订合同；（使）收缩(shrink)；感染(疾病)，染上(恶习)
	例 In general, the *contracts* are often no more than verbal agreements. 一般而言，合同往往不过是口头协议。// The students paid for the meals they *contract* for. 学生们为订的饭付了钱。
	派 contraction(*n.* 收缩；压缩)

contract

divert	*vt.* 转移…的注意力，使分心(distract)；使娱乐(amuse, entertain)；使转向，使改道(或绕道)
[daɪˈvɜːrt]	记 词根记忆：di(离开) + vert(转) → 转移 → 转移…的注意力；使转向
	例 The first publisher to produce books aimed primarily at *diverting* a child audience. 最早的图书出版商出版图书的主要目的是娱乐儿童读者。

revoke	*vt.* 撤销，撤回；取消，废除
[rɪˈvoʊk]	记 词根记忆：re(回) + vok(呼喊) + e → 叫回 → 撤销，撤回
	例 John's work permit was *revoked* after six months. 半年之后，约翰的工作证被吊销了。
	参 provoke(*vt.* 激怒；挑衅)；evoke(*vt.* 引起)

melanin	*n.* 黑色素
[ˈmelənɪn]	例 The skin of the grass mouse contains lots of *melanin*, or dark pigments. 草鼠的皮肤中含有很多黑色素。
	参 melatonin(*n.* 褪黑激素)

zealous	*a.* 狂热的，热烈的，充满激情的(crazy)
[ˈzeləs]	记 来自zeal(*n.* 热情，激情)
	例 Wilton also made a lead equestrian image of King George III that was created in New York in 1770 and torn down by *zealous* patriots six years later. 1770 年，威尔顿在纽约也用铅制作了乔治三世王骑马的塑像，六年后被狂热的爱国者给捣毁了。

31

drawback	*n.* 缺点，障碍，不利条件(disadvantage, shortcoming)；退款，退税
[ˈdrɔːbæk]	记 组合词：draw(拉) + back(向后) → 拖后腿 → 缺点，障碍
	例 The main *drawback* of the new system is that it is hard to operate. 新系统的主要缺点是操作困难。

| **somewhat** | *ad.* 稍微，有点(*rather, slightly) |
| [ˈsʌmwʌt] | 例 What happened to him remains *somewhat* of a mystery. 他到底出了什么事，现在还是个谜。 |

perform	*v.* 做，履行，完成；表演，演出；执行(enact, execute)
[pərˈfɔːrm]	记 联想记忆：per(每) + form(形式) → 表演是各种艺术形式的综合 → 表演
	例 They *perform* their music as a means of individual self-expression. 他们把演奏音乐当做自我表现的一种方式。
	派 performance(*n.* 表演；执行；绩效)；performer(*n.* 表演者)

buddy
[ˈbʌdi]

n. 密友；搭档，伙伴（companion）

搭 buddy movie 伙伴电影

例 We'll use a *buddy* system throughout the ride. 我们将在整个驾车过程中实行一项结伴制。

swallow
[ˈswɑːloʊ]

v. 吞，咽；吞没，侵吞；轻信，轻易接受；默默忍受；使不流露，抑制 *n.* 燕子；吞，咽

记 联想记忆：s + wall(墙) + ow → 燕子在墙角垒窝 → 燕子

例 Chew your food properly before *swallowing* it. 吞咽食物之前要好好咀嚼。

pierce
[pɪrs]

v. 刺穿，刺破（*puncture, penetrate）；穿孔(于)，打眼(于)

记 联想记忆：r 从一片(piece)中穿过 → 刺穿

例 The bullet *pierced* the police officer's vest. 子弹打穿了警官的防弹衣。

recoil
[rɪˈkɔɪl]

vi. 弹回（rebound, resile）；后退，退缩；产生后坐力 *n.* 后退，退缩；反冲，(尤指枪炮的)后坐力

记 词根记忆：re(向后) + coil(卷，盘绕) → 卷回去 → 弹回

搭 recoil from doing sth. 对做某事畏缩不前

例 The girl *recoiled* in horror at the sight of the snake. 那个女孩一见到蛇就吓得后退了。

infrastructure
[ˈɪnfrəˌstrʌktʃər]

n. 基础设施，基础结构

记 词根记忆：infra(在…下面) + struct(建造) + ure → 建在下面的 → 基础设施，基础结构

例 Both the national and state governments developed transportation *infrastructure*. 国家和州政府都发展了运输基础设施。

engraving
[ɪnˈɡreɪvɪŋ]

n. 雕刻术，刻版术；版画（print）

记 来自 engrave(*vt.* 雕刻)

例 Thereafter *engraving* tended to lose ground to etching, which was a much easier technique for the artist to learn. 此后雕刻术让位于蚀刻术，因为对艺术家来说学会蚀刻术要容易得多。

vehicle
[ˈviːəkl]

n. 交通工具，车辆（carriage, conveyance）；工具，手段

记 词根记忆：vehi(运) + cle(表小东西，名词后缀) → 载人的东西 → 交通工具，车辆

例 Private companies built the roads, and collected fees from all the *vehicles* traveling on them. 私营企业修建了道路，向所有路过车辆征收费用。

meteorological
[ˌmiːtiərəˈlɑːdʒɪkl]

a. 气象学的；气象的

记 来自 meteorology(*n.* 气象学)

搭 meteorological data 气象数据；meteorological instrument 气象仪器

例 Scientists spent nearly ten years in studying the *meteorological* records. 科学家花了近十年的时间来研究这些气象记录。

core
[kɔːr]

n. 地核，果心，核心（center）；要点，精髓 *vt.* 去掉…的中心部分

记 词根记忆：cor(心) + e → 核心

搭 to the core 十足，透顶

例 Concern for the disadvantaged groups is at the *core* of the argument. 对弱势群体的关注是争论的核心。

360
□ buddy　　□ swallow　　□ pierce　　□ recoil　　□ infrastructure　□ engraving
□ vehicle　　□ meteorological □ core

strip [strɪp]	*vt.* 剥夺，剥掉(remove)；脱去…的衣服 *n.* 条，带状物；条纹 记 联想记忆：s(音似：死) + trip(旅行) → 死亡剥夺了人的尘世之旅 → 剥夺 搭 comic strip 连环漫画；strip away 揭掉，去掉；清除 例 The man was disgraced and *stripped* of his title. 他名誉扫地，被取消了头衔。
lace [leɪs]	*n.* 蕾丝；缎带；鞋带，系带 *v.* 用带子束紧 记 发音记忆："蕾丝" 例 Fine handmade *lace* is traditionally made of linen thread. 精美的手工蕾丝传统上由亚麻线制成。
kinetic [kɪˈnetɪk]	*a.* 运动的，运动引起的；动力学的 记 词根记忆：kine(动) + tic → 运动的 搭 kinetic art 动态艺术；kinetic molecular theory 分子运动论 例 Each fragment's immense *kinetic* energy was transformed into heat. 每个碎片产生的巨大动能被转化为热能。
premature [ˌpriːməˈtʃʊr]	*a.* 早熟的；过早的；(做法等)不成熟的，仓促的 *n.* 早产儿 记 联想记忆：pre(在…前面) + mature(成熟的) → 没有成熟的 → 早熟的 例 The conclusion seemed to be *premature* that Wilson would be absent from the election. 说威尔逊不会参加竞选好像有点言之过早。
vacation [veɪˈkeɪʃn]	*vi.* 度假 *n.* 假期 记 词根记忆：vac(空的) + ation → 有空 → 度假 搭 on vacation 度假；paid vacation 带薪假期 例 During summer *vacation*, many white-collar people would like to go abroad to take a *vacation*. 夏季假期时，很多白领都想去国外度假。
elementary [ˌelɪˈmentri]	*a.* 初级的，基础的(primary)；基本的；简单的 搭 elementary school 小学 例 You've made an *elementary* mistake. 你犯了一个根本性错误。
stationary [ˈsteɪʃəneri]	*a.* 静止的(immobile)；固定的，稳定的，不变的(*fixed, immovable) 记 联想记忆：station(位置) + ary → 总在同一个位置的 → 静止的 例 The truck collided with a *stationary* car. 卡车撞上一辆停着的小汽车。 参 stationery(*n.* 文具)
notation [noʊˈteɪʃn]	*n.* 符号，记号 记 词根记忆：not(知道) + ation → 使人知道的东西 → 符号，记号 例 She made a *notation* in the margin of the book. 她在书的空白处做了个记号。
prime [praɪm]	*a.* 主要的(*chief)；最初的(original)；最好的；首先的 *n.* 全盛时期，盛年 *vt.* 使准备好；事先指点 记 词根记忆：prim(第一) + e → 主要的；最初的 例 In the railroads' *prime* years, there were few individuals in the United States. 在铁路出现的初期，美国的人口还很少。 派 primer(*n.* 初级读本)

specific [spəˈsɪfɪk]	*a.* 明确的，具体的；特定的，特有的 记 词根记忆：spec(看) + i + fi(做) + c → 按照要求看着做 → 特定的，特有的 例 It's thought that *specific* genes in an animal's body have an influence on anxious behavior. 人们以为动物体内某些特殊基因对焦虑行为有影响。 派 specifically(*ad.* 明确地；特定地) 参 special(*a.* 特别的)；especial(*a.* 特别的，特殊的)
flock [flɑːk]	*vi.* 聚结，成群(gather) *n.* 群(group, crowd)；(鸟、兽等)一群；大量 搭 in flocks 成群结队 例 Many spectators *flocked* to the farm to catch a glimpse of Mrs. Stowe. 很多观众聚集到这个农场来一睹斯托夫人的风采。
nectar [ˈnektər]	*n.* 花蜜；甘美的饮料，琼浆玉液 记 原指希腊和罗马神话中如花蜜般的神酒，后引申为"花蜜" 例 Honeybees communicate the sources of *nectar* to one another by doing a dance in a figure-eight pattern. 蜜蜂通过跳 8 字舞来告知对方花蜜的出处。
enactment [ɪˈnæktmənt]	*n.* (法律、法案、法令等的)制订，颁布(*establishment)；法律，法规 记 词根记忆：en(进入) + act(行动) + ment → 制订行动计划 → 颁布 例 The *enactment* of this law will be a great step backward for the country. 这条法律的颁布对该国来说将是一大退步。
sluggish [ˈslʌɡɪʃ]	*a.* 行动迟缓的(slow)；不活泼的(lethargic, inactive)；无精打采的，怠惰的 记 词根记忆：slugg(=slug 懒散的) + ish → 懒散的 → 行动迟缓的 搭 a sluggish market 不景气的市场 例 I have taken some tablets that can make people feel rather *sluggish*. 我吃了一些会让人感觉不想动的药片。 派 sluggishness(*n.* 萧条；呆滞)
district [ˈdɪstrɪkt]	*n.* 地区，区域；管区，行政区(section, area, region) 例 In Austria, officials on the *district* level are not elected, but appointed by the state government. 在澳大利亚，区级别的官员不是选举产生的，而是由州政府任命。
obsolete [ˌɑːbsəˈliːt]	*a.* 过时的(old-fashioned)；废弃的 例 The astronomers consider the study of cosmic jets to be an *obsolete* scientific field. 天文学家认为关于宇宙喷射流的研究已过时。 obsolete
prestige [preˈstiːʒ]	*n.* 威望(influence)；声望(reputation) 记 联想记忆：pres(看做 president, 总统) + tige(看做 tiger, 老虎) → 总统和老虎两者都是有威望的 → 威望 例 No other colonial artisans rivaled the silversmiths' *prestige*. 在殖民地时期，其他工匠在声望上都无法与银匠相匹敌。

□ specific　　□ flock　　　□ nectar　　□ enactment　□ sluggish　　□ district
□ obsolete　　□ prestige

silicate	*n.* 硅酸盐
[ˈsɪlɪkeɪt]	搭 aluminium silicate 硅酸铝

moral	*a.* 道德(上)的，道义上的(ethical)；有道德的，品行端正的(good)；精神的
[ˈmɔːrəl]	(spiritual) *n.* [常 *pl.*]品行，道德(ethics)
	记 词根记忆：mor(风俗，习惯) + al → 全社会约定俗成的 → 道德(上)的
	例 The movie was considered an affront to public *morals*. 人们认为这部电影冒犯了公众道德。
	派 morality(*n.* 道德)；moralist(*n.* 道德说教者，卫道士)；moralistic(*a.* 是非观念坚定的；说教的)

pigeon	*n.* 鸽子
[ˈpɪdʒɪn]	记 发音记忆："批准" → 非常时期养鸽子也要经过批准 → 鸽子
	例 Seeds and fruit form the major component of the diet of *pigeons*. 鸽子的主要食物是种子和水果。

adaptive	*a.* 适合的，有适应性的
[əˈdæptɪv]	搭 adaptive behavior 适应行为
	例 Most *adaptive* behavior scales are completed by interviewing a parent, a teacher, or another individual who is familiar with the student's daily activities. 大多数适应行为量表是通过采访了解该学生日常行为的父母、老师或其他人来完成的。

raw	*a.* 生的，未烹制的；自然状态的，未经加工的；生疏的，无经验的；粗犷的；原始的，未经处理的
[rɔː]	例 This is only *raw* data and will need further analysis. 这只是原始数据，有待进一步分析。// What does the author imply about the *raw* materials used to make glass? 作者对制造玻璃的原材料有什么暗示？

negotiation	*n.* 商议，谈判(treaty)；流通
[nɪˌɡoʊʃiˈeɪʃn]	记 来自 negotiate(*v.* 商议，谈判)
	例 At the peace *negotiations* with Britain, Americans demanded, and got what they wanted. 与英国和平谈判时，美国人提出了要求并得到了满足。

delectable	*a.* 美味可口的(tasty, delicious)；有吸引力的；令人喜爱的，赏心悦目的
[dɪˈlektəbl]	记 联想记忆：d + elect(选) + able(能…的) → 在众多食物中能被选出来的 → 美味可口的
	例 It is extremely *delectable* for us to have accepted your application for the membership of Student Union. 我们非常高兴接受了你加入学生会的申请。

abrasion	*n.* 表面磨损
[əˈbreɪʒn]	记 词根记忆：ab(离去) + ras(擦) + ion → 擦掉 → 表面磨损
	例 *Abrasion* due to daily wear alters the surface features of beads. 日常佩戴导致的磨损改变了珠子的表面特征。
	参 abrasive(*n.* 磨料 *a.* 研磨的)

31

fiber

['faɪbər]

n. 纤维素；纤维制品；纤维

记 联想记忆：多食富含纤维素（fiber）的食物，有助于消化降火（fire）

搭 man-made fibers 人造纤维制品；muscle fibers 肌肉纤维

例 Dried fruits are especially high in *fiber*. 干水果的纤维素含量特别高。

派 fibrous(*a.* 含纤维的；纤维状的)

---

burrow

['bɜːroʊ]

v. 挖掘，挖地洞（dig, tunnel）；寻找，探索 *n.* 洞穴；地洞

记 联想记忆：借（borrow）钱买了把犁（furrow）来挖（burrow）地

例 The aardvark is a mammal that *burrows* into the ground to catch ants and termites. 土豚是一种哺乳动物，它们挖地洞捕食蚂蚁和白蚁。

---

regular

['regjələr]

a. 规则的，有规律的（orderly）；整齐的，匀称的；频繁的，经常的；正常的（normal）；经常的（usual）；正规的，正式的

记 词根记忆：reg(治理) + ular → 得到治理的 → 规则的，有规律的

例 They occur at *regular* intervals. 它们有规律地间歇发生。

派 regularity(*n.* 规律性；经常性；匀称)；regularly(*ad.* 有规律地；经常；匀称地)

---

sum

[sʌm]

n. 和，总数；金额，数额(*amount)；算术 *v.* 共计，合计，总计(total)

搭 in sum 总而言之；sum up 总结，概括

例 Ask them to work out a *sum*. 让他们算出总额。// We have *summed* up the most important single fact about it at this moment in time. 此时此刻我们已经及时地对与它相关的最重要的一条事实进行了总结。

派 summarize(*v.* 总结，概括)；summary(*n.* 总结，概括 *a.* 总结性的，概括的)

---

defecate

['defəkeɪt]

vi. 排便；澄清

记 词根记忆：de(向下) + fec(做) + ate(动词后缀) → 向下做 → 排便

音频

词根、词缀预习表

val	价值	validate vt. 使有效	leth	死，僵	lethal a. 致命的
vad	走	evade v. 逃避	par	安排	prepare v. 准备
leg	送	relegate vt. 使贬职	term	边界	determine v. 确定
crus	十字形	crusade n. 十字军(远征)	stant	站立	substantial a. 实质的
pos	放	propose v. 建议	viv	生命	revival n. 复兴

---

crust
[krʌst]

n. 地壳；外壳；硬的表面；(一片)面包片
记 联想记忆：这个铁制品的外壳(crust)上布满一层锈(rust)
例 The Earth's *crust* occupies less than 1% of the Earth's volume. 地壳在地球体积中所占的比例不到 1%。
参 mantle(n. 地幔)；core(n. 地核)

---

scholar
[ˈskɑːlər]

n. 学者(academician)；奖学金获得者
记 词根记忆：schol(闲暇) + ar(表人，名词后缀) → 学者(希腊语 schole 指"闲暇"，指一个真正的学者要有闲暇时间看书治学、思考问题、进行学术讨论。)
例 He was the most distinguished *scholar* in his field. 他是其领域中成就最为卓著的学者。
派 scholarly(a. 有学问的；学术的，学术性的)；scholarship(n. 奖学金)

---

validate
[ˈvælɪdeɪt]

vt. 使有效，使生效；证实
记 词根记忆：val(价值) + id + ate(使…) → 使有价值 → 使有效，使生效
例 These two great poems are believed to have been written some time between 800BC and 700BC, partly because the poems refer to the social conditions of that time, conditions that have been *validated* by the findings of archeologists. 这两首伟大的诗篇被认为是写于公元前 800 年到公元前 700 年间，部分原因是诗篇提到当时的社会状况，这些状况已被考古学家的发现证实了。
派 validation(n. 确认)

---

abort
[əˈbɔːrt]

v. (使)夭折，中止(计划等)(cancel)；使流产
记 词根记忆：ab(相反) + ort(=ori 升起) → 无法升起 → (使)夭折，中止(计划等)
例 They had no choice but to *abort* the project. 他们别无选择，只得中止该项目。

---

motive [ˈmoʊtɪv]	*n.* 动机，目的(incentive) *a.* 发动的；导致运动的 记 词根记忆：mot(移动) + ive → 有意向某处移动 → 动机，目的 例 He had an ulterior *motive* in offering to help you. 他主动提出要帮你是有私心的。
evade [ɪˈveɪd]	*v.* 逃避，回避(avoid)；躲开，避开 记 词根记忆：e(出，外) + vad(走) + e → 向外走 → 逃避，回避 例 Father felt humiliated, because his son *evaded* military service. 儿子逃避兵役让父亲觉得很丢脸。
credentialism [krəˈdenʃəlɪzəm]	*n.* 文凭主义 记 来自 credential(*n.* 资格证书)；cred(相信) + ential → 让人相信的东西 → 资格证书 例 This survey is to find out students' views on the aim of education, *credentialism* and the effects of *credentialism* on students' motivation of learning. 这个调查旨在了解学生对教育的目的、文凭主义，以及文凭主义对学生学习动机影响的看法。
arable [ˈærəbl]	*a.* 可耕作的，适于耕作的 *n.* 可耕地 记 联想记忆：ar(看做 art，技术) + able → 通过技术认定可耕 → 可耕作的 例 There will be no more *arable* land, if people cut trees in a destructive manner. 如果人类毁灭性地砍伐树木，就不会有更多的耕地了。
divine [dɪˈvaɪn]	*a.* 神的，神圣的；非凡的，超人的；极好的，极美的 *n.* 牧师 例 My brother and his wife had a perfectly *divine* time in Hawaii. 我哥哥和嫂子在夏威夷度过了一段极美好的时光。
relegate [ˈrelɪgeɪt]	*vt.* 使贬职，使降级；放逐，贬谪 记 词根记忆：re(向后) + leg(送) + ate → 向后送 → 使贬职，使降级 例 The former general manager has been *relegated*, so no one is afraid of him. 前总经理已经降职了，所以现在没人怕他。
vicious [ˈvɪʃəs]	*a.* 危险的，罪恶的；残酷的，凶残的；恶性的 记 来自 vice(*n.* 恶行，恶习；罪行) 例 A *vicious* look came to me, as I caught the thief. 当我抓住小偷时，有一束恶狠狠的目光向我看过来。
cohere [koʊˈhɪr]	*vi.* 连贯，一致；黏合(stick)；齐心协力，团结一致 记 词根记忆：co(共同) + her(黏附) + e → 黏在一起 → 连贯，一致 例 Tina's ideal opinion does not *cohere* with her companions' beliefs. 蒂娜理想的想法与她同事的信念不一致。
shrewd [ʃruːd]	*a.* 敏捷的，机灵的；精明的 记 发音记忆："熟的" → 对某事很熟，所以反应灵敏 → 敏捷的，机灵的 例 Although that *shrewd* businessman is very rich, he doesn't have a happy family. 那个精明的商人尽管腰缠万贯，却没有美满的家庭。

advantageous [ˌædvənˈteɪdʒəs]	*a.* 有利的 记 来自 advantage (*n.* 优势，有利条件) 例 Actually, the new house policy is still not *advantageous* to poor families. 实际上，新的住房政策对贫困家庭还是没有多大好处。
reiterate [riˈɪtəreɪt]	*vt.* 反复说，重申 记 词根记忆：re(再，又) + it(走) + erate → 反复地走 → 反复说，重申 例 Listen carefully, I just say once, no *reiterating*. 仔细听，我只说一次，不会重复。
monogamy [məˈnɑːɡəmi]	*n.* 一夫一妻制 记 词根记忆：mono(单个) + gam(婚姻) + y → 一夫一妻制 例 *Monogamy* is the basic rule among couples in most of the countries. 一夫一妻制是大多数国家夫妻间的基本规则。
tame [teɪm]	*a.* 驯服的；沉闷的，乏味的 *vt.* 驯化；控制并利用 例 Teddy is a *tame* bear, who can play the violin standing on the ball. 泰迪是一只被驯服的熊，能站在球上拉小提琴。
stigma [ˈstɪɡmə]	*n.* 污点，耻辱；烙印；特征 记 词根记忆：stig(刺) + ma → 留在名声上的刺 → 污点，耻辱
outlive [ˌaʊtˈlɪv]	*vt.* 比…长命，比…耐久 记 词根记忆：out(超过) + live(活着) → 比(某人)活得久 → 比…长命，比…耐久 例 The old in this small village *outlive* other old people elsewhere by more than 10 years. 这个小村里的老人要比其他地方的老人多活十多岁。
trivialize [ˈtrɪviəlaɪz]	*vt.* 使显得琐碎；轻视 记 词根记忆：tri(三) + via(路) + lize → 由一条路变成三条路 → 使显得琐碎；轻视 例 Just *trivialize* that problem, because we have something more important to discuss. 先别管那个问题，因为我们还有更重要的事要商量。
resent [rɪˈzent]	*v.* 憎恶，愤恨，怨恨 记 词根记忆：re(再，又) + sent(感觉) → 再一次痛彻心扉的感觉 → 憎恶，愤恨 例 There are some people *resenting* criticism. 有些人很憎恶批评。
degenerative [dɪˈdʒenərətɪv]	*a.* 衰退的，堕落的；(疾病等)变性的 例 The medicine didn't heal him, but produced a *degenerative* effect. 这药不仅没有治愈他，还使他的病情恶化了。
solemn [ˈsɑːləm]	*a.* 庄严的，严肃的；隆重的 记 词根记忆：sol(太阳) + emn → 太阳是神圣庄严的 → 庄严的 例 Once my father has a *solemn* look, there must be something bad. 父亲一旦表情严肃，就一定是有坏事发生。

32

□ advantageous □ reiterate □ monogamy □ tame □ stigma □ outlive
□ trivialize □ resent □ degenerative □ solemn

knit [nɪt]	*v.* 编结，编织；(使)紧密结合，使紧凑；(使折骨)愈合；皱紧，皱(眉) 记 联想记忆：骨头愈合(knit)之后，居然长出了一个节(knot) 例 The girl is *knitting* a scarf for her boyfriend. 女孩正在给她的男朋友织围巾。
glorify ['glɔːrɪfaɪ]	*vt.* 吹捧，美化(beautify)；赞美，赞扬(praise) 记 词根记忆：glor(光荣；赞美) + ify → 使光荣 → 美化；赞美 例 Futurism rejected all traditions and attempted to *glorify* contemporary life by emphasizing the machine and motion. 未来主义拒绝一切传统，并通过强调机器和运动来试图美化现代生活。
recount [rɪ'kaʊnt]	*v.* 讲述，描述(narrate)；重新清点(选票等)，重计 记 词根记忆：re(再，又) + count(数) → 再数 → 重新清点，重计 例 Tom was pleased to *recount* his adventures, because of the playmates' interest. 由于同伴们都感兴趣，汤姆很高兴讲述自己的冒险经历。
financial [faɪ'nænʃl]	*a.* 财政的，财务的，金融的 记 来自 finance(n. 财政，金融) 搭 financial aid 助学金，助学贷款；financial plan 金融计划 例 He received a loan of one million dollars from the bank to tide over his *financial* difficulty. 他收到了银行提供的 100 万美金贷款，以应对财务困难。 派 financially(*ad.* 财政上，金融上)
crusade [kruː'seɪd]	*n.* 十字军(远征)；斗争，运动(movement) *v.* 加入十字军，投身正义运动 记 词根记忆：crus(十字形) + ade → 十字军(远征) 例 They came to perceive the war as a kind of democratic *crusade* against southern society. 他们开始视战争为对抗南部社会的一种民主运动。
grasshopper ['græshɑːpər]	*n.* 蚂蚱，蝗虫(locust) 记 组合词：grass(草地) + hopper(跳跃者) → 草地上的跳跃者 → 蚂蚱
voltage ['voʊltɪdʒ]	*n.* 电压，伏特数 例 The *voltage* drop is the difference between the two readings. 电压降是两个读数之间的差额。
fundamental [ˌfʌndə'mentl]	*a.* 基础的，基本的，根本的 (*integral, *basic, *essential, *primary) *n.* 基本原则；基础 例 Society is undergoing *fundamental* change. 社会正在发生根本性变革。 派 fundamentally(*ad.* 根本上；完全地)
documentary [ˌdɑːkju'mentri]	*a.* 文件的，文献的；记录的，纪实的(realistic) *n.* 纪录片 搭 documentary material 文献资料 例 Most *documentary* filmmakers use neither actors nor studio setting. 大多数纪录片摄制者既不使用演员，也不用摄影棚的背景。// There was a really good *documentary* on television last night about bald eagles. 昨天晚上电视播放的一个纪录片很不错，是关于秃头鹰的。
merchant ['mɜːrtʃənt]	*n.* 商人 记 词根记忆：merc(交易) + hant → 进行交易的人 → 商人 例 Venice was once a city of rich *merchants*. 威尼斯曾是富商云集的城市。

reform
[rɪˈfɔːrm]

n./v. 改革，改造，革新（innovate）；改正，改过自新

记 词根记忆：re（再，又）+ form（形式）→ 给予新形式 → 改革，改造，革新

例 One of many *reforms* came in the area of public utilities. 众多改革中有一项涉及公共设施领域。

派 reformer（*n.* 改革者）

façade
[fəˈsɑːd]

n. 正面（front, face）；表面（surface）

记 联想记忆：faç（看做 face，正面）+ ade → 正面；表面

例 The sound of a person may give a clue to the *façade* or mask of him. 一个人的声音可能是揭露其虚伪外表的线索。

channel
[ˈtʃænl]

n. 频道；渠道，途径；通道（path, way）；海峡；水道，航道

例 Complaints must be made through the proper *channels*. 投诉必须经过正当途径进行。

vibration
[vaɪˈbreɪʃn]

n. 振动，颤动（libration, quiver）

搭 sympathetic vibration 共振

例 Seismic waves are *vibrations* caused by earthquakes. 地震波指地震产生的振动。

参 vibrancy（*n.* 活泼；振动）

perfect

[ˈpɜːrfɪkt]*a.* 完美的，理想的；完全的，十足的（*ideal, flawless）

[pərˈfekt]*vt.* 使完美，使熟练

例 Practice makes *perfect*. 熟能生巧。

派 perfection（*n.* 完美）；perfectly（*ad.* 完美地；完全）

soak
[soʊk]

v. 浸泡，浸湿，浸透

记 联想记忆：把衣服浸泡（soak）在肥皂（soap）水里

搭 soak up 吸收，吸掉；吸取，摄取

例 I'm so *soaked* from the rain. I'd go back to my room to change my clothes if there were more time before the performance. 雨水把我浇透了。演出前要是时间充裕的话，我就回屋换件衣服。

参 soap（*n.* 肥皂）

32

resume
[rɪˈzuːm]

v. （中断后）重新开始，继续（*begin again）

记 词根记忆：re（又，再）+ sum（拿，取）+ e → 再次拿起 → 重新开始

例 She left the hospital and *resumed* her classes. 她出院后，重新开始上课了。

propose
[prəˈpoʊz]

v. 建议，提议（suggest, project）；提名，推荐；打算，计划；求婚

记 词根记忆：pro（在…前面）+ pos（放）+ e → 放在前面 → 在行动之前提出 → 建议，提议

例 A number of schemes were *proposed* for sending pictures by Internet. 人们提出数个用网络发送图片的方案。

派 proposal（*n.* 提案，建议；求婚）

hardy [ˈhɑːrdi]	*a.* 强壮的(strong)；(植物等)耐寒的；能吃苦耐劳的 记 联想记忆：hard(硬的) + y → 强壮的；耐寒的 例 The dachshund is a *hardy*, alert dog with a good sense of smell. 达克斯狗是一种身体强壮且警觉的狗，其嗅觉非常灵敏。

hardy

acid [ˈæsɪd]	*n.* 酸，酸性物质 *a.* 酸的，酸味的；尖刻的，刻薄的 记 本身是词根，意为"酸" 例 It's the *acid* that eventually eats away the paper. 最后让纸腐蚀的正是酸。 派 acidic(*a.* 酸的，酸性的)；acidity(*n.* 酸度，酸性) 参 arid(*a.* 干旱的)；avid(*a.* 渴望的)；avoid(*v.* 避免)

hieratic [ˌhaɪəˈrætɪk]	*a.* 僧侣的；手写草书体的 *n.* 手写草书体 例 At that time *hieratic* was used only for religious texts. 当时手写草书体只用于宗教文本。

thorn [θɔːrn]	*n.* 刺，荆棘；带刺小灌木 记 联想记忆：t + horn(角) → 尖尖的角 → 刺，荆棘 例 *Thorns* are imitated as a means of protection by some of the tropical species. 某些热带物种通过长得像荆棘来保护自己。 派 thorny(*a.* 多刺的)

lethal [ˈliːθl]	*a.* 致命的(deadly)；破坏性极大的，极其有害的 记 词根记忆：leth(死，僵) + al → 致命的 例 Only about 25 kinds of scorpions are *lethal* to humans. 只有 25 种蝎子对人类是致命的。

grab [græb]	*v.* (随便或匆匆地)拿，抓，夺(clutch) 记 联想记忆：螃蟹(crab)用钳子抓(grab)人 例 I'll *grab* a snack at the break. 我会在休息期间吃点东西。

grab

contrary [ˈkɑːntreri]	*a.* 相反的，逆的 (in conflict with, opposite) *n.* 相反，反面 记 词根记忆：contra(反) + ry → 相反的，逆的 例 If there is no evidence to the *contrary*, we ought to believe the witness. 如果没有反面证据，我们就应该相信这个证人。

heritage [ˈherɪtɪdʒ]	*n.* 遗产(legacy)；传统(tradition) 记 词根记忆：her(遗传) + it + age(集体名词后缀) → 遗传下来的东西 → 遗产；传统 搭 World Cultural Heritage 世界文化遗产 例 African Americans were urged by Locke to promote their own cultural *heritage*. 洛克鼓励非洲裔美国人发扬他们自己的文化传统。

cavity [ˈkævəti]	*n.* 腔；洞，穴，窟窿(pit, crater)；龋洞 记 来自 cave(*n.* 洞穴) 搭 cranial cavity 颅腔；abdominal cavity 腹腔 例 There is a *cavity* in her tooth. 她牙上有个洞。

370
□ hardy　　□ acid　　□ hieratic　　□ thorn　　□ lethal　　□ grab
□ contrary　　□ heritage　　□ cavity

astronomical [ˌæstrəˈnɑːmɪkl]	*a.* 天文学的；极大的，庞大的 记 来自 astronomy(*n.* 天文学) 搭 astronomical observation 天文观测 例 The natural colors of *astronomical* objects can be captured. 天体的自然颜色是可以捕捉到的。// Most *astronomical* objects are very remote and the light we receive from them is rather feeble. 大多数天体距离我们都非常遥远，从它们那里接收到的光非常微弱。
likewise [ˈlaɪkwaɪz]	*ad.* 同样(similarly)；也 例 *Likewise*, when a football game was shown on the air, the stands were often empty because fans chose to watch the game at home. 同样，当足球赛被转播时，看台上往往是空的，因为球迷们选择了在家观看比赛。
exterior [ɪkˈstɪriər]	*a.* 外部的，外表的(outside) *n.* 外部，外表 记 词根记忆：ex(外) + terior → 外部的，外表的 例 In day-to-day use, the potter smoothed the *exterior* surface of the pot with wet hands. 在日常使用中，陶工用湿漉漉的手弄平了陶器的外表面。 参 interior(*a.* 内部的 *n.* 内部)
waste [weɪst]	*a.* 无用的，废弃的；荒芜的 *n.* 浪费；废料，废弃物 *vt.* 浪费，消耗 例 *Waste* water is pumped from the factory into the nearby river. 工厂里的废水被抽到了附近这条河里。// A: Growing up we never had a TV. Even now I'm not used to watching it much. B: Well, it's kind of like reading. Some things you find are great, but a few are real *waste* of time. You have to pick and choose. A: 我们从小就没有电视。现在我还不怎么习惯看电视。 B: 嗯，这有点像读书。你会发现有些内容不错，但是有些真的就是浪费时间。你要有所取舍。
fragment	[ˈfrægmənt] *n.* 碎片，断片(*debris, patch) [frægˈment] *v.* (使)分裂，成碎片 例 Snowflakes consist of broken *fragments* and clusters of adhering ice crystals. 雪花是由碎片和粘在一起的冰晶体构成的。 派 fragmentary (*a.* 由碎片组成的); fragmented (*a.* 成碎片的；四分五裂的)
eloquent [ˈeləkwənt]	*a.* 雄辩的(expressive)；动人的(appealing) 记 词根记忆：e + loqu (说) + ent (形容词后缀) → 能说会道的 → 雄辩的 例 Camen Lomas Garza's *eloquent* etchings depict primal images of the rural environment. 卡门·洛马斯·加尔扎生动的铜版画描绘了乡村地区的原貌。 派 eloquence(*n.* 雄辩；雄辩术)

32

fragment

eloquent

primate [ˈpraɪmeɪt]	*n.* 灵长类，灵长目动物；大主教 例 Although *primates* are well studied in comparison to other animal groups, several new species have been recently discovered. 尽管与其他动物群体相比，灵长目动物得到充分的研究，但最近也发现了一些新的灵长目动物。
supply [səˈplaɪ]	*n.* 供应(量)；储备；补给(品) *vt.* 供给，供应(provide)；满足(需要)，弥补(不足) 记 词根记忆：sup(在…下面) + ply(填满) → 在下面填满 → 供给 搭 supply sth. to sb. 给某人提供某物 例 Take water with you. It is available at the relay stations but it helps to have an additional *supply*. 带上水吧。虽然中继站供应水，但是多带些水总是好的。
reluctant [rɪˈlʌktənt]	*a.* 不情愿的，勉强的(unwilling) 记 发音记忆："驴拉坦克" → 不情愿的，勉强的 例 He was *reluctant* to admit he had done something wrong. 他不愿承认自己做了错事。 派 reluctance(*n.* 不情愿，勉强)
convey [kənˈveɪ]	*vt.* 运送，运输(carry, transfer, transport)；传达，表达(communicate, transfer) 记 词根记忆：con(共同) + vey(道路) → 共同用路 → 运送；传达 例 I would *convey* the sense of adventure that cavers share. 我将传达一下洞穴探索者所共有的冒险意识。
garb [ɡɑːrb]	*n.* 服装，装束(costume, dress) *vt.* 穿着，装扮 记 联想记忆：演出时间快到了，那个演员抓起(grab)演出服装(garb)匆匆赶到后台 例 A man in the *garb* of a priest went onto the stage and stood there silently. 一名穿着牧师服的男子走上了台，并默默地站在那里。
stem [stem]	*vt.* 阻止，遏制；起源 *n.* 茎，干(trunk) 搭 stem from 源于 例 Her dance *stemmed* from her soul and spirit. 她的舞蹈源自她的灵魂和精神。
naive [naɪˈiːv]	*a.* 天真的，率真的，质朴的(innocent, artless)；幼稚的，无知的，轻信的；稚拙派的 记 联想记忆：native(原始的，土著的)减去 t → 比土著人懂得还要少 → 天真的，质朴的；幼稚的 例 Her expression is neither *naive* nor instinctive. 她的表情既不天真也不是出于本能。// His works produced *naive* pictures of country life. 他的作品稚拙地描绘了乡村生活。

prepare [prɪˈper]	*v.* 准备，预备 记 词根记忆：pre(在…前面) + par(安排) + e → 提前安排 → 准备，预备 搭 prepare for 为…做准备，准备好 例 The final exam is approaching. Students are busy *preparing* for it. 期末考试快到了。学生们正在忙着备考。// This vein cutting is just one method the beetles used to *prepare* a safe meal. 切断叶脉只是甲虫用来准备安全食物的一种方法。// A: What sorts of changes are you thinking of? B: I'd like to make some changes in the way we *prepare* our food. A: 你在琢磨着怎样改变？ B: 我想改变我们做饭的方式。
underground	[ˌʌndərˈɡraʊnd] *ad.* 在地(面)下，往地(面)下；秘密地，不公开地 [ˈʌndərɡraʊnd] *a.* 地下的(subterranean, buried)；秘密的，不公开的 记 组合词：under(在…下) + ground(地面) → 地下的 搭 underground water 地下水；underground garage 地下停车场 例 Rescuers found victims trapped several feet *underground*. 营救人员发现有受难者被困在地下几英尺深处。 参 underestimate(*vt.* 低估)；understand(*v.* 理解)；undertake(*v.* 承担；从事)
alert [əˈlɜːrt]	*a.* 警觉的，警惕的(*vigilant, watchful) *vt.* 警告，提醒(*ware, remind) *n.* 警戒(期间)；警报 记 联想记忆：Red Alert"红色警戒"，20 世纪 90 年代风靡全球的电脑游戏 搭 alert sb. to sth. 使某人意识到某事；on full alert 全面戒备 例 I want something that will keep me *alert* in class. 我想要能让我在课堂上保持清醒的东西。// Fire ants make use of an alarm pheromone to *alert* workers to an emergency. 火蚁利用一种报警信息素来提醒工蚁有紧急情况。
genetics [dʒəˈnetɪks]	*n.* 遗传学 记 来自 gene(*n.* 基因) 例 He's interested in the *genetics* of mammals. 他对哺乳动物遗传学感兴趣。
creativity [ˌkriːeɪˈtɪvəti]	*n.* 创造力，创造性 例 Some jazz bands started relying on the *creativity* of the instrumentalists to attract audiences. 一些爵士乐队开始依靠乐器演奏家的创意来吸引听众。
girder [ˈɡɜːrdər]	*n.* 主梁，大梁(crossbeam) 记 联想记忆：gird(束，捆) + er → 支撑物 → 大梁 例 Wooden *girders* are more common than steel in light-frame buildings. 木梁比钢梁更常用于轻结构建筑物。

32

allergic [əˈlɜːrdʒɪk]	*a.* 过敏的，(对…)变态反应的；对…讨厌的 记 联想记忆：aller(看做 alert，警报) + gic → 皮肤发出警报 → 过敏的 搭 be allergic to 对…过敏；反感，厌烦 例 Something in this room is making my eyes itch. I must be *allergic* to something. 屋子里有东西让我眼睛发痒，我肯定是过敏了。// A: So are you going over to Cindy's after class? B: I'd like to. But she has a pet cat and I'm very *allergic*. A: 你下课后要去辛迪那里？ B: 我想去。但是她养了只猫，我很讨厌猫。

allergic

bold [bould]	*a.* 大胆的(*daring)；冒失的；粗(字)体的；醒目的 记 联想记忆：b + old(年长) → 年长的人胆大心细 → 大胆的 例 The employee paid for his *bold* remark by getting extra work. 这位员工为他的口无遮拦付出了加班的代价。
determine [dɪˈtɜːrmɪn]	*v.* 查明，确定(*dictate)；决心，决定(decide)；支配，影响 记 词根记忆：de + term(边界) + ine → 划定边界 → 确定 例 We *determined* to make our recycling program work. 我们决心让我们的再循环项目发挥作用。 派 determinant(*a.* 决定的 *n.* 决定因素，决定条件)；determination(*n.* 决心，决定)；indeterminate(*a.* 不确定的)
refreshing [rɪˈfreʃɪŋ]	*a.* 使人耳目一新的(*unusual)；提神的，使人精神振作的 记 来自 refresh(*vt.* 使精神振作) 例 It's so *refreshing* to feel the wind in my hair and the water on my face. 风吹拂着头发，水打在脸上，令人精神振奋。 参 refreshment(*n.* 提神之物；恢复活力；(常 *pl.*)饮料，小食)
vapor [ˈveɪpər]	*n.* 蒸气，潮气(steam) 记 发音记忆："外喷" → 蒸气向外喷 → 蒸气 例 A *vapor* may co-exist with a liquid (or solid). 蒸气可与液体(或固体)共存。 派 vaporize(*vt.* 蒸发，汽化)；vaporization(*n.* 蒸发，汽化)
asymmetrical [ˌeɪsɪˈmetrɪkl]	*a.* 不均匀的，不对称的(unbalanced, uneven) 搭 an asymmetrical haircut 不对称发型 例 Most people's faces are *asymmetrical*. 大多数人的脸是不对称的。
spawn [spɔːn]	*v.* 产卵(fertilize)；产生，促成(*create, bring forth) *n.* (鱼、蛙、贝等的)卵 记 联想记忆：大虾(prawn)产卵(spawn) 例 They could induce oysters to *spawn* not only in summer but also in fall. 他们可以诱使牡蛎不仅在夏天还能在秋天产卵。
epoch [ˈiːpɑːk]	*n.* 新纪元，时代(era) 记 联想记忆：听到时代(epoch)的回声(echo) 例 The death of the emperor marked the end of an *epoch* in the country's history. 皇帝驾崩标志着该国历史上一个时代的结束。

collision [kəˈlɪʒn]	*n.* 碰撞；冲突，抵触 记 来自 collide(*vi.* 碰撞；冲突) 搭 a collision of interests 利益冲突 例 The biggest surprise is the role of air resistance in cushioning the shock of *collision*. 最令人吃惊的是空气阻力在缓冲碰撞中所起的作用。
substantial [sʌbˈstænʃl]	*a.* 实质的；坚固的；可观的，大量的 记 词根记忆：sub(在…下面) + stant(站立) + ial(形容词后缀) → 站在下面的 → 实质的 例 The price reductions in winter clothes are pretty *substantial*. 冬季服装减价幅度非常大。 派 substantially(*ad.* 基本上，大体上；实质上；重大地) 参 substance(*n.* 物质)
revival [rɪˈvaɪvl]	*n.* 复兴，再流行(renewal)；复苏；苏醒，复活；(戏剧等的)重演 记 词根记忆：re(又) + viv(生命) + al → 生命重现 → 复兴 例 Our economy is undergoing a *revival*. 我们的经济在复苏。 派 revive[*v.* (使)苏醒，复活；(使)复苏；重新使用；重演]
galaxy [ˈgæləksi]	*n.* 星系；[G-]银河系，银河；群英 记 源自希腊文 galaxias，词根 gala 意为 "乳汁；乳状物"，古希腊人认为银河是天后赫拉的乳汁流淌而成的。 例 There are three main types of *galaxy*: spiral, elliptical, and irregular. 星系主要有三种类型：螺旋形、椭圆形和形状不规则的星系。
shovel [ˈʃʌvl]	*vt.* 铲；把…大量投入 *n.* 铲，铁铲；挖掘机 记 联想记忆：shove(推) + l → 把泥土推开 → 铲 例 It took some people several days to *shovel* the snow away from their houses. 这些人用了好几天的时间才把房前的雪铲除。
revise [rɪˈvaɪz]	*vt.* 修订，修改(change)；复习 记 词根记忆：re(又，再) + vis(看) + e → 反复看 → 修订，修改 例 Experience led workers to *revise* their techniques. 经验促使工人们改进了技术。 派 revision(*n.* 修订，修改；修订版)
spectacular [spekˈtækjələr]	*a.* 壮观的，引人注目的(striking, remarkable) *n.* 壮观的场面；壮观的演出 记 联想记忆：spectac(le)(景象；奇观) + ular → 壮观的，引人注目的 搭 a spectacular success 巨大的成功 例 The most *spectacular* thing about the sea cucumber is the way it defends itself. 海参最了不起的是它自卫的方式。

32

rely

[rɪ'laɪ]

vi. 依赖，依靠(depend)；信赖，信任

记 联想记忆：re(一再) + ly(音似：lie"撒谎") → 又撒谎了，不值得信赖 → 信赖

搭 rely on 依赖，指望；信任

例 You can *rely* on him to keep your secret. 你可以相信他一定会为你保守秘密的。//

A: I have to borrow enough money to buy a plane ticket. My archaeology class is taking a future trip to Alaska and I may never get another chance like this.

B: Look, when push comes to show, the people you can *rely* on most are your family.

A: 我得借足够的钱去购买机票。我的考古学课要组织去阿拉斯加实地考察，我可能再也不会有这样的机会了。

B: 你瞧瞧，到了关键时刻，最能依靠的还是你的家人。

Few things are impossible in themselves; and it is often for want of will, rather than of means, that man fails to succeed.

事情很少有根本做不成的；其所以做不成，与其说是条件不够，不如说是由于决心不够。

——法国作家 罗切福考尔德(La Rocheforcauld, French writer)

词根、词缀预习表

pond	权衡，考虑	ponder v. 思索	pon	放	postpone v. 延期
rog	要求	arrogant a. 傲慢的	tach	接触	attach vt. 连接
ten	握住	tenet n. 原则	lux	光	luxury n. 奢侈品
vig	生命	vigilance n. 警戒	compl	填满	accomplish vt. 完成
cis	切	precise a. 准确的	vast	空的	devastate vt. 破坏

---

caption
[ˈkæpʃn]

n. (图片等的)说明文字；标题；(电影)字幕 *vt.* 给(图片等)加说明文字

记 词根记忆：cap(抓住；采用) + tion → 为抓住人的注意力 → 给(图片等)加说明文字

例 If you don't understand the picture, take a look at its *caption* below. 如果你看不懂这幅画，就看看下面的文字说明。

---

prolong
[prəˈlɔːŋ]

vt. 拉长，延长(extend)

记 词根记忆：pro(向前) + long(长的) → 向前拉长 → 拉长，延长

例 There is no drug to help *prolong* one's life. 没有什么药能帮助人们延年益寿。

---

detract
[dɪˈtrækt]

v. 减损；贬低，诋毁

记 词根记忆：de(向下) + tract(拉) → 向下拉 → 减损；贬低

例 A little stain *detracts* from the value of the painting. 一块小小的污渍降低了这幅画的价值。

---

scourge
[skɜːrdʒ]

vt. 鞭笞；使受苦，折磨 *n.* 鞭子；祸害；鞭笞

记 联想记忆：要有足够的勇气(courage)，才能面对生活的折磨(scourge)

搭 the scourge of war 战争之苦

例 Little Tommy was *scourged* by guilt. 小汤米深受内疚的煎熬。

---

aberrant
[æˈberənt]

a. 越轨的；异常的

记 词根记忆：ab(离开) + err(徘徊) + ant → 脱离某物徘徊的 → 越轨的；异常的

例 Any *aberrant* behavior was forbidden between men and women in the old days. 在过去，男女之间是不允许有任何越轨行为的。

派 aberrance(*n.* 越轨)

---

disperse [dɪˈspɜːrs]	*v.* 分散，散开；疏散；散布 记 词根记忆：di(分离) + spers(散播) + e → 分开散播 → 分散，散开 例 The wind *dispersed* the clouds, and the Sun came out again. 风吹散了云，太阳又出来了。
compressible [kəmˈpresbl]	*a.* 可压缩的 记 联想记忆：compress(压缩) + ible(能…的) → 可压缩的；可压榨的 例 You should use *compressible* packing materials. 你应该使用可压缩包装材料。
ponder [ˈpɑːndər]	*v.* 思索，沉思 记 词根记忆：pond(权衡，考虑) + er → 反复权衡，仔细考虑 → 思索，沉思 例 I have given you so much time to *ponder*, and it's time for you to respond. 我已经给了你很长时间让你考虑，是你给出答复的时候了。
suspense [səˈspens]	*n.* 担心，焦虑；悬念，不确定 记 词根记忆：sus(在…下面) + pens(悬挂) + e → 下面挂着(一颗心) → 担心，焦虑；悬念，不确定 搭 keep...in suspense 保持悬念 例 Don't keep us in *suspense* any longer, or we are going to go crazy. 别再对我们保密了，否则我们就要疯了。
hesitant [ˈhezɪtənt]	*a.* 犹豫的，吞吞吐吐的，犹豫不定的 记 词根记忆：hes(黏附) + it + ant → 脚像被黏住了 → 犹豫的 例 It seems wrong, because mother was not a *hesitant* person before. 不对劲，妈妈以前不是一个说话吞吞吐吐的人。
immigrate [ˈɪmɪɡreɪt]	*vi.* 移居入境 记 词根记忆：im(向内) + migr(移动) + ate → 移居入境 例 The little boy *immigrated* with his mother to England when he was two, and he has never seen his father. 小男孩两岁时跟母亲移居英国，他从未见过父亲。
charismatic [ˌkærɪzˈmætɪk]	*a.* 蒙受神恩的；有超凡魅力的 记 词根记忆：charis(喜爱) + mat + ic → 深受神的喜爱的 → 蒙受神恩的 例 His *charismatic* personality made him have a lot of friends. 他超凡的个人魅力使他拥有很多朋友。
arrogant [ˈærəɡənt]	*a.* 傲慢的，自大的 记 词根记忆：ar(向) + rog(要求) + ant → 向他人要求的 → 傲慢的，自大的 例 Maggie is so *arrogant* that no one wants to make friends with her. 玛吉太傲慢，以至于没人想和她做朋友。
instantaneous [ˌɪnstənˈteɪnɪəs]	*a.* 瞬间的，即刻的，立即的 记 联想记忆：instant(立即) + aneous → 瞬间的，即刻的，立即的 例 I can't give you an *instantaneous* reply to this issue. 对于这个问题，我不能马上给你答复。

smear [smɪr]	*v.* 胡乱涂抹；弄脏；诽谤，诋毁 *n.* 污迹，污斑；诽谤，诋毁；(显微镜的)涂片 记 联想记忆：遭到诽谤(smear)，发誓(swear)要报复 例 Let's *smear* the paint with the brush on the wall. 让我们用刷子将油漆刷在墙上。
tenet ['tenɪt]	*n.* 原则；信条；教义 记 词根记忆：ten(握住) + et → 牢牢握住的东西 → 原则；信条；教义 搭 central tenets 主要信条 例 The basic *tenets* of the Christian faith are from the *Bible*. 基督教信仰的基本信条源于《圣经》。
wretch [retʃ]	*n.* 不幸的人；恶棍，无赖 记 联想记忆：这个可怜的人(wretch)把身上唯一值钱的手表(watch)弄丢了 例 The *wretch* who stole the purse didn't admit what he had done. 那个偷了钱包的无赖竟不承认他所做的事。
ruthless ['ruːθləs]	*a.* 无情的，残酷的，冷酷的；坚决的，彻底的 记 联想记忆：ruth(怜悯) + less(无) → 毫无怜悯之心的 → 无情的 搭 grim and ruthless 残酷无情 例 Jack believes that to succeed in this world he has to be *ruthless*. 杰克认为想要在这个世界获得成功，他就必须残酷无情。
cohabitation [ˌkoʊˌhæbɪ'teɪʃn]	*n.* 同居(现象或生活)，同住 记 来自 cohabit(*vi.* 同居，同住) 例 With the development of social values, *cohabitation* is being accepted by many young people. 随着社会价值观的发展变化，同居正越来越被年轻人所接受。
synonym ['sɪnənɪm]	*n.* 同义词 记 词根记忆：syn(共同) + onym(字，词) → 同义词 例 *Synonyms* are different words with almost identical or similar meanings. 同义词是指具有相同或相似含义的不同词汇。 派 synonymous(*a.* 同义的)
proportion [prə'pɔːrʃn]	*n.* 比例(ratio)；部分(share)；均衡，相称(equipoise) 记 词根记忆：pro + portion(部分) → 比例；部分 搭 out of proportion 不相称，不协调 例 Scientists have tried to quantify this *proportion* of the solar energy. 科学家们已经尽力量化太阳能的这部分。 派 proportional (*a.* 相称的，成比例的); proportionate (*a.* 相称的，成比例的); disproportionate(*a.* 不成比例的)
reddish ['redɪʃ]	*a.* 微红的 例 They often appear as a solid *reddish* mass when viewed from a ship or from the air. 从船上或空中看过去，它们通常像是一块微红的实体。

33

construction
[kən'strʌkʃn]
n. 构造, 结构(structure); 建筑物
搭 metal-frame construction 金属框架建筑
例 Because of the real risk of losing beaches, many geologists support a ban on all types of stabilizing *construction* on shore lines. 由于存在丧失海滩的实际风险, 很多地质学家对禁止在海岸线建造各类固定建筑这一法令表示支持。
参 instruction(*n.* 说明; 指令)

fellowship
['feloʊʃɪp]
n. 友谊(friendship); 奖学金(scholarship); 团体, 协会
例 I heard Joan was turned down for the graduate *fellowship*. 我听说琼未能申请到研究生奖学金。

architect
['ɑːrkɪtekt]
n. 建筑师; 设计师, 缔造者
记 词根记忆: archi(主要的) + tect(建造) → 主要的建造者 → 建筑师
例 He was one of the principal *architects* of the revolution. 他是那次革命的主要发动者之一。
派 architecture(*n.* 建筑学; 建筑风格; 结构); architectural(*a.* 建筑学的; 建筑方面的)

band
[bænd]
vi. 联合, 集合(unite, ally) *n.* 乐队; 群, 伙; 带; 波段, 频带
记 联想记忆: 乐队(band)成员手(hand)敲键盘
例 Local people *banded* together to fight the drug dealers. 当地人齐心协力打击毒品贩子。

gemstone
['dʒemstoʊn]
n. 经雕琢的宝石
记 组合词: gem(宝石) + stone(石头) → 宝石

flu
[fluː]
n. 流行性感冒
搭 come down with flu 感冒; catch a flu 得了流行性感冒
例 I've got a typical *flu*. I'm usually miserable for a week and it ends up ruining my holidays. 我患了典型流感, 一般要持续一个礼拜, 我的假期就这样毁了。

flu
COUGH
COUGH
COUGH

thesis
['θiːsɪs]
n. 论文(paper); 论题, 论点
例 Now that you've finished writing your *thesis*, do you think you will have time to sit back and take it easy? 既然你把论文写完了, 你觉得有时间放松吗?
参 hypothesis(*n.* 假设)

clan
[klæn]
n. 家族, 宗族, 氏族; 帮派
记 联想记忆: 家族(clan)的形成是因为上帝用泥土(clay)造出了人 → 家族
例 In history, *clan* warfare was always followed by great loss in both population and money. 历史上, 宗族冲突总是伴随着人力和财力的双重损失。

reflect	*v.* 反射，映现；显示，表明(mirror)；仔细考虑，深思
[rɪˈflekt]	记 词根记忆：re(向后) + flect(弯曲) → 向后弯曲 → 反射
	例 What an insulator does is *reflect* back the heat of burning fuel. 隔热装置的作用是反射燃烧燃料的热量。// Partly this decline *reflected* the low level of births during the depression and the war. 这种下降部分反映了大萧条和战争期间的低生育水平。
	派 reflection(*n.* 映像；反射；反映；沉思)；reflective(*a.* 反射的；沉思的)；reflector(*n.* 反光面；反光体)
	参 self-reflective(*a.* 自省的)
deserted	*a.* 荒废的，空无一人的(obsolete, void)；被离弃的，被遗弃的
[dɪˈzɜːrtɪd]	记 来自 desert(*v.* 放弃，遗弃)
	例 Downtown shopping areas became *deserted* after the war. 市中心购物区在战后被废弃了。
lobby	*n.* 休息室，大厅(hall)；游说团 *v.* 游说
[ˈlɑːbi]	记 联想记忆：在旅馆大厅(lobby)里数进进出出的人是他的爱好(hobby)之一
	例 Sally is waiting for the man in the *lobby*. 萨莉正在大厅等待那位男士。
probe	*v.* 探查，探测(explore)；盘问，追问 *n.* 探针；探测器(detector)；探索，调查
[proʊb]	记 词根记忆：prob(检测) + e → 探查；探索
	例 Hummingbirds have stiletto-like bills to *probe* the deepest nectar-bearing flowers. 蜂鸟用钻孔锥一样的喙来探进藏花蜜的花朵的最深处。
thereby	*ad.* 因此，从而
[ˌðerˈbaɪ]	例 Regular exercise strengthens the heart, *thereby* reducing the risk of heart attacks. 经常锻炼可以增强心肌功能，从而减少心脏病发作的危险。
toed	*a.* 有趾的
[toʊd]	例 Although they are quite slow in trees, three-*toed* sloths are agile swimmers. 虽然三趾树懒在树上活动迟缓，但它们在水里很灵活。
vigilance	*n.* 警戒，警惕(watchfulness, alertness, caution)
[ˈvɪdʒɪləns]	记 词根记忆：vig(生命) + il + ance → 有生命的，活动的 → 不睡 → 警戒，警惕
	例 The police cannot afford to relax their *vigilance* for a minute. 警方一刻也不敢放松警惕。
	派 vigilant(*a.* 警惕的，警觉的)
legislature	*n.* 立法机关，立法团体
[ˈledʒɪsleɪtʃər]	记 来自 legislate(*v.* 制定法律)
	例 Senators are designated by their respective state *legislatures* rather than by the voters themselves. 参议员由各自的州立法机构指定，而不是由选民自己决定。
gaseous	*a.* (含)气体的，气态的
[ˈɡæʃiəs]	记 来自 gas(*n.* 气体)
	例 Like Jupiter, Saturn is a large, *gaseous* planet. 土星与木星一样，是个巨大的气态行星。

33

□ reflect □ deserted □ lobby □ probe □ thereby □ toed
□ vigilance □ legislature □ gaseous

artificial [ˌɑːrtɪˈfɪʃl]	*a.* 人工的，人造的，假的（synthetic, false）；矫揉 造作的，假装 记 词根记忆：arti(技巧) + fic(做，制作) + ial(形 容词后缀) → 通过技巧制作的 → 人工的，人造 的，假的 搭 artificial intelligence 人工智能 例 *Artificial* flowers are used for scientific as well as for decorative purposes. 假花既有科学用途， 也有装饰用途。 派 artificially(*ad.* 人工地；人为地)
oxide [ˈɑːksaɪd]	*n.* 氧化物 记 词根记忆：ox(=oxy 氧) + ide → 氧化物 例 Even materials that are considered to be pure elements often contain a coating of *oxides*. 甚至那些被认为不含杂质的材料经常也含有一层氧化物。
precise [prɪˈsaɪs]	*a.* 准确的，精确的（*accurate, exact）；严谨的 记 词根记忆：pre(表加强) + cis(切) + e → 切得 很准 → 准确的，精确的 搭 to be precise 准确的说 例 The definition is not *precise*. 这个定义不准确。 派 precisely(*ad.* 精确地；正好)
debt [det]	*n.* 债务（liability）；负债情况；罪过 记 发音记忆："贷的" → 贷款 → 债务 例 He died heavily in *debt*. 他去世时负债累累。 派 debtor(*n.* 债务人，借方)
glean [gliːn]	*vt.* 点滴搜集，四处收集 记 联想记忆：在歉收的（lean）时候，四处收集 (glean)食物 搭 glean sth. from sb./sth. 从…找到… 例 Most of the methods he *gleaned* were of no practical use in our daily life. 他搜集的大多数方 法对我们的日常生活没有实际用处。 派 gleanings(*n.* 收集到的东西)
rural [ˈrʊrəl]	*a.* 乡村的，农村的（country）；田园的 记 词根记忆：rur(乡村) + al(…的) → 乡村的 例 Composers often write the music in *rural* communities. 作曲家们经常在 乡村创作音乐。
tally [ˈtæli]	*n.* 记录；账 *v.* (使)吻合 搭 tally method 记账方法；keep a tally of 记录 例 The cowboy kept a *tally* book for keeping count of the cattle. 牛仔保留 着一个计数簿来统计牛的数量。

□ artificial □ oxide □ precise □ debt □ glean □ rural
□ tally

curl [kɜːrl]	*v.* (使)卷曲，蜷缩(crouch) *n.* 卷发；卷曲状；卷曲物 搭 curl up 卷起，撅起；蜷曲，蜷缩 例 Although these bats sleep during the day, they do so *curled* up with their heads exposed to the sun. 尽管这些蝙蝠白天睡觉，它们还是会蜷起身体而将头暴露在阳光之下。 参 hurl(*v.* 猛投，猛掷；大声斥责)
snack [snæk]	*n.* 快餐，小吃，点心 搭 snack food 点心，小吃；snack bar 快餐店，小吃店 例 Usually I only have a *snack* at lunchtime. 我中午通常只吃点心。
pursue [pərˈsjuː]	*v.* 继续(hold on)；从事于(engage)；追击，追踪(*chase, trace)；追求 记 联想记忆：钱包(purse)被偷走了，赶忙去追踪(pursue) 例 Few predators fail to *pursue* such obviously vulnerable prey. 很少有食肉动物不能追捕到如此明显易受攻击的猎物。
broadcast [ˈbrɔːdkæst]	*v.* 广播，播放 *n.* 广播，广播节目 例 The school radio station *broadcast* free public service announcements. 学校电台免费播放公共服务通知。
angiosperm [ˈændʒioʊˌspɜːrm]	*n.* 被子植物 例 In the last class we talked about the classification of trees and we ended up with a basic description of *angiosperm*. 上一节课我们谈到了树木的分类，结束时我们对被子植物进行了概述。
cramped [kræmpt]	*a.* (空间)狭小的，狭窄的(limited)；受限制的；(字迹)密小难认的 记 联想记忆：在狭窄的(cramped)纸上写字显得密密麻麻的(crammed) 例 This place is nice but it seems pretty *cramped*. 这个地方不错，但似乎有点挤。
shellfish [ˈʃelfɪʃ]	*n.* 贝类，有壳的水生动物 记 组合词：shell(外壳) + fish(鱼) → 有外壳的鱼 → 贝类 例 *Shellfish* always attach themselves to huge rocks. 贝类经常将自己贴附在大石块上。
postpone [ˌpoʊstˈpoʊn]	*v.* 延期，推迟(delay) 记 词根记忆：post(在…后面) + pon(放) + e → 放在后面 → 延期，推迟 例 The meeting has been *postponed* until further notice. 会议推迟了，召开时间有待进一步通知。
trace [treɪs]	*vt.* 查出，找到；追溯；探索(explore)；描摹(describe)；追述 *n.* 痕迹(*imprint)；微量，少许；扫描线 例 The Anasazi family was matrilinear, that is, descent was *traced* through the female. 阿那萨奇人家庭是母系家庭，也就是说通过女性来传宗接代。 // Scientists believe that when the oceans were young, they contained only a *trace* of salt. 科学家们认为，海洋在最初形成之时只包含少量盐分。

33

gnaw [nɔː]	*v.* 啃，咬(nibble, bite) 搭 gnaw at sb. (长时间)折磨某人 例 The dog was *gnawing* a bone. 那只狗在啃骨头。 派 gnawing(*a.* 咬的；折磨人的)
petition [pəˈtɪʃn]	*n.* 请愿；请愿书；诉状 *v.* (向…)请愿，正式请求(appeal) 记 词根记忆：pet(寻求) + ition → 寻求(帮助) → 请愿；请愿书 搭 sign a petition 签请愿书 例 A *petition* signed by 3,000 hospital doctors was handed to the Minister of Health. 一份由 3000 名医院医生签署的请愿书被递交给了卫生部长。
arrange [əˈreɪndʒ]	*v.* 布置；安排，筹备(plan, prepare) 记 联想记忆：ar(表加强) + range(排列) → 有序地排列 → 布置；安排；筹备 例 Help the man *arrange* his trip. 帮助此人安排他的行程。 派 arrangement(*n.* 布置；安排，筹备)
tribal [ˈtraɪbl]	*a.* 部落的，宗族的；种族的(racial) 记 来自 tribe(*n.* 部落) 例 The girl married a *tribal* leader. 这个女孩嫁给了一个部落首领。
destination [ˌdestɪˈneɪʃn]	*n.* 目的地，终点(terminal, end) 记 联想记忆：destin(e)(预定) + ation → 预定的地方 → 目的地 例 The travel agency will provide a variety of *destinations* and flight times for their customers. 旅行社将为顾客提供到达许多目的地的多时段航班。
reconstruction [ˌriːkənˈstrʌkʃn]	*n.* 复兴；改造，再建 搭 a reconstruction period 复兴时期
attach [əˈtætʃ]	*vt.* 连接(fix, connect)；依附于(affix)；系，贴，连接；使依恋，使喜爱；认为有(重要性、责任等) 记 词根记忆：as + tach (接触) → 接触上 → 连接；依附于 例 They *attach* themselves to the mother's leg. 他们抱着母亲的腿。 派 attached (*a.* 附加的，附属的；爱慕的)；attachment(*n.* 附加装置；依恋)
seismic [ˈsaɪzmɪk]	*a.* 地震的，地震引起的；影响深远的，重大的 记 词根记忆：seism(震动) + ic → 地震的，地震引起的 搭 seismic waves 震波 例 *Seismic* social changes have occurred. 发生了重大的社会变革。
nonetheless [ˌnʌnðəˈles]	*ad.* 虽然如此，但是，依然 例 We're proud of our father's achievement, but *nonetheless* I sometimes find it useless. 我们为父亲的成就感到骄傲，但是有时候我发现那没什么用。

designate [ˈdezɪɡneɪt]	*vt.* 命名(name, appoint)；任命(nominate)；指明，标示 *a.* 已任命但尚未就职的 记 词根记忆：de + sign(标志) + ate → 给出标志 → 命名 例 The founders stipulated that senators be *designated* by their respective state legislatures. 建国者们规定参议员由各个州的立法机构指定。 派 designated(*a.* 指定的)；designation(*n.* 指定，委任；名称)
abstract	[ˈæbstrækt] *a.* 抽象的(unconcrete)；抽象派的(nonrepresentational) *n.* 摘要，梗概(summary) [æbˈstrækt] *vt.* 做…的摘要；提取 记 词根记忆：abs + tract(拉，抽) → 抽象的 搭 in the abstract 抽象地，理论上 例 I really like those *abstract* paintings we saw in our history class today. 我确实很喜欢今天历史课上看到的那些抽象绘画作品。 派 abstracted(*a.* 出神的，心不在焉的)；abstraction(*n.* 抽象概念；抽象；提取)
barren [ˈbærən]	*a.* 贫瘠的，荒芜的(*infertile, unproductive)；不结果实的，不(生)育的 记 发音记忆："巴人" → 巴蜀人民很勤快，不见荒芜景象 → 荒芜的 例 The farmer's soil was overworked and *barren*. 这个农民的土地由于过度使用而变得贫瘠。
sore [sɔːr]	*a.* 疼痛的(painful)；恼火的 *n.* 疮口，痛处 记 联想记忆：做家务(chore)做得腰酸背痛(sore) 搭 a sore point 心病，伤心事 例 My feet were *sore* after the walk. 我走路把脚都走疼了。
familiarize [fəˈmɪliəraɪz]	*vt.* 使熟悉 记 来自familiar(*a.* 熟悉的) 例 They don't *familiarize* themselves with the campus. 他们对校园不熟悉。
dragonfly [ˈdræɡənflaɪ]	*n.* 蜻蜓 例 As a seasonal symbol in Japan, the *dragonfly* is associated with summer and early autumn. 在日本，蜻蜓是季节的象征，与夏季和秋初联系在一起。
descriptive [dɪˈskrɪptɪv]	*a.* 描述性的，叙述的 例 *Descriptive* statistics involves tabulating, depicting, and describing collections of data. 描述性统计包括制表、图示以及描绘系列数据。
setting [ˈsetɪŋ]	*n.* 环境(surroundings)；背景(context)；布景；曲；底座，底板 例 *Setting* can influence literary style. 情节背景能够影响文学风格。
multiply [ˈmʌltɪplaɪ]	*v.* (使)增加(increase)；(使)繁殖(increase, breed)；乘 记 词根记忆：multi(多的) + ply(折叠) → 多重 → (使)增加；(使)繁殖 例 Mosquitoes seem to *multiply* quickly. 蚊子好像繁殖得很快。 派 multiplication(*n.* 增加；繁殖；乘法)

33

□ designate　　□ abstract　　□ barren　　□ sore　　□ familiarize　　□ dragonfly
□ descriptive　　□ setting　　□ multiply

385

luxury [ˈlʌkʃəri]	*a.* 奢华的 *n.* 奢侈，奢华；奢侈品 记 词根记忆：lux(光) + ury → 发出万丈光芒 → 奢侈品 例 Goods that had once been *luxury* items became part of everyday life. 曾经的奢侈品在今天已成为日常生活中的一部分。 派 luxurious(*a.* 奢侈的)
bellows [ˈbeloʊz]	*n.* 风箱 记 联想记忆：和 bellow(*v.* 吼叫)一起记 例 *Bellows* are widely used in industrial and mechanical appliances. 风箱广泛应用于工业和机械。
accomplish [əˈkɑːmplɪʃ]	*vt.* 达到(reach)；完成(complete)；实现(realize) 记 词根记忆：ac(向) + compl(填满) + ish → 给填满 → 完成 例 Human labor could still *accomplish* as much work as the first machines. 人工仍可以完成最初的机器能完成的工作量。 派 accomplishment(*n.* 成就)
ripe [raɪp]	*a.* 熟的；成熟的(*mature) 记 联想记忆：稻熟(ripe)米(rice)香 例 Is the fruit at the snack bar *ripe*? 小吃店的水果是熟的吗? 派 ripen[*v.* (使)成熟]
detective [dɪˈtektɪv]	*n.* 侦探，私人侦探 *a.* 侦探的 搭 a detective story 侦探小说 例 The *detective* solved a jewelry store robbery. 那位侦探破获了一起珠宝店抢劫案。
survive [sərˈvaɪv]	*v.* 幸免，幸存；继续存在，存货；艰难度过；比…长命 记 词根记忆：sur + viv(生活) + e → 活下来 → 幸存 例 The tailed toad may not *survive* without special efforts of conservationists. 没有生态环境保护者付出的特殊努力，有尾蟾蜍可能无法生存。 派 survival(*n.* 生存，存活；残存物)；survivor(*n.* 幸存者，生还者)
merchandise [ˈmɜːrtʃəndaɪs]	*n.* 商品，货物(goods, commodities) *vt.* 买卖，经营 记 词根记忆：merc(贸易) + hand(掌管) + ise → 掌管贸易 → 商品；买卖，经营 例 The Olympic *merchandise* plays a positive role in widely displaying the image of Olympic brands. 奥运商品在广泛展示奥运品牌的形象方面发挥着积极的作用。
temper [ˈtempər]	*n.* 脾气，性情(mood, disposition) *vt.* 缓和，调节(modulate, moderate) 记 联想记忆：情绪(temper)会影响体温(temperature) 例 An excellent movie can lessen the girl's *temper*. 一部好电影能缓和这个女孩的情绪。

devastate [ˈdevəsteɪt]	*vt.* 破坏，毁坏 (*ruin)；令人震惊，使难以承受 记 词根记忆：de (表加强) + vast (空的) + ate (使…) → 使完全变空 →破坏 例 The flood *devastated* countless houses. 洪水破坏了无数房屋。
counterpart [ˈkaʊntərpɑːrt]	*n.* 相对物；职位相当的人；副本 (duplicate) 记 词根记忆：counter (相反地) + part (部分) → 相对物 例 These female writers, like most of their male *counterparts*, were amateur historians. 这些女性作家和大多数男性作家一样，都是业余历史学家。
seal [siːl]	*vt.* 密封 (fasten, close)；确定，使成定局 *n.* 海豹；封铅，封条；印，图章 记 联想记忆：sea (海洋) + l (看做 love，爱) → 喜欢海洋的动物 → 海豹 搭 under seal 密封，加盖印信；set the seal on sth. 使某事万无一失，使某事圆满 例 The oven was *sealed* shut until the bread was fully baked. 烤箱一直密封到面包烤熟为止。

My fellow Americans, ask not what your country can do for you, ask what you can do for your country. My fellow citizens of the world: ask not what American will do for you, but what together we can do for the freedom of man.

美国同胞们，不要问国家能为你们做些什么，而要问你们能为国家做些什么。全世界的公民们，不要问美国将为你们做些什么，而要问我们共同能为人类的自由做些什么。

——美国总统 肯尼迪 (John Kennedy, American President)

33

□ devastate　　□ counterpart　　□ seal

Word List 34

词根、词缀预习表

reg	统治	regulate v. 管理，控制	sid	坐	subsidy n. 津贴
circ	环绕	circulate v. (使)循环	duct	拉	introduction n. 介绍；导言
pet	追求	perpetual a. 永久的	rupt	断裂	abrupt a. 突然的，意外的
secut	跟随	consecutive a. 连续不断的	rig	水	irrigate vt. 灌溉
limin	界限	eliminate vt. 消除	sat	充足	saturate vt. 使饱和

---

bounce
[baʊns]

v. (使)弹起，(使)反弹 n. 弹跳；反弹力
记 联想记忆：弹跳（bounce）起来掀翻一盎司（ounce）酒
例 The basketball *bounced* off the backboard and missed the basket. 篮球从篮板上弹了回来，没进篮筐。

bounce

---

graphics
['ɡræfɪks]

n. 图形，图像；制图法，制图学
记 词根记忆：graph(图) + ics → 图形，图像
搭 graphics card 显示卡
例 Students are asked to prepare texts and *graphics* separately and then combine them. 老师要求学生分别准备课文和图片，然后将两者合并起来。
参 mathematics(n. 数学)；physics(n. 物理学)

---

regulate
['reɡjuleɪt]

v. 管理，控制(control)；调整，调节(adjust)；校准
记 词根记忆：reg(统治) + ul + ate(动词后缀) → 管理，控制
例 They *regulate* their temperature by making a variety of internal adjustments. 它们通过各种体内调节来控制体温。
派 regulation(n. 规章，规则)；regulator(n. 调节器)；regulatory(a. 调整的)

---

pause
[pɔːz]

n./v. 中止，暂停(suspend)
搭 pause to do 停顿做…；give sb. pause 使认真考虑
例 A *pause* gives the listener time to think about what was just said. 停顿给听众时间去思考刚才所说的话。

---

elusive
[iˈluːsɪv]

a. 难以理解的，难懂的；难捕捉的；逃避的
记 来自elude(vt. 逃避；使困惑)
例 A solution to the problem of toxic waste is proving *elusive*. 事实证明，有毒废料这个问题难以解决。

---

giraffe [dʒə'ræf]	*n.* 长颈鹿 例 Although generally quiet and non-vocal, *giraffes* have been heard to communicate with various sounds. 虽然长颈鹿通常很安静，不发出什么声音，但有人听到过它们用各种声音进行交流。
limitation [ˌlɪmɪ'teɪʃn]	*n.* 限制（limit）；局限性 例 Any *limitation* to the king's power could be permanent. 对国王权力的任何限制都可能是永久性的。
assortment [ə'sɔːrtmənt]	*n.* 分类；各种各样（mixture） 例 She was dressed in an odd *assortment* of clothes. 她穿着奇装异服。
predominate [prɪ'dɑːmɪneɪt]	*vi.* 统治，支配，占优势（dominate） 记 联想记忆：pre(在…前面) + dominate(统治) → 处于统治地位 → 统治，支配，占优势 例 Red and yellow *predominate* in these flowers. 这些花朵主要的颜色是红色和黄色。 派 predominant(*a.* 支配的；主要的)
reproach [rɪ'proʊtʃ]	*v./n.* 指责，斥责，批评 记 联想记忆：只要有人靠近(approach)，她就大声斥责(reproach) 例 The girl *reproached* her brothers for ruining her birthday party. 女孩责备哥哥们把她的生日派对搞砸了。
gratify ['grætɪfaɪ]	*vt.* 使满意，使高兴；满足(愿望等) 记 词根记忆：grat(高兴的) + ify → 使高兴 搭 gratify sb.'s taste 满足某人的爱好 例 The parents were very *gratified* at their daughter's growth and progress. 父母对女儿的成长和进步感到非常满意。 派 gratification(*n.* 满足，满意；令人喜悦的事物)
pharaoh ['feroʊ]	*n.* 法老 记 发音记忆："法老" 例 A *pharaoh* in ancient Egypt is the counterpart of Emperor in ancient China. 古埃及的法老相当于古代中国的皇帝。
circulate ['sɜːrkjəleɪt]	*v.* (使)循环；(使)流通；(使)传播，(使)流传 记 词根记忆：circ(环绕) + ul + ate → (使)循环 例 You should keep your feet above your heart a few minutes each day to make blood *circulate* better. 每天应该坚持让脚高于心脏几分钟，这样能促进血液循环。
encroach [ɪn'kroʊtʃ]	*vi.* 侵占；侵蚀，蚕食(土地) 记 词根记忆：en(进入) + croach(=croch 钩子) → 使进入自己的钩子 → 侵占 例 After the old man died, the step-son *encroached* on his whole property. 老人死后，继子侵占了他的全部财产。

34

glorious [ˈɡlɔːriəs]	*a.* 壮丽的，辉煌的；光荣的；令人愉快的，极好的 记 发音记忆："可劳累死" → 光荣的桂冠来之不易 → 光荣的 例 There is always a *glorious* sunset near the sea by poets. 在诗人眼中，海边的日落总是极为瑰丽。 glorious
focal [ˈfoʊkl]	*a.* 焦点的；很重要的 记 来自 focus(*v.* 聚焦) 搭 focal point 焦点；集中点 例 Jack's *focal* point on study in this semester is to take TOEFL and get a high mark. 杰克这学期学习的主要目标是参加托福考试并拿到好成绩。
toady [ˈtoʊdi]	*vi.* 谄媚，奉承 *n.* 谄媚者，马屁精 记 联想记忆：今天(today)遇见一个马屁精(toady) 例 Tom hates to *toady* to others, but he does act as a *toady*. 汤姆讨厌去奉承别人，但他却是个实实在在的马屁精。
hearsay [ˈhɪrseɪ]	*n.* 谣言，传闻，道听途说 记 组合词：hear(听) + say(说) → 听说来的 → 谣言，传闻 例 It's just *hearsay*, so don't believe it. 这只是个谣言，所以不用相信。
ambivalent [æmˈbɪvələnt]	*a.* 对立的，感情矛盾的 记 词根记忆：ambi(双方的) + val(力量) + ent → 双方都有力量的 → 对立的，感情矛盾的 例 People often keep an *ambivalent* attitude towards white lies. 人们对善意谎言的态度通常都很矛盾。
momentary [ˈmoʊmənteri]	*a.* 片刻的，瞬间的，暂时的(temporary) 例 The criminal had a *momentary* hesitation, before he answered the question. 罪犯在回答问题之前，有片刻的迟疑。
lofty [ˈlɔːfti]	*a.* 高耸的；崇高的；高傲的 记 联想记忆：loft(阁楼) + y → 阁楼一般都位于房子的较高处 → 高耸的 例 The mountain climbers are going to conquer this *lofty* mountain. 登山者将要征服这座高山。
scrupulous [ˈskruːpjələs]	*a.* 多顾虑的，谨慎的；一丝不苟的，严谨的；审慎正直的，恪守道德规范的 记 联想记忆：scrup(le)(顾虑，顾忌) + ul + ous(多…的) → 多顾虑的，谨慎的 例 This job requires someone very *scrupulous* and careful. 这个工作需要非常谨慎且细心的人来做。
nimble [ˈnɪmbl]	*a.* 敏捷的，灵活的(agile, deft) 记 联想记忆：猴子的四肢(limb)很敏捷(nimble) 例 The team needs a leader who has a *nimble* mind. 这个团队需要一个头脑灵活的队长。

□ glorious □ focal □ toady □ hearsay □ ambivalent □ momentary
□ lofty □ scrupulous □ nimble

perpetual [pər'petʃuəl]	*a.* 连续不断的；永久的，长期的 记 词根记忆：per(贯穿) + pet(追求) + ual → 始终追求的 → 连续不断的 例 The *perpetual* snow of the Arctic began to melt. 北极终年不化的积雪开始融化了。
antecedent [ˌæntɪ'siːdnt]	*n.* 祖先，先辈 *a.* 先行的 记 词根记忆：ante(在…前面) + ced(走) + ent → 走在前面的 → 先行的 例 It is a great curiosity that who is human being's *antecedent* on earth. 人们一直很好奇，到底谁才是人类的祖先。
extinguish [ɪk'stɪŋgwɪʃ]	*vt.* 熄灭，扑灭；消灭，毁灭，使破灭 记 词根记忆：ex(没有) + ting(刺) + uish → 用针刺使没有 → 熄灭，扑灭；消灭 例 Please *extinguish* your cigarette, because this is a non-smoking zone. 请将烟熄灭，这是无烟区。
dote [dəʊt]	*vi.* 溺爱(spoil) 记 联想记忆：溺爱(dote)就是集万千宠爱于一点(dot)，而不顾其他 搭 dote on/upon 溺爱，宠爱 例 It is common that grandparents *dote* on their grandchildren. 爷爷奶奶溺爱孙子孙女是很平常的事。
consecutive [kən'sekjətɪv]	*a.* 连续不断的，连贯的 记 词根记忆：con(共同) + secut(跟随) + ive → 一个接一个的 → 连续不断的 例 I am very tired, because this is the third *consecutive* weekend that I worked overtime. 我实在太累了，因为我已经连续三个周末加班了。
liberal ['lɪbərəl]	*a.* 自由的，开明的；慷慨的；不严格的；人文(教育)的 记 词根记忆：liber(自由) + al → 自由的 例 Tom's *liberal* thoughts brought him much inspiration. 汤姆自由的思想为他带来许多灵感。
rental ['rentl]	*a.* 租用的；出租(业)的 *n.* 租金额；租赁，出租 搭 rental service 出租服务 例 I'll get in contact with a *rental* house company to rent an apartment. 我要联系一家房屋租赁公司租一间公寓。
skeletal ['skelətl]	*a.* 骨骼的，骸骨的；梗概的；轮廓的 记 来自 skeleton(*n.* 骨骼；梗概；轮廓) 例 I have written only a *skeletal* plot for the book. 那本书我目前只写了一个情节梗概。
tough [tʌf]	*a.* 坚韧的；棘手的，困难的(hard)；强健的，吃苦耐劳的；粗暴的(rough)；严格的；(肉等食物)老的 记 发音记忆："塔夫" → 像塔一样的壮夫 → 强健的 搭 a tough job 棘手的工作；tough luck 真倒霉 例 He's as *tough* as nails — a good man to have on the mountain rescue team. 他很能吃苦——是山区营救队的得力成员。 参 rough(*a.* 粗糙的；粗暴的)

34

rental

clump [klʌmp]	*n.* 丛，簇，束；块，团；群，组 *v.* 聚集，成群(cluster)；以沉重的脚步行走 例 He got a *clump* of soil from the edge of a cow pasture. 他从奶牛牧场的边缘处取了一块土。
poetry [ˈpoʊətri]	*n.* 诗歌；诗集；诗意 记 来自 poet(*n.* 诗人) 搭 modern poetry 现代诗 例 He knows how to appreciate *poetry*. 他知道如何欣赏诗歌。
repertoire [ˈrepərtwɑːr]	*n.* (剧团等的)常备剧目，保留剧目；(剧团、演员等的)可表演节目；全部才能 记 词根记忆：re(再，又) + pert(带) + oire → 反复带着的剧目 → (剧团等)的常备剧目 例 All teachers have a variety of techniques and activities that they regularly use — their *repertoire*. 所有老师都有着多种常用的讲课技巧和课堂活动，这是他们的常备技能。
imitate [ˈɪmɪteɪt]	*vt.* 模仿，效仿(*copy)；仿制，仿造 记 词根记忆：imit(模仿) + ate(动词后缀) → 模仿，效仿 例 The author indicates that children *imitate* their parents. 作者指出儿童模仿其父母。 // He had been trained to *imitate* the artist's style. 他受过训练去模仿这个艺术家的风格。 派 imitation(*n.* 模仿，效法；仿制品)
exploit	[ɪkˈsplɔɪt] *vt.* 开发(tap)；利用(make use of)； 剥削 [ˈeksplɔɪt] *n.* 英勇行为，业绩，功绩 记 词根记忆：ex(出) + plo(折叠) + it → 向外折 → 开发；利用 例 As preeminent generalists, members of this species *exploit* a great range of habitats and resources. 作为著名的多面手，这个物种的成员开发多种栖息地和资源。 派 exploitation(*n.* 开发)；over-exploitation(*n.* 过度开采)
proof [pruːf]	*n.* 证据，证明(evidence)；证词；检验，证实；校样 *a.* 耐…的，防…的 例 These results are a further *proof* of her outstanding ability. 这些成果进一步证明了她的杰出才干。 参 soundproof(*a.* 隔音的)；fireproof(*a.* 防火的)；waterproof(*a.* 防水的)；rustproof(*a.* 不生锈的)
rally [ˈræli]	*v.* 集合，召集；恢复(健康等)，重新振作 *n.* 集会，(群众)大会(assembly) 记 联想记忆：r + all(所有) + y → 所有人都参加的大会 → 集会 例 They have *rallied* a great deal of support for their campaign. 他们为竞选活动征得了大量的支持。

specify [ˈspesɪfaɪ]	*vt.* 使具体化；明确规定，详细说明 记 词根记忆：spec(看) + ify → 认真地看 → 使具体化 例 The regulations *specify* that calculators may not be used in the examination. 考试规则明确规定考试时不得使用计算器。 派 specific(*a.* 明确的，具体的；特定的); specifically(*ad.* 明确地，具体地；特意); specification(*n.* 详述；规格，规范)
genetic [dʒəˈnetɪk]	*a.* 基因的，遗传(学)的 记 来自 gene(*n.* 基因) 搭 genetic code 遗传密码；genetic engineering 遗传工程(学) 例 What type of amber is probably the most valuable for *genetic* research? 哪种琥珀可能对基因研究最有价值？
eliminate [ɪˈlɪmɪneɪt]	*vt.* 消除(*eradicate, remove)；淘汰 记 词根记忆：e(出) + limin(界限) + ate → 划在界限之外 → 消除；淘汰 例 Certain species may be *eliminated* and others may survive for no particular reason. 不知什么原因，某些物种可能被淘汰，而其他的则可能存活。 派 elimination(*n.* 消除，除去)
scatter [ˈskætər]	*v.* 使分散，驱散，散开(*irregularly distribute, disperse)；撒播 例 Over 25,000 islands are *scattered* across the surface of the Pacific. 太平洋上散布着 2.5 万多座岛屿。 派 scattered(*a.* 分散的，零散的) scatter
desperate [ˈdespərət]	*a.* 绝望的(despairing)；不顾死活的，拼命的；极度渴望的 记 词根记忆：de(去掉) + sper(希望) + ate → 去掉希望 → 绝望的 例 His failure made him *desperate*. 失败令他绝望了。 参 prosperous(*a.* 繁荣的，富裕的)
proliferate [prəˈlɪfəreɪt]	*vi.* 激增，迅速繁殖(multiply, propagate, reproduce) 记 词根记忆：prol(i)(子孙) + fer(带来) + ate → 带来子孙后代 → 迅速繁殖 例 Books on this subject have *proliferated* over the last year. 过去一年，有关该主题的书籍大量涌现。 派 proliferation(*n.* 激增，涌现；增殖)
errand [ˈerənd]	*n.* 差事，差使(assignment, task) 记 词根记忆：err(漫游) + and → 跑来跑去 → 差使 例 I have to pick up my car and do a couple of *errands*. 我得去取车，跑一些差事。
horde [hɔːrd]	*n.* 一大群人(crowd, swarm)；游牧部落 例 There are *hordes* of traders at the jumble sale today. 今天的旧货义卖会上有很多交易者。

34

□ specify   □ genetic   □ eliminate   □ scatter   □ desperate   □ proliferate
□ errand   □ horde

literacy
[ˈlɪtərəsi]

n. 有文化，有教养；读写能力

记 词根记忆：liter（文字）+ acy → 识字 → 读写能力

例 Franklin's newspaper was especially significant because *literacy* was increasing at the time. 富兰克林的报纸尤其重要，因为当时识字的人数在增多。

literacy

coverage
[ˈkʌvərɪdʒ]

n. 新闻报道；覆盖范围

记 联想记忆：cover(覆盖)+ age(集体名词后缀) → 覆盖范围

例 Channel 5 will provide live *coverage* of tonight's hockey game. 第五频道将现场直播今晚的曲棍球赛。

subsidy
[ˈsʌbsədi]

n. 补助金，津贴(*financing, allowance)

记 词根记忆：sub（在…下面）+ sid（坐）+ y → 坐在下面(给予帮助) → 补助金

例 The government decided to reduce the level of agricultural *subsidies*. 该政府决定降低农业补贴标准。

evidence
[ˈevɪdəns]

vt. 证明(*indicate) *n.* 证据(proof)；迹象；根据(basis)

记 词根记忆：e + vid(看见) + ence → 看见的人或物 → 证据；迹象

例 Emotional health is *evidenced* in the voice by free and melodic sounds of the happy. 快乐的人畅所欲言，音调悠扬，这证明其情绪健康。

vivid
[ˈvɪvɪd]

a. 清晰的；鲜明的(bright)；生动的(lively)；活泼的

记 词根记忆：viv(生命) + id → 有生命力的 → 鲜明的；生动的

例 Garlen gave a *vivid* description of Julie Peterson. 加林生动地描写了朱莉·彼得森。

派 vividly(*ad.* 生动地；鲜明地)

suspension
[səˈspenʃn]

n. 暂停(pause)；暂缓，推迟，延期；悬架；悬浮液

搭 suspension bridge 吊桥

例 The *suspension* of trading on the Grain Exchange was justified. 谷物交易所暂停交易是有道理的。

suspension

cape
[keɪp]

n. 海角，岬；斗篷，披肩

例 The need for ships to round the *Cape* Horn was greatly reduced by the opening of the Panama Canal in 1914. 自 1914 年巴拿马运河开通以来，船只绕经合恩角的需求大大降低了。

generalize
[ˈdʒenrəlaɪz]

v. 概括，归纳(sum up, conclude)；推广

记 来自 general(*a.* 概括的)

例 Algebra *generalizes* certain basic laws. 代数学总结一些基本的法则。

派 generalization(*n.* 归纳，概括；推广)；generalized(*a.* 广泛的，普遍的)

sled [sled]	*n.* 雪橇(sledge); 摘棉机 *v.* 乘雪橇, 用雪橇运 例 We were hoping we could go *sledding*. 我们本来希望能去乘雪橇。
current ['kɜːrənt]	*n.* (液体、气体的)流(stream); 潮流, 趋势(tendency) *a.* 现行的, 当前的 (ongoing); 流通的; 最近的 搭 current price 时价 例 Birds use warm air *currents* to help their flight. 鸟利用暖气流助飞。 派 currently(*ad.* 现在, 目前; 普遍地); concurrent(*a.* 同时发生的); currency(*n.* 货币; 通行, 流行)
vital ['vaɪtl]	*a.* 生死攸关的 (mortal); 至关重要的 (of the utmost importance); 精力充沛的, 有活力的 记 词根记忆: vit(生命) + al → 有关生命的 → 生死攸关的 例 This temperature gradient may be *vital* to successful hatching. 这种温度梯度可能对孵化的成功至关重要。 派 vitalism (*n.* 生机论); vitalist (*n.* 生机论者); vitality(*n.* 生命力; 活力)
besiege [bɪˈsiːdʒ]	*vt.* 包围(surround); 使应接不暇 记 联想记忆: be + siege(包围) → 包围 例 Almost daily the public is *besieged* by claims for no-aging diets, new vitamins, and other wonder foods. 公众几乎每天都被宣称为 "驻颜" 膳食、新维生素和其他特效食品的东西所包围。
media ['miːdiə]	*n.* 媒介, 媒体 记 词根记忆: medi(中间) + a → 在中间起作用 → 媒介 搭 mass media 大众传媒 例 Popular *media* often distort such stories. 大众媒体经常扭曲这种故事。
commodity [kəˈmɑːdəti]	*n.* 商品(article); 日用品 记 词根记忆: com(共同) + mod(样式) + ity → 样式繁多 → 商品 例 By the 1940s her paintings had become a very precious *commodity*. 到 20 世纪 40 年代, 她的画作已成为非常珍贵的商品。
introduction [ˌɪntrəˈdʌkʃn]	*n.* 介绍; 传入, 引进; 导言, 绪论 记 词根记忆: intro(入内) + duct(拉) + ion(名词后缀) → 向内拉 → 介绍; 传入 例 I've got to take an *introduction* to poetry before. 我之前接触过诗歌。
scout [skaʊt]	*v.* 侦察; 寻找; 搜索 *n.* 侦察员; 侦察机; 童子军 记 联想记忆: sc + out(外面) → 在外面巡逻的人 → 侦察员 例 We *scouted* the village for somewhere to stay the night. 我们在这个村子里四处查看, 想找个过夜的地方。

34

herd [hɜːrd]	*n.* 牧群，兽群；人群，芸芸众生 *v.* 放牧；成群，聚集 记 联想记忆：牧群(herd)逐水草(herb)而居 搭 a herd of 一群 例 Don't follow the *herd*. 不要随波逐流。
abrupt [əˈbrʌpt]	*a.* 突然的，意外的(unexpected)；(举止、言谈等)唐突的，鲁莽的 记 词根记忆：ab(离去) + rupt(断裂) → 突然的，意外的 例 Most paleontologists suspect that *abrupt* changes in climate led to the mass extinctions. 大多数古生物学家怀疑气候的剧变导致了古生物的大规模灭绝。
sew [soʊ]	*v.* 缝(纫)，做针线活；缝补，缝上 记 联想记忆：男人在田里播种(sow)，女人在家缝缝补补(sew) 搭 sew up 缝合，缝补；安排妥帖，使万无一失 例 My grandmother taught me how to *sew* when I was very young. 我很小的时候，奶奶就教我做针线活了。 参 sewage(*n.* 污水，污物)
buck [bʌk]	*v.* 猛然弓背跃起；猛然震荡；抵制，反抗 *n.* 美元；雄鹿 例 He admired her willingness to *buck* the system. 他赞赏她反抗现存体制的主动性。
avert [əˈvɜːrt]	*vt.* 避免，规避(avoid)；转移(目光、注意力等) 记 词根记忆：a + vert(转) → 转开 → 避免，规避 例 A fresh tragedy was narrowly *averted* yesterday. 昨天差点又发生了一场悲剧。 派 aversion(*n.* 厌恶，反感)
graph [græf]	*n.* 图表(diagram) 记 本身为词根，意为"写；图" 例 They should look for another *graph* immediately. 他们应该立刻去找另一张图表。
shuttle [ˈʃʌtl]	*v.* 穿梭往返；短程往返运送 *n.* 航天飞机；(织机的)梭子；(短程穿梭于两地的)航班(或火车、汽车) 记 联想记忆：shut(关闭) + tle → 封闭的空间 → 航天飞机 搭 space shuttle (往返于地球和太空站之间运载人和物资的)航天飞机 例 A bus *shuttles* passengers back and forth from the station to the terminal. 一辆公共汽车在火车站和公共汽车终点站之间往返运送旅客。
transparent [trænsˈpærənt]	*a.* 透明的；明显的，显而易见的；直率的 记 词根记忆：trans(穿过) + par(平等，相等) + ent → (光)均匀地穿过 → 透明的 例 Jellyfish may be large enough to be seen, but they are *transparent*. 有些水母很大，能被看到，但它们是透明的。 派 transparency(*n.* 透明；透明度)

sake [seɪk]	*n.* 缘故，理由(purpose)；好处 **搭** for the sake of 为了 **例** I believe education for its own *sake*. 我相信教育本身是有价值的。
flap [flæp]	*n.* 拍打；(鸟)振翅(飞行)；封盖，袋盖 *v.* (使)摆动(sway)；拍打(lap) **记** 联想记忆：f(看做 fly，飞) + lap(拍打) → 拍打 **例** The flags are *flapping* in the breeze. 旗帜在微风中摆动。
horizon [həˈraɪzn]	*n.* 地平线(skyline)；[常 *pl.*]眼界，视野(sight, eyeshot) **记** 联想记忆：ho + riz(看做 rise，升起) + on → 太阳从地平线上升起 → 地平线 **例** The farmers' broader *horizons* and greater self-respect were reflected to some degree in their behavior. 农民们更开阔的视野和更强烈的自尊在一定程度上通过其行为反映了出来。
sauce [sɔːs]	*n.* 调味汁，佐料(condiment, relish) **记** 联想记忆：调味汁(sauce)是菜肴美味的来源(source) **例** *Sauces* are an essential element in cuisines all over the world. 在全世界，调味汁都是烹饪中必不可少的元素。
adjunct [ˈædʒʌŋkt]	*n.* 附加物，附件(*addition, accessory)；附加语，修饰语 **记** 词根记忆：ad + junct(结合，连接) → 连在上面的东西 → 附加物 **例** The garage is an *adjunct* to the house. 车库是房子的附加物。
wasp [wɑːsp]	*n.* 黄蜂 **例** The various species of *wasps* fall into two main categories: solitary *wasps* and social *wasps*. 各种各样的黄蜂可归为两大类：独居黄蜂和群居黄蜂。
foment [foʊˈment]	*vt.* 煽动，挑起，激起(instigate) **记** 联想记忆：fom(看做 form，形成) + ent → 帮助形成 → 煽动 **例** Three sailors were *fomenting* a mutiny on the ship. 三名船员在船上煽动兵变。
stalk [stɔːk]	*n.* 茎，梗，柄(stem) *v.* 偷偷接近；跟踪；趾高气扬地走 **记** 联想记忆：他一句话不说(talk)，趾高气扬地走(stalk)了 **例** Its *stalk* is not strong enough to support its weight. 它的茎秆不够强壮，无法支撑起自身的重量。
part-time [ˈpɑːrtˌtaɪm]	*a.* 兼职的；部分时间的 **搭** part-time worker 兼职工作者 **例** I want to look for a *part-time* job. 我想找份兼职工作。
harbor [ˈhɑːrbər]	*vt.* 窝藏；藏有 *n.* 港口(port) **搭** natural harbor 天然港 **例** *Harboring* the killer is illegal. 窝藏杀人犯是违法的。

flap

34

irrigate [ˈɪrɪɡeɪt]	*vt.* 灌溉；冲洗(伤口或身体部位) 记 词根记忆：ir(进入) + rig(水) + ate → 把水引入 → 灌溉 例 The irrigation system was built in 256 BCE to *irrigate* an enormous area of farmland. 该灌溉系统建于公元前 256 年，用来灌溉大片农田。 派 irrigation(*n.* 灌溉)
communicate [kəˈmjuːnɪkeɪt]	*v.* 交流，沟通；传达，传播(express, convey)；通信 例 They will use satellites to *communicate* with mountain climbers. 他们将通过卫星与登山者进行联络。 派 communication(*n.* 交流；传播；通信)
portion [ˈpɔːrʃn]	*n.* 部分(part, share)；一份 *vt.* 划分，分配 记 联想记忆：port(看做 part, 部分) + ion → 部分 例 Why do squirrels eat only a *portion* of each acorn they retrieve? 松鼠为什么只吃它重新得到的每个橡子的一部分？
authority [əˈθɔːrəti]	*n.* 权力(power), 管辖权；[*pl.*]官方，当局；权威，专家 记 联想记忆：作家(author)有权(authority)主宰主人公的命运 例 He's an *authority* on energy sources. 他是能源方面的权威。// Your professor should have the *authority* to get something done about it. 你的教授应该有权让人对此采取措施。
clinic [ˈklɪnɪk]	*n.* 门诊部，诊所(dispensary) 例 In America, patients have to make an appointment with doctors in the *clinic* first. 在美国，病人看病时需要先和诊所的医生预约。
sanctuary [ˈsæŋktʃueri]	*n.* 禁猎区，动物保护区 (reserve)；庇护所，避难所(shelter, refuge)；圣所，圣殿 记 词根记忆：sanct(神圣) + (u)ary(表地方，名词后缀) → 神圣的地方 → 圣所，圣殿；避难所 搭 a natural sanctuary 自然保护区；a bird sanctuary 鸟类保护区 例 Hunters are forbidden from hunting in wildlife *sanctuaries* of this region. 狩猎者不得在这一带的野生动物保护区捕猎。
linguist [ˈlɪŋɡwɪst]	*n.* 语言学家；通晓数国语言的人 记 词根记忆：lingu(语言) + ist(表人，名词后缀) → 语言学家 例 Historical *linguists* study how languages evolve over time. 历史语言学家研究随着时间的推移语言是如何演变的。
closet [ˈklɑːzət]	*vt.* 把…关在房间里（尤指为了进行密谈）*n.* 橱，壁橱(cabinet) *a.* 隐蔽的(closely private)；私下的，秘密的(confidential) 例 He had *closeted* himself away in the room after failing the exam. 考试失利后，他把自己关在房间里不见任何人。
bookstore [ˈbʊkstɔːr]	*n.* 书店(bookshop) 例 I have to get a check cashed to pay my *bookstore* bill. 我要兑现一张支票来支付书店的账单。

remind [rɪˈmaɪnd]	*vt.* 提醒(inform); 使想起; 使发生联想 例 He'll drive more slowly only if you *remind* him. 只有你提醒他, 他才会开慢点。
candidate [ˈkændɪdət]	*n.* 候选人(nominee); 投考者 记 联想记忆: can(能) + did(做) + ate → 踏实能干才能成为候选人 → 候选人 例 The crowd was overwhelmed by the *candidate's* speech. 人群被候选人的演说震撼了。
speculate [ˈspekjuleɪt]	*v.* 推测(*hypothesize); 深思, 沉思; 投机, 做投机买卖 记 词根记忆: spec(看) + ulate → 仔细地看 → 推测; 深思, 沉思 例 Although scientists can *speculate* about its nature, neither humans nor machines will ever be able to visit it. 尽管科学家们能推测其性质, 但人类和机器永远都不可能造访那里。 派 speculation(*n.* 推测); speculative(*a.* 推测的; 投机的); speculator(*n.* 投机者)
abiding [əˈbaɪdɪŋ]	*a.* 持久的, 永久的(enduring, permanent) 记 来自 abide(*v.* 停留; 容忍) 搭 abiding friendship 持久的友谊 例 The old man has an *abiding* love for music and drama. 这位老人一直热爱音乐和戏剧。 参 temporal(*a.* 短暂的, 暂时的); temporary(*a.* 临时的)
yield [jiːld]	*v.* 生产, 出产(*provide); 屈服, 顺从; 让出, 放弃; 变形, 弯曲 *n.* 产量(output); 收益(income) 记 联想记忆: 这片田地(field)出产(yield)西瓜 例 His well begins to *yield* 20 barrels of crude oil a day. 他的油井开始每天产 20 桶原油。// Crop *yields* have increased dramatically. 农作物产量有了显著的增长。
continuity [ˌkɑːntəˈnjuːəti]	*n.* 连贯性, 连续性(consistency, succession) 例 Some experts argue that school vacations interrupt the *continuity* of the school year. 一些专家辩称学校的假期打断了学年的连续性。 派 discontinuity(*n.* 不连续, 中断)
saturate [ˈsætʃəreɪt]	*vt.* 使湿透(soak); 使饱和(fill) 记 词根记忆: sat(充足) + ur + ate(使…) → 使足够 → 使饱和 例 The ocean *saturates* the atmosphere with water. 海洋使大气中充满水分。 派 saturated(*a.* 湿透的; 饱和的)

选谁呢?

candidate

34

Word List 35

rodeo [ˈroʊdioʊ]	*n.* 牛仔竞技表演 例 *Rodeos* have provoked opposition from animal rights and animal welfare advocates. 牛仔竞技表演引起了那些动物权利以及动物福利拥护者的反对。
loan [loʊn]	*n.* 贷款；出借，借出；暂借的东西 *vt.* 借出；贷给 记 发音记忆："漏" → 因为把钱借出去了，所以账本有漏洞 → 出借，借出 搭 student loan 学生贷款；loan application 贷款申请 例 Martin is looking into the possibility of getting a *loan*. 马丁正在调查获得贷款的可能性。// A: Janet, here's the book you *loan* me. I'm a bit embarrassed I can't seem to find the jacket for it. B: I would never even notice this. You are the few people who actually returned books to me. A: 珍妮特，这是你借给我的书。不好意思，我好像找不到书套了。 B: 我都没注意到。你是少数几个把书还给我的人之一。 参 moan(*n./v.* 呻吟)
collaborator [kəˈlæbəreɪtər]	*n.* 合作者，协作者；通敌者 记 词根记忆：col(共同) + labor(工作) + at + or(表人，名词后缀) → 合作者，协作者 例 I need a *collaborator* to help me with the task. 我需要一个人来协作我完成这项任务。

phase [feɪz]	*n.* 相位，月相；阶段，时期（period）*vt.* 分阶段实行，逐步做 **搭** phase out 逐步废除 **例** The *phases* of the Moon have served as primary divisions of time for thousands of years. 几千年来，月相一直主要用于区分时间。 **参** phrase（*n.* 短语）
specimen [ˈspesɪmən]	*n.* 标本，样本（sample）；范例；抽样 **记** 词根记忆：spec（看，观察）+ imen → 观察时用来参照的 → 标本，样本；范例 **例** Astronauts have brought back *specimens* of rock from the Moon. 宇航员从月球带回了岩石标本。
deficient [dɪˈfɪʃnt]	*a.* 不足的，缺乏的（*inadequate）；有缺陷的，不完善的 **记** 词根记忆：de（分离）+ fic（做）+ ient → 做得不好的 → 不足的，缺乏的；有缺陷的 **例** John's diet is *deficient* in fiber and Vitamin E. 约翰的饮食中缺少纤维和维生素 E。
slide [slaɪd]	*v.* 滑动（glide, slip）*n.* 滑动（slippage）；滑坡，滑道；幻灯片 **记** 联想记忆：s + lid（盖子）+ e → 盖子太滑，从桌子上掉了下去 → 滑动 **搭** slide projector 幻灯机 **例** They *slide* on a more yielding layer at the base of the lithosphere. 它们在岩石圈底部更柔软的一层滑动。 **派** slider（*n.* 滑行者；滑动器）；sliding（*a.* 滑行的）
legible [ˈledʒəbl]	*a.* 清楚的（distinct）；易读的（readable） **记** 词根记忆：leg（读）+ ible → 易读的 **例** The song she had written for the contest wasn't *legible*. 她为比赛所写的歌不容易懂。 **派** illegible（*a.* 难辨认的）
complicated [ˈkɑːmplɪkeɪtɪd]	*a.* 难懂的，复杂的（complex） **例** This type of engine is expensive and *complicated*. 这种引擎昂贵且复杂。 **派** uncomplicated（*a.* 不复杂的，简单的）
limb [lɪm]	*n.* 肢，臂；（树的）主枝 **记** 联想记忆：没有四肢（limb）不能攀爬（climb） **例** For a while, she lost the use of her *limbs*. 好一会儿她四肢都动弹不得。 **参** limp（*vi.* 跛行）
subsequent [ˈsʌbsɪkwənt]	*a.* 随后的（*later）；并发的（successive） **记** 词根记忆：sub（在…下面）+ sequ（跟随）+ ent → 随后的 **例** *Subsequent* reforms have made these notions seem quite out-of-date. 随后的改革使这些观念显得颇为过时。 **派** subsequently（*ad.* 后来，随后） **参** consequent（*a.* 随之发生的，作为结果的）

35

by-product	*n.* 副产品；副作用，意外结果
[ˈbaɪˌprɑːdʌkt]	例 A *by-product* can be useful and marketable, or it can be considered waste. 有些副产品有用并可出售，有些则是废品。
dorsal	*a.* 背部的，背脊的(back)
[ˈdɔːrsl]	记 词根记忆：dors(背) + al(形容词后缀) → 背部的
	例 The fishes' *dorsal* fins are usually cut off by the fishermen. 鱼类的背鳍通常被渔民切掉。
zinc	*n.* 锌
[zɪŋk]	搭 zinc oxide 氧化锌
cable	*n.* 缆绳，钢索；电缆(wire)；电报(telegraph) *v.* 给…发电报，用电报传送
[ˈkeɪbl]	搭 wire cable 多股缆；钢丝绳
	例 In electrical engineering *cables* are used to carry electric currents. 在电机工程中，电缆用于传输电流。
politics	*n.* 政治；政纲，政见；政治事务(或活动)；权术；政治学
[ˈpɑːlətɪks]	记 联想记忆：政治(politics)要讲政策(policy)
	例 He is a major figure in British *politics*. 他是英国政坛的风云人物。
	参 political(*a.* 政治的；政党的；争权夺利的)
bloom	*n.* 花；开花(期)；青春焕发(的时期) *v.* (使)开花(blossom)
[bluːm]	记 联想记忆：杜鹃花开(bloom)鲜红如血(blood)
	例 The sun is shining, and the flowers are *blooming*. 阳光灿烂，花儿绽放。
reputation	*n.* 名声，声望，名誉(fame)
[ˌrepjuˈteɪʃn]	记 词根记忆：re(再，又) + put(想) + ation → 值得反复考虑 → 非常看重的 → 名声，声望，名誉
	搭 a good/bad reputation 好/坏名声；earn/gain/establish a reputation as sth. 以…获得/建立名声
	例 Professor Howl does have a good *reputation* in the political science department. 豪尔教授在政治科学系的声誉的确不错。
overcharge	*v.* 讨价过高，索价过高；(使)过量装填；渲染，夸张 *n.* 过高的要价；超载
[ˌoʊvərˈtʃɑːrdʒ]	记 联想记忆：over(过度) + charge(收费) → 索价过高
	例 Some car mechanics, if they think that someone doesn't know much about cars, may try to *overcharge* that person. 当一些汽车修理工认为某人对车不太了解时，就会设法多收这个人的钱。
invade	*v.* 侵入，侵略(*move into, intrude)；侵扰
[ɪnˈveɪd]	记 词根记忆：in(进入) + vad(走) + e → 未经允许走进来 → 侵入，侵略
	例 We are going to talk about a special way some plants respond to being *invaded* by pests. 我们要谈论一些植物应对害虫入侵的一种特殊方式。
	派 invader(*n.* 侵略者)；invasion(*n.* 侵略，入侵)

mansion
[ˈmænʃn]

n. 公寓，府邸(dwelling)；大厦

记 联想记忆：mans(e)(牧师的住宅) + ion → 府邸

例 The family lived in an 18th century country *mansion*. 这家人住在一座18世纪的乡村宅邸里。

---

aquarium
[əˈkweriəm]

n. 养鱼缸；水族馆

记 词根记忆：aqu(a)(水) + arium(表场所，名词后缀) → 水族馆

例 It was estimated that in 1999 over nine million US households owned an *aquarium*. 据估计，1999年美国有900多万家庭拥有养鱼缸。

aquarium

---

wholesome
[ˈhoʊlsəm]

a. 健康的，有利健康的(healthful)；有道德的

记 联想记忆：whole(整体) + some → 能保存一个整体的 → 有利健康的

例 Bitter pills may have *wholesome* effects. 良药苦口利于病。

---

melodrama
[ˈmelədrɑːmə]

n. 情节剧，通俗剧；戏剧性的事件

例 Instead of tragedy, we got *melodrama*. 我们看的是情节剧，而不是悲剧。

派 melodramatic(*a.* 情节剧式的；夸大的，耸人听闻的)

---

haircut
[ˈherkʌt]

n. 理发

搭 have/get a haircut 剪头发

例 Have you noticed that Mr. Wilson got a *haircut*? 你注意到威尔逊先生理发了吗？

---

predator
[ˈpredətər]

n. 捕食性动物，食肉动物；掠夺者，剥削者

记 词根记忆：pred(掠夺) + at + or(表人或物，名词后缀) → 掠夺肉食 → 捕食性动物，食肉动物

例 The government has adopted a firm policy to protect the domestic industry from foreign *predators*. 该政府采取了严厉的政策来保护本国工业不受外来剥削。

派 predatory(*a.* 捕食性的，食肉的；压榨他人的)

---

awesome
[ˈɔːsəm]

a. 使人敬畏的；使人恐惧的

记 联想记忆：awe(敬畏) + some(充满…的) → 使人敬畏的

例 The image of gods and kings on the surface of the columns was a little bit *awesome*. 柱子上神和国王的形象有点令人敬畏。

参 handsome(*a.* 英俊的)；wholesome(*a.* 健康的，有利健康的)

35

---

lichen
[ˈlaɪkən]

n. 青苔，地衣

例 *Lichens* are famous for their ability to survive a water shortage. 青苔以其在缺水环境下仍富有顽强的生命力而著称。

---

ongoing
[ˈɑːngoʊɪŋ]

a. 正在进行的；不间断的；继续存在的 *n.* 前进，发展

记 联想记忆：on + going(进行中的) → 正在进行的

例 Both limitations and problems will quite likely be encountered during the *ongoing* transition to the market economy. 正在进行的市场经济转型将很可能遇到限制和问题。

gospel [ˈɡɑːspl]	*n.* 准则，信条（principle）；绝对真理；[G-]福音；福音音乐；训示 记 来自《圣经·新约》中的福音书（Gospel）；可能来自 god + spell → 上帝的话 → 福音；信条 例 Mahalia Jackson's powerful, joyous *gospel* music style had gained her an international reputation. 马哈莉亚·杰克逊欢快有力的福音音乐风格使她享誉世界。
reservation [ˌrezərˈveɪʃn]	*n.* 预约，预订；保留意见，疑惑；（美国为土著美洲人划出的）居留地 记 来自 reserve（*vt.* 预订；保留） 搭 make a reservation 预订；confirm a reservation 确认预订 例 I'm sorry. I need to work late tonight. So you should probably cancel our *reservation* at the restaurant. 对不起，今晚我得工作到很晚。你或许应该取消我们在饭店的预订。
advertise [ˈædvərtaɪz]	*vt.* 为…做广告，宣传（promote）；（在报刊、电视、广播中）公告，公布 记 词根记忆：ad(=to) + vert(转) + ise(使…) → 使人们的注意力转向某一方 → 宣传 例 I'd like to enroll in the free seminar you *advertised* in the newspaper. 我想报名参加你在报纸上宣传的免费研讨会。 派 advertisement(*n.* 广告；公告)
mesmerize [ˈmezməraɪz]	*vt.* 施催眠术；使入迷，迷住（fascinate） 例 We were *mesmerized* by her performance. 我们都被她的表演迷住了。 mesmerize
groan [ɡroʊn]	*vi.* 呻吟（moan）；叹息（sigh）；发出呻吟般的声音 *n.* 呻吟；抱怨；呻吟声，叹息声 记 联想记忆：人长大后（grown）似乎更爱叹息（groan） 搭 groan at 对…抱怨；groan with 充满，堆满 例 The trees creaked and *groaned* in the wind. 树在风中嘎吱作响。
modest [ˈmɑːdɪst]	*a.* 谦虚的；适度的（mild, decent） 记 词根记忆：mod（适合）+ est → 适合的 → 谦虚的；适度的 例 The national debt had shot up from a *modest* 65 million dollars in 1861. 国债在 1861 年从适度的 6500 万美元猛增。 派 modestly(*ad.* 谨慎地；适度地) 过奖… modest

along [ə'lɔːŋ]	*ad.* 向前；一起 *prep.* 沿着 搭 come along 与…一起 例 Houses had been built *along* both sides of the river. 沿河两岸已盖起了房屋。// A: What a relationship Steven and his father have! B: Don't they? I only hope my daughter and I can get *along* like that when she's Steven's age. A: 史蒂文和他父亲的关系多融洽啊! B: 难道不是吗? 我只希望我女儿到了史蒂文的年纪，能和我像他们父子那样相处。
magnificent [mæg'nɪfɪsnt]	*a.* 极好的(wonderful)；宏伟的，华丽的(gorgeous)；崇高的，高尚的(lofty) 记 词根记忆：magn(大) + if(使) + icent → 做得很大 → 华丽的；高尚的 例 Financier Andrew Mellon donated most of his *magnificent* art collection to the National Gallery of Art. 金融家安德鲁·梅隆把他收藏的大部分精美艺术品捐献给了国家艺术馆。// The temple is so grand and *magnificent* with so many features. 这座寺庙规模宏大，华丽壮观，颇具特色。
hike [haɪk]	*v./n.* 徒步旅行，远足(walkabout) 记 联想记忆：穿着 Nike 鞋去远足(hike) 例 Her sister's children love to *hike* in the mountains. 她姐姐的孩子喜欢去山里徒步旅行。
overall	[ˌoʊvər'ɔːl] *a.* 全面的，综合的 *ad.* 总共 ['oʊvərɔːl] *n.* (套头)工作服，工装裤 记 组合词：over(从头到尾) + all(所有的) → 全面的，综合的 例 A creative architect can find ways to incorporate natural landscape into the *overall* design. 富有创意的建筑师能把自然景观融入整体设计中。// In the experiment, the *overall* growth of algae and the number of species dropped. 在实验中，藻类的整体生长速度和物种数量都降低了。
scurry ['skɜːri]	*vi./n.* 急跑，疾行(*rush, scamper, scuttle) 记 联想记忆：上课时间快到了，妈妈催促(hurry)孩子跑(scurry)去学校 例 Ants *scurried* around the pile of rotting wood. 蚂蚁围着那堆腐烂的木头快速爬来爬去。
indigestion [ˌɪndɪ'dʒestʃən]	*n.* 消化不良(症) 记 来自 digest(*v.* 消化)
boom [buːm]	*vi.* 迅速发展，激增；发出低沉有力的声音 *n.* 激增，繁荣(*expansion)；繁荣昌盛期 搭 baby boom 生育高峰 例 Agriculture *boomed*, with machinery doing the job of farm workers drawn into the army. 机器替代被应召入伍的农民工作，农业迅速发展了起来。 派 booming(*a.* 急速发展的)

35

perpetuate [pərˈpetʃueɪt]	*vt.* 使永存，使持续（last） 记 词根记忆：per（贯穿）+ pet（追求）+ uate → 永远追求 → 使永存，使持续 例 Insects have many enemies, but they must *perpetuate* their kind. 昆虫有很多敌人，但是它们必须延续后代。 参 perpetual（*a.* 连续不断的；永久的，长期的）
companion [kəmˈpæniən]	*n.* 同伴，共事者（partner, comrade） 记 词根记忆：com（共同）+ pan（面包）+ ion → 共享面包的人 → 同伴，共事者 例 Pierre and his *companions* did in fact reach the near vicinity of the North Pole. 皮埃尔和他的同伴的确到达了北极附近。
twine [twaɪn]	*n.* 细绳（rope, string）*v.* (使某物)缠绕，盘绕，围绕 记 联想记忆：大家应该像双胞胎（twins）一样拧成一股绳（twine），齐心协力把这件事做好 例 The reaper gathered the stalks and bound them with *twine*. 收割者把秸秆收了起来，并用细绳把它们捆绑住。
resident [ˈrezɪdənt]	*a.* 常驻的；(在某地)居住的 *n.* 居民（dweller）；住宿者，旅客；住院实习医生 记 来自 reside（*vi.* 居住于，定居于） 例 Each nest has a distinct odor that allows its inhabitants to distinguish foreign ants from *resident* ants. 每个蚁穴都有独特的气味，使居住在其中的蚂蚁能够分辨外来蚂蚁和常住蚂蚁。 派 residential（*a.* 居住的；住宅的；提供住宿的）
concede [kənˈsiːd]	*v.* 承认（grant）；让步（yield）；允许 记 词根记忆：con（带着）+ ced（走）+ e → 带着某物走 → 承认；让步 例 The author *conceded* that individual chimpanzees may have a preference for certain companions. 作者承认某些猩猩可能会偏爱特定的同伴。 参 cede（*vt.* 割让，放弃）；accede（*vi.* 同意）；recede（*vi.* 后退）；precede（*v.* 先于，领先）
float [fləʊt]	*v.* (使)漂浮，(使)浮动（drift）；飘动 记 联想记忆：船（boat）在水面漂浮（float） 例 Some small local canals are able to *float* only small rafts of timber. 本地一些小运河只能浮起小木筏。 派 floating（*a.* 漂浮的；不固定的，浮动的）
rod [rɑːd]	*n.* 杆，棒（bar） 记 联想记忆：拿着木棒（rod）去打劫（rob） 例 The fireplace had pivoting metal *rods* to hang pots. 壁炉有绕轴旋转的金属棒用做挂锅。

classical ['klæsɪkl]	*a.* 经典的，古典(文学)的 记 来自 classic(*n.* 经典著作) 例 Professor Lee will give a speech on *classical* literature in the hall this Friday. 李教授将于本周五在礼堂做关于古典文学的讲座。
principle ['prɪnsəpl]	*n.* 原则(fundamentals)；原理(theory)；道德准则，行为规范；信念 记 词根记忆：prin(第一) + cip(取) + le → 需第一位选取的 → 原则；原理 搭 in principle 原则上，理论上；大体上，基本上 例 You should stick to your *principles.* 你应该恪守自己的原则。 参 principal(*a.* 最重要的，主要的 *n.* 负责人)
outspoken [aʊt 'spoʊkən]	*a.* 直言不讳的，坦率的(frank) 例 He was *outspoken* in his criticism of the government's handling of the disaster. 他直言不讳地批评了政府对灾难的处理方式。
factual ['fæktʃuəl]	*a.* 实际的，真实的，事实的 记 来自 fact(*n.* 事实，真相) 例 The story of the train may not be completely *factual.* 关于这列火车的故事可能并非完全符合事实。
prize [praɪz]	*vt.* 珍视(value) *n.* 奖品(award)；奖金(premium)；难能可贵的东西 *a.* 应获奖的；优秀的，典范性的 例 Sturgeons are *prized* for their blackish roe. 鲟鱼因其黑色的鱼卵而受到珍视。
formidable ['fɔːrmɪdəbl]	*a.* 难对付的(*difficult, rough)；强大的(mighty, powerful)；令人敬畏的 记 词根记忆：formid(害怕) + able(能…的) → 令人害怕的 → 难对付的；强大的 例 They faced *formidable* difficulties in their attempt to reach the mountain summit. 他们在试图抵达山顶的过程中面临着巨大的困难。
obedience [oʊ 'biːdiəns]	*n.* 服从，顺从(submittal, compliance) 记 来自 obey(*v.* 服从，顺从) 例 The unruly children showed no *obedience* to their parents. 任性的孩子们不服从他们的父母。 派 disobedience(*n.* 不服从，违抗)
persist [pər 'sɪst]	*vi.* 坚持(stick to)；持续(*continue) 记 词根记忆：per(始终) + sist(站立) → 始终站着 → 坚持；持续 例 John won't give up. He *persists* in repeating his opinion. 约翰不愿放弃，他坚持重复自己的观点。 派 persistence(*n.* 坚持；持续)；persistent(*a.* 坚持不懈的；持久的) 参 subsist(*vi.* 存货；生存)；consist(*vi.* 在于；由…组成)
skeptical ['skeptɪkl]	*a.* 怀疑的(suspicious) 记 词根记忆：skep(检查) + tical → 因为怀疑而进行检查 → 怀疑的 例 We are *skeptical* about her chances of winning. 我们对她获胜的可能性表示怀疑。 派 skepticism(*n.* 怀疑论；怀疑态度)

35

□ classical   □ principle   □ outspoken   □ factual   □ prize   □ formidable
□ obedience   □ persist   □ skeptical

dearth [dɜːrθ]	*n.* 缺乏，短缺 记 联想记忆：物以稀（dearth）为贵（dear） 例 There is a *dearth* of good young actors at the moment. 目前，优秀的年轻男演员太少了。
invitation [ˌɪnvɪˈteɪʃn]	*n.* 邀请；请柬；吸引，诱惑 例 She'll consider the man's *invitation*. 她会考虑这位男士的邀请。
sequence [ˈsiːkwəns]	*n.* 一系列，一连串；顺序，次序，序列（order）*vt.* 按顺序排列 记 词根记忆：sequ（跟随）+ ence → 顺序，次序，序列 例 Number the pages in *sequence*. 按顺序标出页码。
humble [ˈhʌmbl]	*a.* 谦卑的；卑贱的；简陋的，低劣的 *vt.* 降低，贬抑 记 词根记忆：hum（地）+ ble → 接近地面的 → 谦卑的；卑贱的 例 In my *humble* opinion, you should listen to others first and then decide. 依我拙见，你应该先听听别人的意见，再做决定。 派 humbleness（*n.* 谦逊；卑贱）
overflow [ˌoʊvərˈfloʊ] [ˈoʊvərfloʊ]	*v.* （使）泛滥，（使）溢出 *n.* 溢出；容纳不下的物（或人） 记 组合词：over（超过）+ flow（流）→ 流到外面来 → 溢出 搭 overflow with 充满，洋溢 例 Once Christmas comes, streets, shops and everywhere else *overflow* with the crowds. 一到圣诞节，大街小巷、商场商店乃至其他任何地方都人满为患。
glimmer [ˈglɪmər]	*n.* 闪烁的微光；隐约的迹象；一丝，一线 *vi.* 发微光；隐约出现 记 联想记忆：glim（灯光）+ mer → 灯光摇曳 → 闪烁的微光 例 There is a *glimmer* of light through the mist in the forest. 薄雾弥漫的森林里微光闪烁。
staunch [stɔːntʃ]	*a.* 坚定的，忠诚的（loyal） 记 词根记忆：st（站）+ aunch → 始终站在某人的身后 → 坚定的，忠诚的 例 The President is a *staunch* supporter of free trade. 该总统是自由贸易的坚定拥护者。
traverse [trəˈvɜːrs]	*v.* 横穿，横渡 记 词根记忆：tra（穿过）+ vers（转）+ e → 横穿 例 The motor cyclist tried to *traverse* over the Yellow River on his motorbike. 这个摩托车手试图骑摩托车飞渡黄河。 traverse
malice [ˈmælɪs]	*n.* 恶意，怨恨 记 词根记忆：mal（坏，恶）+ ice → 恶意 例 I think he certainly bears you no *malice*, so don't worry. 我想他对你肯定没有恶意，不用担心。

sneaky [ˈsniːki]	*a.* 偷偷摸摸的，鬼鬼祟祟的 记 词根记忆：sn(悄悄地行进) + eak + y → 偷偷摸摸地靠近 → 偷偷摸摸的 例 At the party, Tiffany took a *sneaky* glance at the boy beside her. 派对上，蒂凡尼偷偷看了一眼她身边的那个男孩。
uphold [ʌpˈhoʊld]	*vt.* 支持，维护；维持(原判等) 记 联想记忆：up(向上) + hold(举起) → 举起来 → 支持，维护 例 Some ancient traditions and customs should be well *upheld*. 一些古老的传统和习俗应该被好好地保持下来。
forsake [fərˈseɪk]	*vt.* 遗弃，放弃，抛弃(abandon) 记 联想记忆：for(为了) + sake(理由) → 年轻的妈妈出于某种无奈的理由不得不遗弃了她的孩子 → 遗弃 例 The brother *forsook* his education and went to work for his whole family. 哥哥为了整个家庭放弃了学业，出去工作。
vow [vaʊ]	*v.* 发誓 *n.* 誓约 记 联想记忆：在寺院里，人们排着队(row)去发誓(vow) 例 The woman *vowed* to her husband's photo that she would take revenge on his enemy. 那个女人对着丈夫的照片发誓，她一定会找他的敌人报仇的。
embargo [ɪmˈbɑːrgoʊ]	*n.* 禁止贸易令；禁运 *vt.* 禁止(船只等)出入港口，禁运；禁止…贸易 记 联想记忆：em + bar(阻挡) + go(去) → 不让(船只)进入 → 禁运 例 The house agent places the apartments under an *embargo* between the house owner and the lodger. 房屋中介禁止房东和房客对公寓进行交易。
ordeal [ɔːrˈdiːl]	*n.* 折磨；严峻考验 记 发音记忆："恶地儿" → 险恶之地 → 严峻考验 例 She was suffering the *ordeal* of divorce. 当时，她正深受离婚之痛的折磨。
deflect [dɪˈflekt]	*v.* (使)偏斜，(使)转向 记 词根记忆：de(离开) + flect(弯曲) → 弯到一边 → (使)偏斜 例 The ship *deflected* from its course, because of the heavy storm. 狂风暴雨使轮船偏离了航线。
abhor [əbˈhɔːr]	*vt.* 憎恨，厌恶(loathe) 记 词根记忆：ab(表加强) + hor(发抖) → 令人发抖 → 憎恨，厌恶 例 The history teacher *abhors* all forms of racism and segregation. 那个历史老师憎恨各种形式的种族歧视和种族隔离。
pernicious [pərˈnɪʃəs]	*a.* 有害的，恶性的 记 词根记忆：per(完全) + nic(=noc 伤害) + ious → 完全伤害的 → 有害的 例 Puppy love is seen to have a *pernicious* influence on students in school. 人们认为早恋会对在校学生产生不好的影响。

35

suspicious [sə'spɪʃəs]	*a.* 可疑的，令人怀疑的；不信任的，猜疑的，多疑的 搭 be suspicious of 对…起疑 例 It's *suspicious* that Tom didn't come home last night, and didn't call back. 汤姆昨天晚上没回家，也没打电话回来，这很可疑。 suspicious
venturesome ['ventʃərsəm]	*a.* 敢于冒险的(daring)；有危险的 记 联想记忆：venture(冒险) + some(充满…的) → 敢于冒险的 例 To climb Mount Everest is a *venturesome* trip for amateur climbers. 对于业余登山者来说，攀登珠穆朗玛峰充满危险。
diagnose [ˌdaɪəg'nous]	*v.* 诊断；判断 记 词根记忆：dia(穿过) + gnos(知道) + e → 古时医生通过望、闻、问、切诊断病情，透过表面看实质 → 诊断 例 She was *diagnosed* with cancer when she was 30. 她30岁时被诊断患有癌症。 派 diagnosis(*n.* 诊断；判断); diagnostic(*a.* 诊断的；判断的) diagnose
regiment ['redʒɪmənt]	*n.* 团；一大群人 *vt.* 组团；管制 记 词根记忆：reg(统治) + iment → 统治的一群人 → 团；一大群人 例 After the earthquake, a whole *regiment* of volunteers rushed to the disaster-hit areas. 地震发生后，大批志愿者奔赴灾区。
smelting ['smeltɪŋ]	*n.* 冶炼，熔炼 例 *Smelting* represented a major technological achievement. 冶炼代表着技术上的重大进步。
cartilage ['kɑːrtɪlɪdʒ]	*n.* 软骨(组织) 例 The *cartilage* in John's nose was broken when it was hit. 约翰鼻子里面的软骨在受到撞击后断了。

词根、词缀预习表

sculp	雕刻	sculpture *n.* 雕像	ev	时间	medieval *a.* 中世纪的
tol	支撑	tolerable *a.* 可忍受的	clam	叫喊	clamor *n.* 吵闹
flu	流	affluent *a.* 丰富的	tect	遮盖	detect *vt.* 察觉
gest	搬运	congest *v.* (使)充满	ton	声音	monotonous *a.* 单调的
vag	漫游	vague *a.* 模糊的	sting	刺	distinguish *v.* 区别

fold [fould]	*n.* 褶，褶层；(地壳岩石层中的)褶皱(pleat)；褶痕，褶缝；羊栏，畜栏 *v.* 折叠；合拢(bend)；包，裹；倒闭 例 Many butterflies can suddenly disappear from view by *folding* their wings. 很多蝴蝶合起翅膀就能突然从(人们的)视线里消失。
discrete [dɪˈskriːt]	*a.* 分离的，个别的(*separate)；离散的 记 词根记忆：dis(分离) + cret(=cern 观察) + e → 分离的 例 Lisa's plan contains several *discrete* ideas. 莉萨的计划包括几个独立的想法。 参 discreet(*a.* 小心的，谨慎的)
courier [ˈkʊriər]	*n.* 送急件的人，信使(messenger)；旅游服务员 记 词根记忆：cour(跑) + ier(表人) → 跑着的人 → 送急件的人 例 A *courier* can deliver the parcels and letters to our office. 信使可以将包裹和信件递送到我们办公室。
sculpture [ˈskʌlptʃər]	*n.* 雕像，雕塑品(carving)；雕刻术(engraving) 记 词根记忆：sculp(雕刻) + ture → 雕像，雕塑品；雕刻术 搭 a marble sculpture of Venus 维纳斯的大理石雕像 例 In Japan, countless paintings and *sculptures* were made under governmental sponsorship. 在日本，不计其数的画和雕塑品是在政府的资助下创作出来的。
polygamy [pəˈlɪgəmi]	*n.* 一夫多妻制，一妻多夫制，多配偶制 记 词根记忆：poly(多) + gam(婚姻) + y → 一夫多妻制，一妻多夫制 例 In ancient China, *polygamy* acted for a couple of thousand years. 在古代中国，一夫多妻制实行了几千年。

despise [dɪˈspaɪz]	***vt.*** 鄙视，看不起 (look down upon) 记 联想记忆：尽管 (despite) 受蔑视 (despise)，他还是坚持自己的意见 例 A tattletale is often *despised* by his classmates. 爱打小报告的人常常为其同学所不齿。 参 despite (*prep.* 尽管)
trumpet [ˈtrʌmpɪt]	***v.*** 鼓吹，宣扬 *n.* 小号，喇叭 例 Mothers often like to *trumpet* their own way to nurture and educate their children. 妈妈们经常喜欢宣扬自己养育孩子的方法。
convene [kənˈviːn]	***v.*** 召集，召开 (正式会议)；聚集，集合 记 词根记忆：con (共同) + ven (来) + e → 来到一起 → 召集；聚集 例 The chairman *convened* all the members to the meeting room. 主席召集所有会员到会议室。
babble [ˈbæbl]	***v.*** 胡言乱语；含糊不清地说；喋喋不休 记 联想记忆：婴儿 (baby) 学说话时，说得含糊不清 (babble) 例 I hate people *babbling*, so please speak out loud and clear. 我讨厌别人说话含糊不清，所以请你大声清晰地说出来。 参 bubble (*n.* 水泡，气泡)
canopy [ˈkænəpi]	***n.*** 天篷；罩盖，遮篷 (awning, covering)；天篷似的树阴 记 联想记忆：can (能) + opy (看做 copy，复制) → 能被复制的遮篷 → 遮篷；来自希腊语 konopeion (蚊帐)，后指天篷 例 The trees formed a *canopy* over the yard. 树木覆盖着庭院。
reproduce [ˌriːprəˈduːs]	***v.*** 繁殖，生育；复制 (*copy)；再现 记 联想记忆：re (再，又) + produce (生产) → 不断生产 → 繁殖；复制 例 They've learned how to *reproduce* these cells. 他们已经学会了如何复制这些细胞。 派 reproduction (*n.* 繁殖；复制品)；reproductive (*a.* 生殖的；再生的)
notable [ˈnoʊtəbl]	***a.*** 值得注意的，明显的；显著的；著名的；重要的 *n.* 名人，要人 记 词根记忆：not (知道) + able (能…的) → 能为人所知的 → 值得注意的；显著的 例 The *notable* writer will visit a big bookstore to publicize his new book. 这位知名作家将莅临一个大书店宣传他自己的新书。
subjective [səbˈdʒektɪv]	***a.*** 主观的，个人的 记 联想记忆：subject (主题) + ive → 主观的 例 You might deal with something in a *subjective* way, but you must analyze it in an objective way first. 你可以主观处理一件事情，但你必须先客观地分析这件事情。

tolerable [ˈtɑːlərəbl]	*a.* 可忍受的，可容忍的(endurable)；尚好的，过得去的 记 词根记忆：tol（支撑）+ er + able（能…的）→ 能支撑自我的 → 可忍受的；可容忍的 例 Although the man can't earn so much money, his loving wife and lovely daughter make his life *tolerable*. 尽管这个男人没有赚很多钱，但他深爱的妻子和可爱的女儿让他的生活还说得过去。 参 intolerable(*a.* 无法忍受的，难耐的)
exclaim [ɪkˈskleɪm]	*v.* 惊叫，呼喊 记 词根记忆：ex(外) + claim(叫喊) → 惊叫 例 The widow *exclaimed* helplessly and nobody knew what had happened to her. 那个寡妇无助地呼喊着，没人知道发生了什么。

exclaim

安红！
我想你！

contradictory [ˌkɑːntrəˈdɪktəri]	*a.* 对立的，矛盾的；反驳的 *n.* 对立物；矛盾因素 记 词根记忆：contra(相反) + dict(说话；断言) + ory → 说反话的 → 对立的，矛盾的 例 The opinions the manager received from his employees were *contradictory*. 经理从员工那得到的意见是互相矛盾的。
anomalous [əˈnɑːmələs]	*a.* 异常的；不规则的(irregular) 记 联想记忆：a(不) + nomal(看做 normal，正常的) + ous → 异常的；不规则的 例 The transfer student was *anomalous*, because he was the only boarder in the class. 这个转校生很特别，因为他是班上唯一的寄宿生。
dissent [dɪˈsent]	*vi.* 不同意，持异议 *n.* 不同意见，异议 记 词根记忆：dis(分离) + sent(送) → 往不同的地方送 → 不同意，持异议 例 Two sides from the debate have their strong *dissents* to each other's opinions. 辩论双方对对方的观点都持强烈的反对意见。
tender [ˈtendər]	*a.* 嫩的；脆弱的；温柔的，亲切的 *v.* (正式)提出；投标 *n.* 投标 记 联想记忆：婴儿很脆弱(tender)，需悉心照料(tend) 搭 tender for 投标 例 A flock of sheep are roaming on the ground and looking for *tender* grass. 一群羊在草地上漫步，寻找着嫩草。
derivative [dɪˈrɪvətɪv]	*a.* 派生的，引出的；无创意的 *n.* 派生词，衍生词；派生物 例 Petroleum is not original, and it's an organic *derivative*. 石油不是原本就有的，而是一种有机衍生物。
bolt [boʊlt]	*v.* 逃跑；闩上 *n.* 插销，门闩；闪电 记 联想记忆：只有大胆的(bold)人才敢逃跑，冲出去(bolt) 搭 a bolt from/out of the blue 晴天霹雳，意外事件 例 The accident on her birthday is like a *bolt* from the blue to her parents. 她生日那天发生的事故对她父母来说简直就是晴天霹雳。

36

calamitous [kə'læmɪtəs]	*a.* 灾难性的(disastrous) 记 来自 calamity(*n.* 灾难) 例 The underground space collapsed in the explosion, with *calamitous* results. 在爆炸中，地下空间坍塌了，造成了灾难性的后果。
surmise	['sɜːrmaɪz] *n.* 推测，猜测(conjecture) [sər'maɪz] *v.* 推测，猜测 记 词根记忆：sur(在…之上) + mis(放) + e → 放在事情之上 → 推测，猜测 例 All of these reasons are pure *surmise* on Joe's part. 所有这些原因纯粹是乔的猜测。
affluent ['æfluənt]	*a.* 丰富的；富裕的 记 词根记忆：af(表加强) + flu(流) + ent → 不断流出的 → 丰富的 例 The man is not a lounge lizard, although he lives in an *affluent* family. 尽管这个男人生活在富裕的家庭，但他并不是一个纨绔子弟。
superimpose [ˌsuːpərɪm'poʊz]	*vt.* 使重叠，使叠加；添加 记 联想记忆：super(在…上面) + impose(强加于) → 强加于上面 → 使重叠，使叠加 例 Father *superimposed* the newspaper on the keys, so mother couldn't find them. 爸爸把报纸放在了钥匙上面，所以妈妈找不到钥匙了。
congest [kən'dʒest]	*v.* (使)充满，拥塞；(使)充血 记 词根记忆：con(共同) + gest(搬运) → 搬运到一起 → (使)充满，拥塞 例 The buses and private cars *congested* in rush hour. 交通高峰期，公交车和私家车挤成一团。 派 congestion(*n.* 拥塞，拥挤；充血)
recollection [ˌrekə'lekʃn]	*n.* 记忆力；回忆，记忆(memory, remembrance)；回想起来的事 记 词根记忆：re(回) + col(一起) + lect(送) + ion(名词后缀) → 将过去的事全部送回 → 回忆 搭 beyond recollection 不记得；within one's recollection 在…的记忆中 例 After the accident, the little boy had no *recollection* at all of his childhood. 这起事故之后，那个小男孩全然回忆不起他的童年了。 派 recollect(*v.* 回忆起，想起)
congratulation [kənˌgrætʃu'leɪʃn]	*n.* 祝贺，道喜 例 Please accept my *congratulation* on your marriage. 请接受我对你们婚礼的祝贺。
ageism ['eɪdʒɪzəm]	*n.* 年龄歧视 例 *Ageism* has significant effects on the elderly and young people. 年龄歧视对老年人和年轻人都有着重大的影响。 参 sexism(*n.* 性别歧视)；racism(*n.* 种族歧视)
pilot ['paɪlət]	*a.* 试验性的 *n.* 飞行员，领航员；领导人 *vt.* 驾驶，领航；试行，试用；使通过，引导 例 In a *pilot* reclamation project, they tested the growth possibilities of eight species of plants. 在一个试验性开垦项目中，他们检测了八个植物物种生长的可能性。

□ calamitous □ surmise □ affluent □ superimpose □ congest □ recollection
□ congratulation □ ageism □ pilot

debut [deɪ'bjuː]	*n.* 首次演出；初次亮相 记 法语词：开始 → 首次演出；初次亮相 搭 film debut 电影首映式 例 He made his *debut* album in 2000. 他于 2000 年推出第一张专辑。
script [skrɪpt]	*n.* 剧本，脚本，广播稿；笔迹（writing, manuscript）；字母表（alphabet） *vt.* 为电影（或戏剧等）写剧本 记 本身为词根，意为"写" 搭 cuneiform script 楔形文字 例 That line isn't in the original *script*. 原剧本中没有那句台词。
consent [kən'sent]	*vi./n.* 同意，赞成，准许（approve, agree） 记 词根记忆：con（共同）+ sent（感觉）→ 有共同的感觉 → 同意，赞成，准许 例 We are fortunate that he's *consented* to share some of his experiences with us. 我们很幸运，他已经同意与我们分享他的一些经历了。
directory [də'rektəri]	*n.* 人名地址录，电话号码簿；目录 记 联想记忆：direct（指引）+ ory（表物）→ 指引人们查询的东西 → 人名地址录 搭 a telephone directory 电话号码簿 例 The 20-page *directory* was issued in November of 1878, just two years after Alexander Graham Bell invented the telephone. 这本长达 20 页的号码簿发行于 1878 年 11 月，仅在亚历山大·格雷厄姆·贝尔发明电话的两年后。
orchid ['ɔːrkɪd]	*n.* 兰，兰花 记 联想记忆：or + chid（看做 child，孩子）→ 孩子天真纯洁像兰花 → 兰花 例 The leaves of some *orchids* are considered ornamental. 一些兰科植物的叶子具有观赏性。
convince [kən'vɪns]	*vt.* 使确信，说服（persuade, assure） 记 词根记忆：con（表加强）+ vinc（征服，克服）+ e → 彻底征服对方 → 使确信，说服 例 She *convinced* the man to apply to graduate school. 她说服了这名男子向研究生院提出申请。 派 convincing（*a.* 令人信服的）；unconvincing（*a.* 不令人信服的）
ardent ['ɑːrdnt]	*a.* 热心的，热情洋溢的（enthusiastic, ardent） 记 词根记忆：ard（燃烧）+ ent → 热心的，热情洋溢的 例 Christina was extremely *ardent* in her admiration for the professor. 克里斯蒂娜对她的教授崇拜得五体投地。 参 impassive（*a.* 无动于衷的，无感情的，冷漠的）
convection [kən'vekʃn]	*n.* 对流；传送（conveying, transmission） 记 词根记忆：con（共同）+ vect（搬运）+ ion → 一起搬运 → 对流 例 A heater is using *convection* when it warms the air in a room. 加热器给屋子里的空气加热时利用的是对流原理。

36

hollow [ˈhɑːloʊ]	*a.* 空心的，中空的；凹陷的；空洞的，虚伪的(false)；(声音)沉闷的，空响的 *n.* 凹陷处，洼地；洞，孔(hole) *vt.* 挖空，凿空 例 The man is destroyed by his own *hollow* values. 这个人被自己虚伪的价值观给毁了。
vague [veɪɡ]	*a.* 模糊的(obscure)；不明确的 记 词根记忆：vag(漫游) + ue → 思路四处漫游 → 模糊的；不明确的 例 A *vague* air of mystery envelops them. 一种模糊的神秘感笼罩着他们。// The language of the charters was *vague*. 许多章程中的语言含混不清。 派 vaguely(*ad.* 含糊地)；vagueness(*n.* 含糊，不明确)
antibiotic [ˌæntibaɪˈɑːtɪk]	*n.* [常 pl.]抗生素 *a.* 抗菌的 记 词根记忆：anti(反) + bio(生命) + tic → 抗生素 例 Now we have lots of *antibiotics* that kill bacteria. 现在我们有很多能消灭细菌的抗生素。
rinse [rɪns]	*vt.* (用清水)冲洗，漂洗，冲刷 *n.* 漂洗，冲洗，洗涤；染发剂 记 联想记忆：rin(=rain 下雨) + se → 雨水冲刷着地面 → (用清水)冲洗 例 *Rinse* the cup out before use. 使用前请将杯子冲洗一下。
nevertheless [ˌnevərðəˈles]	*ad.* 然而，不过(*however, still) 例 She *nevertheless* urged men to educate their daughters and to treat their wives as equals. 然而，她还是督促男性要教育自己的女儿并平等对待妻子。
insult	[ɪnˈsʌlt] *vt.* 侮辱，凌辱(*affront, humiliate) [ˈɪnsʌlt] *n.* 侮辱，凌辱 记 联想记忆：in(在…里面) + sult(看做 salt，盐)→ 灌盐水 → 侮辱，凌辱 例 He *insulted* her by calling her a stupid fool. 他侮辱了她，说她是个笨蛋。
cabin [ˈkæbɪn]	*n.* 小屋(hut, cottage)；机舱，船舱 例 Nineteenth-century *cabins* used as dwellings were occasionally plastered on the interior. 19 世纪用于居住的小木屋，有时候会在内部被涂上灰泥。
gourmet [ˈɡʊrmeɪ]	*a.* 美味的 *n.* 美食家 搭 gourmet food 美味佳肴 例 Over the last few years, a trend has been developing to introduce blended coffees known as *gourmet* coffee into the American market. 近几年兴起了一个潮流，人们把被称做极品咖啡的混合咖啡引入了美国市场。
insect [ˈɪnsekt]	*n.* 昆虫，虫 例 Some *insects* are considered ecologically beneficial and a few provide direct economic benefit. 一些昆虫被认为具有生态价值，还有一些(被认为)能带来直接的经济效益。 insect
productivity [ˌprɑːdʌkˈtɪvəti]	*n.* 生产力，生产率(fertility) 记 来自 product(*n.* 产物，产品) 例 Wage rates depend on levels of *productivity*. 工资水平取决于生产量的多寡。

416
□ hollow   □ vague   □ antibiotic   □ rinse   ■ nevertheless   □ insult
□ cabin   □ gourmet   □ insect   □ productivity

surgeon	*n.* 外科医师
[ˈsɜːrdʒən]	记 联想记忆：surge(波动) + on → 做外科医师，情绪不能太波动 → 外科医师
	例 Although a large number perform general surgery, many *surgeons* choose to specialize in a specific area. 虽然很大一部分外科医师做的是普通外科，但也有很多选择专攻某一领域。
	参 surgery(*n.* 外科学；外科手术；手术室)

govern	*v.* 统治，治理，管理(administrate)；决定，支配；控制，影响
[ˈgʌvərn]	例 Laws are *governing* the printing industry. 依法治理印刷行业。
	派 governing(*a.* 统治的，管理的；控制的)；government(*n.* 政府；政体；统治，治理)

strategy	*n.* 战略，策略(tactics)
[ˈstrætədʒi]	记 联想记忆：str(看做 strange, 奇怪的) + ate(吃) + gy → 用奇怪的方法吃掉对手 → 战略，策略
	例 It's all part of an overall *strategy* to gain promotion. 这都不过是一个获得晋升的完整计划的一部分。
	派 strategic(*a.* 战略性的)；strategist(*n.* 战略家)

average	*a.* 平均的；一般的；平庸的 *n.* 平均水平；平均数 *v.* 平均为
[ˈævərɪdʒ]	搭 an average person 常人；on average 平均起来
	例 The new designed train runs at an *average* speed of 120 miles per hour. 新设计的火车平均时速 120 英里。

postcard	*n.* 明信片
[ˈpoʊstkɑːrd]	例 I received a *postcard* from London. 我收到了一张寄自伦敦的明信片。

mount	*v.* 增加(increase)；登上，攀登；骑上，乘上；发起，组织，开展 *n.* 山，山峰(mountain)；支架，底座
[maʊnt]	例 Blankets of snow and ice grains *mounted* layer upon layer. 厚厚的雪与冰粒层层相叠。

corporate	*a.* 法人的，公司的(incorporated)；共同的，全体的
[ˈkɔːrpərət]	记 词根记忆：corp(身体) + or + ate → 全体的
	例 Sarah used to teach psychology, but now she is a *corporate* statistician. 萨拉过去教心理学，不过她现在是一个公司的统计员。

distasteful	*a.* 令人反感的，讨厌的(displeasing, disagreeable)；味道不佳的
[dɪsˈteɪstfl]	例 The teacher's manners were *distasteful* to every student in the class. 班上的每个学生都不喜欢这个老师的行为举止。

medieval	*a.* 中世纪的，中古的
[ˌmiːdˈiːvl]	记 词根记忆：medi(中间) + ev(时间) + al → 中世纪的，中古的
	例 The museum had an exhibit of *medieval* armor last month. 博物馆上个月展出了中世纪的铠甲。

36

clamor

[ˈklæmər]

n. 吵闹，喧哗(noise)

记 词根记忆：clam(叫喊) + or → 吵闹，喧哗

例 The *clamor* from the backyard drew us out of the house. 后院的喧哗把我们引出了房子。

参 claim(*n.* 要求); proclamation(*n.* 宣言); reclamation(*n.* 回收；开垦)

relevance

[ˈreləvəns]

n. 有关，相关(性)；中肯，适当；重大关系，意义；实用性

记 词根记忆：re(再，又) + lev(举) + ance → 一再举起 → 相关(性)

例 As you prepare to become elementary school teachers, you'll be hearing a lot of discussion about the *relevance* of teaching penmanship. 在准备成为小学老师时，你们会听到很多关于是否应该教授书法的讨论。

biochemical

[ˌbaɪoʊˈkemɪkl]

a. 生物化学的，生化的

例 Enzymes are what make many of the body's *biochemical* reactions possible. 酶使身体内很多生化反应成为可能。

second

[ˈsekənd]

a. 第二的；次等的，二等的 *n.* 秒；瞬间，片刻 *v.* 赞成，附和 *num.* 第二

搭 at second hand 间接地

例 Since I got the news at *second* hand, I cannot vouch for its veracity. 这消息是我间接得来的，我不能保证它的真实性。 //

A: I want to buy two tickets. Is there a discount if I take a student ID card?

B: Oh, let me see. I need to check it. Just a *second*.

A: 我想买两张票，如果我用学生证是否能打折？

B: 让我看看，我需要核实一下，请稍片刻。

assistance

[əˈsɪstəns]

n. 帮助，援助(help, aid)

记 来自 assist(*v.* 帮助，援助)

例 The old man can walk only with the *assistance* of crutches. 那个老人只能靠拐杖走路。 //

A: I'm really having trouble with this calculus course. If I can't start doing better soon, I'm going to have to drop it.

B: Why don't you get some help from the graduate *assistance*? That's what it is there for.

A: 微积分课真难。如果不能很快学好，我打算放弃它了。

B: 你为何不从研究生援助会那里寻求帮助呢？为学生提供帮助就是设立援助会的目的啊。

modeling

[ˈmɑːdlɪŋ]

n. 立体感(third dimension); 建模，造型

例 In sculpture the term "*modeling*" denotes a way of shaping clay, wax, or other pliable materials. 在雕塑艺术中，"造型"一词表示使黏土、蜡或其他可塑材料成形的方式。

laundry

[ˈlɔːndri]

n. 洗衣店，洗衣房；洗好的衣服；待洗的衣服

记 词根记忆：lau(洗) + nd + (o)ry(表地点，名词后缀) → 洗衣店，洗衣房

例 The dormitory *laundry* service gives out clean sheets each week. 宿舍洗衣服务部每周都会发干净的床单。

spew [spjuː]	*v.* 喷涌 (exude, vomit); 射出; 呕吐, 呕出 *n.* 喷出物 例 We assume that volcanoes *spewed* out the same gasses. 我们认为火山喷出了同样的气体。
orbital [ˈɔːrbɪtl]	*a.* 轨道的 记 来自 orbit (*n.* 轨道) 例 *Orbital* resonances greatly enhance the mutual gravitational influence of the bodies. 轨道共振能大幅提高天体间相互的重力影响。
generalization [ˌdʒenrəlaɪˈzeɪʃn]	*n.* 概括, 归纳 例 The speech is full of sweeping *generalizations*. 这篇发言满是泛泛之论。
inheritance [ɪnˈherɪtəns]	*n.* 遗产, 继承物 (heritage); 继承; 遗传 (特征) 搭 historic inheritance 历史遗产 例 Demone and his twin brother entered on their *inheritance* when they were only 21. 德蒙和他的孪生兄弟仅 21 岁时就继承了遗产。
detect [dɪˈtekt]	*vt.* 发现, 察觉 (*discover); 探测 (explore); 查明 记 词根记忆: de (去掉) + tect (遮盖) → 去除遮盖 → 发现, 觉察 例 These experiments were designed to *detect* consciousness. 设计这些实验是为了探测意识。 派 detectable (*a.* 可发觉的); detector (*n.* 探测器)
preference [ˈprefrəns]	*n.* 偏爱 (favoritism); 优先 (权) (superiority) 搭 preference for/to 偏爱 例 He has no reading *preferences*. 他在阅读方面没有特别的喜好。 参 preferred (*a.* 首选的)
subliminal [ˌsʌbˈlɪmɪnl]	*a.* 下意识的, 潜意识的 记 联想记忆: sub (在…下面) + limin (=limen 最小限度的神经刺激) + al → 下意识的, 潜意识的 例 The form of *subliminal* advertising is illegal in some countries in Europe. 在一些欧洲国家, 隐性广告这种形式是非法的。
blame [bleɪm]	*vt.* 谴责, 责备 (condemn, rebuke) *n.* 过失, 责备 (condemnation, reprehension); 责任 搭 be to blame (for sth.) (对某事) 负有责任; take the blame for sth. 对某事承担责任 例 The report *blames* leaders' neglect of duty for milk powder with poor quality. 报道谴责领导人在劣质奶粉问题上玩忽职守。
shape [ʃeɪp]	*n.* 形状, 外形, 样子 (form); 体形, 身材; 形式; 幻象; 情况, 状况 *vt.* 使成为…形状, 塑造; 决定…的形成 搭 in the shape of 呈…的样子; out of shape 变形的, 走样的; take shape 成形; shape up 进展 (顺利); 改善 例 The government provides money in the *shape* of grants and student loans. 政府以助学金和学生贷款的形式提供资金。 参 shame (*n.* 羞耻, 羞愧)

36

hemisphere [ˈhemɪsfɪr]	*n.* (地球或天体的)半球；大脑半球(*side) 记 词根记忆：hemi(半) + spher(球) + e → 半球 例 Columbus returned to Spain from the western *hemisphere*. 哥伦布从西半球返回西班牙。
squirrel [ˈskwɜːrəl]	*n.* 松鼠 例 However some *squirrels* also consume meat, especially when faced with hunger. 然而，一些松鼠也会吃肉食，尤其是在面临饥饿时。
enforce [ɪnˈfɔːrs]	*vt.* 实施，生效，执行(carry out)；强迫，迫使(compel) 记 联想记忆：en(使…) + force(力量) → 使有力量 → 实施；强迫 例 Dr. White *enforces* strict deadlines on lab work. 怀特博士对实验室的工作执行着严格的截止日期限制。
pollen [ˈpɑːlən]	*n.* 花粉 例 The individual *pollen* grains are small enough to require magnification to see details. 单个花粉颗粒太小了，需要放大才能看到细节。
institute [ˈɪnstɪtjuːt]	*vt.* 设立(establish)；制定；开创(initiate) *n.* 研究所，学院 记 词根记忆：in + stit(站立) + ute → 设立 例 The government *instituted* a 35-hour workweek. 政府制定了每周工作35小时的制度。 派 institution(*n.* 机构；风俗习惯；制度；设立)
spark [spɑːrk]	*v.* 激发，引发，触发(blaze, bring about)；冒火花 *n.* 火花，火星(flash) 记 联想记忆：s + park(公园) → 公园经常是擦出爱情火花的地方 → 火花 例 The proposal will *spark* a storm of protest on campus. 这一提案将在校园内引起抗议热潮。
chain [tʃeɪn]	*n.* 链(条)；[*pl.*]镣铐；一连串，一系列(serial)；连锁店 *vt.* 用链条拴住；联号，连锁店 搭 chain reaction 连锁反应 例 Algae are the base of the aquatic food *chain*, which means the other organisms depend on them for food. 水藻是水生食物链的基础，也就是说其他生物依靠它们获得食物。// With bicycle *chains* covered, cyclists would need to clean and oil their chains only once every six months instead of once a week. 盖住自行车链条，骑车的人只需半年而非一周给链条清洗并上油一次。// If that toad became extinct, we'd lose an important link in the *chain* of revolution. 如果那种蟾蜍灭绝了，我们将失去进化链上重要的一环。
monotonous [məˈnɑːtənəs]	*a.* 单调的，无聊的(*boring, *tedious) 记 词根记忆：mono(单个) + ton(声音) + ous → 一个声音的 → 单调的 例 Factory work is less creative and more *monotonous*. 在工厂工作更缺乏创意，更加单调。

rattle [ˈrætl]	*v.* (使)发出咔嗒声；使紧张，使恐惧 *n.* 咔嗒声； 拨浪鼓 例 Every time a train went past, the windows *rattled*. 每逢火车经过，窗户都格格作响。 参 rattlesnake(*n.* 响尾蛇)
similar [ˈsɪmələr]	*a.* 相似的，类似的 (alike) 记 词根记忆：simil(相同) + ar → 相似的 例 We have very *similar* interests. 我们兴趣相仿。 派 similarity(*n.* 类似；类似点)
embarrass [ɪmˈbærəs]	*vt.* 使尴尬，使困窘；使困惑 记 联想记忆：em + barr (看做 bar，酒吧) + ass (蠢驴) → 在酒吧喝醉了表现得像一头驴 → 使尴尬 例 The question about private life *embarrassed* the movie star. 那个关于私生活的问题令电影明星很尴尬。// It *embarrassed* me to speak in front of a group of people. 在一群人面前说话令我感到尴尬。
outfit [ˈaʊtfɪt]	*n.* 全套装备；全套服装 记 联想记忆：out(完全) + fit(合适的) → 里里外外都合适的 → 全套服装 例 I wish these shoes matched my *outfit*. 我希望这双鞋子与我的全套服装相配。
brand [brænd]	*vt.* 铭刻；打烙印于；丑化，败坏名声 *n.* 商标，品牌；类型；烙印 搭 name brand 名牌；brand image 品牌形象 例 The newspaper *branded* the President a dictator. 报纸指责该总统是独裁者。
economical [ˌiːkəˈnɑːmɪkl]	*a.* 经济的，实惠的；节俭的，节约的 (thrifty)；精打细算的 记 词根记忆：eco(家) + nom(管理) + ical → 管理家庭开支的 → 节俭的，节约的 例 My mother is *economical* in all areas of her life. 我母亲在生活的各个方面都很节俭。// A: Currently the only way to stop the books from decaying is to remove the binding and treat each page individually to remove the acid. B: That doesn't sound very *economical*. A: 目前唯一一使书不腐烂的方法就是去掉封面，然后将每一页的酸性物质去掉。 B: 那听起来可不经济。

36

distinguish [dɪˈstɪŋgwɪʃ]	*v.* 区别，辨别(*discriminate, differentiate)；使有别于，成为…的特征；看清，听出；使杰出，使著名 记 词根记忆：di(分开) + sting(刺) + uish → 用刺将…分开 → 区别，辨别 搭 distinguish from 区别，识别；distinguish oneself 使自己脱颖而出 例 These three kinds of meteorites can usually be *distinguished* by density. 这三种陨星通常可以通过密度来区别。 派 distinguishable(*a.* 可区别的；易辨认的)；distinguished(*a.* 著名的；高贵的)
artisan [ˈɑːrtəzn]	*n.* 工匠，手艺人(workman, craftsman) 记 词根记忆：arti(技术) + s + an (表人，名词后缀) → 有技术的人 → 工匠，手艺人 例 *Artisans* were the dominant producers of goods before the Industrial Revolution. 在工业革命发生之前，工匠是物品生产的主力军。
elliptical [ɪˈlɪptɪkl]	*a.* 椭圆(形)的；隐晦的；省略的，简略的 记 来自 ellipse(*n.* 椭圆，椭圆形) 例 The motion of stars in *elliptical* galaxies is predominantly radial. 椭圆星系里的星体主要呈放射状运动。
mint [mɪnt]	*v.* 铸造(硬币)(coin) *n.* 薄荷；造币厂；大量的钱 搭 in mint condition 崭新；完美，完好无缺 例 They identified the city where the penny was *minted*. 他们确定了铸造硬币的城市。

In our efforts to adjust differences of opinion we should be free from intolerance of passion, and our judgements should be unmoved by alluring phrases and unvexed by selfish interests.

在我们努力协调意见的分歧时，应当抛弃偏执与意气用事；我们的判断不应当被花言巧语蒙骗，也不应被个人私利扰乱。

——美国总统 克利夫兰(Grover Cleveland, American President)

van	空	vanish *vi.* 消失	juven	年轻的	rejuvenate *vt.* 使年轻
speci	种类	species *n.* 种类	not	知道	annotation *n.* 注释
grad	走	gradual *a.* 逐步的	spic	看	conspicuous *a.* 显眼的
sit	食物	parasite *n.* 寄生物	pon	放	exponent *n.* 解释者
ol	气味	olfactory *a.* 嗅觉的	clin	倾斜	recline *v.* 斜倚

vanish [ˈvænɪʃ]	*vi.* 消失(disappear, fade); 灭绝(die out) 记 词根记忆: van(空) + ish → 消失; 灭绝 例 Some oyster beds have *vanished* entirely. 一些牡蛎养殖场彻底消失了。
overwhelm [ˌouvərˈwelm]	*vt.* 淹没, 漫过(submerge); 压倒, 击败, 制服(overcome); (感情上)使难以忍受; 使应接不暇 记 组合词: over(在…之上) + whelm(淹没) → 淹没; 压倒 例 Extensive falls of volcanic ash and coarser particles *overwhelm* and bury all forms of life. 火山灰和较粗颗粒大量降落, 淹没并埋葬了所有生命。 派 overwhelming(*a.* 压倒性的, 无法抗拒的)
sequoia [sɪˈkwɔɪə]	*n.* 美洲杉, 红杉(redwood) 例 Most visitors come to the National Park only to see some *sequoias*, but these trees are found in a relatively small area. 大多数游客来国家公园只为了看红杉, 但这些树只在相对较小的区域可见。
prairie [ˈpreri]	*n.* 大草原 记 联想记忆: pr + air(空气) + ie → 大草原上空气好 → 大草原 例 The tallgrass *prairie* has been converted into one of the most intensive crop producing areas in North America. 在北美, 高草草原已成为农作物生产最密集的区域之一。
canal [kəˈnæl]	*n.* 运河, 沟渠 *vt.* 开运河 记 发音记忆: "可难啰" → 完全靠双手开挖运河可是件难事 → 运河 例 *Canal* building was revived in this age because of commercial expansion. 在这一时期, 因为商业扩张, 运河开凿又得以复兴。

exact [ɪgˈzækt]	*a.* 精确的，准确的（precise）；严谨的，严格的；精密的 *vt.* 要求，索取；强迫，迫使 记 联想记忆：ex(出) + act(做) → 做出精确的结果 → 精确的 搭 to be exact 准确说来 例 To be *exact*, the assignments must be handed in on time by the end of next Monday. 准确地说，必须在下周一前准时交作业。
retail [ˈriːteɪl]	*n.* 零售 *v.* 零售；以…价格销售 *ad.* 以零售方式 记 词根记忆：re + tail(切割) → 切割成小块出售 → 零售 例 *Retail* merchants were not willing to sell goods at low prices. 零售商不愿意低价出售商品。 派 retailer(*n.* 零售商；零售店)
hypothesis [haɪˈpɑːθəsɪs]	*n.* 假设，假说（assumption, theory）；前提 记 联想记忆：hypo(在…下面) + thesis(论点) → 在论点之下，非真正论点 → 假设，假说 例 Professor Brown's *hypothesis* was that whales ate polluted fish, and this caused their death. 布朗教授的假设是鲸鱼食用了受到污染的鱼而死亡。
selection [sɪˈlekʃn]	*n.* 选择，挑选（choice）；精选（assortment）；被挑选出来的人（或物），精选品；可供选择的事物 例 In other words, natural *selection* is an important process （though not the only process） by which evolution takes place within a population of organisms. 换句话说，自然选择是生物种群一个重要(尽管不是唯一)的进化过程。
tug [tʌg]	*v.* (用力地)拖，拉 *n.* 牵引（pull）；猛拉；拖船 记 联想记忆：蚂蚁拖着(tug)虫子(bug)的尸体 例 A little girl *tugged* at my sleeve to get my attention. 一个小女孩拽了拽我的袖子，想引起我的注意。
overdue [ˌoʊvərˈduː]	*a.* 过期未付的，逾期的；过度的，过火的；迟到的，延误的 记 组合词：over(超过) + due(预期的) → 超过期限的 → 逾期的 例 I have to take these magazines back to the library — they're *overdue*. 我得把这些杂志带到图书馆去还了——它们已经过期了。
frustrate [ˈfrʌstreɪt]	*vt.* 使感到灰心，挫败（confound）；阻止 记 联想记忆：frust + rate （费用） → 出去玩只带了一部分钱，费用不够，很有挫败感 → 挫败 例 The rescue attempt was *frustrated* by bad weather. 营救行动因天气恶劣而受阻。 派 frustration(*n.* 懊丧，懊恼；挫折); frustrating(*a.* 令人沮丧的)

outline ['aʊtlaɪn]	*n.* 轮廓(profile)；概要(summarization)，**大纲** *vt.* 描绘；略述 记 联想记忆：out(外面的) + line(线条) → 轮廓；概要 例 She hasn't prepared the course *outline* yet. 她尚未准备好课程大纲。
species ['spiːsiːz]	*n.* **种类，类群**(group, class) 记 词根记忆：speci(种类) + es → 种类，类群 例 Only a few of the many *species* at risk of extinction actually make it to the lists and obtain legal protection like pandas. 事实上，在许多濒临灭绝的物种中，只有很少一部分进入了名单，像熊猫一样得到了法律保护。
negate [nɪ'ɡeɪt]	*vt.* **取消；否定**(deny) 记 词根记忆：neg(否定) + ate → 取消；否定 例 The new law *negated* the possibility of a reduction in taxes. 新的法律否定了减少税收的可能性。
consequence ['kɑːnsəkwens]	*n.* **结果**(outcome)；**影响**(influence)；**推理**(inference)；**重要(性)，重大** 记 词根记忆：con + sequ(跟随) + ence → 跟随其后 → 结果；影响 搭 in consequence of 由于…的缘故 例 The extinction of a few species is a *consequence* of human progress. 一些物种的灭绝是人类进步带来的结果。// The relative importance of each consideration or *consequence* is determined. 每种考虑或后果的相对重要性都是确定的。 派 consequent(*a.* 随之发生的)
overcome [ˌoʊvər'kʌm]	*vt.* **战胜，克服**(conquer, defeat) 记 来自词组 come over(战胜，克服) 例 Fortunately, scientific and technological advances have *overcome* most of these problems. 幸运的是，科技进步已经克服了其中的大部分问题。
adjacent [ə'dʒeɪsnt]	*a.* **邻近的，毗连的**(*nearby, adjoining, bordering) 记 词根记忆：ad(近) + jac(扔) + ent(形容词后缀) → 扔得很近的 → 邻近的，毗连的 例 Only in Pennsylvania and *adjacent* areas was stone widely used in dwellings. 只有在宾夕法尼亚州及其附近地区石头才广泛应用于建造住所。
gradual ['ɡrædʒuəl]	*a.* **逐渐的，逐步的；坡度平缓的，不陡的** 记 词根记忆：grad(走) + ual → 一步步地行走 → 逐渐的，逐步的 例 They grow by the *gradual* transformation of snow into glacier ice. 当雪逐渐转化为冰川时，它们得到增长。 派 gradually(*ad.* 逐渐地，逐步地)

37

□ outline   □ species   □ negate   □ consequence □ overcome   □ adjacent
□ gradual

425

puppet [ˈpʌpɪt]	*n.* 木偶(marionette); 玩偶(doll); 傀儡，受人操纵的人(或集团) 记 联想记忆: pup(小狗) + pet(宠物) → 宠物小狗 → 木偶; 玩偶 例 The occupying forces set up a *puppet* government. 占领军建立了一个傀儡政府.
accounting [əˈkaʊntɪŋ]	*n.* 会计学; 会计 例 Management *accounting* is concerned primarily with providing a basis for making management or operating decisions. 管理会计主要是为(决策者们)做管理或业务上的决策提供根据.
roll [rəʊl]	*v.* (使)滚动，转动; 卷，绕; (使)摇摆，(使)摇晃 *n.* (一)卷; 卷形物; 名单，花名册 例 Icebergs may *roll* over unexpectedly. 冰山有可能会出人意料地滚动. 派 roller(*n.* 滚筒，滚轴); rolling(*a.* 旋转的; 起伏的)
irony [ˈaɪrəni]	*n.* 反话，讽刺，嘲弄; 具有讽刺意味的事 记 联想记忆: iron(铁) + y → 像铁一样冷冰冰的话 → 反话，讽刺 例 There was a hint of *irony* in her voice. 她的声音里有一丝讽刺之意.
parasite [ˈpærəsaɪt]	*n.* 寄生物; 食客 记 词根记忆: para(在…旁边) + sit(食物) + e → 坐在旁边白吃的 → 寄生物 例 The tachinid fly is a *parasite* of harmful insects. 寄蝇是一种有害的寄生昆虫. 派 parasitic(*a.* 寄生的)
clumsy [ˈklʌmzi]	*a.* 笨拙的(awkward); 不得体的，冒犯人的; 复杂难懂的，难处理的 例 Her *clumsy* fingers couldn't untie the knot. 她笨手笨脚的，解不开这个结.
recession [rɪˈseʃn]	*n.* (经济的)衰退，衰退时期，萧条时期; 撤回，退回 记 词根记忆: re(反) + cess(行走) + ion → 向后走 → 衰退; 撤回 例 What they are hoping to do is to come up with a coordinated plan to ease the *recession*, get their economies back on track and put in place regulatory measures to try to prevent similar crises in the future. 他们希望提出一项统筹规划来减缓经济衰退并使经济重回轨道，还希望拟出调整措施以避免相同危机的再次爆发.

inaccessible [ˌɪnækˈsesəbl]	*a.* 难达到的，不可及的(unreachable)；不能得到的(unattainable) 记 联想记忆：in(不) + accessible(易达到的) → 难达到的，不可及的 例 In the west only a small part of the region has been surveyed because most of the lands are *inaccessible*. 在西部只有一小部分地区得到了勘察，因为大多数地区人们难以到达。
deduct [dɪˈdʌkt]	*vt.* 扣除，减去(subtract)；推论，演绎 记 词根记忆：de(向下) + duct(拉) → 向下拉 → 扣除，减去 例 The tax will be *deducted* from your salary later. 税稍后会从你的工资里扣掉。 派 deduction(*n.* 推论，演绎；扣除)；deductive(*a.* 推论的，演绎的) 参 conduct(*v.* 引导 *n.* 行为)
philosophy [fəˈlɑːsəfi]	*n.* 哲学；哲学体系，思想体系；人生观，人生哲学 记 词根记忆：philo(爱) + soph(聪明，智慧) + y(名词后缀) → 爱智慧的学问 → 哲学 搭 metaphysical philosophy 形而上学哲学 例 Her *philosophy* of life is to take it one day at a time. 她的人生哲学是做一天和尚撞一天钟。 派 philosopher(*n.* 哲学家；善于思考的人)；philosophic(*a.* 哲学的；达观的) 参 psychology(*n.* 心理学)；philology(*n.* 语文学) philosophy 禅
reptile [ˈreptaɪl]	*n.* 爬行动物，爬虫类；卑鄙的人 记 词根记忆：rept(爬) + ile(表物，名词后缀) → 爬行动物 例 Not until the beginning of the 19th century did it become clear that *reptiles* and amphibians are in fact quite different animals. 到了19世纪初，人们才清楚爬行动物和两栖类动物实际上是完全不同的两类动物。 派 reptilian(*a.* 爬虫类的)
admit [ədˈmɪt]	*v.* 承认(confess)；准许…进入，接纳(*let in) 记 词根记忆：ad(向，往) + mit(送) → 往里送 → 接纳 搭 admit of 容许，有…可能 例 I must *admit* that my performance was bad. 我必须承认我表现不佳。 派 admittance(*n.* 进入；进入权)；admittedly(*ad.* 诚然；公认地)
swamp [swɑːmp]	*n.* 沼泽地，湿地(marsh) *vt.* 使陷入，淹没；使应接不暇，使疲于应对(overwhelm) 例 Slogging through a *swamp* in the rain is not funny. 在大雨中穿过沼泽地可不是闹着玩的。// I have been *swamped* with other things. 我一直忙着别的事。 派 swampy(*a.* 沼泽的，湿地的)
germinate [ˈdʒɜːrmɪneɪt]	*v.* (使)发芽，萌芽；(使)发展 记 词根记忆：germ(芽) + in + ate → (使)发芽 例 The idea of establishing her own enterprise started to *germinate* in her mind when she was just a college student. 上大学期间她就萌生了自己创业的想法。

37

□ inaccessible   □ deduct   □ philosophy   □ reptile   □ admit   □ swamp
□ germinate

procedure
[prəˈsiːdʒər]

n. 程序，手续，步骤(approach, course)

例 You should follow the graduate school application *procedures*. 你应该遵循研究生院申请程序。

encase
[ɪnˈkeɪs]

vt. 包住(*embed)

记 联想记忆：en(进入) + case(容器) → 被装入容器中 → 包住

例 Floating on the oceans every year are 7 quadrillion 659 trillion metric tons of ice *encased* in 10,000 icebergs. 每年有 1 万座冰山包裹着 7659 兆公吨的冰漂浮在海洋上。

restoration
[ˌrestəˈreɪʃn]

n. 恢复；整修，修复；复位，复原；归还

例 The common citizens in the country demand a *restoration* of the right to vote. 这个国家的普通民众要求恢复选举权。

olfactory
[ɑːlˈfæktəri]

a. 嗅觉的

记 词根记忆：ol(气味) + fact(制作，做) + ory → 使有气味的 → 嗅觉的

例 The poisonous gas damaged my *olfactory* nerves. 毒气破坏了我的嗅觉神经。

canvas
[ˈkænvəs]

n. 画布；油画；帆布

搭 under canvas 在帐篷里

例 There will be a sale of the artist's early *canvases* this Sunday. 本周日将举办那位画家早期油画的拍卖会。

pique
[piːk]

vt. 激怒(provoke)；激起，引起(arouse) *n.* 恼怒，生气；怨恨

记 词根记忆：piqu(刺激) + e → 因受刺激而不悦 → 激怒

搭 pique one's interest/curiosity 激起某人的兴趣/好奇心

例 When he realized nobody was listening to him, he left in a fit of *pique*. 发觉无人听他的话，他愤然离去了。

downside
[ˈdaʊnsaɪd]

n. 缺点，负面；底侧；下降趋势

例 The *downside* of my part-time job is that the company is too far away from my dorm. 我的兼职工作不好的一点是公司离宿舍太远了。

参 upside(*n.* 上边，上面)

locate
[ˈloʊkeɪt]

vt. 使坐落于(situate)；找出，定位(orient)

记 词根记忆：loc(地点) + ate → 找到地点 → 找出，定位

例 Her hotel is *located* far from the conference center. 她的酒店距会议中心很远。// She'd be able to *locate* where the man was seated. 她能够找到那个男子的座位。

派 location(*n.* 位置；场所)

anecdote
[ˈænɪkdoʊt]

n. 秘闻；轶事，趣闻

记 词根记忆：an(不) + ec(=ex 外) + dot(给予) + e → 没有向外给的 → 未公开的 → 秘闻

例 There is a memoir of *anecdotes* of the family on the bookshelf. 书架上有一本家庭轶事录。

turbulent [ˈtɜːrbjələnt]	*a.* 动乱的(disorderly); 狂暴的, 汹涌的(violent) 记 词根记忆: turb(搅动) + ul + ent → 搅动得厉害 → 动乱的; 狂暴的, 汹涌的 例 The weather patterns are so *turbulent* here. 这里的天气非常多变。
sophisticated [səˈfɪstɪkeɪtɪd]	*a.* 老练的, 见多识广的(worldly-wise); 精密的(exact); 复杂的, 先进的(complex, developed); 高雅的, 有教养的 记 来自 sophisticate(*n.* 久经世故的人) 例 Computer systems are becoming more *sophisticated* all the time. 计算机系统日益复杂先进。 派 unsophisticated(*a.* 不懂世故的; 单纯的) 参 sophistication(*n.* 世故; 精密, 复杂)
draw [drɔː]	*v.* 吸引, 招引(attract, entice); 画, 描绘; 拖, 拉; 引起, 激起; 拨出, 抽出; 提取, 支取; 推断出; 打成平局 *n.* 平局, 和局; 抽签 例 The plan has *drawn* a lot of criticism. 这个计划引来众多批评。
rejuvenate [rɪˈdʒuːvəneɪt]	*vt.* 使年轻; 使恢复活力(refresh) 记 词根记忆: re(再, 又) + juven(年轻的) + ate(使…) → 使年轻; 使恢复活力 例 Music can help *rejuvenate* or soothe the patient. 音乐有助于患者恢复活力, 或减轻痛苦。
tentacle [ˈtentəkl]	*n.* 触角, 触须, 触手(antenna) 记 词根记忆: tent(感觉) + acle(表物, 名词后缀) → 用于感知的东西 → 触角 例 The *tentacles* drag this prey into the sea anemone's mouth. 触角把捕获物拉进海葵的嘴里。
furious [ˈfjʊriəs]	*a.* 狂怒的, 狂暴的(angry); 强烈的, 猛烈的 搭 be furious with sb. at sth. 因某事对某人大发雷霆 例 He was *furious* with himself for letting things get so out of control. 他生自己的气, 怪自己竟把事情搞得如此不可收拾。 参 curious(*a.* 好奇的)
annotation [ˌænəˈteɪʃn]	*n.* 注释, 注解 记 词根记忆: an(加) + not(知道) + ation → 加上文字以让人知道 → 注释, 注解 例 The book will be published with *annotations* and the index. 这本书出版时将附有注释和索引。
rage [reɪdʒ]	*v.* (暴风雨、火势、战斗等)猛烈地继续, 激烈进行; 发怒, 怒斥; (流行病等)迅速蔓延, 猖獗 *n.* 风靡一时的事物, 时尚(fashion); 狂怒(anger, fury) 记 联想记忆: r + age(时代) → 不同的时代有不同的时尚 → 时尚 例 Forest fires were *raging* out of control. 森林大火迅速蔓延, 失去了控制。 派 enrage(*vt.* 激怒)

37

fiery [ˈfaɪəri]	*a.* 似火的；易怒的，暴躁的 记 联想记忆：fier(看做 fire，火) + y → 似火的 例 After some drinking, my father's temper became *fiery*. 喝了点酒之后，我爸爸的脾气变得火爆了。
grouse [graʊs]	*v.* 发牢骚，抱怨 *n.* 松鸡；怨言 记 联想记忆：松鸡(grouse) 抱怨(grouse) 说，它总是在清早被唤醒(arouse) 例 The husband is *grousing* about his wife always chattering about tiny things. 丈夫抱怨妻子总是唠叨一些琐碎的事情。
afloat [əˈfloʊt]	*a.* 漂浮的；有偿债能力的，能维持下去的 *ad.* 漂浮地 记 联想记忆：a + float(漂浮) → 漂浮的 例 The paper was *afloat* in the water without sinking like a stone. 纸在水中漂浮着，而没有像石头一样沉下去。
scruple [ˈskruːpl]	*n./vi.* 踌躇，顾忌，顾虑 记 联想记忆：scrup(看做 scrub，矮小的人) + le → 矮小者时常不自信，顾忌很多 → 顾忌 搭 not scruple to do sth. 肆无忌惮地做某事 例 Tina lent her boyfriend one thousand dollars to help him out without any *scruple*. 蒂娜毫不犹豫地借给男友 1000 美金帮他渡过难关。
rob [rɑːb]	*vt.* 抢夺，抢掠；剥夺，使失去(plunder) 搭 rob sb. blind 骗取某人大量钱财；rob sb. of sth. 从某人那抢走某物 例 A last-minute goal *robbed* the team of victory. 最后一分钟的进球使这支球队与胜利擦肩而过。
dissimulate [dɪˈsɪmjuleɪt]	*v.* 掩盖，掩饰，假装(dissemble) 记 词根记忆：dis(不) + simul(相同) + ate → 不和本来面目相同 → 掩盖，掩饰 例 The little boy was *dissimulating* his sorrow of losing his mother. 那个小男孩一直掩饰着自己的丧母之痛。
aboriginal [ˌæbəˈrɪdʒənl]	*a.* (人、生物等)原始的(native)；土著的，土生土长的 *n.* 土著 记 联想记忆：ab + original(最初的) → 原始的；土著的 例 This group of *aboriginal* people used to live in the tribe. 这些土著人过去生活在部落中。
expedient [ɪkˈspiːdiənt]	*n.* 权宜之计，应急办法，临时手段 *a.* (行动等)得当的，可取的 记 词根记忆：ex(外) + ped(脚) + ient → 将脚向外迈 → 权宜之计 例 After hearing the story, the government resorted to various *expedients* to raise money. 听到这个报道之后，政府采取各种应急办法筹款。
superstitious [ˌsuːpərˈstɪʃəs]	*a.* 迷信的，受迷信思想支配的 记 词根记忆：super(在…之上) + stit(站立) + ious → 站在他物之上的 → 迷信的 例 Some foreigners are *superstitious* about opening umbrellas in the room. 一些外国人迷信在屋里撑伞是不吉利的。

430 □ fiery   □ grouse   □ afloat   □ scruple   □ rob   □ dissimulate
□ aboriginal   □ expedient   □ superstitious

elapse [ɪˈlæps]	*vi.* (时间)消逝，流逝 记 词根记忆：e(外) + laps(掉) + e → 向外掉落 → (时间)消逝 例 Ten years have *elapsed* since we graduated from college. 从我们大学毕业至今，已经十年了。
auspicious [ɔːˈspɪʃəs]	*a.* 吉兆的，吉利的；幸运的 记 词根记忆：au(=avi 鸟) + spic(看) + ious → 看见传说中的青鸟 → 吉兆的 例 We are very happy to have an *auspicious* start to the new year. 我们很高兴新年有个好彩头。
plow [plaʊ]	*n.* 犁 *v.* 耕田，犁田，耕作(cultivate, till) 记 联想记忆：牛(cow)在耕田(plow) 搭 plow sth. into sth. 把…大量投资于…，把…大量投入于…；plow through 艰难地进行；猛冲过 例 The *plowed* fields had been sown with wheat. 犁过的田地已经种上了小麦。
categorize [ˈkætəgəraɪz]	*vt.* 将…分类，把…加以分类 记 来自 category(*n.* 种类) 例 The music albums are *categorized* into Chinese, English and Japanese. 音乐专辑被分成中文、英文和日文三类。
despondent [dɪˈspɑːndənt]	*a.* 垂头丧气的，沮丧的 例 The whole team was so *despondent*, because they didn't get the project. 因为没有拿到这个项目，整个团队都很沮丧。
espouse [ɪˈspaʊz]	*vt.* 支持，拥护，赞成 记 词根记忆：e(出) + spous(约定) + e → 给出约定 → 支持，拥护，赞成 例 Mary is the chairman of the group which *espouses* feminism. 玛丽是那个拥护女权主义组织的主席。
conspicuous [kənˈspɪkjuəs]	*a.* 显眼的，明显的 记 词根记忆：con(共同) + spic(看) + uous → 大家都能看到的 → 显眼的 例 A blond girl in a Chinese school is very *conspicuous*. 一个金发碧眼的女孩在中国学校里是很显眼的。
hind [haɪnd]	*a.* 后面的，在后的(back) 记 联想记忆：后面的(behind)后面(hind) 例 The *hind* legs of the gerbil are particularly well adapted to leaping across its desert habitat. 沙鼠的后腿尤其适应于在沙漠栖息地跳跃。
untapped [ˌʌnˈtæpt]	*a.* 未开发的，未使用的 记 来自 tap(*vt.* 开发，利用) 例 Three quarters of the Earth's fresh water supply are still tied up in glacial ice, a reservoir of *untapped* fresh water. 地球上四分之三的淡水供应仍存在于冰川中，那里蕴藏着未开发的淡水。

37

ambush [ˈæmbʊʃ]	*n./vt.* 埋伏，伏击 记 联想记忆：am(上午) + bush(灌木丛) → 一上午躲在灌木丛里 → 埋伏 例 The team was *ambushing* in the bush. 一队人马正埋伏在灌木丛里。
exponent [ɪkˈspoʊnənt]	*n.* 解释者；倡导者，拥护者(advocator)；指数，幂 记 词根记忆：ex(出) + pon(放) + ent → 将内心想法放出的人 → 解释者 例 She was a leading *exponent* of free trade during her political career. 她从政期间是自由贸易的主要倡导者。 派 exponential(*a.* 指数的，幂的)
confusion [kənˈfjuːʒn]	*n.* 困惑；混乱，混淆 记 来自 confuse(*vt.* 使困惑；弄乱) 搭 lead to confusion 导致混乱；in confusion 困惑地 例 There is some *confusion* about what the exact definition of the theory should be. 关于这个理论的确切定义是什么还存在着一些困惑。
resist [rɪˈzɪst]	*v.* 抵抗(withstand)；耐(热等)，抗(病等) 记 词根记忆：re(反) + sist(站) → 反着站 → 抵抗 例 It *resists* breaking when heated. 加热时它能够防裂。 派 resistance(*n.* 反抗；阻力；电阻)；resistant(*a.* 抵抗的)
moth [mɔːθ]	*n.* 蛾 记 发音记忆："莫死" → 不畏死 → 飞蛾扑火不畏死 → 蛾 例 *Moths* frequently appear to circle artificial lights, although the reason for this behavior remains unknown. 飞蛾经常绕着人造灯光飞，但这一行为背后的原因尚不为人所知。
shame [ʃeɪm]	*n.* 羞耻，羞愧，耻辱；可耻的人(或事物) *vt.* 使羞愧；玷辱 搭 put…to shame 使自愧不如，使相形见绌 例 My failure has brought *shame* on my family. 我的失败使家人蒙羞。 // A: Just as Sarah was opening the present, I realized the camera wasn't working. B: What a *shame*! A: 萨拉正要打开礼物时，我发现相机不能用了。 B: 真遗憾! 参 ashamed(*a.* 羞愧的，惭愧的；羞耻的)；shave(*v.* 刮)
biologist [baɪˈɑːlədʒɪst]	*n.* 生物学家 例 Cantor, at the age of 50, had a world-wide reputation as a cell *biologist*. 康托尔在 50 岁时成为举世闻名的细胞生物学家。 参 anthropologist(*n.* 人类学家)；archaeologist(*n.* 考古学家)；sociologist(*n.* 社会学家)
disaster [dɪˈzæstər]	*n.* 灾难(*catastrophe)；彻底的失败 记 词根记忆：dis(离开) + aster(星星) → 星位不正，预示有灾难 → 灾难 例 The Mandans protected themselves against the *disaster* of crop failure and accompanying hunger. 曼丹人保护自己免遭作物歉收以及由此引发的饥饿所带来的灾难影响。 派 disastrous(*a.* 灾难性的)

incessant

[ɪnˈsesnt]

a. 不断的，不停的(unceasing)

记 词根记忆：in(不) + cess(走) + ant → 走个不停 → 不断的，不停的

例 I'm tired of his *incessant* complaining. 他无休止的抱怨让我厌烦。

派 incessantly(*ad.* 不断地，不停地)

skull

[skʌl]

n. 颅骨，头骨；脑袋；头脑

记 联想记忆：据说脑袋(skull)大的人掌握技能(skill)比较快

例 In some animals, the *skull* also has a defensive function. 一些动物的头骨也具有防御功能。

infant

[ˈɪnfənt]

n. 婴儿，幼儿(baby) *a.* 婴儿的；初期的

例 Usually anything that is shiny, has sharp contrasting colors, or has complex patterns will catch an *infant's* eye. 通常只要是闪闪发亮的，或色彩对比鲜明的，或有着复杂图案的东西都能抓住婴儿的视线。

commune

[kəˈmjuːn] *vi.* 与…亲密地交谈 [ˈkɑːmjuːn] *n.* 群体，公社

记 词根记忆：com(共同) + mun(服务) + e → 为大家服务 → 群体，公社

例 The man spent much of his time *communing* with nature. 那个男人许多时间里都沉浸在大自然中。

recline

[rɪˈklaɪn]

v. 向后倚靠，斜倚

记 词根记忆：re(向后) + clin(倾斜) + e → 向后斜 → 斜倚

例 If anyone is tired during the visit, he or she can *recline* on the lounge chair for tourists. 如果有人在参观期间感到疲惫，可以斜躺在为游客准备的沙发椅上。

参 incline[*v.* (使)倾斜]

available

[əˈveɪləbl]

a. 可得到的，可找到的(*accessible, obtainable)；有空的(free)

记 联想记忆：avail(有用) + able(能…的) → 可利用的 → 可得到的

例 Evening wear isn't *available* in those shops. 那些商店不卖晚装。// I'll be *available* on Tuesday and Friday afternoons to discuss your papers with you. 我周四下午和周五下午有空和你讨论你的论文。

派 availability(*n.* 可得到性)；unavailable(*a.* 不可获得的)

environmental

[ɪnˌvaɪrənˈmentl]

a. 有关环境的，自然环境的，生态环境的；环境的

搭 environmental influences 环境影响

例 Let's talk about an *environmental* issue that has something to do with how common household products have changed. 我们来谈论一个环境问题，这个问题与普通家庭用品如何发生了改变有关。//

A: Hi, Jim. What are you doing?

B: Hi, Linda. I'm working on a report on energy resources for my *environmental* science class.

A: 你好，吉姆。你在干什么？

B: 你好，琳达。我在为环境科学课写一份能源资源报告。

37

tableland

[ˈteɪbllænd]

n. 高原，台地(plateau)

例 The *tableland* was once a hive of volcanic activity. 该高原曾是火山活动活跃地。

433

erect [ɪˈrekt]	*a.* 直立的(upright) *vt.* 建立(establish)；竖立 记 词根记忆：e(向上) + rect(直) → 直立的；建立 例 Many buildings in this style were *erected* nationwide through government programs during the Depression. 在大萧条时期，很多这种风格的建筑物通过政府立项在全国各地修建了起来。
illuminate [ɪˈluːmɪneɪt]	*vt.* 照亮(lighten)；启发，启迪；阐明，说明 记 词根记忆：il(向内) + lumin(光) + ate → 向内投入光 → 照亮；启发 例 The light *illuminates* the scales of the fish at the bottom of the boat. 灯照亮了船底处的鱼的鳞片。 派 illuminating(*a.* 照亮的；启蒙的，富有启发性的)
spheroid [ˈsfɪrɔɪd]	*n.* 球状体，椭球体 记 词根记忆：spher(球) + oid → 球状体 例 On closer examination I saw it was really a *spheroid*. 进一步观察后，我发现它实际上是个椭球体。
fatigue [fəˈtiːɡ]	*n.* 劳累(tiredness)；(金属材料等的)疲劳 记 联想记忆：fat(胖的) + igue → 胖人容易劳累 → 劳累 例 Metal *fatigue* is the tendency of metal to break under repeated stress. 金属疲劳是指金属在反复受压后容易断裂。
climate [ˈklaɪmət]	*n.* 气候；气候区，地带；风气，氛围；思潮 例 Economic globalization has become a trend in the current economic *climate*. 经济全球化已成为当前经济气候的一个趋势。
novice [ˈnɑːvɪs]	*n.* 生手，新手(tyro)；新信徒 记 联想记忆：no(不) + vice(副的，第二的) → 连副的都不是 → 生手，新手 例 Selina is a complete *novice* as a journalist. 塞利娜作为记者完全是个新手。
recall [rɪˈkɔːl]	*v.* 回忆起，回想起(recollect)；召回，叫回；收回，撤销 *n.* 记忆力，记性；召回 记 联想记忆：re(再，又) + call(叫喊) → 再次喊起旧日的小名 → 回忆起 例 I seem to *recall* that the festival got started in the 1930s. 我好像记得20世纪30年代才开始庆祝这个节日。

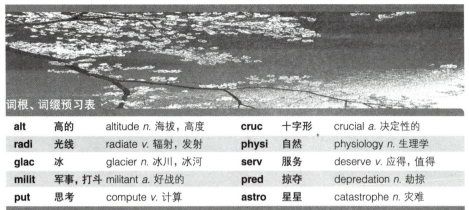

词根、词缀预习表

alt	高的	altitude n. 海拔，高度	cruc	十字形	crucial a. 决定性的
radi	光线	radiate v. 辐射，发射	**physi**	自然	physiology n. 生理学
glac	冰	glacier n. 冰川，冰河	**serv**	服务	deserve v. 应得，值得
milit	军事，打斗	militant a. 好战的	**pred**	掠夺	depredation n. 劫掠
put	思考	compute v. 计算	**astro**	星星	catastrophe n. 灾难

external [ɪk'stɜːrnl]	*a.* 外部的，外面的(exterior)；外来的；对外的 记 词根记忆：ex(外) + ternal → 外部的，外面的 例 A combination of internal and *external* factors caused the company to close down. 内外因素结合导致了该公司的倒闭。
altitude ['æltɪtjuːd]	*n.* 海拔，高度(height)；[常 *pl.*] 高处 记 词根记忆：alt(高的) + it + ude(表状态，名词后缀) → 海拔，高度 例 Plants cannot move water to high *altitudes*. 工厂无法把水输送到高海拔地区。
pursuit [pər'suːt]	*n.* 追求；[常 *pl.*]花时间和精力等做的事；消遣 例 The peregrine falcon has been clocked at 140 to 200 miles per hour in successful *pursuit* of pray. 游隼成功追捕猎物时被记录的飞行速度为每小时 140-200 英里。
vertical ['vɜːrtɪkl]	*a.* 垂直的，竖直的(upright, erect) *n.* 垂直线 记 联想记忆：电影《垂直极限》*Vertical Limit* 例 There are both horizontal and *vertical* movements in air. 空气中既有水平运动也有垂直运动。 派 vertically(*ad.* 垂直地)
rigid ['rɪdʒɪd]	*a.* 严格的(strict)；刚硬的，不易弯曲的(stiff)；死板的，刻板的；僵硬的 记 联想记忆：rig(=rog 要求) + id → 不断要求 → 严格的 例 The curriculum was too narrow and too *rigid*. 课程设置过于狭窄和死板。 派 rigidity(*n.* 坚硬；死板)
flavor ['fleɪvər]	*n.* 风味，滋味(taste)；调味品 *vt.* 给…调味 搭 a bitter flavor 苦味；a strong flavor 口味重；flavor of …的风味 例 This salad needs something to give it more *flavor*. 这个沙拉需要加点东西才更有味道。 // I wonder what this new *flavor* of ice cream tastes like. 我想知道这种新风味的冰激凌口味如何。

priority
['praɪ'ɔːrəti]

n. 优先权，优先 (privilege)；优先考虑的事，最重要的事

记 来自 prior (*a.* 在前的)

例 The system gives *priority* to the students who have been here the longest. 该制度给在这里时间最久的学生以优先权。

radiate
['reɪdieɪt]

v. (光、热等)辐射，发射；流露，显示；自中心向各方伸展

记 词根记忆：radi (光线) + ate → 发出光线 → 辐射，发射

例 He *radiated* self-confidence. 他显得很自信。

派 radiation (*n.* 辐射；放射线)；radiator (*n.* 散热器，暖气片)；radiant (*a.* 光芒四射的；辐射的)

radiate

glacier
['gleɪʃər]

n. 冰川，冰河

记 词根记忆：glac (冰) + ier → 冰川，冰河

例 The *glaciers* that reached the Pacific Coast were valley *glaciers*. 延伸到太平洋沿岸的冰川是山谷冰川。

position
[pə'zɪʃn]

vt. 安置 (install) *n.* 位置 (location)；职位 (*job)；立场 (*status)；姿势，姿态；见解

记 词根记忆：pos (放) + ition → 位置；安置

例 In the rising wind, the boys have *positioned* themselves to counterbalance the tilt of the boat as it speeds along in a choppy sea. 风越来越大，男孩们摆好姿势，以平衡船在波浪起伏的大海中急速行驶时产生的倾斜。

beach
[biːtʃ]

n. 海滩，湖滩，河滩

搭 a beach person 常去海滩的人，海滩迷

例 Geologists have found that seawalls actually speed up the destruction of the *beaches*. 地质学家们发现，海堤其实会加速对海滩的破坏。

参 reach (*v.* 到达)

assistant
[ə'sɪstənt]

a. 辅助的，助理的；副的 *n.* 助手，助教 (helper, aide)

搭 teaching assistant 助教；personal assistant 私人助理；sales assistant 销售助理

例 Bob was quickly sacked, and one week later Friedman chose Joe as *assistant* general manager. 鲍勃很快被开除了，一周之后弗里德曼选择了乔为副总经理。

派 assist (*v.* 帮助，援助)；assistance (*n.* 帮助，援助)

参 tutor (*n.* 指导教师)；professor (*n.* 教授)；instructor (*n.* 讲师)

comedy
['kɑːmədi]

n. 喜剧；喜剧性 (事件)，滑稽，幽默

例 The 1950s saw the decline of past *comedy* stars and a certain paucity of new talent in Hollywood. 在 20 世纪 50 年代，好莱坞过去的那些喜剧明星日益减少，而新的天才也寥若晨星。

□ priority   □ radiate   □ glacier   □ position   □ beach   □ assistant
□ comedy

overlap	[ˌoʊvərˈlæp] v. (使)交叠，部分重叠 [ˈoʊvərlæp] n. 重叠；重叠的部分
	例 The end of the first scene *overlapped* the beginning of the second. 第一幕的结尾与第二幕的开始重合了。
	派 overlapping(*a.* 重叠的) overlap
nurture [ˈnɜːrtʃər]	*vt.* 养育，养护，培养；扶植，支持 (support)；滋长，助长 *n.* 养育，培养
	记 联想记忆：大自然(nature)像母亲一样养育(nurture)着人类
	例 We want to *nurture* the new project, not destroy it. 我们想支持新项目，而不是破坏它。
militant [ˈmɪlɪtənt]	*a.* 好战的，好暴力的 *n.* 激进分子
	记 词根记忆：milit(军事，打斗) + ant → 好战的
	例 The leader of a *militant* group was arrested by the police. 警方逮捕了一个好战团伙的领头人。
continuum [kənˈtɪnjuəm]	*n.* 统一体(a coherent whole)
	例 The development of jazz can be seen as part of the larger *continuum* of American popular music, especially dance music. 爵士乐的发展可被视为美国流行音乐，尤其是舞蹈音乐这一大的连续统一体中的一部分。
virtuous [ˈvɜːrtʃuəs]	*a.* 有道德的，品行端正的，品德高的；〈贬〉自命清高的，自以为是的
	记 来自 virtue(*n.* 美德)
	例 If we are going to discuss goodness and justice — what makes an individual good or a society just or *virtuous* — then we need to start with the ancient Greeks. 如果我们要讨论善良与正义——能使一个人品德高尚或使一个社会正义的东西——我们需要从古希腊人讲起。
addictive [əˈdɪktɪv]	*a.* 使人上瘾的；使人沉醉的，醉心的
	记 来自 addict(*n.* 瘾君子；对…入迷的人)
	例 It is said that Marijuana is psychologically though not physically *addictive*. 据说大麻使人在心理上上瘾，而非生理上。
omit [əˈmɪt]	*vt.* 省略，删去；遗漏，忽略(neglect)
	记 联想记忆：om(音似："呕") + it(它) → 把它呕出去 → 省略
	搭 omit doing/to do 忘记…
	例 You'd better check the name list again to make sure there is no one *omitted* from it. 你最好再查看一下名单，确保没有遗漏任何人。
	参 vomit(*v.* 呕吐)
illusion [ɪˈluːʒn]	*n.* 幻觉，错觉(delusion)；幻想中的事物
	记 词根记忆：il(不，无) + lus(=lust 光) + ion → 看到根本没有的光 → 幻觉，错觉
	例 They brush away *illusions* and second-hand opinions. 他们不理会幻觉和二手评论。// Many workers are seduced by rosy *illusions* of life as a telecommuter. 很多员工被远程办公生活的美好幻觉所诱惑。
	派 disillusion(*vt.* 使醒悟，使理想破灭)；illusionist(*n.* 幻术师，魔术师)
	参 allusion(*n.* 提及；暗示)；elusion(*n.* 逃避)

38

household [ˈhaʊshoʊld]	*a.* 家庭的，家用的；家喻户晓的 *n.* 家庭（family） 记 组合词：house（房屋）+ hold（拥有）→ 有房屋才像个家 → 家庭 搭 household appliances 家用电器；household word 家喻户晓的词语 例 She was almost *household* throughout much of her lifetime because of her prolific literary output. 她创作了大量的文学作品，所以她一生大部分时间几乎都是个家喻户晓的人物。
chronical [ˈkrɑːnɪkl]	*a.* 慢性的，延续很长的（inveterate） 记 词根记忆：chron（时间）+ ical → 长时间的 → 慢性的 例 Asthma is *chronical* and very common. 哮喘是慢性病，而且非常常见。 参 chronology（*n.* 年代学）；synchronous（*a.* 同步的，同时的）；chronicle（*n.* 编年史）
methane [ˈmeθeɪn]	*n.* 甲烷，沼气（firedamp） 例 The relative abundance of *methane* makes it an attractive fuel. 甲烷含量相对丰富，这使得它成为一种受人欢迎的燃料。
ironic [aɪˈrɑːnɪk]	*a.* 说反话的，讽刺的（sarcastic）；出乎意料的 记 来自 irony（*n.* 反话，讽刺） 例 Maybe the most *ironic* example of human behavior that can lead to desertification is irrigation. 或许导致沙漠化的最具讽刺意味的人类行为就是灌溉。
compute [kəmˈpjuːt]	*v.* 计算，估算（calculate, reckon） 记 词根记忆：com（表加强）+ put（思考）+ e → 一再思考 → 计算 例 The losses caused by the drought were *computed* at $2 million. 旱灾造成的损失估算为 200 万美元。
preponderance [prɪˈpɑːndərəns]	*n.* 优势（superiority, dominance） 记 来自 preponderant（*a.* 占优势的） 例 The New World butterflies make up the *preponderance* of examples because they are the most familiar species. 在这些标本中新大陆的蝴蝶占多数，因为它们是最为人所熟知的物种。
reschedule [ˌriːˈskedʒuːl]	*vt.* 重新计划，重订…的时间表 例 The international conference had to be *rescheduled* due to several countries' absence. 由于数个国家缺席，这次国际会议不得不重新安排时间。
genuine [ˈdʒenjuɪn]	*a.* 真的，非人造的（actual, true）；真诚的，诚实的 记 词根记忆：gen（出生，产生）+ uine → 生来就有的 → 真的 例 Only *genuine* refugees can apply for asylum. 只有真正的难民才能申请政治避难。 派 genuinely（*ad.* 真正地） 参 genius（*n.* 天才）
leak [liːk]	*v.* (使)漏，(使)渗出，(使)泄漏 *n.* 漏洞，裂缝；泄露；(消息等的)走漏 例 The faucet started *leaking*. 水龙头开始漏水了。

grazing [ˈɡreɪzɪŋ]	*n.* 放牧；牧场(pasture) 搭 over grazing 过度放牧 例 *Grazing* is very beneficial to the ecosystem. 放牧对生态系统大有益处。
crucial [ˈkruːʃl]	*a.* 至关重要的，决定性的(*important, essential) 记 词根记忆：cruc(十字形) + ial(形容词后缀) → 十字路口 → 决定性的 例 How salt became so *crucial* to our metabolism is a mystery. 盐如何变得对我们的新陈代谢如此重要仍是个未解之谜。
instance [ˈɪnstəns]	*n.* 例子，事例(*case) 记 联想记忆：in + stance(看做 stand，站立) + ce → 模特站在那就是最好的例子 → 例子 搭 for instance 例如，比如；in the first instance 第一，首先 例 The report highlights a number of *instances* of injustice. 这篇报道重点列举了一些不公正的事例。
overtime [ˈoʊvərtaɪm]	*ad.* 加班 *a.* 超时的，加班的 例 My boss keeps asking me to work *overtime*. 我的老板不断要求我加班。
physiology [ˌfɪziˈɑːlədʒi]	*n.* 生理学；生理机能 记 词根记忆：physi(自然) + ology(…学) → 研究身体的自然状态的学科 → 生理学 例 Anatomy and *physiology* are closely related fields of study. 解剖学和生理学这两个研究领域密切相关。 派 physiological(*a.* 生理的)
lava [ˈlɑːvə]	*n.* 岩浆，熔岩(magma) 记 联想记忆：幼虫(larva)被岩浆(lava)熔化掉了 例 Evidence of this is the molten *lava* that flows out of volcanoes. 火山喷出的熔岩证实了这一点。
deserve [dɪˈzɜːrv]	*v.* 应得，值得(be entitled to, merit) 记 词根记忆：de + serv(服务) + e → 花钱享受应得的服务 → 应得，值得 例 The man *deserves* the grade he received. 这个人获得的级别是他应得的。 派 deserved(*a.* 应得的)；deserving(*a.* 理应获得的)；undeserved(*a.* 不应得的) 参 desert(*n.* 沙漠)
grocery [ˈɡroʊsəri]	*n.* 杂货店；杂货 例 It was sold in *grocery* stores and door to door. 它在杂货店有售，也上门售货。
captivity [kæpˈtɪvəti]	*n.* 囚禁，拘留(confinement) 记 词根记忆：capt(抓住) + iv + ity(表状态，名词后缀) → 被抓住 → 囚禁 例 The bird had escaped from *captivity*. 那只鸟已逃离樊笼。

38

pronounced [prəˈnaʊnst]	*a.* 显著的(marked, distinct)；明确的(definite) 记 来自 pronounce(*v.* 宣称；发音) 例 A *pronounced* division of labor exists, leading to the establishment of many specialized professions. 因为存在明显的分工，从而出现了很多专门的职业。
bouquet [buˈkeɪ]	*n.* 花束(bunch)；香味，芬芳 搭 bouquet garni 香料包 例 The students put a large *bouquet* of roses and lilies in front of the monument. 学生们在纪念碑前献了一大束玫瑰和百合花。 参 banquet(*n.* 宴会，盛宴)
	bouquet
endeavor [ɪnˈdevər]	*vi./n.* 努力，尽力(strive, effort) 记 联想记忆：end(尽头) + eav(看做 eager, 热情) + or(看做 our, 我们的) → 用尽了我们的热情 → 努力，尽力 例 Susan *endeavors* to get better grades in college. 苏珊努力在大学取得更好的成绩。
submission [səbˈmɪʃn]	*n.* 屈服，服从；提交，呈递；提交物；(向法官提出的)看法，意见 例 I was so excited to finally see my work in print. It was my third *submission*. 终于看到我的作品印刷出来了，我特别兴奋。这是我第三次投稿了。
ware [wer]	*n.* 陶器(pottery)；器皿(vessel)；[*pl.*](尤指小商贩在市场里出售的)物品 例 He traveled from town to town selling his *wares*. 他走乡串镇出售自己的货品。 参 glassware(*n.* 玻璃器具)
conclusive [kənˈkluːsɪv]	*a.* 确定的，确凿的，不容置疑的(*definitive)；结论性的 例 Is the research about the link between coffee and heart disease *conclusive*? 关于咖啡和心脏病之间存在联系的研究是确定的吗？ 参 inclusive(*a.* 包含的，包括的)；inconclusive(*a.* 非决定性的)
jaw [dʒɔː]	*n.* 颌，颚；[常 *pl.*]嘴(包括颌骨和牙齿) 记 发音记忆："嚼" → 他下颌脱臼了，没法嚼东西 → 颌
retreat [rɪˈtriːt]	*vi.* 退却，撤退(retire)；退缩 *n.* 退却，撤退；隐退处 例 She and her tribe had to *retreat* to Canada. 她和她的部落不得不撤退到加拿大。// Those log buildings are the mountain *retreats* of wealthy New Yorkers. 那些圆木建筑是富有的纽约人的山间隐居所。
squid [skwɪd]	*n.* 鱿鱼，枪乌贼 参 squib(*n.* 小爆竹)

440　□ pronounced　□ bouquet　□ endeavor　□ submission　□ ware　□ conclusive
□ jaw　□ retreat　□ squid

adventure [əd'ventʃər]	*n.* 奇遇(happening); 冒险活动 记 词根记忆：ad(to) + vent(来) + ure → 一步步地靠近危险 → 冒险活动 例 He has had many *adventures* along the way — lost instruments, missed connections, no hotel room, and so on. 他一路上经历了很多冒险的事情——仪器丢了，和他人失去了联系，没住上旅馆等。 派 adventurer(*n.* 冒险家); adventurous(*a.* 喜欢冒险的)
denote [dɪ'nout]	*v.* 表示，意指(represent); 标示，预示，象征(indicate) 记 词根记忆：de(向下) + not(知道) + e → 深究 → 表示 例 A very high temperature often *denotes* a serious illness. 高烧常常说明病得很重。 参 connote(*v.* 意味着；暗示); notify(*vt.* 通报)
stew [stjuː]	*n.* 炖菜；不安，担忧 *v.* 炖，煨；思考；不安，担忧 记 发音记忆："死丢" → 拼命往锅里丢东西 → 炖 例 I've been *stewing* over the problem for a while. 这个问题我已经考虑了一会儿了。 派 stewed(*a.* 太酽的，泡苦了的)
incoming ['ɪnkʌmɪŋ]	*a.* 引入的；新任的；正来临的，刚收到的 *n.* 进来，到来；[常 *pl.*]收入；进来之物，新来的东西 记 来自 income(*n.* 收入，所得) 例 The traffic accident happened when a bus collided with an *incoming* truck. 公交车与迎面驶来的卡车相撞，造成了这起交通事故。 参 forthcoming(*a.* 即将来临的)
rupture ['rʌptʃər]	*v.* (使)破裂(*burst); (关系)决裂，断绝 记 词根记忆：rupt(断裂) + ure → (使)破裂 例 The change in volume may cause the lungs to distend and even *rupture*. 容量的变化可能会导致肺肿胀甚至破裂。
patriarchic ['peɪtriɑːrkɪk]	*a.* 家长的，族长的；德高望重的 记 词根记忆：patri(父亲) + arch(统治) + ic → 男性统治的 → 家长的，族长的 例 The dominance of *patriarchic* structures in Kenyan politics and society is well illustrated by the low number of women among the members of parliament (MPs). 在肯尼亚社会和政治中，家长制结构大为盛行，议会中女性成员数量之低充分体现了这一点。
suppress [sə'pres]	*vt.* 抑制，阻止(restrain); 镇压，压制；禁止发表，查禁；阻止…的生长(或发展) 记 词根记忆：sup(向下) + press(压) → 向下压 → 抑制，阻止 例 Alder trees can *suppress* the growth of nearby trees. 桤木会抑制其周边树木的生长。 参 depress(*vt.* 使沮丧); oppress(*vt.* 压迫)

38

depredation [ˌdeprəˈdeɪʃn]	*n.* 劫掠，掠夺，破坏(plunder, robbery) 记 词根记忆：de(表加强) + pred(掠夺) + ation → 完全掠夺 → 劫掠 例 The *depredations* of war can still be seen several years after the event. 战争蹂躏的痕迹在事后数年仍显而易见。
racing [ˈreɪsɪŋ]	*a.* 比赛的 *n.* 比赛，竞赛(game) 例 He was one of the greatest *racing* drivers of all time. 他是有史以来最伟大的赛车手之一。
handle [ˈhændl]	*v.* 处理(deal)；对待(treat)；操纵；触，摸 *n.* 柄，把手，拉手 记 联想记忆：hand(手) + le → 方便手操作的东西 → 柄，把手 例 I'm taking six classes and doing a part-time job. That's about all I can *handle* right now. 我现在上六节课，做一份兼职。目前我只能应付这么多了。// To start the machine, you need first read the handbook and then turn the *handle* left. 要想启动机器，首先需要阅读手册，然后再把手柄往左转。 参 candle(*n.* 蜡烛)
operate [ˈɑːpəreɪt]	*v.* 运转，开动(run)；(on)动手术；经营，管理；起作用 记 词根记忆：oper(工作) + ate → 工作着的 → 运转 搭 operate the machine 操作机器 例 It's important that you all understand that quartz heaters *operate* on a totally different principle with common convection heaters. 重要的是，你们要理解石英加热器与普通对流加热器的运行原理完全不同。
hue [hjuː]	*n.* 颜色(*color)；色度，色调；信仰，观点；形式，样子 搭 hue and cry 强烈抗议 例 They may be glassy blue, or in darker *hues*. 它们可能是玻璃蓝或更深的颜色。
rhythm [ˈrɪðəm]	*n.* 节奏，韵律 记 本身为词根，意为"节奏" 例 The boat rocked up and down in *rhythm* with the sea. 小船随着波浪起伏有致。 派 rhythmic(*a.* 有韵律的，有节奏的)
permission [pərˈmɪʃn]	*n.* 允许，同意(consent)；许可证，书面许可 记 词根记忆：per(贯穿，自始至终) + miss(送) + ion → 自始至终都发送 → 允许，同意 搭 special permission 特许；permission slip 请假条 例 You must ask *permission* for all major expenditures. 一切重大开支均须申报批准。//

A: I'm really disappointed; there are a couple of required courses I have to take before I can take the history class I'm interested in.

B: Don't be disappointed yet. You may be able to get special *permission* from the professor.

A: 我真的很失望；要修我感兴趣的历史课之前得先上几门必修课程。

B: 先别失望。你可以从教授那里得到特殊许可。

catastrophe
[kə'tæstrəfi]

n. 灾难，灾祸(disaster, tragedy)；困难

记 词根记忆：cat(a)(落下) + astro(星星) + phe → 星星坠落(古人观天象，认为星星坠落预示着大难临头) → 灾难

例 A senior UN official says there is still time to avert a *catastrophe* in the Horn of Africa where eight million drought victims are threatened with famine. 联合国一位高级官员表明仍有时间阻止发生于"非洲之角"的一场灾难。在那里，800万干旱受害者面临着饥荒的威胁。

派 catastrophic(*a.* 灾难性的)

deliberate

[dɪ'lɪbərət] *a.* 故意的，蓄意的；审慎的，深思熟虑的(*careful, cogitative)
[dɪ'lɪbəreɪt] *v.* 深思熟虑

记 词根记忆：de(表加强) + liber(权衡) + ate → 反复权衡 → 审慎的

例 Every step in the process was slow and *deliberate*. 这个过程的每一步都是稳扎稳打，并且经过深思熟虑的。

派 deliberately(*ad.* 故意，蓄意；深思熟虑地)

presidency
['prezɪdənsi]

n. (总统的)职位(position)；(总统的)任期(term)

例 The Whig party decided to nominate him for the *presidency*. 辉格党决定提名他为总统候选人。

independent
[ˌɪndɪ'pendənt]

a. 独立的，自主的；自立的(*autonomous)；不相干的，不受影响的；无偏见的，中立的；私立的；有主见的；无党派的

例 Two *independent* research bodies reached the same conclusion. 两个彼此不相干的研究部门得出了相同的结论。// She is very *independent*. 她非常有主见。

派 independently(*ad.* 独立地)

handful
['hændfʊl]

n. 一把；少数人(或物)

例 Only a *handful* of people attended the meeting. 只有少数几个人参加了会议。

yelp
[jelp]

v. 尖叫 *n.* (发出)短而尖的叫声

记 联想记忆：发出尖叫(yelp)，寻求帮助(help)

例 The kid likes to tread on his puppy's paw, which always makes it *yelp*. 小孩喜欢踩小狗的爪子，这总让小狗尖叫。

fortify
['fɔːrtɪfaɪ]

vt. 支持，给…以勇气；加强，增强；筑防御工事于

记 词根记忆：fort(强大) + ify(使…) → 使强大 → 加强

搭 fortify against 加强防卫

例 Father wore a heavy coat to *fortify* the cold weather. 父亲穿了一件厚大衣来抵御寒冷的天气。

38

□ catastrophe □ deliberate □ presidency ■ independent □ handful □ yelp
□ fortify

muse [mjuːz]	*n.* 灵感 *v.* 沉思，冥想 记 联想记忆：Muse(希腊神话中的缪斯女神) 例 The famous writer felt that his *muse* had deserted him. 那位著名作家觉得自己已失去了创作灵感。
tickle ['tɪkl]	*v.* (使)发痒；使高兴，逗乐 *n.* 痒 记 联想记忆：买张电影票(ticket)让她高兴(tickle) 例 My father used to *tickle* my feet when I was young. 我小的时候，父亲常常在我的脚上挠痒痒。
contemplate ['kɑːntəmpleɪt]	*v.* 思量，考虑，思忖；注视，凝视；打算 记 联想记忆：con + templ(看做 temple，寺庙) + ate → 庙里的和尚常常打坐 → 思量 例 The boss is *contemplating* a visit to Mexico this vacation. 老板正盘算着这个假期去墨西哥旅游。 派 contemplation(*n.* 沉思，思考；凝视); contemplative(*a.* 沉思默想的；冥想的)
intelligible [ɪn'telɪdʒəbl]	*a.* 聪明的，理智的；易懂的，易理解的 记 词根记忆：intel(在…之间) + lig(选择) + ible(能…的) → 能作出选择的 → 聪明的 例 The story he told was hardly *intelligible*. 他讲的故事极其难懂。
mortify ['mɔːrtɪfaɪ]	*vt.* 使蒙受屈辱，使难堪 记 词根记忆：mort(死亡) + ify(使…) → 使达到死亡 → 使蒙受屈辱 例 The boy was beaten by his little brother, so he felt *mortified*. 男孩让他弟弟给打了，他感到很屈辱。
deviant ['diːviənt]	*a.* 不正常的，越出常规的 *n.* 不正常的人 记 词根记忆：de(偏离) + vi(路) + ant → 偏离正路 → 不正常的 例 Mark is a *deviant*, so he has no friends. 马克是一个不正常的人，所以他没有什么朋友。
patriarchy ['peɪtriɑːrki]	*n.* 父权制，父系社会，家长统治 例 Feminists are against *patriarchy*. 女权主义者反对父权制。
entreat [ɪn'triːt]	*v.* 乞求，恳求，请求 记 词根记忆：en(在…里面) + treat(拉) → 在里面拉 → 乞求，恳求 例 This is the first and also the last time I *entreat* a favor from you. 这是我第一次也是最后一次求你帮我。
loath [loʊθ]	*a.* 不情愿的，勉强的 例 Unlike other children in his age, Tom is *loath* to go out to play with friends. 与同龄人不同，汤姆不喜欢出去和朋友们玩耍。
cordial ['kɔːrdʒəl]	*a.* 亲切的，热诚的(heartfelt) 记 词根记忆：cord(心脏) + ial → 发自内心的 → 亲切的，热诚的 例 Everybody likes Honey, because she keeps a *cordial* smile on her face all the time. 每个人都喜欢哈尼，因为她总是面带热情的笑容。

loath

derivation [ˌderɪˈveɪʃn]	*n.* (尤指词语的)起源，发源(source, origin)；派生 记 来自 derive(*v.* 起源)；de + rive(r)(河) → 黄河是中华文明的摇篮 → 起源 例 The *derivation* of many Japanese words are from Chinese characters. 很多日本文字源自汉字。
gleam [gliːm]	*n.* 微光；一丝，一线；表露 *vi.* 闪光，闪烁(glitter)；流露出 搭 gleam with 流露 例 A young couple took a walk by the seashore with the *gleam* of moonlight. 一对年轻夫妇在洒满月光的海边散步。
clench [klentʃ]	*v./n.* 握紧，抓牢；咬紧(牙关等) 例 The strong man was *clenching* his fists and trembling with rage. 那个强壮的男人紧握着拳头，气得直哆嗦。
provocative [prəˈvɑːkətɪv]	*a.* 挑衅的，煽动性的；惹人讨厌的；挑逗的 记 词根记忆：pro(向前) + voc(叫喊) + ative → 向前叫喊的 → 挑衅的 例 Although Tim gave his *provocative* remarks on this issue, no one wanted to respond to him. 尽管蒂姆对这件事情发表了挑衅的言论，但没有人想要回应他。
quash [kwɑːʃ]	*vt.* 撤销，废止；镇压；平息 记 词根记忆：qu + ash(灰) → 使成灰 → 平息 例 Finally, the judge *quashed* a verdict. 最终，法官宣布裁决无效。
filial [ˈfɪliəl]	*a.* 子女的；子孙后代的 记 词根记忆：fil(儿子) + ial → 儿子的 → 子女的 例 *Filial* piety is considered the first virtue in Chinese culture, and it is the main concern of a large number of stories. 孝是中国文化中的第一美德，也是大量故事的主要关注点。
tempo [ˈtempoʊ]	*n.* (乐曲的)速度，节奏；行进速度(pace) 例 The *tempo* of life in big cities is so fast that my grandpa is not used to it. 大城市的生活节奏太快，我爷爷不习惯。
rouse [raʊz]	*vt.* 唤起，唤醒；激起，鼓舞；激怒 记 发音记忆："扰死" → 唤起，唤醒 例 The alarm doesn't seem to work, because I am always *roused* by my mother's yelling. 闹钟好像不起作用，因为我总是被妈妈的叫声唤醒。
brochure [broʊˈʃʊr]	*n.* 小册子，说明书(pamphlet, booklet) 记 发音记忆："不用求" → 说明书在手，再不用求人了 → 说明书 例 This *brochure* provides you with accurate information about the new services. 这本小册子提供有关新服务的精确信息。
conduct	[kənˈdʌkt] *v.* 引导(guide)；传导(transmit)；进行(progress)；管理，指挥；(行为)表现 [ˈkɑːndʌkt] *n.* 行为(behavior)；管理(方式)，实施(方式) 记 词根记忆：con(表加强) + duct(拉) → 用力拉 → 引导 例 He found the copper used was not effective in *conducting* heat. 他发现所使用的铜在导热方面没有效果。 // I'll be *conducting* my psychology experiment this Saturday. 我将在本周六开展我的心理实验。

38

□ derivation   □ gleam   □ clench   □ provocative   □ quash   □ filial
□ tempo   □ rouse   □ brochure   □ conduct

faculty ['fæklti]	*n.* 学院；全体教职员工；能力（ability, capacity） 搭 the faculty of law 法学院 例 The old man has a *faculty* for saying the right things. 这位老人有能力说出正确的话。
hint [hɪnt]	*n.* 暗示，提示（cue）；[常 *pl.*]忠告（advice）；征兆，迹象；少量，少许；窍门 *v.* 暗示，示意 记 联想记忆：hi(嗨) + nt → 向你打招呼，给你提示 → 提示 例 Our counselors will give you *hints* about successful interviewing. 我们的顾问将给你一些关于成功采访的建议。

Every man's work, whether it be literature of music, of pictures or architecture of anything else, is always a portrait of himself.

每个人的工作，不管是文学、音乐、美术、建筑还是其他工作，都是自己的一幅画像。

——美国教育家 勃特勒.S.（Samuel Brtler, American educator）

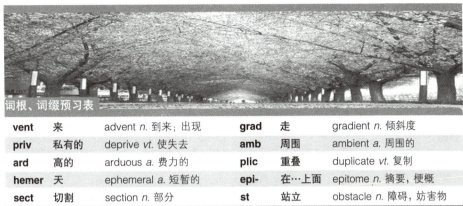

词根、词缀预习表

vent	来	advent n. 到来；出现	grad	走	gradient n. 倾斜度
priv	私有的	deprive vt. 使失去	amb	周围	ambient a. 周围的
ard	高的	arduous a. 费力的	plic	重叠	duplicate vt. 复制
hemer	天	ephemeral a. 短暂的	epi-	在…上面	epitome n. 摘要，梗概
sect	切割	section n. 部分	st	站立	obstacle n. 障碍，妨害物

---

chill
[tʃɪl]

n. 寒冷，寒意(coldness) *a.* 寒冷的 *v.* (使)变冷，冷却

记 联想记忆：c + hill(小山) → 山上高处不胜寒 → 寒冷

例 A small fire was burning to take the *chill* off the room. 房间里生着小火炉驱寒。

---

sweeping
['swiːpɪŋ]

a. 彻底的，广泛的(extensive)；〈贬〉(过于)笼统的，一概而论的 *n.* 清扫，扫除；垃圾

例 The Arts and Crafts Movement in the United States was responsible for *sweeping* changes in attitudes toward the decorative arts. 美国的工艺美术运动彻底改变了人们对装饰艺术的态度。

---

moist
[mɔɪst]

a. 潮湿的(damp, humid)；多雨的(rainy)

记 联想记忆：薄雾(mist)中湿漉漉的(moist)城市

例 Warm and *moist* air from the Pacific Ocean is forced upward as it crosses the Sierra Nevada. 来自太平洋的暖湿气流在经过内华达山脉时被迫向上移动。

派 moisten[*v.* (使)变得湿润，变得潮湿]

---

henceforth
[ˌhensˈfɔːrθ]

ad. 从此以后(*from that time on)

记 组合词：hence(因此) + forth(往前) → 从此以后

例 In 1926 he announced that *henceforth* his factories would close for the entire day on Saturday. 1926 年，他宣布自己的工厂从此以后在周六全天停工。

---

advent
['ædvent]

n. 到来，来临(*arrival)；出现(emergence)

记 词根记忆：ad + vent(来) → 到来，来临；出现

例 With the *advent* of power-driven machinery, home industry began to give way to production in mills and factories. 随着动力驱动机器的出现，家庭工业开始让位于磨坊和工厂的生产。

---

foreshorten [fɔːˈʃɔːrtn]	*vt.* (绘画、摄影等)用透视法缩小；缩短，节略(curtail) 记 组合词：fore(在前面) + shorten(缩短) → 用透视法缩小 例 To get the perspective you want, you need to *foreshorten* the objects. 要得到你想要的透视图，你需要用透视法将物体缩小。
internal [ɪnˈtɜːrnl]	*a.* 内在的，内部的(interior)；国内的，内政的；内心的 例 There are two categories of reasons: *internal* factors and external factors. 存在两类原因：内部原因和外部原因。 派 internally(*ad.* 在内，在中心) 参 external(*a.* 外在的，外部的)
yogurt [ˈjoʊɡərt]	*n.* (=yoghurt)酸奶(酪) 例 *Yogurt* is a rich source of calcium — a mineral that contributes to colon health and decreases the risk of colon cancer. 酸奶含有丰富的钙。钙这种矿物质有利于结肠健康，并能降低得结肠癌的风险。
remodel [ˌriːˈmɑːdl]	*vt.* 重新塑造，改造(remake)；改编(军队、剧本)；改变(行为等) 例 The Philadelphia Museum of Art was *remodeled*. 费城艺术博物馆被重新改造了。
infrared [ˌɪnfrəˈred]	*a.* 红外线的；产生红外线的 *n.* 红外线 记 联想记忆：infra(在…下面) + red(红色) → 在红色之下 → 红外线的 例 The quartz crystal's energy is turned into *infrared* radiation. 石英晶体的能量可以转换成红外辐射。
spiny [ˈspaɪni]	*a.* 长满刺的，多刺的，带刺的；棘手的 例 Starfish are not really fish, and they belong to the family of echinoderms which are *spiny* skinned sea animals. 海星其实不是鱼，它属于棘皮动物，一种全身长满刺的海洋动物。
haul [hɔːl]	*v.* (用力)拖，拖运(pull, drag) *n.* 拖，拉，拖运；一次获得(或偷得)的数量；旅行的距离 记 联想记忆：用力拖(haul)个大箱子，不时停下来(halt)休息 例 Farm women had to *haul* large quantities of water into the house from wells. 农妇不得不大量地从井里打水，然后挑回家。
noticeable [ˈnoʊtɪsəbl]	*a.* 明显的，值得注意的(*conspicuous, outstanding, remarkable) 记 联想记忆：notice(注意) + able(能…的) → 值得注意的 例 Red lettering on signs is much more *noticeable* than blue. 标识用红色字母比蓝色字母更引人注目。
decompose [ˌdiːkəmˈpoʊz]	*v.* (使)分解(disintegrate)；(使)腐烂(decay, rot) 记 联想记忆：de(分离) + compose(组成) → 把组合在一起的东西分开 → (使)分解 例 The Earth's surface is basically rock, and it is this rock that gradually *decomposes* into clay. 地球表面主要是岩石，正是这些岩石逐渐分解成了黏土。 派 decomposition(*n.* 分解；腐烂)

improve [ɪmˈpruːv]	*v.* 改善，改进，增进；好转，进步 例 Coffee in this restaurant is really *improved*. They must have changed suppliers. 这家饭店的咖啡的确更好喝了。他们肯定换了供应商。 参 approve(*v.* 赞成，批准)
minute [maɪˈnuːt]	[maɪˈnuːt] *a.* 细微的，极小的(*tiny*)；细致入微的，详细的 [ˈmɪnɪt] *n.* 分，分钟；一会儿，片刻；时刻 例 The snowfall consists of myriads of *minute* ice crystals that fall to the ground. 无数落到地上的极小的冰晶体构成了降雪。
deprive [dɪˈpraɪv]	*vt.* 使失去，剥夺(take away) 记 词根记忆：de(去掉) + priv(私有的) + e → 使某物离开某人 → 使失去，剥夺 例 Plant stems die when *deprived* of water. 植物茎秆缺水会枯死。 派 deprivation(*n.* 剥夺，丧失；缺失)
orchestra [ˈɔːrkɪstrə]	*n.* 管弦乐队(band) 记 联想记忆：or + chest(胸腔) + ra → 管弦乐队的成员需借助胸腔的力气演奏乐器 → 管弦乐队 搭 symphony orchestra 交响乐队 例 The 20th-century *orchestra* was far more flexible than its predecessors. 在 20 世纪，管弦乐队比以前的管弦乐队要灵活得多。 派 orchestral(*a.* 管弦乐的); orchestration(*n.* 管弦乐编曲) chest orchestra
arduous [ˈɑːrdʒuəs]	*a.* 费力的，艰巨的(laborious) 记 词根记忆：ard(高的) + uous(多…的) → 很高的，难以攀登的 → 费力的，艰巨的 例 The tasks of the coming year of the market department are very *arduous*. 未来一年市场部的工作异常艰巨。
transaction [trænˈzækʃn]	*n.* 交易，业务(deal)；办理，处理 记 词根记忆：trans(变换) + act(行为) + ion → 交易 例 There has been a sharp decrease in commercial *transactions* between companies since the financial crisis. 金融危机以来，公司之间的商业交易急剧减少。 参 transfer(*v.* 转移); transport(*vt.* 运输); transmit(*v.* 传输)
ephemeral [ɪˈfemərəl]	*a.* 短暂的，转瞬即逝的(transient) 记 词根记忆：ep(在) + hemer(天) + al → 历时一天的 → 短暂的 例 Often happiness is described as being *ephemeral*. 人们通常将幸福描述为转瞬即逝的。
superintendent [ˌsuːpərɪnˈtendənt]	*n.* 主管，负责人(principal)；指挥者，管理者；警长 记 联想记忆：super(上等的) + intend(计划) + ent(表人) → 身处上级，做计划的人 → 主管，负责人 例 At the time of the Revolution, the *Superintendent* of Indian Affairs had little power. 在革命时期，印第安人事务负责人几乎没什么权力。

39

□ improve　　□ minute　　□ deprive　　□ orchestra　　□ arduous　　□ transaction
□ ephemeral　　□ superintendent

brush [brʌʃ]	*v.* 刷，拂(wipe)；轻碰 *n.* 画笔；刷子；轻碰；小冲突 搭 brush up on sth. 快速提高；重温(生疏了的技术等) 例 I really need to *brush* up on my math. 我确实需要复习数学。
incredible [ɪnˈkredəbl]	*a.* 惊人的，难以置信的(unbelievable) 记 词根记忆：in(不) + cred(相信) + ible(能…的) → 难以置信的 例 He must get an *incredible* phone bill every month. 他每个月的电话费账单数目肯定很惊人。 派 incredibly(*ad.* 惊人地)
encompass [ɪnˈkʌmpəs]	*vt.* 包含(*include)；环绕(encircle) 记 词根记忆：en(进入) + compass(范围) → 进入范围 → 包含；环绕 例 The term "art deco" has come to *encompass* three distinct but related design trends of the 1920s and 1930s. "装饰艺术"这个词涵盖了20世纪二三十年代三个明显不同但又相关的设计潮流。 出去 进去 encompass
section [ˈsekʃn]	*n.* 部分(part)；地区(region)；部门(division)；(文章等的)段落，章节；截面，剖面 记 词根记忆：sect(切割) + ion → 部分 例 Our library has a reserve *section* of fine books. 我们的图书馆有一个精品图书存放区。
faucet [ˈfɔːsɪt]	*n.* 龙头，旋塞 例 Did you fix the leaky *faucet*? 你修好那个漏水的水龙头了吗？ 参 fauces(*n.* 咽喉)
gradient [ˈɡreɪdiənt]	*n.* 坡度；倾斜度，斜率；梯度 记 词根记忆：grad(走) + ient → 倾斜度，斜率；梯度 搭 temperature gradient 温度梯度 例 Steep *gradients* limit the size of load that a locomotive can haul, including the weight of the locomotive itself. 陡峭的坡度限制了机车的运载量，也限制了机车本身的重量。
absorption [əbˈsɔːrpʃn]	*n.* 吸收(assimilation, reception)；全神贯注，专心致志 例 Bosses really appreciate Jim's complete *absorption* in his work. 老板们很赏识吉姆对工作的全身心投入。
chimpanzee [ˌtʃɪmpænˈziː]	*n.* 黑猩猩 例 In some *chimpanzee* communities, the young females may inherit high status from a high-ranking mother. 在一些黑猩猩群落里，年轻的雌性黑猩猩能从它地位尊贵的母亲那里继承高贵的身份。
temporary [ˈtempəreri]	*a.* 暂时的，临时的(*existing) 记 词根记忆：tempor(时间) + ary(形容词后缀) → 时间很短的 → 暂时的 例 She must have been a *temporary* worker. 她肯定是个临时工。 派 temporarily(*ad.* 临时地，暂时地)

aggression [əˈɡreʃn]	*n.* 侵略(invasion); 敌对的情绪或行为 记 词根记忆: ag(表加强) + gress(行走) + ion → 不断行走, 四处闯荡 → 侵略 例 Within this colony, there is little *aggression* among ants from different nests. 在这个蚁群当中, 来自不同蚁巢的蚂蚁之间很少有攻击行为。
project [prəˈdʒekt] [ˈprɑːdʒekt]	[prəˈdʒekt] *v.* 放映(show, screen); 规划(plan, figure); 预测, 推想 [ˈprɑːdʒekt] *n.* 方案(scheme); 课题, 项目(item); 工程 记 词根记忆: pro(向前) + ject(投, 掷) → 向前投 → 放映 例 The unemployment rate has been *projected* to fall. 据预测, 失业率将下降。 派 projection(*n.* 预测, 推想; 放映; 放映的影像); projector(*n.* 放映机)
satire [ˈsætaɪər]	*n.* 讽刺文学, 讽刺作品; 讽刺(irony) 记 源自拉丁语, 意为"讽刺杂咏", 现在在英语中多指"讽刺"或"讽刺文学" 例 The movie is a stinging *satire* on the middle class. 这部电影是对中产阶级的尖锐讽刺。 派 satirist(*n.* 讽刺作家; 惯于讽刺的人)
chagrin [ʃəˈɡrɪn]	*n.* 懊恼, 失望(embarrassment, disappointment) 记 联想记忆: cha(拼音: 茶) + grin(苦笑) → 喝茶苦笑 → 懊恼, 失望 例 The man feels *chagrin* at being fired. 那个男人因被解雇而感到懊恼。
batch [bætʃ]	*n.* 一批, 一组, 一群; 一批生产的量 *v.* 分批处理 记 联想记忆: bat(蝙蝠) + ch → 蝙蝠都是成群生活 → 一群 例 They deliver the goods in *batches*. 他们分批交付货物。
grovel [ˈɡrɑːvl]	*vi.* 摇尾乞怜, 奴颜婢膝 记 联想记忆: 居然为了一双手套(glove)摇尾乞怜(grovel) 例 You don't need to *grovel* to the bank manager for a loan. 你不必为了贷款而向银行经理低声下气。
ambient [ˈæmbiənt]	*a.* 周围的, 周围环境的; (音乐)产生轻松氛围的 记 词根记忆: amb(周围) + ient → 周围的 例 Margaret was bathing with the *ambient* music. 玛格丽特边听着氛围音乐边洗澡。
duplicate [ˈduːplɪkət] [ˈduːplɪkeɪt]	[ˈduːplɪkət] *a.* 完全相同的; 副本的 *n.* 复制品; 副本 [ˈduːplɪkeɪt] *vt.* 复写; 复制; 使加倍 记 词根记忆: du(两, 双) + plic(重叠) + ate → 做成双重 → 复制 搭 in duplicate 一式两份 例 The form has to be handed in in *duplicate*. 这个表格需要一式两份上交。
transcendent [trænˈsendənt]	*a.* 卓越的, 出众的 记 来自 transcend(*vt.* 超越, 胜过) 例 Joe is a pianist of *transcendent* genius in his town. 乔是他们镇上杰出的天才钢琴师。

39

harmonious [hɑːrˈmoʊniəs]	*a.* 和谐的，协调的；和睦的，融洽的 记 词根记忆：harmon(连接) + ious → 连接在一起的 → 和谐的，协调的 例 The government is trying to commit itself to build a *harmonious* community. 政府正致力于打造一个和谐社会。
prostitution [ˌprɑːstəˈtjuːʃn]	*n.* 卖淫；出卖灵魂，堕落；滥用 例 Poverty and miserable destiny drove some young girls to *prostitution*. 贫穷和悲惨的命运迫使一些年轻女子从事卖淫。
impenetrable [ɪmˈpenɪtrəbl]	*a.* 不能穿透的；不可理解的，高深莫测的 记 联想记忆：im(不) + penetrable(可穿透的) → 不可穿透的 例 You can't drive there because of the *impenetrable* fog outside. 外面雾太大，你不能开车去那儿。
verge [vɜːrdʒ]	*vi.* 接近，濒临 *n.* (路边的)草地 记 联想记忆：和 edge(*n.* 边缘)一起记 搭 verge on 濒于，行将；on the verge of 接近于，濒临于 例 Father was on the *verge* of sleeping, because he had worked for three days. 父亲马上就要睡着了，因为他已经工作了三天。
kinship [ˈkɪnʃɪp]	*n.* 血缘关系，亲属关系 记 联想记忆：kin(亲属) + ship(表性质、状态，名词后缀) → 血缘关系，亲属关系 例 *Kinship* is one of the most basic principles for organizing individuals into social groups. 血缘关系是将独立个体组织成社会群体时最基本的原则之一。
groove [gruːv]	*n.* 沟；槽；唱片上的纹路 记 联想记忆：注意不要和 grove(*n.* 小树林)相混 搭 be stuck in a groove 墨守成规 例 The coach was stuck in a *groove*, so the team couldn't make progress. 教练墨守成规，所以球队没取得什么进步。
epitome [ɪˈpɪtəmi]	*n.* 摘要，梗概；典型，典范 记 词根记忆：epi(在…上面) + tom(切) + e → 切下来放在上面 → 摘要，梗概；典型 例 Every family is the *epitome* of the whole society. 每个家庭都是整个社会的缩影。
illusory [ɪˈluːsəri]	*a.* 虚幻的，幻觉的 记 词根记忆：il(=in) + lus(闹着玩) + ory → 头脑对某事闹着玩 → 虚幻的 例 A big mirror in the room gives people an *illusory* sense of more space. 室内的大镜子会让人产生空间变大了的幻觉。
anomie [ˈænəmi]	*n.* 社会道德沦丧，失范；混乱 例 When a social system is in a state of *anomie*, common values are no longer understood or accepted, and new values have not developed. 社会秩序处于失范状态即意味着普通价值观不再被理解或接受，而新的价值观尚未确立。

negligible [ˈneglɪdʒəbl]	*a.* 可以忽略的，微不足道的；无关紧要的 记 词根记忆：neg(不) + lig(选择) + ible → 不用选择的 → 可以忽略的 例 Bob has learnt Japanese only for two weeks, so it was *negligible*. 鲍勃只学了两个星期的日语，可以忽略不计了。
emigrate [ˈemɪgreɪt]	*v.* 移民，移居国外 记 词根记忆：e(出) + migr(移动) + ate → 向外移动 → 移居国外 例 It is popular for Chinese movie stars to *emigrate* to Western countries. 中国电影明星移民到西方国家是司空见惯的事。
slick [slɪk]	*a.* 光滑的；熟练的；圆滑的，口齿伶俐的；精巧的，巧妙的 例 Jimmy always has a *slick* excuse for being late. 吉米总有巧妙的原因来解释迟到。
prelude [ˈpreluːd]	*n.* 前奏曲，序幕 记 词根记忆：pre(在…前面) + lud(演奏) + e → 前奏曲 例 The first strike was just a *prelude* of the revolution. 第一次的罢工事件只是这场革命的序曲而已。
immerse [ɪˈmɜːrs]	*vt.* 使浸没于；使沉浸于，使陷入 记 词根记忆：im(内) + mers(浸没) + e → 向内浸 → 使浸没于；使沉浸于 搭 immerse in (使)沉浸在，专心于 例 Please *immerse* the vegetables in water for three minutes before washing them. 洗菜之前，先把蔬菜放在水中浸泡三分钟。
cluster [ˈklʌstər]	*n.* 簇，团，串，丛；群(*group) *vi.* 成群，成串；丛生；群集(*concentrate, assemble) 记 词根记忆：clust(=clot 凝块) + er → 凝成块 → 丛生；群集 例 The plant bears its flowers in *clusters*. 这种植物开花成簇。
barber [ˈbɑːrbər]	*n.* 理发师(haircutter) *v.* 为…理发；当理发师 记 发音记忆："爸爸" → 爸爸是理发师 → 理发师 例 I remembered asking the *barber* not to cut my son's hair too short. 我记得告诉过理发师不要把我儿子的头发剪得太短。
ruin [ˈruːɪn]	*vt.* 破坏，毁灭(destroy)；使破产 *n.* 毁灭，毁坏；[常 *pl.*]废墟，遗迹(relic) 记 联想记忆：一场大雨(rain)毁了(ruin)庄稼 例 A little rain never *ruined* a good picnic. 下一点雨从来不会破坏一次好的野餐。

39

cluster

爸！你又给我剃秃了

barber

auxiliary

[ɔːɡˈzɪliəri]

a. 辅助的，补助的，补充的(aiding; supplementary)；备用的，后备的

记 词根记忆：aux(=aug 提高) + ili + ary(形容词后缀) → 使提高的 → 辅助的

搭 auxiliary machinery 辅助机器

例 The factories in the region always have an *auxiliary* generator in event of power cuts. 这个地区的工厂总有一台备用发动机，以防断电。

distress

[dɪˈstres]

n. 痛苦，忧伤(pain, grief)；贫困，窘迫；遇难 *vt.* 使痛苦，使悲伤，使忧虑

记 联想记忆：dis(分开) + tress(看做 dress, 衣服) → 分开后，看到衣服睹物思人，悲从中来 → 痛苦，忧伤

例 Two in *distress* makes sorrow less. 同病相怜。

pole

[poʊl]

n. 地极；磁极，电极；柱，杆，杖；极端

例 Their opinions were at opposite *poles* of the debate. 在这场辩论中，他们的意见截然相反。

vicinity

[vəˈsɪnəti]

n. 邻近，附近

记 词根记忆：vicin(邻居) + ity → 邻近的地区 → 邻近，附近

例 It's concluded that Pierre and his companions did in fact reach the near *vicinity* of the North Pole on April 6th, 1909. 结论表明，皮埃尔及其同伴的确于 1909 年 4 月 6 日到达了北极附近地区。

metallic

[məˈtælɪk]

a. 金属般的；金属制的；含金属的

记 来自 metal(*n.* 金属)

例 The engineers are creating exotic new *metallic* substances. 工程师们正在创造奇异的新金属物质。

term

[tɜːrm]

n. 学期(semester)；期限，期间；条件，条款(clause)；术语 *vt.* 把…称为

搭 in terms of 按照，依据

例 If you compare the Earth and the Moon in *terms* of substance, you will find the Moon isn't much like the Earth. 如果从物质的角度比较地球和月球，你会发现月球和地球不太像。

chief

[tʃiːf]

a. 主要的(*primary)；总的(total)；首席的 *n.* 首领(leader, head)；酋长，族长

例 The *chief* reason why he couldn't come is that he is ill. 他不能来的主要原因是他病了。

exaggerate

[ɪɡˈzædʒəreɪt]

v. 夸张，夸大(overstate)

记 词根记忆：ex(出) + ag(表加强) + ger(搬运) + ate → 运了太多出来 → 夸张，夸大

例 I tend to discount anything that Sally says. She *exaggerates* so much! 萨莉说什么我都不会那么相信了。她太夸张了！

派 exaggerated(*a.* 夸张的，夸大的)；exaggeration (*n.* 夸张)

hinder [ˈhɪndər]	*vt.* 阻碍，妨碍(*inhibit, obstruct) 记 联想记忆：hind(后面的) + er → 落在后面，拖后腿 → 阻碍，妨碍 例 The government shouldn't create regulations that might *hinder* business growth. 政府不应该制定会妨碍商业发展的规定。 派 unhindered(*a.* 不受妨碍的，不受阻碍的)
shatter [ˈʃætər]	*v.* (使)粉碎，破碎(destroy, smash)；(使希望等)破灭；(使)散开，吹散；给予极大打击 记 发音记忆："筛它" → (使)粉碎，破碎 例 This is why glass *shatters* so easily. 这就是玻璃如此容易碎的原因。 参 shutter(*n.* 百叶窗，快门)
instruction [ɪnˈstrʌkʃn]	*n.* 教导；[常 *pl.*]用法说明(directions)；指示(indication) *a.* 说明用法的 搭 an instruction manual 用法说明手册 例 The students must follow the *instructions* exactly. 学生必须准确按照说明进行操作。
prehistoric [ˌpriːhɪˈstɔːrɪk]	*a.* 史前的；陈旧的 记 联想记忆：pre(在…前面) + historic(历史的) → 史前的 例 Archaeology has long been an accepted tool for studying *prehistoric* cultures. 考古学长期以来都是研究史前文化时所普遍使用的工具。
address [əˈdres]	*n.* 地址；讲话(speech) *v.* 作(正式)讲话；写姓名地址 例 Dean Williams was invited by the college president to *address* the faculty. 学院院长邀请威廉斯系主任给教职员工讲话。
ripen [ˈraɪpən]	*v.* (使)成熟 记 来自 ripe(*a.* 熟的，成熟的) 例 The fruit turns from green to yellow to red as it *ripens*. 水果成熟时颜色会由绿转黄再变红。 派 ripener(*n.* 催熟剂)
infectious [ɪnˈfekʃəs]	*a.* 传染性的，传染病的(contagious)；有感染力的 搭 infectious disease 传染病 例 Colds are *infectious*, and so are some eye diseases. 感冒会传染，有些眼疾也会传染。
garbage [ˈɡɑːrbɪdʒ]	*n.* 垃圾，废物(rubbish, waste)；废话，无聊的东西；垃圾箱 例 We're going to be cleaning up all of the *garbage* here at the lake area. 我们要清理干净湖区的所有垃圾。
bundle [ˈbʌndl]	*n.* 捆，束(package, bale)；包袱 *vt.* 收集，归拢；把…塞入 记 发音记忆："绑到" → 把散的东西捆到一起 → 捆，束 例 Mary gave a *bundle* of clothes to charity. 玛丽捐给了慈善组织一包衣服。 // The farmers *bundled* the husks of corn together for fuel. 农民们把玉米皮绑起来用做燃料。

infectious

别喝，我有肝炎

bundle

39

forerunner [ˈfɔːrʌnər]	*n.* 先驱者，开路人；先兆，预兆 记 组合词：fore(在前面) + runner(跑步者) → 跑在前面的人 → 先驱者 例 William Blake is regarded as the *forerunner* of Romanticism in English literature. 威廉·布莱克被誉为英国浪漫主义文学的先驱。
provision [prəˈvɪʒn]	*n.* 供应，供应品；(法律等的)条款；准备，预备(preparation) 记 来自provide(*v.* 供应，提供) 例 Standard music notation makes no *provision* for these innovations. 标准乐谱没有为这些创新做好准备。
meaningful [ˈmiːnɪŋfl]	*a.* 意味深长的(significant, important)；有目的的，有用意的；有意义的 记 来自meaning(*n.* 含意，意义) 例 Learning to communicate with people from other countries was the most *meaningful* experience I had in London. 学会与其他国家的人交流是我在伦敦最有意义的经历。 参 meaningless(*a.* 无意义的，无价值的)
accompany [əˈkʌmpəni]	*vt.* 为…伴奏；陪伴，陪同(attend)；伴随，和…一起发生 记 联想记忆：ac(表加强) + company(同伴；陪伴) → 陪伴，陪同 例 She will *accompany* the man to the restaurant. 她会陪那男子去饭店。// I need someone to *accompany* me while I play the piano. 我弹钢琴时需要人伴奏。 派 accompaniment(*n.* 伴奏；伴随物)
linen [ˈlɪnɪn]	*n.* 亚麻织品；亚麻布 记 联想记忆：line(线) + n → 用亚麻线一根根织成的 → 亚麻织品 例 Fine handmade lace is traditionally made of *linen* thread. 精美的手工蕾丝传统上是用亚麻线织成的。
quartz [kwɔːrts]	*n.* 石英 记 联想记忆：quart(看做quarter，一刻钟) + z → 钟表，石英钟 → 石英 例 Not all varieties of *quartz* are naturally occurring. 并非所有种类的石英都是天然形成的。
uppermost [ˈʌpərmoʊst]	*a.* 最高的，最上面的；最重要的 *ad.* 在最上面，在最重要的位置 记 组合词：upper(较高的) + most(最) → 最高的 例 Small mammals suffered hardship in the exposed and turbulent environment of the *uppermost* trees. 小型哺乳动物在树顶无遮蔽和混乱的环境里经受了磨难。
defense [dɪˈfens]	*n.* 防御，防卫(protection) 记 来自defend(*v.* 防御，防护) 搭 defense mechanism 防卫机制；defense against 对…的防御 例 Strengthening national *defense* is a strategic task in the country's modernization drive, and a key guarantee for safeguarding the country's security and unity. 加强国防是该国现代化建设中一项具有战略意义的任务，也是国家安全和统一的重要保障。 派 defenseless(*a.* 无防御的)；defensible(*a.* 可辩解的，合乎情理的；可防御的)；defensive(*n.* 防御 *a.* 防御的，保卫的；戒备的)

sacred [ˈseɪkrɪd]	*a.* 宗教(性)的(religious)；上帝的，神圣的(holy) 记 词根记忆：sacr(神圣的) + ed → 神圣的 例 Cows are *sacred* to Hindus. 印度教徒把牛奉为圣物。
extent [ɪkˈstent]	*n.* 程度，范围(*magnitude, *scale, *scope) 例 These innovations in manufacturing boosted output and living standards to an unprecedented *extent*. 这些生产创新把产量和生活水平提高到了前所未有的程度。 参 extend(*v.* 延伸)；extant(*a.* 现存的，尚存的)
classify [ˈklæsɪfaɪ]	*vt.* 分类(categorize, sort)；分等(arrange in classes) 记 联想记忆：class(类别) + ify(使…) → 分类 例 We have difficulty in *classifying* all of the varieties of owls. 我们很难给所有猫头鹰分类。 派 classification(*n.* 分类；级别)
realistic [ˌriːəˈlɪstɪk]	*a.* 现实(主义)的；逼真的 记 来自 real(*a.* 真的，真实的) 搭 realistic movement 现实主义运动 例 After reading the fiction, you'll get a *realistic* picture of the hard life people had on the American frontier. 读完这篇小说后，你会对人们在美国边疆的艰苦生活有真实的了解。 派 unrealistic(*a.* 不切实际的，不实在的)
sense [sens]	*n.* 感官，官能；感觉；判断力；意义，意思(meaning) *v.* 觉得，意识到 记 词根记忆：sens(感觉) + e → 感觉 搭 make sense 明白，理解；解释清楚；言之有理；in a sense 从某种意义上说 例 Bees use their *sense* of smell to recognize whether another bee is related to them. 蜜蜂通过嗅觉来判断另一只蜜蜂是否跟它们有关系。// A: I'm getting worried about Jennifer. All she talks about these days is her volleyball team and all she does is practice. B: Her grades will fall for sure. Let's try to find her after dinner and talk some *sense* into her. A: 我开始担心珍妮弗了。这些天她只谈论她所在的排球队，什么都不干，只练球。 B: 她的成绩肯定会下滑的。晚饭后咱们去找找她，给她讲讲道理。
obstacle [ˈɑːbstəkl]	*n.* 障碍，妨害物(handicap, barrier, obstruction) 记 词根记忆：ob(反) + st(=stand 站立) + acle(表小东西) → 反着站的物体 → 障碍，妨害物 例 Shortage of materials posed the biggest *obstacle* to the development of military forts. 原料短缺构成了军事堡垒建设的最大障碍。
whereby [werˈbaɪ]	*ad./conj.* 借以，凭 例 There should be a compensation arrangement *whereby* workers cooperate. 应该有一个补偿安排，以使员工们相互合作。

39

□ sacred　　　□ extent　　　□ classify　　　□ realistic　　　□ sense　　　□ obstacle
□ whereby

Word List 40

词根、词缀预习表

friv	破碎，弄碎	frivolous *a.* 琐碎的	quea	说	bequeath *vt.* 遗赠；流传
tend	拉扯	contender *n.* 竞争者	nunci	说	enunciate *v.* 清晰地发音
gen	产生	indigenous *a.* 本地的	post	放	postulate *vt.* 假定，假设
arti	技巧	artifice *n.* 诡计，奸计	cern	区别	discern *vt.* 洞悉；识别
feit	做	counterfeit *vt.* 伪造	cad	落下	cascade *vi.* 倾泻

---

inform
[ɪnˈfɔːrm]

vt. 通知，通告；了解，熟悉；告发，检举，告密
记 联想记忆：in(进入) + form(形式) → 进入形式，公告于众 → 通知，通告；了解
例 You should have *informed* me earlier. 你应该早点告诉我。
派 informant(*n.* 提供信息的人；告密者)；informative(*a.* 提供有用信息的；给予知识的)

sturdy
[ˈstɜːrdi]

a. (人、动物等)健壮的，结实的(strong)；稳固的(stable)；顽强的
记 联想记忆：健壮的(sturdy)身体是学习(study)的本钱
例 The small village has always maintained a *sturdy* independence. 这个小村子始终顽强地保持着独立。

momentous
[moʊˈmentəs]

a. 重大的，重要的
记 联想记忆：moment(瞬间) + ous(形容词后缀) → 瞬间就能产生影响的 → 重大的
例 Which university one chooses is a *momentous* decision for every student. 选择哪所大学对每个学生来说都是一个重大的决定。

enslave
[ɪnˈsleɪv]

vt. 奴役
记 联想记忆：en(使…) + slave(奴隶) → 使成为奴隶 → 奴役
例 The early settlers tried their best to *enslave* the local people. 早期殖民者尽其所能去奴役当地人。

frivolous
[ˈfrɪvələs]

a. 琐碎的，无关紧要的；愚蠢的，可笑的；无聊的，不严肃的，轻佻的
记 词根记忆：friv(破碎，弄碎) + olous → 琐碎的，无关紧要的
例 Tim is seen as a *frivolous* man because he often changes girlfriends. 蒂姆被视为是一个轻佻的人，因为他经常换女朋友。

contender [kənˈtendər]	*n.* 竞争者，争夺者，对手(competitor, opponent, rival) 记 词根记忆：con(共同) + tend(拉扯) + er(表人，名词后缀) → 互相拉扯的人 → 竞争者 例 Peter is a strong *contender* for the gold medal of the 100-metre race. 彼得是 100 米赛跑金牌的有力竞争者。
indigenous [ɪnˈdɪdʒənəs]	*a.* 本地的，本土的；土产的；土著的 记 词根记忆：indi(内部) + gen(产生) + ous → 内部产生的 → 本地的 例 Pandas which are widely loved by people are *indigenous* to China. 广受人们喜爱的大熊猫原产于中国。
artifice [ˈɑːrtɪfɪs]	*n.* 诡计，奸计；策略 记 词根记忆：arti(技巧) + fic(做) + e → 用技巧来做 → 诡计，奸计；策略 例 Asking for a sick leave is just an *artifice* to avoid practicing the violin. 请病假不过是不想练习小提琴的小诡计罢了。
maze [meɪz]	*n.* 迷宫；复杂难懂的细节；困惑，迷惘 *vt.* 使混乱；使困惑，迷惑 记 联想记忆：令人惊讶(amaze)的东西去掉 a 成了迷宫(maze) 例 Ron and his friends are lost in the *maze*. 罗恩和他的朋友们在迷宫里迷路了。
spellbind [ˈspelbaɪnd]	*vt.* 用妖术迷惑；迷住，使入迷 记 组合词：spell(咒语) + bind(绑住) → 用咒语将人绑住 → 用妖术迷惑；迷住 例 The old witch tried to *spellbind* the princess staying in the high tower. 那个老巫婆设法用妖术迷惑公主待在高塔里。
counterfeit [ˈkaʊntərfɪt]	*a.* 伪造的，假冒的 *n.* 赝品 *vt.* 伪造，仿造 记 词根记忆：counter(反) + feit(做) → 反着做 → 伪造，仿造 例 Producing the *counterfeit* currency is illegal. 制造假币是违法的。
upsurge [ˈʌpsɜːrdʒ]	*n.* (情绪)高涨；激增 记 联想记忆：up(向上) + surge(喷涌) → 向上喷涌 → (情绪)高涨 例 There is always an *upsurge* in sales during Spring Festival holiday. 春节期间，销售额总会出现激增。
bequeath [bɪˈkwiːð]	*vt.* 遗赠；流传 记 词根记忆：be + quea(说) + th → 说出来把东西留给谁 → 遗赠；流传 例 Grandma *bequeathed* her granddaughter a box of books and drawings. 奶奶将一箱书画遗赠给了孙女。
conceivable [kənˈsiːvəbl]	*a.* 可能的(possible)；可信的，可想象的 例 It is hardly *conceivable* that the little boy should do such a thing. 难以想象那个小男孩会干这种事。
enunciate [ɪˈnʌnsieɪt]	*v.* 清晰地发音；表达，阐明 记 词根记忆：e(出) + nunci(说) + ate → 说出来 → 清晰地发音；表达 例 Every actor is required to *enunciate* quite well. 每个演员说话时发音都必须非常清晰。

40

prejudice	*n.* 偏见，成见 *vt.* 使产生偏见；使…受到损害，有损于
[ˈpredʒudɪs]	记 词根记忆：pre(在…前面) + jud(判断) + ice → 预先作出判断 → 偏见，成见
	搭 without prejudice (to) (对…)没有不利，无损(于)
	例 *Pride and Prejudice* is Lily's favorite novel.《傲慢与偏见》是莉莉最喜欢的一部小说。

shred	*n.* 碎片，细条；些许，少量 *vt.* 切碎，撕碎
[ʃred]	记 联想记忆：精明的(shrewd)人连小碎纸片(shred)也不会随便丢
	搭 in shreds 破破烂烂的
	例 The wedding veil was torn to *shreds* by the bride. 新娘把婚纱撕碎了。

chivalrous	*a.* 有骑士精神的；(尤指对女人)彬彬有礼的，殷勤的(gallant)
[ˈʃɪvlrəs]	记 词根记忆：chival(=caval 马) + rous → 骑马的 → 骑士的 → 有骑士精神的；殷勤的
	例 Mr. Black is famous for his *chivalrous* manner to women. 布莱克先生以对女士彬彬有礼而闻名。

heed	*n./v.* 注意，留心(attention, notice)
[hiːd]	记 联想记忆：上课的时候，要(need)格外留心(heed)老师讲了些什么
	例 The small investors paid little *heed* to future land users. 小投资者很少关注未来的土地使用者。

betray	*vt.* 出卖，泄露(机密等)；辜负，对…不忠；流露情感
[bɪˈtreɪ]	记 发音记忆："被踹" → 被人暗地里踹了一脚 → 出卖
	例 As an agent, although Tom is not on purpose, *betraying* the state secrets is not forgivable. 作为一名特工，尽管汤姆不是故意的，但泄露国家机密是不可饶恕的。

admire	*vt.* 钦佩，仰慕；欣赏(appreciate)
[ədˈmaɪər]	记 词根记忆：ad(表加强) + mir(惊奇) + e → 让人很惊奇 → 钦佩；欣赏
	例 I really *admire* your dedication. 我确实钦佩你的献身精神。
	派 admiration(*n.* 钦佩；赞美，赞赏)

haphazard	*a.* 偶然的，任意的；无计划的，无秩序的
[hæpˈhæzərd]	记 联想记忆：hap(运气) + hazard(冒险) → 运气加冒险就获得了成功 → 偶然情况 → 偶然的
	例 I read these books in a *haphazard* way. 我读这些书没有什么计划。

spearhead	*n.* 先锋，前锋，先头部队 *vt.* 为…作先锋；带头做
[ˈspɪrhed]	记 组合词：spear(矛) + head(头) → 矛头 → 先锋
	例 Britain was the *spearhead* of the Industrial Revolution. 英国是工业革命的先锋。

postulate	*vt.* 假定，假设
[ˈpɑːstʃəleɪt]	记 词根记忆：post(放) + ul + ate → 放出问题 → 假定，假设
	例 The teacher *postulated* that all of the students in his class would pass the final exam. 老师假设他班上所有的学生都能通过期末考试。

□ prejudice □ shred □ chivalrous □ heed □ betray □ admire
□ haphazard □ spearhead □ postulate

rainbow [ˈreɪnboʊ]	*n.* 彩虹 记 组合词：rain(雨) + bow(弓) → 雨后天上出现的弓状物 → 彩虹 例 In Greek mythology, the *rainbow* was considered to be a path made by a messenger between Earth and Heaven. 在希腊神话里，彩虹被认为是由往来于天地之间的信使制造的通道。
humanitarian [hjuːˌmænɪˈteriən]	*a.* 人道主义的，慈善的 *n.* 人道主义者，博爱者，慈善家 搭 humanitarian aid 人道主义援助 例 They are calling for the release of the hostages on *humanitarian* grounds. 他们站在人道主义立场要求释放人质。
inactive [ɪnˈæktɪv]	*a.* 不活动的；怠惰的(idle) 例 Although the states dominated economic activity during this period, the federal government was not *inactive*. 尽管这个时期各州政府掌控着经济活动，但联邦政府也并非无所作为。
block [blɑːk]	*vt.* 阻塞(back up)；阻碍，妨碍 *n.* 大块；街区；障碍物 搭 block up 塞住 例 He should stop *blocking* the doorway. 他不应该堵着门口。
recycle [ˌriːˈsaɪkl]	*vt.* 回收利用，再应用 记 联想记忆：re(再，又) + cycle(循环) → 再循环 → 回收利用 例 Old buildings in many cities were *recycled* for modern use. 很多城市的旧建筑在现代又被重新利用了起来。
adobe [əˈdoʊbi]	*n.* 泥砖，土坯 记 联想记忆：a + do + be → 一次做完的土坯 → 土坯，泥砖 例 A well-planned *adobe* wall of the appropriate thickness is very effective at controlling inside temperature. 土坯墙如果厚度适当且设计得好，能极有效地控制室温。 参 abode(*n.* 住处，住所)
frost [frɔːst]	*v.* (使)结霜，蒙上霜 *n.* 霜；霜冻；严寒 记 联想记忆：霜冻(frost)一来，暖意顿失(lost) 例 The car windows had *frosted* over. 车窗上结满了霜。
longitude [ˈlɑːngətjuːd]	*n.* 经度，经线 记 词根记忆：long(长的) + it + ude → 连接南北两极的长线 → 经线 搭 longitude zone 经度带 例 Each of the satellites is constantly sending out signals, and each signal contains important information that can be used to determine the *longitude*, latitude and elevation at any point on the Earth's surface. 每颗卫星都一直在发送信号，每个信号都包含着重要的信息，这些信息可用来确定地球表面任何一点的经纬度和海拔。 参 attitude(*n.* 观点，态度)；latitude(*n.* 纬度)；altitude(*n.* 海拔，高度)

40

adequate [ˈædɪkwət]	*a.* 适当的(proper); 足够的(*sufficient); 适当的，胜任的 记 词根记忆: ad(表加强) + equ(平等) + ate(形容词后缀) → 比平等多的 → 足够的 例 There is little evidence that people lacked *adequate* wild food resources. 鲜有证据表明人们缺少足够的野生食物来源。 派 adequately(*ad.* 充分地); inadequate(*a.* 不充分的，不足的)
kingdom [ˈkɪŋdəm]	*n.* 王国(realm, domain); 领域，界 记 联想记忆: king(国王) + dom(表领域) → 国王统治的领域 → 王国 例 Many insects live in a colony in the *kingdom* of animals. 动物王国中很多昆虫都是群居动物。 参 The United Kingdom 联合王国
intersection [ˌɪntərˈsekʃn]	*n.* 交点; 十字路口，道路交叉口(crossroad) 记 词根记忆: inter(在…中间) + sect(切割) + ion(名词后缀) → 在路面中间切割 → 十字路口 例 There was no left turn at the last *intersection*. 最后一个十字路口没有左转弯。
religion [rɪˈlɪdʒən]	*n.* 宗教; 宗教信仰(belief); 宗派，教派 记 词根记忆: re(再，又) + lig(绑) + ion → 一再用思想束缚 → 宗教 例 The law states that everyone has the right to practice their own *religion*. 法律规定每个人都有宗教信仰自由。 派 religious(*a.* 宗教的; 虔诚的)
surge [sɜːrdʒ]	*v.* 涌动; 蜂拥而出; 飞涨，激增 *n.* 汹涌，澎湃; 猛涨(*sharp increase); (感情等)奔放 记 词根记忆: surg(升起) + e → 涌动 例 In June 1986, the glacier *surged* ahead as much as 47 feet a day. 1986 年 6 月，冰川每天最多向前挺进了 47 英尺。// They are having trouble keeping up with the recent *surge* in consumer spending. 对于近期出现的消费开支的猛增，他们难以应对。 派 upsurge(*n.* 高涨; 激增)
discern [dɪˈsɜːrn]	*vt.* 洞悉(ascertain); 识别(identify) 记 词根记忆: dis(分开) + cern(区别) → 区别开来 → 洞悉; 识别 例 The weather data allows computers to *discern* the subtle atmospheric changes. 气象资料使电脑可以识别天气的细微变化。 派 discernible(*a.* 可识别的)
method [ˈmeθəd]	*n.* 方法，办法，措施(*means); 秩序(system) 例 We should find out a new *method* to solve the problem. 我们应该找出新方法来解决这个问题。 派 methodical(*a.* 有办法的; 有条不紊的); methodology(*n.* 方法; 方法论)

intent
[ɪnˈtent]

n. 意图，目的(*purpose, *goal) *a.* (on)专心的，专注的；(on)急切的

记 联想记忆：in(进入) + tent(帐篷) → 深夜摸进帐篷，有何图谋 → 意图

例 The man was charged with *intent* to kill. 那个男人被指控蓄意谋杀。

派 intention(*n.* 意图，目的)；intentional(*a.* 存心的，故意的)；intentionally
(*ad.* 故意地，存心地)

maintain
[meɪnˈteɪn]

vt. 维持，保持 (*keep, *preserve)；维修，保养；
主张，坚持；赡养，负担

记 词根记忆：main(手) + tain(拿) → 用手牢牢
拿住 → 维持，保持

例 Some consumers believe organic foods can
maintain health. 一些消费者认为有机食品能维持
健康。

acronym
[ˈækrənɪm]

n. 首字母缩写词(abbreviation)

记 词根记忆：acro(顶端) + (o)nym(字，词) → 把单词最顶端的字母放在
一起 → 首字母缩写词

例 *Acronyms* and initialisms are used most often to abbreviate names of
organizations and long or frequently referenced terms. 首字母缩写词最常
用来缩略一些机构的名称以及一些特别长或被频繁提及的术语。

vegetation
[ˌvedʒəˈteɪʃn]

n. 植物(plant)；植被

例 They feed almost exclusively on dead *vegetation*. 它们几乎只吃死了的
植物。

参 vegetable(*n.* 蔬菜；植物)

possess
[pəˈzes]

vt. 具有，拥有(own)

记 联想记忆：poss(看做 boss，老板) + ess →
老板有很多财产 → 具有，拥有

例 They *possess* detailed knowledge of the
rules of jazz performers. 他们对爵士乐演奏者的
惯常做法了如指掌。

派 possessed(*a.* 着迷的，疯狂的)；possession(*n.* 具有，拥有；财产)

interplay
[ˈɪntərpleɪ]

n./vi. 相互作用，相互影响(interact)

记 联想记忆：inter(在…之间) + play(担任角色) → 在两者之间担任角色
→ 相互作用

例 She combines cultural documentation with invention in an *interplay* of
fact and fiction. 她通过事实与虚构的相互作用，把文化记录与杜撰结合了
起来。

40

recurring
[rɪˈkɜːrɪŋ]

a. 往复的，反复的，再次发生的(repeated, recurrent, repetitious)

例 Some scientists believe one can control *recurring* bad dreams. 一些
科学家认为人可以控制反复做的噩梦。

cascade
[kæˈskeɪd]

vi. 倾泻，流注 *n.* 小瀑布；倾泻

记 词根记忆：cas(落下) + cad(落下) + e → 水一再落下 → 倾泻

例 Water *cascaded* down the mountainside. 水从山腰倾泻而下。

□ intent   □ maintain   □ acronym   □ vegetation   □ possess   □ interplay
□ recurring   □ cascade

assembly [ə'sembli]	*n.* 集会；集会者；装配，安装；立法机构，议会 搭 assembly line 装配线；assembly room 礼堂 例 People in the country used to fight for freedom of speech and freedom of *assembly*. 这个国家的人们过去常常为言论自由和集会自由而斗争。
investigate [ɪn'vestɪɡeɪt]	*v.* 研究，调查(*check, probe) 记 联想记忆：invest(投资) + i + gate(大门) → 想入投资大门得先做市场调查 → 调查 例 The program will *investigate* how the brain functions and malfunctions. 这个项目将研究大脑如何运作以及如何失控。 派 investigation(*n.* 调查，研究) 麻烦您填个调查问卷！ investigate
mercantile ['mɜːrkəntaɪl]	*a.* 贸易的，商业的(commercial)；重商主义的 记 词根记忆：merc(贸易) + ant + ile → 贸易的，商业的 例 Beads can often be used to designate the degree of *mercantile*, technological, and cultural sophistication. 珠子工艺经常被用来体现商业、技术和文化方面的高超水平。
renovate ['renəveɪt]	*vt.* 修复(restore)；更新，翻新 记 词根记忆：re(重新) + nov(新的) + ate → 修复；更新，翻新 例 They have completely *renovated* the restaurant. 他们已经彻底整修了这家饭店。 派 renovation(*n.* 修复；翻修，整修)
attractive [ə'træktɪv]	*a.* 吸引人的，有魅力的 (*tempting, *appealing, *inviting, *intriguing, charming)；引起注意的 例 American children's books are almost always *attractive* and interesting to children. 美国的儿童读物趣味盎然，总能吸引孩子们。 派 attractiveness(*n.* 魅力，吸引力)；unattractive(*a.* 不引人注意的)
postage ['poʊstɪdʒ]	*n.* 邮资，邮费 记 联想记忆：post(邮寄) + age(集体名词后缀) → 邮资，邮费 例 How much is the *postage* for a letter to Vancouver? 往温哥华寄封信邮资是多少？
coexist [ˌkoʊɪɡ'zɪst]	*vi.* 共存 搭 coexist with 与…共存 例 Different traditions *coexist* successfully side by side. 不同的传统和谐共存着。 派 coexistence(*n.* 共处，共存)
lasting ['læstɪŋ]	*a.* 持久的，永久的(permanent) 例 The rise of industrialization brought widespread and *lasting* change to the United States society. 工业化的崛起给美国社会带来了广泛而持久的变化。

foster [ˈfɔːstər]	*v.* 鼓励，促进，助长(encourage)；培养，抚育 (nurture)；领养 *a.* 代养的
	记 联想记忆：fost(看做 fast，快速的) + er → 使 变得更快速 → 鼓励，促进，助长
	例 The sole purpose of the American Academy of Arts and Letters is to "*foster*, assist and sustain an interest" in literature, music, and art. 美国艺术文学院的唯一目的是培养、帮助和维持 人们对文学、音乐和艺术的兴趣。

foster

aloft [əˈlɔːft]	*ad.* 在高处；在空中
	记 联想记忆：a + loft(阁楼) → 空中楼阁 → 在空中
	例 As the bell is ringing, the kids are immediately sent *aloft* to bed. 铃声 一响，孩子立刻被打发上楼睡觉。

manifestation [ˌmænɪfeˈsteɪʃn]	*n.* 显示，表明(indication)；[常 *pl.*]清楚表明某事的言行；(鬼魂等的)显灵
	记 词根记忆：mani(手) + fest(打) + ation → 用手打开 → 显示，表明
	例 What Watson did was to observe muscular habits because he viewed them as a *manifestation* of thinking. 沃森特别观察了(那个人的)肌肉的(运 动)习惯，因为他认为肌肉运动能体现人的思维活动。
	参 manifestative(*a.* 显然的，明白的)

date [deɪt]	*n.* 日期，日子；时期，年代；约会；约会对象 *v.* 注明日期(mark the time of)； 确定…的年代；与…约会
	搭 to date 迄今为止，直到现在；date back to 追随到，始于
	例 We haven't set a *date* for the wedding yet. 我们尚未确定婚期。

surround [səˈraʊnd]	*v.* 包围，圈住；围绕，环绕(circle)
	记 联想记忆：sur + round(圆) → 在圆的外边 → 包围；围绕
	例 Nowadays we are constantly *surrounded* by news and information. 现在，我们每时每刻都被新闻和信息所包围。
	参 surrounding(*n.* 环境)

limestone [ˈlaɪmstoʊn]	*n.* 石灰石
	记 组合词：lime(石灰) + stone(石头) → 石灰石
	例 The solubility of *limestone* in water and weak acid solutions leads to karst landscapes. 石灰石在水和弱酸中的可溶性造就了喀斯特地貌。

exert [ɪgˈzɜːrt]	*vt.* 运用，行使；施加(*cause, *influence)；努力，竭力
	记 词根记忆：ex(出，外) + ert(=sert 放置) → 把 力量放出去 → 运用；施加
	例 The pressure *exerted* on the human body increases by an atmosphere for every 10 meters of depth in seawater. 人体在海水中每下降十米，所受的压强就增加一个大 气压。
	派 exertion(*n.* 运用，行使；努力)

exert

converge [kən'vɜːrdʒ]	*vi.* 汇聚，聚集，聚合(assemble, aggregate)；相交，会合；趋于一致 记 词根记忆：con(共同) + verg(转) + e → 转到一起 → 汇聚，聚集，聚合 例 Small pieces of floating ice *converge* and form icebergs. 小块的浮冰聚集在一起形成冰山。 派 convergence(*n.* 汇聚，聚合)
prerequisite [ˌpriː'rekwəzɪt]	*n.* 先决条件，前提(precondition) *a.* 必备的，作为先决条件的 记 联想记忆：pre(在…前面) + requisite(必需品) → 先决条件 例 There is plenty room, but there is a *prerequisite*. 空间很大，但是有一个先决条件。
squeeze [skwiːz]	*v.* 挤压；挤入(press, crush)；挤过，塞入；压榨，榨取；削减 *n.* 挤；拮据，紧缺；压榨，榨取 记 联想记忆：s + quee(看做 queen，女王) + ze → 很想挤进去与女王握手 → 挤入 搭 squeeze into 挤进 例 She felt as if every drop of emotion had been *squeezed* from her. 她觉得自己的激情似乎已经被榨尽了。
lengthen ['leŋθən]	*v.* 延长，(使)变长(extend, elongate) 记 来自 length(*n.* 长度) 例 The daylight is *lengthening* as summer approaches. 随着夏天的临近，白天在变长。
atrophy ['ætrəfi]	*n.* 萎缩(症)(shrinkage) 记 词根记忆：a(无) + troph(营养) + y → 没有营养，无法生长 → 萎缩(症) 例 There are many diseases and conditions which cause muscular *atrophy*. 很多疾病和生理状况都会导致肌肉萎缩。
employ [ɪm'plɔɪ]	*vt.* 用，使用；雇用(hire) *n.* 受雇，雇用 例 For the past several years many graduates have been *employed* as sales men or sales women. 过去几年，很多毕业生都被雇用为销售人员。
coil [kɔɪl]	*v.* (使)盘绕，卷(wind, roll) *n.* 卷；线圈(wire) 记 联想记忆：c + oil(油) → 油烧开了会出现一圈一圈的波纹 → 线圈 例 Mist *coiled* around the tops of the hills. 薄雾盘绕着山巅。
repel [rɪ'pel]	*v.* 击退，驱逐；排斥(exclude)；抵制，拒绝；使反感，使厌恶 记 词根记忆：re(向后) + pel(推) → 向后推 → 击退；排斥 例 The gravitational force makes stars *repel* each other rather than attract. 万有引力使恒星相互排斥而非吸引。

applicant [ˈæplɪkənt]	*n.* 申请者 记 来自 apply(*v.* 申请) 例 There are more than 1,000 *applicants* for the job advertised on the newspaper. 有 1000 多人申请报上刊登的这份工作。 参 application(*n.* 申请); applicability(*n.* 适用性)
gourd [ɡʊrd]	*n.* 葫芦;葫芦制成的容器 例 Give me a *gourd* so I can bail. 把葫芦瓢给我,我好把水舀出去。 参 gourmand(*n.* 大肚汉;喜欢吃喝的人)
concern [kənˈsɜːrn]	*vt.* 涉及,关系到;使关心,使担忧 *n.* 关心,挂念;(利害)关系;有关的事,负责的事;公司,企业 记 词根记忆:con(表加强) + cern(搞清) → 弄得很清楚 → 关心 搭 concern oneself with/about 关心 例 What *concerns* me most is our lack of preparation for the change. 最让我担心的是我们对事态的变化缺乏准备。// This matter is not my *concern*. 这件事不由我负责。 派 concerned(*a.* 担忧的;关切的,关注的); unconcerned(*a.* 不关心的,不关注的); concerning(*prep.* 关于,涉及)
mechanize [ˈmekənaɪz]	*vt.* 使机械化(automate) 记 词根记忆:mechan(机器) + ize → 使机械化 例 *Mechanized* farming required more capital and fewer laborers. 机械化农业需要投入更多的资本,使用更少的劳动力。 派 mechanization(*n.* 机械化)
harmony [ˈhɑːrməni]	*n.* 和声;和谐,融洽,协调(accord);相符,一致 记 词根记忆:harmon(连接) + y → 和声;和谐 搭 in harmony (with) (与…)协调一致,和睦相处 例 The piano is able to play both the melody and its accompanying *harmony* at the same time. 钢琴能同时演奏音乐和伴奏的和声。 派 harmonize[*v.* (使)协调;配和声]; harmonious(*a.* 和睦的;协调的)
theoretical [ˌθiːəˈretɪkl]	*a.* 不切实际的(unrealistic);理论(上)的(abstract) 例 They devoted a lot of time to *theoretical* problems. 他们在理论问题上投入了大量时间。 派 theoretically(*ad.* 理论上)
ancestor [ˈænsestər]	*n.* 祖先,祖宗(forefather);原种;原型 记 词根记忆:ance(在…前面) + cest(走) + or(表人,名词后缀) → 走在前面的人 → 祖先 例 In some cultural contexts, some people seek providence from their deceased *ancestors*. 在一些文化里,一些人向他们的已故祖先寻求庇护。 参 ancestry(*n.* 祖宗,祖先;世系,血统); ancestral(*a.* 祖先的;祖传的)

40

ancestor

---

huddle [ˈhʌdl]	*n.* (尤指杂乱地)挤在一起的人(或东西) *vi.* 聚集在一起,挤作一团(crowd together);蜷缩,缩成一团,蜷缩 记 联想记忆:聚集在一起(huddle)处理(handle)问题 例 People stand around in small *huddles* to shelter from the rain. 人们三五成群地挤在一起避雨。
congenial [kənˈdʒiːniəl]	*a.* 情投意合的;相宜的,适宜的(kindred);适当的,合适的 记 词根记忆:con(带着)+ gen(出生)+ ial → 带着某物一同出生的 → 天生拥有的 → 相宜的 例 Political liberty was *congenial* to the development of art taste. 政治自由有利于培养艺术品位。
overlook [ˌoʊvərˈlʊk]	*vt.* 俯瞰,眺望;忽略(disregard, neglect);对…不予考虑 记 来自词组 look over(从…上面看) 例 We'll have our lunch in a garden restaurant *overlooking* a small park. 我们将在一个能够俯瞰小公园的花园酒店共进午餐。// She *overlooked* my paper by mistake. 她因失误而忽略了我的论文。
textile [ˈtekstaɪl]	*n.* 纺织品(fabric) 记 词根记忆:text(编织)+ ile → 纺织品 例 The European *textile* industry increased its demand for American export products then. 当时,欧洲纺织业增加了对美国出口产品的需求。
ratio [ˈreɪʃioʊ]	*n.* 比,比率(proportion) 记 词根记忆:rat(清点)+ io → 比,比率 例 The school has a very high teacher-student *ratio*. 这所学校的师生比例很高。
idle [ˈaɪdl]	*a.* 懒散的(*inactive, lazy);没有工作的,闲散的;空闲的(vacant);漫无目的的;无用的,无效的 *v.* 无所事事,虚度(光阴) 记 发音记忆:"爱斗" → 无所事事的人才爱斗 → 懒散的;无所事事 例 Over 8 percent of the workforce is now *idle*. 现在有超过8%的劳动力闲置。 参 idol(*n.* 偶像)
execute [ˈeksɪkjuːt]	*vt.* 执行,履行,实施(*create, perform);将…处死,处决;完成(complete) 记 词根记忆:ex(表加强)+ ecut(追踪)+ e → 加强追踪 → 执行 例 They drew up and *executed* a plan to reduce fuel consumption. 他们制订并实施了一项降低燃料消耗的计划。 派 execution(*n.* 执行;处决;完成);executive(*a.* 决策的 *n.* 执行者;经理人员)

| **reciprocity** | *n.* 互惠，互助；互惠主义 |
| [ˌresɪˈprɑːsəti] | 例 It can be approached only when the agreement is based on the *reciprocity*. 只有当协议基于互惠互利原则时，这个问题才能得以解决。 |

shortage	*n.* 不足，缺乏(scarcity, deficiency)
[ˈʃɔːrtɪdʒ]	记 联想记忆：short(缺乏的) + age(集体名词后缀) → 不足，缺乏
	例 In South Asia, the data indicate that food *shortage* remains a key issue, even where per capita food production has continued to rise along with population increase. 数据显示，在南亚，尽管伴随着人口增长，人均粮食产量也在不断增加，但食物短缺仍是个主要问题。

existence	*n.* 存在，实在；生存，生活(方式)
[ɪɡˈzɪstəns]	记 来自 exist(*vi.* 存在，生存)
	例 People generally want portraits as evidence of their *existence* for future generations. 人们通常都想把画像留给后代，以证明自己曾存在过。// Scientists have established the *existence* of planets outside our own solar system. 科学家们已经证实我们所在的太阳系外存在着行星。

terminate	*v.* (使)停止，结束(stop, end)
[ˈtɜːrmɪneɪt]	记 词根记忆：termin(边界) + ate → (使)停止，结束
	例 In America, a woman's decision to *terminate* the pregnancy is involved in human rights and moral problems. 在美国，女性终止妊娠的决定涉及人权和道德问题。
	派 termination(*n.* 终止，结束)

terminate

influential	*a.* 有影响力的；有权势的
[ˌɪnfluˈenʃl]	记 来自 influence(*n./vt.* 影响)
	例 Who was the most *influential* watercolor painter in the mid-1800s? 谁是 19 世纪中叶最有影响力的水彩画画家？

standard	*n.* 标准，准则(model, rule) *a.* 标准的(*customary, normative)
[ˈstændərd]	记 联想记忆：stand(站立) + ard → 站立的规矩 → 标准，准则
	搭 up to standard 合格
	例 They are working hard to meet these *standards*. 他们正努力地工作以满足这些标准。
	派 standardize(*vt.* 使标准化，使符合标准)；standardization(*n.* 标准化)

40

reveal	*vt.* 暴露，揭露(disclose)；展现(*show)
[rɪˈviːl]	记 联想记忆：re(相反) + veal(看做 veil，面纱) → 除去面纱 → 暴露，揭露
	例 Glassmakers did not want to *reveal* the methods they used. 玻璃工人不想展示他们所用的方法。

打死我也不说

reveal

□ reciprocity　　□ shortage　　□ existence　　□ terminate　　□ influential　　□ standard

□ reveal

Word List 41

音频

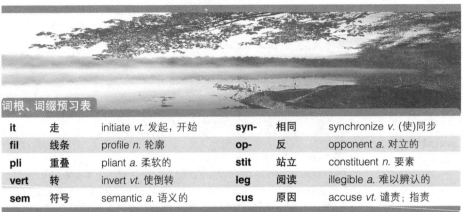
initiate	[ɪˈnɪʃieɪt] *vt.* 发起，开始，创始(*begin)；接纳(新成员)，让…加入 [ɪˈnɪʃiət] *n.* 新加入组织的人 记 词根记忆：in(向内) + it(走) + iate → 向内走 → 发起，开始 例 Those organizations *initiated* a rescue program. 那些组织开始了一项援救计划。
autonomy [ɔːˈtɒnəmi]	*n.* 自治，自治权；自主，自主权 记 词根记忆：auto(自己) + nom(法律) + y → 自己制定法律进行统治 → 自治 例 *Autonomy* is the inviolable right possessed by a country. 自主权是一个国家拥有的不可侵犯的权利。
contemporary [kənˈtempəreri]	*a.* 当代的(*existing, current)；同时代的 *n.* 同代人，当代人 记 词根记忆：con(共同) + tempor(时间) + ary → 同时代的 例 Her style is imitative of other *contemporary* authors. 她的风格模仿了当代其他作者。 // At Harvard, he was a *contemporary* of Santayana. 在哈佛大学，他是与桑塔亚纳同时代的人。
wagon [ˈwæɡən]	*n.* 四轮马车(或牛车)；货车(carriage) 例 *Wagons* are pulled by animals such as horses, mules or oxen, and are used for transporting goods, agricultural materials or sometimes people. 四轮马车由马、骡或公牛等动物来拉，用于运输货物、农业物料，有时也载人。 参 coach(*n.* 四轮大马车)；stagecoach(*n.* 公共马车)

profile [ˈproʊfaɪl]	*n.* 人物专访；概述，传略，人物简介；面部的侧影；轮廓，外形 *vt.* 扼要介绍，概述 记 词根记忆：pro(在…前面) + fil(线条) + e → 在前面看到的线条 → 外部线条 → 轮廓 例 The girl didn't catch the prince's face, but his handsome *profile*. 女孩没有看见王子的正面，却看到了他英俊的侧脸。
adjust [əˈdʒʌst]	*v.* 调整，调节(alter, rectify)；适合，适应(adapt)；校正，校准 记 词根记忆：ad + just(正确的) → 使正确 → 调整，调节；适合 例 The basic idea is that insect pests cannot *adjust* to temperatures much above normal. 基本的观点是害虫不能适应超出正常温度太高的温度。 派 adjustment(*n.* 调整，调节；适应)
obituary [oʊˈbɪtʃueri]	*n.* 讣闻，讣告 记 词根记忆：ob(=to 向，往) + it(走，离去) + uary → 到某地去再相见(是去世的委婉说法) → 讣闻，讣告 例 The chairman wrote an *obituary* on the blackboard of the community. 主席在社区的黑板上写了一则讣闻。
lessen [ˈlesn]	*v.* (使)变小，变少，减轻 记 联想记忆：less(更少的) + en → (使)变小，变少，减轻 例 The pain on Jacky's leg was *lessening* and he could walk carefully step by step. 雅基腿上的疼痛正在减轻，能够小心地一步一步走了。
bilateral [ˌbaɪˈlætərəl]	*a.* 有两边的；双边的 记 词根记忆：bi(双，两) + later(侧面，边) + al → 有两边的；双边的 例 These two countries are planning to sign the *bilateral* agreement. 两国计划签署双边协议。
racism [ˈreɪsɪzəm]	*n.* 种族主义，种族歧视 记 联想记忆：rac(e)(种族) + ism(表主义，抽象名词后缀) → 种族主义，种族歧视 例 In certain areas of America, *racism* still exists. 在美国的某些地区，种族主义仍然存在。
smirk [smɜːrk]	*vi.* 假笑，得意地笑 记 联想记忆：smi(le)(微笑) + rk(看做 clerk，店员) → 店员的微笑 → 假笑 例 The way Mr. White *smirks* makes me nervous. 怀特先生假笑的方式让我很紧张。
pliant [ˈplaɪənt]	*a.* 柔软的；温顺的；易受影响的 记 词根记忆：pli(=ply 重叠) + ant → 能重叠的 → 柔软的 例 It's not a good thing for children to be too *pliant*. 对孩子来说，过于温顺也不是件好事。

41

trample [ˈtræmpl]	*v.* 踩碎；践踏，摧残(人权、心灵等) 记 发音记忆："穿破" → 走路太用力，把鞋都穿破 → 踩碎；践踏 例 Don't *trample* on the lawn. It's what we can do and should do. 不要践踏草坪，这是我们能做的，也是我们应该做到的。
fraudulent [ˈfrɔːdʒələnt]	*a.* 欺诈的，欺骗性的 例 *Fraudulent* advertisements are increasing, so celebrities are more cautious when being spokespersons. 欺诈性广告越来越多，所以名人做代言人时要更加小心。
zigzag [ˈzɪɡzæɡ]	*vi.* 曲折行进 *a.* 之字形的，弯弯曲曲的 *n.* 之字形 记 组合词：zig(急转弯) + zag(急转弯) → 一路上都是急转弯 → 弯弯曲曲的；曲折行进 例 The driver should pay extra attention to the *zigzagging* roads. 司机驾驶时要格外注意弯弯曲曲的道路。
deploy [dɪˈplɔɪ]	*vt.* 部署，调度(军队等)；利用 记 联想记忆：de(表加强) + ploy(策略) → 运用策略 → 部署，调度；利用 例 The meeting aims to *deploy* the works in the coming year. 会议的主要目的是部署来年的工作。
memorize [ˈmeməraɪz]	*vt.* 记住，记忆，熟记 记 词根记忆：memor(记忆) + ize → 记住，记忆 例 To *memorize* the lines is the basic request for an actor. 熟记台词是对一个演员最基本的要求。
stereotype [ˈsteriətaɪp]	*n.* 陈规；固定形式，老套；刻板印象 *vt.* 对…形成固定看法 记 词根记忆：stereo(固定的) + typ(形状) + e → 有着固定的形状 → 陈规；固定形式 例 Our boss is not a *stereotype* of the strict, careful and smileless man. 我们老板不是那种人们一般印象中严厉、认真、不苟言笑的人。
invert [ɪnˈvɜːrt]	*vt.* 使倒转，使倒置，使颠倒 记 词根记忆：in(反) + vert(转) → 反转 → 使倒转，使倒置，使颠倒 例 If you *invert* a full glass of water sealed with paper, the water will not leak. 如果你用纸封住满满的一杯水，然后倒置杯子，水不会漏出来。 invert
obscene [əbˈsiːn]	*a.* 淫秽的，下流的；骇人听闻的；可憎的，可恶的 记 联想记忆：ob(反，逆) + scene(场合) → 跟这种严肃场合极为不符 → 下流的 例 The boys wandering about the backstreet often speak some *obscene* language. 流连后街的那几个男孩经常口出污言秽语。

paradox [ˈpærədɑːks]	*n.* 似非而是的论点；自相矛盾的话 记 词根记忆：para(相反的) + dox(观点) → 自相矛盾的话 例 It's a *paradox* that he wants to get a higher score but doesn't want to study harder. 他想得高分，又不想努力学习，这真是自相矛盾。
wedge-shaped [ˈwedʒˌʃeɪpt]	*a.* 楔形的 例 There are pointed, square and *wedge-shaped* bridge supports. 桥墩有尖的、圆形的，还有楔形的。
semantic [sɪˈmæntɪk]	*a.* 语义的 记 词根记忆：sem(符号) + ant + ic → 有关符号的 → 语义的 例 The *semantic* meaning of this sentence is not simple. 这个句子在语义上的含义并不简单。
preach [priːtʃ]	*v.* 布道，讲道；竭力鼓吹，宣讲，宣传(生活方式、体制等)；说教 记 联想记忆：布道(preach)是想达到(reach)让他人信服的目的 例 The President *preached* against racism, sexism and violence. 总统竭力宣传反对种族歧视、性别歧视和暴力行为。
readability [ˌriːdəˈbɪləti]	*n.* 可读性 记 联想记忆：read(阅读) + abil(能…的) + ity(名词后缀) → 能被阅读的 → 可读性 例 *Readability* is an important factor of history books, but that students' interests of them are also important. 可读性是历史书一个重要的因素，但学生们对这些书的兴趣也很重要。
moderate	[ˈmɑːdərət] *a.* 适度的(mild)；温和的(temperate)；普通的(ordinary) [ˈmɑːdəreɪt] *v.* 缓和，使适中 *n.* 持温和意见的人 记 词根记忆：mod(适合) + erate → 使适合的 → 适度的 例 Flies breed prolifically when temperatures are warm, food is abundant, and humidity is *moderate*. 当天气暖和、食物充足、湿度适宜时，苍蝇会大量繁殖。// It is a common experience in people that appetite is lost even under conditions of *moderate* thirst. 人们经常有这种体验，那就是有些口渴的时候也会没有胃口。 派 moderately(*ad.* 一般地；适度地)；moderation(*n.* 适度，合理)
poverty [ˈpɑːvərti]	*n.* 贫穷，贫困(poorness) 搭 poverty line 贫困线 例 These writers often focused on economic hardship, studying people struggling with *poverty*. 这些作家经常专注于经济困难，研究那些与贫困作斗争的人们。

41

sanitation [ˌsænɪˈteɪʃn]	*n.* 卫生(*health)；卫生设施, 卫生设备 记 词根记忆：san(健康) + it + ation → 要想健康, 得讲卫生 → 卫生 例 Inadequate *sanitation* is a major cause of disease and improving *sanitation* is known to have a significant impact on health both in households and across communities. 卫生设施不足是导致疾病的主要原因, 众所周知, 改善卫生状况对家庭内部和全社会的健康都有着重大的影响。
tantalizing [ˈtæntəlaɪzɪŋ]	*a.* 诱人的 tantalizing 例 It was really a *tantalizing* night together with my classmates in the resort. 和同学们在度假胜地共度的那个夜晚真是美妙。
minor [ˈmaɪnər]	*a.* 较小的(lesser)；次要的(subordinate) *n.* 未成年人；辅修科目 *vi.* 辅修 记 词根记忆：min(小) + or → 较小的；次要的 例 Typing the essay is only a *minor* problem for me. 打论文对我来说只是个小问题。
coupon [ˈkuːpɑːn]	*n.* 礼券, 优惠券(gift certificate)；配给券, 票证 记 联想记忆：coup(出乎意料的行动) + on → 意外得到的 → 礼券, 优惠券 例 I've got a *coupon* for a half-off dinner at that new restaurant down the street. 我拿到了街头那家新餐厅的半价优惠券。
base [beɪs]	*vt.* 把(总部等)设在；以…为根据 *n.* 基础, 底部；基地, 根据地 *a.* 卑鄙的, 不道德的 记 词根记忆：bas(底部) + e → 基础 搭 base on/upon 基于… 例 For most social insects, membership in a colony is *based* on how closely related they are genetically. 对大多数群居昆虫而言, 一个群落里的成员身份是以他们之间在基因上的亲密关系为基础的。
synchronize [ˈsɪŋkrənaɪz]	*v.* (使)同步, 同时发生 记 词根记忆：syn(相同) + chron(时间) + ize(动词后缀) → 有着相同的时间 → (使)同步, 同时发生 例 The titles in a movie should *synchronize* with the action. 电影的字幕应该与剧情同步。
extravagant [ɪkˈstrævəɡənt]	*a.* (言行等)放肆的, 过分的(excessive)；奢侈的, 铺张的 记 词根记忆：extra(超过的) + vag(走) + ant → 走出正常的范围 → 放肆的, 过分的 例 Residents were warned not to be *extravagant* with water, in view of the low rainfall this year. 鉴于今年降雨量少, 居民被告诫不得浪费用水。 派 extravagantly(*ad.* 挥霍无度地)

cafeteria [ˌkæfə'tɪriə]	*n.* 自助餐厅，自助食堂 记 联想记忆：cafe(咖啡馆) + teria → 自助餐厅 例 At one time, upscale *cafeteria*-style restaurants dominated the culture of the Southern United States. 高消费阶层的自助餐厅式餐馆曾盛行于美国南部。
powder ['paʊdər]	*n.* 粉，粉末(dust)；散剂；火药，炸药 例 A wide range of cleaning fluids and *powders* is available. 有各种各样的清洁剂和去污粉供应。
devote [dɪ'voʊt]	*vt.* (to)为…付出(时间、精力等)；献身于(dedicate) 记 联想记忆：de(表加强) + vote(投票) → 把票全给了某个人 → 献身于 例 They could *devote* themselves entirely to "prose literature". 他们能完全投入到"散文"的创作中。// This room is *devoted* to electric fish. 这个房间是用来养电鱼的。 派 devoted(*a.* 投入的)；devotion(*n.* 热爱；献身；投入)
monopoly [mə'nɑːpəli]	*n.* 垄断，专卖；垄断商品，专卖商品；独占，专利(品) 记 词根记忆：mono(单个) + poly(多) → 独占多数市场份额 → 垄断 例 A good education should not be the *monopoly* of the rich. 良好的教育不应该成为富人的专利。
opponent [ə'poʊnənt]	*n.* 敌手，对手，反对者(adversary, objector) *a.* 对立的，反对的，对抗的 记 词根记忆：op(反) + pon(放) + ent → 放在相反位置的 → 对立的 例 Our football team's *opponents* won the game. 我们足球队的对手赢得了比赛。
idyllic [aɪ'dɪlɪk]	*a.* 田园诗般的，田园风光的，牧歌的 记 来自 idyll(*n.* 田园诗) 例 They lead an *idyllic* existence in the countryside. 他们在乡下过着诗情画意的生活。
constituent [kən'stɪtʃuənt]	*n.* 选民(electorate)；要素，成分(*component, element) *a.* 有宪法制定或修改权的；组成的，构成的 记 词根记忆：con(共同) + stit(=stat 站立) + uent → 站在一起 → 要素，成分 例 Vitamins became recognized as essential food *constituents* necessary for health. 维生素成为健康所需的重要食物成分。
epitomize [ɪ'pɪtəmaɪz]	*vt.* 成为…的缩影；摘要，概括，缩写 记 词根记忆：epi(在…上) + tom(切) + ize → 剪切下来放在上面 → 成为…的缩影 例 The novel seems to *epitomize* the 1960s. 这部小说似乎就是 20 世纪 60 年代的缩影。

41

genesis [ˈdʒenəsɪs]	*n.* 起源，开端（origin） 记 词根记忆：gen（出生，产生）+ esis → 起源，开端 例 Like many fundamental problems in science, the *genesis* of earthquakes is controversial. 如同科学上的许多基本问题一样，人们对地震发生的原因也存在争议。
indifference [ɪnˈdɪfrəns]	*n.* 冷漠，不关心（disinterest） 记 来自 indifferent（*a.* 不关心的，冷漠的） 例 What they feared most was *indifference*. 他们最害怕的是冷漠。
convex [ˈkɑːnveks]	*a.* 凸出的（bulgy） 搭 convex lens 凸透镜 例 *Convex* mirrors reflect light outwards, therefore they are not used to focus light. 凸镜向外反射光线，因此它们不用来聚光。
distinctive [dɪˈstɪŋktɪv]	*a.* 出众的，有特色的（unique） 记 来自 distinct（*a.* 明显的，有区别的） 搭 distinctive feature 特色 例 American elms have *distinctive* dark green leaves that look lopsided. 美国榆树深绿色的叶子颇具特色，看上去两侧是不均衡的。// Green pepper has a very *distinctive* flavor. 青椒的味道很独特。
enlightenment [ɪnˈlaɪtnmənt]	*n.* 启发，教化，启迪（illumination）；[the E-]启蒙运动 记 来自 enlighten（*vt.* 启发，启蒙） 例 The *Enlightenment* was not a single movement or school of thought, for these philosophies were often mutually contradictory or divergent. 启蒙运动不是一次单一的运动，也不限于某一思想流派，因为那些思想家们的思想经常互相矛盾或有分歧。
rustic [ˈrʌstɪk]	*a.* 乡村的；淳朴的；用粗糙木材制作的 记 词根记忆：rus（乡村）+ tic → 乡村的；用粗糙木材制作的 例 The *rustic* floor is quite dirty. 木地板非常脏。
facial [ˈfeɪʃl]	*a.* 面部的；面部用的 例 Fear, happiness, sadness, and surprise are universally reflected in *facial* expressions. 恐惧、开心、悲伤和惊讶一般都由面部表情所反映。
medium [ˈmiːdiəm]	*a.* 中等的；平均的 *n.* [*pl.* media]媒介，媒体；方法，手段（*technique, way, means） 记 词根记忆：medi（中间）+ um → 媒介，媒体 例 A man of *medium* height robbed me of my wallet. 一个中等身材的男人抢走了我的钱包。
drain [dreɪn]	*v.* (使)流走，流出（flow away）；使耗尽 *n.* 下水道，排水沟；排放；消耗（expenditure） 记 联想记忆：d（看做 dig，挖）+ rain（雨水）→ 挖一条排雨水的沟 → 排水沟 例 Water is let in or *drained* out until it reaches approximately the same level as the water ahead. 水被引进来或排出去，直至达到与前面的水差不多的高度。 派 drainage（*n.* 排水；排水装置）

poetic
[poʊˈetɪk]

a. 诗歌的；诗意的(lyrical)

例 The *poetic* output of this famous poet is over 200. 这位著名诗人著有 200 多篇诗作。

require
[rɪˈkwaɪər]

vt. 需要(need)；要求，命令(demand)

记 词根记忆：re(再，又) + quir(=quest 追求) + e → 需要

例 The condition *requires* urgent treatment. 这种情况需要紧急处理。

派 required(*a.* 必需的，必备的)；requirement(*n.* 要求，需要)

diplomatic
[ˌdɪpləˈmætɪk]

a. 外交的，从事外交的；有策略的，有手腕的，老练的(tactful)

记 来自 diplomat(*n.* 外交家，外交官)

例 Betty really lost her temper at that meeting. She has to learn to be a lot more *diplomatic* than that. 贝蒂在那次会议上真的发脾气了。她应该学着更讲究策略一些。

diplomatic

oral
[ˈɔːrəl]

a. 口头的，口述的(spoken)；口腔的

记 词根记忆：or(说) + al(形容词后缀) → 口头的，口述的

例 He was interested in *oral* history. 他对口述历史感兴趣。

lament
[ləˈment]

n. 挽歌，悼词 *vt.* 抱怨(*complain)；痛惜(moan)

记 联想记忆：lam(看做 lame，瘸的) + ent → 瘸了腿所以抱怨 → 抱怨

例 In many oral traditions, both early and modern, *lament* has been a genre usually performed by women. 在很多口头传统中，不管是早期的还是现代的，挽歌一般由女性吟唱。

braid
[breɪd]

n. 穗带，饰带；发辫 *vt.* 编织(weave)；编成辫子

例 The general's uniform was trimmed with gold *braid*. 将军的制服饰有金色穗带。

daisy
[ˈdeɪzi]

n. 雏菊；一流的人物

搭 daisy chain 雏菊花环；as fresh as a daisy 精力充沛的

例 She looked as fresh as a *daisy* after her short sleep. 她睡了一会儿以后，看上去精神饱满。

epic
[ˈepɪk]

n. 史诗；史诗般的电影(或书籍等)；壮举 *a.* 史诗般的；艰苦卓绝的；壮丽的，宏大的

例 What they demonstrated was that oral *epics* tended to be constructed in short episodes. 他们表明，口传史诗往往由简短的片段构成。

catalog
[ˈkætəlɔːg]

n. (=catalogue)目录(list)

记 词根记忆：cata(完全地) + log(说话) → 完整列出将说的话 → 目录

例 Some libraries have eliminated their card *catalog* in favour of the OPAC for the purpose of saving space for other use. 一些图书馆为节省空间以作他用，不再使用卡片目录，而采用联机公共目录查询系统。

□ poetic   □ require   □ diplomatic   □ oral   □ lament   □ braid
□ daisy   □ epic   □ catalog

muscle [ˈmʌsl]	*n.* 肌肉(brawn); 体力, 力量, 实力; 影响力 记 发音记忆: "马瘦" → 瘦马没有肌肉 → 肌肉 例 He is an intelligent player but lacks the *muscle* of older competitors. 他是个聪明的选手, 但缺乏老对手的体力。 派 muscular(*a.* 肌肉的; 强健的)
ooze [uːz]	*v.* 渗出, 慢慢流出(leak, seep); 洋溢着, 充满 *n.* 泥浆; 缓慢渗出 记 联想记忆: oo(形似泥浆冒的泡泡) + ze → 渗出; 泥浆 例 The resin *oozes* out of the tree and the spider or leaf gets encased in it. 树脂从树里渗出来, 把蜘蛛或树叶裹在了里面。
individual [ˌɪndɪˈvɪdʒuəl]	*a.* 单独的(separate); 独特的(special) *n.* 个人, 个体(unit) 记 联想记忆: in + divid(e)(分割) + ual → 分割开的 → 单独的; 个人 例 How do *individual* ants adapt to specialized tasks? 蚂蚁个体如何适应特定工作? 派 individually(*ad.* 个别地); individuality(*n.* 个性); individualize(*vt.* 赋予个性, 使个性化)
withstand [wɪðˈstænd]	*vt.* 经受住, 耐(*tolerate, endure); 抵挡 记 联想记忆: with(与…一起) + stand(站) → 手牵手站在一起抵挡洪流 → 抵挡 例 A desert animal can *withstand* high body temperatures. 沙漠动物能耐高温。
apartment [əˈpɑːrtmənt]	*n.* 公寓套房(flat, suite); 房间 记 联想记忆: a + part(部分, 局部) + ment → 分成一套一套的 → 公寓套房 例 For *apartment* landlords, each vacancy represents a loss of income. 对公寓住宅屋主而言, 房屋空置意味着收入受损。
porous [ˈpɔːrəs]	*a.* 有孔的, 多孔的; 能渗透的 记 词根记忆: por(开口) + ous → 有开口的 → 有孔的, 多孔的 例 Some bones are not *porous* enough to be effectively grafted. 有些骨头渗透性不强, 无法对其进行有效移植。
relevant [ˈreləvənt]	*a.* 相关的, 有关的(relative); 中肯的, 贴切的; 有价值的, 有意义的 记 词根记忆: re(再, 又) + lev(举) + ant → 一再举起的 → 相关的 例 He doesn't have *relevant* resource material. 他没有相关材料。 派 relevance(*n.* 相关性)
elaborate	[ɪˈlæbərət] *a.* 精心制作的(*detailed), 复杂精美的(*ornate, complex) [ɪˈlæbəreɪt] *v.* 详述; 详细制订, 精心制作 记 联想记忆: e(出) + labor(劳动) + ate → 辛苦劳动做出来 → 精心制作的 例 They developed *elaborate* ceremonies and religious rituals to bring rain. 他们设计了复杂的典礼和宗教仪式来求雨。 派 elaborately(*ad.* 精巧地); elaboration(*n.* 详尽阐述)

through [θruː]	*prep.* 穿过，通过；从头到尾，自始至终；经由，以；因为，由于 *ad.* 从头到尾，自始至终；直达，径直；彻底，完全 *a.* 完成的，结束的；直达的，直通的
	搭 plough through 费力地阅读；through and through 彻底，完全
	例 The broadcast can be heard by wireless operators on ships with a radio *through* several hundred miles. 在配有无线电的船只上，无线电报员能听到几百英里外的广播。//
	A: At the rate of its being used, the copier is not going to make it *through* the rest of the year.
	B: The year? It's supposed to be good for five.
	A: 照现在的使用速度，复印机撑不过今年就会用坏。
	B: 今年？它应该能用五年呢。
	参 thorough (*a.* 彻底的；完全的)
vacancy ['veɪkənsi]	*n.* 空房间；空位，空缺(opening)；(头脑)空虚
	记 词根记忆：vac(空的) + ancy(表状态，名词后缀) → 处于空的状态 → 空缺
	例 The Cliffside Inn is not so near the campus but it always has a few *vacancies*. 崖边旅店离校园不是很近，但总会有一些空房间。
establish [ɪ'stæblɪʃ]	*vt.* 建立，设立(*set, *enact)；安置，使定居(settle)；确定，证实
	记 词根记忆：e(出) + st(站立) + abl(能…的) + ish(使…) → 使能站出来 → 建立
	例 She helped *establish* peace between her tribe and the colonists. 她帮助自己的部落与殖民者建立了和平的局面。// How long does it take for lichens to *establish* themselves? 青苔多长时间才能扎根？
	派 established (*a.* 确定的；著名的，公认的)；establishment (*n.* 建立；机构)
platitude ['plætɪtjuːd]	*n.* 陈词滥调，老生常谈
	记 词根记忆：plat(平的) + itude → 平庸之词 → 陈词滥调
	例 My advisor's hollow *platitudes* aren't very helpful. 我的指导教师空洞的陈词滥调用处不大。
	派 platitudinous (*a.* 陈腐的；乏味的)
dimensional [daɪ'menʃnl]	*a.* …度空间的
	搭 three-dimensional image 三维图像
	例 One distinctive feature of Moore's sculpture is his use of holes or openings to emphasize that he is indeed working in a three-*dimensional* medium. 摩尔的雕塑作品有一个鲜明的特色，那就是他通过使用孔穴来强调他是在一个三维的环境中进行创作的。
crazy ['kreɪzi]	*a.* 疯狂的，不理智的(insane, deranged)；狂热的，热衷的；精神失常的
	例 I know it sounds *crazy* but it just might work. 我知道这听起来有点疯狂，但或许有效。
	派 craze (*n.* 狂热；风行一时的东西)

41

illegible [ɪˈledʒəbl]	*a.* 难以辨认的，(字迹)模糊的 记 词根记忆：il(不) + leg(阅读) + ible(能…的) → 无法阅读的 → 难以辨认的 例 The letter on the monument was seriously worn and *illegible*. 纪念碑上的字母严重磨损，难以辨认。
sidebar [ˈsaɪdbɑːr]	*n.* 补充报道 记 组合词：side(旁边) + bar(条) → 在旁边提供信息的条框 → 补充报道
drowsy [ˈdraʊzi]	*a.* 昏昏欲睡的；催眠的 搭 make sb. drowsy 使某人昏昏欲睡 例 The stuff the nurse gave me seemed to have helped. But it was making me awfully *drowsy*. 护士给我的药好像有效，却让我感觉特别困。
ridge [rɪdʒ]	*n.* 脊；山脊，山脉；高压脊；隆起物 记 联想记忆：桥梁(bridge)去掉 b 就只剩下脊(ridge) 例 We drove up a hill side and finally stopped on a high *ridge*. 我们沿着山腰往上开，最后停在一个高高的山脊上。
bonanza [bəˈnænzə]	*n.* 富矿带；带来好运的事；兴盛，繁荣 例 The movie proved to be a *bonanza* for its lucky backers. 事实证明，这部电影为它幸运的赞助者带来了好运。
alike [əˈlaɪk]	*ad.* 一样地，相似地；同样程度地 *a.* 相同的，相似的(same, similar) 记 联想记忆：a + like(相似的) → 相似的 搭 look alike 看起来像 例 Good management benefits employers and employees *alike*. 良好的管理对雇主和雇员同样有利。 派 alikeness(*n.* 相像)
pedagogy [ˈpedəɡɑːdʒi]	*n.* 教育学，教学法(education) 记 词根记忆：ped (儿童) + agog (引导) + y → 引导儿童 → 教育学 例 However, during the second half of the twentieth century social *pedagogy* became increasingly associated with social work and notions of social education in a number of European countries. 然而在 20 世纪下半叶，在众多欧洲国家，社会教育学与社会工作和社会教育理念越来越密切相关。 派 pedagogic(*a.* 教育学的) "…第三章 别打孩子" pedagogy
material [məˈtɪriəl]	*n.* 材料，原料(stuff)；素材，资料 *a.* 物质的，身体上的(physical)；重要的(crucial)；实质性的，客观存在的 搭 raw materials 原料 例 She had to collect *material* for her latest movie. 她得为其最新电影收集素材。

dot [dɑːt]	*v.* 星罗棋布于(scatter across)；打点于；点缀 *n.* 点，圆点；小数点 记 联想记忆：壶(pot)上有很多可爱的小圆点(dot) 例 The fantastic island, *dotted* with tropical plants, attracts tens of thousands of tourists abroad every year. 这个海岛长满了热带植物，每年都吸引着数以万计的国外游客。
notorious [noʊˈtɔːriəs]	*a.* 臭名昭著的，声名狼藉的 记 词根记忆：not(知道) + or + ious → 广为人知的 → 臭名昭著的，声名狼藉的 搭 be notorious for 因…而臭名昭著 例 The short story showed what was kind and what was evil through the contrast between two brothers, one famous and one *notorious*. 这个短篇小说通过兄弟俩的对比——一个享誉盛名，另一个臭名昭著，告诉人们何为善何为恶。
habitat [ˈhæbɪtæt]	*n.* (动物或植物的)自然环境，栖息地(home) 记 词根记忆：hab(生活，居住) + it + at → 住的地方 → 栖息地 搭 natural habitat 天然栖息地 例 One reason why the number of amphibians is declining is that their *habitats* have been destroyed. 两栖动物数量减少的原因之一是它们的栖息地遭到了破坏。
chew [tʃuː]	*v.* 咀嚼；思量，熟思 搭 chew over 深思熟虑；详细讨论 例 I'll *chew* your proposal over for a few days and then let you know my answer. 对你的建议我会仔细考虑几天再给你答复。
educated [ˈedʒukeɪtɪd]	*a.* 受过教育的，有教养的(informed, learned) 例 Gifford, a highly *educated* man who suffered from inward struggle, died of depression at last. 吉福德是个很有教养的人，他遭受着内心挣扎的折磨，最终抑郁而死。
accuse [əˈkjuːz]	*vt.* 谴责(condemn)；指责，归咎(blame)；指控，控告(charge) 记 词根记忆：ac(反，逆) + cus(=caus 原因) + e → 谴责；指责 例 I *accused* John of hitting my dog. 我指责约翰打了我的狗。 // The police *accused* Bill of being at the scene of the crime. 警方指控比尔曾在犯罪现场。 派 accusation(*n.* 谴责；责备；控告)
reckless [ˈrekləs]	*a.* 轻率的，鲁莽的，无所顾忌的(*irresponsible, rash) 记 联想记忆：reck(顾忌) + less(无) → 无所顾忌的 → 轻率的，鲁莽的 例 The young girl has always been *reckless* with money. 那个年轻女孩花钱总是大手大脚。

41

Word List 42

音频

词根、词缀预习表

log	说	slogan n. 口号	sed	坐	sedentary a. 久坐的
par	相等	comparative a. 比较的	dow	给予	endow vt. 赋予
don	给予	donate vt. 捐赠	acu	尖的	acumen n. 敏锐
scrib	写	subscribe v. 订阅	ceed	走	proceed vi. 进行下去
solv	松开	absolve vt. 赦免	vok	叫喊	evoke vt. 唤起

---

rendition
[ren'dɪʃn]

n. 表演，演唱（performance）；提供，给予；翻译
例 Her *rendition* of the song was excellent. 那首歌她唱得好极了。

---

drift
[drɪft]

v. (使)漂流，漂移；漂泊，游荡 *n.* 漂流(物)；漂泊；大意，主旨；倾向，趋势
搭 drift apart 逐渐疏远；continental drift 大陆漂移
例 The drift wood could have been *drifting* in the ocean currents for months or even years. 这块浮木可能已在洋流中漂流了数月甚至数年。
参 draft(*n.* 草稿)

---

haven
['heɪvn]

n. 港口；庇护所，避难所(shelter)；栖息处(habitat)
记 联想记忆：与天堂(heaven)只有一(e)步之遥的地方 → 庇护所(haven)
例 Maine's abundant forests and rivers have made it a *haven* for many kinds of wildlife. 缅因州森林茂盛，河流众多，成为多种野生动植物的栖息地。

---

slogan
['sloʊɡən]

n. 标语，口号；广告语
记 词根记忆：s + log(说) + an → 标语，口号
例 "For all human beings" is the *slogan* of this event. "为了全人类"是这次活动的口号。

---

affinity
[ə'fɪnəti]

n. 密切关系；吸引力；喜爱
记 词根记忆：af(=ad, to) + fin(末端) + ity → 靠近末端 → 密切关系
例 There is an *affinity* between the cultures of the two countries. 两国文化之间存在着密切关系。
参 infinity(*n.* 无限，无穷)

slogan

---

stun [stʌn]	*vt.* 使昏迷；使震惊；使…目瞪口呆，给以深刻印象 **记** 联想记忆：太阳(sun)里面多了一个 t，使人震惊(stun) **例** They were *stunned* by the view from the summit. 在峰顶看到的景色给他们留下了深刻的印象。 **派** stunning(*a.* 让人惊叹的；极好的，绝妙的)
comparative [kəm'pærətɪv]	*a.* 比较的(relative)；比较级的；相对的(relative) *n.* 比较级 **记** 词根记忆：com（共同）+ par（相等）+ ative → 放在一起看看是否等同 → 比较的 **搭** comparative linguistics 比较语言学 **例** Bill is a *comparative* stranger in the town as he just moved here. 比尔刚搬到这个镇上，相当于一个陌生人。 **参** compatible(*a.* 协调的，一致的；兼容的)
fulfill [fʊl'fɪl]	*vt.* 履行(perform, execute)；实现(achieve)；符合，具备 **记** 联想记忆：ful(看做 full，充满的) + fil(看做 fill，装满) → 做得圆满，实现了梦想 → 履行；实现 **例** He has *fulfilled* his graduation requirements. 他已符合毕业要求。
paste [peɪst]	*v.* 粘贴；拼贴 *n.* 面团；糨糊 **记** 联想记忆：糨糊(paste)的味道(taste)不太好 **例** The children were busy cutting and *pasting* paper hats. 孩子们忙着剪裁和拼贴纸帽子。
ally	['ælaɪ] *n.* 同盟国；结盟者，支持者 [ə'laɪ] *v.* (使)结盟 **记** 联想记忆：all(所有) + y → 所有人站在一起 → (使)结盟 **例** The *Allies* in World War II contain Britain, France, America, China and so on. 第二次世界大战中的同盟国包括英、法、美、中等国。
scandal ['skændl]	*n.* 丑事，丑闻；恶意诽谤，流言蜚语；可耻的行为 **记** 联想记忆：scan(扫描) + dal → 扫描时事，揭露丑闻 → 丑闻 **例** The Watergate *Scandal* is known nationwide in the 1970s. 水门事件在 20 世纪 70 年代传遍全国。
inactivate [ɪn'æktɪveɪt]	*vt.* 使不活动，使不活跃 **记** 联想记忆：in(不) + activate(使活动) → 使不活动 **例** Glycoproteins in plant cell walls may *inactivate* enzymes that degrade cell walls. 植物细胞壁的糖蛋白可以抑制酶的活动，这种酶会损害细胞壁。
explode [ɪk'spləʊd]	*v.* (使)爆炸(burst)；激增；冲动，发怒 **记** 联想记忆：探险(explore)时遭遇爆炸(explode) **例** How a star becomes unstable and *explodes* as a supernova is not known. 人们不了解恒星是如何变得不稳定并爆炸成超新星的。 **派** explosion(*n.* 爆炸)；explosive(*n.* 炸药 *a.* 爆炸的)
utility [juː'tɪləti]	*n.* 功用，效用(function, avail)；公用事业 **搭** utility company 公用事业公司 **例** His *utility* bills are low. 他的公用事业账单费用不高。

42

filter

[ˈfɪltər]

v. 过滤(percolate, screen)；筛选；(消息等)走漏；渗入，透过 *n.* 过滤器 (strainer)；筛选

例 Springwater is clean, since it has been *filtered* through permeable rocks. 天然泉水是经过具有渗透性的岩石过滤的，所以很干净。

receptive

[rɪˈseptɪv]

a. (对⋯)接受快的；善于接受的，能接纳的

记 词根记忆：re(再，又) + cept(拿，取) + ive → 能一再拿住的 → (对⋯)接受得快的

例 Peter is a *receptive* person, who learns much faster than any other student in his class. 彼得接受能力很强，他比班上其他同学学得都快。

donate

[ˈdoʊneɪt]

vt. 捐赠(contribute)；赠送(present)

记 词根记忆：don(给予) + ate → 捐赠；赠送

例 A local business has *donated* these "Do Not Litter" signs to the club. 当地一家公司给俱乐部赠送了这些"请勿乱丢杂物"的标识。

派 donation(*n.* 捐款，捐赠物)

riddle

[ˈrɪdl]

n. 谜；谜语；难解之谜；粗筛 *vt.* 使布满窟窿

记 联想记忆：谜(riddle)底在中间(middle)

例 Mary knows the answer to the *riddle*, but she doesn't tell. 玛丽知道谜底，却不说出来。

schematic

[skiːˈmætɪk]

a. 图解的；纲要的；严谨的

记 联想记忆：schema(图表，计划) + tic → 图解的；纲要的

例 The play has a very *schematic* plot. 这出戏的剧情非常严谨。

pottery

[ˈpɑːtəri]

n. 陶器；陶器厂，制陶作坊；制陶工艺，陶器制造术

例 The chief handicrafts of this country are *pottery* and wood carving. 这个国家的主要手工艺是制陶和木雕。

参 lottery(*n.* 彩票)

acquit

[əˈkwɪt]

vt. 宣告无罪；表现

记 联想记忆：ac + quit(离开) → 让人离开监牢 → 宣告无罪

例 The court *acquitted* the old man of the charge of shoplifting. 法庭宣判对这个老人在商店行窃的指控不成立。

discount

[ˈdɪskaʊnt] *n.* 折扣

[dɪsˈkaʊnt] *vt.* 把⋯打折扣；不全信，漠视，低估

记 联想记忆：dis(分离) + count(计算) → 不计算在内的部分 → 折扣

例 She could stay at a hotel at a *discount*. 她可以待在打折酒店。

discount

50% off　30% off

semiotics

[ˌsemiˈɑːtɪks]

n. 符号学

记 词根记忆：semi(符号) + ot + ics(⋯学) → 符号学

例 He made a wide audience aware of *semiotics* by various publications. 他通过多种出版物使更多的人对符号学有所了解。

edible [ˈedəbl]	*a.* 可食用的 (eatable) **记** 词根记忆：ed(吃) + ible(能…的) → 可食用的 **例** Codfish is a kind of *edible* fish that lives in cold water. 鳕鱼是一种生活在冷水中的可食用鱼。 **派** inedible(*a.* 不能吃的)
subscribe [səbˈskraɪb]	*v.* 订购, 订阅; 申请, 预订; 捐助, 赞助 **记** 词根记忆：sub(在…下面) + scrib(写) + e → 在下面写上名字 → 订阅, 订购 **搭** subscribe to 订阅, 订购; 同意, 赞成 **例** My mother is used to *subscribing* to the morning newspaper every year. 妈妈习惯了每年都订早报。
verbalize [ˈvɜːrbəlaɪz]	*v.* 用言语(或文字)表达 **记** 词根记忆：verb(言语) + al + ize(动词后缀) → 用言语(或文字)表达 **例** The woman was very excited and difficult to *verbalize* her thanks. 这个女人非常激动, 难以用言语来表达她的感激之情。
align [əˈlaɪn]	*v.* (使)结盟; 排整齐; 校准; 使一致 **记** 联想记忆：a + lign(看做 line, 线) → 排成一条线 → (使)结盟 **例** Two rows of trees *aligned* with each side of the main road will drop leaves every autumn. 主干道两旁排成直线的树木每年秋天都会落叶。 **派** alignment(*n.* 排成直线; 结盟)
purchase [ˈpɜːrtʃəs]	*n.* 购买; 购买的物品 *vt.* 购买(buy, shop) **记** 联想记忆：pur + chase(追逐) → 为了得到紧俏的商品而竞相追逐 → 购买 **例** He is very pleased with his *purchase*. 他对购买的东西很满意。// She *purchased* a product for cleaning rugs. 她买了一个清洗地毯的产品。
syntactic [sɪnˈtæktɪk]	*a.* 句法的; 按照句法的 **记** 词根记忆：syn(共同) + tact(排列) + ic → 把句子排列在一起 → 句法的 **例** A *syntactic* theory that sheds light on human linguistic abilities ought to explain why such patterns do not occur in human languages. 能够阐明人类语言能力的句法理论应该解释人类语言为什么不存在这些句式。
verbiage [ˈvɜːrbiɪdʒ]	*n.* 冗词, 赘言, 废话 **记** 联想记忆：verb(词语) + i + age(年龄) → 一个词说了一辈子 → 冗词, 赘言 **例** Tom is tired of Tim's *verbiage*. 汤姆受够了蒂姆的废话。
drag [dræg]	*v.* 拖动(pull, move, haul); 缓慢而费力地移动(或行进); 拖沓地进行, 拖延 *n.* 累赘, 障碍; 一吸, 一抽, 一饮 **记** 本身是词根, 意为"拉" **例** I managed to *drag* myself out of bed. 我总算硬撑着从床上爬了起来。

42

absolve [əbˈzɑːlv]	*vt.* 赦免；免除(责任、义务等)；宽恕 词根记忆：ab(分离) + solv(松开) + e → 放开(使脱离责任、罪责等) → 赦免 例 The king *absolved* the young man of his disrespect to the kingdom. 国王宽恕了这个年轻人对王国的不敬。 派 absolution(*n.* 赦免，免罪)
sensational [senˈseɪʃənl]	*a.* 轰动性的，引起哗然的，耸人听闻的；〈口〉极好的，绝妙的 搭 sensational headlines 耸人听闻的头条新闻 例 The *sensational* news attracted the mayor's attention. 这条轰动性的新闻引起了市长的注意。
paucity [ˈpɔːsəti]	*n.* 极小量，少量 词根记忆：pauc(少的) + ity → 极小量，少量 例 When he came to undertake analysis in adulthood, the *paucity* of these early memories caused his therapist to wonder whether some painful memories were being repressed. 当他开始对成年期进行分析时，关于这段时期他记得的很少，这使得他的治疗师怀疑是否有些痛苦的记忆被压抑了。
geology [dʒiˈɑːlədʒi]	*n.* 地质学；地质概况 词根记忆：geo(地球，地) + logy(…学) → 地质学 例 I'm really looking forward to this trip with our *geology* class. 我非常盼望着与地质学班上的同学一起参加的这次旅行。 派 geologist(*n.* 地质学者)；geological(*a.* 地质的，地质学的)
allege [əˈledʒ]	*vt.* 断言，宣称 词根记忆：al(向) + leg(送) + e → (把话)向某人送去 → 断言，宣称 例 The detective *alleged* the murderer was still at large. 这名侦探断言凶手仍逍遥法外。
rhyme [raɪm]	*v.* (使)押韵；和…同韵 *n.* 押韵；同韵词，押韵词 联想记忆：r + hyme(看做 hymn，赞美诗) → 赞美诗一般都押韵 → 押韵 例 A poem usually *rhymes*. 诗通常都会押韵。 派 rhyming(*n.* 押韵)
given [ˈɡɪvn]	*a.* 规定的，特定的(specified)；假定的(supposed) *prep.* 考虑到，鉴于 例 A few birds awake at any *given* moment to give the alarm. 一些鸟可以在特定时间醒来发出警报。
sedentary [ˈsednteri]	*a.* 久坐的，固定不动的；土生的，不迁徙的(*unchangeable, settled)；沉积的 词根记忆：sed(坐) + ent + ary → 久坐于此的 → 久坐的；不迁徙的 例 These incursions disrupted the old European *sedentary* farming lifestyle that had existed for 3,000 years. 这些入侵打断了已持续了 3000 年的欧洲老式农业生活方式。

periodical [ˌpɪriˈɑːdɪkl]	*n.* 期刊, 杂志 *a.* 周期的, 定期的 记 来自 period(*n.* 时期, 周期) 例 The young lady published articles on two different *periodicals*. 这个年轻的女士在两份不同的期刊上发表了文章。
endow [ɪnˈdaʊ]	*vt.* 使天生具有, 赋予; 资助, 捐赠 记 词根记忆: en(内) + dow(给予) → 向里边给予 → 使天生具有, 赋予 例 Nature *endowed* Jane with a pleasant smile. 简天生有着迷人的笑容。 派 endowment(*n.* 天赋; 捐赠)
adversary [ˈædvərseri]	*n.* 对手, 敌手(enemy) 记 词根记忆: ad(反, 逆) + vers(转) + ary → 转向反方 → 对手, 敌手 例 Having a qualified *adversary* is a happy thing to make a progress. 有一个强劲的对手是一件能让你取得进步的高兴事。
offspring [ˈɔːfsprɪŋ]	*n.* 子孙, 后代(descendant); (动物的)崽 记 联想记忆: off(出来) + spring(春天) → 像春天一样带来希望 → 子孙, 后代 例 How many *offspring* does a tiger usually have? 老虎通常一窝能生几只幼崽?
suburb [ˈsʌbɜːrb]	*n.* 市郊, 郊区 记 词根记忆: sub(在…下面) + urb(城市) → 市郊, 郊区 例 The growth of *suburbs* was facilitated by the development of zoning laws and numerous innovations in transport. 分区制度和交通上的无数创新加速了郊区的发展。 派 suburban(*a.* 郊区的, 城外的; 平淡乏味的); suburbanite(*n.* 郊区居民)
evaporation [ɪˌvæpəˈreɪʃn]	*n.* 蒸发; 消失, 不存在 记 来自 evaporate(*v.* 蒸发; 消失); e(出) + vapor(水汽) + ate(使…) → 使水汽出去 → 蒸发 例 *Evaporation* is an essential part of the water cycle. 蒸发是水循环极其重要的一环。
bony [ˈboʊni]	*a.* 瘦骨嶙峋的; 似骨的; 多骨的 记 联想记忆: 有些女孩认为瘦骨嶙峋(bony)就是美的(bonny) 例 The three-toed sloth has hook-like claws at the ends of its long *bony* arms. 三趾树懒瘦长的手臂末端长有钩状爪。
polar [ˈpoʊlər]	*a.* (南、北)极的, 极地的; 磁极的; 正好相反的, 截然对立的 搭 polar expedition 极地探险 例 The *polar* bear is found in the Arctic Circle and adjacent land masses. 北极熊被发现于北极圈内以及邻近陆地地区。 派 polarity(*n.* 极性; 两极化); polarize(*vt.* 使极化; 截然对立)
compose [kəmˈpoʊz]	*v.* 创作(*create, devise); 组成(constitute); 使安定(calm, pacify) 记 词根记忆: com(共同) + pos(放) + e → 放到一起 → 组成 例 She began to *compose* original paintings at an early age. 她年轻时就开始创作绘画作品了。

42

debate [dɪˈbeɪt]	*v./n.* 辩论(argue); 讨论, 争论(discuss, dispute) 记 词根记忆: de(表加强) + bat(打, 击) + e → 加强打击 → 辩论 例 The two parties are *debating* politics on the radio. 这两个党派正在广播电台就政治议题进行辩论。 派 debatable(*a.* 有争议的)
integrate [ˈɪntɪɡreɪt]	*v.* (使)合并, (使)成为一体 记 词根记忆: in(不) + tegr(触摸) + ate → 未被触摸 → (使)合并, (使)成为一体 例 She *integrated* dance and plot. 她把舞蹈和情节合成一体。 派 integrated(*a.* 综合的; 完整的); integration(*n.* 融合, 综合)
simile [ˈsɪməli]	*n.* 明喻 记 词根记忆: simil(相同) + e → 相同的东西 → 明喻 例 *Simile* is not equal to metaphor. 明喻和隐喻是不一样的。
comparable [ˈkɑːmpərəbl]	*a.* 可比较的, 类似的(similar, like); 比得上的 记 词根记忆: com(共同) + par(相等) + able(能…的) → 能等同的 → 可比较的 例 The potters replaced the imports with *comparable* domestic goods. 制陶工人用类似的国内产品替代了进口产品。
decent [ˈdiːsnt]	*a.* 体面的 (honorable); 适当的, 得体的 (suitable); 令人满意的 (satisfactory); 正派的 记 词根记忆: dec(变得恰当) + ent → 体面的; 适当的 例 What I'd like to do is to find a *decent* job. 我想做的就是找到一份体面的工作。// It's hard work, but I get to be outdoors and the pay is *decent*. 这是个辛苦活, 但是我可以在户外, 而且报酬也不错。
rug [rʌg]	*n.* (小)地毯(carpet); 围毯 搭 a hearth rug 壁炉前的小地毯 例 The *rug* tones in well with the wallpaper and furniture. 这地毯与墙纸和家具很协调。
complacence [kəmˈpleɪsns]	*n.* 自满, 满足(satisfaction) 记 词根记忆: com(表加强) + plac(快乐的) + ence → 很快乐 → 自满 例 Despite signs of an improvement in the economy, there is no room for *complacence*. 尽管在经济方面有改善的迹象, 但仍不容自满。
unbridgeable [ʌnˈbrɪdʒəbl]	*a.* 不能架桥的; 不能逾越的(impassable, insurmountable) 例 Because of the deep and *unbridgeable* differences between the two countries in terms of their political values, conceptions of international order and geopolitical interests, constant frictions, even minor conflicts, should be the rule. 由于两国在政治价值、对国际秩序的认识以及地理政治利益方面深刻且不可调和的分歧, 经常性的摩擦甚至一些小冲突是必然会存在的。

extol [ɪkˈstoʊl]	*vt.* 赞美，颂扬(*praise, compliment) 记 词根记忆：ex(外) + tol(举) → 向外举 → 赞美，颂扬 例 The little boy was *extolled* as a genius. 那个小男孩被誉为天才。
quote [kwoʊt]	*v.* 引用(cite)；报价 *n.* 引文(quotation)；报价 记 联想记忆：记录(note)报价(quote) 例 The author *quotes* public opinion to support the argument for farming plankton. 作者引用舆论来支持养殖浮游生物的论点。 派 quotation(*n.* 引文；报价)
immigrant [ˈɪmɪɡrənt]	*a.* (从国外)移来的，移民的 *n.* (外来)移民；侨民 记 词根记忆：im(向内) + migr(移动) + ant(表人) → 向内迁移的人 → 移民 例 Looking after the house and family was familiar to *immigrant* women. 料理家务、照顾家人对移民女性而言很平常。 派 immigration(*n.* 移民入境) 参 emigrant(*n.* 移居外国者)
asteroid [ˈæstərɔɪd]	*n.* 小行星 记 词根记忆：aster(星星) + oid(形状) → 小行星 例 Many *asteroids* have been placed in groups and families based on their orbital characteristics. 人们根据轨道特征对许多小行星进行分类。
haste [heɪst]	*n.* 急忙，急速，匆忙(hurry) *v.* 赶快，匆忙 例 In my *haste* I forgot my books. 我一着急就把书给忘了。 派 hasten(*v.* 催促；加速)
suitcase [ˈsuːtkeɪs]	*n.* 手提箱，衣箱 记 组合词：suit(一套衣服) + case(箱子) → 衣箱 例 Leather also became a popular material for *suitcases*. 皮革也广泛用于制作手提箱。
acumen [ˈækjəmən]	*n.* 敏锐，聪明(acuteness, brightness) 记 词根记忆：acu(尖的，锐利的) + men → 敏锐 例 The public were much impressed by the political *acumen* of the President. 总统的政治才干给民众留下了极其深刻的印象。
translation [trænsˈleɪʃn]	*n.* 翻译；译文，译本 例 The book loses something in *translation*. 这本书在翻译过程中丢掉了一些原意。
meantime [ˈmiːntaɪm]	*n./ad.* 其时，同时(meanwhile) 例 That will be fine, and in the *meantime* you should try to take it easy. 那不会有问题，同时你应该尽量放松。

42

□ extol   □ quote   □ immigrant   □ asteroid   □ haste   □ suitcase
□ acumen   □ translation   □ meantime

senate [ˈsenət]	*n.* 参议院(parliament); 上院(Upper House) 记 词根记忆: sen(老的) + ate → 元老院 → 参议院; 上院 例 *Senate* membership can be determined either through elections or appointments. 参议员资格可通过选举或任命获得。 派 senator(*n.* 参议员)
chance [tʃæns]	*n.* 机会(opportunity); 可能性, 偶然性; 偶然的事 *v.* 碰巧, 偶然发生; 冒…的险 搭 by any chance 可能, 或许; by chance 偶然 例 There is no *chance* that he will change his mind. 他不大可能改变主意。
overseas [ˌoʊvərˈsiːz]	*ad.* 在海外, 在国外(abroad) *a.* 海外的, 国外的 例 The product is sold both at home and *overseas*. 这个产品行销海内外。
indispensable [ˌɪndɪˈspensəbl]	*a.* 必不可少的(necessary) 记 联想记忆: in(不) + dispensable(可有可无的) → 不是可有可无的 → 必不可少的 例 Surveys sometimes are *indispensable* sources of information. 调查有时是信息必不可少的来源。
proceed [proʊˈsiːd]	*vi.* 进行下去, 继续做(progress); 发生(occur); 继续下去; (沿特定路线)行进, 前往 记 词根记忆: pro(向前) + ceed(走) → 向前走 → 进行下去, 继续做 例 As one *proceeds* toward the Southeast, broadleaf vegetation becomes dominant. 越往东南地区走, 宽叶植被越多。
alien [ˈeɪliən]	*n.* 外星人; 组织之外的人; 外国人, 外侨 *a.* 外国的, 异域的(foreign); 陌生的; 不相容的, 格格不入的 例 Many movies have been made about *aliens* coming to Earth. 很多电影都是关于造访地球的外星人的。// Someone introduced an *alien* plant into the Florida swamp. 有人向佛罗里达的沼泽引入了一种外来植物。
envision [ɪnˈvɪʒn]	*vt.* 想象, 展望, 预想(imagine) 记 词根记忆: en(在…之内) + vis(看) + ion → 在内部看 → 想象 例 It wasn't until the 1920s that someone *envisioned* mass appeal for radio. 直到20世纪20年代, 才有人预见广播对大众的吸引力。
proper [ˈprɑːpər]	*a.* 正确的(accurate, correct); 合乎体统的, 适当的(fitting); 固有的, 特有的(peculiar) 记 本身为词根, 意为"适当的" 例 The biologists did not have the *proper* equipment or the skill to handle the eggs. 生物学家没有合适的设备或技能来处理这些蛋。 派 properly (*ad.* 正确地; 适当地); improperly (*ad.* 错误地; 不适当地)
sewage [ˈsuːɪdʒ]	*n.* 污水, 污物(waste) 例 The city needs a new *sewage* disposal system. 这个城市需要一套新的污水处理系统。 越洗越脏 sewage

490
☐ senate ☐ chance ☐ overseas ☐ indispensable ☐ proceed ☐ alien
☐ envision ☐ proper ☐ sewage

residue [ˈrezɪduː]	*n.* 剩余物，残余物（remnant） 记 词根记忆：re(再，又) + sid(坐) + ue → 一直坐在那里 → 剩余物，残余物 例 The water can be drawn off and evaporated, leaving a *residue* of clay. 水可以排出来，然后挥发，留下黏土残余。
analysis [əˈnæləsɪs]	*n.* 分析（study）；分析报告；分解 记 词根记忆：ana(贯穿) + lys(分开) + is → 整个分开 → 分析；分解 例 They conducted a computer *analysis* of photographs. 他们对照片进行了电脑分析。 参 analyst(*n.* 分析家)
relative [ˈrelətɪv]	*a.* 相对的；有关的（related）*n.* 亲属，亲戚 例 She has produced a surprising amount of fictions in a *relative* short time. 她在相对较短的时间里创作了数量惊人的小说。
maximum [ˈmæksɪməm]	*a.* 最大（或高、多）的，最大限度的（*peak, highest）*n.* 最大量，极限（an upper limit） 记 词根记忆：max(大的，高的) + imum → 最大的，最高的 例 The *maximum* speed of this car is 150 miles per hour. 这辆车的最高时速为 150 英里。
poster [ˈpoʊstər]	*n.* 海报，招贴画（placard）；(在网络留言板上)发布消息的人 记 来自 post(*v.* 张贴) 例 Many people also collect and sell posters, and some famous *posters* have become quite valuable. 很多人也收集和出售海报，一些著名的海报变得相当值钱。
fascinate [ˈfæsɪneɪt]	*v.* 深深吸引，迷住（attract, charm） 记 联想记忆：fasc(看做 fast，彻底) + in(里面) + ate → 彻底陷在里面 → 迷住 例 He is so *fascinated* by meteorology. 他被气象学深深吸引住了。 派 fascination(*n.* 魅力，吸引力；迷恋)；fascinating(*a.* 有吸引力的，迷人的)
stereo [ˈsterioʊ]	*n.* 立体声(装置) *a.* 立体声的 记 本身是词根，意为"三维的，立体的" 例 He wonders what kind of *stereo* equipment the woman has. 他想知道这个女子有哪种立体声设备。
gin [dʒɪn]	*n.* 杜松子酒；弹棉机，轧棉机 *v.* 轧(棉) 搭 the cotton gin 轧棉机 例 I'd like a *gin*. 我要一杯杜松子酒。
confederacy [kənˈfedərəsi]	*n.* 联盟，同盟，联邦（alliance）；私党 记 词根记忆：con(共同) + feder(相信) + acy → 互相相信 → 联盟 例 She may have exerted even more influence on the *confederacy* than he did. 她对联盟产生的影响可能比他还大。 派 confederate(*n.* 同伙 *a.* 联盟的，同盟的)

42

desolate	[ˈdesələt] *a.* 荒凉的，无人烟的(deserted)；不幸的，忧伤的 [ˈdesəleɪt] *vt.* 使感到悲惨，使感到凄凉；使荒芜 記 词根记忆：de(表加强) + sol(单独) + ate → 荒凉的 例 At the South Pole lies Antarctica, the coldest and most *desolate* region on Earth. 南极洲位于南极，是地球上最寒冷、最荒凉的地区。 参 solitude(*n.* 孤独)；solo(*n.* 独唱)
conservative [kənˈsɜːrvətɪv]	*a.* 保守的，守旧的(traditional, conventional)； (式样等)不时新的，传统的 *n.* 保守派 記 来自 conserve(*vt.* 保存) 搭 Conservative Party (英国的)保守党；conservative views 保守的观点；a dark conservative suit 一套黑色的传统西服；conservative society 守旧的社会 例 At a *conservative* estimate, the visit to Paris for five days will cost about £2,000. 保守估计，到巴黎旅游五天大约要花费 2000 英镑。
evoke [ɪˈvoʊk]	*vt.* 唤起，引起，激起(*stimulate, arouse) 記 词根记忆：e(出) + vok(叫喊) + e → 喊出来 → 唤起，引起，激起 例 The purpose of a poem need not be to inform the reader of anything, but rather to *evoke* feelings. 诗的目的不一定是要让读者了解什么，而是要激发情感。 参 invoke(*vt.* 援引；恳求)；provoke(*vt.* 激怒)；revoke(*vt.* 撤回)
receptor [rɪˈseptər]	*n.* 感受器；受体 記 词根记忆：re(表加强) + cept(拿，取) + or → 用力拿住 → 感受器 例 The liver is the *receptor* of dietary fat. 肝脏是食用脂肪的接受者。
ability [əˈbɪləti]	*n.* 能力，才干(capacity) 記 联想记忆：abil(看做 able, 能…的) + ity(名词后缀) → 能力 搭 academic ability 学习能力，研究能力 例 You will be given the *ability* to recognize your own apprehension, to analyze and to draw a conclusion. 你将被给予能力来认识自己的见解，进行分析并得出结论。 参 liability(*n.* 责任，义务；债务；可能性)；reliability(*n.* 可靠性)
brass [bræs]	*n.* 铜管乐器；黄铜(器) 記 联想记忆：铜管乐器(brass)声音低沉(bass) 例 *Brass* has a muted yellow color, which is somewhat similar to gold. 黄铜呈柔和的黄色，与金子的颜色略为相似。
vestige [ˈvestɪdʒ]	*n.* 遗迹，残余(remnant, remains, trace)；丝毫，一点儿 記 词根记忆：vestig(脚印) + e → 留下的脚印 → 痕迹，遗迹 搭 the last vestiges of …的最后残余 例 There's not a *vestige* of truth in the rumor. 这个谣言毫无真实性可言。

gymnasium [dʒɪmˈneɪziəm]	*n.* 体育馆；健身房 记 该词源自希腊语 *gymnasion*（赤身训练），古希腊运动员训练时要求赤身裸体，据说这样能使全身最大限度地自由活动。 例 In December of 2001, the *gymnasium* was closed to begin a $30 million renovation. 2001 年 12 月，该体育馆被关闭，开始进行耗资 3000 万美元的整修工作。
maize [meɪz]	*n.* 玉米 记 发音记忆："麦子" → 麦子和玉米都属于农作物 → 玉米 例 *Maize* is the most widely grown crop in a number of countries. 在很多国家，玉米都是最广泛种植的作物。
magnesium [mægˈniːziəm]	*n.* 镁 参 magnesia(*n.* 镁砂)
disposal [dɪˈspoʊzl]	*n.* 清除，处理，处置(getting rid of)；变卖 搭 garbage disposal 垃圾处理；at one's disposal 任由某人处理 例 Environmentalists think recycling should be promoted as the best answer to waste *disposal*. 环保主义者认为应该促进回收利用，这是处理废物的最佳方案。

Growth and change are the law of all life. Yesterday's answers are inadequate for today's problems—just as the solutions of today will not fill the needs of tomorrow.

生长与变化是一切生命的法则。 昨日的答案不适用于今日的问题——正如今天的方法不能解决明天的需求。

——美国总统 罗斯福 .F.（Franklin Roosevelt, American President）

42

Word List 43

音频

词根、词缀预习表

vapor	水汽	evaporate v. (使)蒸发	**sist**	站立	resistant a. 抵抗的
cod	心	concord n. 和睦	**ven**	来	souvenir n. 纪念品
cree	分开	decree v. 判决	**liev**	举起	relieve vt. 缓解
rupt	断裂	corrupt a. 腐化的	**tag**	接触	contagious a. 传染性的
cid	掉落	incident n. 事件	**vent**	来	inventory n. 目录

---

descend
[dɪˈsend]

v. 遗传(inherit); 下降(fall); 起源(于); 降临, 来临
记 词根记忆: de(向下) + scend(爬) → 向下爬 → 下降
搭 be descended from 是…的后裔
例 The octopus and the squid *descended* from earlier creatures with shells. 章鱼和鱿鱼是早期有壳生物的后代。
派 descendant(*n.* 后代, 后裔)
参 decent(*a.* 正派的); descent(*n.* 下降; 血统, 出身)

---

annul
[əˈnʌl]

vt. 宣布无效, 取消, 废除
记 词根记忆: an(接近) + n(=ne 没有) + ul → 使接近没有 → 宣布无效
例 The signature in the agreement was fake, so the judge *annulled* the contract. 由于协议中的签名是假的, 因此法官宣判合约无效。

---

mail
[meɪl]

n. 邮件 *vt.* 邮寄(post)
搭 a mail carrier 邮差; internal mail 内部邮件; by mail 通过邮件
例 I hear the post office hired two more students to work in the *mail* room. 我听说邮局又雇了两个学生在邮件室工作。

---

bill
[bɪl]

n. 账单; 纸币, 钞票; 议案, 法案; 节目单; 招贴, 海报 *vt.* 用招贴(或广告、报纸等)宣布; 给…开账单
例 She always pays her *bills* on time. 她总是按时支付账单。

---

enrich
[ɪnˈrɪtʃ]

vt. 使充实; 使肥沃(fertilize); 使富裕, 使富有
记 联想记忆: en(使…) + rich(充足的; 肥沃的) → 使充实; 使肥沃
例 Plant growth greatly *enriched* our atmosphere with oxygen. 植物的生长大大丰富了大气中的氧气。
派 enrichment(*n.* 丰富; 肥沃)

---

march [mɑːrtʃ]	*n.* 行进，行军；示威游行；进行曲；进行，进展 *v.* 前进，进发；行进，齐步走；游行示威 例 The band played a military *march*. 乐队演奏了军队进行曲。// The front ranks *marched* toward the enemy line. 前锋朝敌方的防线行进了。
hormone [ˈhɔːrmoʊn]	*n.* 激素，荷尔蒙 记 词根记忆：horm(冲动) + one → 激素，荷尔蒙 例 The short child of tall parents very likely had a *hormone* deficiency early in life. 如果父母高个子而孩子身材矮小，那么这个孩子很可能在小时候缺乏荷尔蒙。 派 hormonal(*a.* 激素的，荷尔蒙的)
sapphire [ˈsæfaɪər]	*n.* 蓝宝石，青石；蔚蓝色 *a.* 天蓝色，蔚蓝色的 例 *Sapphires* are commonly worn as jewelry. 蓝宝石常被用做首饰佩戴。
coalition [ˌkoʊəˈlɪʃn]	*n.* 联盟，同盟；结合，联合(combination) 记 词根记忆：co(共同) + alit(变成) + ion → 变成一体 → 结合，联合 搭 in coalition with 与…联合 例 I'm going door to door tonight to tell people about the student action *coalition*. 我今晚要挨家挨户告诉人们关于学生行动同盟的事情。// The environmental groups advocate healthy life in *coalition* with consumer groups. 环保组织与消费者组织联合倡导健康的生活方式。
hockey [ˈhɑːki]	*n.* 曲棍球 记 联想记忆：一只猴子(monkey)在玩曲棍球(hockey) 例 Why didn't you go to the *hockey* finals last weekend? 上个周末你怎么没去看曲棍球决赛？
evaporate [ɪˈvæpəreɪt]	*v.* (使)蒸发；消失，不复存在(disappear, vanish) 记 词根记忆：e(出) + vapor(水汽) + ate(使…) → 使水汽出去 → (使)蒸发 例 Ices have *evaporated* from its outer layers to leave a crust of nearly black dust all over the surface. 冰已经从外层开始融化，在表面留下一层几乎是黑色的灰尘。 派 evaporation(*n.* 蒸发；消失)；evaporated(*a.* 浓缩的，脱水的)；evaporating(*a.* 蒸发作用的)
culpable [ˈkʌlpəb]	*a.* 有罪的；该谴责的，难辞其咎的 记 词根记忆：culp(指责) + able(能…的) → 应该受到指责的 → 该谴责的，难辞其咎的 例 As his elder sister, Mary was *culpable* about Jay's suffering. 作为杰伊的姐姐，玛丽对杰的遭遇是难辞其咎的。
linger [ˈlɪŋgər]	*vi.* 徘徊，流连(hover)；继续存留；缓慢消失 记 联想记忆：那位歌手(singer)徘徊(linger)于曾经的舞台 例 The faint smell of her perfume *lingered* in the room. 房间里仍残留着她那淡淡的香水味。

43

linger

从白天到黑夜 我不愿离开

function [ˈfʌŋkʃn]	*n.* 机能，功能，作用；函数 *v.* 运行；起作用(*serve) 搭 function as sb./sth. 起…作用，具有…功能 例 The *function* of the heart is to pump blood through the body. 心脏的功能是把血液输往全身。 派 multifunctional(*a.* 多功能的)；malfunction(*n.* 故障)
troupe [truːp]	*n.* 剧团；马戏团；芭蕾舞团 记 联想记忆：部队(troop)里的一群(group)人组建了一个剧团(troupe) 例 Cheryl usually doesn't travel with the dance *troupe*. 谢里尔一般不和舞蹈团一同旅行。
mock [mɑːk]	*v.* 嘲笑，嘲弄(ridicule)；(为了取笑)模仿；蔑视，不尊重 *a.* 模拟的，演习的；假装的 *n.* 模拟考试 记 联想记忆：和尚(monk)没头发常受到嘲笑(mock) 例 These achievements were *mocked* by the artistic elite of Paris as expensive and ugly follies. 巴黎艺术精英嘲笑这些成就是昂贵且丑陋的愚蠢行为。 参 mockingbird(*n.* 嘲鸟)
texture [ˈtekstʃər]	*n.* 质地(character)；纹理(vein)；结构(structure) 记 词根记忆：text(编织) + ure → 质地；纹理 例 Igneous rocks vary in *texture* as well as chemistry. 火成岩在质地和化学成分上各不相同。
enroll [ɪnˈroʊl]	*v.* 登记，注册(check in, register)；招收 记 联想记忆：en(进入) + roll(名单) → 上了名单 → 登记；注册 例 He didn't know that she was *enrolled* in a linear algebra course. 他不知道她选了线性代数课程。
confiscate [ˈkɑːnfɪskeɪt]	*vt.* 没收，充公，征用 记 词根记忆：con (和) + fisc (箱；金库) + ate → 使和金库分开 → 没收，充公，征用 例 The monitor *confiscated* the mp3-player which Tina was listening to in the class. 班长没收了蒂娜在上课时听的 mp3 播放器。
amend [əˈmend]	*vt.* 修正，修订(法律文件等) 记 联想记忆：a(表加强) + mend(修理) → 修正，修订 例 The tutor told his student to *amend* the final edition of his paper and hand it in next Monday. 导师让他的学生再修改一下论文终稿，下周一上交。
concord [ˈkɑːŋkɔːrd]	*n.* 和睦；公约 记 词根记忆：con(共同) + cord(心) → 心与心相连 → 和睦 例 It's strange that cats and dogs can live in *concord*. 很奇怪猫和狗竟能和睦相处。
brighten [ˈbraɪtn]	*v.* (使)更明亮；(使)快活起来；(使)有希望 例 The flowers in the window really *brighten* my spirits. 橱窗里的花确实让我精神振奋。

vascular [ˈvæskjələr]	*a.* 血管的，脉管的 记 词根记忆：vas(管) + cul + ar → 血管的 例 Research in treating *vascular* disease is exploring new areas, such as minimally invasive techniques which are less risky and speed a patient's recovery time. 血管疾病的治疗研究正在探测新的领域，比如切入程度最低的治疗技术，这种技术风险性更低，且能缩短病人的康复时间。 参 muscular(*a.* 肌肉的)
aristocratic [ˌærɪstəˈkrætɪk]	*a.* 贵族(统治)的，有贵族气派的 记 词根记忆：aristo(最好的) + crat(统治) + ic → 贵族(统治)的 例 Most people in the street envy the *aristocratic* lifestyle. 大多数普通人都羡慕贵族的生活方式。
fracture [ˈfræktʃər]	*n.* 骨折；断裂；破裂 *v.* (使)断裂，折断(*crack)；(使)分裂 记 词根记忆：fract(打碎) + ure → (使)断裂，折断 例 *Fracture* on tools also indicates that a majority of ancient people were right-handed. 工具上的破裂也表明古时大部分人都用右手。
decree [dɪˈkriː]	*n.* 政令，法令；裁定，判决 *v.* 判决；颁布 记 词根记忆：de + cree(分开) → 判决 例 The local government issued a new *decree* to solve the problems of education. 当地政府颁布了一项新法令来解决教育问题。
scarf [skɑːrf]	*n.* 围巾，披巾(shawl)，头巾 记 联想记忆：为了遮住脖子上的伤疤(scar)，围了条围巾(scarf) 例 He bought a silk *scarf* for her as a birthday present. 他给她买了条丝巾作为生日礼物。
authoritative [əˈθɔːrəteɪtɪv]	*a.* 官方的；权威性的，可信的；专断的，命令式的 例 The mayor has announced the *authoritative* instructions. 市长已经宣读了官方指示。
impersonal [ɪmˈpɜːrsənl]	*a.* 没有人情味的，冷淡的(indifferent)；客观的(objective) 记 联想记忆：im(不) + personal(个人的) → 不带个人感情的 → 没有人情味的，冷淡的；客观的 例 The relationships tend to be *impersonal*. 这种关系往往会很冷淡。
autonomous [ɔːˈtɑːnəməs]	*a.* 自治的；独立自主的 记 词根记忆：auto(自己) + nom(法律) + ous → 自己制定法律的 → 自治的；独立自主的 例 There are three *autonomous* states in this country. 这个国家有三个自治州。
canvass [ˈkænvəs]	*v.* 游说，拉选票；细查 记 联想记忆：在帆布(canvas)上写上标语来拉选票(canvass) 例 The candidate has to go on the street and *canvass* for votes in every campaign season. 每个竞选季，候选人都要去街上为自己拉选票。

43

conspiracy [kən'spɪrəsi]	*n.* 密谋；阴谋(plot) 例 Some innocent people were involved in this *conspiracy*. 一些无辜的人被卷入这场阴谋当中。
corrupt [kə'rʌpt]	*a.* 堕落的，腐化的；腐败的，贪污的 *v.* 使腐化，腐蚀，使堕落；破坏，损坏 记 词根记忆：cor(表加强) + rupt(断裂) → 完全断裂 → 腐化的 例 From ancient times to present day, *corrupt* officials still exist. 从古到今，腐败的官员一直存在。
default [dɪ'fɔːlt]	*n.* 违约；弃权；(计算机)缺省 *vi.* 不履行义务，违约 记 联想记忆：de(表加强) + fault(过失) → 过失进一步恶化 → 违约 搭 in default of 因缺少；by default 缺席 例 The village is rich in coal, but it doesn't put it into good use in *default* of advanced technology. 这个村子盛产煤，却因为缺少先进的技术而不能充分利用。
pivot ['pɪvət]	*n.* 枢轴；中心点；核心 *v.* (使)在枢轴上旋转 例 The *pivot* on which the old system turned had disappeared. 维系旧制度的支柱已经消失了。
seminar ['semɪnɑːr]	*n.* 研讨会(workshop)；研讨班 记 联想记忆：semin(播种) + ar → 研讨会播下思想的种子 → 研讨会 例 Teaching is by lectures and *seminars*. 教学形式为讲座和研讨课。
depose [dɪ'pouz]	*vt.* 革除，罢免，废黜 记 词根记忆：de(向下) + pos(放) + e → (将人)向下放 → 革除，罢免 例 The official was *deposed* by the superior governor because of his negligence. 这个官员因为渎职而被上一级主管罢免了。
identical [aɪ'dentɪkl]	*a.* 相同的(*exactly alike)；同一的(selfsame) 例 The director wants the songs in the Broadway version to be *identical* to the songs in the film. 导演想让百老汇版的歌曲与电影版的歌曲完全相同。
desegregate [ˌdiː'segrɪɡeɪt]	*v.* 废除种族隔离 记 词根记忆：de(反) + se(分离) + greg(群) + ate → 反对分离群体 → 废除种族隔离 例 To *desegregate* allows both black and white children to go to the same school and study in the same class. 废除种族隔离可以让黑人孩子和白人孩子在同一个学校学习，在同一个班里上课。
assassinate [ə'sæsəneɪt]	*vt.* 暗杀，行刺；诋毁 记 联想记忆：ass(蠢人) + ass(蠢人) + in + ate → 不停地骂人是蠢人 → 诋毁 例 Many activists in this revolution were *assassinated* by the reactionaries. 这次革命中的许多积极分子被反动派暗杀了。

superior	*a.* （级别、地位等）较高的；（质量、价值等）更好的；有优越感的，高傲的；超群的 *n.* 上级，长官
[suːˈpɪriər]	记 词根记忆：super(在…上面) + ior → 较高的
	例 Natural vitamins are *superior* to synthetic ones. 天然维生素优于合成维生素。
	派 superiority[*n.* 优越(性)，优势；优越感]

photograph	*n.* 照片 *v.* 拍照
[ˈfoʊtəɡræf]	搭 take a photograph 拍照
	例 Our professor took *photographs* of small oceanic snails. 我们的教授给小型海洋蜗牛拍了照。
	参 paragraph(*n.* 段)

muscular	*a.* 肌肉的；肌肉发达的；强健的，强壮的(strong, well-built)
[ˈmʌskjələr]	记 来自 muscul(e)(*n.* 肌肉)
	搭 muscular cell 肌细胞；muscular tissue 肌肉组织；muscular dystrophy 肌肉萎缩
	例 The athletes kept their *muscular* bodies in shape with three hours' swimming every morning. 运动员每天上午游泳三个小时以保持强健的体魄。

| **amino** | *a.* 氨基的 |
| [əˈmiːnoʊ] | 搭 amino acid 氨基酸 |

disarm	*v.* 解除武装；裁军；消除(疑虑)，消解(怒气等)
[dɪsˈɑːrm]	记 联想记忆：dis(分离) + arm(武器) → 解除武装
	例 The troop captured and *disarmed* more than 100 rebels. 部队逮捕了100多名叛逃者并缴获了他们的武器。

scarce	*a.* 缺乏的(lacking)；稀有的，罕见的(*rare)
[skers]	记 联想记忆：scar(伤疤) + ce → 有伤疤，不完整的 → 缺乏的
	例 Watches and clocks were *scarce* in the United States until the late 1850s. 19世纪50年代末之前钟表在美国很少见。
	派 scarcely(*ad.* 几乎不；刚刚)；scarcity(*n.* 缺乏，不足)
	参 scare(*v.* 惊吓，恐吓)

incident	*n.* 事情，事件(happening)；摩擦，冲突
[ˈɪnsɪdənt]	记 词根记忆：in + cid(掉落) + ent(表物，名词后缀) → 忽然掉落的东西 → 事件
	例 She isn't upset about the *incident*. 此事并没有让她不安。
	派 incidental(*a.* 附带发生的，次要的；偶然的)

curiosity	*n.* 好奇心，求知欲(desire to know)；罕见而有趣之物，珍品
[ˌkjʊriˈɑːsəti]	记 词根记忆：cur(注意) + ios + ity → 多加注意 → 好奇心
	例 You really pick my *curiosity*. 你确实激起了我的好奇心。

43

atmosphere [ˈætməsfɪr]	*n.* 大气，大气层；空气（*air）；气氛，氛围（tone） 记 词根记忆：atmo(蒸汽) + spher(球体) + e → 地球周围的气体 → 大气，大气层 例 There was an *atmosphere* of mutual trust between them. 他们之间有一种互相信任的气氛。 派 atmospheric(*a.* 大气的，空气的)
instinct [ˈɪnstɪŋkt]	*n.* 本能，直觉；生性，天性（nature） 记 词根记忆：in(内) + stinct(刺) → 内在的刺激 → 本能；天性 例 *Instinct* drives green turtles to always return to the beach where they were hatched. 绿海龟总能在本能的驱使下回到它们的孵化地所在的海滩。 派 instinctive(*a.* 本能的，直觉的；天生的)；instinctively(*ad.* 本能地) 参 extinct(*a.* 灭绝的)；distinct(*a.* 清楚的)；extinguish(*vt.* 熄灭)
vacuum [ˈvækjuəm]	*n.* 真空；真空状态，空白，空虚 *v.* 用吸尘器清扫 记 词根记忆：vac(空的) + uum → 真空 搭 vacuum cleaner 真空吸尘器；in a vacuum 与世隔绝，脱离实际 例 His resignation has created a *vacuum* which cannot easily be filled. 他的引退造成了难以填补的空白。
antique [ænˈtiːk]	*n.* 古物，古董 *a.* 古老的，古时的 记 词根记忆：anti(在…前面) + que → 以前的 → 古老的 例 Invaluable *antiques* were destroyed in the fire. 价值连城的古董在大火中被焚毁。 参 antiquity(*n.* 古老；古迹；古物)
resistant [rɪˈzɪstənt]	*a.* 抵抗的，有抵抗力的；抵制的；抗…的，耐…的 记 词根记忆：re(反) + sist(站立) + ant(形容词后缀) → 站在对立面的 → 抵抗的 搭 be resistant to 对…有抵抗力；acid resistant 抗酸的 例 Scientists found that a number of damaging insects were *resistant* to pesticide. 科学家们发现许多害虫对杀虫剂有抵抗力。 杀虫灵 resistant
ideomotor [ˌaɪdiəˈmoʊtər]	*a.* 观念运动的 搭 ideomotor theory 念动说 例 As we all know, *ideomotor* action is a term of psychology. 众所周知，观念运动是一个心理学术语。
breathing [ˈbriːðɪŋ]	*n.* 呼吸（respiration） 例 When you feel nervous, the best way to relax is deep *breathing* exercises. 当你感觉紧张时，最好的放松方式是练习深呼吸。
dent [dent]	*vt.* 使凹下；挫伤，损害 *n.* 缺口，凹痕（cavity） 例 It seemed that nothing could *dent* her confidence. 似乎没有什么事会挫伤他的信心。

□ atmosphere   □ instinct   □ vacuum   □ antique   □ resistant   □ ideomotor
□ breathing   □ dent

intrinsic [ɪnˈtrɪnsɪk]	*a.* 固有的，本质的，内在的(inherent) 记 联想记忆：intr(看做 intro，向内) + insic(看做 inside，内部) → 内在的 例 During their growing period, many parents failed to teach children the *intrinsic* value of good behavior. 在孩子的成长阶段，很多家长未能教导他们认识到良好品行的内在价值。
skeleton [ˈskelɪtn]	*n.* 梗概，提纲(sketch)；骨架，骨骼；框架(framework) 例 The human *skeleton* consists of 206 bones. 人的骨骼由 206 块骨头组成。
disease [dɪˈziːz]	*n.* 疾病(illness, sickness)；弊端，恶疾 记 联想记忆：dis(不) + ease(安心) → 身心不安 → 疾病 搭 viral disease 病毒病；heart disease 心脏病 例 *Diseases* usually affect people not only physically, but also emotionally. 疾病常常不仅在身体上还会在情绪上给人造成影响。 派 diseased(*a.* 有病的，患病的；病态的)
concentric [kənˈsentrɪk]	*a.* 同心的 记 词根记忆：con(共同) + centr(中心) + ic → 有着共同中心的 → 同心的 例 Many *concentric* circles were formed in the pond. 池塘里形成了很多同心圆。 派 concentricity(*n.* 同心；集中)
racket [ˈrækɪt]	*n.* (网球等的)球拍；喧嚷，吵闹；勒索，诈骗 例 What a *racket* the children are making! 这些孩子真是太吵了。 派 racketeer(*n.* 诈骗者，非法获取钱财者)
earnest [ˈɜːrnɪst]	*a.* 认真的；真诚的 *n.* 诚挚；认真 记 联想记忆：earn(挣钱) + est → 要想挣钱就得认真地工作 → 认真 搭 in earnest 严肃地，认真地；当真 例 Despite her *earnest* efforts, she could not find a job. 尽管她已尽心竭力，但仍找不到工作。
instrument [ˈɪnstrəmənt]	*n.* 仪器，器械，工具；乐器 搭 musical instruments 乐器 例 Some alarmists believe these new *instruments* will bring an end to classical music. 一些杞人忧天的人认为这些新乐器会给古典音乐带来灭顶之灾。 派 instrumental(*a.* 有帮助的；乐器的)；instrumentalist(*n.* 器乐演奏者，器乐家) 参 percussion (*n.* 打击乐器)
hibernation [ˌhaɪbərˈneɪʃn]	*n.* 冬眠(状态)(dormancy)；休眠，蛰伏 记 来自 hibernate(*vi.* 冬眠)；hibern(冬天) + ation → 冬眠 例 Mammals vary their body temperatures during *hibernation*. 哺乳动物在冬眠时体温会发生变化。

43

fatal [ˈfeɪtl]	*a.* 致命的（*deadly）；毁灭性的（destructive）；命中注定的 记 联想记忆：fat（看做 fate，命运）+ al → 致命的；命中注定的 例 High temperatures are also *fatal* to the growing embryo. 高温对成长中的胚胎也有致命的危险。
nominate [ˈnɑːmɪneɪt]	*vt.* 任命，指定；提名，推荐（designate, name, propose） 记 词根记忆：nomin（名字）+ ate → 任命；提名 例 You've been *nominated* for the committee. 你已经被提名为委员会成员了。 派 nomination（*n.* 任命；提名） 任命你为经理！ nominate
cholesterol [kəˈlestərɔːl]	*n.* 胆固醇 记 词根记忆：chole（胆，胆汁）+ ster（固体的）+ ol（油）→ 胆固醇 例 Avoiding animal products may decrease the *cholesterol* levels in the body. 避免吃动物产品能降低体内的胆固醇水平。
articulate	[ɑːrˈtɪkjələt] *a.* 善于表达的；发音清晰的，口齿清楚的 [ɑːrˈtɪkjuleɪt] *v.* 明确表达，清楚说明（utter distinctly）；清晰地吐（字），清晰地发（音）；用关节连接 记 词根记忆：art（技巧）+ icul + ate → 说话有技巧 → 明确表达 例 Some species, such as ants, seem to be very *articulate* creatures. 一些物种，比如蚂蚁，似乎是非常有表达能力的动物。
souvenir [ˌsuːvəˈnɪr]	*n.* 纪念品，纪念物（reminder, memento） 记 词根记忆：sou（=sub 在某地）+ ven（来）+ ir → 在某地游玩带回来的东西 → 纪念品，纪念物 搭 as a souvenir of 作为…的纪念；a souvenir shop 纪念品商店 例 The shop along the street sells the *souvenirs* of the famous tourist attraction. 沿街商店出售著名旅游景点的纪念品。
relieve [rɪˈliːv]	*vt.* 缓解，减轻（ease）；使轻松，使宽慰；调剂；接替，换班 记 词根记忆：re（再，又）+ liev（=lev 举起）+ e → 再次举起 → 缓解，减轻 例 We played cards to *relieve* the boredom of the long wait. 长时间等待很无聊，我们打牌来解闷。 派 relieved（*a.* 放心的，感到宽慰的）；reliever（*n.* 缓解物）
medication [ˌmedɪˈkeɪʃn]	*n.* 药物治疗；药物（medicine） 记 词根记忆：med（医疗，治疗）+ ic + ation（表物，名词后缀）→ 药物 搭 be on medication（for ...）（为…病而）吃药 例 I thought your doctor gave you *medication* for your allergies last week. 我以为你的医生上周给你开过过敏药了。

electrode [ɪˈlektroʊd]	*n.* 电极 例 If you put *electrodes* on the throat and measure muscle activity, you will discover that when people are thinking, there is muscular activity in the throat. 如果你把电极放到喉咙上测量肌肉活动的话，会发现人们思考时喉部肌肉在活动。 参 electronic(*a.* 电子的); electrical(*a.* 电的，有关电的)
contagious [kənˈteɪdʒəs]	*a.* 传染性的；有感染力的(catching) 记 词根记忆: con(通过) + tag(接触) + ious → 通过接触传播的 → 传染性的 例 A hobby like collecting classical music can be *contagious* and expensive. 像收集古典音乐这样的嗜好具有感染力，花销也很大。 参 contiguous(*a.* 邻近的)
thread [θred]	*v.* 穿(针、线等); (使)穿过，通过 *n.* 线；线索；思路 例 It took me a long time to *thread* my way through the crowd. 我花了很长时间才从人群中挤过去。 派 threadlike(*a.* 线状的)
sponge [spʌndʒ]	*n.* 海绵；寄生虫(parasite) *v.* 用海绵(或湿布)擦，揩 记 发音记忆: "死胖子" → 海绵吸饱水活像个死胖子 → 海绵 例 His mind was like a *sponge*, ready to absorb anything. 他的脑子像海绵，什么都能吸收。 派 spongy(*a.* 柔软的)
automobile [ˈɔːtəməbiːl]	*n.* 汽车，机动车(motor) 记 联想记忆: auto(自动) + mobile(可移动的) → 汽车 例 Benz was the largest *automobile* company in the world at that time. 当时，奔驰是世界上最大的汽车公司。 参 immobile(*a.* 固定的；不活动的)
republic [rɪˈpʌblɪk]	*n.* 共和国；共和政体 记 联想记忆: re + public(公共的) → 公共利益的代表 → 共和国 例 Both modern and ancient *republics* vary widely in their ideology and composition. 现代共和国和古代共和国在意识形态和构成上都相去甚远。 派 republican(*a.* 共和的，共和党的 *n.* 共和党人)
dominant [ˈdɑːmɪnənt]	*a.* 统治的，支配的，占优势的(important, outweighing, predominant); 有统治权的 记 词根记忆: domin(统治) + ant(形容词后缀) → 统治的，支配的 搭 dominant position 支配地位; dominant philosophy 主流哲学; dominant theme 主题，主旨; dominant in 主宰… 例 Aristotle considered an object's downward or upward motion to be the result of the *dominant* nature of the object. 亚里士多德认为，物体的上下运动是物体本身所具有的支配性所产生的结果。 派 predominant(*a.* 卓越的；支配的)

43

ritual
['rɪtʃuəl]

n. 典礼，(宗教等的)仪式；例行公事，老规矩 *a.* 仪式的(ceremonial)；习惯的，例行的

记 来自 rite(*n.* 典礼，仪式)

例 *Ritual* ceremonies were conducted by the brother or son. 典礼仪式由兄弟或儿子主持。

periphery
[pə'rɪfəri]

n. 外围，边缘(circumference, boundary)

记 词根记忆：peri(周围) + pher(带来) + y → 带到周围 → 外围，边缘

例 The company will locate its headquarters on the *periphery* of the city. 该公司将把总部设在城市周边地区。

immediate
[ɪ'miːdiət]

a. 即刻的；当前的；最接近的(proximal)；紧接的，紧靠的

记 联想记忆：im(不，无) + mediate(居中的) → 省去中间过程 → 即刻的

例 Reaction from the public and press was *immediate*, and derisive. 公众和媒体立即作出了反应并进行嘲讽。

参 intermediate(*a.* 中间的；中级的)

delirium
[dɪ'lɪriəm]

n. 精神错乱，神志失常(insanity, madness)

例 The *delirium*-sufferer loses the capacity for clear and coherent thought. 精神错乱者无法清晰连贯地思考。

insistence
[ɪn'sɪstəns]

n. 坚持，坚决主张(adherence)

记 来自 insist(*v.* 坚持)

例 There is much democratic *insistence* on the worthiness of every level of birth and work. 很多民众坚持认为每个层次的出身和工作都值得尊重。

botany
['bɑːtəni]

n. 植物学；植物

记 联想记忆：bot(看做 about，关于) + any(任何) → 关于任何(植物) → 植物学

例 The practice and use of *botany* for medical purposes is still common to this day in some areas. 现在，在一些地区，将植物用于医疗的做法仍很普遍。

派 botanical(*a.* 植物学的)；botanist(*n.* 植物学家)

quarterly
['kwɔːrtərli]

ad. 按季度，一季一次 *n.* 季刊 *a.* 季度的，每季一次的

记 来自 quarter(*n.* 季度)

例 We hope to pay the rent *quarterly*. 我们希望按季支付租金。

stage
[steɪdʒ]

n. 阶段(period)；步骤(phase)；舞台(platform)；戏剧(drama) *vt.* 上演；筹划(arrange)

记 联想记忆：st + age(年龄；时代) → 俗话说：台上一分钟，台下十年功 → 舞台

例 The product is still at the design *stage*. 该产品尚处于设计阶段。

legislative
['ledʒɪsleɪtɪv]

n. 立法机关 *a.* 立法的，有立法权的；根据法规执行的

例 Members of congress have to spend most of their time in Washington taking care of their *legislative* duties. 国会议员大部分时间要待在华盛顿履行立法职责。

combination [ˌkɑːmbɪˈneɪʃn]	*n.* 结合(体)，混合(体)(mixture)；化合；组合(compounding) 记 来自 combine(*v.* 联合，结合) 例 The company decided to work on a new product in *combination* with several overseas partners. 这家公司决定联合几家海外合伙人制造新产品。
inventory [ˈɪnvəntɔːri]	*n.* 目录，清单；库存(stock) 记 词根记忆：in(里) + vent(来) + ory(表物，名词后缀) → 对所有进来的货物进行清查 → 目录 例 In the 1800s, store owners sold everything from a needle to a plow, trusted everyone, and never took *inventory*. 在 19 世纪初，商店店主从针到犁什么都卖，他们相信每一个人，从来不搞存货清单。
denounce [dɪˈnaʊns]	*vt.* 谴责，公开指责，抨击；告发 记 词根记忆：de(向下) + nounc(宣布) → 向不好的方面宣布 → 谴责，公开指责 例 The expert *denounced* the stupid villagers as they destroyed their living environment. 专家谴责那些愚蠢的村民破坏了他们的生活环境。

The brotherly spirit of science, which unites into one family all its votaries of whatever grade, and however widely dispersed throughout the different quarters of the globe.

科学的博爱精神把分散在世界各地，各种热心科学的人联结成一个大家庭。

——美国总统 罗斯福 .F.（Franklin Roosevelt, American President）

43

Word List 44

音频

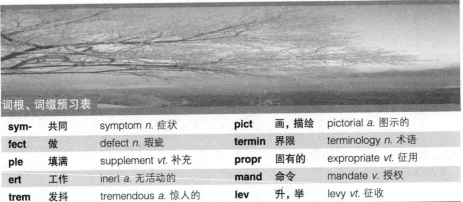

词根、词缀预习表

sym-	共同	symptom *n.* 症状	**pict**	画,描绘	pictorial *a.* 图示的
fect	做	defect *n.* 瑕疵	**termin**	界限	terminology *n.* 术语
ple	填满	supplement *vt.* 补充	**propr**	固有的	expropriate *vt.* 征用
ert	工作	inert *a.* 无活动的	**mand**	命令	mandate *v.* 授权
trem	发抖	tremendous *a.* 惊人的	**lev**	升,举	levy *vt.* 征收

---

squirt
[skwɜːrt]

v. (使)喷射,喷(spout, spurt);向…喷射 *n.* (液体、粉末等的)喷射;〈口,贬〉无名小辈
记 联想记忆:往裙子(skirt)上喷(squirt)香水
例 The snake can *squirt* poison from a distance of a meter. 这种蛇能将毒液喷射到一米外远。

---

resin
['rezn]

n. 树脂
例 Many compound *resins* have distinct and characteristic odors. 很多复合树脂气味很独特。

---

context
['kɑːntekst]

n. 上下文;背景(setting);环境(environment)
记 词根记忆:con(共同) + text(编织) → 共同编织在一起 → 上下文
例 Beads are often valuable in their original cultural *context* as well as in today's market. 珠子项链无论是在最初的文化背景下还是在当今的市场上通常都很值钱。

---

symptom
['sɪmptəm]

n. 症状;征兆(sign)
记 词根记忆:sym(共同) + pto(掉下) + m → 一起掉下来的东西 → 症状;征兆
例 Much of the focus of the class was on the recognition of vitamin deficiency *symptoms*. 这节课的重点主要是辨识缺乏维生素的症状。

---

interrupt
[ˌɪntəˈrʌpt]

v. 打扰;中断;阻碍(hinder)
记 词根记忆:inter(在…之间) + rupt(断裂) → 在中间断裂 → 中断;阻碍
例 When you *interrupted* me, you made me lose my train of thought. 你打断我的时候,让我思绪尽失。
派 interruption(*n.* 打扰)

---

defect	[ˈdiːfekt] *n.* 瑕疵，缺陷(flaw)；过失
	[dɪˈfekt] *vi.* 变节，叛变
	记 词根记忆：de(离开) + fect(做) → 没做好 → 瑕疵，缺陷；过失
	例 The sweater could be a manufactures' *defect*, and we'll exchange it for you. 这件运动衫有个生产上的瑕疵，我们会为你换一件新的。

defect

velocity	*n.* 速度，速率(speed, rate)；迅速
[vəˈlɑːsəti]	记 词根记忆：velo(快的) + city → 速度，速率；迅速
	例 The *velocity* of a river is determined by the slope, the depth, and the roughness of the riverbed. 河流的速度取决于河床的坡度、深度和粗糙程度。

dormitory	*n.* 宿舍(hostel)
[ˈdɔːrmətɔːri]	记 词根记忆：dorm(睡眠) + it + ory(表地点，名词后缀) → 睡觉的地方 → 宿舍
	搭 dormitory room 宿舍
	例 Most of the freshmen of this university live in *dormitories*. 这所大学的大多数大一新生都住宿舍。

freight	*n.* 货运；运费 *vt.* 运送，货运；使充满
[freɪt]	记 联想记忆：运费(freight)一般是按照货物(freight)的重量(weight)来计算的
	例 The fish was shipped in a refrigerated *freight* car. 鱼用冷藏货车运输。
	派 freighter(*n.* 货船；运输飞机)

tread	*v.* 踏，践踏(trample)；行走 *n.* 轮胎面；脚步声；步法
[tred]	搭 tread on sb.'s heels 步某人后尘
	例 Please *tread* very quietly as the baby is asleep. 孩子睡觉呢，脚步轻一点。
	参 treadmill(*n.* 踏车；枯燥无味的生活或工作)

ascribe	*vt.* (to)把…归于(attribute)；归咎于
[əˈskraɪb]	记 词根记忆：a + scrib(写) + e → 把…写上去 → 把…归于
	例 Tradition *ascribes* these works to a man named Homer. 一直以来人们都认为这些作品是一个叫荷马的人写的。

supplement	[ˈsʌplɪmənt] *n.* 补充(物)，增补(物)(*extension)；增刊；(书籍的)补遗，附录 [ˈsʌplɪment] *vt.* 补充，增补(*add to)
	记 词根记忆：sup(在…下面) + ple(填满) + ment → 在下面填满 → 补充，增补
	例 Some countries define dietary *supplements* as foods, while in others they are defined as drugs or natural health products. 一些国家将补充饮食定义为食物，另一些国家则将其定义为药物或保健产品。// She *supplements* her income by writing articles for magazines. 她通过为杂志写文章来增加收入。

44

equation
[ɪˈkweɪʒn]

n. (数学)等式,方程式;等同,相等;均衡

记 词根记忆:equ(相等的,平等的) + ation → 等式

例 As economists put it, the industry forms a crucial part of a country's economic *equation*. 正如经济学家所言,工业是一个国家经济均衡的关键部分。

参 equal(*a.* 平等的)

---

copper
[ˈkɑːpər]

n. 铜;铜币

记 联想记忆:cop(警察) + per → 警察制服上的铜扣 → 铜

例 Like silver and gold, *copper* is easily worked, being both ductile and malleable. 与金、银一样,铜易延展,可塑性强,锻造起来很容易。

---

rear
[rɪr]

vt. 养育,抚养,培养;饲养(*raise) *n.* 后部,后方;臀部 *a.* 后部的,后面的

搭 bring up the rear 落在最后,殿后;rear sb./sth. on sth. (以…)娱乐,培养

例 Later they developed a technique for feeding the larvae and *rearing* them to spat. 后来他们开发出一种喂养幼虫并培育成蚝卵的技术。

---

distinct
[dɪˈstɪŋkt]

a. 明显的,清楚的(*visible);确实的;截然不同的(*separate, *different)

记 词根记忆:di(分开) + stinct(刺) → 用刺分开 → 明显的,清楚的

例 Two *distinct* processes are involved in molting. 蜕皮包括两个明显不同的过程。

---

accede
[əkˈsiːd]

vi. 即位,就任;同意

记 词根记忆:ac(靠近) + ced(走) + e → 走近(职位等) → 即位,就任

例 The Queen Elizabeth II *acceded* to the throne officially in 1952. 女王伊丽莎白二世于 1952 年正式即位。

---

mosquito
[məˈskiːtoʊ]

n. 蚊子(skeeter)

记 发音记忆:"貌似黑头" → 像鼻子上的黑头 → 蚊子

例 Some scientists believe that eradicating *mosquitoes* would not have serious consequences for any ecosystems. 一些科学家认为,消灭蚊子不会对任何生态系统造成严重后果。

---

numerous
[ˈnuːmərəs]

a. 许多的(many);无数的(countless)

记 词根记忆:numer(数) + ous(多…的) → 数目众多的 → 许多的;无数的

例 Cosmic rays consist of rapidly moving particles of *numerous* different kinds. 宇宙射线由无数种快速移动的粒子构成。

---

livestock
[ˈlaɪvstɑːk]

n. 〈总称〉家畜,牲畜

记 组合词:live(活的) + stock(东西) → 活物 → 家畜

例 At the time Quebec was a major market for *livestock*, crops and fish. 当时魁北克是牲畜、谷物和鱼类交易的主要市场。

---

inert
[ɪˈnɜːrt]

a. 无活动的,惰性的(inactive);不活泼的,迟钝的

记 词根记忆:in(不) + ert(工作) → 不工作的 → 无活动的,惰性的

搭 inert element 惰性元素

例 Viruses are *inert* outside living cells, but within the appropriate cells they can replicate. 病毒在活体细胞外呈惰性,但是在合适的细胞里它们能够复制。

□ equation   □ copper   □ rear   □ distinct   □ accede   □ mosquito
□ numerous   □ livestock   □ inert

prescription [prɪˈskrɪpʃn]	*n.* 处方，药方；开处方，开药方 记 词根记忆：pre(在…前面) + script(写) + ion → 提前写下的 → 处方，药方 搭 prescription drugs 处方药 例 Pharmacists fill drug *prescriptions*, keep records of the drugs their patients are taking to make sure that harmful combinations are not prescribed. 药剂师填写医药处方，记录病人要服用的药物，确保没有开出有害的药物组合。 参 infirmary(*n.* 医务室)
awkward [ˈɔːkwərd]	*a.* 别扭的(unnatural)；笨拙的(clumsy)；难处理的，棘手的；难操纵的 记 发音记忆："拗口的" → 别扭的 例 Tom was always a bit *awkward* when meeting new people. 汤姆见到生人时都会感到有点别扭。// The tennis racket was too big and *awkward* for Jane. 网球拍对简来说太大了，很不好用。 派 awkwardly(*ad.* 别扭地；笨拙地)
collective [kəˈlektɪv]	*a.* 集体的，共同的(common) *n.* 集体，共同体 记 词根记忆：col(共同) + lect(收集) + ive → 为生活而一起去收集食物 → 集体的 例 The decision, made by the board of directors, is the result of *collective* agreement. 董事会作出的决定是经过集体同意的。
invertebrate [ɪnˈvɜːrtɪbrət]	*n.* 无脊椎动物 *a.* 无脊椎的 记 词根记忆：in(无) + vertebr(椎骨) + ate → 无脊椎动物 例 *Invertebrates* make up a large proportion of all life in the sea. 无脊椎动物占了所有海洋生物的很大一部分。 参 vertebrate(*n.* 脊椎动物 *a.* 有脊椎的)
barge [bɑːrdʒ]	*v.* 冲撞，乱闯 *n.* 驳船 记 发音记忆："八只" → 八只驳船 → 驳船 搭 barge in on 闯入；插嘴，打岔 例 They *barged* their way through the crowds. 他们横冲直撞地挤过人群。
snap [snæp]	*v.* 猛咬；(使咔嚓)折断，断裂(*break, burst)；打开，关上；呵斥，厉声说；拍照 *n.* 啪嗒声；照片 *a.* 仓促的，匆忙的 记 联想记忆：s + nap(小睡) → 上课睡觉时被老师抓住，遭到呵斥 → 呵斥 搭 snap out 厉声说出；snap up 抢购 例 He *snapped* a twig off a bush. 他啪地从灌木上折下一小枝。
feat [fiːt]	*n.* 功绩，壮举(achievement, act, deed) 记 联想记忆：f + eat(吃) → 取得了功绩，好好吃一顿犒劳一下 → 功绩 例 Acquiring their language is a most impressive intellectual *feat* for children. 习得语言是孩子们最了不起的一项智力成就。

44

conservation [ˌkɑːnsərˈveɪʃn]	*n.* 守恒；保存；（对自然资源的）保护（preservation） 记 来自 conserve（*vt.* 保存） 例 Biological diversity has become widely recognized as a critical *conservation* issue only in the past two decades. 生物多样性在过去 20 年才开始被广泛认为是重要的环保议题。 派 conservationist（*n.* 环保主义者）；conservatism（*n.* 保守主义）
smother [ˈsmʌðər]	*vt.* 使窒息而死；厚厚地覆盖；抑制，扼杀；把（火）闷熄 记 联想记忆：s（看做 she，她）+ mother（母亲）→ 她快被母亲的爱弄得窒息 → 使窒息 例 The voices of the opposition were effectively *smothered*. 反对者的声音被有效地压制了下去。
blur [blɜːr]	*v.* (使)变模糊，难以区分（make indistinct）；玷污（smear）*n.* 模糊形状；模糊的记忆；污点 例 The differences between art and life seem to have *blurred*. 艺术和生活之间的差别似乎已变得模糊不清。
mantle [ˈmæntl]	*n.* 覆盖物（cloak）；披风，斗篷；（煤气灯）纱罩；【地】地幔 记 联想记忆：man（词根：手）+ tle → 一手遮天 → 覆盖物 例 He concluded that the depth marked the boundary between a solid *mantle* and the liquid core. 他断定这个深度标志着固态地幔和液态地核之间的界限。
demonstrate [ˈdemənstreɪt]	*v.* 论证，证明；表现，显露（show）；示范，演示；游行示威 记 词根记忆：de（完全）+ monstr（展示）+ ate → 完全展示 → 论证；表现 例 The researchers have sought to *demonstrate* that their work can be a valuable tool of science. 研究人员试图证明他们的工作可以成为科学的宝贵工具。 派 demonstration（*n.* 游行示威；示范；证明；显露）；demonstrative（*a.* 感情外露的；指示的）
additive [ˈædətɪv]	*n.* 添加剂 *a.* 添加的；加法的 记 联想记忆：add（加）+ itive → 添加剂；添加的 搭 food additives 食品添加剂 例 With the advent of processed foods in the second half of the 20th century, many more *additives* have been introduced, of both natural and artificial origin. 在 20 世纪下半叶，随着加工食品的出现，更多的添加剂被用于食品，包括自然添加剂和人工添加剂。
lithosphere [ˈlɪθəsfɪr]	*n.* 岩石圈 记 词根记忆：litho（石）+ spher（球体）+ e → 岩石圈 例 The *lithosphere* is divided into a few dozen plates of various sizes and shapes. 岩石圈分为尺寸和形状不同的几十个岩层。

demonstrate

□ conservation　□ smother　□ blur　□ mantle　□ demonstrate　□ additive
□ lithosphere

dam [dæm]	*n.* 坝，堤 *vt.* 筑坝；控制 记 发音记忆："担" → 堤坝担负着阻隔洪水的责任 → 坝 例 It is considered to be the oldest *dam* still in use. 它被认为是仍在使用的最古老的堤坝。
steep [stiːp]	*a.* 陡的，陡峭的；急剧的(sharp)；(价格等)过高的 *v.* 浸泡；沉浸 记 联想记忆：本来挺陡的台阶(step)中又加一个 e 就更陡峭(steep)了 搭 be steeped in 深深浸淫；饱含(某品质)；steep oneself in 沉浸于，潜心于 例 The traditional organizations went into *steep* decline during the 1950s and 1960s. 在 20 世纪五六十年代，传统组织急剧衰退。
exhaust [ɪgˈzɔːst]	*n.* 废气；排气管 *vt.* 用尽，耗尽(drain)；使非常疲倦；详尽讨论 搭 exhaust emissions 尾气排放 例 Don't give up until you have *exhausted* all the possibilities. 只要还有可能就别放弃。 派 exhaustive (*a.* 详尽的，彻底的)；exhausted (*a.* 精疲力竭的；耗尽的)；exhausting(*a.* 令人疲惫不堪的)；inexhaustible(*a.* 无穷无尽的) exhaust
cardiac [ˈkɑːrdiæk]	*a.* 心脏的；心脏病的 记 词根记忆：card(心) + iac → 心脏的 搭 cardiac muscle 心肌 例 *Cardiac* arrest is an abrupt cessation of pump function in the heart. 心脏停搏是指心脏忽然停止输送血液。
Easter [ˈiːstər]	*n.* 复活节 例 This led to the American custom of *Easter* parades all over the world. 这使得美国人庆祝复活节的习俗盛行于全世界。
Latin [ˈlætn]	*a.* 拉丁的；拉丁语的 *n.* 拉丁语 例 The term virus is derived from the *Latin* word for poison or slime. Virus(病毒)这个词起源于拉丁文，原指毒药或黏液。
minimum [ˈmɪnɪməm]	*a.* 最小的，最低的 *n.* 最小值，最低限度 记 词根记忆：min(小) + im + um → 最小的；最小值 例 You seem to meet our *minimum* qualifications. 你看上去满足我们对资历的最低要求。
raise [reɪz]	*v.* 举起，提升(lift)；(使)直立；增加；募集；饲养，养育；引起；提出 *n.* (工资、薪金的)提升，增加 搭 raise the roof （在屋内）大声喧闹，闹翻天；raise sb.'s spirits 使振奋 例 They're going to *raise* the dorm fees again. 他们又要提高住宿费。 // I'm really glad our club decided to *raise* money for the children's hospital, and most of the people we'd phoned seemed happy to contribute. 我很高兴我们的俱乐部决定为儿童医院募集资金，接到我们电话的大多数人都乐意捐赠。 参 rise(*v.* 升起，上升) 知道的请举手 raise

amateur [ˈæmətər]	*n.* 业余爱好者；外行（non-professional）*a.* 业余爱好的；业余的 记 词根记忆：amat(=amor 爱) + eur(表人) → 业余爱好者 例 The competition is open to both *amateurs* and professionals. 这次比赛业务选手和职业选手均可参加。
prior [ˈpraɪər]	*a.* 在…前的（*preceding, former）；优先的 记 词根记忆：pri(=prim 第一的，首要的) + or → 优先的 例 *Prior* to this report, Seattle's park development was very limited and short of funds. 在这个报告之前，西雅图公园的开发非常有限，资金匮乏。
sheer [ʃɪr]	*a.* 陡峭的（steep）；完全的，十足的，全然的（utter）；绝对的；极薄的 *ad.* 垂直地，陡峭地 *vi.* 急转，偏离 记 联想记忆：绵羊(sheep)在陡峭的(sheer)山上吃草 搭 sheer away/off from 急拐以避开 例 The decade of the 1870s was a period in which the *sheer* number of newspapers doubled. 在 19 世纪 70 年代，报纸的绝对数量增长了一倍。
measure [ˈmeʒər]	*n.* [常 *pl.*]措施(step)；标准，程度；衡量；度量单位 *v.* 测量；估量，判断(assess) 搭 measure up 测量；衡量 例 The biologists realized that if new *measures* were not taken, oysters would become extinct. 生物学家们意识到，如果不采取新的措施，牡蛎就会灭绝。// The energy content of food is *measured* in calories. 食物所含的能量用卡路里来度量。 派 measurement(*n.* 测量；尺寸)
engaging [ɪnˈgeɪdʒɪŋ]	*a.* 迷人的(charming) 记 来自 engage(*v.* 吸引) 例 Fanny Buice had an *engaging* personality that delighted audiences for nearly half a century. 范妮·布斯个性迷人，在近半个世纪里一直给观众带来欢笑。 参 engagement(*n.* 约定)
convert [kənˈvɜːrt]	*v.* (使)改变(信仰、观点等)；(使)转变，转化（*change, transform） 记 词根记忆：con(完全) + vert(转) → 完全转变 → (使)转变，转化 例 He was soon *converted* to the socialist cause. 他不久便转而献身于社会主义事业了。 派 converter(*n.* 转化器；变流器)；convertible(*a.* 可改变的，可转换的)

tremendous [trə'mendəs]	*a.* 惊人的(striking); 巨大的 记 词根记忆: trem(发抖) + end + ous(多…的) → 多得让人发抖的 → 惊人的 例 He has a *tremendous* skill in placing his buildings in harmony with nature. 他技艺高超，能使他的建筑与自然和谐统一。// *Tremendous* amounts of food supplies and artifacts have been found there. 那里发现了大量的食物给养和手工艺品。 派 tremendously(*ad.* 巨大地; 非常地)
bunch [bʌntʃ]	*n.* 簇, 束, 捆; 帮, 伙(gang) *v.* 捆成一束; 聚集(pack; crowd) 记 联想记忆: 一帮(bunch)人在吃午餐(lunch) 例 A *bunch* of us are going out for pizza. 我们一帮人要出去吃比萨饼。 参 bundle(*n.* 捆, 束)
pictorial [pɪk'tɔːriəl]	*a.* 图示的, 有图片的; 绘画的, 图画的 *n.* 画报, 画刊 记 词根记忆: pict(画, 描绘) + orial → 起描绘作用的 → 图示的 例 The East Asian Library has an impressive collection of *pictorial* works about China. 东亚图书馆藏有数量惊人的有关中国的图示作品。
enlist [ɪn'lɪst]	*v.* 征募, 从军, 参军; 谋取(帮助、支持等) 记 联想记忆: en(=in 进入) + list(名单) → 进入名单 → 征募 例 Being *enlisted* in the army turns him from an innocent boy into a real man. 入伍当兵使他从一个无知的男孩蜕变成一个真正的男人。
stuff [stʌf]	*n.* 原料, 材料(material) *vt.* 填满, 塞满; 让…吃饱 记 联想记忆: 不能把职员(staff)当做材料(stuff)来用 例 Did you learn about this *stuff* in cooking school? 你在烹饪学校学过这个吗? 参 staff(*n.* 员工)
rumor ['ruːmər]	*n.* 传闻, 谣言 记 联想记忆: rum(看做 run, 跑) + or → 好事不出门, 坏事传千里 → 传闻, 谣言 例 Many of the stories are based on *rumor*. 这些说法很多都是道听途说。
trigger ['trɪɡər]	*vt.* 引发, 导致(cause, kindle) *n.* 扳机 搭 trigger a war 引发战争 例 Pheromones are chemical signals *triggering* behavioral responses. 信息素是引发行为反应的化学信号。
agency ['eɪdʒənsi]	*n.* 代理处, 经销机构; (政府等的)专门机构 搭 travel agency 旅行社; government agency 政府机构; through the agency of 由于…的作用 例 The country has created a public employment *agency* as a way to combat unemployment. 为解决失业问题，该国成立了一个公共职业介绍所。 参 agent(*n.* 代理人; 原动力)

44

| **packed** [pækt] | *a.* 拥挤的（crowded）；压紧的（compressed） |
| | 例 The subway is *packed* this morning. 今天早上地铁里很挤。 |

resign [rɪˈzaɪn]	*v.* 辞去，辞职；放弃；顺从，听从
	记 联想记忆：re（回）+ sign（签名）→ 不再签到 → 辞去，辞职
	搭 resign from 从…辞职
	例 Aged 15, Edward *resigned* himself to the fact that he'd never be a first-class musician. 15 岁的爱德华自认为永远都无法成为一名一流的音乐家。
	派 resignation（*n.* 辞职；放弃）

resign

他可以做担保人！

guarantee

guarantee [ˌɡærənˈtiː]	*v.* 保证（pledge）；担保（assure）*n.* 保证，担保；保证书
	记 联想记忆：guar（看做 guard，保卫）+ ant（蚂蚁）+ ee → 蚁后保证要开展一场保卫战 → 保证
	例 We have a priority service that would *guarantee* delivery in three days. 我们提供优先服务，保证三日内到货。

coordinate	[koʊˈɔːrdɪneɪt] *v.* 协调，相配合（harmonize, cooperate）
	[koʊˈɔːrdɪnət] *n.* 同等物；坐标
	记 词根记忆：co（共同）+ ordin（顺序）+ ate → 顺序一致 → 协调
	例 Political parties in the United States help to *coordinate* the campaigns of their members that mark election years. 美国的政党帮助协调其候选人在选举年的竞选。

terminology [ˌtɜːrməˈnɑːlədʒi]	*n.* （某学科的）专门用语，术语（term）；术语学
	记 词根记忆：termin（界限）+ (o)logy（…学）→ 仅限于一部分人使用的语言 →（某学科的）专门用语，术语
	例 You're familiar with basic film *terminology*. 你熟悉基本的电影术语。

inaugurate [ɪˈnɔːɡjəreɪt]	*vt.* 为…举行就职典礼；为…举行开幕式；开始，开创
	记 词根记忆：in（进入）+ augur（占卜，预测）+ ate → 进入预测好的未来 → 开创
	例 The woman was *inaugurated* as president in March. 那位女士在三月就职总裁。
	派 inauguration（*n.* 就职，就职典礼）

composer [kəmˈpoʊzər]	*n.* 作曲家，作曲者
	记 词根记忆：com（共同）+ pos（放）+ er（表人，名词后缀）→ 把不同的东西放到一起的人 → 作曲家
	例 He doesn't know many *composers* of classical music. 他并不了解很多古典音乐的作曲家。// The director got a South African *composer* to write songs with a distinct African sound. 导演找了一位南非作曲家来创作带有非洲独特风格的歌曲。

trade

[treɪd]

n. 贸易，商业；交易；职业，行业 *v.* 交易，买卖；互相交换

搭 international trade 国际贸易；the drug trade 毒品交易；the slave trade 奴隶贸易；make a trade 做交易；restraint of trade 贸易管制

例 *Trade* between the two countries has increased. 两国间的贸易额增长了。// He refused to *trade* with that company again. 他拒绝再次与那家公司做生意。

参 trace(*vt.* 追踪)；fade(*v.* 褪色；衰弱；凋谢)

empower

[ɪmˈpaʊər]

v. 授权，准许(authorize)；使控制局势

记 联想记忆：em + power(权力) → 使有权力 → 授权，准许

例 The new law *empowered* the citizens to have the right of hearing. 新法令使公民有听证的权利。

injurious

[ɪnˈdʒʊərɪəs]

a. 侮辱的，诽谤的；造成伤害的，有害的

记 来自 injury(*v.* 伤害，侮辱)

例 Everybody knows that smoking is *injurious* to health, but there are still many people smoking. 每个人都知道吸烟有害健康，但还是有很多人抽烟。

confine

[kənˈfaɪn]

vt. 限制(*restrict, *limit)；禁闭

记 词根记忆：con(表加强) + fin(界限) + e → 限制

例 The other early apartment buildings were *confined* to the typical New York building lot. 其他早期的公寓楼必须建于典型的纽约建筑用地内。

派 confinement(*n.* 限制；禁闭)

faction

[ˈfækʃn]

n. 派别，派系，小集团；派系斗争

例 The party was divided by endless *faction* and intrigue. 那个政党被派系斗争和阴谋诡计搞得四分五裂。

lapse

[læps]

n. 失误；失足 *vi.* (合同、协议等)期满终止，失效；衰退；背弃

记 词根记忆：laps(掉) + e → 掉下 → 失误；失足

搭 lapse into (逐渐)陷入，进入(…状态)

例 Every husband hopes that his wife will forgive his *lapse*. 每个丈夫都希望妻子可以原谅他们的不忠。

enact

[ɪˈnækt]

v. 制定法律，颁布；扮演(角色)

记 联想记忆：en(使…) + act(法令) → 使成为法令 → 制定法律

例 Kate dreams to *enact* Snowwhite in a drama. 凯特梦想着能在话剧中扮演白雪公主。

allay

[əˈleɪ]

vt. 减轻，减少(*reduce, alleviate)

例 Maria wrote stories interesting enough to attract children and morally instructive enough to *allay* adult distrust of fiction. 玛丽亚写的故事非常有趣，能吸引儿童，也相当具有道德指导意义，可以减轻成年人对小说的怀疑。

expropriate

[eksˈproʊprieɪt]

vt. 征用，没收(私有财产)

记 词根记忆：ex(出) + propr(固有的) + iate → 使人失去自身所固有的 → 征用，没收(私有财产)

例 The army *expropriated* the farmer's warehouse as their temporary shelter. 部队征用农民的仓库作为临时的栖身之处。

44

mandate [ˈmændeɪt]	*n.* 授权；委托书，授权令；任期 *v.* 强制执行；授权 记 词根记忆：mand(命令) + ate → 发出命令 → 授权；强制执行 例 The local government gave the customs a *mandate* to further crack down on smuggling. 当地政府授权海关以便进一步打击走私活动。
fraud [frɔːd]	*n.* 骗子，冒名顶替者；冒牌货；欺骗(行为) 记 发音记忆："富饶的" → 骗子专挑富人区行骗 → 骗子 例 The handsome man was a notorious *fraud* in his circle. 这个英俊的男人在他的社交圈里是个臭名昭著的骗子。

现在投资就有100倍回报！

fraud

imperial [ɪmˈpɪriəl]	*a.* 帝国的，帝王的；至尊的(sovereign)；专横的 记 词根记忆：im（表加强）+ per（安排）+ ial → 有着完全的安排权力的 → 帝国的 例 Conservatives and liberals alike also pushed for *imperial* expansion. 保守主义者和自由主义者均强烈要求进行帝国扩张。
empress [ˈemprəs]	*n.* 女皇，皇后 搭 the Empress of Egypt 埃及女王 例 An American painter is commissioned to paint the *Empress's* portrait. 一位美国画家受委托为女皇画像。
dramatic [drəˈmætɪk]	*a.* 戏剧的；引人注目的(*striking*)；突然的，巨大的；戏剧性的(theatrical) 记 来自 drama(*n.* 戏剧) 例 He made a *dramatic* shift from the classical tradition to the arts and crafts movement. 他作出了一个从古典传统到工艺美术运动的巨大转变。// *Dramatic* activities require the use of costumes. 戏剧活动需要使用戏装。 派 dramatically(*ad.* 戏剧性地；引人注目地)
levy [ˈlevi]	*vt.* 征收(税等) *n.* 征收额；税款；征兵 记 词根记忆：lev(升，举) + y → 命令将钱物上交 → 征收；征税 例 The officials *levied* on the landlord's estates. 政府官员扣押了地主的地产。
apply [əˈplaɪ]	*v.* 申请，请求；适用；应用，运用；涂，敷，施 记 词根记忆：ap(=ad 向，靠近) + ply(折叠) → 折得很近的 → 适用 搭 apply to 适用于；apply for 申请 例 I would like to *apply* for one of the security guard positions you advertised in the local paper. 我想申请你在本地报纸上刊登的保安职位。 参 supply(*vt.* 提供)
interrogate [ɪnˈterəɡeɪt]	*vt.* 审问，讯问，盘问 记 词根记忆：inter（在…之间）+ rog（问）+ ate → 在中间问 → 审问，讯问，盘问 例 The policeman was *interrogating* a prisoner who was accused of cheating. 警察正在审问那个涉嫌诈骗的犯人。 派 interrogation(*n.* 审问，讯问，盘问)

□ mandate □ fraud □ imperial □ empress □ dramatic □ levy
□ apply □ interrogate

forfeit [ˈfɔːrfət]	*vt.* 被没收，丧失 *n.* 罚款；没收物 记 词根记忆：for(出，外) + feit(=fact 制作，做) → 没有做的权力 → 被没收，丧失 例 You will *forfeit* your deposit, if you break the furniture. 如果你弄坏了家具，你的押金将不会退还。
juridical [dʒʊˈrɪdɪkl]	*a.* 法律的，司法的 记 词根记忆：jur(正确的) + id + ical → 法律的，司法的 例 The rights and responsibilities of a *juridical* person are distinct from those of the natural person. 在享有的权利和承担的责任上，法人和自然人截然不同。
lawsuit [ˈlɔːsuːt]	*n.* 诉讼 记 组合词：law(法律) + suit(诉讼) → 诉讼 例 The poor girl lost the *lawsuit* as she was out of money. 那个可怜的女孩因为没有钱输掉了官司。
mandatory [ˈmændətɔːri]	*n.* 强制的，法定的，义务的 (imperative, obligatory) *n.* 受托人；代理人 记 词根记忆：mand(命令) + at + ory → 强制的，法定的，义务的 例 The offence carries a *mandatory* life sentence. 这种罪行依照法律要判无期徒刑。
endangered [ɪnˈdeɪndʒərd]	*a.* 濒危的，将要灭绝的 (extinct) 搭 endangered species 濒危物种 例 Stork believes climate change is the major issue as to why species are becoming *endangered*. 斯托克认为气候变化是造成物种面临灭绝危险的主要因素。

44

Word List 45

音频

farce [fɑːrs]	*n.* 笑剧(剧本), 滑稽剧(剧本); 闹剧 记 联想记忆: 别小看了滑稽剧(farce), 有时它也很有批判的力量(force) 例 Japan has a centuries-old tradition of *farce* plays. 日本有着长达数世纪的滑稽剧表演史。
lubricant [ˈluːbrɪkənt]	*n.* 润滑剂 记 词根记忆: lubr(光滑的) + ic + ant(表物, 名词后缀) → 使变光滑的东西 → 润滑剂 例 During that special period, *lubricant* was not available to common people. 在那段特殊时期, 普通民众买不到润滑剂。
dairy [ˈderi]	*n.* 牛奶场; 乳品店; 奶制品 *a.* 乳品的 记 联想记忆: 每天(daily)吃乳品(dairy)来强身健体 搭 dairy products 乳制品; dairy farming 乳品业; dairy cattle 乳牛 例 While most countries produce their own milk products, the structure of the *dairy* industry varies in different parts of the world. 大多数国家都自产乳品, 但世界上不同地方的乳品业结构各不相同。
microwave [ˈmaɪkrəweɪv]	*n.* 微波; 微波炉 例 *Microwave* ovens became common kitchen appliances in Western countries in the late 1970s. 在 20 世纪 70 年代后期, 微波炉成为西方国家常见的厨房用具。
legislate [ˈledʒɪsleɪt]	*v.* 制定法律; 通过立法 记 词根记忆: leg(法律) + isl + ate(使…) → 使成为法律 → 制定法律; 通过立法 例 The state government promised to *legislate* against drug trade. 州政府承诺制定相关法律来制止毒品交易。

indict [ɪnˈdaɪt]	*vt.* 控诉，起诉，控告 记 词根记忆：in(逆，反) + dict(说) → 逆着某人说 → 控诉，起诉，控告 例 The boy was *indicted* for murdering his mother. 男孩被控告谋杀了他的母亲。
tube [tjuːb]	*n.* 管(pipe)；管状物；管状器官 记 联想记忆：立方形(cube)的管道(tube) 搭 vacuum tube 真空管，电子管；bronchial tube 支气管 例 In 1919 he invented the first multiple-grid vacuum *tube*, the tetrode. 1919年，他发明了最早的多极真空管，即四极管。
distort [dɪˈstɔːrt]	*vt.* 弄歪(形状等)(twist)；扭曲，歪曲(misrepresent) 记 词根记忆：dis(分开) + tort(卷缠) → 把原本缠在一起的分开 → 歪曲 例 Mark *distorted* the story, trying to place the blame on his sister. 马克歪曲事实，想把责任推到姐姐身上。 派 distorted(*a.* 变形的)；distortion(*n.* 歪曲，变形) 参 contort(*vt.* 扭弯，扭曲，曲解)；retort(*v.* 反驳，反击)
cancel [ˈkænsl]	*v.* 取消，废除(abolish)；删去，删除(revoke, call off)；抵消 记 源自拉丁文 cancelli(斜条格钩)，据说古罗马书写员在抄写错误时会用斜条格钩状来表明注销，后引入英语，作"取消"讲 搭 cancel out 抵偿，抵消 例 I had to *cancel* my appointment with my dentist. I couldn't fit it in. 我得取消与牙医的预约，安排不过来了。 派 cancellation(*n.* 取消；废除)
industry [ˈɪndəstri]	*n.* 勤劳，勤奋；工业，行业 例 His *industry* and literary achievement are beginning to be recognized and appreciated. 他的勤奋和文学成就开始得到人们的认可和赏识。
dispute [dɪˈspjuːt]	*n.* 争论(*argument)；纠纷 *v.* 争论(debate)；对…表示异议 记 词根记忆：dis(分开) + put(思考) + e → 分开思考 → 争论 例 The village chief dealt with land *disputes* and religious affairs. 村长负责处理土地纠纷和宗教事务。 参 disrepute(*n.* 坏名声) dispute
essay [ˈeseɪ]	*n.* 散文，随笔(prose)；短文；评论(comment) 记 联想记忆：散文(essay)看似很随意(easy)，其实不然 例 We'll begin our study by reading the first *essay* listed in the syllabus. 我们将通过阅读大纲列出的第一篇文章来开始我们的学习。
sieve [sɪv]	*n.* 筛子(boult)；漏勺(strainer) *vt.* 筛，滤(sift) 记 联想记忆：用筛子(sieve)过一下是为了保留(save)精华 例 The old woman's mind feels like a *sieve* these days. 近来那个老妇人的记性很差。

45

□ indict   □ tube   □ distort   □ cancel   □ industry   □ dispute
□ essay   □ sieve

commit	*vt.* 承诺(promise); 犯错; 犯罪; 忠于
[kə'mɪt]	记 词根记忆: com(共同) + mit(送) → 共同送出 → 承诺
	搭 commit crimes 犯罪
	例 The college is *committed* to selecting more faculty members. 这所学院致力于挑选出更多的教职人员。
	派 committed(*a.* 忠于…的; 坚定的)
auditorium	*n.* 礼堂(hall); 观众席
[ˌɔːdɪ'tɔːriəm]	记 词根记忆: aud(听) + it + orium(表场所、地点, 名词后缀) → 听讲座等的地方 → 礼堂
	例 No smoking in the *auditorium*. 礼堂里禁止吸烟。
transportation	*n.* 运输; 运输系统, 运输工具
[ˌtrænspɔːr'teɪʃn]	搭 public transportation 公共交通
	例 Today I want to mention an even earlier form of *transportation*, one that brought the first European settlers to America. 今天我想讲一种更早的交通形式, 是它把第一批欧洲殖民者带到了美洲。
dilute	*a.* 冲淡的, 稀释的 *vt.* 冲淡, 稀释 (water down); 淡化, 削弱
[daɪ'luːt]	记 词根记忆: di(=dis 分离) + lu(冲洗) + te → 冲开 → 冲淡, 稀释; 淡化
	例 The doctor told him to bathe his eyes with a very *dilute* solution of boric acid. 医生让他用稀释的硼酸溶液清洗眼睛。
plastic	*n.* 塑料 *a.* 塑料的; 可塑的 (malleable); 做作的, 虚伪的
['plæstɪk]	搭 the plastic industry 塑料工业; plastic arts 造型艺术
	例 The doors are made of *plastic*. 这些门是由塑料做的。
stack	*n.* 堆(pile, heap) *v.* 堆积, 堆放(pile)
[stæk]	记 联想记忆: 库存(stock)一堆(stack)商品
	搭 stack up 堆起, 积聚成一堆
	例 There's room to *stack* up the cans of coffee. 这里有地方堆放咖啡罐。
oval	*a.* 卵形的, 椭圆形的(elliptic) *n.* 卵形, 椭圆形
['oʊvl]	记 联想记忆: o(音似: 喔) + val(音似: 哇哦) → 发"哇"、"哦"这些声音, 嘴都要张成椭圆形 → 椭圆形的
	例 The island has the shape of an elongated *oval*. 该岛呈拉长椭圆形。
fabric	*n.* 布料, 织品(cloth, textile); 构造, 结构(framework)
['fæbrɪk]	例 Mass transportation revised the social and economic *fabric* of the American city in three fundamental ways. 公共交通以三种基本方式改变了美国城市的社会与经济结构。

portray
[pɔːr'treɪ]

vt. 描绘 (picture, depict)；扮演(某角色)，饰演
记 联想记忆：por(看做 pour，倒) + tray(碟) → 将(颜料)倒在碟子上 → 描绘
例 Bret Harte achieved fame with stories that *portrayed* local life in the California mining camps. 布雷特·哈特因其描写加州矿区生活的小说而成名。
派 portrayal(*n.* 描述，表现)

Babylonian
[ˌbæbɪ'ləʊniən]

a. 巴比伦的；奢华的 *n.* 巴比伦人
例 A considerable amount of *Babylonian* literature was translated from Sumerian originals. 巴比伦文学作品中的很大一部分译自苏美尔文学。

capacity
[kə'pæsəti]

n. 能力(ability)；容量；职责，职位(role)；生产力
记 词根记忆：cap(拿住) + ac + ity(表状态、情况，名词后缀) → 能拿住 → 能力；容量
例 Does human mental *capacity* have limitations? 人类的脑容量有限度吗？

capacity

blast
[blæst]

v. 爆炸(burst)；发出尖响；猛烈抨击 *n.* 一阵(大风、气流等)；爆炸；冲击波；响声
记 联想记忆：b + last（最后） → 最后一声 b → 爆炸
搭 blast furnace 鼓风炉；at full blast 最大马力地；最大音量地
例 He *blasted* his stereo all night. 他整夜都高放着立体声音响。

dispersal
[dɪ'spɜːrsl]

n. 疏散；散布，散开
记 词根记忆：di(分开) + spers(散播) + al → 分散开 → 疏散；散布
例 The police received a lot of training in crowd *dispersal*. 警察在疏散人群方面受过大量训练。

partnership
['pɑːrtnərʃɪp]

n. 合伙；伙伴关系；合伙人身份
记 联想记忆：partner(伙伴) + ship(表身份) → 合伙人身份
例 Henry built up his own business in *partnership* with an American expert. 亨利与一个美国专家合伙创办了自己的公司。
参 relationship(*n.* 关系)

relic
['relɪk]

n. 遗物，遗迹，遗风
记 词根记忆：re(回) + lic(=linqu 留下) → 留下来的东西 → 遗物，遗迹
例 The building stands as the last remaining *relic* of the village's cotton industry. 这座建筑物是这个村子棉纺业仅存的遗迹。

irreverent
[ɪ'revərənt]

a. 不敬的
记 词根记忆：ir(不) + re(再) + ver(感到敬畏) + ent → 不再感到敬畏的 → 不敬的
例 The young girl has an *irreverent* attitude towards marriage. 那个年轻女孩对婚姻持无所谓的态度。
派 irreverence(*n.* 不敬；不敬的行为)

irreverent

45

meteorology [ˌmiːtiə'rɑːlədʒi]	*n.* 气象学(aerography) 记 词根记忆：meteor(陨石；天气) + ology(…学) → 古代根据陨石判断天气 → 气象学 例 *Meteorology* has application in many diverse fields such as military, energy production, transport, agriculture and construction. 气象学应用于许多不同领域，如军事、能源生产、运输、农业和建筑。 派 meteorological(*a.* 气象学的)；meteorologist(*n.* 气象学者)
circumference [sər'kʌmfərəns]	*n.* 周围，周边(periphery)；圆周；周长 记 词根记忆：circum(周围) + fer(带来) + ence → 带来一圈 → 圆周 例 They have calculated the approximate *circumference* of the Earth. 他们已经计算出了地球圆周的大概长度。
publicize ['pʌblɪsaɪz]	*vt.* 宣传，推广，宣扬(advertise, promote) 记 联想记忆：public(公众) + ize → 使广为公众所知 → 宣传，推广 例 He travels around to *publicize* his writings. 他四处游走宣传他的作品。// After a theory has been *publicized*, scientists design experiments to test the theory. 一个理论公布之后，科学家们设计实验来测试该理论。
device [dɪ'vaɪs]	*n.* 装置，设备(equipment, apparatus)；手法，策略(technique) 记 词根记忆：de(向下) + vic(看) + e → 向下观看时所借助的东西 → 装置 例 Allegory is a literary *device* by which another level of meaning is concealed within what is usually a story. 寓言是一种文学手法，即另外一层意思通常被隐藏在一个故事里面。 参 devise(*vt.* 设计)
beak [biːk]	*n.* 鸟嘴，喙 例 The gull held the fish in its *beak*. 海鸥嘴里叼着鱼。
premier [prɪ'mɪr]	*n.* 首相，总理 *a.* 第一的，首要的；最著名的 记 词根记忆：prem(=prim 首先) + ier → 首要的 例 The *premier* is reporting on the work of the government in the next year. 总理正在做明年的政府工作报告。
codify ['koʊdɪfaɪ]	*vt.* 把…编成法典，使法律成文化；整理，系统化(systematize) 记 来自 code(*n.* 法典，法规) 例 The country is trying to *codify* the rules on outsourcing. 这个国家正在努力把外部采办规则编成法典。
dismal ['dɪzməl]	*a.* 阴沉的，阴郁的(gloomy)；忧郁的，沮丧的(blue, gloomy)；差劲的 记 来自拉丁语 dies mail，意为"不吉利的日子"，后引申为"阴沉的；忧郁的" 例 The *dismal*, cold day depressed every one. 阴郁寒冷的天气使每个人都觉得压抑。

harsh [hɑːrʃ]	*a.* 恶劣的，严酷的(severe); 刺耳的(raspy); 粗糙的，毛糙的 记 联想记忆：har(看做 hard, 坚硬的) + sh → 态度强硬 → 恶劣的 例 They believe that iron offers less resistance to fire and *harsh* weather than traditional materials. 他们认为铁在抵抗火和恶劣天气方面不如传统材料。 派 harshness(*n.* 恶劣，严酷；粗糙)
volunteer [ˌvɑːlənˈtɪr]	*n.* 志愿者；志愿军 *v.* 自愿做 *a.* 志愿的，义务的 记 词根记忆：volunt(意愿) + eer → 志愿者 例 I'm never going to *volunteer* to help Janet with the party again. 我再不会自愿帮助珍妮特搞派对了。 参 voluntary(*a.* 自愿的，志愿的); involuntary(*a.* 非自愿的；不知不觉的)
diffuse	[dɪˈfjuːz] *v.* 散播，传播(*travel); (光等)漫射，扩散(spread) [dɪˈfjuːs] *a.* 扩散的，漫射的；冗长的 记 词根记忆：dif(分开) + fus(流) + e → 分流 → 传播；漫射 例 A gas forms no free surface but tends to *diffuse* throughout the space available. 气体并不形成自由的表面，而是会在现有的空间扩散。 派 diffusely(*ad.* 广泛地); diffusion(*n.* 传播；扩散)
chubby [ˈtʃʌbi]	*a.* 丰满的，圆胖的(plump, fat) 例 He has a *chubby* baby face, which makes him appear younger than his age. 他长了一张圆胖的娃娃脸，这让他看起来比实际年龄小。 参 skinny(*a.* 极瘦的); slim(*a.* 苗条的)
intimate	[ˈɪntɪmət] *a.* 亲密的，密切的(close); 详尽的，精通的；个人隐私的(personal) *n.* 至交，密友 [ˈɪntɪmeɪt] *v.* 暗示，透露 记 联想记忆：in + ti + mate(伙伴) + ate → 互为好伙伴 → 亲密的 例 The boss has *intimate* knowledge of the client's requirements. 老板非常熟悉客户的要求。 派 intimacy(*n.* 熟悉；亲密，密切)
transcend [trænˈsend]	*vt.* 超越(exceed, surpass) 记 词根记忆：trans(越过) + (s)cend(爬) → 超越 例 Murray's essays *transcended* the boundaries of her world in recognizing the need for training women to earn their own living. 默里的论文超越了她所在世界的边界，她认识到了需要对女性进行培训以便其能自谋生计。
hurry [ˈhɜːri]	*v.* 使加快，催促；赶快，匆忙 *n.* 急忙，匆忙，仓促 搭 hurry up (使)赶快，急忙；in a hurry 迅速，赶快 例 We were *hurried* into making an unwise choice. 我们在催促之下作出了不明智的选择。

45

venom
[ˈvenəm]

n. (蛇等分泌的)毒液(poison);恶意,怨恨

记 词根记忆:ven(=venen 毒药) + om → (蛇等分泌的)毒液

例 The animals most widely known to use *venom* are snakes. 最广为人知的使用毒液的动物是蛇。

---

monarchy
[ˈmɑːnərki]

n. 君主制;君主国

记 词根记忆:mon(单个) + archy(统治) → 君主制

例 There are several constitutional *monarchies* in Europe. 欧洲有若干个君主立宪国。

---

paraphrase
[ˈpærəfreɪz]

n. 释义(meaning) *v.* 解释(explain);改写(rewrite)

记 词根记忆:para(旁边) + phras(说) + e → 在一旁说起解释作用 → 释义;解释

例 The reporter *paraphrased* the President's comments. 记者解释了总统的评论。

---

worth
[wɜːrθ]

a. 值…的,价值…的,值得…的 *n.* 价值(value);财产

例 We are thinking of taking the kids to the new aquarium this weekend. Do you think it's *worth* the trip? 我们想这个周末带孩子去新的水族馆。你觉得值得一去吗?

---

erratic
[ɪˈrætɪk]

a. 古怪的,反复无常的(eccentric);不规则的;不稳定的

记 词根记忆:err(徘徊) + at + ic(形容词后缀) → 在某地徘徊的 → 反复无常的

例 The water supply in this city is quite *erratic*. 这个城市的水供应相当不稳定。

---

loyal
[ˈlɔɪəl]

a. 忠诚的,忠贞的(faithful)

记 联想记忆:对皇家的(royal)事情很忠诚(loyal)

例 We should be *loyal* to our duty. 我们应该忠于自己的职责。

派 loyalty(*n.* 忠诚,忠心);loyalist(*n.* 忠诚分子)

---

dinosaur
[ˈdaɪnəsɔːr]

n. 恐龙

记 词根记忆:dino(恐怖的) + saur(蜥蜴) → 恐龙

例 Although known for their large size, many *dinosaurs* were human-sized or smaller. 尽管恐龙因其庞大的体积为人所知,但很多恐龙只有人体大小,或者更小。

参 tyrannosaur(*n.* 霸王龙);pterosaur(*n.* 翼龙)

---

hazard
[ˈhæzərd]

n. 危险(*danger);风险(risk) *vt.* 尝试着做(或提出);冒…风险,使处于危险

记 发音记忆:"骇死人的" → 危险

例 Coral reefs have always been one of the greatest *hazards* to ships sailing in tropical seas. 珊瑚礁对在热带海洋航行的船只来说一直是最大的威胁之一。

派 hazardous(*a.* 危险的,冒险的)

legitimate [lɪˈdʒɪtɪmət]	*a.* 合法的，法定的（legal）；正当合理的，合情合理的 记 词根记忆：leg(法律) + itim + ate → 合法的，法定的 例 It seems a perfectly *legitimate* question. 这似乎是完全合乎情理的问题。// A: It's the third time this week my roommate had a party in our room. This is really starting to affect my class work. I wonder if I should talk to someone at the housing office about changing rooms. B: Sounds like you've got a *legitimate* reason. You two are just not compatible at all. A: 这是我的室友本周在宿舍开的第三次派对了。这真的开始影响我的功课了。我想是否应该和住宿办谈谈换宿舍的事情。 B: 听起来好像你有个正当的理由。你俩根本就处不到一块儿。
recreation [ˌrekriˈeɪʃn]	*n.* 娱乐，消遣（amusement） 记 来自 recreate（*v.* 得到娱乐） 例 There is a need to improve facilities for leisure and *recreation*. 有必要改进休闲娱乐设施。 派 recreational（*a.* 娱乐的，消遣的）
swindle [ˈswɪndl]	*vt./n.* 诈骗，骗取（con） 记 联想记忆：s + wind(风) + le → 四处吹风，搞诈骗 → 诈骗，骗取 例 The bad guy *swindled* 1,000 dollars from the old woman. 那个坏人从那个老妇人那骗取了 1000 美元。
collide [kəˈlaɪd]	*vi.* 碰撞，互撞；冲突，抵触（conflict） 例 What happens when electrons and gas *collide* in space? 电子和气体在空间中相撞时会发生什么？ 派 collision（*n.* 碰撞；冲突）
oxygen [ˈɑːksɪdʒən]	*n.* 氧，氧气 记 词根记忆：oxy(酸；氧) + gen(产生) → 产生酸的东西 → 氧，氧气 例 Liquid *oxygen* may also be produced by condensation out of air. 液态氧也可通过冷凝空气而生成。 参 hydrogen（*n.* 氢）
gem [dʒem]	*n.* 宝石，珍品；美丽绝伦的事物 例 This picture is the *gem* of his collection. 这幅画是他收藏中的极品。
combat [ˈkɑːmbæt]	*v./n.* 战斗，格斗（conflict, battle） 记 词根记忆：com(共同) + bat(打，击) → 共同打 → 战斗，格斗 例 San Antonio, Texas, offers an important lesson for numerous other cities *combating* urban decay. 得克萨斯州的圣安东尼奥市给其他很多与城区衰落作斗争的城市上了重要的一课。

recreation

45

□ legitimate   □ recreation   □ swindle   □ collide   □ oxygen   □ gem
□ combat

lower [ˈloʊər]	*v.* 降低(reduce) *a.* 较低的；下级的，下等的(inferior) 例 Your heart rate is *lowered*. 你的心率降低了。// The study of *lower* animals gives insight into the form and structure of the nervous system of higher animals. 研究低等动物让人们能进一步了解高等动物神经系统的形状和结构。
avalanche [ˈævəlæntʃ]	*n./v.* 雪崩(snowslide)；山崩(landslide) 例 In mountainous terrain *avalanches* are among the most serious hazards to life and property. 在多山地带，山崩是生命和财产面临的最严重的危害之一。
fierce [fɪrs]	*a.* 凶猛的，残忍的(cruel)；狂热的，强烈的；激烈的，猛烈的(violent) 记 联想记忆：强迫(force)人大冷天光脚，真是残忍(fierce) 例 Human population near the equator has evolved dark skin over many generations because of exposure to the *fiercest* rays of the sun. 由于暴露在最强烈的日光下，赤道附近的人们经过数代的进化，形成了深色的肤色。
sponsor [ˈspɑːnsər]	*vt.* 主办；赞助(patronize) *n.* 发起者(source)；赞助者(benefactor) 记 联想记忆：spons（音似：四帮四）+ or → 以四帮四的形式资助别人 → 赞助 例 Our museum membership will be *sponsored* by the professor. 我们的博物馆会员费将由教授赞助。
cuneiform [ˈkjuːnɪfɔːrm]	*n.* 楔形文字 *a.* 楔形的；楔形文字的 例 These inscriptions were written in *cuneiform* and in two other ancient languages. 这些碑文是用楔形文字和其他两种古老文字写成的。
manifesto [ˌmænɪˈfestoʊ]	*n.* 宣言，声明 记 词根记忆：mani(手) + fest(打) + o → 用手打，怒意很明显 → 宣言，声明 例 The candidate declared a *manifesto* announcing that he would quit this afternoon. 那个候选人今天下午发表声明，宣布退出竞选。
outlaw [ˈaʊtlɔː]	*vt.* 宣布…为非法 *n.* 罪犯，歹徒，亡命之徒；被剥夺法律权益者 记 联想记忆：out(出) + law(法律) → 越出法律范围 → 罪犯 例 Although Robin was an *outlaw*, he stole from the rich and helped the poor. 虽然罗宾是名罪犯，但是他劫富济贫。
pact [pækt]	*n.* 协议，条约，公约 记 联想记忆：p + act(行为) → 签订契约来约束行为 → 契约 例 The two sides have made a *pact* to keep the secret of the boy's birth. 双方达成了协议，要对男孩的身世保密。
reign [reɪn]	*n.* 统治，支配；任期 *vi.* 当政，统治；占主导地位，占优势 记 词根记忆：reig(=reg 统治) + n → 统治 搭 reign over 统治 例 Leo is an ambitious man, who wants to *reign* over the country. 利奥是一个有野心的人，他想统治整个国家。

summon [ˈsʌmən]	*v.* 传唤，传讯(出庭)；召集，召开(会议)；鼓起(勇气)，振作(精神) 记 词根记忆：sum(=sub 在…之下) + mon(警告) → 在警告下来到 → 传唤 搭 summon up 鼓起(勇气)，奋起 例 *Summon* the staff on the board to talk about how to deal with pirates. 召集全体船员到甲板上，讨论对付海盗的方法。
latent [ˈleɪtnt]	*a.* 潜在的，隐伏的(hidden)；潜伏的；休眠的 记 联想记忆：late(晚的) + nt → 晚到的 → 潜在的，隐伏的 搭 latent disease 潜伏性疾病；latent period 潜伏期 例 The term "*latent* heat" refers to the energy that has to be used to convert liquid water to water vapor. "潜热"这个词指把液态水转化成水蒸气时吸收的能量。
wield [wiːld]	*vt.* 支配，掌权，行使(权力等) 记 联想记忆：支配(wield)不放弃(yield) 例 The chairman *wielded* much power of the party. 主席掌握着该党的大部分权力。
penalty [ˈpenəlti]	*n.* 处罚，惩罚；罚金；(运动、比赛)犯规的处罚 记 词根记忆：pen(惩罚) + al + ty → 处罚，惩罚 例 The death *penalty* has been abolished in some countries. 一些国家已经废除了死刑。
verdict [ˈvɜːrdɪkt]	*n.* 裁定；判断；意见 记 词根记忆：ver(真实的) + dict(说) → 说出事实 → 裁定 例 When the judge announced the *verdict* of not guilty, the defendant wept for joy. 当法官宣布裁定无罪时，被告喜极而泣。
reconcile [ˈrekənsaɪl]	*vt.* 使协调；使和解；使顺从 记 联想记忆：re(再，又) + concile(看做 council，委员会) → 一再召开委员会 → 使协调；使和解 搭 reconcile oneself to 将就，妥协 例 The two companies were *reconciled* after one side apologized in public. 在一方公开道歉后，两个公司又言归于好了。 派 reconciliation(*n.* 调解，和解；协调)
hurl [hɜːrl]	*v.* 猛投(fling)；大声斥责 记 联想记忆：不要大声斥责(hurl)孩子，以免伤害(hurt)他 例 The luxury express trains that *hurl* people over spots spotlight the romance of railroading. 把乘客载往各处的豪华快车突出了铁路旅行的浪漫气息。

penalty
迟到五次
奖金全扣

45

527

sovereign
['sɑːvrən]

a. 君主的；至高无上的；独立自主的 *n.* 君主，元首，最高统治者

记 词根记忆：sover（=super 在…之上）+（r)eig（=reg 统治）+ n → 拥有最高统治权的 → 君主的；至高无上的

例 The emperor holds the *sovereign* power in the country. 皇帝掌握着这个国家的最高权力。

派 sovereignty(*n.* 主权；最高统治权；独立自主)

prosecute
['prɑːsɪkjuːt]

v. 起诉，控告，检举；担任控方律师；继续从事

记 词根记忆：pro(在…前面) + secut(跟随) + e → 在大家采取行动前跟随 → 事先追踪行迹 → 起诉

例 The man was *prosecuted* for drunk driving. 这个男人因酒后驾驶而被起诉。

派 prosecutor(*n.* 公诉人，检察官；控方律师)

blade
[bleɪd]

n. 刀刃，刀片；叶片；草叶；桨叶

记 联想记忆：热门电影《刀锋战士》英文为 *Blade*

例 The *blades* of the electric fan are covered with dust. 电扇的叶片上全是灰。

tyrannical
[tɪ'rænɪkl]

a. 专制的，残暴的，专横的

记 联想记忆：tyran(看做 tyrant，暴君) + nical → 专制的，残暴的，专横的

例 It is said that the new general manager is a *tyrannical* person. 据说新来的总经理是个专横的人。

verifiable
['verɪfaɪəbl]

a. 可证实的，可核实的

记 来自 verify(*v.* 证实)

例 Claiming something is true misses the point, while presenting *verifiable* fact proves its correctness. 声称某样东西是正确的没有什么意义，而提出可证实的事实才能证明它的正确性。

suborn
[sə'bɔːrn]

vt. 收买，买通(使作伪证等)，唆使

记 联想记忆：被收买(suborn)了去杀人放火，真是够笨的(stubborn)

例 The suspect tried to *suborn* the witness in order to escape from charges. 嫌疑犯试图收买证人，以摆脱指控。

warrant
['wɔːrənt]

n. 授权，批准；许可证；委任状，执行令 *vt.* 保证，担保；使正当

记 联想记忆：warr(看做 war，战争) + ant(蚂蚁) → 战争中杀人如蚁也是不正当的 → 使正当

例 Vehicles can get into the city during the Spring Festival period, but they must have a travel *warrant*. 车辆可以在春节期间进入这个城市，但必须要有通行证。

irritable
['ɪrɪtəbl]

a. 急躁的，易怒的；易受刺激的；过敏的

记 词根记忆：ir(进入) + rit(擦) + able → 进入摩擦 → 急躁的，易怒的

例 She is *irritable* when she is unhappy. 她不开心时容易急躁。

notion [ˈnoʊʃn]	*n.* 概念，观念(concept)；想法(thought) 记 词根记忆：not(知道) + ion(名词后缀) → 知道 → 有了概念和想法 → 概念，观念；想法 例 Subsequent reforms have made these *notions* seem quite out-of-date. 随后的改革使这些观念看上去颇为落伍。
migrate [ˈmaɪɡreɪt]	*v.* 迁徙(flight)；移居(transplant) 记 词根记忆：migr(移动) + ate → 迁徙；移居 例 When these people *migrated* from the countryside, they carried their fears and suspicion with them. 这些人迁出乡村时，心里不乏担忧和疑虑。 派 migrant(*n.* 移居者)；migratory(*a.* 迁移的；流浪的)
preside [prɪˈzaɪd]	*vi.* 担任主席；主持(会议等)；掌管 记 词根记忆：pre(在…前面) + sid(坐) + e → 坐在前面 → 担任主席 搭 preside at/over 主持，主管 例 The teacher who will *preside* hasn't arrived at the meeting, and everybody is worried about her. 主持会议的老师还没有到，每个人都很担心。
slander [ˈslændər]	*n.* 诽谤(罪)，中伤，诋毁 *vt.* 诽谤，诋毁 记 词根记忆：sland (=scandal 障碍物) + er → 设障碍物，使人绊倒 → 诽谤，诋毁 例 Ross was involved in a case of *slander*. 罗斯被卷入一起诽谤案中。
reservoir [ˈrezərvwɑːr]	*n.* 水库，蓄水池；(知识、人才等的)储备，储藏 记 词根记忆：re(再，又) + serv(维持) + oir → 保存 → 水库 例 The book is a *reservoir* of information about English literature. 这本书是英语文学的知识宝库。

45

Word List 46

词根、词缀预习表

puls	推	pulse *n.* 脉搏	tract	拉	attract *vt.* 吸引
min	突出	eminent *a.* 显著的	ben	好的	benign *a.* 有利的
ject	扔	eject *v.* 逐出	vi	道路	previous *a.* 先前的
fid	相信	fidelity *n.* 忠诚	cis	切	excise *vt.* 切除
tor	转动	torrent *n.* 洪流	pli	弯, 折	pliable *a.* 柔韧的

---

scheme
[ski:m]

n. 计划, 方案(plan, design); 阴谋; 体系, 体制 *v.* 密谋, 秘密策划, 图谋
记 联想记忆: sch(看做 school, 学校) + eme(看做 theme, 论文) → 学校让学生为论文拟定写作计划 → 方案; 注意不要和 schema(*n.* 图解)相混
搭 propose a scheme 拟定计划
例 One of the earliest of the *schemes* was patterned on the human eye. 最初的一个方案就是模仿人类的眼睛。

---

consult
[kənˈsʌlt]

v. 请教; 商议(counsel, confer); 参考, 翻阅(refer to)
记 联想记忆: 不顾侮辱(insult), 不耻请教(consult)
例 She is *consulting* with the reference librarian. 她正在向参考书阅览室的图书管理员请教。
派 consultant(*n.* 顾问)
参 result(*n.* 结果); assault(*n.* 攻击, 袭击)

---

dispose
[dɪˈspəʊz]

v. 安排, 布置; 使倾向于
搭 dispose of 清除, 销毁; 应付, 解决; 击败
例 Contemporary readers are easily *disposed* to think of "literature" only as something written. 当代读者很容易认为"文学"只指书面的东西。// Irresponsible people often *dispose* of the waste in ponds. 没有责任感的人经常把垃圾扔到池塘里。
派 disposal (*n.* 处理, 清除); disposable (*a.* 一次性的; 可动用的); disposed(*a.* 乐意的); disposition(*n.* 排列, 布置; 处置)

---

pulse
[pʌls]

n. 脉搏, 脉率(throb); 脉冲(an electromagnetic wave)
记 词根记忆: puls(推) + e → 脉搏, 脉率; 脉冲
搭 electronic pulse 电冲
例 The doctor took my *pulse*. 医生给我量了脉搏。

---

furnace
['fɜːrnɪs]

n. 火炉，熔炉(oven, kiln)；锅炉

记 联想记忆：fur（毛皮）+ nace → 坐在火炉旁边就像披着温暖的毛皮 → 火炉

例 It's like a *furnace* here. 这里热得像火炉。

realization
[ˌriːəlaɪˈzeɪʃn]

n. 实现(fulfillment)；意识(awareness)

例 Expectation is better than *realization*. 期望比实现更美好。

dilemma
[dɪˈlemə]

n. 困境，进退两难的局面

记 发音记忆："地雷嘛" → 陷入雷区 → 进退两难的局面

例 I have the *dilemma* of choosing a new car or a computer. 我面临选择新车还是电脑的两难局面。

peculiar
[pɪˈkjuːliər]

a. 独特的(*distinctive)；罕见的(unusual)；奇怪的，古怪的

例 Each product had its own *peculiar* characteristics. 每个产品都有其特性。

派 peculiarity(*n.* 特性；怪癖)

morale
[məˈræl]

n. 士气，斗志(spirit)

记 联想记忆：和moral(*n.* 道德)一起记

搭 raise morale 提高士气

例 Throughout the wilderness, post bands provided entertainment and boosted *morale*. 四周一片荒芜，哨所乐队提供了娱乐，鼓舞了士气。

eminent
['emɪnənt]

a. 显著的，杰出的(outstanding, distinguished)

记 词根记忆：e(出)+ min(突出)+ ent → 显著的，杰出的

例 An *eminent* architect will give a lecture to us this afternoon. 今天下午那位著名的建筑师将给我们做讲座。

派 preeminent(*a.* 卓越的)

参 imminent(*a.* 即将到来的，迫切的)；prominent(*a.* 卓越的，显著的)

screen
[skriːn]

vt. 掩蔽(shield)；审查(censor)；筛选 *n.* 屏幕

例 She methodically *screened* and cultured scores of soil samples, which she then sent to her partner. 她有条不紊地筛选并培养了几十个土壤样品，然后送给了她的合伙人。

valid
['vælɪd]

a. 有根据的，合理的(well-founded)；有效的(effective)

记 词根记忆：val(价值)+ id → 有价值的 → 有效的

例 The data in your report seems to be *valid* to me. 你的报告里的数据在我看来好像是有根据的。// The main point of the passage is that oral narratives are a *valid* form of literature. 这篇文章的主要观点是口述是一种有效的文学形式。

派 validate(*vt.* 证实，确认)；validity(*n.* 合法性；符合逻辑)

eject
[iˈdʒekt]

v. 逐出，驱赶(expel)；喷出，喷射(erupt)；弹出

记 词根记忆：e(出来)+ ject(扔) → 扔出来 → 逐出；喷出

例 Some artists came to truly embrace the life in small towns and to *eject* city life in so called "sophisticated society". 一些艺术家开始真正接受小镇的生活，拒绝所谓"复杂社会"的城市生活。

参 reject(*vt.* 拒绝)；object(*v.* 反对)；inject(*vt.* 注射)；deject(*vt.* 使沮丧)

fidelity [fɪˈdeləti]	*n.* 忠诚，忠实 (loyalty, allegiance)；精确，逼真 记 词根记忆：fid(相信) + elity → 值得相信 → 忠诚，忠实 例 With *fidelity* to real life and accurate representation without idealization, the authors studied local dialects. 作者们研究当地方言时，忠于现实生活，准确反映现实，不带任何理想化成分。
partial [ˈpɑːrʃl]	*a.* 部分的，不完全的 (incomplete)；偏爱的，癖好的；偏袒的 记 来自 part(*n.* 部分) 例 It was only a *partial* solution to the problem. 那只是部分地解决了问题。 派 partially(*ad.* 部分地，不完全地)；impartially(*ad.* 公平地)；partiality (*n.* 偏袒；酷爱)
skip [skɪp]	*v.* 跳 (jump, leap)；跳过，略过，漏过；不出席 (absent) *n.* 跳；跳过 例 I'd like to *skip* the meeting, but I can't just not go. 我不想参加这个会议，但不能不去。
regenerate [rɪˈdʒenəreɪt]	*v.* (使)复兴，(使)振兴 (restore)；(使)再生 记 词根记忆：re(再，又) + gen(产生) + er + ate → 使再次产生 → (使)再生 例 The sea cucumber will *regenerate* itself if it is attacked. 海参被袭击后能自我修复。 派 regeneration(*n.* 复兴；再生)
bump [bʌmp]	*n.* 肿块；撞击；碰撞声 *v.* 碰撞 (hit) 记 发音记忆：物体碰撞的声音 例 Starfish's skin is covered with thorny *bumps*. 海星的皮肤上布满了带刺的疙瘩。// I *bumped* into her at the market just last week. 我上周刚在市场遇到她。 参 dump(*v.* 倾倒)；damp(*a.* 潮湿的)
submarine [ˌsʌbməˈriːn]	*n.* 潜水艇 *a.* 水下的，海底的 记 联想记忆：sub(在…下面) + marine(船舶) → 水下船舶 → 潜水艇 例 Two *submarines*, both launched in September 1888, marked the maturing of naval *submarine* technology. 1888 年下水的两艘潜水艇标志着海军潜艇技术的成熟。 submarine
promising [ˈprɑːmɪsɪŋ]	*a.* 有希望的 (hopeful)；有前途的 记 来自 promise(*v.* 承诺) 例 The award subsidizes a *promising* American writer's visit to Rome. 这个奖项会资助一位有前途的美国作家访问罗马。
domesticate [dəˈmestɪkeɪt]	*vt.* 驯养，驯化 (cultivate)；使精于家务，使喜爱家居 记 来自 domestic(*a.* 家庭的) 例 In ancient times, wild animals were caught and *domesticated* to serve human beings. 在古代，人们捕捉野生动物并将其驯化，使其为人类服务。 派 domesticated(*a.* 驯养的，家养的)；domestication(*n.* 驯养，驯服)

□ fidelity □ partial □ skip □ regenerate □ bump □ submarine
□ promising □ domesticate

staff [stæf]	*n.* 全体职工(crew, personnel)；行政人员；棍棒 *vt.* 为…配备人员；任职于 记 联想记忆：明星(star)后面往往跟着一群工作人员(staff) 例 A congressional representative needs a large *staff*. 一名国会代表需要一大批工作人员。
motion ['moʊʃn]	*n.* 运动，移动(*movement)；动作；提议，动议 *v.* (向…)做动作，示意 记 词根记忆：mot(移动) + ion(名词后缀) → 运动，移动 例 The fish pushes water aside by the forward *motion* of its head and with a curve of its body and its flexible tail. 鱼通过头部的向前运动以及身体游动和灵活的尾巴而把水推向两侧。 派 motionless(*a.* 不动的，静止的)
pathology [pə'θɑːlədʒi]	*n.* 反常，变态(abnormality)；病理学；病状 记 词根记忆：path(病) + ology(…学) → 病理学 例 The boundary lines between normality and *pathology* are often clearly delineated by medical science. 医学往往能清楚地给出正常与反常之间的界限。
torrent ['tɔːrənt]	*n.* 洪流，急流；爆发，迸发(rush) 记 词根记忆：tor(=torn 转动) + rent → 水流转动不停地前进 → 洪流，急流；迸发 例 His article brought a *torrent* of criticism. 他的文章招来很多非议。 派 torrential(*a.* 奔流的，湍急的)
concentration [ˌkɑːnsn'treɪʃn]	*n.* 专注，专心；浓度，含量；集中，聚集 例 The music can help relieve depression and improve *concentration*. 音乐有助于缓解抑郁情绪，提高注意力。// It's important to have the soil tested regularly to determine the lead *concentration*. 要定期检测土壤，确定铅含量，这很重要。

concentration

pocketbook ['pɑːkɪtbʊk]	*n.* 钱袋，皮夹(purse, wallet)；财政状况，财力 例 Many foreign goods are too expensive for American *pocketbooks*. 许多外国货都太贵，一般美国人承受不起。
kerosene ['kerəsiːn]	*n.* 煤油，火油 例 *Kerosene* was used to light lamps. 过去煤油用来点灯。
smoothly ['smuːðli]	*ad.* 顺利地(successfully)；平稳地；平静地 例 The interview went *smoothly*. 面试进展顺利。
bulb [bʌlb]	*n.* (植物的)鳞茎；鳞茎状物；灯泡 例 The *bulb* has burned out. 灯泡烧坏了。

46

□ staff　　　□ motion　　　□ pathology　　　□ torrent　　　□ concentration　□ pocketbook
□ kerosene　□ smoothly　　□ bulb

533

reasonable

['riːznəbl]

a. 合理的，适当的(fair)；通情达理的；(价钱)公道的

记 联想记忆：reason(道理) + able(能…的) → 能讲道理的 → 通情达理的

搭 a reasonable excuse 合理的借口

例 What do you think would be a *reasonable* price to pay for a new computer? 你觉得一台新电脑付多少钱合理? //

A: The job sounds great, but I'm a little worried about how much time it might take.

B: It's pretty *reasonable*. It never took me more than five hours a week to do all the grading and then another thirty to forty minutes to record the grades on the computer.

A: 这份工作听起来不错，但是我有点担心它会占用太多时间。

B: 时间上很合理。我每周花在评分上的时间不超过 5 个小时，然后再用 30 到 40 分钟把分数输入电脑。

派 unreasonable(*a.* 不合理的；不讲理的；过度的)

---

captive

['kæptɪv]

a. 被监禁的，被困住的；受控制的 *n.* 俘虏，战俘(prisoner)

记 词根记忆：capt(抓) + ive → 俘虏

例 They were the size of a grain of rice at birth and were the first babies to be produced under the *captive* breeding program. 它们刚出生时只有谷粒大小，是人工捕获饲养计划培育出来的第一批幼体。

派 captivity(*n.* 监禁，关押)

---

hospitable

[hɑːˈspɪtəbl]

a. (气候、环境等)宜人的(pleasant)；好客的，殷勤的；开通的

记 词根记忆：hosp(=host 主人) + it + able(能…的) → 能胜任主人一职的 → 好客的

例 The climate is more *hospitable* in the sea. 海洋的气候更加宜人。

参 hospital(*n.* 医院)

---

attract

[əˈtrækt]

vt. 吸引(*lure, *draw)

记 词根记忆：at + tract(拉) → 拉过来 → 吸引

例 The songs *attracted* only the young people in the community. 这些歌曲只吸引了社会上的年轻人。

派 attraction(*n.* 吸引，诱惑)；attractant(*n.* 引诱物)

attract

---

pipe

[paɪp]

vt. 用管道输送；用线路系统传输 *n.* 管子，管道(tube, hose)；烟斗

例 The speech was *piped* over a public address system. 讲话经广播系统传送出去。

---

crumple

['krʌmpl]

v. (使)变皱，起皱(rumple)；破裂；崩溃，垮台

搭 crumple zone 防撞缓冲区

例 Jane *crumpled* the letter up, torn it into pieces and in the end threw it on the fire. 简把信揉成一团，撕成碎片，最后扔进了火里。

派 crumpled(*a.* 皱巴巴的)

reliance [rɪ'laɪəns]	*n.* 依靠，依赖(dependance)；信任 例 Such learning methods encourage too great a *reliance* upon the teacher. 这样的学习方法会造成对老师的过分依赖。
bald [bɔːld]	*a.* 光秃的，秃头的(uncovered, hairless)；简单的，单调的 例 He's *bald* and doesn't need a haircut. 他是秃头，不需要理发。 参 bold(*a.* 大胆的)
extraordinary [ɪk'strɔːrdəneri]	*a.* 特别的(*exceptional, special)；非凡的(*remarkable) 记 组合词：extra(以外的) + ordinary(平常的) → 平常之外的 → 特别的 例 Nitinol is one of the most *extraordinary* metals to be discovered last century. 镍钛诺是上世纪发现的最特别的金属之一。
checked [tʃekt]	*a.* 格子花纹的；棋盘状的 例 A *checked* shirt won't look good on the man. 这个人穿格子衬衫不好看。
jeans [dʒiːnz]	*n.* 牛仔裤 例 It's all right to wear *jeans* for a class presentation. 在课堂做报告时可以穿牛仔裤。
stimulate ['stɪmjuleɪt]	*vt.* 刺激；激励，激发(*motivate, evoke) 记 词根记忆：stim(刺) + ul + ate(动词后缀) → 刺激；激励 例 The lecture *stimulated* her to study the subject in more depth. 那个讲座激发她进一步深入研究那个课题。
benign [bɪ'naɪn]	*a.* (疾病)良性的(innocuous)；有利的；善良的，和蔼的(kind) 记 词根记忆：ben(好的) + ign → 良性的；有利的 搭 a benign tumor 良性肿瘤 例 The *benign* climate conditions brought this region a bumper crop. 有利的气候条件给这个地区带来了丰收。
insurance [ɪn'ʃʊrəns]	*n.* 保险；保险费；保险业 记 来自insure(*v.* 为…保险；买卖保险) 例 You can see how *insurance* helped encourage international trade. 你可以看到保险在促进国际贸易上的作用。
economic [ˌiːkə'nɑːmɪk]	*a.* 经济的；经济上的；经济学的；合算的 记 词根记忆：eco(家) + nom(管理) + ic → 管理家庭开支的 → 经济的 搭 economic conditions 经济情况 例 In order to comprehend the operation of an *economic* system, we must deal not only with the things that can be seen, but we also have to give our attention to the things which cannot be perceived directly. 为全面理解经济体制的运作，我们不但要面对可见的问题，而且要关注不能直接被察觉的问题。// In the *economic* sense, laisser faire meant that while the government should be responsible for things like maintaining peace and protecting property rights, it should not interfere with private business. 从经济学上讲，自由主义指政府应该在为诸如维护秩序和保护产权这些事务负责的同时，不应干预私营企业。 派 uneconomic(*a.* 不经济的，浪费的)

46

maritime [ˈmærɪtaɪm]	*a.* 海的，海事的；航海的 **记** 联想记忆：mari(海) + time(时间) → 海上的时间 → 航海的 **例** The peopling of the Pacific Islands has been described as the greatest feat of *maritime* colonization in human history. 人类在太平洋岛屿上定居被描述为人类海洋殖民史上最伟大的壮举。
continent [ˈkɑːntɪnənt]	*n.* 大陆，陆地(mainland)；洲 **例** We are going to spend a weekend on the African *continent*. 我们要去非洲大陆度周末。 **派** continental(*a.* 大陆性的)
fungi [ˈfʌŋɡaɪ]	*n.* [fungus的复数]真菌 **记** 发音记忆："房盖" → 真菌的形状像房盖 → 真菌 **例** Eatable mushroom, a kind of *fungi*, has a high value of nutrition and is good for our health. 可食用蘑菇是一种真菌，具有很高的营养价值，有益健康。 **参** bacteria(*n.* 细菌)；virus(*n.* 病毒)
belie [bɪˈlaɪ]	*vt.* 给人以错觉(misrepresent)；掩饰(disguise)；证明…不正确 **记** 联想记忆：be + lie(谎言) → 使…成谎言 → 给人以错觉 **例** The boy's cheerful manner *belied* his real thoughts. 男孩开心的样子掩饰了他真实的想法。
documentation [ˌdɑːkjumenˈteɪʃn]	*n.* 文件(file)；归档，文献记录 **例** The researcher is faced with the problem of primary materials that have little *documentation*. 这个研究人员面临的问题是原始资料很少有文件记载。
gender [ˈdʒendər]	*n.* 性别(sex)；(语法中的)性 **记** 联想记忆：和 tender(*a.* 温柔的)一起记 **搭** gender differences 性别差异 **例** Feminists challenge the dominant ideologies concerning *gender* roles. 女权主义者质疑有关性别角色的主流意识形态。
clue [kluː]	*n.* 线索(*information)；提示(cue, hint) **例** Diet may hold the *clue* to the cause of migraines. 饮食习惯有可能揭示偏头痛的起因。
plague [pleɪɡ]	*vt.* 困扰，使苦恼；纠缠 *n.* 鼠疫；传染病(epidemic)；祸患，灾害 **记** 联想记忆：pla(看做 PLA，人民解放军) + gue(音似：go) → 解放军一走灾祸就来了 → 祸患，灾害 **例** Financial problems are *plaguing* the company. 财政问题困扰着这家公司。
aggravate [ˈæɡrəveɪt]	*vt.* 恶化，加重；激怒 **记** 词根记忆：ag(表加强) + grav(重的) + ate(使…) → 使变重 → 恶化，加重 **例** The doctor told the patient not to get angry easily, or it would *aggravate* the condition of his illness. 医生告诉病人不要轻易生气，否则病情会恶化。 **派** aggravation(*n.* 恶化，加重；烦恼)

surpass [sərˈpæs]	*vt.* 超过，超越，胜过(*exceed) 词 联想记忆：sur(在…上面) + pass(通过) → 在上面通过 → 超过 例 Canada *surpassed* the United States in transportation improvements. 加拿大在运输改良方面超过了美国。
curative [ˈkjʊrətɪv]	*a.* 有助于治疗的，有疗效的 *n.* 药物 记 词根记忆：cur(治疗) + ative → 有疗效的 例 The *curative* power of the antibiotics introduced in the 1950s was amazing at the time. 20世纪50年代引进的抗生素在当时疗效惊人。
previous [ˈpriːviəs]	*a.* 先前的，在前的(*past, preceding) 记 词根记忆：pre(在…前面) + vi(道路) + ous → 走路走在前面的 → 先前的，在前的 例 A library notice was sent to him at his *previous* address. 图书馆给他的通知寄到了他以前的地址。 派 previously(*ad.* 先前，以前)
hereditary [həˈredɪteri]	*a.* 遗传(性)的；可继承的，世袭的 记 词根记忆：her(继承人) + edit + ary(形容词后缀) → 继承下来的 → 遗传(性)的 例 Asthma is *hereditary* in his family. 哮喘是他们家族的遗传病。
bosom [ˈbʊzəm]	*n.* 胸部，乳房；胸怀，内心 例 The mother pressed her baby to her *bosom*. 妈妈把婴儿紧紧抱在怀里。
calculus [ˈkælkjələs]	*n.* 微积分；结石 记 词根记忆：calcul(计算；石头) + us → 微积分；结石 例 *Calculus* is also used to gain a more precise understanding of the nature of space, time, and motion. 人们也通过微积分来更精确地理解空间、时间和运动的本质。
invalid	[ɪnˈvælɪd] *a.* 无效的；无可靠根据的，站不住脚的 [ˈɪnvəlɪd] *n.* 病弱者，残疾者 记 词根记忆：in(无) + val(价值) + id → 无价值的 → 无效的 例 The treaty was declared *invalid* because it had not been ratified. 条约没有得到批准，因此被宣布无效。
cerebral [səˈriːbrəl]	*a.* 大脑的；理智的(intellectual) 记 词根记忆：cer(头顶) + ebr + al → 大脑的 例 The old man died from the *cerebral* haemorrhage. 那位老人死于脑溢血。
dosage [ˈdoʊsɪdʒ]	*n.* 剂量 记 词根记忆：dos(给予) + age(集体名词后缀) → 医生给予的量 → 剂量 例 Do not exceed the recommended *dosage*. 切勿超过规定剂量。

46

excise ['eksaɪz]	*vt.* 切除；删去 记 词根记忆：ex(出) + cis(切) + e → 切除 例 The lump in her brain was successfully *excised* by the surgeon this afternoon. 今天下午她大脑里的肿块被外科医生成功地切除了。 派 excision〔*n.* 切除(术)〕
balm [bɑːm]	*n.* 香脂油，药膏；镇痛剂，安慰剂 记 联想记忆：镇痛剂(balm)能让人镇静(calm)下来 例 Tom's excellent performances on work was truely a *balm* to his mother. 汤姆在工作上的优秀表现对他妈妈来说确实是一种安慰。
holistic [hoʊ'lɪstɪk]	*a.* 整体的，全面的；功能整体性的 记 词根记忆：hol(=holo 全部) + istic → 整体的，全面的 搭 holistic medicine 整体医学 例 The *holistic* solutions are required for the environmental problems. 环境问题需要整体性的解决方案。
infirm [ɪn'fɜːrm]	*a.* 虚弱的；不坚定的 记 联想记忆：in(不) + firm(结实的；坚定的) → 虚弱的；不坚定的 例 The doctor warned him that he was too *infirm* to go to work. 医生警告他，他太虚弱了，不能去工作。
patient ['peɪʃnt]	*a.* 有耐心的，能忍耐的 *n.* 病人，患者 例 The teacher was so *patient* that all the students liked her. 这位老师很有耐心，所以学生们都很喜欢她。
myopic [maɪ'oʊpiə]	*a.* 近视的；缺乏远见的 记 词根记忆：my(闭上) + op(眼睛) + ic → 闭上眼睛的 → 缺乏远见的 例 Their parents' *myopic* attitude towards gifted education might be responsible for their misconception. 也许是他们的父母对资优教育缺乏远见的态度造成了他们的误解。
optic ['ɑːptɪk]	*a.* 眼的；视觉的；光学上的 *n.* 光学仪器 记 词根记忆：opt(眼睛) + ic → 眼的 例 The lump in his brain pressed the *optic* nerve, so the patient was blind temporarily. 大脑中的肿块压迫着视觉神经，所以病人暂时失明了。
pathological [ˌpæθə'lɑːdʒɪkl]	*a.* 病态的；病理学的；不理智的，无道理的 例 She has a *pathological* fear of heights. 她无道理地恐高。
capillary ['kæpəleri]	*n.* 毛细血管 *a.* 毛状的；毛细血管的 记 词根记忆：capill(毛发) + ary → 毛状的 例 *Capillaries* also supply blood to the organs. 毛细血管也会向器官输送血液。

538
□ excise   □ balm   □ holistic   □ infirm   □ patient   □ myopic
□ optic   □ pathological   □ capillary

trench [trentʃ]	*n.* 沟渠，壕沟（ditch）；战壕 *v.* 挖沟 记 联想记忆：掉进沟渠（trench），全身湿透（drench） 例 The oceanic crust is remelted beneath the ocean *trenches*. 洋壳在海沟下又一次融化。
deny [dɪ'naɪ]	*v.* 否认（negate）；拒绝承认；拒绝给予（refuse） 记 发音记忆："抵赖" → 否认 例 Access to the information was *denied* to them. 他们无法得到这个情报。
costume ['kɑːstjuːm]	*n.* 服饰（dress）；服装，装束；戏装 例 The actors were still in *costume* and make-up. 这些演员仍是戏装打扮。
rampant ['ræmpənt]	*a.* 猖獗的，肆虐的（wild, extravagant）；蔓生的 记 联想记忆：ramp（坡道）+ ant → 坡道上长满草 → 蔓生的 搭 rampant inflation 无法控制的通货膨胀 例 Due to the climate, the serious disease is *rampant* in this region. 由于气候原因，这种严重的疾病在这个地区不断蔓延。
generate ['dʒenəreɪt]	*vt.* 产生（produce）；引起，导致（*cause） 记 词根记忆：gen（产生）+ er + ate → 产生；引起 例 The smoke it *generated* went out through the main chimney. 它所产生的烟通过主烟囱飘出去了。 派 generator（*n.* 发电机）
cassette [kə'set]	*n.* 盒式录音（或录像）带 搭 a cassette player 盒式磁带放音机 例 Always put the *cassette* back in its case before storage. 存放之前，记得要将录音带放回盒中。
Neolithic [ˌniːə'lɪθɪk]	*a.* 新石器时代的 记 词根记忆：neo（新的）+ lith（石头）+ ic → 新石器的 → 新石器时代的 例 *Neolithic* peoples were skilled farmers, manufacturing a range of tools necessary for the tending and harvesting of crops. 新石器时代的人是熟练的农民，他们制造了一系列工具，这些工具是种植和收割农作物所必需的。
fumigate ['fjuːmɪgeɪt]	*vt.* 烟熏，香薰（以灭虫或消毒） 记 词根记忆：fum（烟）+ ig（开动）+ ate → 烟熏 例 The Environmental Protection Agency recommended that the room should be *fumigated* with chlorine dioxide gas. 美国环境保护局建议应该用二氧化氯气体熏蒸该房间。
innovative ['ɪnəveɪtɪv]	*a.* 革新的，创新的（*novel）；富有革新精神的（inventive） 例 Another *innovative* use for cold ocean water is to cool buildings. 冷海水的另一种创新用途是给建筑物降温。// The art community is *innovative*. 这个艺术团体富有创新精神。 参 innovator（*n.* 创新者）

46

counter [ˈkaʊntər]	*ad.* 相反地 *a.* 相反的 *n.* 柜台；计数器 *v.* 反对，反击；抵制 记 来自 count(*v.* 计算) 搭 baggage counter 行李存放柜台 例 It may seem to run *counter* to common sense to say that introducing water into an area can cause it to become more like a desert. 往一个地区引水会导致该地更像沙漠，这话好像有违常理。// Sometimes when it really gets busy, I work at the check-out *counter*. 有时真忙起来，我就在收银台工作。 参 encounter(*n./v.* 相遇)
flag [flæg]	*n.* 旗帜(banner)；标记(sign) *v.* 标记 例 The black and white *flag* went down, and the race began. 黑白旗落下，比赛开始了。

flag

explosive [ɪkˈsploʊsɪv]	*a.* 爆炸(性)的，爆发(性)的；使人冲动的 *n.* 炸药 搭 explosive news 爆炸性新闻；explosive device 引爆装置；an explosive situation 一触即发的形势 例 The balloon was inflated with hydrogen and unbeknown to the pilot, potentially *explosive*. 这个气球充的是氢气，而飞行员不知道它有可能会爆炸。
pliable [ˈplaɪəbl]	*a.* 易弯曲的，柔韧的(flexible, supple)；易受影响的；顺从的 记 词根记忆：pli(=ply 弯，折) + able → 能弯曲的 → 易弯曲的，柔韧的 例 The sheet of plastic becomes very *pliable* when it is warmed. 塑料片加热后会变得非常柔韧。
recipe [ˈresəpi]	*n.* 食谱(cookbook)；方法，秘诀，诀窍(formula) 记 词根记忆：re + cip(拿，取) + e → 抓住关键 → 诀窍 例 His *recipe* for success is perseverance. 他成功的秘诀是坚持不懈。

Word List 47

音频

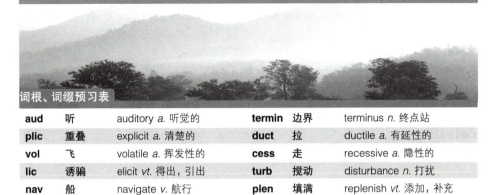

词根、词缀预习表

aud	听	auditory *a.* 听觉的	termin	边界	terminus *n.* 终点站
plic	重叠	explicit *a.* 清楚的	duct	拉	ductile *a.* 有延性的
vol	飞	volatile *a.* 挥发性的	cess	走	recessive *a.* 隐性的
lic	诱骗	elicit *vt.* 得出，引出	turb	搅动	disturbance *n.* 打扰
nav	船	navigate *v.* 航行	plen	填满	replenish *vt.* 添加，补充

---

precautionary
[prɪˈkɔːʃəneri]

a. 预防的
记 来自 precaution(*n.* 预防)
例 She was kept in the hospital overnight as a *precautionary* measure. 为谨慎起见，她被安排整夜留院观察。

---

compact
[kəmˈpækt]

a. 紧凑的；简洁的(concise) *vt.* 压缩(compress)
记 词根记忆：com(表加强) + pact(系紧) → 紧凑的
搭 the compact industrial city 工业密集型城市
例 Native plants in these areas are becoming more *compact*. 这些地区的本土植物变得更加密集。
参 impact(*n.* 碰撞；冲击)

---

sap
[sæp]

vt. 使衰竭(drain, exhaust)；削弱，逐渐破坏 *n.* 液，汁(fluid)；精力；笨蛋
例 Years of failure have *sapped* us out of confidence. 连年失败使得我们逐渐丧失了信心。

---

auditory
[ˈɔːdətɔːri]

a. 耳的；听觉的
记 词根记忆：aud(听) + it + ory(形容词后缀) → 听觉的
例 The car accident last year hurt the girl's *auditory* nerves. 去年的那场车祸使女孩的听觉神经受损了。

---

explicit
[ɪkˈsplɪsɪt]

a. 清楚的(clear)；直率的(direct)
记 词根记忆：ex(外) + plic(重叠) + it → 把重叠在一起向外展开 → 清楚的
例 The directions Jane gave me to get to her house were very *explicit*. 简十分清楚地向我指明了去她家的路。
参 implicit(*a.* 含蓄的)

---

lens [lenz]	*n.* 透镜；镜头；镜片 记 联想记忆：透镜(lens)借(lend)给你 例 Convex *lenses* can be used to concentrate the sun's rays. 凸透镜可用来聚焦太阳光。
volatile [ˈvɑːlətl]	*a.* 挥发性的，易挥发的；不稳定的(unstable)；反复无常的 记 词根记忆：vol(飞) + atile → 容易飞走的 → 挥发性的 例 These bacteria release *volatile* substances. 这些细菌会释放挥发性物质。 派 volatility(*n.* 挥发性)
celestial [səˈlestʃl]	*a.* 天空的，天上的(*astronomical, heavenly) 记 词根记忆：cel(天空) + est + ial → 天空的，天上的 例 Stars may be spheres, but not every *celestial* object is spherical. 星星可能是球体，但并非每个天体都是球形的。
behaviorism [bɪˈheɪvjərɪzəm]	*n.* 行为主义 例 Many people consider John Watson to be the founder of *behaviorism*. 很多人认为约翰·沃森是行为主义的创始人。
semester [sɪˈmestər]	*n.* 学期(term) 记 联想记忆：se(看做 see，看) + mester(看做 master，老师) → 在新学期又能看到老师了 → 学期 例 I have to attend five courses this *semester*. 这个学期我必须上五门课。
equator [ɪˈkweɪtər]	*n.* 赤道 记 词根记忆：equ(相等) + at + or → 将地球进行等分 → 赤道 例 Near the *equator* there is little distinction between summer, winter, autumn, or spring. 在赤道附近，一年四季区别甚微。
productive [prəˈdʌktɪv]	*a.* 生产(性)的；能产的，多产的；富有成效的 记 词根记忆：pro(向前) + duct(拉) + ive → 不断向前拉的 → 多产的 搭 expand productive forces 发展生产力；a productive writer 多产的作家；a productive meeting 卓有成效的会议 例 Health is important to me as a means to a *productive* life. 健康对我很重要，健康能让我的人生有所建树。 参 conductive(*a.* 传导的)
elicit [iˈlɪsɪt]	*vt.* 得出，引出(*bring out, educe)；诱出 记 词根记忆：e(出) + lic(诱骗) + it → 诱骗到外面来 → 得出，引出；诱出 例 Even questions that are less structured must be carefully phrased in order to *elicit* the type of information desired. 甚至设置得较差的问题都必须措辞严谨，以得到想要的信息类型。
newsletter [ˈnjuːzletər]	*n.* 时事通讯 记 组合词：news(消息，新闻) + letter(文字) → 传递消息的文字 → 时事通讯 例 The *newsletter* is published two times a month. 时事通讯一周发行两次。

salon [səˈlɑːn]	*n.* 营业性的厅(或院等);沙龙;客厅,会客厅 记 发音记忆:"沙龙" → 营业性的厅 搭 a hairdressing salon 美发厅;a literary salon 文化沙龙
afford [əˈfɔːrd]	*v.* 买得起,担负得起;冒险做;提供,给予(*provide, supply) 记 联想记忆:af + ford(看做 Ford,美国福特家族) → 财大气粗 → 买得起 例 Most landless farmers could not *afford* the necessary tools in that country. 在那个国家,大多数无地的农民买不起所需的工具。 派 affordable(*a.* 负担得起的)
magma [ˈmægmə]	*n.* 岩浆 例 All *magma* consists basically of a variety of silicate minerals. 所有的岩浆基本上都由各种硅酸盐矿物质构成。
utilize [ˈjuːtəlaɪz]	*vt.* 利用(make use of) 记 词根记忆:ut(用) + ilize → 利用 例 The body takes in and *utilizes* food substances. 身体吸收并利用食物。 派 utilization(*n.* 利用) utilize
hieroglyph [ˈhaɪərəglɪf]	*n.* 象形文字,象形符号 例 Scholars generally believe that Egyptian *hieroglyphs* came into existence a little after Sumerian script, and, probably were, invented under the influence of the latter. 学者们普遍认为,古埃及象形文字出现于苏美尔文字之后,而且很可能是在苏美尔文字的影响下产生的。 派 hieroglyphic(*a.* 象形文字的) hieroglyph
sporadic [spəˈrædɪk]	*a.* 偶发的,间或出现的,零星的 记 联想记忆:spor(看做 sport,体育) + ad(广告) + ic → 体育广告不定时出现 → 偶发的,间或出现的 例 *Sporadic* violence continued across the country, despite a large deployment of security forces by the government. 尽管该国政府部署了大量的安全部队,但暴力事件在全国境内仍时有发生。
Jupiter [ˈdʒuːpɪtər]	*n.* 木星 例 The world anxiously watched as a hurtling chunk of comet plunged into the atmosphere of *Jupiter*. 全世界忧虑地看着一颗疾飞的彗星落入木星的大气层。
qualify [ˈkwɑːlɪfaɪ]	*v.* (使)具有资格,(使)合格;(使)有权,限定,修饰 例 The man *qualified* as a dentist last month. 此人上个月获得了牙医资格。 派 qualification(*n.* 资格;限定条件);qualified(*a.* 有资格的,合格的)

授予你职业资格证书!

qualify

47

parameter [pəˈræmɪtər]	*n.* 参量，参数；界限，范围 记 词根记忆：para(旁边) + meter(测量) → 在一旁辅助测量 → 参量，参数 例 We must work within the ***parameters*** of budget and time this year. 我们今年必须在预算和时间规定的范围内工作。
contradict [ˌkɑːntrəˈdɪkt]	*v.* 反驳(refute)；同…矛盾，相抵触 记 词根记忆：contra(反) + dict(说话；断言) → 说反话 → 反驳 例 Newton's idea of gravity ***contradicted*** the idea of a universe that was static, unchanging. 牛顿的引力观与宇宙是静止不变的观点相抵触。 派 contradictory(*a.* 反驳的，反对的)
thaw [θɔː]	*v.* (使)融化，解冻(melt, defrost)；(使冷冻食品)化冻；(使)变暖；变得友善 *n.* 解冻时期；缓和 记 联想记忆：t + haw(看做 hoe，锄地) → 冰雪融化便可以锄地了 → (使)融化，解冻 例 Even when the ice ***thaws***, the stones do not return to their original positions. 甚至冰融化了，石头也不会回到原来的位置。
walnut [ˈwɔːlnʌt]	*n.* 胡桃；胡桃木 例 As a matter of fact there is a plaque identifying the black ***walnut*** as the tallest black ***walnut*** in the state. 事实上，有块牌匾说明这就是该州最高的黑胡桃木。 参 peanut(*n.* 花生)
square [skwer]	*n.* 正方形；广场(plaza)；平方 *a.* 正方形的(foursquare)；成直角的，方的；平方的 *vt.* 使成正方形；求平方；使打成平局 例 The hotel is just off the main ***square***. 旅馆就在主广场附近。 派 squarely(*ad.* 正对着地；明确无误地)
policy [ˈpɑːləsi]	*n.* 政策，方针；原则；保险单 记 联想记忆：警察(police)贯彻国家方针(policy) 搭 insurance policy 保险单 例 Honesty is the best ***policy***. 诚实为上。
obstruct [əbˈstrʌkt]	*vt.* 妨碍，阻挠；阻塞(impede, block) 记 词根记忆：ob(反) + struct(建造) → 反着建造 → 妨碍，阻挠 例 Skyscrapers and television reception ***obstruct*** air traffic. 摩天大楼和电视接收装置妨碍空中交通。 派 obstruction (*n.* 阻碍；障碍物); unobstructed (*a.* 畅通的)
loathsome [ˈloʊðsəm]	*a.* 令人厌恶的，讨厌的(repulsive) 例 There is a ***loathsome*** smell in the kitchen. 厨房里有一股令人作呕的气味。

loathsome

swing [swɪŋ]	*v.* (使)摆动, 摇荡; (使)突然转向, 突然转身(turn around) *n.* 摆动, 摇摆; 秋千 记 联想记忆: s + wing(翅膀) → 摆动翅膀, 在风中盘旋 → 摆动 搭 swing music 摇摆舞音乐 例 The signal it receives causes it to *swing* to the left. 接收到的信号使它向 左转。
molecule ['mɑːlɪkjuːl]	*n.* 分子 记 词根记忆: mol(颗粒) + e + cule(小的) → 小颗粒 → 分子 例 Most *molecules* are far too small to be seen with the naked eye, but there are exceptions. 大多数分子都很小, 肉眼不可见, 但也有例外。 派 molecular(*a.* 分子的; 分子组成的)
navigate ['nævɪgeɪt]	*v.* 航行, 横渡(海、河等); 导航; 设法完成 记 词根记忆: nav(船) + ig(开动) + ate(动词后缀) → 开动船只 → 航行 例 Researchers have found that migrating animals use a variety of inner compasses to help them *navigate*. 研究人员发现迁徙的动物通过各种体内 指南针来实现导航。 派 navigation(*n.* 航行; 导航); navigable(*a.* 可航行的; 适于航行的)
tangle ['tæŋgl]	*n.* 混乱(mess); 纠纷, 不和 *v.* (使)缠结, 纠结(*twist) 记 联想记忆: 两人缠结(tangle)在一起跳探戈(tango) 搭 tangle with sb. 与某人争吵 例 Her financial affairs are in a *tangle*. 她的财务状况一塌糊涂。
opposite ['ɑːpəzət]	*a.* 对面的; 对立的; 相反的(contrary) *n.* 对立面; 对立物 *prep.* 在…对面 例 She tried her best to calm him down but it seemed to be having the *opposite* effect. 她尽力想让他平静下来, 却似乎适得其反了。// The window is *opposite* the heater. 窗户对着加热器。 派 opposition(*n.* 反对; 对手)
far-fetched [fɑːrˈfetʃt]	*a.* 牵强的 例 Her excuse for being late sounds a bit *far-fetched* to me. 在我听来, 她 迟到的理由有点牵强。
senator ['senətər]	*n.* 参议员 记 来自 senate(*n.* 参议院) 例 He has served as a Democratic *senator* for the State of New York since 1998. 自 1998 年以来, 他一直是纽约州的民主党参议员。
anarchist ['ænərkɪst]	*n.* 无政府主义者 例 The man established an *anarchist* society in the region. 此人曾在该地 区建立了一个无政府主义社会。 派 anarchistic(*a.* 无政府主义的)
contributor [kənˈtrɪbjətər]	*n.* 投稿者; 贡献者; 捐助者; 促成物 例 Sulfur dioxide is a pollutant and a major *contributor* to acid rain. 二氧化 硫是一种污染物, 是酸雨形成的主要因素。

47

nitrogen [ˈnaɪtrədʒən]	*n.* 氮 记 词根记忆：nitro(硝酸) + gen(产生) → 产生硝酸 → 氮 搭 nitrogen dioxide 二氧化氮 例 *Nitrogen* composes 80 percent of the air we breathe. 我们呼吸的空气中 80% 为氮气。
terminus [ˈtɜːrmɪnəs]	*n.* (火车、汽车等的)终点站(terminal, end) 记 词根记忆：termin(边界) + us → 终点站 例 We arrived at the *terminus*. 我们到终点站了。
compromise [ˈkɑːmprəmaɪz]	*n./v.* 妥协，折中(yield) 记 联想记忆：com + promise(保证) → 相互保证 → 妥协，折中 例 The two parties made an effort to reach a *compromise*. 两党努力达成妥协。
eligible [ˈelɪdʒəbl]	*a.* 符合条件的，合格的(qualified)；适合的 记 词根记忆：e(出) + lig(=lect 选择) + ible(能…的) → 能被选出来的 → 符合条件的，合格的 例 Members of the Academy and Institute are not *eligible* for any cash prizes. 研究院的成员没有资格获得任何奖金。 派 ineligible(*a.* 不合格的)
specialize [ˈspeʃəlaɪz]	*v.* 专攻；(使)专用于 搭 specialize in 擅长于；专攻 例 The shop *specializes* in hand-made hats. 这家商店专营手工制作的帽子。 派 specialization(*n.* 专门化，特殊化)
accelerate [əkˈseləreɪt]	*v.* (使)加快，加速(*increase, quicken) 记 词根记忆：ac(表加强) + celer(快速的) + ate (使…) → (使)加快，加速 例 Exposure to the sun can *accelerate* the ageing process. 暴露在日光下会加快老化过程。 派 acceleration(*n.* 加速，加快；加速能力；加速度) 参 deceleration(*n.* 减速) accelerate
ductile [ˈdʌktaɪl]	*a.* 有延性的，韧性的(plastic)；易引导的，易受影响的 记 词根记忆：duct(拉) + ile → 易拉长的 → 有延性的，韧性的 搭 ductile metals 韧性金属 例 Another unusual feature of glass is the manner in which its viscosity changes as it turns from a cold substance into a hot, *ductile* liquid. 玻璃具有另一个不寻常的特性，那就是当其从冰冷的固态变成炽热的、易延展的液体时，其黏性会发生变化。
comparison [kəmˈpærɪsn]	*n.* 比较，对比；比拟，比喻 例 The professor mainly discussed a *comparison* of urban and rural life in the early twentieth century. 教授主要探讨了 20 世纪初城市与乡村生活的对比。// The *comparison* is quite appropriate. 这个比喻很恰当。

symphony [ˈsɪmfəni]	*n.* 交响乐，交响曲；(色彩等的)和谐，协调
	记 词根记忆：sym(共同) + phon(声音) + y → 奏出共同的声音 → 交响乐
	搭 symphony orchestra 交响乐团
	例 The orchestra played Beethoven's *Fifth Symphony*. 这个管弦乐团表演了贝多芬的《第五交响曲》。
	派 symphonic(*a.* 交响乐的)
plaster [ˈplæstər]	*n.* 灰浆，灰泥，石膏 *v.* 在…上抹灰泥，厚厚地涂
	记 联想记忆：plaste(看做 paste，粘贴) + r → 贴石膏 → 在…上抹灰泥
	例 These rough places on the wall could be *plastered* over. 可以在墙面的这些粗糙之处抹上灰泥。
dazzling [ˈdæzlɪŋ]	*a.* 令人眼花缭乱的，耀眼的
	记 来自 dazzle〔 *v.* (使)目眩，眼花〕
	例 Louis is playing the trumpet with *dazzling* originality. 路易斯在以令人眼花缭乱的技艺演奏小号。
compare [kəmˈper]	*v.* 比较，相比，对比
	记 词根记忆：com(共同) + par(相等) + e → 放在一起看是否相等 → 比较，相比，对比
	搭 compare with 与…比较，对照；compare to 比喻为，把…比做
	例 *Compared* with lunar space suits, Martian space suits will require smaller air tanks. 与登月太空服相比，火星太空服所需的气罐将更小。
anatomy [əˈnætəmi]	*n.* 解剖(学)(dissection)；解剖构造；剖析
	记 词根记忆：ana(分开) + tomy(切) → 切开 → 解剖(学)
	例 We will discuss other features of the Neanderthal *anatomy*. 我们将讨论穴居人解剖构造的其他特点。
	派 anatomical(*a.* 解剖的)
radiation [ˌreɪdiˈeɪʃn]	*n.* 放射；辐射；放射物，放射线；辐射的热(或能量等)
	记 词根记忆：radi(光线) + ation(名词后缀) → 射出光线 → 放射；辐射
	搭 solar radiation 太阳辐射；radiation therapy 放射疗法
	例 Because it spends a lot of time in the intense tropical sun, the grass mouse has also evolved two separate safeguards against the sun's ultraviolet *radiation*. 由于长时间待在强烈的热带阳光下，草鼠进化出了两套防止紫外线辐射的安全措施。
evaluate [ɪˈvæljueɪt]	*vt.* 评价，估计(assess, estimate)
	记 词根记忆：e(出) + val(价值) + uate → 给出价值 → 评价，估计
	例 What I expect you to do with your revision is to *evaluate* and improve the overall effectiveness of your paper. 我期望你修改时能客观评价并加强论文的整体效果。
	派 evaluation(*n.* 评估，评价)；evaluative(*a.* 可评估的)
recessive [rɪˈsesɪv]	*a.* 隐性的
	记 词根记忆：re(向后) + cess(走) + ive(形容词后缀) → 向后走的 → 隐性的
	例 A good manager could help improve the staff's *recessive* quality. 一个好的管理者可以帮助员工提高隐性素质。

47

□ symphony   □ plaster   □ dazzling   □ compare   □ anatomy   □ radiation
□ evaluate   □ recessive

scrutinize
['skru:tənaɪz]

v. 仔细检查，细察

记 词根记忆：scrut(检查) + in + ize(动词后缀) → 仔细检查，细察

例 The lawyer stayed up all night to *scrutinize* all the documents in order to find more proof. 律师熬通宵仔细检查了所有文件，以期找到更多证据。

:scrutinize

wan
[wæn]

a. 苍白的，无血色的；憔悴的

例 She gave me a *wan* smile. 她勉强向我一笑。

electrolysis
[ˌɪˌlek'trɑːləsɪs]

n. 电解作用；电解术

记 词根记忆：electro(电流) + lys(松开) + is → 用电来进行分解 → 电解作用

literary
['lɪtəreri]

a. 文学(上)的；文人的，书卷气的

记 词根记忆：liter(文字) + ary → 文字上的 → 文学(上)的

例 Mark Twain drew on his own experiences and used dialect and common speech instead of *literary* language. 马克·吐温从亲身经历取材，使用方言和日常用语进行写作，而不是使用文学语言。

参 literacy(*n.* 读写能力；有文化)；illiterate(*a.* 文盲的，缺乏教育的)

subconscious
[ˌsʌb'kɑːnʃəs]

n. 下意识，潜意识 *a.* 下意识的，潜意识的

记 联想记忆：sub(在…下面) + conscious(意识的) → 下意识的

搭 subconscious desires 下意识的欲望

例 Our *subconscious* takes control of much of our life. 我们的潜意识控制着我们生活中的很多东西。

needy
['niːdi]

a. 贫穷的，贫困的(poor)

记 联想记忆：need(需要) + y → 什么都需要 → 贫穷的

例 The two financially *needy* writers would receive enough money so they could devote themselves entirely to "prose literature". 两位经济拮据的作家会得到足够的资金，这样他们就能完全投入"散文"的创作中。

trauma
['trɑːmə]

n. 精神创伤；外伤；痛苦经历

记 发音记忆："筹码" → 老想着筹码和赌博，使精神受到损伤 → 精神创伤

例 We felt exhausted after the *traumas* of recent days. 经受了近日来的种种痛苦经历，我们都感到筋疲力尽。

cortex
['kɔːrteks]

n. 皮层，皮质

记 联想记忆：cor(共同) + tex(看做 text，编织) → 层层编织而成 → 皮层

搭 the cerebral cortex 大脑皮层

syndrome
['sɪndroʊm]

n. 综合征；典型表现

记 词根记忆：syn(共同) + drom(跑) + e → 疾病的症状同时发生 → 综合征

搭 This *syndrome* is associated with frequent coughing. 这种综合征与经常咳嗽有关。

wrench [rentʃ]	*v.* 扭伤；猛拉，猛扭；使痛苦 *n.* 扭伤；(离别的)痛苦，难受；扳手 记 发音记忆："润湿" → 地湿，很滑，扭伤脚 → 扭伤 例 He managed to *wrench* himself free. 他终于设法挣脱了出来。
amphibious [æmˈfɪbiəs]	*a.* 两栖的；水陆两用的 记 词根记忆：amphi(两的) + bio(生活，生命) + us → 以两种方式生存的 → 两栖的 例 Since the 1920s development of *amphibious* vehicles has greatly diversified. 自 20 世纪 20 年代以来，水陆两用车辆的发展大大多样化了。
carbohydrate [ˌkɑːrboʊˈhaɪdreɪt]	*n.* 碳水化合物 记 词根记忆：carbo(碳) + hydr(水) + ate → 碳水化合物
quench [kwentʃ]	*vt.* 扑灭，熄灭(extinguish, put out)；解(渴)(slake, satisfy one's thirst) 记 联想记忆：quen(看做 queen，女王) + ch → 扑灭女王的嚣张气焰 → 扑灭，熄灭 搭 quench a fire/flames 灭火 例 Mineral water is the best way to *quench* one's thirst. 喝矿泉水是解渴的最佳方式。 派 quenchable(*a.* 可熄灭的)；quenching(*n.* 淬火，熄灭)
degenerate	[dɪˈdʒenəreɪt] *vi.* 退化，衰退 [dɪˈdʒenərət] *a.* 堕落的；退化的 记 词根记忆：de(去掉) + gen(产生) + erate → 毁掉所产生的东西 → 退化 例 Her health *degenerated* quickly. 她的健康状况迅速恶化。
executive [ɪgˈzekjətɪv]	*n.* 执行者；管理人员；行政负责人 *a.* 执行的，实施的；行政的 搭 Chief Executive Officer 首席执行官；local business executive 本地商务主管 例 Kate, a former teacher, is now an *executive* for a charity. 凯特以前是个教师，现在是一个慈善团体的管理者。
trance [træns]	*n.* 恍惚；昏睡状态 例 The old man fell into a *trance*. 这个老人陷入了昏睡状态。
disturbance [dɪˈstɜːrbəns]	*n.* 打扰(interference)；骚动(stir)；心神不安，烦恼 记 词根记忆：dis(分开) + turb(搅动) + ance → 搅开 → 打扰 例 Noise, in the technical sense, implies a random chaotic *disturbance*. 从专业知识层面讲，噪音是指无序杂乱的干扰。
plankton [ˈplæŋktən]	*n.* 浮游生物 例 Most *planktons* have transparent tissues as a protective camouflage. 大多数浮游生物都有透明的组织作为保护性伪装。
instructor [ɪnˈstrʌktər]	*n.* 导师，(大学)讲师(teacher)；教练，指导员 例 Fred was asked to submit his term paper to the *instructor* in advance. 弗雷德被要求提前把学期论文交给导师。 参 coach(*n.* 教练)；tutor(*n.* 家庭教师)

47

lack [læk]	*n./vt.* 缺乏，不足(deficiency) 搭 lack of 缺乏，没有；lack (for) nothing 什么都不缺 例 Studies show that *lack* of patience has a serious impact on one's success. 研究显示缺乏耐心对一个人的成功有严重的影响。// It's the *lack* of moisture that causes the problem. 正是缺少水分导致了这个问题。 参 lake(*n.* 湖)
slice [slaɪs]	*n.* 薄片(flake)；部分，份额(segment) *vt.* 把⋯切成片 记 联想记忆：sl + ice(冰) → 把冰块切碎 → 把⋯切成片 例 Our company is well placed to grab a large *slice* of the market. 我们公司处境有利，足以获得巨大的市场份额。
career [kəˈrɪr]	*n.* 生涯，经历；职业(profession) 记 联想记忆：和同音词 Korea(*n.* 韩国)一起记 例 The *career* advisory service here on campus can help you prepare your cover letters. 校园里的职业咨询服务能帮助你准备求职信。 参 cancer(*n.* 癌症)
inconspicuous [ˌɪnkənˈspɪkjuəs]	*a.* 不引人瞩目的，不显眼的(unapparent) 例 It is said that the grand spectacle of a comet develops from a relatively small and *inconspicuous* chunk of ice and dust. 据说巨大壮观的彗星起初只是由较小而不起眼的冰和灰尘组成的块状物。
replenish [rɪˈplenɪʃ]	*vt.* 添加，补充(supplement) 记 词根记忆：re(再，又) + plen(填满) + ish → 添加，补充 例 The body needs to be *replenished* with nutrients in order to maintain a high level of energy throughout the day. 身体需要补充营养才能全天保持饱满的活力。
optimal [ˈɑːptɪməl]	*a.* 最佳的，最理想的(optimum) 记 词根记忆：optim(最好的) + al → 最佳的，最理想的 例 This is the *optimal* time for harvesting apples. 这是收获苹果的最佳时节。
fibrous [ˈfaɪbrəs]	*a.* 含纤维的；纤维状的 记 来自 fibre(*n.* 纤维) 搭 fibrous tissue 纤维组织 例 Collagen is a kind of *fibrous* protein that holds the body together. 胶原蛋白是一种纤维蛋白质，将人体各组织结合在一起。
buffalo [ˈbʌfəloʊ]	*n.* 水牛；(北美)野牛 例 The Native Americans followed the wounded *buffalo* until it fell dead. 这些印第安人紧追着这头受伤的水牛不放，直到它倒地死去。
hybrid [ˈhaɪbrɪd]	*a.* 杂交产生的；混合的，合成的 *n.* 杂交植物(或动物)；混合物，合成物 例 They suggest small low-emission cars for urban use and larger *hybrid* or lean-burn cars for use elsewhere. 他们建议在城市中使用低排量的小型车，而将那些较大的双动力汽车和稀燃车应用在其他地方。

willow ['wɪloʊ]	*n.* 柳，柳树；柳木制品 记 联想记忆：把枕头(pillow)晒在柳树(willow)上 例 The *willow* is a famous subject in many East Asian nations' cultures. 在东亚很多国家的文化里，柳树是一个著名的主题。 参 basketry(*n.* 篮筐，篓编织品；编制工艺)
induce [ɪn'djuːs]	*vt.* 引起，导致(*cause)；诱使，劝诱；感应 记 词根记忆：in(向内) + duc(拉) + e → 向内拉 → 引起，导致 例 The marine biologists could *induce* oysters to spawn not only in the summer but also in the fall. 海洋生物学家可以诱使牡蛎在夏、秋两季都产卵。 派 inducement(*n.* 劝诱；诱因); inducible(*a.* 可诱导的，可诱发的) 参 educe(*vt.* 得出，引出); deduce(*vt.* 推论)
rayon ['reɪɑːn]	*n.* 人造丝，人造纤维 例 Recommended care for regular *rayon* is dry-cleaning only. 常规人造丝在保养时推荐只用干洗。
scale [skeɪl]	*n.* 鳞；规模；比例(proportion)；刻度；【音】音阶；等级，级别 *vt.* 攀登(*climb) 记 词根记忆：scal(登，爬) + e → 攀登 搭 on a large scale 大规模地；in scale 成比例，相称 例 Even in this current era of large *scale*, the interrelationships involved in this process are frequently misunderstood. 甚至在目前这个大规模的时代，这个过程涉及的相互关系也常常被误解。// Foxes can't *scale* the sheer rocks. 狐狸不能攀上陡峭的岩石。

Education is a progressive discovery of our ignorance.
教育是一个逐步发现自己无知的过程。
——美国历史学家 杜兰特(Durant, American historian)

47

Word List 48

音频

词根、词缀预习表

cit	叫喊	recital *n.* 音乐演奏会	ceiv	拿，抓	deceive *v.* 欺骗
man	流	emanate *v.* 散发	spond	回答，约定	correspond *vi.* 相一致
pel	推	compel *vt.* 驱使	leg	送	delegate *n.* 代表
meter	测量	diameter *n.* 直径	isol	岛屿	isolate *vt.* 使隔离
flour	花	flourish *vi.* 繁荣	ple	填满	implement *vt.* 使生效

recital [rɪˈsaɪtl]	*n.* 音乐演奏会；诗歌朗诵会；赘述 记 词根记忆：re(再，又) + cit(叫喊) + al → 反复叫喊 → 音乐演奏会 例 The famous pianist will give a piano *recital*. 那位著名钢琴家将举办一场钢琴演奏会。 参 solo(*n.* 独唱)
flank [flæŋk]	*n.* 肋腹；侧面；(军队等的)侧翼 *vt.* 位于…的侧面 记 联想记忆：军队侧翼(flank)空着(blank)，没人守护，很危险 例 He left the courtroom *flanked* by armed guards. 她在武装警卫的护送下离开了法庭。
silt [sɪlt]	*n.* 淤泥(sullage) *v.* (用淤泥)阻塞 记 联想记忆：小心别坐上(sit)淤泥(silt) 例 The river delta was *silted* up by the sand. 这条河的三角洲被泥沙淤塞了。
ample [ˈæmpl]	*a.* 富足的，充足的，丰富的(abundant, enough)；宽敞的 记 联想记忆：市场上苹果(apple)很充足(ample) 例 The state of New Jersey offers *ample* opportunities for bicyclists of all abilities. 新泽西州给各种水平的骑自行车的人提供了大量的机会。 参 trample(*v.* 踩碎，践踏)；amble(*vi.* 缓行，漫步)
converse [kənˈvɜːrs]	*vi.* 交谈，会话(talk, discuss) *a.* 逆向的，相反的 *n.* 相反的事物；反面 记 词根记忆：con(共同) + vers(转) + e → 共同转换方向 → 交谈，会话 例 Pairs of deaf people are able to *converse* freely over television. 成对的听障人士能通过电视自由交谈。

patriot [ˈpeɪtrɪət]	*n.* 爱国者 记 词根记忆：patr(父亲，引申为"祖国") + iot → 把祖国当父亲看待的人 → 爱国者 例 He was a fervent *patriot*. 他是名热情的爱国者。 派 patriotic(*a.* 爱国的); patriotism(*n.* 爱国主义，爱国精神)
oak [oʊk]	*n.* 橡树，橡木 例 This deck is made of solid *oak*. 这块甲板是用实心橡木制作的。
emanate [ˈeməneɪt]	*v.* 散发(声音、气味、热等); 表现，显示 记 词根记忆：e(出，外) + man(流) + ate → 向外流 → 散发 搭 emanate form 起源于，发源于 例 Once the delicious smells *emanated* from the kitchen, I was the first one that rushed into the dining room. 一闻到从厨房里飘出的香味，我就第一个冲到了饭厅。
sparse [spɑːrs]	*a.* 稀疏的，稀少的(rare); 贫乏的 记 联想记忆：稀疏的(sparse)火花(spark) 例 The information available on this subject is *sparse*. 有关这个课题的资料匮乏。 派 sparsely(*ad.* 稀少地，稀疏地)
encrust [ɪnˈkrʌst]	*v.* (使)在表面形成硬壳，结壳; 用…装饰外层 记 联想记忆：en(使…) + crust(外壳) → 使有外壳 → (使)在表面形成硬壳 例 The crown was *encrusted* with diamonds. 王冠上镶满了钻石。
propagate [ˈprɑːpəɡeɪt]	*v.* 繁殖(raise, reproduce); 散布，传播(spread, disperse) 记 词根记忆：pro(向前) + pag(扎牢，系牢) + ate → 向前系牢 → 让自己的血统一代代地牢固下去 → 繁殖 例 Some tropical plants can only be *propagated* from seeds. 一些热带植物只能通过种子进行繁殖。
herbivore [ˈhɜːrbɪvɔːr]	*n.* 食草动物 记 词根记忆：herb(i)(草) + vor(吃) + e → 食草动物 例 *Herbivores* form an important link in the food chain. 食草动物是食物链中重要的一环。
floral [ˈflɔːrəl]	*a.* 花的，像花的; 饰以花的，绘有花的 记 词根记忆：flor(花) + al → 花的 例 He devoted much time to *floral* design in his study room, with the inspiration from a cartoon. 他花费了很多时间对书房进行花饰设计，创作灵感来源于一幅漫画。

48

track [træk]	*n.* 跑道；小路(path)；轨迹；足迹 *v.* 跟踪，追踪 🔖 联想记忆：原声大碟 Original Sound Track 📝 I have a lot of clocks because I have trouble keeping *track* of the time. 我有很多钟表，因为我老忘时间。 📌 trace(*n.* 痕迹，踪迹 *v.* 追踪)
sprain [spreɪn]	*n./vt.* 扭伤 🔖 联想记忆：sp + rain(雨)→雨天路滑，扭伤了脚→扭伤 📝 I stumbled and *sprained* my ankle. 我摔了一跤，把脚踝扭了。
constant ['kɑːnstənt]	*a.* 坚定的；稳定的(stable)；不变的，持续的(*consistent, continued, continuous) *n.* 常数，恒量 🔖 词根记忆：con（共同）+ stant（站立）→ 站在一起 → 坚定的；稳定的；不变的 🔍 constant temperature 恒温 📝 The tuition remained *constant* in the past five years. 学费在过去五年保持不变。 📌 instant(*a.* 立即的)
hoof [huːf]	*n.* (牛、马等的)蹄 🔖 发音记忆："舒服"→有蹄的动物走路很舒服→蹄 📝 There is a visible impression made by the *hoof* of an animal. 那儿有一个动物留下的蹄印清晰可见。
adopt [ə'dɑːpt]	*v.* 采用(assume)；收养，领养；正式通过，批准 🔖 词根记忆：ad + opt(选择)→采用 📝 Iron was rapidly *adopted* for the construction of bridges. 铁很快被用来建造桥梁。 🔧 adoption(*n.* 采用；收养)
sustainable [sə'steɪnəbl]	*a.* 不破坏生态平衡的，可持续的；足可支撑的；可忍受的 🔖 联想记忆：sustain(支持，支撑)+ able(能…的)→足可支撑的 📝 *Sustainable* development is to attain a perpetual balance between population, economic growth and the environment. 可持续发展就是要实现人口、经济增长和环境三者之间的持久平衡。
compel [kəm'pel]	*vt.* 驱使，强迫(drive) 🔖 词根记忆：com(共同)+ pel(推)→驱使，强迫 📝 Beads come in shapes, colors, and materials that almost *compel* one to handle them and to sort them. 珠子形状多样，色彩丰富，材质各不相同，驱使人们把玩挑选。 🔧 compelling(*a.* 引人注目的) 📌 dispel(*vt.* 驱散)；impel(*vt.* 推动)；repel(*vt.* 击退)；expel(*vt.* 驱逐；开除)

bound [baʊnd]	*a.* 被束缚的，有义务的（*obligated, enclose）*n.* [常 *pl.*]界限（*limit, boundary）；跳跃 *v.* 跳跃；弹回；形成…的界线，给…划界 例 Music was closely *bound* up with religious beliefs. 音乐与宗教信仰紧密相连。// Education knows no *bounds*. 教育无止境。 派 unbound(*a.* 未装订的；被释放的)
molecular [məˈlekjələr]	*a.* 分子的；摩尔的；由分子组成的 记 联想记忆：molecul(e)(分子) + ar → 分子的 例 The determination of *molecular* structure requires a multitude of experimental methods. 要通过很多实验性方法来确定分子结构。
diameter [daɪˈæmɪtər]	*n.* 直径 记 词根记忆：dia(穿过) + meter(测量) → 穿过圆的中心进行测量 → 直径 例 The tree trunk is one meter in *diameter*. 树干直径达一米。
linguistic [lɪŋˈgwɪstɪk]	*a.* 语言的，语言学的 记 词根记忆：lingu(语言) + istic → 语言的，语言学的 例 She was going to analyze the differences between the two distinct *linguistic* systems in the next class. 她将在下节课分析这两种显著不同的语言系统之间的差异。
rancher [ˈræntʃər]	*n.* 牧场主；大农场(或牧场)工人 例 Rodeos at agricultural fairs became so popular that *ranchers* and business people began to organize rodeos as independent events, separate from fairs. 农展会的牛仔竞技表演变得如此流行，以至于大农场主和商人们都开始组织与展会分开的独立竞技表演。
heyday [ˈheɪdeɪ]	*n.* 全盛期(climax) 记 组合词：hey(惊喜声) + day(日子) → 充满惊喜声的日子 → 全盛期 搭 in one's heyday 在…的全盛时期 例 In his *heyday*, David was a great movie director. 戴维在他的事业顶峰期是位了不起的电影导演。
bleach [bliːtʃ]	*n.* 漂白剂 *v.* (使)变白，漂白 例 His hair was *bleached* by the sun. 他的头发被太阳晒得发白。 参 beach(*n.* 海滩)；breach(*n.* 违背)
nap [næp]	*n.* 小睡，打盹(doze) 例 I have to take a *nap*; I am too tired. 我太累了，得小睡一下。
clog [klɑːg]	*v.* (使)堵塞，阻塞(congest, jam) *n.* 障碍 记 联想记忆：一段圆木(log)搁在路中间，使交通堵塞(clog) 例 The narrow streets were *clogged* with traffic. 狭窄的街道上交通堵塞。
sulfur [ˈsʌlfər]	*n.* 硫；硫黄 记 联想记忆：吸入过多的硫(sulfur)让人十分痛苦(suffer) 例 *Sulfur* is an essential element for all life, and is widely used in biochemical processes. 硫是所有生命必需的元素，并被广泛用于生化过程。 派 sulfuric(*a.* 硫的，含硫黄的)

48

□ bound □ molecular □ diameter □ linguistic □ rancher □ heyday
□ bleach □ nap □ clog □ sulfur

apprenticeship [əˈprentɪʃɪp]	*n.* 学徒的身份；学徒的年限 例 During their mid teens a number of young people leave home to serve as an *apprenticeship* in the factories. 许多年轻人在十五六岁时就离家去工厂当学徒。
prevailing [prɪˈveɪlɪŋ]	*a.* 普遍的（*most frequent, universal）；流行的（popular）；（指风）一地常刮的，盛行的 记 来自 prevail（*vi.* 流行，盛行） 例 The *prevailing* winds in the Great Basin are from the west. 大盆地的盛行风来自西边。
discipline [ˈdɪsəplɪn]	*vt.* 训练（drill）；惩罚（punish）*n.* 纪律；学科（subject） 记 联想记忆：dis(不) + cip + line(线) → 不站成一条线就要受惩罚 → 惩罚 例 They give orders and may *discipline* group members who inhibit attainment of the group's goals. 他们发号施令，还会处罚阻碍实现团队目标的成员。 派 disciplined（*a.* 受过训练的；遵守纪律的）
hop [hɑːp]	*v.* (人)单足跳行；(鸟等)齐足跳行；跳上(汽车、火车、飞机等) *n.* 蹦跳；(尤指乘飞机的)短程旅行 记 联想记忆：憋足气一下跳(hop)到顶部(top) 例 He *hopped* on the next bus. 他跳上了下一辆公交车。
subversive [səbˈvɜːrsɪv]	*a.* 颠覆性的，破坏性的 *n.* 颠覆分子 记 词根记忆：sub(在…下面) + vers(转) + ive(形容词后缀) → 在下面翻转的 → 颠覆性的 例 The *subversive* nature of Gluck's revisions of the classical myths is shown in the way she rewrites the myths. 格卢克对古典神话的改写所具有的颠覆性本质体现在她对这些神话改写的方式上。
grind [graɪnd]	*v.* 打磨（polish）；磨(碎)，碾(碎)（*crush）*n.* 磨碎，碾碎；苦差事 记 联想记忆：将一块大(grand)石头磨碎(grind) 搭 grind down sb. 虐待某人，欺压某人；grind out sth. 大量生产 例 The windmill has been used to pump water and *grind* grains. 磨坊被用来泵水和碾谷子。 派 grinder（*n.* 磨工）
objective [əbˈdʒektɪv]	*n.* 目标，目的（target, aim）*a.* 客观的 记 联想记忆：和 object（*n.* 目标）一起记 搭 achieve the objective 达到目的；objective reality 客观事实 例 Many people would not have been able to meet their *objectives* if not for government support. 要是没有政府支持，很多人根本不可能实现他们的目标。 派 objectivity（*n.* 客观性；客观现实） 参 subjective（*a.* 主观的）；optimistic（*a.* 乐观的）；neutral（*a.* 中立的）；critical（*a.* 批评的）；doubtful（*a.* 怀疑的）；approving（*a.* 赞成的）

flourish [ˈflɜːrɪʃ]	*vi.* 繁荣，茂盛（*thrive, boom）；挥舞，挥动 记 词根记忆：flour(=flor 花) + ish → 像花一样绽放 → 繁荣，茂盛 例 The art movement really *flourished* in the 1930s, during the depression years. 艺术运动在 20 世纪 30 年代的大萧条时期真正兴盛了起来。
peripheral [pəˈrɪfərəl]	*a.* 不重要的（unimportant）；外围的 记 词根记忆：peri(周围的) + pher(带来) + al → 外围的 搭 peripheral nerves 末梢神经 例 However, the dispute between the colonists and England was *peripheral*. 然而，殖民者和英国之间的争议并不重要。
bulletin [ˈbʊlɪtɪn]	*n.* 新闻简报；公告，布告；(机构或组织的)简报 记 联想记忆：bullet(子弹) + in → 新闻简报传播的速度如子弹 → 新闻简报 搭 bulletin board 公告牌；news bulletin 新闻 例 There is lots of information on the *bulletin* board. 公告牌上有很多信息。
plight [plaɪt]	*n.* 困境，苦境 记 联想记忆：p(音似：不) + light(轻松的) → 不轻松的处境 → 困境，苦境 例 Mark sympathized with Bill, who was in a horrible *plight*. 马克同情深陷于可怕困境的比尔。
stock [stɑːk]	*vt.* 储备，储存（store）*n.* 库存，现货；备用物；股份，股票（share）；世系，血统；家畜，牲畜 *a.* 常用的，常备的；老一套的，陈腐的 搭 stock market 股票市场；stock exchange 证券交易所；on the stock 在制作中；stock up 备货，囤积 例 The farmer *stocked* his ponds with fish. 这个农民在他的鱼塘里养了鱼。
disseminate [dɪˈsemɪneɪt]	*v.* 散布，传播（*spread） 记 词根记忆：dis(分开) + semin(种子) + ate → 把种子播种在不同的地方 → 散布，传播 例 The film *disseminated* an image of the good life in Southern California. 这部电影展现了南加州美好生活的景象。
crow [kroʊ]	*n.* 乌鸦 *v.* 啼叫，打鸣；(因成功而)得意洋洋 记 联想记忆：一只乌鸦(crow)停在牛(cow)背上 例 He cannot stop *crowing* about his victory. 他滔滔不绝地夸耀自己的胜利。
hawk [hɔːk]	*n.* 鹰，隼（eagle）；主战分子 *vt.* 叫卖，兜售 记 联想记忆：美国的两个党派：鹰派(Hawk)和鸽派(Dove) 例 The *hawk* swooped on its prey. 老鹰猛扑向猎物。
response [rɪˈspɑːns]	*n.* 回答；反应，响应 记 词根记忆：re(再，又) + spons(回答，约定) + e → 再次给出回答 → 回答；反应 例 The news provoked an angry *response*. 这条消息引起了人们的愤怒。 派 responsive(*a.* 响应的)
dismay [dɪsˈmeɪ]	*vt.* 使气馁，使沮丧（discourage, deject）；使诧异 *n.* 灰心，气馁；诧异 记 联想记忆：dis(不) + may(可能) → 不可能做到 → 使气馁 例 I was *dismayed* by the news in the paper. 报纸上的消息让我十分沮丧。

48

□ flourish   □ peripheral   □ bulletin   □ plight   □ stock   □ disseminate
□ crow   □ hawk   □ response   □ dismay

557

haunt [hɔːnt]	*vt.* (鬼魂等)出没于;(思想,回忆等)萦绕在心头;长期缠扰 *n.* 常去的地方 记 联想记忆:姑妈(aunt)常去的地方(haunt)是商店 例 People were *haunted* by the prospect that unprecedented change in the nation's economy would bring social chaos. 国民经济前所未有的变化将导致社会动乱的可能性萦绕在人们心头。
traditional [trəˈdɪʃənl]	*a.* 传统的,惯例的(conventional);口传的,传说的 搭 traditional view 传统观点 例 The elevation of Mount Everest was determined many years ago using *traditional* surveying methods. 珠穆朗玛峰的海拔是多年前使用传统勘测手段测定的。// I understand your troupe performs *traditional* music and dance from many different native American cultures. 我知道你的剧团可以表演源自美国不同土著文化的传统音乐和舞蹈。
protein [ˈprəʊtiːn]	*n.* 蛋白质 记 词根记忆:prot(首先) + ein → 维持生命最需要之物 → 蛋白质 例 Peas are a good source of vegetable *protein*. 豌豆是植物蛋白质的一个优质来源。
deceive [dɪˈsiːv]	*v.* 欺骗(trick) 记 词根记忆:de(分离) + ceiv(拿,抓) + e → 拿走 → 欺骗 例 Mary *deceived* the interviewer about her past experience. 玛丽就她过去的经历欺骗了面试官。 派 deceptive(*a.* 欺骗性的)
sprout [spraʊt]	*v.* 发芽,抽条,生长(grow);迅速出现,涌现出(flourish) *n.* 新芽,嫩枝,苗 记 联想记忆:spr(看做 spring,春天) + out(出) → 春天来了,柳树发芽了 → 发芽;新芽 例 Its seeds cannot *sprout* on their own. 这些种子不能自己发芽。
compass [ˈkʌmpəs]	*n.* 罗盘,罗盘仪;[*pl.*]圆规;范围(range, scope) 记 词根记忆:com(共同) + pass(脚步) → 共同通过脚步丈量,进行均分 → 范围 例 The television station broadcasts over a wide *compass*. 电视台播送节目的范围很广。
theory [ˈθɪəri]	*n.* 理论,原理;学说;见解,看法(notion) 记 词根记忆:the(看,考虑) + ory → 做事时要考虑、参考的东西 → 理论 搭 in theory 理论上;按理说 例 According to the *theory* of relativity, nothing can travel faster than light. 根据相对论,任何东西都无法超越光速。// It sounds great in *theory*; my concern is in practice. 这在理论上来说确实不错,但我担心的是实践问题。 派 theorize(*v.* 理论化,形成理论); theoretical(*a.* 理论的,理论上的)

atom [ˈætəm]	*n.* 原子；微粒，微量 例 Coal contains fewer hydrogen *atoms* than oil. 煤所含的氢原子比石油的要少。
luster [ˈlʌstər]	*n.* 光亮，光泽(gloss)；荣耀 记 词根记忆：lus(光) + ter → 光亮，光泽 例 Turquoise is opaque with a waxy *luster*, varying in color from greenish gray to sky blue. 绿宝石不透明，具有蜡质的光泽，颜色从绿灰到天蓝都有。
review [rɪˈvjuː]	*vt./n.* 审查；复习；回顾；评论(comment)；检阅 记 联想记忆：re(又，再) + view(看) → 又看一遍 → 复习；回顾 例 The woman needs to *review* the report again. 这个女子需要审查一下这份报告。 派 reviewer(*n.* 评论家；审查者)
correspond [ˌkɔːrəˈspɑːnd]	*vi.* 相一致，符合(accord)；相当于(match)；通信 记 词根记忆：cor(共同) + re(再，又) + spond(回答，约定) → 又给出相同的回答 → 相一致 例 The majority of films made after 1927 *corresponded* to specific musical compositions. 1927 年以后摄制的大部分影片都配有特定的音乐作品。 派 correspondence(*n.* 通信；相关，相似)；corresponding(*a.* 符合的；相应的，相当的)
hydrothermal [ˌhaɪdrəˈθɜːml]	*a.* 热液的 记 词根记忆：hydro(水) + therm(热) + al → 热液的 例 There are *hydrothermal* vents, which are small cracks on the sea floor. 那儿有热液排放口，也就是海床上的小裂缝。 参 thermal(*a.* 热的，热量的)
perceive [pərˈsiːv]	*vt.* 感知，察觉(see, observe)；理解 记 词根记忆：per(全部) + ceiv(拿住) + e → 全部拿住 → 感知，察觉 例 Art deco in its many forms was largely *perceived* as thoroughly modern. 很多形式的装饰艺术在很大程度上都被认为是完全现代的。 参 perceptive(*a.* 感知的)
strand [strænd]	*n.* (线等的)股，缕；部分，方面 *vt.* 使滞留；使搁浅 记 联想记忆：只有一股(strand)绳是站(stand)不起来的 搭 strand wire 绞合线，绳索 例 The strike left hundreds of tourists *stranded* at the airport. 这场罢工使成百上千的游客滞留在机场。
alternative [ɔːlˈtɜːrnətɪv]	*n.* 可供选择的事物(*option)；选择的自由，选择的余地 *a.* 可供替代的；非传统的 搭 alternative energy 替代能源 例 So far the electric car seems to be the best *alternative*. 到目前为止，电动车好像是最好的替代品。

alternative

erupt [ɪˈrʌpt]	*v.* 突然发生，爆发(burst out)；(岩浆等)喷出 记 词根记忆：e(出) + rupt(断) → 断裂后喷出 → 爆发 例 Kilauea is one of the world's most active volcanoes, having *erupted* dozens of times since 1952. 基拉韦厄火山是世界上最活跃的火山之一，自1952 年以来已爆发过几十次。 派 eruption(*n.* 火山爆发，喷发)
chlorine [ˈklɔːriːn]	*n.* 氯 派 chlorinate(*vt.* 加氯消毒) 参 chloride(*n.* 氯化物)
scrape [skreɪp]	*v.* 刮掉，擦掉（rub, brush）；（使）发出刺耳的刮擦声；勉强获得 *n.* 擦痕（abrasion）；刮，擦；刮擦声 搭 scrape off 擦去；scrape by/along (on…)（靠…）艰难度日 例 They *scraped* a living by playing music on the streets. 他们靠在街头演奏音乐勉强维持生活。 派 scraping(*n.* 刮削下的碎屑)
conceive [kənˈsiːv]	*v.* 构思，构想，设想(design, imagine)；怀孕 记 词根记忆：con(共同) + ceiv(抓) + e → 一起抓住(思想) → 构思，构想，设想 例 Gertrude had *conceived* it as a part of her mission. 格特鲁德认为这是她使命的一部分。 // Mercy Warren *conceived* her plan to write a history of the American Revolution. 默西•沃伦构想了撰写美国革命历史的计划。 参 deceive(*v.* 欺骗)；perceive(*vt.* 感知，察觉)
delegate	[ˈdelɪɡət] *n.* 代表(representative) [ˈdelɪɡeɪt] *vt.* 委派…为代表，授权(authorize) 记 词根记忆：de(分离) + leg(送) + ate → 外派出去 → 代表 例 The town elected two *delegates* to attend the conference. 这个城镇选了两名代表参加会议。 // John *delegated* the job of mowing the lawn to his daughter. 约翰把割草的工作交给了他女儿。
process [ˈprɑːses]	*vt.* 加工，处理(dispose) *n.* 过程(*circle)；程序，手续(procedure)；工序，制作法 记 词根记忆：pro（向前）+ cess（走）→ 向前走 → 过程 例 The women used their tools to *process* all of the fish and marine mammals brought in by the men. 女人用她们的工具加工男人带回来的所有的鱼和海洋哺乳动物。 派 processing(*n.* 处理)
corps [kɔːr]	*n.* 军团，兵团；特种部队；(从事某工作或活动的)一群人，一组人 记 词根记忆：corp(身体) + s → 团队 → 军团，兵团 例 A *corps* of trained and experienced doctors had been sent into the flood-striken area. 一队训练有素且经验丰富的医生被派往了受洪水袭击的地区。

isolate [ˈaɪsəleɪt]	*vt.* 使隔离，使孤立（separate） 记 词根记忆：isol(=insul 岛屿) + ate(使…) → 使成为孤岛 → 使隔离，使孤立 搭 isolate from 与…隔离 例 Studies show that non-readers tend to *isolate* themselves from the community. 研究表明不会阅读的人倾向于把自己从社会中隔离开来。 派 isolated(*a.* 隔离的，孤立的)
anecdotal [ˌænɪkˈdoʊtl]	*a.* 轶话的，逸闻趣事的 记 来自 anecdote(*n.* 趣闻，轶事) 例 The scholar's findings are based on *anecdotal* evidences rather than formal researches. 这个学者的发现是基于轶事类证据，而非正式的研究。
emit [iˈmɪt]	*vt.* 发出(*give off, *produce)；放射(radiate)；排放 记 词根记忆：e(出，外) + mit(放) → 发出；放射；排放 例 The plants react by *emitting* a chemical signal, which acts like a call for help. 植物们的反应是发出化学信号，就像发出求助一样。 龟派气功 emit
capability [ˌkeɪpəˈbɪləti]	*n.* 能力(ability, potentiality)；性能；容量；潜质 记 词根记忆：cap(拿住) + abil(=able 能…的) + ity(名词后缀) → 有能力拿住 → 能力 例 The limited mining *capability* made iron very expensive. 有限的矿产容量致使铁非常昂贵。
diction [ˈdɪkʃn]	*n.* 措辞，用语(expression) 记 词根记忆：dict(说话) + ion → 措辞，用语 例 To practice *diction* by oneself is useful. 自己练习措辞十分有用。 参 dictation(*n.* 听写)
opaque [oʊˈpeɪk]	*a.* 不透明的，不透光的(impenetrable)；难懂的，晦涩的 记 词根记忆：opa(不透明) + que → 不透明的，不透光的 搭 an opaque finish 一种绝光的涂料 例 Quartz may be transparent, translucent, or *opaque*. 石英可以是透明的、半透明的或不透明的。
tow [toʊ]	*vt./n.* 拖，牵引(pull) 记 联想记忆：拉(tow)弓(bow)射箭 例 Could you please give me a *tow*? 你能拉我一把吗？ tow
imply [ɪmˈplaɪ]	*vt.* 意味着，暗示(suggest)；说明，表明；使有必要 记 词根记忆：im(在…里面) + ply(重叠) → 在里面重叠 → 暗示 例 The project *implies* an enormous investment in training. 这个项目需要在培训方面做巨大的投资。

48

glaze [gleɪz]	*n.* 釉料；糖浆 *v.* 上釉(gloss)；给…装玻璃 记 联想记忆：师傅给陶器上釉(glaze)的时候，双眼盯着(gaze)陶器，生怕出错 例 It was created by adding a brown *glaze* to the fired clay. 这是通过给烧制好的黏土上褐色的釉而制成的。 派 glazing(*n.* 上釉)；glazed(*a.* 上过釉的；木然的)
organic [ɔːˈgænɪk]	*a.* 有机的；器官的；有机体的 搭 organic chemistry 有机化学；organic being 有机体 例 Improve the soil by adding *organic* matter. 通过加入有机物来改良土壤。 参 organism(*n.* 生物，有机体；有机组织)
ailment [ˈeɪlmənt]	*n.* 小病(sickness, illness) 记 词根记忆：ail(痛苦) + ment(名词后缀) → 小病 例 Thanks to the medical reforms, the poor man got timely treatment for his *ailment*. 多亏了医疗改革，这个穷人的疾病得到了及时的医治。
camouflage [ˈkæməflɑːʒ]	*n./vt.* 掩饰，伪装(hide, disguise) 例 Mammals rarely use this type of *camouflage*, but many fish and invertebrates do. 哺乳动物很少使用这种伪装，但是很多鱼和无脊椎动物会用。
implement [ˈɪmplɪment]	[ˈɪmplɪment] *vt.* 使生效，执行，实施(carry out) [ˈɪmplɪmənt] *n.* [常*pl.*]工具，器具(*tool) 记 词根记忆：im(在…里面) + ple(填满) + ment → 在里面填满 → 使生效，执行，实施 例 It took the company a year to *implement* the plan. 公司用了一年时间来实施这个计划。// They began using improved *implements*. 他们开始使用改良的工具。 派 implementation(*n.* 执行)
unadorned [ˌʌnəˈdɔːnd]	*a.* 未装饰的，朴实的(plain, unembellished) 例 The works written by the female poet are all *unadorned* and simple. 这位女诗人的作品朴实而简练。
resource [ˈriːsɔːrs]	*n.* [常*pl.*]资源，财力；资料；谋略 记 联想记忆：re(一再) + source(源泉) → 可一再使用的源泉 → 资源 例 The freedom from foreign invasion enables a country to develop its natural *resources* steadily. 不受外来侵略可以使一国的自然资源得到稳定的开发。 派 resourceful(*a.* 足智多谋的，机敏的) 参 source(*n.* 来源，源头)；sauce(*n.* 酱油)；saucer(*n.* 茶托)；recourse(*n.* 求援)
curve [kɜːrv]	*v.* 弄弯，成曲线形(bend) *n.* 曲线；曲线图；弯曲 记 联想记忆：在雕刻(carve)时，曲线(curve)很难处理 例 The ballerina *curves* her arms above her head. 芭蕾舞女演员把胳膊弯到头顶。

twinkling [ˈtwɪŋklɪŋ]	*n.* 瞬间，一眨眼 *a.* 闪光的
	例 Opportunities appear unexpectedly, and disappear in the *twinkling* of an eye. 机会不期然地出现，而后转瞬即逝。
hominid [ˈhɑːmɪnɪd]	*n.* 原始人类；人科动物 *a.* 灵长目的
	记 词根记忆：homi(=hom 人) + nid → 原始人类；人科动物
	例 His study involves the dietary habits of *hominids*. 他的研究涉及原始人类的饮食习惯。

Experience is a hard teacher because she gives the test first, the lesson afterwards.

经验是一位先行测试然后才授课严厉的教师。

——英国作家 弗农 .L.(Law Vernon, British writer)

索　引

careless / 298
cargo / 173
caribou / 222
carnivore / 204
cart / 30
cartilage / 410
carve / 220
cascade / 463
cascara / 105
cashier / 162
cassette / 539
cast / 224
casual / 135
casualty / 51
catalog / 477
catalyst / 340
catastrophe / 443
categorize / 431
category / 295
cater / 223
caterpillar / 98
catholic / 62
causal / 110
cautious / 351
cavern / 286
cavity / 370
cease / 246
celebrate / 59
celestial / 542
cell / 34
cellist / 103
cement / 302
censor / 280
census / 334
centennial / 298
centigrade / 251
centric / 219
ceramic / 338
cereal / 171
cerebral / 537
ceremonial / 150
ceremony / 182
certificate / 106
certitude / 15
chafe / 272
chagrin / 451
chain / 420
challenge / 163
chamber / 285
champion / 128

championship / 177
chance / 490
channel / 369
chant / 157
chaos / 124
chaotic / 4
chapel / 96
characteristic / 190
characterize / 348
charcoal / 97
charisma / 74
charismatic / 378
chart / 315
charter / 336
chaste / 145
check / 27
checked / 535
cherish / 88
chew / 481
chief / 454
chill / 447
chilly / 143
chimpanzee / 450
chip / 134
chivalrous / 460
chlorine / 560
choir / 332
cholesterol / 502
choppy / 285
choreograph / 339
chorus / 244
chromosome / 191
chronical / 438
chronicle / 200
chronological / 344
chubby / 523
chunk / 266
cider / 76
cipher / 146
circuit / 193
circular / 41
circulate / 389
circumference / 522
circumstance / 188
citadel / 291
cite / 90
civil / 230
claim / 218
clam / 113
clamor / 418

clan / 380
clarify / 298
clasp / 226
classic / 25
classical / 407
classify / 457
clay / 274
clench / 445
client / 141
cliff / 288
climate / 434
cling / 306
clinic / 398
clip / 226
clipper / 43
clog / 555
clone / 252
closet / 398
clue / 536
clump / 392
clumsy / 426
cluster / 453
clutch / 335
coalition / 495
coarse / 341
code / 133
codify / 522
coefficient / 313
coexist / 464
cognition / 103
cognitive / 178
cohabitation / 379
cohere / 366
coherent / 173
cohesion / 228
cohesive / 74
coil / 466
coincide / 220
collaborate / 254
collaborative / 256
collaborator / 400
collapse / 339
colleague / 305
collective / 509
collide / 525
collision / 375
colonial / 180
colonization / 4
colonize / 267
colony / 240

column / 18
combat / 525
combination / 505
combine / 21
combustible / 207
comedy / 436
comet / 78
comic / 182
command / 46
commemorate / 183
comment / 274
commentary / 80
commerce / 206
commission / 102
commit / 520
committee / 111
commodity / 395
commonplace / 229
communal / 83
commune / 433
communicate / 398
community / 40
commute / 221
compact / 541
companion / 406
comparable / 488
comparative / 483
compare / 547
comparison / 546
compass / 558
compatible / 263
compel / 554
compensate / 71
compensation / 321
competence / 83
compile / 66
complacence / 488
complain / 241
complaint / 88
complement / 310
complementary / 184
completion / 325
complex / 85
complicated / 401
compliment / 25
comply / 57
component / 169
compose / 487
composer / 514
compound / 64

diminish / 275
diminution / 111
dinosaur / 524
dioxide / 295
diplomat / 87
diplomatic / 477
directory / 415
disadvantage / 267
disappoint / 41
disarm / 499
disaster / 432
disastrous / 88
discard / 86
discern / 462
discharge / 6
disciple / 317
discipline / 556
disclose / 132
disconcert / 74
discord / 180
discount / 484
discourage / 119
discourse / 252
discredit / 145
discrete / 411
discriminate / 16
disease / 501
disguise / 50
disgust / 118
disintegrate / 122
disinterest / 144
disinterested / 325
dismal / 522
dismay / 557
dismiss / 255
disorder / 139
disparate / 356
dispatch / 257
dispel / 192
dispersal / 521
disperse / 378
displace / 151
display / 137
disposal / 493
dispose / 530
disproportionate / 3
disprove / 268
dispute / 519
disquiet / 28
disrepute / 232

disrupt / 112
disseminate / 557
dissent / 413
dissenter / 68
dissimulate / 430
dissipate / 52
dissolute / 133
dissolve / 278
dissuade / 179
distant / 284
distasteful / 417
distinct / 508
distinctive / 476
distinguish / 422
distort / 519
distract / 91
distress / 454
distribute / 77
district / 362
disturb / 262
disturbance / 549
dive / 27
diverge / 51
diverse / 299
diversify / 344
diversion / 58
diversity / 99
divert / 359
dividend / 313
divine / 366
division / 151
divorce / 294
doctrine / 217
documentary / 368
documentation / 536
dogged / 333
dolphin / 232
domain / 349
domestic / 197
domesticate / 532
domicile / 227
dominant / 503
dominate / 42
donate / 484
doodle / 110
dormancy / 199
dormant / 90
dormitory / 507
dorsal / 402
dosage / 537

dot / 481
dote / 391
downside / 428
downtown / 64
downward / 55
dozen / 236
draft / 137
drag / 485
dragonfly / 385
drain / 476
dramatic / 516
dramatize / 16
drastic / 92
draw / 429
drawback / 359
drench / 286
drift / 482
drill / 224
drought / 114
drowsy / 480
dual / 166
dubious / 93
ductile / 546
due / 10
dull / 117
dump / 177
dupe / 166
duplicate / 451
durable / 46
dwarf / 25
dwindle / 227
dye / 141
dynamical / 302
eager / 185
earnest / 501
ease / 92
Easter / 511
eccentric / 287
eclecticism / 68
eclipse / 46
ecological / 151
ecology / 184
economic / 535
economical / 421
ecosystem / 219
edge / 125
edible / 485
edifice / 205
editorial / 311
educated / 481

effective / 159
efficiency / 79
efficient / 188
effluent / 297
eject / 531
elaborate / 478
elapse / 431
elasticity / 38
elective / 70
electricity / 8
electrode / 503
electrolysis / 548
electron / 10
elegant / 204
element / 251
elementary / 361
elevate / 358
elicit / 542
eligible / 546
eliminate / 393
elite / 120
ellipse / 313
elliptical / 422
elm / 250
elongate / 254
eloquent / 371
elusive / 388
emanate / 553
emancipate / 154
embargo / 409
embark / 227
embarrass / 421
embed / 200
embellish / 51
emblem / 131
embody / 69
embrace / 4
embryo / 318
emerald / 354
emerge / 91
emergent / 101
emigrate / 453
eminent / 531
emission / 115
emit / 561
emotion / 115
emotional / 84
emphasize / 223
empiricism / 89
employ / 466

570

empower / 515
empress / 516
enact / 515
enactment / 362
encase / 428
enclose / 240
encompass / 450
encounter / 55
encourage / 329
encroach / 389
encrust / 553
endanger / 134
endangered / 517
endeavor / 440
endless / 300
endorse / 330
endow / 487
endure / 58
energetic / 180
enforce / 420
engage / 11
engaging / 512
engineering / 127
engrave / 16
engraving / 360
engulf / 10
enhance / 143
enlighten / 256
enlightenment / 476
enlist / 513
enormous / 107
enrich / 494
enroll / 496
enrollment / 165
ensconce / 191
enslave / 458
ensue / 202
ensure / 63
entail / 342
enterprise / 123
entertain / 290
enthusiasm / 129
enthusiastic / 192
entitle / 31
entity / 302
entourage / 201
entreat / 444
entrench / 191
entrepreneur / 352
enunciate / 459

envelop / 50
envelope / 262
environmental / 433
envision / 490
enzyme / 274
ephemeral / 449
epic / 477
epidemic / 136
episode / 222
epitome / 452
epitomize / 475
epoch / 374
equal / 132
equation / 508
equator / 542
equitable / 45
equivalent / 43
era / 224
eradicate / 202
erect / 434
erode / 326
erosion / 156
errand / 393
erratic / 524
erupt / 560
eschew / 354
espouse / 431
essay / 519
essence / 1
essential / 284
establish / 479
estate / 278
esteem / 192
estimate / 79
eternal / 35
ethic / 127
ethical / 21
ethnic / 139
ethnology / 103
etiquette / 144
evacuate / 144
evacuation / 140
evade / 366
evaluate / 547
evaporate / 495
evaporation / 487
even / 188
evergreen / 277
evidence / 394
eviscerate / 160

evoke / 492
evolution / 303
evolve / 56
exact / 424
exaggerate / 454
exalt / 65
exalted / 112
excavate / 238
excavation / 326
exceed / 77
exception / 175
excess / 178
exchange / 184
excise / 538
exclaim / 413
exclude / 187
exclusive / 16
excursion / 104
execute / 468
executive / 549
exemplary / 59
exemplify / 357
exempt / 305
exert / 465
exhale / 57
exhaust / 511
exhibit / 317
exhilarating / 124
exhort / 356
existence / 469
exodus / 64
exorbitant / 180
exotic / 347
expand / 247
expansion / 148
expect / 14
expedient / 430
expedition / 204
expeditious / 357
expel / 10
expenditure / 226
experimental / 157
expertise / 37
expire / 275
explicit / 541
explode / 483
exploit / 392
explore / 30
explosion / 96
explosive / 540

exponent / 432
expose / 123
exposition / 5
exposure / 142
expressive / 301
expropriate / 515
extend / 177
extension / 337
extensive / 344
extent / 457
exterior / 371
external / 435
externality / 331
extinct / 35
extinguish / 391
extol / 489
extort / 180
extract / 182
extraordinary / 535
extrapolate / 314
extravagant / 474
extreme / 358
extremity / 211
extrinsic / 267
fable / 87
fabric / 520
fabricate / 124
fabulous / 193
façade / 369
facet / 149
facial / 476
facilitate / 8
facility / 265
faction / 515
factor / 312
factual / 407
faculty / 446
fade / 67
Fahrenheit / 327
faint / 136
fake / 15
falcon / 184
falter / 89
familiarize / 385
famish / 227
fantastic / 177
fantasy / 50
farce / 518
fare / 281
far-fetched / 545

gloss / 75
glossy / 161
glow / 289
glue / 106
gnaw / 384
gorge / 261
gorgeous / 303
gorilla / 80
gospel / 404
gossip / 237
Gothic / 282
gouge / 100
gourd / 467
gourmet / 416
govern / 417
grab / 370
gradient / 450
grading / 175
gradual / 425
grain / 350
granite / 194
grant / 126
granular / 290
graph / 396
graphics / 388
graphite / 329
grasp / 290
grasshopper / 368
gratify / 389
gravel / 273
gravitational / 59
gravity / 38
graze / 154
grazing / 439
gregarious / 272
grid / 212
grievous / 3
grill / 121
grimly / 316
grind / 556
grip / 85
groan / 404
grocery / 439
groom / 45
groove / 452
gross / 125
grouse / 430
grovel / 451
grudge / 184

grump / 237
guarantee / 514
guideline / 113
guilty / 271
gulf / 293
gull / 337
gush / 63
gymnasium / 493
habit / 69
habitat / 481
hail / 255
haircut / 403
halt / 127
hammer / 334
hamper / 297
handful / 443
handle / 442
handy / 318
haphazard / 460
harbor / 397
hardly / 251
hardware / 171
hardy / 370
harmonic / 268
harmonious / 452
harmony / 467
harness / 198
harsh / 523
haste / 489
hatch / 291
haul / 448
haunt / 558
haven / 482
havoc / 143
hawk / 557
hay / 18
hazard / 524
hazel / 188
heading / 81
healing / 92
healthful / 26
hearsay / 390
hedge / 355
heed / 460
hemisphere / 420
hemp / 21
henceforth / 447
herald / 71
herb / 73

herbivore / 553
herd / 396
hereditary / 537
heritage / 370
hesitant / 378
heyday / 555
hibernation / 501
hide / 33
hierarchy / 90
hieratic / 370
hieroglyph / 543
highlight / 67
hike / 405
hind / 431
hinder / 455
hint / 446
hinterland / 349
hitch / 237
hitherto / 78
hive / 263
hoard / 234
hockey / 495
hoe / 66
holistic / 538
hollow / 416
homage / 16
homestead / 19
homing / 22
hominid / 563
homogeneous / 124
homosexuality / 356
hoof / 554
hook / 249
hop / 556
horde / 393
horizon / 397
horizontal / 324
hormone / 495
horn / 151
hospitable / 534
hostile / 306
household / 438
hover / 275
huddle / 468
hue / 442
hull / 238
humanitarian / 461
humanity / 170
humble / 408

humid / 183
humidity / 229
hummingbird / 277
humorous / 90
hurl / 527
hurricane / 289
hurry / 523
husbandry / 38
husk / 2
hustle / 15
hybrid / 550
hydraulic / 303
hydrogen / 59
hydrothermal / 559
hygiene / 162
hypertext / 212
hypocritical / 212
hypothesis / 424
hypothesize / 196
hypothetical / 259
iceberg / 180
idealize / 8
identical / 498
identification / 98
identify / 54
identity / 11
ideology / 47
ideomotor / 500
idiom / 219
idle / 468
idyllic / 475
igneous / 20
ignite / 356
ignorant / 115
ignore / 73
illegible / 480
illuminate / 434
illusion / 437
illusory / 452
illustrate / 355
illustrative / 259
image / 293
imaginary / 228
imaginative / 3
imagist / 254
imbibe / 134
imitate / 392
imitation / 66
immature / 306

immediate / 504
immense / 276
immerse / 453
immigrant / 489
immigrate / 378
immune / 219
immunity / 183
immutable / 350
impact / 271
impair / 326
impart / 351
impede / 134
impel / 201
impending / 259
impenetrable / 452
imperative / 338
imperial / 516
impermeable / 174
impersonal / 497
impetus / 80
implement / 562
implication / 177
implicit / 250
implore / 154
imply / 561
import / 330
impose / 304
imprecise / 296
impressive / 324
imprint / 56
improve / 449
improvise / 109
impulse / 246
inaccessible / 427
inactivate / 483
inactive / 461
inanimate / 57
inanity / 181
inaugurate / 514
incapacitate / 258
incense / 230
incentive / 46
inception / 207
incessant / 433
incessantly / 41
incident / 499
incidental / 52
incinerate / 130
inclination / 61

incline / 3
incoming / 441
incompatible / 123
incongruity / 210
inconspicuous / 550
inconvenient / 122
incorporate / 258
incredible / 450
incredulous / 75
increment / 153
incubate / 81
incur / 39
incursion / 147
indecipherable / 212
independent / 443
indicate / 185
indict / 519
indifference / 476
indigenous / 459
indigent / 237
indigestion / 405
indignant / 119
indispensable / 490
individual / 478
indolent / 132
induce / 551
induct / 74
industry / 519
inert / 508
inertia / 311
inevitably / 132
infancy / 21
infant / 433
infatuate / 16
infection / 265
infectious / 455
inferior / 173
infest / 242
infiltrate / 312
infirm / 538
inflammation / 23
inflate / 243
inflation / 106
influential / 469
influenza / 269
influx / 9
inform / 458
informant / 93
informative / 182

informed / 104
infrared / 448
infrastructure / 360
infuriate / 51
ingenious / 357
ingredient / 23
inhabit / 44
inherent / 325
inherit / 347
inheritance / 419
inhibit / 176
initial / 198
initiate / 470
inject / 248
injurious / 515
innate / 328
inner / 20
innocent / 12
innovate / 211
innovative / 539
inquire / 314
insanity / 116
inscribe / 55
insect / 416
insert / 268
insight / 86
insist / 161
insistence / 504
insolvent / 331
inspect / 325
inspire / 103
install / 195
instance / 439
instantaneous / 378
instead / 276
instill / 63
instinct / 500
instinctual / 14
institute / 420
instruct / 80
instruction / 455
instructor / 549
instrument / 501
insufficient / 174
insulate / 215
insulin / 30
insult / 416
insurance / 535
intact / 226

integral / 319
integrate / 488
integrity / 297
intellect / 114
intelligence / 42
intelligent / 247
intelligible / 444
intense / 189
intent / 463
intentionally / 160
interact / 289
interactive / 74
interest / 177
interface / 213
interfere / 346
interim / 39
interior / 13
intermediate / 134
intern / 260
internal / 448
internship / 33
interplay / 463
interpret / 133
interrelate / 29
interrogate / 516
interrupt / 506
intersection / 462
interstellar / 333
interval / 353
intervening / 53
interweave / 168
intimate / 523
intoxication / 239
intrepid / 7
intricate / 22
intrigue / 28
intriguing / 81
intrinsic / 501
introduction / 395
intrude / 130
intrusion / 174
intuitive / 225
invade / 402
invalid / 537
invasion / 275
invasive / 100
inventory / 505
inverse / 29
invert / 472

invertebrate / 509
investigate / 464
invitation / 408
inviting / 70
involve / 223
ironic / 438
irony / 426
irregular / 165
irresistible / 135
irreverent / 521
irrigate / 398
irritable / 528
irritate / 52
isolate / 561
issue / 8
item / 85
ivory / 342
jar / 297
jaw / 440
jeans / 535
jelly / 189
jeopardize / 56
jewelry / 335
jog / 322
joint / 136
jolt / 78
jot / 47
journal / 229
journalism / 104
juice / 194
jumble / 214
junction / 114
Jupiter / 543
juridical / 517
justice / 270
justify / 278
juvenile / 84
keen / 125
kennel / 32
kernel / 9
kerosene / 533
kiln / 216
kindle / 202
kinetic / 361
kingdom / 462
kinship / 452
knack / 237
knit / 368
label / 151

laboratory / 322
laborious / 192
labyrinth / 165
lace / 361
lack / 550
lament / 477
landing / 261
landmark / 158
landmass / 218
landscape / 217
landslide / 286
languish / 64
lapse / 515
larva / 149
larynx / 203
laser / 54
lash / 107
lasting / 464
latent / 527
lateral / 202
Latin / 511
latitude / 255
latter / 323
laudable / 39
launch / 341
laundry / 418
laureate / 231
lava / 439
lavish / 168
lawn / 176
lawsuit / 517
lax / 140
lay / 49
layer / 196
layout / 208
leach / 312
lead / 18
league / 342
leak / 438
leap / 208
lease / 55
least / 72
ledge / 164
leftover / 59
legend / 181
legible / 401
legislate / 518
legislative / 504
legislature / 381

legitimate / 525
leisure / 6
lengthen / 466
lens / 542
lessen / 471
lethal / 370
lethargy / 299
lettuce / 83
level / 17
levy / 516
liable / 355
libel / 139
liberal / 391
liberate / 324
librarian / 162
license / 228
lichen / 403
lighthearted / 237
lightning / 32
likewise / 371
limb / 401
limestone / 465
limitation / 389
lineage / 52
linear / 242
linen / 456
linger / 495
linguist / 398
linguistic / 555
lipid / 74
liquefy / 311
liquid / 32
listless / 44
literacy / 394
literary / 548
literature / 339
lithosphere / 510
litter / 234
livelihood / 241
livestock / 508
lizard / 272
load / 211
loan / 400
loath / 444
loathsome / 544
lobby / 381
locality / 240
locate / 428
locomotion / 308

locomotive / 171
lodge / 80
lofty / 390
log / 129
logical / 80
longevity / 150
longitude / 461
loose / 227
lope / 262
lore / 118
lost-and-found / 351
lounge / 250
lower / 526
loyal / 524
lubricant / 518
lucrative / 331
lumber / 235
luminosity / 308
luminous / 99
lunar / 171
lunge / 40
lure / 7
lush / 20
lust / 89
luster / 559
luxurious / 279
luxury / 386
lyric / 31
machinery / 14
maglev / 127
magma / 543
magnesium / 493
magnet / 93
magnetic / 214
magnificent / 405
magnify / 340
magnitude / 32
mail / 494
mainstream / 133
maintain / 463
maize / 493
major / 204
male / 124
malice / 408
malicious / 131
malleable / 168
malnutrition / 208
mammal / 61
mammoth / 24

manage / 262
mandate / 516
mandatory / 517
maneuver / 104
mania / 325
manifest / 248
manifestation / 465
manifesto / 526
manipulate / 334
manner / 272
mannerism / 230
mansion / 403
mantle / 510
manual / 170
manufacture / 172
mar / 169
marble / 205
march / 495
margin / 267
marine / 306
maritime / 536
marked / 66
marsh / 45
marvel / 350
mask / 78
mason / 81
mass / 135
mast / 57
mat / 244
match / 181
mate / 191
material / 480
maternal / 192
mathematics / 193
matrimony / 217
mature / 207
maturity / 298
maximum / 491
maze / 459
meager / 177
meaningful / 456
meantime / 489
measure / 512
mechanic / 218
mechanics / 316
mechanize / 467
medal / 54
media / 395
mediate / 5

medication / 502
medieval / 417
meditate / 63
medium / 476
melanin / 359
mellow / 192
melodic / 92
melodious / 88
melodrama / 403
melody / 341
melt / 6
membrane / 284
memo / 195
memorize / 472
mental / 53
mention / 183
mercantile / 464
merchandise / 386
merchant / 368
mercury / 128
mercy / 30
mere / 263
meridian / 207
mesmerize / 404
Mesolithic / 168
mess / 288
metabolic / 162
metallic / 454
metaphor / 111
meteor / 317
meteorite / 299
meteorological / 360
meteorologist / 264
meteorology / 522
methane / 438
methanol / 295
method / 462
meticulous / 118
metric / 147
metropolis / 123
metropolitan / 205
microbe / 19
microorganism / 271
microprocessor / 116
microscope / 138
microscopic / 19
microwave / 518
middleman / 191
midterm / 281

mighty / 23
migrate / 529
mild / 64
milieu / 42
militant / 437
military / 240
millennium / 342
mime / 79
mimic / 322
mine / 232
mingle / 39
minimal / 323
minimize / 281
minimum / 511
minor / 474
minority / 31
mint / 422
minus / 319
minute / 449
miracle / 108
mischievous / 201
miserable / 187
mismanage / 89
missile / 286
mission / 148
mobile / 242
mock / 496
mode / 85
modeling / 418
modem / 71
moderate / 473
modernity / 101
modest / 404
modify / 99
modulate / 329
moist / 447
moisture / 38
mold / 92
molecular / 555
molecule / 545
molten / 299
momentary / 390
momentous / 458
momentum / 312
monarch / 136
monarchy / 524
monastery / 149
monetary / 332
monitor / 262

monogamous / 212
monogamy / 367
monopoly / 475
monotonous / 420
monotony / 179
monster / 81
monument / 345
monumental / 346
moor / 286
moral / 363
morale / 531
morgue / 145
morphology / 280
mortality / 26
mortgage / 331
mortify / 444
mosaic / 268
mosquito / 508
moss / 281
moth / 432
motif / 95
motion / 533
motivate / 22
motive / 366
motor / 161
mottled / 240
motto / 321
mound / 287
mount / 417
mountainous / 241
muggy / 25
multiple / 27
multiplicative / 319
multiply / 385
multitude / 351
mundane / 194
municipal / 176
mural / 314
muscle / 478
muscular / 499
muse / 444
mushroom / 44
musical / 223
musician / 24
mutual / 87
myopic / 538
myriad / 153
mythology / 92
nail / 6

naive / 372
naked / 132
nap / 555
narrate / 94
narrative / 211
nationalism / 81
naturalist / 216
nauseous / 233
naval / 250
navigate / 545
necessitate / 237
necessity / 331
nectar / 362
needy / 548
negate / 425
neglect / 102
negligent / 88
negligible / 453
negotiate / 331
negotiation / 363
neoclassical / 142
Neolithic / 539
neon / 281
nest / 164
neuron / 45
neutral / 288
neutron / 103
nevertheless / 416
newsletter / 542
newsprint / 272
niche / 69
nickel / 232
nicotine / 113
nightmare / 24
nimble / 390
nitrogen / 546
nocturnal / 283
nomadic / 41
nominal / 15
nominate / 502
nominee / 7
nonetheless / 384
nonsense / 244
nonverbal / 215
normally / 247
nostalgia / 330
nostalgic / 178
nosy / 3
notable / 412

notate / 289
notation / 361
notch / 160
noted / 86
noteworthy / 120
noticeable / 448
notify / 61
notion / 529
notorious / 481
notwithstanding / 146
nourish / 10
nourishment / 346
novel / 109
novelty / 203
novice / 434
noxious / 126
nucleus / 106
nude / 29
numeric / 320
numerous / 508
nurture / 437
nutrient / 161
nutrition / 239
oak / 553
oasis / 292
obedience / 407
obituary / 471
objective / 556
obligate / 133
obliterate / 4
oblivious / 254
oblong / 320
obscene / 472
obscure / 231
observatory / 301
observe / 221
obsess / 60
obsolete / 362
obstacle / 457
obstruct / 544
obtain / 272
occasional / 122
occupy / 49
occur / 123
oceanographer / 116
octopus / 112
odd / 87
odorous / 312
offensive / 91

offer / 98
officious / 167
offset / 62
offspring / 487
olfactory / 428
omit / 437
ongoing / 403
onslaught / 113
ooze / 478
opal / 219
opaque / 561
operant / 202
operate / 442
opponent / 475
opportunity / 198
oppose / 17
opposed / 193
opposite / 545
oppressive / 134
optic / 538
optimal / 550
optimistic / 65
optimize / 212
optional / 232
oral / 477
oratorio / 144
orbit / 216
orbital / 419
orchestra / 449
orchid / 415
ordeal / 409
ordinal / 321
ordinate / 320
ore / 137
organic / 562
organism / 72
orient / 300
orientation / 306
origin / 183
originate / 73
ornament / 145
ornamental / 110
ornate / 279
ornithology / 245
orthodox / 15
otherwise / 73
outbreak / 109
outcome / 291
outcry / 310

outermost / 308
outfit / 421
outgas / 145
outlaw / 526
outline / 425
outlive / 367
outlying / 149
output / 306
outrage / 28
outrageous / 101
outrageously / 61
outspoken / 407
outstanding / 173
outweigh / 168
oval / 520
overact / 143
overall / 405
overcharge / 402
overcome / 425
overdue / 424
overflow / 408
overgraze / 345
overhaul / 328
overlap / 437
overload / 58
overlook / 468
overnight / 89
overrun / 29
overseas / 490
oversleep / 95
overt / 62
overtime / 439
overview / 157
overwhelm / 423
owl / 276
oxide / 382
oxygen / 525
oyster / 47
pack / 335
packed / 514
pact / 526
paddle / 243
painstaking / 170
palatable / 245
palate / 262
pale / 293
Paleolithic / 166
pamphlet / 140
pancreas / 282

potential / 203
pottery / 484
pound / 171
poverty / 473
powder / 475
practicable / 101
practical / 41
pragmatic / 237
prairie / 423
preach / 473
precautionary / 541
precede / 44
precious / 352
precipitate / 172
precise / 382
precursor / 348
predation / 75
predator / 403
predecessor / 27
predict / 291
predispose / 63
predominant / 140
predominate / 389
preeminent / 178
prefer / 256
preference / 419
prehistoric / 455
prejudice / 460
preliminary / 333
preliterate / 15
prelude / 453
premature / 361
premier / 522
premise / 332
preoccupation / 82
prepare / 373
preponderance / 438
prerequisite / 466
prescribe / 194
prescription / 509
presentation / 316
preserve / 185
preside / 529
presidency / 443
president / 9
press / 195
prestige / 362
pretension / 315
pretentious / 54
pretext / 39

prevail / 226
prevailing / 556
prevalent / 187
previous / 537
prey / 172
primal / 149
primary / 292
primate / 372
prime / 361
primitive / 182
primordial / 248
principal / 33
principle / 407
prior / 512
prioritize / 201
priority / 436
privilege / 315
prize / 407
proactive / 50
probe / 381
procedure / 428
proceed / 490
process / 560
proclaim / 17
prodigious / 65
productive / 542
productivity / 416
profession / 18
proficient / 107
profile / 471
profound / 244
progressive / 9
prohibit / 16
prohibitive / 168
project / 451
projector / 188
proliferate / 393
prolific / 43
prolong / 377
prolonged / 147
prominent / 137
promising / 532
promote / 84
prompt / 222
prone / 167
pronounced / 440
proof / 392
proofread / 216
propagate / 553
propel / 66

propensity / 87
proper / 490
property / 247
prophet / 133
proponent / 94
proportion / 379
proposal / 158
propose / 369
proprietor / 171
prose / 337
prosecute / 528
prospect / 134
prospector / 301
prosper / 339
prosperity / 211
prostitution / 452
protagonist / 146
protein / 558
protest / 347
prototype / 162
protrude / 153
provincialism / 267
provision / 456
provocative / 445
provoke / 344
prudent / 47
psychoanalysis / 72
psychology / 50
publication / 252
publicize / 522
puddle / 94
Pueblo / 228
puff / 63
pulp / 132
pulse / 530
pump / 305
punch / 39
punctual / 333
puncture / 46
pupil / 121
puppet / 426
purchase / 485
pure / 194
puritanical / 76
purity / 146
purple / 244
pursue / 383
pursuit / 435
puzzle / 248
pyramid / 355

quadruple / 319
quaint / 140
qualify / 543
quality / 326
quantify / 45
quantitative / 320
quantum / 213
quarry / 108
quarterly / 504
quartz / 456
quasar / 90
quash / 445
quell / 155
quench / 549
query / 75
questionnaire / 31
quiescent / 173
quilt / 220
quit / 349
quiver / 279
quiz / 126
quota / 197
quotation / 31
quote / 489
quotient / 319
racing / 442
racism / 471
racket / 501
radar / 340
radiate / 436
radiation / 547
radical / 176
radioactive / 258
radius / 209
raft / 248
rage / 429
rainbow / 461
rainfall / 194
raise / 511
rally / 392
ramble / 238
rampant / 539
ranch / 220
rancher / 555
rancorous / 4
random / 249
range / 115
rank / 349
rape / 75
rare / 194

rash / 98
rate / 104
ratify / 47
ratio / 468
ration / 244
rationality / 28
rattle / 421
ravage / 64
raven / 46
ravine / 264
raw / 363
rayon / 551
reactor / 338
readability / 473
readily / 53
realistic / 457
realization / 531
realm / 334
realtor / 236
reapply / 212
rear / 508
reasonable / 534
rebate / 329
rebel / 347
rebellious / 30
recall / 434
recede / 202
receiver / 265
receptacle / 9
reception / 161
receptive / 484
receptor / 492
recess / 357
recession / 426
recessive / 547
recharge / 44
recipe / 540
recipient / 281
reciprocal / 320
reciprocity / 469
recital / 552
reckless / 481
recline / 433
recognition / 178
recognize / 265
recoil / 360
recollection / 414
recommend / 263
reconcile / 527
reconstruction / 384

recount / 368
recoup / 331
recover / 1
recreation / 525
recruit / 146
rectangle / 32
rectify / 193
recurring / 463
recycle / 461
reddish / 379
redeem / 332
redundant / 29
reef / 9
refer / 129
reference / 354
refine / 138
reflect / 381
reflection / 227
reform / 369
refraction / 86
refrain / 132
refreshing / 374
refrigerate / 324
refund / 72
refurbish / 316
refute / 120
regardless / 197
regenerate / 532
regiment / 410
region / 58
register / 123
regular / 364
regulate / 388
rehabilitate / 91
rehearse / 105
reign / 526
reinforce / 78
reiterate / 367
reject / 321
rejuvenate / 429
rekindle / 317
relate / 349
relative / 491
relay / 299
release / 87
relegate / 366
relevance / 418
relevant / 478
reliable / 206
reliance / 535

relic / 521
relief / 108
relieve / 502
reliever / 211
religion / 462
reluctant / 372
rely / 376
remainder / 309
remains / 314
remark / 32
remarkable / 257
remind / 399
remnant / 346
remodel / 448
remote / 207
removal / 174
renaissance / 2
render / 269
rendition / 482
renew / 31
renovate / 464
renown / 4
rental / 391
repel / 466
repertoire / 392
repertory / 107
repetition / 357
replace / 358
replenish / 550
replica / 39
replicate / 188
represent / 159
representative / 303
repress / 51
reproach / 389
reproduce / 412
reptile / 427
republic / 503
reputation / 402
repute / 26
request / 57
require / 477
reschedule / 438
rescue / 20
resemble / 81
resent / 367
reservation / 404
reserve / 58
reservoir / 529
reside / 231

resident / 406
residue / 491
resign / 514
resilience / 336
resin / 506
resist / 432
resistant / 500
resolute / 52
resolve / 307
resonance / 223
resort / 264
resource / 562
respect / 296
respective / 346
respire / 280
respond / 36
respondent / 272
response / 557
responsible / 298
restoration / 428
restore / 218
restraint / 308
restrict / 274
resume / 369
retail / 424
retain / 311
retire / 229
retract / 132
retreat / 440
retrieval / 213
retrieve / 356
retrospect / 143
retrospective / 62
reunion / 49
reveal / 469
revenue / 165
revere / 8
reverse / 253
reversible / 285
revert / 125
review / 559
revise / 375
revitalize / 113
revival / 375
revive / 30
revoke / 359
revolt / 150
revolution / 43
reward / 188
rhinoceros / 71

rhyme / 486
rhythm / 442
ribbon / 161
riddle / 484
ridge / 480
ridicule / 201
ridiculous / 85
righteous / 191
rigid / 435
rigor / 85
rigorous / 260
rim / 189
rinse / 416
rip / 133
ripe / 386
ripen / 455
ripple / 120
rite / 248
ritual / 504
rival / 136
rivalry / 347
roam / 235
rob / 430
robust / 284
rod / 406
rodent / 333
rodeo / 400
roe / 92
roll / 426
romantic / 270
roost / 160
rotate / 239
rotational / 302
rough / 27
rouse / 445
routine / 7
rub / 23
rudimentary / 309
rug / 488
rugged / 221
ruin / 453
rumor / 513
rupture / 441
rural / 382
rush / 69
rust / 283
rustic / 476
rustproof / 18
ruthless / 379

sac / 266
sacred / 457
sacrifice / 143
sacrificial / 347
saddle / 121
sage / 155
sake / 397
salamander / 318
salient / 20
salmon / 204
salon / 543
sample / 241
sanction / 142
sanctuary / 398
sanitation / 474
sap / 541
sapphire / 495
sardonic / 41
satellite / 335
satire / 451
satiric / 42
saturate / 399
saturation / 104
Saturn / 268
sauce / 397
saucy / 3
saunter / 279
savage / 76
scale / 551
scan / 315
scandal / 483
scar / 129
scarce / 499
scarf / 497
scatter / 393
scavenger / 351
scene / 122
scent / 219
schedule / 323
schematic / 484
scheme / 530
scholar / 365
scholarship / 274
scientific / 152
scoff / 134
scope / 130
scorch / 325
score / 296
scorn / 39

scornful / 134
scourge / 377
scout / 395
scrape / 560
scratch / 266
screen / 531
script / 415
scroll / 4
scrub / 27
scruffy / 208
scruple / 430
scrupulous / 390
scrutinize / 548
scuba / 156
scuffle / 193
sculpt / 340
sculpture / 411
scurry / 405
seal / 387
seashore / 177
season / 158
seasoning / 150
secede / 28
seclusion / 205
second / 418
secrete / 8
section / 450
secular / 191
secure / 10
sedentary / 486
sediment / 205
sedimentary / 81
seem / 146
seep / 11
segment / 10
segregate / 215
seismic / 384
seismograph / 172
seismology / 125
selection / 424
selective / 169
semantic / 473
semester / 542
seminar / 498
semiotics / 484
senate / 490
senator / 545
senior / 60
sensational / 486

sense / 457
sensible / 335
sensitive / 5
sensory / 251
sensual / 316
sentimental / 277
separate / 161
sequence / 408
sequential / 213
sequoia / 423
series / 298
session / 255
setback / 238
setting / 385
settle / 327
severe / 203
sew / 396
sewage / 490
sewerage / 188
sexism / 154
shade / 170
shallow / 135
shame / 432
shape / 419
sharpen / 199
sharply / 267
shatter / 455
shear / 75
sheath / 124
shed / 89
sheer / 512
shell / 176
shellfish / 383
shelter / 230
shield / 24
shift / 158
shipwright / 216
shirk / 90
shore / 95
shortage / 469
shortly / 149
shovel / 375
shower / 336
shred / 460
shrewd / 366
shrimp / 311
shrink / 54
shrivel / 21
shroud / 287

shrub / 299
shuffle / 329
shuttle / 396
sidebar / 480
sidewalk / 205
siege / 40
sieve / 519
signal / 113
significant / 235
signify / 93
silica / 86
silicate / 363
silicon / 228
silt / 552
silversmith / 34
similar / 421
simile / 488
simmer / 190
simplicity / 216
simplify / 236
simply / 296
simulate / 268
simultaneous / 108
singular / 192
sinuous / 13
situated / 68
skeletal / 391
skeleton / 501
skeptical / 407
skim / 260
skip / 532
skull / 433
skyscraper / 25
slacken / 133
slander / 529
slash / 120
sled / 395
sledding / 249
sleek / 285
sleigh / 238
slender / 126
slice / 550
slick / 453
slide / 401
slight / 308
slip / 259
slog / 227
slogan / 482
slope / 181
sloth / 307

slough / 179
sluggish / 362
slumber / 309
smear / 379
smelting / 410
smirk / 471
smoothly / 533
smother / 510
snack / 383
snap / 509
sneaker / 229
sneaky / 409
snide / 88
snowflake / 175
soak / 369
sober / 201
so-called / 32
soccer / 137
sociable / 220
sociology / 79
soda / 226
sodium / 297
soft / 41
solar / 80
solder / 173
sole / 241
solemn / 367
solicit / 6
solid / 220
solitary / 209
solitude / 280
solo / 287
soloist / 146
soluble / 65
solution / 8
solvent / 285
somber / 110
somewhat / 359
soothe / 284
sophisticated / 429
soprano / 301
sore / 385
sound / 131
sour / 323
source / 222
souvenir / 502
sovereign / 528
sow / 231
soybean / 311
spacecraft / 118

spaghetti / 310
span / 217
spare / 17
spark / 420
sparse / 553
spatial / 302
spawn / 374
spear / 51
spearhead / 460
specialize / 546
species / 425
specific / 362
specify / 393
specimen / 401
speckle / 40
spectacle / 112
spectacular / 375
spectator / 174
spectrum / 327
speculate / 399
spellbind / 459
spew / 419
sphere / 5
spherical / 293
spheroid / 434
spice / 230
spike / 239
spill / 232
spin / 326
spinet / 139
spinning / 203
spiny / 448
spiral / 78
splash / 337
split / 265
spoil / 33
sponge / 503
sponsor / 526
spontaneity / 57
spontaneous / 108
sporadic / 543
spot / 309
sprain / 554
sprawl / 135
spray / 148
spread / 252
spring / 345
sprinkle / 15
sprout / 558
spun / 336

spur / 47
spurn / 356
squabble / 263
squander / 154
square / 544
squash / 190
squeeze / 466
squid / 440
squirrel / 420
squirt / 506
stable / 62
stack / 520
stadium / 41
staff / 533
stage / 504
stagecoach / 138
staggered / 250
staggering / 115
stagnant / 332
stain / 27
stake / 35
stalk / 397
stampede / 89
standard / 469
stanza / 117
staple / 128
starch / 33
stardom / 204
stark / 225
startling / 338
stash / 243
state / 327
statesman / 165
static / 214
station / 348
stationary / 361
statistic / 351
statue / 185
stature / 240
status / 84
staunch / 408
steady / 73
steep / 511
steer / 353
stellar / 350
stem / 372
stereo / 491
stereotype / 472
sterile / 168
stew / 441

variable / 303
variant / 285
varied / 97
varnish / 278
vary / 5
vascular / 497
vast / 190
vault / 79
vegetarian / 18
vegetation / 463
vegetative / 308
vehicle / 360
veil / 242
vein / 335
velocity / 507
venom / 524
venomous / 285
vent / 322
ventilation / 214
venture / 244
venturesome / 410
verbal / 11
verbalize / 485
verbiage / 485
verdict / 527
verge / 452
verifiable / 528
verify / 160
versatile / 196
verse / 19
version / 267
versus / 24
vertebrate / 115
vertical / 435

vestige / 492
veto / 217
viable / 199
vibrant / 343
vibrate / 128
vibration / 369
vice / 47
vicinity / 454
vicious / 366
vigilance / 381
vigor / 279
violate / 353
violent / 124
viral / 323
virtual / 213
virtue / 96
virtuous / 437
virus / 327
viscous / 286
visible / 193
visual / 27
visualize / 354
vital / 395
vivid / 394
vivify / 356
vocal / 354
vocalize / 155
vocation / 264
vogue / 280
volatile / 542
volcano / 103
voltage / 368
volume / 287
volunteer / 523

voracious / 298
vow / 409
voyage / 112
vulgar / 155
vulnerable / 160
waggle / 313
wagon / 470
walnut / 544
wan / 548
wane / 160
wanna / 26
ware / 440
warehouse / 206
warp / 155
warrant / 528
wary / 231
wasp / 397
waste / 371
watercourse / 185
wax / 72
wear / 152
weathering / 314
weave / 337
wedge / 74
wedge-shaped / 473
weed / 21
weird / 51
welfare / 125
well-heeled / 343
whereby / 457
whim / 280
wholesome / 403
wick / 283
widespread / 133

wield / 527
willful / 86
willow / 551
wintry / 302
wipe / 162
wispy / 296
wit / 205
withdraw / 345
wither / 176
withhold / 3
withstand / 478
wonder / 278
worship / 179
worth / 524
wrap / 342
wreck / 130
wrench / 549
wretch / 379
wrinkle / 67
X-ray / 85
yarn / 251
yeast / 130
yelp / 443
yield / 399
yogurt / 448
yoke / 254
yolk / 286
zealous / 359
zest / 144
zigzag / 472
zinc / 402
zone / 297

《新托福考试写作高分速成》

陈向东 著

◎ 详细阐述托福综合写作解答的7大步骤及5大写作原则，给出独立写作3大写作策略和5大解题原则

◎ 深刻剖析写作思路，并提供解题策略及思维训练，解读真题

◎ 精心打造托福写作题型、解答原则与黄金模板

定价：35元 开本：16开 页码：280页

《TOEFL 写作/口语论证论据素材大全》 韦晓亮 编著

◎ 全面性：全面补充TOEFL写作和口语英文论证论据素材

◎ 权威性：汇集世界优秀外文期刊、报纸、书籍、检索数据库和权威新闻网站的英文内容

◎ 指导性：汇集新东方TOEFL考试培训项目数年教学经验和写作、口语教学成果

定价：25元 开本：16开 页码：248页

《新托福考试核心语法》

（含光盘1张）

Nancy Gallagher 编著

◎ 全书涵盖20个重要的英语语法点，紧扣新托福考试语法要点

◎ 结合经典的例子，对各个语法点进行精辟深入的讲解

◎ 提供大量模考练习，设有计时测验

定价：50元 开本：16开 页码：308页

《新托福考试阅读特训》

（第二版） **Ji-Yeon Lee** 著

◎ 62篇精选文章，题材广泛，全面满足备考需求

◎ 特设仿真阅读试题，体验真实考试情境

◎ 全书结构编排科学合理，实用性强

定价：55元 开本：16开 页码：472页

《托福考试口语特训》

（第二版）（附MP3）

Ji-Yeon Lee 著

◎ 68个单元精练详解，6大题型逐个突破

◎ 提供多种练习方式，逐步掌握答题技巧

◎ 特设口语模拟试题，体验真实考试情景

定价：65元 开本：16开 页码：520页

《新托福考试听力特训》

（第二版）（含光盘1张）

Ji-Yeon Lee 著

◎ 59篇精选听力练习语料，题材广泛，全面满足备考需求

◎ 提供多种练习方式，逐步掌握答题技巧

◎ 特设听力模拟试题，体验真实考试情景

定价：58元 开本：16开 页码：452页

《新托福考试写作特训》

（第二版）（含光盘1张）

Ji-Yeon Lee 著

◎ 三个章节精练详解，两种题型各个击破

◎ 提供多种练习方式，逐步掌握写作技巧

◎ 特设仿真写作测试，体验真实考试情境

定价：46元 开本：16开 页码：304页

《TOEFL 巴朗词表》（附MP3）

Steven J. Matthiesen 编著

◎ 系统研究真题，提炼高频词汇

◎ 收录双语释义，遴选同义派生

◎ 提供经典例句，加深理解记忆

定价：35元 开本：16开 页码：256页

《托福词组必备》

俞敏洪 编著

◎ 紧扣真题，选词科学
◎ 例句经典，原汁原味
◎ 收录同义词组，扩充词汇量
◎ 幽默插图，巧妙助记

定价：22元 开本：32开 页码：256页

《TOEFL iBT 口语词汇小伴侣》

张洪伟 翟少成 编著

◎ 应试导向——紧扣新托福口语考试趋势，给出三类词汇供考生掌握
◎ 科学统计——所涉及学术类专业词汇来自真实词频统计数据

定价：15元 开本：32开 页码：280页

《TOEFL词汇词根＋联想记忆法：45天突破版》

俞敏洪 编著

◎ "词根＋联想记忆法"实用有趣，有效提升词汇量
◎ 甄选重点词汇，紧跟TOEFL考试趋势
◎ 增加单词返记菜单，有助于复习和自测
◎ 再现真题例句，直击TOEFL考试要点

定价：45元 开本：32开 页码：520页

《TOEFL iBT 阅读词汇小伴侣》

张洪伟 蔡青 编著

◎ 针对性强——囊括托福阅读全部话题及学科领域词汇
◎ 实用性佳——精选托福阅读词汇及同义词，在语境中真正融会贯通
◎ 分类清晰——囊括托福阅读基础、核心、高频及次高频分类词汇

定价：15元 开本：32开 页码：204页

《TOEFL iBT 词汇10000》

（含光盘1张）张洪伟 戴云 编著

◎ 源于真题目——收录托福真题的必备词汇与经典例句
◎ 奉献真经典——凝结托福名师的教学感悟与智慧结晶

定价：45元 开本：16开 页码：444页

《托福写作词汇小伴侣》

张洪伟 戴云 编著

◎ 针对性强——浓缩托福独立写作和综合写作最常用词汇
◎ 实用性佳——精选鲜活的托福写作常用短语与习惯搭配

定价：16元 开本：32开 页码：332页

《TOEFL iBT 听力词汇小伴侣》邱政政 戴懿德 编著

◎ 紧跟TOEFL考试趋势，权威指点
◎ 精选常考核心词汇，针对性强
◎ 分类词汇专业全面，重点突出
◎ 精选TOEFL常用短语与习惯搭配，实用性佳

定价：18元 开本：32开 页码：388页

《TOEFL 词汇词根＋联想记忆法》 俞敏洪 编著

◎ "GRE红宝书"姊妹篇，"词根＋联想"实用有趣
◎ 500个常考习语短语，打通听力，阅读经脉
◎ 释义精准并配真题例句，直击TOEFL考试要点

定价：32元 开本：32开 页码：424页

《词以类记：TOEFL iBT 词汇》 张红岩 编著

◎ TOEFL iBT 最新词汇：覆盖听说读写

◎ 按学科和意群分类：细分至最小同义词区间

定价：35元 开本：32开 页码：424页

《新托福考试专项进阶——初级听力》（附 MP3 光盘）

定价：42元 开本：16开 页码：288页

《新托福考试专项进阶——中级听力》（附 MP3 光盘）

定价：45元 开本：16开 页码：344页

《新托福考试专项进阶——高级听力》（附 MP3 光盘）

定价：45元 开本：16开 页码：348页

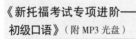

《新托福考试专项进阶——初级口语》（附 MP3 光盘）

定价：42元 开本：16开 页码：296页

《新托福考试专项进阶——中级口语》（附 MP3 光盘）

定价：38元 开本：16开 页码：248页

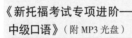

《新托福考试专项进阶——高级口语》（附 MP3 光盘）

定价：42元 开本：16开 页码：288页

《新托福考试专项进阶——初级阅读》

定价：35元 开本：16开 页码：308页

《新托福考试专项进阶——中级阅读》

定价：38元 开本：16开 页码：344页

《新托福考试专项进阶——高级阅读》

定价：40元 开本：16开 页码：368页

《新托福考试专项进阶——阅读模拟试题（上）》

定价：36元 开本：16开 页码：252页

《新托福考试专项进阶——阅读模拟试题（下）》

定价：36元 开本：16开 页码：252页

《新托福考试专项进阶——初级写作》（附 MP3 光盘）

定价：40元 开本：16开 页码：268页

《新托福考试专项进阶——中级写作》（附 MP3 光盘）

定价：38元 开本：16开 页码：248页

《新托福考试专项进阶——高级写作》（附 MP3 光盘）

定价：42元 开本：16开 页码：304页

《新托福考试专项进阶——听力模拟试题（上）》（附 MP3 光盘）

定价：40元 开本：16开 页码：256页

《新托福考试专项进阶——听力模拟试题（下）》（附 MP3 光盘）

定价：36元 开本：16开 页码：220页

◎ 《新托福考试专项进阶》系列丛书从托福考试所考查的听、说、读、写四项技能入手，为考生提供了详尽的考试指导，并将各技能分为初、中、高三级，通过独特的"进阶训练"方式，再辅以大量练习，让考生逐步掌握托福实考的技巧，同时切实提高英语实际运用能力，从而在短期内轻松取得托福高分。本丛书内容编排由易到难，循序渐进，实战性强，是不可多得的托福备考资料。

◎ 本丛书引进自韩国多乐园出版社。该社成立于1977年，在韩国英语教育出版领域始终处于领军地位。本丛书被韩国众多学校和培训机构指定为课堂教材，在托福考生中享有较高声誉。

书名	《TOEFL词汇词根+联想记忆法:乱序版》(以下简称"乱序版")	《TOEFL词汇词根+联想记忆法》(以下简称"正序版")	《TOEFL词汇词根+联想记忆法:45天突破版》(以下简称"45天版")	《TOEFL词汇词根+联想记忆法:便携版》(以下简称"便携版")
出版社/定价	西安交通大学出版社/58.00元	西安交通大学出版社/28.00元	群言出版社/45.00元	北京语言大学出版社/22.00元
页数/开本	600/特16开 (170*230)	424/32开 (145*210)	520/32开 (145*210)	392/32开 (120*185)
首版年份	2013年10月	2013年8月	2013年8月	2011年3月
篇章结构	48个Word List	核心单词(35个Word List),核心词组	45个Word List	基础词汇(21个Word List),主题词汇(11大主题),场景词汇(3大场景)
配套MP3	对英文主词及英文例句进行录音	对英文主词及其中文释义进行录音	对英文主词及其中文释义进行录音	登录http://www.dogwood.com.cn/下载录音,对英文主词及其中文释义进行录音
词汇量	约4500个核心词汇,800多个核心词组,派生词、同义词等,补充大量的同反义词,形近词等	约2700个核心词汇,500多个核心词组,派生词等,补无大量的同义词	约3900个核心词汇,670多个核心词组,派生词,派近词等,补充大量的同反义词,形近词等	约4500个核心词汇,800多个核心词组
适用的学生层次	所有准备参加TOEFL考试的考生			
相同点	1. 紧扣TOEFL考试,收录TOEFL考试核心词汇,精选中文释义。 2. 以"词根+联想"记忆法为主,辅以谐音、拆分、形近等多种记忆方法。 3. 为单词提供丰富的同义词,并以*标注已考同义词。 4. 归纳TOEFL考试核心词组。			
不同点	1. 编排方式 　乱序版:全书所有单词乱序编排 　正序版:单词按A-Z字母顺序排列 　45天版:全书乱序,每个单元内按A-Z字母顺序编排,乱中有正 　便携版:基础词汇乱序编排,分类词汇按A-Z字母顺序编排 　前三本均收录大量真题例句。 2. "正序版"标注听力词汇,专设核心词组一节,收录历年真题中考过的重点词组,并标注考试时间。 3. "乱序版"和"45天版"每个单元前有词根、词缀预习表,系统学习本单元重点词汇,词组,词缀。 4. "乱序版"和"45天版"每个单词前有词根,图帮助考生加深对单词的理解和记忆。			
学习建议	有的考生认为以正序为方便查阅,符合已有的背单词习惯,容易有成就感;有的考生认为以乱序排编不容易形成上下单词的提示记忆,能保证背词的均匀性,效率更高。TOEFL"正序版"、"乱序版"和"便携版"可作为以上三者的有力补充。词缀、词组,例句以及收录单词内容各不相同,考生可以根据自己的学习习惯选择其中之一进行学习。在每页下方返返记录单,有助于复习和自测;并有大量生动有趣的插图,有助于记忆。			